Arkady YERUSALIMSKY

*

GERMAN IMPERIALISM: ITS PAST AND PRESENT

*

PROGRESS PUBLISHERS
MOSCOW

TRANSLATED FROM THE RUSSIAN BY VIC SCHNEIERSON

А. ЕРУСАЛИМСКИЙ

**Германский империализм:
история и современность**

На английском языке

First printing 1969

CONTENTS

GREAT CARTHAGE WAGED THREE WARS.
IT WAS STILL POWERFUL AFTER THE FIRST,
STILL INHABITED AFTER THE SECOND,
NO LONGER TO BE FOUND AFTER THE THIRD.

Bertolt Brecht

This book is not an orderly account of the history of German imperialism. It does not contain a chronological analysis of all the pertinent problems. It is a selection of works on the development of German imperialism in the 20th century, on its home, foreign and colonial policy, its ideology and historiography. They were written over a long period beginning in the mid-twenties and ending in the present. Each had its own, often limited, purpose. Some are independent studies of Soviet, German, British and French documents and of documents from archives in the Soviet Union, the German Democratic Republic and the scientific institutions of the Weimar Republic. Others are studies of the more significant trends in the historiography and ideology of German imperialism. Still others were written "in the make of the events" and are journalistic in complexion.

Briefly, some of the topics, treated as objects of scientific investigation, have a solid documentary foundation, while others were dealt with in a journalistic vein. These latter are now an echo of past history even where the author succeeded as historian and contemporary to size up the events more or less correctly.

The writer always had a liking for historical journalism, to which he devoted himself before the war and after it was over, but especially in his capacity of war correspondent. He has accumulated a vast amount of notes (regrettably irregular) taken in Moscow, in the front lines and abroad, recording facts and impressions, and events indicating the influence exerted by the Soviet Union and the other members of the anti-nazi coalition on international affairs. The bulk of the notes are related to the military and political aspects of Hitler Germany, to nazi propaganda, etc. They were the meat for articles in *Krasnaya Zvezda*, *Pravda* and *Izvestia*, and radio broadcasts (chiefly beamed abroad).

The writer hopes that they will be of interest to the reader as the record of a Soviet historian's view of nazi Germany.

The collection is arranged in chronological order by subjects. The various works have thus been converted into chapters and grouped in four parts. Some are presented as originally written. Others have been touched up, but no amendments or additional facts were inserted even where new documentary material has come to hand, for the writer wished to preserve the original interpretation of events, save where they contradicted contemporary research. Some chapters, on the other hand, have been considerably expanded and partly revised. Besides, a few new chapters have been added.

The date at the end of every chapter indicates the time of writing of the original text. Two dates are given where the account was expanded or brought up to date at a later time.

Much changed in the world in the years encompassed by this collection. Much also changed in the writer's scientific interests. However, having devoted the greater part of his conscious life to the study of international relations in the 19th and 20th centuries, he invariably concentrated on the problem of German imperialism and militarism. The hard facts prompted him to do so. Indeed, it is impossible to dismiss the subject, seeing that 50 years after the outbreak of the First World War and 25 years after the Second, and less than 20 years after the collapse of the nazi empire, a revived German militarism again beclouds the political horizons of Europe.

The generation born in the early 20th century has experienced the aggressive powers of German imperialism in a most tragic manner in two world wars fought with an interval of a mere 20 years. Each of these wars—and the Second immeasurably more than the First—has impregnated itself on the minds of men. Future generations as well as our contemporaries will long ponder these military disasters, these horrid nightmares that descended on the peoples of Europe, on all mankind, in the 20th century.

The causes behind the world wars generated by imperialism are still one of the most important and exciting problems, although historians have done much to pinpoint them, especially with regard to the First World War. Though the responsibility for the two wars falls squarely on all the imperialist powers, with German imperialism and militarism the chief instigator, influential forces in the reactionary camp have a political stake in concealing the facts. However, the progressive forces have an equally big stake in learning all the facts as conclusively as possible. The matter is not one of merely educational interest. It will provide the knowledge essential for preventing a new war.

The young generation has not experienced war. The hundreds of thousands of young people who set out to quench their thirst for knowledge and travel, are drawn not only to unique monuments of architecture and art. At Piskarevsky Cemetery in Leningrad, beside the ovens of Auschwitz, the monument to the Warsaw ghetto uprising, at Lidiče, at Buchenwald and other death camps, they are shocked more intensely than the elder generation, and ask the burning question of who is responsible for the monstrous war crimes that eclipse the practices of the medieval Inquisition. They seek the answer not only to the moral aspect, though that, too, is important. They wonder about the underlying meaning, the social mainsprings and the historical milieu. They want to know the motive forces of aggression, to draw the due political conclusions and to adopt decisions in tune with the balance of forces now prevailing in the world. The point at issue is to pick the path in history that would prevent the German militarists from starting a third war in the name of their revanchist plans.

A third war: it is a possibility we must never forget. This does not go to say that history is cyclical or repetitious. Nor does recognition of the possibility of a third war bear the stamp of doom preached by the atomic ideologists. There is no such thing in history as a complete revival of the past. Even the restoration of the Bourbons after the collapse of the Napoleonic empire was not a restoration in the precise sense of the word. The revival of German militarism, too, cannot follow a closed historical circuit, that is, repeat with precision all the stages and forms from the time of the Prussian army of Frederick II, the militarist system of Moltke and Ludendorff, to the fascist war machine of Hitler, Keitel and Heusinger. Yet past traditions, and still more past experience, have not been flung overboard. The rebirth of German militarism, even as a quasi-democratic "renovation" within the NATO framework, is a grave threat to world peace. Besides, it is not really a "renovation". It is much more an adaptation to the new situation in the world and in Germany.

The situation has, indeed, changed. Take a retrospective glance at the early 20th century. Compare it with its latter half. You will see that the changes were impelled by the emergence of a world system of socialist states, whose increasing influence on international affairs can hardly be exaggerated. Due to the objective regularities governing the development of the socialist community, due to the disintegration of colonialism and, last but not least, due to the growth of the working-class and democratic movement in the capitalist countries, the tempo of the historical process increased immensely after the Second World War, and doubly so due to the indelible impact on this process of scientific thought and new technology.

We cannot overlook the fact that this complex historical process has wrought a change in mentality, that the idea of peace, of the necessity of fighting for peace, has gained much greater currency than in the early 20th century or the brief interval between the two world wars. The atomic and space age has opened up unexplored horizons, but it has also created new dangers which have to be assessed and removed in the interest of our own and future generations.

In Germany, too, far-reaching changes have taken place after the Second World War. Much time has passed, more than embraces the history of the Weimar Republic or that of the Hitler Reich. If the basic principles of the Potsdam Conference, envisaging the extirpation of big monopolies and militarism, had been implemented throughout Germany, the country's peaceful development would have been ensured. But the abandonment of these principles by the Western powers and the revival of monopoly capital in West Germany split the country in two, creating a new political situation in Central Europe.

Two sovereign German states—the Federal Republic and the German Democratic Republic—came into being on German soil. The first, which remained in the system of capitalist states, set out to revive militarism and entered NATO. The second is developing along socialist lines and has become a member of the community of socialist countries and of the Warsaw Treaty Organisation. The German Democratic Republic has no territorial claims. It recognises the Oder-Neisse and the other frontiers established after the Second World War. It adheres to the policy of the peaceful coexistence of states with different socio-economic systems. The aggressive elements in the Federal Republic, on the other hand, have continuously urged frontier revision, generating international tension and sowing the seeds of a new war.

After the experience of two world wars, whereby German imperialism aspired to gain world domination, the imperialists have understood—and contemporary German reactionary historiography admits it at last—that their world ambitions are unrealistic and should be abandoned by reason of the balance of forces. The times for *Weltpolitik* in the traditional sense are over. The old slogan, "our future is on the seas", is no longer tenable. The idea of a "German mission", evolved in the past century during the formative period of the Reich, has been modified by the new situation. The resources of German militarism have shrunk. But now, too, employing new forms of economic expansion through "European integration" and the Common Market, and through neo-colonialism, the German militarists have set out to gain supremacy in Western Europe and to extend their political and military influence in NATO. What is more, they are bent on territorial expansion in Central and Eastern Europe. Their top spokesmen have declared that the cardinal task is to restore the 1937 borders, the borders of the 1871 Bismarckian empire. Of all things, they insist on the legality of Hitler's Munich deal partitioning Czechoslovakia.

Not only does this programme of territorial expansion deliberately ignore the principal results of the Second World War and the realities of post-war development in Eastern and Central Europe. It is designed to accomplish the revenge-seeking goals at the expense of the German Democratic Republic, Poland, Czechoslovakia and the Soviet Union.

In this context, the treaty of friendship, mutual assistance and co-operation concluded in Moscow by the Soviet Union and the German Democratic Republic (on June 12, 1964) is a factor stabilising the situation in Central Europe. While West German militarism is seeking to gain control over atomic weapons through NATO or the Bonn-Paris "axis", the German Democratic Republic has, for the first time in history, proclaimed a "German doctrine of peace", a realistic programme envisaging the conversion of Central Europe into a denuclearised zone.

Two Germanys exist on German soil, each embodying different historical traditions. Certainly, these traditions are refracted through the prism of the modern times. Take the militarist ideology as associated, say, with the Prussianism of Heinrich von Treitschke or the aggressive nationalism of the Pan-Germanic Union, or yet the outspoken racialism of Rosenberg and his "20th-century myth". All of them have dropped into the background, giving place to the more up-to-date "Atlantic idea", the "European idea", and the "Christian idea of the West", a special favourite of the existing politico-clerical regime. The militarist ideas peddled as "European" are highly varied and of many hues, including the cosmopolitan, but are pervaded all the same by the traditional aggressive German nationalism.

Militarism is unavoidably one of the focal problems in the ideological life of the two German states, and understandably so, for today the attitude towards it is a measure not only of public leaders and statesmen, but also of historical, even philosophical, thought.

However, while the German Democratic Republic has effected a total rupture with militarism and has revived and advanced anti-militarist traditions, the very reverse is true of the Federal Republic, where the matter is at once more complex, because it is not confined to simply reproducing the traditional ideas of the old-time pugnacious Prusso-German militarism.

Militarist ideas are discredited in the eyes of the public in countries that twice in this century have had to fight Germany, though they are today allies of Federal Germany within NATO. They are discredited in the eyes of the young generation, too, which has escaped the wholesale nazi brainwashing. Besides, the defeats of 1918 and of 1945 hold up the lie conclusively to the myth of German militarism's invincibility, its identity with the interests of the German people, its positive role.

"One of the foremost duties of political history," said Gerhard Ritter, the most eminent representative of the German historical school, in 1954, "is to determine the historical place of modernity by cognising the past." This was said at the time when the Adenauer government enlisted the help of former Hitlerite generals in building up the Bundeswehr as a foundation for the militarist system of which the newly enunciated plan of psychological warfare is a component. Soon enough the collective effort of the ideologists of reviving militarism was put together in a catechism of historico-political ideas: *Questions of the Destiny of Modernity* (vols. 1-4, 1957-59). But even earlier, answering the troublesome question about German militarism's responsibility for the world wars and for the damage they caused the German nation, Ritter arrived at the following conclusion:

"Nobody is responsible any longer, because the giant war machine with its eternal frictions has become much too big to consider anybody responsible for what it does." This ushered in the concept of military automatism as an irrational force that defies control and self-control at critical times. In substance, militarism's historical responsibility was replaced by a concept of historical irresponsibility and, consequently, historical rehabilitation.

Later, Ritter extended his concept in various directions and came to the conclusion that the problem of militarism in German history is a problem only in the highly relative and technical sense of "warcraft", historically necessary and justified, save in those exceptional cases when, personified by such figures as Ludendorff, it opposed itself to "statesmanship" and required that politics serve war or when it became the tool of such figures of "demoniac power" as Hitler. In a certain sense, Ritter referred the ideal of "statesmanship" to Bismarck. As for the anti-militarist forces and traditions (which he describes as "radical pacifism"), Ritter totally denies them any historical credibility and, since "state leadership" cannot espouse them without exposing itself to "the danger of self-destruction", he denies them the right of existing.

Such, in general terms, are the zigzags of the historical

thinking that endeavours to splice the old-time ideas of German militarism with its revival in modern conditions. However, though it is the most traditional and reactionary variant, it is not the only one. There are others, more radical on the face of it and seemingly hostile to ossified concepts, which ignore the past and search for new philosophico-historical ideas. "The economic miracle and the Wehrmacht are splendid," writes Karl Jaspers, one of the most prominent West German existentialist philosophers, in his book, *Vital Questions of German Politics* (1963), "but entirely insufficient to ensure the prolonged existence and stability of a free state." In search of stability he turns to what he describes as positive and negative experiences of history. He treats Bismarck as the initiator of modern German history, the embodiment of the Prusso-German national image. Nor does he convert that image into an embodiment of the "European idea", as is fashionable in modern West German historiography (particularly after Winston Churchill compared Adenauer to Bismarck). On the face of it, he refers to the Iron Chancellor in relation to the problem of German militarism. He recalls Bismarck's phrase, "Once Germany is put in the saddle, it will learn to ride by itself", and adds: "No, Bismarck did not teach the people to ride; on the contrary, he denied the people such training. After Bismarck resigned, the consequences began to tell: the people, uninstructed in the art of horseback riding, and the ruling group consisting of the Kaiser, the officials and generals, who knew nothing except sitting in the saddle but could not ride either, caused the mount to make ridiculous leaps. It came to pass that the world treated the horse not as a horse but as a mad dog, which it destroyed. Such was our situation in 1945."

Identifying the German people with German militarism, Jaspers thus produced a quasi-explanation for Germany's historical destiny, garbed in the fetching habit of a radical rupture with the past.

As we see, a legend is being created in different quarters by means of different arguments—now conservative, now seemingly critical and intolerant of the old scheme—that the German nation has never had anti-militarist forces and traditions. This is why, for all the difference in points of departure, reactionary German historiography and German existentialist philosophy arrive at the same political conclusions. "Today," say Jaspers, "the big job is to learn to ride under the protection of, and in solidarity with, the West."

Yet what the nation needs most after the two world wars and the calamities German militarism has inflicted on it, is to revive its anti-militarist traditions. What it needs is to unify its anti-militarist forces, to wipe out the reviving militarism and the danger of a third war, which in our nuclear age will put in doubt the very existence of the German nation. Anti-militarist democratic traditions came into being a long time ago. Though much too often the Germans became the tools of reactionary and aggressive elements, there always were forces in their midst who championed their true interests. Those were people, groups and parties conscious of their duty, who had the courage to stand up in adversity for the life-asserting philosophy of their nation, to advocate progressive ideas, who fructified culture and called for action. This blending of thought and action has been a feature of the progressive movement since the German Renaissance.

The growth of the working class, the development of scientific communism in the works of Marx and Engels, marked a new phase in German history. The fight against the reactionary militarist forces gained a scientific foundation and a profoundly conceived aim. It drew the whole of the working class into the battle, which now represented the true national and democratic interest of the German people. The German workers and all German democratic forces may be proud that Frederick Engels, a German, was the first to draft a project for universal disarmament in face of a fresh round of arming at the end of the 19th century. It was not a utopian project either, but entirely realistic, even in the capitalist environment. Such veteran Social-Democrats as August Bebel, Wilhelm Liebknecht and Paul Singer were convinced anti-militarists. So were their successors, Franz Mehring, Clara Zetkin, Karl Liebknecht and Rosa Luxemburg, who contributed deep-going theoretical research to the struggle against militarism.

Today, many bourgeois historiographers and sociologists admit that the 1914-18 holocaust had been an imperialist war, a war for pre-eminence in world markets. Yet Karl Liebknecht and Rosa Luxemburg paid with their lives for this conception, scientifically developed by Vladimir Lenin, and for their opposition to the forces that spawned the imperialist war.

Today, probing the origins of the Second World War, bourgeois historiographers maintain that nobody in the Weimar Republic had anticipated the rise to power of the nazis, let alone the war. Yet the Communist Party of Germany, which acted on the scientific theory of Marxism-Leninism, kept saying over and over for all to hear: "Who votes for Hindenburg, votes for Hitler; who votes for Hitler, votes for war." In retrospect this may be described as prophetic, but was viewed by many people at the time as "communist propaganda". The Germans paid dearly for ignoring the warning, which was at once a summons to fight nazism, militarism and war. A great many people, Communists and non-Communists alike, who joined in the fight, were steeled ideologically in the savage struggle.

"Genius develops in quiet places, character out in the full current of human life," wrote Goethe. The character of the communist leaders developed in this full current as they stood at the head of the anti-militarist and anti-fascist movement. The minds of many Social-Democrats, too, grew lucid in this current. They realised like Rudolf Breitscheid, somewhat belatedly it is true, that if anything could deliver Germany from nazism and war it was united action by the working class and all the other democratic forces. The best of the German intellectuals realised it too. Though they were not Communists, they represented the spirit and aspirations of the "other Germany". This is true particularly of Carl von Ossietzky. Early in his life, he understood the evil of militarism in German history and laboured to expose the demagogy and practice of militarism and national-socialism. Like a pure fount, his works distinguished by a Nobel Peace Prize in 1935, quenched the intellectual thirst of the numerous honest people in Germany and other West European countries who sensed the perils of militarism, who thought nazism repulsive and made it their life's work to do battle against these monstrous products of German imperialism. This is true, among others, of Kurt Tucholsky, a gifted, perspicacious and fearless anti-fascist writer. To use the phrase of Leonhard Frank, a democrat and humanist, their orientation was "left, where the heart is".

Though this book deals mainly with German imperialism and militarism, the writer never lost sight of the "other

Germany", the Germany of the working class, of broad democratic circles, of progressive intellectuals and a humane culture, which has earned the deepest respect of all men and contributed eminently to world culture.

During the nazi nightmare, when the bulk of the German people was addled by chauvinism or terrorised into submission and became the blind tool of nazism and militarism, quite a few people in Germany either went deep underground or emigrated in order to fight fascism, militarism and war. The incredibly arduous struggle steeled them. It took deep faith and will-power to pull through. The antifascists fought as best they could, pondering on the past and pinning their hopes on the future, determined to salvage the honour of the German nation.

Contemporary reactionary historiography has invented the legend (how easily legends are made and how slowly are they dissipated!) that the plotters of July 20 had been the only patriotic Resistance force in Hitler Germany. It ignores the Communist Party, the Resistance movement and the Free Germany Committee, the struggle of the democratic elements against fascism and war. At the same time, it misrepresents the patriotic, democratically-minded section of the July 20 plotters. Goerdeler, one of the chief personalities in the plot, whose politico-philosophical and religious views are described as having anticipated the modern "Christian ideas" and West German "European thinking", is held up as a hero. Yet the reactionary nature of his ideas is as indisputable as his impotence after the plot failed is puzzling. He surrendered and called on the other plotters to give themselves up as well. The letter he wrote is, in this sense, truly unique. "We must consider July 20 as God's final judgement," he wrote. "The Führer escaped almost certain death. God did not wish the existence of the Germany I wanted to be bought at the price of a bloody crime. Once more, he entrusted the task to the Führer. This is an old German principle. Every German who took part in the plot is now obliged to join the Führer, who was saved by God."

The real heroes of the Resistance did not think, feel or act as Goerdeler did. Theirs was a different philosophy, forged in the arduous struggle, a life-asserting philosophy of profound ideas, free thoughts, a sense of duty to their contemporaries and to history. In early 1944, some six months before the generals essayed their plot, in a death cell at Bautzen a prisoner wrote his comrade a farewell letter which will always rank among the finest specimens of epistolary writing, a monument to the grandeur of the human spirit. In this letter, addressed in a way to all contemporaries and future generations, Ernst Thälmann set out his historico-philosophical beliefs. "There is historical truth," he wrote, "and there is such a thing as political conscience which requires that this truth be served. Truth cannot be falsified for long, because there is nothing more irrevocable than facts. Always remember that our conscience is clear, that it is not tarnished in any way in respect to the working people of Germany. It is not burdened by any war crimes, by predatory imperialist policy, by tyranny, terrorism, dictatorship, coercion of anybody's mind, infringements on the freedom of others or by abuse, by quasi-socialism and fascist racial theories, by Rosenbergian philosophising, arrogance, haughtiness, boasting, etc. We are untarnished."

Thälmann had every reason to be proud of his Party, whose traditions the Communists of West Germany cherish today and which inspire the workers of the German Democratic Republic who are building the new, socialist society. At all times, in success and in failure, Thälmann checked and re-checked his own and his Party's course, the better to see the way ahead. "To be sure," he wrote in his cell, "we are not blameless angels either. We have also committed big, sometimes even grave, political blunders. Regrettably, we have overlooked and left in abeyance some of the things that had to be done ... to block the nazi rise to power."

Acknowledgement of blunders cleared the path for fresh effort. The anti-fascists made staggering sacrifices. In 1944 alone the Gestapo seized about half a million people. The anti-fascist front of the "other Germany" was politically broad. The Communist Party, which charted strategy and tactics at its Brussels and Berne conferences, stood in the van. Yet the names of Communists stand alongside those of Social-Democrats, Christians, many tens of thousands of workers, students and intellectuals who all did their bit for the anti-fascist cause. A group of genuinely anti-fascist patriots was also involved in the July 20 plot. The head of this group, Colonel Claus Schenk von Stauffenberg, and the members of the Kreisau circle (Graf Helmuth von Moltke, Adam von Trott zu Solz, etc.), sought contacts with the democratic anti-fascist and anti-militarist forces of the nation.

Today, two Germanys exist. One acts on the long-standing democratic anti-militarist traditions in ideology, historiography and the struggle for the future of the German nation. But traditions have a way of disregarding frontiers. They are alive also in the Federal Republic, where they rouse people to the dangers implicit in the aggressive, revisionist and militarist course pushed forward under the anti-communist banner.

The understanding of this peril has not yet penetrated into the thick of the masses, but has already come into evidence in various ways and, above all, as a reawakening of political realism. People are coming to understand that the anti-communist ideology combined with the strategic "sword and shield" conception is a battering-ram in the hands of the West German militarists, who are using it in their efforts to get a front seat at the control board of atomic war. Sooner or later, the facts and lessons of history will reveal to the people of the Federal Republic that their co-existence with the aggressive militarist forces imperils the German nation to the point of disaster and that nothing save the peaceful coexistence of states with different socio-economic systems will reconcile the two German states and secure peaceful development for the people of Germany, of Europe, of the world. The far-reaching changes in the contemporary world, the realities of our age, offer for the first time in history the optimistic possibility of averting a new world-wide conflagration and securing peace.

Briefly, the choice is between peaceful coexistence and nuclear disaster. It is a choice we have to reckon with by virtue of the terrible consequences anti-communist policy wrought on the eve of the Second World War and of the stains of blood German militarism has already left on the chronicle of the 20th century. One can only regret that this choice is not the figment of an imagination inclined to minimise one set of facts, that has already become past history, in order to exaggerate another that belongs to the hypothetical future. No, it is a bitter but unavoidable choice fraught with untold dangers in our nuclear age. It has got to be apprehended in the historical context and the comprehension of it has got to be politically active, not contemplative, denuding the dialectical core of the multiformity and complexity of current developments. This will help to appreciate the lessons of the past in the present for the sake of a peaceful future.

In this sense, historical thinking is never focused on remote ages or past decades to the exclusion of the present. The historian is a child of his times and cannot as he studies the distant or recent past divest himself of responsibility, moral as well as professional, for the present and future. No matter how modest his contribution, he cannot confine himself to merely recapitulating events. His labours must be at least a drop in the general current of life and struggle known as history and modernity.

Need it be said that creative Marxism-Leninism has always been, and always will be, the historian's compass. Just as Karl Marx had, in writing *Capital*, studied the history and economy of Britain, which he regarded as the home of the most clearly delineated mature capitalism, so did Lenin, in writing *Imperialism, the Highest Stage of Capitalism*, study the economic and political features and peculiarities of German imperialism for identical reasons.

His *Notebooks on Imperialism* offer the historian a welcome glimpse of Lenin's creative laboratory, of some of the aspects of the methodology he employed in studying imperialism in general and its German variety in particular.

Now that this book, written in the course of nearly a lifetime, is completed, the writer is most acutely conscious of its many oversights and omissions. What is more, if there were time, he would write it all over again. This is natural. Science, like life, is motion, and the science of history is no exception to the rule.

August 1964

Part One

"WELTPOLITIK"—
ROAD TO WAR AND DEFEAT

GERMAN FOREIGN POLICY
AT THE BEGINNING OF THE TWENTIETH CENTURY

(Problems and Sources)

Our contemporary will hardly picture the unjustified optimism and unbridled self-applause the ruling classes in the principal capitalist countries lavished upon themselves as they prepared to welcome in the 20th century. The industrial boom generated the most radiant hopes. The World's Fair, opening in Paris in 1900, would, it seemed, mark the beginning of a new era of capitalist prosperity. The declarations signed in The Hague by a 26-nation conference on the "laws and customs of war on land" inspired the bourgeois press to hold forth on the possibility of collective efforts buttressing peace. But it was all a magnificent illusion. The Hague declarations did not prevent U.S. imperialism from gaining a foothold in Cuba and completing the seizure of the Philippines, a strategic outpost at China's front door, while the British imperialists started a war against the Boer republics in South Africa and the German imperialists took possession of the Caroline and Marshall islands and a slice of Samoa, launched an expansion scheme in Turkey and China, and drew up a new naval programme. Neither did they prevent the French imperialists from redoubling their efforts in Africa and Indo-China, and the Russian imperialists from setting their sights on Manchuria, while the Japanese tightened their hold on Korea, enhanced their influence at the court in Peking and began priming for a war with Russia. The principal imperialist powers were hell-bent on completing the economic and political division of the world while already poised for a violent redivision. No major power, non-European as well as European, was willing to act the indifferent onlooker. All were immersed in the arms race.

Yet bourgeois historians, journalists and political writers trumpeted far and wide that the peace efforts of the capitalist powers had succeeded, for no military conflicts had shaken Europe in the thirty years since the Franco-Prussian war. Not surprisingly, each of the powers claimed credit for this. The zealous ideologists of German imperialism created the legend that Europe owed its peace to the increasing military strength and active foreign policy of the German empire—a legend later brilliantly exposed by Lenin, who demonstrated in his study of the laws governing world history during the emergence and development of imperialism that the relative peace in Europe was due most of all to the ceaseless wars in the colonial territories.[1]

The events at the turn of the century bore no resemblance to the idyllic picture painted by the bourgeois ideologists. The contention that the peace efforts of the principal capitalist powers were bearing fruit, stridently advertised during The Hague conference (not only by pacifists), was exploited by the powers for entirely different ends. When the U.S. imperialists, for example, precipitated a war over Cuba and the Philippines, German diplomacy used peace as a pretext to try and organise collective action to stave off the U.S. aggression. That it was unsuccessful is a different matter. The Spanish-American war created a complex welter of imperialist contradictions and made a collective intervention by the European powers unthinkable. Furthermore, it was soon obvious that the German imperialists, the promoters of the scheme, were least interested in salvaging the peace and much more in using the collective effort to wrest from the United States territorial concessions at the expense of Spanish colonies.

They got what they wanted, and certainly not by intervening in behalf of peace, but by warlike threats and demonstrations of German naval strength.[2]

The idea of a diplomatic intervention against the Boer War collapsed just as ignominiously. When the British imperialists began preparing for the war, no other imperial-

---

[1] See Lenin, *Collected Works*, Vol. 24, p. 401.

[2] See A. S. Yerusalimsky, *Vneshnauga politika i diplomatiya germanskogo imperializma v kontse XIX veka*, Moscow, 1951, pp. 459-78 (Russ. ed.).

ist power stirred a finger. What each of them wanted was to create additional difficulties for Britain and extract therefrom certain economic and political advantages. The only major European power that did not wish its British rival to swallow the Boer republics with their gold and diamond mines, was Germany. Influential German financial groups associated with the Deutsche Bank and the Disconto Gesellschaft were themselves casting a greedy eye on the Boer republics and tried at first to discourage the British aggression. But British finance capital, notably the Rothschilds, Joseph Chamberlain and Cecil Rhodes, offered the Deutsche Bank financial and diplomatic support in the Middle East (the Baghdad railway project, etc.) on the condition that the powerful German alignment abandon the Boers to their fate. The Pan-Germanic Union, which had for years peddled racist ideologies and plans of a German South Africa, campaigned against the government's "betrayal" of "blood-brothers", but did it half-heartedly and uninspiringly. Not until 1900, when Boer resistance created grave military and political difficulties for the British, did it become somewhat livelier.

Not content with London's support of their economic expansion in Turkey, the German imperialists wanted to take advantage of their British rival's difficulties and step up expansion elsewhere, notably in China. Britain's other rivals, such as France and especially tsarist Russia, were also itching to exploit her difficulties, each in her own interest. Nicholas II indulged himself in the notion that he held the keys to the whole international situation. He went to the length of secretly planning how he would mass his troops in Central Asia and challenge Britain's colonial power.[1] Obtuse though he was, he realised in time, however, that he lacked the essentials—troops, money, communications and transport, and the assurance that other powers would take his side. German diplomacy alone goaded him on, for Germany's rulers and monopoly press, who had candidly proclaimed the *Drang nach Osten* policy and dreamed of penetrating into Asia Minor up to the Persian Gulf, believed that tension between Britain and Russia would benefit them more even than the Boer War.

---

[1] See *Krasny arkhiv*, 1934, Vol. 2 (63), p. 125, "Letter of Nicholas II, Nov. 2 (Oct. 21), 1899" (Russ. ed.).

Nicholas II, for his part, endeavoured to set Kaiser Germany on Britain.[1] But German diplomacy suddenly decided to revert to the idea of collective efforts in behalf of peace in South Africa, hoping to create additional difficulties for Britain and exact fresh tribute from her in the way of colonial plunder. Undercover negotiations were begun with the governments of tsarist Russia and France. The delicate parleys were conducted with the utmost caution, for the conferees did not trust each other, expecting their partners to betray them and put them at odds with Britain, whose financial and naval power, coupled with her diplomatic weight in world politics, were still rated rather highly. In the end, however, word of the negotiations did reach the British, and German diplomacy attempted in abject cowardice to shift the blame for the talks on the Russian tsar, who, for his part, blamed them on the Kaiser. So the new attempt at diplomatic intervention also proved unsuccessful.

In the meantime, a world economic crisis broke out. It began in 1900 in Russia and spread gradually to most of the West European countries, primarily Germany. Its effects were felt instantly in two associated directions: first, it stimulated concentration of capital and growth of monopolies and, second, it whetted the expansionist ambitions of the powers.

When the twentieth century came and the old "free" capitalism gave way to monopoly capitalism, the imperialist contradictions which grew precipitously and enmeshed the whole world, created the danger of a world war. German imperialism swelled into the most powerful expansionist force with a big stake in a redivision of the world.

For our generation the story of German imperialism is, above all, a story of expansionism and of the two world wars it has unleashed. The importance of knowing the foreign policy and diplomacy of the German imperialists in the various historical phases is, therefore, self-evident. It has attracted the interest of historians in the Soviet Union,[2]

---

[1] See B. A. Romanov, *Ocherki diplomaticheskoi istorii russko-yaponskoy voiny, 1895-1907*, Moscow-Leningrad, 1955, p. 116 (Russ. ed.).

[2] Valuable Soviet studies are available, which outline in general form the history of the foreign policy and diplomacy of German imperialism in the early 20th century. See Y. V. Tarle, "Yevropa v epokhu imperializma", *Works*, Vol. V, Moscow, 1958 (Russ. ed.); V. M. Khvostov, *Istoriya diplomatii*, Vol. II, Moscow, 1963 (Russ. ed.);

the German Democratic Republic[1] and elsewhere.[2]

The subject has many aspects and an extensive specifically historical content. I should like to show how the investigator is impelled to search for new as yet untapped sources, and how, on the other hand, his scrutiny of such new sources of diverse origin compels him to deal with problems transcending the traditional notions of this most important phase in the history of German imperialism and militarism.

The traditional notions are limited in general terms to the following—the "Bülow era", the era of the "policy of unifying" the Junkerdom and the bourgeoisie, and the naval development programme. This, in the field of German home policy, and in the field of foreign policy, the 1900 Anglo-German agreement on spheres of influence in China, the Anglo-German negotiations of an alliance against Russia in 1901, Germany's penetration into Turkey and culmination of talks concerning a Baghdad railway concession, German diplomacy during the Russo-Japanese war.

Mezhdunarodniye otnosheniya na Dalnem Vostoke (1840-1949), ed. Y. M. Zhukov, Moscow, 1956 (Russ. ed.). An interesting paper by I. Goldstein and R. Levina, *Germansky imperializm* (Moscow, 1947, Russ. ed.), probes the socio-economic peculiarities of German imperialism. In addition, G. V. Yefimov, *Vneshnaya politika Kitaya 1894-1899,* Moscow, 1958 (Russ. ed.); G. L. Bondarevsky, *Bagdadskaya doroga i proniknoveniye germanskogo imperializma na Blizhny Vostok (1888-1903),* Tashkent, 1955 (Russ. ed.); B. A. Romanov, *Ocherki diplomaticheskoi istorii russko-yaponskoi voiny, 1895-1907,* Moscow-Leningrad, 1955 (Russ. ed.); Y. I. Rubinstein, *Politika germanskogo imperializma v zapadnykh polskikh zemlyakh v kontse XIX-nachale XX v.,* Moscow, 1953 (Russ. ed.). Concerning the anti-imperialist struggle of the German working class see B. A. Aizin, *Podyom rabochego dvizheniya v Germanii v nachale XX veka (1903-1906),* Moscow, 1954 (Russ. ed.); B. A. Aizin, "Borba Karla Libknekhta protiv militarizma v nachale XX veka (1903-1907)" in the collection *Imperializm i borba rabochego klassa,* Moscow, 1960 (Russ. ed.).

[1] See A. Schreiner, *Zur Geschichte der deutschen Aussenpolitik 1871-1945,* Bd. I, Berlin, 1952; J. Kuczynski, *Studien zur Geschichte des deutschen Imperialismus,* Bd. I-II, Berlin, 1950-52; V. Markov, L. Ratman, "Proniknoveniye germanskikh monopoly v Yegipet" in the collection *Imperializm i borba rabochego klassa,* Moscow, 1960 (Russ. ed.); H. Stoecker, *Deutschland und China im XIX. Jahrhundert,* Berlin, 1958; G. Heidorn, *Monopole-Presse-Krieg. Die Rolle der Presse bei der Vorbereitung des 1. Weltkrieges,* Berlin, 1960.

[2] G. Badia, *Histoire de l'Allemagne contemporaine (1917-1962),* t. 1, 1917-33; t. 2, 1933-62; Paris, 1962. Interesting observations occur in A. Taylor's *The Struggle for Mastery in Europe. 1848-1918,* Oxford-Toronto, 1955.

Anglo-German naval rivalry, beginning of the "policy of encircling" Germany, the Moroccan crisis, and the emergence of the Entente as a major setback for Germany's policy of exploiting the contradictions between her rivals—Britain, France and Russia.

These traditional themes, which German bourgeois historiography[1] refuses to transcend, dealing with issues of foreign policy and diplomacy in isolation from questions of economic history, the class struggle and domestic policy, have their origin firstly in the German bourgeois historians' desire to obscure the true goals of the "national" foreign policy, especially the mechanics of the growing influence of the German and international monopolies, and also the resistance to this mechanism of the other socio-economic and political forces, and, secondly, in the fact that *Die Grosse Politik der Europäischen Kabinette 1871-1914*, the chief source of bourgeois investigations, is a collection of exclusively diplomatic documents.[2] German bourgeois historians were in a somewhat conflicting situation. Though they portrayed Germany's foreign policy at the beginning of the 20th century as "world politics", they reduced it in effect to European and Asia Minor politics, dealing with the Far East and the Moroccan questions only insofar as these affected the situation of the German empire in Europe. This extended "Europocentrism" had its roots in German militarism, which harped doggedly on *Weltpolitik*, that is, German world domination achieved by war in Europe.

---

[1] See E. Brandenburg, *Von Bismarck zum Weltkriege*, Berlin, 1924; J. Haller, *Die Ära Bülow. Eine historisch-politische Studie*, Stuttgart-Berlin, 1922; F. Hartung, *Deutsche Geschichte vom Frankfurter Frieden bis zum Vertrag von Versailles, 1871-1919*, Bonn-Leipzig, 1924; E. Reventlow, *Deutschlands Auswärtige Politik 1888-1914*, Berlin, 1918; J. Ziekursch, *Politische Geschichte des neuen deutschen Kaiserreiches*, Bd. 3, Frankfurt a/M, 1930; H. Oncken, *Das Deutsche Reich und die Vorgeschichte des Weltkrieges*, Bd. I-II, Leipzig, 1933; H. Lohmeyer, *Die Politik des Zweiten Reiches 1871-1918*, Bd. I-II, Berlin, 1939; W. Schüssler, *Deutschland zwischen Russland und England*, Leipzig, 1940; E. Eyck, *Das persönliche Regiment Wilhelms II. Politische Geschichte des deutschen Kaiserreiches von 1890 bis 1914*, Erlenbach-Zürich, 1947; F. Haselmayer, *Diplomatische Geschichte des Zweiten Reiches von 1871-1918*, Bd. I-V, München, 1955-62. Among the latest works whitewashing militarism in Kaiser Germany see G. Pitter, *Staatskunst und Kriegshandwerk. Das Problem des "Militarismus" in Deutschland*, Bd. I, II, München, 1954-60.

[2] See below, "The Versailles Thesis and Its Revision".

Bourgeois historians (pre- and post-war) leave the subject of the subsurface processes of German expansion and the motive powers behind Germany's imperialist foreign policy and diplomacy well enough alone. Friedrich Meinecke, one of the stalwarts of German historiography, it is true, once endeavoured to define the problem. "Everything was closely interrelated," he wrote, "export industrialism, naval building, the Tirpitz naval laws and the unification policy designed to unite employers in town and country against the proletariat and gain support for the naval armament plan, making the state a servant of their interest [the Junkerdom and the bourgeoisie.—*A. Y.*], thus accentuating the social division of the nation."[1]

However, German bourgeois historiography did not go a step farther than this general formula. G. W. F. Hallgarten[2] in *Imperialismus vor 1914* and E. Kehr in *Schlachtflottenbau und Parteipolitik* endeavoured to break out of the vicious circle in a bid to bare the "sociological basis" of imperialist foreign policy, Germany's in particular. Their investigations, which embrace considerable historico-economic data, are of unquestionable interest but lack the vitality of Lenin's theory of imperialism. Although Hallgarten, whose work merits the closest attention, referred favourably to my work, *Vneshnaya politika i diplomatiya germanskogo imperializma v kontse XIX veka (The Foreign Policy and Diplomacy of German Imperialism at the End of the Nineteenth Century)*[3], and although Renouvin[4] maintained in his paper at the 10th International Congress of Historians in Rome that both our works are contiguous and represent a new trend, I am inclined to think that they are essentially different not only in presentation but above all in approach to the basic problem of imperialism and the influence exerted by the class struggle in the metropolitan country and the national liberation struggle of the colonial peoples on the foreign policy and diplomacy of the German imperialism.

---

[1] F. Meinecke, *Geschichte des deutsch-englischen Bündnisproblems 1890 bis 1901*, München-Berlin, 1927, S. 6.

[2] G. W. F. Hallgarten, *Imperialismus vor 1914. Soziologische Darstellung der deutschen Aussenpolitik bis zum ersten Weltkrieg*, Bd. I-II, München, 1951; E. Kehr, *Schlachtflottenbau und Parteipolitik 1894-1901, Berlin*, 1930.

[3] Hallgarten, op. cit.

[4] See *Voprosy istorii* No. 7, 1956, pp. 207-08 (Russ. ed.).

A Soviet historian who sets out to describe German foreign policy and show German diplomacy in action on key issues of inter-state relations, particularly its role and methods in provoking European crises, has more than enough concrete historical material to go by—the voluminous *Staatsarchiv*, the volumes of *Die Grosse Politik der Europäischen Kabinette*, *British Documents*, *Documents diplomatiques français*, *Krasny arkhiv*, a vast number of memoirs, the numerous investigations and, last but not least, the wealth of material in the Archive of Russian Foreign Policy at the Foreign Ministry of the U.S.S.R. Interesting details and additional information are also available in the recently published personal archive of Friedrich von Holstein,[1] the Grey Eminence of the German diplomatic school who had helped topple Bismarck and pursued a "pendulum" policy between Russia and Britain.

Critically and discerningly used, these sources provide an idea of the devious roads and by-roads of German foreign policy and diplomacy at the end of the 19th and in the early 20th centuries up to the outbreak of the First World War. They should make the background for an exposition of the influence exercised on foreign policy by Junker and bourgeois imperialism—the various groups of the financial oligarchy, the industrial monopolies and the Junkerdom—and reveal the inner mechanics of the struggle of classes and parties over matters of foreign and colonial policy.

It seems to me that a simultaneous synchronised examination of German domestic policy and the class struggle, the foreign policy and diplomacy of German imperialism in association with its colonial policy and that of other imperialist powers, offers a number of advantages. Firstly, it enables the investigator to unfurl the historic panorama. Secondly, the historian is then able to examine the domestic and foreign policy in close association with the general system of states, which, never stabile, is in constant flux.[2] Thirdly, it brings out in bold relief the uneven development of capitalism from country to country, one of the principal laws most distinctly visible in the period of capitalism's

---

[1] F. v. Holstein, *Die geheimen Papiere Friedrich von Holsteins*, Bd. I-IV, Göttingen-Berlin-Frankfurt a/M, 1957-63; G. W. F. Hallgarten, "Fritz von Holsteins Geheimnis. Neues Licht auf die Lebensgeschichte der 'Grauen Eminenz'", *Historische Zeitschrift*, 1954, Bd. 177, S. 75-83.
[2] Lenin, *Collected Works*, Vol. 24, p. 401; Vol. 35, p. 264.

entry into the imperialist stage.[1] The problems of German foreign policy and diplomacy in the early 20th century are, in a way, the same as those of the preceding years, but contain many new elements both in the theoretical and the concrete historical contexts. Not the change of chancellors —the resignation of Hohenlohe and advent of Bülow—but the world economic crisis of 1900-03 should be the point of departure in our study.

The crisis, which followed different paths from country to country, had far-reaching consequences. Its economic aspect has been examined exhaustively.[2] But, as Lenin put it, it occurred "entirely ... within a cartel economy",[3] particularly so in Germany, and had tremendous domestic and international political consequences. To probe the deep interconnections, it is therefore essential to invoke sources of different origins.

The economic and political influence of the monopolies is a highly important problem and I considered it pertinent to locate material about the history of the German banks, cartels and trusts, the war concerns like Krupp's, the German Union of Industrialists, the Union of Landholders and the various colonial organisations, which exerted a tremendous influence on the policy of the German government. The documents I needed were discovered partly in the Central German Archive in Potsdam, partly in the former Prussian Archive in Merseburg and partly in the collections of the German Economic Institute in Berlin, where, by the way, I found some of the papers of the Deutsche Bank. Cumulatively, these materials bear out Lenin, who said the monopolies gained a bigger, essentially new role at the time of the 1900-03 crisis. They also reveal the immense and direct influence of the Junkerdom and the monopolies on the internal policies of the state,[4] especially in respect to

---

[1] See A. S. Yerusalimsky, *Vneshnaya politika i diplomatiya germanskogo imperializma v kontse XIX veka*, p. 555 (Russ. ed.).

[2] *Miroviye ekonomicheskiye krizisy 1848-1935*, Vol. 1, ed. Y. Varga, 1937 (Russ. ed.); I. Trakhtenberg, *Denezhniye krizisy (1821-1938)*, Moscow, 1939 (Russ. ed.); L. A. Mendelson, *Teoriya i istoriya ekonomicheskikh krizisov i tsyklov*, Vol. 1-3, Moscow, 1959-64 (Russ. ed.).

[3] Lenin, *Collected Works*, Vol. 39, p. 72.

[4] See DZA Potsdam, *Akten der Reichskanzlei betreffend die Mittellandskanale*; DZA Merseburg, *Staatsministerium, Sitzungsprotokolle; Die Polenpolitik; Zolltarifberatungen*, etc.

the working class[1] and to the Polish problem, as well as their influence on foreign policy directly and indirectly through the bourgeois and Junker parties inside and outside the Reichstag.[2] Besides they reveal the influence exerted on the press inside and outside Germany.[3]

Of special interest is the political role of the Pan-Germanic Union, the ideological headquarters of the more aggressive German imperialist elements. Bourgeois literature tends to distort the issue.[4] The *Alldeutsche Blätter*, the principal mouthpiece of the Union, its pamphlets and archives, enable the Marxist investigator to substantiate the connection between the Union and the big monopolies, the leadership of the bourgeois and Junker parties and certain government quarters. This is important, because it reveals the specific content of the imperialist *Mitteleuropa* concept,[5] and even more so because it exposes the far-reaching expansionist designs of the German imperialists in Europe and on other continents.

Archive material enables the investigator to outline more specifically the struggles within the ruling class—between the Junkers, who held the key posts in the government and army, and the bourgeoisie, between the various groups of the financial oligarchy, and between individual monopo-

---

[1] DZA Potsdam, *Akten der Reichskanzlei betreffend Sozialdemokraten.*

[2] West German historians are obviously tendentious on this score. See O. E. Schüddekopf, *Die deutsche Innenpolitik im letzten Jahrhundert und der konservative Gedanke. Die Zusammenhänge zwischen Aussenpolitik, innerer Staatsführung und Parteigeschichte, dargestellt an der Geschichte der Konservativen Partei von 1807 bis 1918*, Braunschweig, 1951; K. Buchheim, *Geschichte der christlichen Parteien in Deutschland*, München, 1953.

[3] See G. Heidorn, *Monopole-Presse-Krieg. Die Rolle der Presse bei der Vorbereitung des 1. Weltkrieges*, Berlin, 1960; P. R. Anderson, *The Background of Anti-English Feeling in Germany. 1890-1902*, Washington, 1939; E. M. Carrol, *Germany and the Great Powers. 1866-1914. A Study in Public Opinion and Foreign Policy*, New York, 1938; O. J. Hale, *Publicity and Diplomacy. With Special Reference to England and Germany, 1890-1914*, New York-London, 1940.

[4] See L. Werner, *Der Alldeutsche Verband 1890-1918*, Berlin, 1935; A. Kruck, *Geschichte des Alldeutschen Verbandes 1890-1939*, Wiesbaden, 1954.

[5] See H. C. Meyer, *Mitteleuropa in German Thought and Action 1815-1945*, The Hague, 1955; J. Pajewski, *Mitteleuropa*, Poznań, 1959.

lies and groups of monopolies that made their appearance in certain branches of industry (e.g., coal, steel, shipbuilding). It reveals the substance of the so-called *Sammlungspolitik*, a reactionary policy of "unifying" the bourgeoisie and Junkerdom for joint action against the working class and the Social-Democratic Party, promoting militarism,[1] carrying through mammoth naval arming[2] and aggressive foreign policy. The voluminous minutes of the German Reichstag[3] and the Potsdam and Merseburg archives, particularly the unpublished minutes of the Prussian Ministry, give a fairly conclusive picture of the realignment of Junker and bourgeois parties,[4] the struggle between and within them over the further growth of militarism,[5] particularly the building of a navy,[6] and over other aspects of their *Weltpolitik*.

No less important is it that the above sources illustrate the expansion of German finance capital. Not always did German capital operate under the flag of its own state; it takes a detailed study to reveal under what signboard it acted—that of, say, a British financial institution or even under the cosmopolitan guise of an international monopoly —while beating the propaganda drums for a *Deutschland, Deutschland über alles*. A closer look will reveal that what it held *über alles* were dividends and that it forced the government time and again, as Bülow put it, "to beat the national drums" in their behalf.

It should be stressed specially that the collision of British and German capital, a struggle between individual groups within the existing international monopolies coupled with

---

[1] See G. Craig, *The Politics of the Prussian Army. 1640-1945*, Oxford, 1955.

[2] West German historians show a renewed interest in this subject. See W. Hubatsch, *Die Ära Tirpitz, Studien zur deutschen Marinepolitik 1890-1918*, Göttingen-Berlin-Frankfurt a/M, 1955; W. Hubatsch, *Der Admiralstab und die Obersten Marinebehörden in Deutschland 1848-1945*, Frankfurt a/M, 1958; *Weltmachtstreben und Flottenbau*, Witten-Ruhr, 1956.

[3] See *Stenographische Berichte über die Verhandlungen des deutschen Reichstages*.

[4] DZA Merseburg, *Akten der Reichskanzlei betreffend politische Parteien*.

[5] DZA Potsdam, *Akten der Reichskanzlei betreffend Friedenspräsenzstärke des deutschen Heeres*.

[6] DZA Potsdam, *Akten der Reichskanzlei betreffend Flottengesetz*.

rivalry in both the principal and secondary theatres of world politics in all the continents of the world (excepting Austrialia), was the dominant imperialist antagonism in the early 20th century, which largely conditioned the general alignment of strength in the world arena. It should be borne in mind, however, that this antagonism did not develop in a straight line. Though the two world rivals kept clashing, in many cases their interests blended. This is true of both the economic sphere (international monopolies) and political sphere (combating the colonial and semi-colonial peoples), and sometimes even of the diplomatic sphere (isolating a common rival).

The fact remains, however, that the Anglo-German imperialist antagonism at the turn of the 20th century is an historical fact, and the only ones to question it are the contemporary West-oriented ideologists of German imperialism and NATO policy.[1] The way this antagonism developed casts light in many respects on the Anglo-German diplomatic negotiations of an alliance against Russia. The talks went on throughout 1901 and anteceded the Anglo-Japanese alliance of 1902. Today, even bourgeois historians no longer take seriously the formerly widespread belief that the parleys had failed due chiefly to "Holstein's big No".[2] Even Meinecke, Ritter[3] and certain other stalwarts, despite their divergent views, arrived at the conclusion that it is essential to pinpoint the objective conditions leading to the collapse of the Anglo-German alliance project and the subsequent growth of Anglo-German rivalry.

But the answer to this question should not be sought in the history of diplomacy,[4] for it is rooted in the deep-going processes that prevailed in the economic and political relations of the ruling classes of Britain and Germany, particularly those between the German and British monopolies.

---

[1] H. Aubin, "Abendland, Reich, Deutschland und Europa", *Schicksalsfragen der Gegenwart. Handbuch politisch-historischer Bildung,* Bd. I., Tübingen, 1957, S. 29 ff.

[2] E. Fischer, *Holsteins grosses Nein. Die deutsch-englischen Bündnisverhandlungen 1898-1901*, Berlin, 1925.

[3] F. Meinecke, *Geschichte des deutsch-englischen Bündnisproblems 1890-1901*, München-Berlin, 1927; G. Ritter, *Die Legende von der verschmähten englischen Freundschaft 1898-1901*, Freiburg, 1929.

[4] See O. Hauser, *Deutschland und der englisch-russische Gegensatz 1900-1904*, Göttingen, 1958.

R. J. Hoffman's[1] useful volume describes the commercial rivalry, but his account does not disclose the imperialist contradictions. E. Kehr,[2] for his part, probes the role played by the German monopolies in the growth of maritime rivalry and the political struggle over naval armament. However, his book is limited in subject matter and chronology, and by some of Kehr's methodological approaches. One ought to go farther afield in the manner outlined by Lenin in his *Notebooks on Imperialism*. Monographic investigation and study of new archive material will broaden our specific concepts of this complicated problem.

The events of 1900, when ambitions were galvanised afresh by the economic crisis and the search for ways of coping with it, show how complex the Anglo-German contradictions were, provided the problem is approached not in the general but the concrete historical context. German imperialism took advantage of the Boer War to penetrate deeper into Turkey and China, where, under the pretext of co-operation, even agreement, it endeavoured to elbow out Britain. On the excuse of combating the "yellow peril", Germany joined in the international armed intervention against the popular I-ho T'uan movement and the subsequent rape of China.[3] But who inspired the intervention? Whose interests did it serve? What immediate and long-term goals did it pursue? To obtain the answer to these questions one would first have to study other questions, such as the foothold in China of the German monopolies and their methods, aims and plans for further penetration.

This is made doubly difficult by the fact that the big German collection of diplomatic documents, in which a whole volume is devoted to the "disturbances in China",[4] goes out of its way (as has now been conclusively established) to conceal or falsify documents in order to obscure the true role played by the German imperialists and mili-

---

[1] R. J. Hoffman, *Great Britain and the German Trade Rivalry 1875-1914*, Philadelphia-London, 1933.

[2] E. Kehr, *Schlachtflottenbau und Parteipolitik 1894-1901*, Berlin, 1930.

[3] See A. S. Yerusalimsky, "Germansky imperializm i podgotovka mezhdunarodnoy interventsii v Kitaye v 1900 godu", *Narody Azii i Afriki* No. 4, 1961; "Pokhod Seymoura i yego proval", *Mezhdunarodniye otnosheniya. Politika. Diplomatiya XVI-XX vv.*, Moscow, 1964 (Russ. ed).

[4] GP, Bd. XVI, Berlin, 1927.

tarists in the rape of China.[1] I was very fortunate to have the use of new archive material, above all documents from the archives of German imperial missions and consulates in China, which I discovered in a still unarranged state in Potsdam.[2] Technically, I had my work cut out poring through them, but the sense of satisfaction I derived from the results made it worth the trouble. To begin with, I obtained a good idea of the intricate way the German monopolies penetrated into China and determined the true role of the Shantung Syndicate, behind which were the major German banks, partly connected, by the way, with British capital, as well as Krupp and other industrial tycoons. These and other materials[3] helped me to establish what groups of German finance capital were seeking, by agreement with Britain, to penetrate into the fabulously wealthy Yangtze basin. The archives of the German mission and consulates also informed me about the domestic situation (the I-ho T'uan movement, the rivalry of various groupings at the Chinese imperial court, the attitude of provincial governors, etc.). To be sure, the information they contained was insufficient, and I had had to look into Soviet archives as well—the Archive of Russian Foreign Policy at the Foreign Ministry of the U.S.S.R., the Central Archive of Military History, and in Leningrad—the Central Historical Archive and Central Naval Archive. Various historical documents published in China were also of considerable help.[4]

By and large, these sources give the investigator a good idea of the imperialist scuffle over China and of the extent to which the German monopolies penetrated into that country, the part played by the German imperialists in the diplomatic spadework preceding the international intervention in China, the part played by the German militarists and the opposition of the German working class, the German

---

[1] See F. Klein, "Über die Verfälschung der historischen Wahrheit in der Aktenpublikation 'Die Grosse Politik der Europäischen Kabinette 1871-1914'", *Zeitschrift für Geschichtswissenschaft*, 1959, Heft 2, S. 318-30; "Zur Chinapolitik des deutschen Imperialismus im Jahre 1900", *Zeitschrift für Geschichtswissenschaft*, 1960, Heft 4, S. 817-43.

[2] DZA Potsdam, *Die deutsche Gesandschaft in China.*

[3] DZA Potsdam, Auswärtiges Amt, Bd. 3533, 8466, 12976, 12991 u.a.; DZA Merseburg, Rep. 89H, Auswärtige Sachen.

[4] *I-ho T'uan tanang shi-liao*, Vol. I, Shanghai, 1959.

monopolies and the "peace" negotiations of the terms on which China was enslaved and, last but not least, China's place in the *Weltpolitik* of the German imperialists. The part played by the German monopolies in China's enslavement and their influence on the government's foreign policy and diplomacy have now therefore been exhaustively studied.

The more difficult thing was to spot the threads connecting the militarists, especially the General Staff, with the monopolies and the government. The official report on the armed expedition to China in 1900-01[1] was drawn up by the naval authorities, not the General Staff, which naturally affected its content. According to second-hand information, namely the memoirs of Colonel-General K. Einem, once the Prussian War Minister,[2] the plan of an armed expedition to China had reposed for years in the files of the General Staff and the Prussian War Ministry, waiting for a suitable occasion to be put to use. The top men in the Foreign Chancellory, too, were straining at the leash. The all-powerful Holstein, the wizard diplomat who secretly played the stock market with consummate skill (holding stocks and shares of banks with a vested interest in Chinese affairs), was in a state of flurry which Bülow likened to that of "an old warhorse that hears the bugle call".[3] By the way, Holstein was closely associated with Alfred von Schlieffen, Chief of the General Staff,[4] although the latter's part in the China intervention was still obscure. The necessary documented facts are unavailable in *Die Grosse Politik*, while the archive of the Prussian General Staff and war ministry was burned to ashes in 1945 and the files of the Foreign Chancellory, extant at Potsdam, deal solely with the technical aspects and personnel of the expedition. It is not likely, however, that the General Staff, the brain of German militarism, escaped the atmosphere of greed and adventurism that afflicted the élite of German finance capital and diplomacy.

---

[1] *Die Deutsche Marine während der Chinawirren*, Berlin, 1903.
[2] Generaloberst K. Einem, *Erinnerungen eines Soldaten 1853-1933*, Leipzig, 1934.
[3] B. v. Bülow, *Denkwürdigkeiten*, Bd. I., Berlin, 1930, S. 367.
[4] See A. S. Yerusalimsky, op. cit., p. 70; H. Lohmeyer, *Die Politik des Zweiten Reiches 1871-1918*, Bd. I, S. 220, Bd. II, S. 87; P. Rassow, "Schlieffen und Holstein", *Historische Zeitschrift*, 1952, Bd. 173, S. 297-313.

"If we want to be honest with ourselves," General Moltke confessed in a letter to his wife, "it was greed that made us cut into the big Chinese pie. We want to make money, build railways, found mining companies and be the bearers of European culture. All this is encompassed by the one word enrichment. We are no better in this sense than the British in Transvaal."[1] However, this did not prevent the future Chief of the General Staff from being annoyed when someone else was chosen to head the armed expedition. Field-Marshal Alfred von Waldersee, a former Chief of the General Staff, left a stain of blood on China's history. This is common knowledge. But what only few people know is that his three-volume memoirs[2] appeared in print with considerable deletions and that the war contribution Waldersee was charged to wrest from China was to finance the building of a German navy, the instrument for winning world domination, just as the earlier contribution by France had financed the army. What still fewer people know is the part played in all this by General Schlieffen, then Chief of General Staff and still the idol of the militarists.[3]

Our searches in German archives were in vain. All we found out, and this only indirectly, was that General Schlieffen had met Count Nostitz, the Russian military agent in Berlin, at the time of the China intervention. This prompted us to continue our search in the Central Archive of Military History in Moscow, where we finally discovered Schlieffen's personal letters forwarded by Nostitz to the Russian General Staff. These revealed that Schlieffen, who was hatching plans for a war on two fronts against France and Russia, was also involved in organising the armed intervention in China. They also revealed that despite the growing contradictions between Russian and German militarists, they were invariably willing to co-operate in crushing a national liberation movement.

The national liberation movement of colonial and semi-colonial peoples has to be dealt with independently. This

---

[1] H. v. Moltke, *Erinnerungen, Briefe, Dokumente 1877-1916*, Stuttgart, 1922.
[2] Waldersee, *Denkwürdigkeiten*, Hrsg. v. H. O. Meisner, Bd. I-III, Stuttgart-Berlin, 1923-25.
[3] G. Ritter, *Der Schlieffen-Plan. Kritik eines Mythos*, München, 1956.

holds true not only in China's case, but also in that of other areas of German monopoly expansion.

A close look at the specific forms and trends of this expansion will show that the *Weltpolitik* idea was much more than a clarion call or programme for the future. It had concrete content and a real foundation already at the beginning of the century. This applies primarily to German economic, political and military influence in Turkey and the rest of Asia Minor, especially in connection with the Baghdad railway project.[1] The plans of a German empire in South Africa or South America, outlined at length in *Alldeutsche Blätter*, the mouthpiece of the Pan-Germanic Union,[2] may sound like the raving of maniacs, and doubly so since the official collection of diplomatic documents gives no indication of German policy in these regions. But a closer glance at the German archives is very revealing. While pushing into China, the Balkans and Asia Minor, and also into Morocco and partly into other North African countries, the German monopolies had "support points" in South Africa and Latin America as well.

This applies not only to the possessions Germany had seized in Africa at the close of the 19th century, but to some degree to the colonial possessions of Britain and Portugal. Newly discovered documents indicate that influential German capitalist groups acting in concert with the Pan-Germanic Union, had far-reaching plans in South Africa. They were highly active there after the Boer War ended.[3] This explains, among other things, their behaviour in Portuguese Angola, which they hoped to share with Britain. Thus, new knot of Anglo-German antagonism appeared in the area, though less distinctly than in North Africa (Morocco).[4]

In Morocco the German imperialists had to reckon with Britain and France, who brought to bear every possible

---

[1] Archive of Russian Foreign Policy, f. Kantselaria, doc. 17, 27, 38, etc., f. Politarkhiv, doc. 231, etc.; DZA Potsdam, Auswärtiges Amt. *Akten betreffend die Beteiligung deutschen Kapitals bei der Orientei-senbahn und die wirtschaftliche Bedeutung Kleinasiens.*

[2] See *Alldeutsche Blätter*, 1898, 1899, 1900.

[3] DZA Potsdam, *Reichskanzlei. Südwestafrika 1905-07*; Auswärtiges Amt, Bd. 5342. *Handelsverhältnisse mit den britischen Besitzungen in Südafrika.*

[4] DZA Potsdam, Reichskanzlei. *Akten betreffend Flottengesetz. Kriegsmarine.*

financial and diplomatic pressure and finally achieved Germany's isolation at the international conference in Algeciras.[1] In South Africa they were resisted by the colonial peoples, whose rising impaired German prestige throughout the African continent. The papers concerning the heroic uprising of the Hereros found in German archives[2] are no credit to German colonialism inspired by influential German monopolies and the *Kolonialgesellschaft*. They show the effective resistance oppressed peoples, even the most backward, are able to marshal. The African peoples fought with stirring courage at the beginning of the century against inhuman exploitation and oppression. These developments shed light on the relations that prevailed then between Britain and Germany in Africa, both northern and southern.

Latin America was the other coveted prize at the beginning of the 20th century. The Venezuelan crisis of 1902, precipitated by the decision of the German monopolies to get their dividends and interest on loans by means of an armed intervention, was no casual or local occurrence. The fact that only one naval training vessel was despatched to the Venezuelan shore is no reason to underrate the far-reaching plans nurtured at the time by the German imperialists. The place of the Venezuelan crisis in history will be clearer to us if we examine its causes and effects in association with Germany's general policy towards Britain, the United States and the Latin American countries. A. Vagts's ponderous, all but unreadable, fact-rich investigation studies German-American relations chiefly in the economic context. Accordingly, he relies most of all on the economic press and on Congress and Reichstag minutes.[3] Soviet and German archives yield additional facts, leading to more profound conclusions on political issues as well. Sources show that in prompting the German Government and its diplomats to provoke the Venezuelan crisis[4], the big German firms, banks and monopolies were impelled by the ambition to penetrate also into other

---

[1] See further, "Diplomatic Preparations for World War 1914-1918".
[2] DZA Potsdam, Auswärtiges Amt. *Kolonialabteilung. Kolonialgesellschaft*; Reichskanzlei: *Akten betreffend militärische Expedition nach Südwestafrika*; Reichskanzlei. *Südwestafrika*.
[3] A. Vagts, *Deutschland und die Vereinigten Staaten in der Weltpolitik*, Bd. I-II, London, 1935.
[4] Archive of Russian Foreign Policy, f. Kantselariya, doc. 14; Central Historical Archive in Leningrad, f. 40, file 1, doc. 89.

Latin American countries, above all Argentina, Brazil and even Mexico.[1] The expansion took unique forms. In some cases, reluctant to act openly, the German monopolies worked through international monopolies, with the support of British and United States monopolies, or against them. The struggle between them, and within them, obviously had a bearing on Anglo-German and German-American relations and contradictions, whose economic and political implications were not confined to Latin America alone. This gives a new historical dimension to the problem, and since our interest here is focused on the main imperialist contradiction of the early 20th century, that between Britain and Germany, we cannot but relegate the German-American relations of the time to the background, thus simplifying the problem of the origin of the First World War, which is tied up closely not only with the problem of political alliances, but also with that of the economic division of the world. Lenin wrote: "The epoch of the latest stage of capitalism shows us that certain relations between capitalist associations grow up, *based* on the economic division of the world; while parallel to and in connection with it, certain relations grow up between political alliances, between states, on the basis of the territorial division of the world, of the struggle for colonies, of the 'struggle for spheres of influence'."[2]

Lenin attached the utmost importance to this problem. His interest was not merely historical, it was also theoretical. In *Imperialism, the Highest Stage of Capitalism* he quoted the following example of how growing concentration of capital led up to the division of the world by the biggest international shipping monopoly:

"In Germany two powerful companies have come to the fore: the Hamburg-Amerika and the Norddeutscher Lloyd, each having a capital of 200 million marks.... On the other hand, in America, on January 1, 1903, the International Mercantile Marine Co., known as the Morgan trust, was formed; it united nine American and British steamship companies.... As early as 1903, the German giants and this American-British trust concluded an agreement to divide the world with a consequent division of profits. The German

---

[1] DZA Potsdam, Auswärtiges Amt, Bd. 21, No. 8462.
[2] Lenin, *Collected Works*, Vol. 22, p. 253.

companies undertook not to compete in the Anglo-American traffic. Which ports were to be 'allotted' to each was precisely stipulated; a joint committee of control was set up, etc. . . .

"International cartels show to what point capitalist monopolies have developed, and the *object* of the struggle between the various capitalist associations. This last circumstance is the most important; it alone shows us the historico-economic meaning of what is taking place; for the *forms* of the struggle may and do constantly change ... but the *substance* of the struggle, its class *content*, positively *cannot* change while classes exist."[1]

When we began our study of the German-American relations of the early 20th century, we were naturally hoping to discover documents shedding light on the history of this first major international monopoly, which, as Lenin demonstrated, was so very influential. Our long search was successful.[2] The documents we found bear out the existence of an international agreement between the major German and American monopolies on shipping in the Atlantic and, much more, its general appraisal by Lenin as a typical product of the imperialist struggle. The documents also add to our knowledge in the chronological plane and as regards intrinsic content. They show that negotiations of the agreement concluded in 1903 had begun in 1901. They reveal differences not only between the German group and Morgan's American group, but also within the German group between the Hamburg-America Line and the North-German Lloyd. They prove that the Kaiser, the German Government and German diplomacy participated in this monopoly deal and that the campaign against the "American menace" in the German press was inspired by the government and the German monopolies.

Whatever we may think in the economic context of the establishment of the big German-American monopoly, which also involved British capital, there are at least two important conclusions to be drawn. First, the Morgan-Ballin monopoly referred to by Lenin was not the only one in existence at the time; German archives reveal that other

[1] Lenin, *Collected Works*, Vol. 22, pp. 251, 253.
[2] DZA Potsdam, Auswärtiges Amt. Plan des Pierpont Morgan, Bd. I-X.

international monopolies were formed, dissolved, and re-
formed early in the century and that German capital
meant to use them to break into the U.S. financial market,
while American capital hoped to invade Germany. This
gave rise to a serious economic and political reaction inside
Germany. The agrarians were naturally opposed to any
expansion of U.S. farming and raised many new issues in
foreign trade (accent on protectionism, etc.). For economic
grounds, the interests of the agrarians coincided with those
of some sections of the financial oligarchy. To a certain
extent and at certain times, these seesawing combinations
of economic interest affected the struggle of classes and
parties in Germany in matters of foreign, as well as domestic
policy. The pattern of economic and political relations between the two young imperialist powers, Germany and the
United States,[1] was fast developing into an essential factor
in the general balance of world strength. This applied not
only to Europe, but also to Asia and South America.

As we see, therefore, the problem of German-American
contradictions has to be included in our overall analysis
of international relations. In our opinion the general set of
problems relating to the origins of the world war of 1914-18
should be widened, and substantially so, for the war
stemmed from antagonisms on a world scale.

This will not be a departure from the established set
of problems concerning imperialist Germany's relations
with the *European* powers—its allies Austria-Hungary and
Italy,[2] on the one hand, and such members of the hostile
military bloc as Russia and France. On the contrary, study
of all world-wide imperialist antagonisms at the beginning
of the 20th century will yield a deeper knowledge of the
historical roots of the war. It broke out on the *European*
continent, but its genesis is to be sought in imperialism's
world-wide contradictions. The imperialist blocs that
emerged in Europe at the turn of the century were brought
into being not only by European, but also by world contradictions. The problem of these military blocs is still a vital
one, politically as well as historically, and the history of the

---

[1] DZA Potsdam, Auswärtiges Amt. *Handelsverhältnisse mit den
Vereinigten Staaten von Amerika*, Bd. 70 u.a.
[2] Archive of Russian Foreign Policy, f. Kantselariya, doc. 17, 105,
106, etc.

German alignment has still to be written. It should be borne in mind that the German militarists had completed planning a war on two fronts when they began building their large navy.

On the other hand, it was precisely in the early 20th century, at the time of the Russo-Japanese war and the Russian revolution of 1905-07 that a far-reaching realignment of states occurred in the world, which, among other things, also affected Russo-German relations. The diplomatic side of these relations is amply illustrated by materials in Soviet and German archives, collections of documents, and certain investigations.[1] Materials of the Central Historical Archive in Leningrad (especially the papers of the Ministry of Trade and Industry), the Pan-Germanic Union and German organisations of industrialists offer evidence of a class struggle over the question of relations with Russia. For one thing, the history of the Russo-German commercial treaty of 1904,[2] ignored by the German collection of diplomatic documents, casts considerable light on the dialectics of the relationship between the German monopolies and the Junkerdom, on their contradictions and their community of interest in combating the German working class and carrying forward eastward expansion.

The economic and diplomatic aspects of the realignment of states in the early 20th century, particularly the flux in Russo-German relations, are not all there is to the problem. We must consider the tremendous revolutionary outbursts which affected Russia's role in the system of states. Her defeat in the Crimean War initiated a process which weakened autocratic Russia as the citadel of European reaction. The Franco-Prussian war, which culminated in the unification of the German empire and the annexation by Germany of two French provinces, Alsace and Lorraine, changed tsarist Russia's international position. It confronted Russia's rulers with the real, though not quite appreciated fact that an economically stronger militarist state had appeared on her western frontier. On the other hand, the tsarist government gained a favourable position for manoeuvre and for exploiting the Franco-German anta-

---

[1] See B. A. Romanov, *Ocherki diplomaticheskoi istorii russko-yaponskoi voiny, 1895-1907*, Moscow-Leningrad, 1955.

[2] Central Historical Archive in Leningrad, f. 40, file 1, doc. 89.

gonism for its own ends in matters of foreign policy and colonial expansion. Here is how Lenin described the situation back in 1895: "The extraordinarily favourable international position enjoyed by Russia as a result of the war of 1870, which for a long time sowed discord between Germany and France, of course only enhanced the importance of autocratic Russia as a reactionary force."[1] Tsarism thrived on the hostility of France and Germany, which brought Europe to the brink of war more than once in the seventies and eighties. But at the beginning of the 20th century, when imperialism came of age in Germany and the other big capitalist countries, the international position of tsarist Russia changed again. Lenin wrote: "Tsarism has manifestly and indisputably ceased to be the chief mainstay of reaction, first, because it is supported by international finance capital, particularly French, and, secondly, because of 1905. At that time [i.e., before imperialism came into being.— A. Y.] the system of big national states—the democracies of Europe—was bringing democracy and socialism to the world in spite of tsarism.... The system now [i.e., at the beginning of the 20th century.—A.Y.] is a handful of imperialist 'Great' Powers (five or six in number), each oppressing other nations.... Today, the socialist proletariat ... is confronted by an *alliance* of tsarist imperialism and advanced capitalist, European, imperialism, which is based on their common oppression of a number of nations.

"Such are the concrete changes that have taken place in the situation."[2]

The investigator has therefore to look into the role of Russia's proletariat, whose revolutionary energy reshaped Russia's destiny and modified the system of international relations. Three other questions are associated with this one, relating directly to the foreign policy of the German imperialists at the beginning of the century: firstly, the influence of the 1905 Russian revolution on the socialist working-class movement in Germany,[3] secondly, German preparations to intervene against the Russian revolution and, thirdly, opposition of the international working class

---

[1] Lenin, *Collected Works*, Vol. 2, p. 27.
[2] Ibid., Vol. 22, p. 342.
[3] *Die Auswirkungen der ersten russischen Revolution von 1905-1907 auf Deutschland*, Bd. I-II, Hrsg. von L. Stern, Berlin, 1954-56.

to the threat of an imperialist world war, particularly of the German workers and the Social-Democratic Party to the foreign policy of the German imperialists. Lastly, in the context of big politics, it is also tied up with the relations between Russian tsarism and France and Britain, the leading imperialist powers of Western Europe. Defeated in the Far East and weakened by the revolution, the Russian imperialists were compelled to seek a rapprochement with British imperialism, their old rival. The Anglo-French and later the Anglo-Russian agreements betokened a defeat for the foreign policy of the German imperialists who had alienated all their rivals, real and potential, by their frantic expansionism in Europe and elsewhere.

The foregoing does not exhaust the problems related to the main topic, nor the list of principal sources. It is no more than a general guideline. I want to stress that Marxist-Leninist historians cannot confine themselves to just relating the diplomatic, purely external order of events. They must probe deep into the rockbottom processes, study the events and facts of economic development, examine the various forms of expansion, delve into the class struggle, the national movements, the foreign policy and even the ideology of imperialism, establishing their dialectical connection and inter-dependence with the system of states, which is never stable and is subject to change under the effect of a variety of factors.

Lenin's *Notebooks on Imperialism*,[1] which offer us a glimpse of the research laboratory of that brilliant scientist and revolutionary, the founder of the truly scientific theory of imperialism, serve us as a guide in studying these heterogeneous, specific and complex grass-root processes not only with respect to methodology, but also method. Lenin worked out his theory during the 1914-18 war after scrutinising economic, social, political and diplomatic sources, and demonstrated that "for Europe, the time when the new capitalism *definitely* superseded the old can be established with fair precision; it was the beginning of the twentieth century".[2]

Our study of Lenin's work convinced us that his scientific conception of imperialism, based on a generalisation of vast

---

[1] Lenin, *Collected Works*, Vol. 39.
[2] Ibid., Vol. 22, p. 200.

information, is foreign, and in spirit hostile, to all revision-ist distortions and dogmatist formulas which are blind to the deep dialectical stream of living history. Even after he produced a precise definition of imperialism, Lenin warned his successors and future historians that "very brief defini-tions, although convenient, for they sum up the main points, are nevertheless inadequate, since we have to deduce from them some especially important features of the phenomenon that has to be defined".[1]

On setting out the principal features of imperialism and producing an adequate definition of this complex historical phenomenon by deep critical study of vast material in his *Imperialism, the Highest Stage of Capitalism*, Lenin emphasised "the conditional and relative value of all definitions in general, which can never embrace all the concatenations of a phenomenon in its full development".[2]

Therefore, the task of the historian dealing with the foreign policy of the German imperialists is to lay bare the mechanics of the growing and determinative influence of the monopolies, their interlacing and rivalry, and the resist-ance of the other socio-economic and political forces, in-cluding, high up on the list, the working class. This is not easy. But that is what makes it all the more attractive.

1961

---

[1] Ibid., p. 266.
[2] Ibid.

DIPLOMATIC PREPARATIONS FOR WORLD WAR
1914-1918

The diplomatic preparations for war began long before 1914. The economic and political contradictions between the major capitalist powers, which gave rise to diverse military alliances, prompted a new alignment of forces in Europe, and also a new system of states, all the more unstable because a frantic arms race and increasing colonial expansionism kept tilting the scales to and fro, creating the peril of armed conflicts. Britain, then the biggest colonial and naval power, elected for a time to stay out of all alliances, but its weight in the system of states had a decisive bearing on the international situation.

The existing system of states was known as the "system of armed peace". This contradictory concept was meant to screen and justify the mounting antagonisms bred by economic and commercial competition, colonial rivalry and the arms race.[1]

Soon after the period of wars for the national reunification of bourgeois states, notably the German empire and Italy, when there emerged in Europe a system of military alliances, Frederick Engels predicted the likelihood of a war—not a local one, not even all-European, but world-wide—and its inevitable result: a general crisis of the capitalist system. Here is what he wrote (in 1887): "This would be a world-wide war on a new scale and of unprecedented vehemence. Between eight and ten million

---

[1] See latest investigation by V. M. Khvostov, *Istoriya diplomatii*, Vol. II, Moscow, 1963.

soldiers will be at each other's throats, while feeding on Europe so consumingly that no host of locusts could match them. The devastation of the Thirty Years' War compressed into three or four years and embracing the whole continent, coupled with hunger, disease, brutalisation of the troops and of the peoples caused by the acute want, a hopeless disorganisation of our artificial mechanism in trade, industry and credit; all this ending in universal bankruptcy; collapse of the old states and of their stereotyped statesmanship—a collapse that will see the crowns of monarchs lying in the streets by the dozen, with no one wishing to pick them up; it is absolutely impossible to anticipate how it will all end and who will emerge the victor; just one outcome is absolutely certain: universal exhaustion and a situation in which the working class can gain its ultimate victory."[1]

It is untrue, however, that the founders of Marxism believed war by capitalist powers to be the sole or even the main condition for socialist victory. On the contrary, they worked steadfastly against aggression and exposed the methods and purposes of capitalist statesmanship of which diplomacy was regarded the supreme embodiment. Though diplomacy was in many countries still the exclusive domain of the old aristocracy, it could not escape the influence of the new forces and interests of the big industrial and, later, finance capital. Marx and Engels counterweighed the aggressively expansionist and nationalist foreign policy of these forces, based on militarism, with the peace-loving foreign policy of the working class based on internationalism and socialist solidarity.

At the time when the old, pre-monopoly capitalism was giving way to imperialism, militarism developed at a high rate. Struggle for a redivision of markets and sources of raw materials and, most of all, struggle for spheres of investment and new colonies or, in brief, struggle for a redivision of the world, became one of the most salient factors in shaping the foreign policy and diplomacy of the big imperialist powers. The basic world-wide imperialist antagonisms were driving the nations inexorably towards a world-wide military cataclysm.

The transition of "free" capitalism to the imperialist stage

---

[1] Marx and Engels, *Works*, Vol. 21, p. 361 (Russ. ed.).

bred insatiable ambitions in the main European capitals. The English nourished plans of a still greater Great Britain, wielding her influence over vast new territories in Asia, Africa and Oceania. The German banking and industrial tycoons, the Junkers and militarists nourished the ambition of a Great Germany or a Central Europe (*Mitteleuropa*) embracing an immense territorial conglomerate in Europe and Asia Minor; besides, they craved for a German colonial empire in Africa and the Pacific and an extensive sphere of German influence in South America. The French financial oligarchy, which was whipping up revanchist sentiment in the country, was determined to regain Alsace-Lorraine, seize the Ruhr basin and expand its colonial empire in Africa. The bourgeoisie and the landowners of tsarist Russia yearned for political and military dominance in the Balkans, for Constantinople and the Straits, and for a greater sphere of influence in Iran. Besides, they did not abandon their ambitions in the Far East despite Russia's humiliation by Japan. The rulers of Austria-Hungary were not content with their political and economic influence over Bulgaria and, partly, Rumania, and dreamed of crushing Serbia, turning her into a vassal and consolidating their rule over the eastern, as well as the western, part of the Balkan Peninsula. Last but not least, the Italian imperialists, who took inspiration from the glory of ancient Rome, yearned for Tirol, Trieste and Albania, for a slice of Asia Minor, colonial possessions in Africa and Italian supremacy in the Mediterranean.

The imperialists of non-European powers, too, were nurturing extensive plans of conquest. U.S. Senator Albert Jeremiah Beveridge, for one, said in the early twentieth century that God made Americans "the master organisers of the world to establish system where chaos reigns. . . . He has marked the American people as His chosen nation to finally lead in the regeneration of the world." The first thing the U.S. imperialists were intent on was to consolidate their pre-eminent influence over the Western Hemisphere and expedite penetration into China.

The capitalists and militarists of Japan were toying with the idea of ruling all East Asia and the adjoining part of the Pacific.

The preparations launched for these plans and, much more, the actual attempts of putting them into effect here and there, deepened the existing contradictions and created new ones.

By the turn of the 20th century Britain was rudely awakened to the fact that it had to reckon with German imperialism as an increasingly dangerous rival exporter and investor who would not confine his dealings to Europe and was stretching out his arm for colonies. The German imperialists harassed Britain, long accustomed to being the industrial hegemon and colonial monopolist, in China and South America, the Balkans and Africa, in Asia Minor and Oceania. They made it clear that it was high time for quickly aging Britain to abandon the stage to her younger German rival. "Britain," Wilhelm II declared, "must get used to the idea that Germany will be a great colonial power." While building up their land armies, the German imperialists also launched naval armament according to a plan worked out by Admiral Tirpitz, and their motto, "Our future is on the seas!", was a direct challenge to Britain.

On the threshold of the imperialist era, Britain was in the zenith of her power, although the first signs of decline were beginning to show. No longer was she the "world's workshop", though ranking as the foremost industrial country. She was still the leading exporter of capital, which gave her immense strength. She possessed a vast colonial empire, the biggest of all, which was an economic pillar of her world power. She had numerous strategic support points all over the world—naval bases, coaling stations, etc., which guarded her ramified communication lines. Besides, she had the world's mightiest navy, which ruled the seas and had no equal in prowess and was, moreover, superior or at least equal to the combined navies of any two other European powers.

With this economic, political and naval strength, Britain could afford her "splendid isolation" for some time yet, controlling the power balance of countries scrimmaging for world influence. She was able to create "equilibrium" when it profited her, and made the most of the antagonisms plagueing the European continent. But very soon a search began for a new foreign policy. New factors had appeared in the world to challenge British supremacy. New rivals entered the scene alongside the old—more powerful than tsarist Russia and France and more insistent about a "place in the sun". The law of the uneven development of capitalism was making itself felt. Britain was quickly losing her status of first industrial power. Germany and the United States were breathing down her neck. They figured more prominently than before in exporting capital and were scrambling for control over colonial and semi-colonial countries. The old and new rivals—save the United States— had a larger and stronger army than Britain's. Furthermore, some of them, not Germany alone, had begun to enlarge their navies.

Britain was hard put to it to keep her naval supremacy, but the possibility of her imperialist rivals pooling their strength made her position precarious. Britain, like all other imperialist countries, was fired by visions of new conquest. So she did not limit her task to merely maintaining the *status quo*. For some time still, her traditional policy of "splendid isolation" made sense, but its "splendour" soon faded. It became a screen for a "free hand" policy, designed to single out the main adversary among the welter of rivals and construct a system of alliances against him.

The crisis of Britain's "splendid isolation" gave impetus to an acute controversy among her rulers over her future orientation. Hence the numerous, often synchronic attempts to associate with Russia against Germany and with Germany against Russia—usually sweetened by promises of sharing influences in the colonial and semi-colonial countries. The first such attempt was made in 1898, when British-French tension was mounting rapidly in Africa, attaining its peak in the conflict over Fashoda (Kodok), which almost caused a war. Fresh attempts followed in the succeeding years, and were by no means mere diplomatic manoeuvres to set one rival against another. They reflected a desire to adapt Britain's policy to the new conditions with the greatest profit. Britain's diplomatic overtures in Russia failed. Tsarism still felt strong enough to pursue its expansionist plans in the Middle and Far East. Following the example set by Japan, Britain and Germany, which had begun a series of armed conquests in the Far East, tsarist Russia was priming for a military venture of her own, and since Japan, too, was preparing to come to grips with Russia, an armed conflict between them became unavoidable.

German diplomacy viewed the situation as highly favourable. Starting negotiations of an alliance with Britain today, then refusing to talk tomorrow, it was bent, as the Kaiser said, on "squeezing" out of Britain colonial, diplomatic and other compensations. Throughout 1901 certain influential British quarters negotiated with Germany an alliance against Russia, or against France, or both of them at once. The German diplomats, knowing that Britain was aiming to embroil their country in a war on two fronts, kept raising the price. Furthermore, since there was a chance of letting Japan come into the Anglo-German alliance, they hoped to avoid involvement on two fronts and, moreover, to frighten Russia with the prospect of fighting in the Far East and in the West at the same time. In any case, Holstein declared in March 1902 that "it is in our interest to retain a free hand" and "in the long run to exact an appropriate compensation not only for support, but even for neutrality". The ambitious plans made in Britain and Germany collapsed, as they were bound to collapse. Both were intent on winning world supremacy and no common ground existed for an agreement. The negotiations were broken off for good. Soon, the world learned that the British Government had concluded a politico-military alliance with Japan, which it hoped to exploit as a striking force against Russia, while its negotiations with Germany had been a convenient screen. This enabled it to transfer part of the British navy from the Pacific to the North Sea, where a German navy was growing fast. Nor did Britain lose time to improve relations with France.

In the circumstances, German diplomacy endeavoured to operate in three directions at once: firstly, it sought to weaken the Franco-Russian alliance, secondly, to whet Anglo-Russian rivalries and, thirdly, to hasten a Russo-Japanese conflict in the Far East.

Wilhelm II, who styled himself Admiral of the Atlantic, attached considerable hopes to the imminent clash between Nicholas II, whom he styled the Admiral of the Pacific, and Japan. Knowing that Japan had Britain behind her, the German diplomats were secretly prompting the Japanese to attack Russia. German imperialist and militarist quarters, with the General Staff as their brain, were certain that a Russo-Japanese war, whatever its outcome, would divert their rivals' strength and enable them to proceed unhampered with their economic expansion, diplomatic juggling, colonial demands and pressure, possibly even a preventive war, against France. But things did not shape out as they wished.

New processes came into operation, involving a realignment of strength in the system of imperialist powers, spurred by the economic and diplomatic struggle of all against all. The territorial division of the world was complete, and the early phase of redivision had set in, marked by a succession of local wars and international complications impelled by the growth of ground and naval armaments. The Russo-Japanese war, which marked the consolidation of imperialism, did not relieve the international contradictions in Europe, nor the world-wide economic, political and colonial rivalries of the principal imperialist powers. On the contrary, it added to them and, as it were, brought about a new round of economic clashes, diplomatic conflicts and local wars. This made the situation more complicated still and to a great extent conditioned the alignment of forces in the forthcoming general imperialist collision.

By virtue of the uneven economic and political development typical of capitalism, especially in its imperialist stage, the various agreements reached by any two powers were no more than a postponement of the affray, or a form of preparation for joint struggle against a third country or group of countries. Uneven development could not but affect the politico-military blocs formed earlier: some tended to solidify, others to lose their cohesion, and others still to fall apart. New groupings appeared, and were gradually afflicted by the same ills. In some cases, even a member of one grouping would link up with one or more members of an opposite grouping.

The highlight of this process was Britain's final abandonment of her "splendid isolation". Soon after the Russo-Japanese war started or, more precisely, on April 8, 1904, Britain and France concluded an agreement recognising Britain's "right" to Egypt and France's "right" to press her claims in Morocco. This was regarded as a major British concession, because much of Morocco's trade was controlled by British, notably Liverpool, merchants. Considering, however, that Moroccan trade was an insignificant fraction of Britain's world-wide commercial interests, the concession was not a very big one. Besides, it was offset by France's acceptance of the "open door" principle. For Britain the transaction held primarily political promise.

In January 1906, the British and French General Staffs met in secret to discuss military affairs. This raised the curtain on the *Entente cordiale*. Having earlier concluded a politico-military alliance with Japan, directed chiefly against Russia, Britain now had France on her side against Germany.

In the meantime, German imperialism expected to profit by the Russo-Japanese war and Russia's setbacks in at least three ways. First, it hoped to saddle Russia with a one-sided commercial treaty that would, in the interest of the Prussian Junkers, hinder exports of Russian farm products to Germany and expand German interests in Russia. Second, it intended to subvert the Franco-Russian alliance and thus isolate France on the European continent. Third, it set out to create a favourable climate for deeper penetration in the Middle East, facilitated by the Baghdad railway concession finalised in 1903.

Russia's difficulties in the Far East created by her military setback, did indeed offer certain prospects of success. German diplomacy made the most of the situation to win Russia to its side and pry her away from France. This was done on the wishes of the militarists who, though they had a plan ready for war on two fronts, preferred to grapple with France alone, with their eastern frontiers safe. After defeating France, the situation would lend itself to striking against Russia. In brief, they intended to smash their continental rivals singly. There was also the alternative scheme of possible rapport with Russia. Holstein, for one, figured that a Russo-German rapprochement may undermine the Franco-Russian alliance and pave the way for a revival of the Continental League against Britain. This was a pipe-dream. But it reveals the frame of mind of German diplomacy and that of the German imperialists, particularly the biggest monopolies and the naval and colonialist quarters, who considered Britain their chief rival and enemy.

The fall of Port Arthur was much more than a military defeat for the Russian tsar. It entailed serious political consequences. As Lenin had predicted, it touched off a tidal wave of revolutionary sentiment among Russia's working class. On the other hand, the European bourgeoisie was alarmed, at least in the beginning, by the "collapse of Russia's military power, which for a long time had been considered the bulwark of European reaction". The European bourgeoisie, Lenin wrote at the time, "had grown so accustomed to identify Russia's moral strength with the military strength of the gendarme of Europe. In its eyes the prestige of the young Russian race was inseparably bound up with that of tsarism, that unshakable authority, which strongly safeguarded the existing 'order of things'. . . .

"Indeed, the European bourgeoisie has cause for alarm. The proletariat has cause for rejoicing. The disaster that has overtaken our mortal enemy not only signifies the approach of freedom in Russia, it also presages a new revolutionary upsurge of the European proletariat."[1]

Petersburg's Bloody Sunday (January 9, 1905) and the "revolutionary days"[2] that followed frightened the Western bourgeoisie and their governments. They prepared to "save Russia from revolution and tsarism from utter ruin".[3] They feared that if the tsar were overthrown, there would be revolutionary ferment in Europe and more ferment among the Eastern peoples. Moreover, it would be robbed of a military ally and likely political partner in international affairs. Germany's rulers also feared that revolutionary developments in Russia would spark a national liberation movement in the western Polish regions under their control.

Loans became an instrument of political pressure on tsarist Russia. At the beginning of the Russo-Japanese war, the Petersburg government discovered that it needed a big loan. It hoped to obtain the necessary funds on the international financial market. On learning that certain tsarist bureaucrats intended for political reasons to postpone the transaction until victory over Japan was made secure, Kokovtsov, the tsar's minister of finance, wrote: "It would be a good thing if only it did not remind me of a sated man talking to a hungry one about the advantages of this or that cuisine." Soon, Foreign Minister Lamsdorf had no choice but to agree. "In view of the vast sums of money consumed by this terrible war," he wrote, "we shall have to look for gold at all costs in the very near future. When the time comes to choose between the opinion of those responsible for foreign policy and those responsible for the state of the treasury, the latter will be more likely to win."

Early in 1905, the tsarist government approached French

---

[1] Lenin, *Collected Works*, Vol. 8, pp. 47-48.
[2] Ibid., pp. 101-23.
[3] Ibid., p. 272.

bankers for a loan. The money was sorely needed to carry on the war and suppress the revolution. The bankers, however, who wanted the tsar to make peace with Japan and also with the Russian liberal bourgeoisie, turned down the request. They committed themselves to a gamble which Lenin described as being "in pursuance of anti-proletarian and anti-revolutionary interests".[1] The German Government, for its part, acted in behalf of the same anti-revolutionary interests but in a direction diametrically opposite to the French in the hope of gaining immediate politico-strategic advantages. It suggested to the banking house of Mendelssohn and Sons to grant a large loan to the tsarist government, hoping thereby to shore up the tsarist autocracy and encourage it to fight on against Japan. It also hoped to drive a wedge between Russia and France, undermine their weakening alliance and, ultimately, after expanding relations with Russia, to isolate France internationally. Just in case the revolutionary situation in Russia got out of hand, imperiling the reign of the tsar and not least of all the semi-autocratic regime in Germany herself, which already had to face up to an aroused working class, the government and General Staff envisaged a possible armed intervention.

But for the time being, German diplomacy set out to use the situation and win Russia to its side. In his conversation with Wilhelm in Björkö at the end of July 1905, Nicholas II vented his fury at the French who were celebrating their agreement with the British at the height of the Russo-Japanese war. "The French," he told the Kaiser, "are acting like scoundrels. My ally refused me help because Britain so wished. Now look at Brest: they are fraternising there with the English. What am I supposed to do in the circumstances?"

The Kaiser told the tsar what exactly he was "supposed to do". He prevailed on him to sign a "trifling document"— a secret treaty of alliance and mutual assistance in the event of a clash with one of the other European powers. At the Kaiser's suggestion, the treaty was to be signed by a minister. So Nicholas ordered his naval minister Birilyov, to sign it without reading what stood in it. "By the grace of God," Wilhelm rejoiced, "the morning of July 24 in Björkö has become a turning point in European history and a big

---

[1] Ibid., p. 268.

consolation to my fatherland, which is at last delivered from the terrible grip of the Gauls and Russians."

However, despite the plea to God, German diplomacy failed to break the tsarist army's bonds with the French General Staff. It could not be entirely sure of Russia's armed forces in its ventures against Britain. On learning that the tsar had concluded an alliance with Germany in Björkö, Foreign Minister Lamsdorf and Witte did their utmost to nullify its effects and salvage the Franco-Russian alliance. "The principal if not the only purpose Wilhelm has," Lamsdorf commented, "is to cause a quarrel between ourselves and France, and thus break his own isolation at our expense." But the Björkö treaty was stillborn. The crowned head of the German imperialists raved in vain, reviling Nicholas for going back on commitments.

The German attempt to break up Russia's alliance with France by a treaty of alliance is revealing in many respects. It shows, for one thing, what importance the German rulers, on the one hand, and those of France, on the other, attached to Russia in the coming war. Kaiser Wilhelm's diplomats and General Staff expected an alliance with Russia to isolate France in Europe. Reichschancellor Bülow and the naval command thought the alliance would be justified if it encompassed more than just Europe and worked primarily against Britain. Yet the imperialist powers had to reckon with an entirely new factor: the working-class movement in the Russian empire was undermining tsarism and weakening it as a military and reactionary force in Europe and Asia. Her imperialist rivals, Britain, Germany, Austria-Hungary and even allied France, kept a wary eye on events, poised to seize upon the slightest economic, diplomatic or strategic advantage accruing from the diminishing role Russia was beginning to play in international affairs.

The scramble for Russia's favours continued, but it was not until a new international crisis broke out over Morocco that its outcome became clear.

At the end of 1904 French financiers and industrialists (the Schneider-Creusot firm included) set up a committee for Moroccan affairs, enlisted the support of influential politicians and granted a fairly large loan to the Sultan of Morocco. They were determined to seize the opportunities deriving from France's recent agreement with Britain. The loan was made conditional on French control over the customs and police in the key ports and French instructors in the Moroccan army. What these conditions meant in effect was the death of Moroccan independence. Prompted by monopolies and financial groups who had plans of their own, the German Government decided to intervene. Also, it hoped to impair the Anglo-French agreement and show France that Britain would leave her in the lurch. With Russia occupied against Japan, Schlieffen, then Chief of the General Staff, and most of the top diplomats believed the situation favourable for a war against France.

On March 31, 1905, Wilhelm II declared publicly while on a visit in Tangier that Germany would not tolerate, and would resist, the domination of Morocco by any foreign power. The German Government refused to negotiate with French Foreign Minister Théophile Delcassé (one of the architects of the Entente) on the grounds that he was hostile to Germany.

However, the German manoeuvre evoked an instantaneous British reaction. The British Government advised Pierre Rouvier, the French Premier, to stand firm on Morocco and not dismiss Delcassé. It promised to field an army of 100 to 115 thousand on the continent if Germany attacked.

Fortified by these even if not entirely official assurances of the British Government, Delcassé suggested at a stormy session of the French cabinet to reject the German claims. But in view of losses by Russia, France's closest ally (a Russian fleet was reported sunk at Tsushima by the Japanese), the cabinet decided on a retreat. Delcassé had to resign in June 1905 and France consented to submit the Moroccan problem to an international conference. The Germans, who had only a short time before endeavoured to provoke a war with France, thought better of it in face of the firm British stand, and agreed to the parleys. Their decision was partly prompted by pressure from U.S. President Theodore Roosevelt and, to some extent, by the hope that they would ultimately break up the Russo-French alliance and win Russia to their side.

The conference convened at Algeciras in the south of Spain early in 1906 and revealed the new alignment of strength in world affairs. "British diplomacy," said Arthur Nicolson, Britain's delegate to the conference, "was more French than the French." This affirmed the strength of the

Anglo-French *Entente cordiale*. The German military attaché in London learned that the British General Staff had alternative plans worked out for shipping an expeditionary army against Germany if the conference fell through and a war began. Moreover, the British military attaché in Brussels Barnardiston was reported to be negotiating with Ducarne from the Belgian General Staff concerning joint operations in the event a German army would cross into Belgian territory. According to the Russian consul in Bombay, the colonial and military quarters there followed the conference "with close attention". "An armed clash between France and Germany," he wrote, "is discussed quite candidly... and one can, as it were, read the question on all faces: is France the new benefactor who will pull the chestnuts out of the fire for Britain, that is, weaken hateful and economically dangerous Germany?"

"The military quarters believe," the consul went on, "that the hour is most favourable for an assault on Germany; it would paralyse her world trade and colonial policy for a long time to come."

On several occasions the conference reached the point of breaking up. Nicolson was instructed by London that "if the Conference is to break up France must not be manoeuvred into the position of appearing to be to blame". Concerted Anglo-French pressure forced German diplomacy, which sensed that it was isolated, to retreat.

Russia's attitude was an important factor at the Algeciras conference. Weakened by her war with Japan and the revolutionary actions of her working class, facing financial disaster and fishing for foreign loans, the tsarist government attempted to mediate between the Anglo-British side and Germany. It was eager for the conference to end, thinking that this would expedite a loan from either France or Germany, or both. The chief Russian plea was the necessity for suppressing "the revolutionary movement, which has already caused echoes in the neighbouring monarchies committed to joint action against the looming danger".

The annoyed German diplomats reminded Russia that appeals for joint effort against the revolutionary movement did not relieve the tsarist government, moved by its sense of self-preservation, of the need to rely primarily on its own resources. This was, in effect, a form of pressure to compel the tsarist government to support Germany's colonialist designs in Morocco. The French Government, for its part, told Petersburg in no uncertain terms that in the event of further vacillation Russia need not expect any loan. So, at the decisive stage of the Algeciras conference, the tsarist government threw its diplomatic support behind France. Paris bankers were instantly allowed to grant Russia the desired loan, deliberately withheld until the closing of the conference.

Even Italy, who was Germany's ally, backed France at the conference, and for a simple reason. Despite her involvement in the Triple Alliance, Italy had concluded a secret agreement with France in 1900 concerning spheres of influence in North Africa. By recognising French interests in Morocco, it obtained the promise that France would not obstruct the seizure of Tripolitania, then part of the Ottoman empire. Two years later, Italy signed another secret agreement with France on mutual neutrality. This move was an indication of Italy's gradual withdrawal from the Triple Alliance.

The Franco-Italian relationship did not escape the notice of the German diplomats. But they were helpless. Reichschancellor Bülow tried to make light of it. The man whose blood rushed to his head every time his wife danced an extra waltz with someone else, he quipped, was not worth his salt. But it came out at Algeciras that this flippancy about Italy's comportment was ill-advised. Austria-Hungary, too, which had considerable dealings with the French banks and still hoped for British diplomatic backing in the event of a clash with Russia in the Balkans, was anything but firm in her support of her German ally.

As a result, France celebrated a diplomatic victory: the conference formally recognised the equality of the economic interests of all the "great powers" in Morocco, but awarded France the function of maintaining "internal order" in the country and controlling the Moroccan police. For the French imperialists this paved the way for the subsequent seizure of Morocco.

The tidal wave of revolution in Russia had a far-reaching effect on the existing system of states. The tsar's international standing was somewhat shaken, while the role of the Western capitalist powers was proportionately elevated. This was when other changes in the system of major European powers came to the surface. Britain's "splendid isolation" was entirely a thing of the past. The Anglo-French Entente grew stronger and, what was more, indicated clearly that it meant to expand by coming to terms with other powers. The Franco-Russian alliance, which hung in the balance during the Russo-Japanese war, was recovering strength, especially after Russia was compelled to climb off the fence and seek closer relations with the Entente. Germany, which had hoped to rip Russia away from France, and then France from Britain, in order to isolate each of them, was herself all but isolated. This was a fact the German imperialists did not instantly grasp, and never fully appreciated, though it was crucial for drawing the appropriate political conclusions. British diplomacy, too, had to let the lessons of its collision with Germany during the Moroccan crisis sink in. In a secret memorandum to his government, Eyre Crowe, a prominent Foreign Office official, pointed to the aggressive claims of imperialist Germany and arrived at the conclusion that it was impossible for Britain to come to terms with her rival. Germany, he wrote, gave Britain no amity, though time and again she pocketed what she asked as the price for amity. Crowe brushed away the notion, still current among some British politicians, that Germany could be appeased by generous British concessions and made more receptive to offers of friendship.

The change in Anglo-Russian relations dates to this particular time. Having humiliated tsarist Russia in the Far East through Japan, the British imperialists were now eager to come to terms with what could be a valuable ally in combating the national liberation movement in the East and in a war with Germany. The tsar, too, gravitated towards Britain. He had had the advantage of West European financial and political support and had survived the revolutionary tornado; the Portsmouth peace had been signed, bringing his war with Japan to an end, and what he wanted now were safeguards against Germany. German expectations that the Russo-Japanese war would strain Anglo-Russian contradictions of which Germany could take advantage in carrying on her fight for world supremacy, misfired.

The arduous negotiations between Britain and Russia yielded a compromise on controversial colonial problems, culminating in an agreement signed on August 31, 1907, which specified the respective spheres of influence in Asia.

Iran was divided into three zones—the northern being Russia's sphere of influence, the south-eastern Britain's, and the central "neutral", that is, a zone of "free" competition. Afghanistan was recognised, in effect, as a British sphere of influence, with both signatories pledging neutrality as to the internal government of Tibet. This Anglo-Russian accord was preceded by an agreement between tsarist Russia and Japan, establishing respective spheres of influence in North-East China.

The Anglo-Russian agreement laid the foundation for the Triple Entente—a military and diplomatic imperialist alliance of Britain, France and Russia, counter-balancing the Triple Alliance, the other European imperialist alignment of Germany, Austria-Hungary and Italy. This formalised Europe's division into two hostile military blocs.

Some Second International leaders hailed the Anglo-Russian agreement, an accord of two old rivals, as a "guarantee of peace". Lenin objected to this opportunist view. Less than a year after the inauguration of the Triple Entente, he called attention to the "inflammable material" that had piled up in imperialist world politics and warned the working class that all overt and covert treaties, agreements, etc., would touch off a war at the slightest provocation by any of the powers.[1]

The emergence of the Entente brought the world a step closer to war. It had no co-ordinated military mechanism at first, no common military conventions or strategic plans. The British General Staff, it is true, parleyed in secret with the general staffs of France and Belgium after the conclusion of the Anglo-French *Entente cordiale*, and then during the Moroccan crisis and the Algeciras conference. It promised to ship four divisions to the continent in the event of a war. There were also negotiations concerning naval co-operation, but the British Government accepted no specific commitments in this respect. All French efforts to obtain such commitments—a military alliance treaty or something to the same effect—were in vain. The military mechanism of the Franco-Russian alliance, on the other hand, functioned unintermittently. It was repeatedly renovated and had a distinctly strategic orientation.

In April 1906 the French and Russian chiefs of staff

---

[1] Lenin, *Collected Works*, Vol. 15, p. 191.

reached an understanding on mobilisation if a clash should occur with the Triple Alliance or any of its signatories. The earlier agreement, signed in 1901, also contained provisions applying to a possible conflict with Britain. Now these were unnecessary. The alliance envisaged war against the Austro-German bloc only. The French imperialists were anxious to buttress the Russian armed forces, badly mauled by the Japanese and the succession of revolutionary upheavals.

All the same, neither the Triple Entente nor the Triple Alliance were stable, let alone close-knit. Having blossomed on the uncertain soil of common imperialist interests, both were harrassed by the differences prevailing among their members, which tended on and off to burst to the surface, causing now one and now another country to come to terms with a member of the opposite group. Sometimes, these honeymoons were casual and short-lived, sometimes they were more enduring. Always, they were an indication of the instability of the system of inter-state relationships, provoking local conflicts that were liable to expand into a universal European diplomatic crisis and, ultimately, a world war. Only one thing brought the powers together: the need to combat the national liberation movement in Asia, roused to active political life. The interests here, too, were not homogeneous. They had a dual basis. When revolutionary unrest gripped Iran and Turkey in 1908, attracting world-wide attention, Lenin observed that there were "two mainsprings of all European policy" ... first, "rivalry among the capitalist powers, anxious to 'bite off' as big a piece as they can and extend their possessions and colonies", and, second, "fear of an independent democratic movement among the nations dependent on or 'protected' by Europe".[1] This was the contradictory foundation for the invisible political contacts maintained by all the major European powers, regardless of the bloc they belonged to. After the tsar put down the revolution in Russia, the West European powers turned their attention elsewhere. Britain and tsarist Russia went into each other's embraces as the revolutionary tide mounted in Iran. Lively diplomatic exchanges occurred between the two powers in September 1908. Apart from the differences, these revealed certain common interests. Lenin quickly spotted the underlying sense and objective outcome of the negotiations. "Today," he wrote, "*all* the biggest

[1] Lenin, *Collected Works*, Vol. 15, pp. 221-22.

European powers ... mortally afraid as they are of any extension of democracy at home because it would benefit the proletariat, are *helping* Russia play the gendarme in Asia. There cannot be the slightest doubt that 'freedom of action' for Russia against the Persian revolution was *part of the September reactionary conspiracy* of Russia, Austria, Germany, Italy, France and Britain."[1]

This conspiracy against the liberation movement in Asia did not, however, inhibit the contradictions between the powers concerned and not even the contradictions within the existing blocs, as the crisis created in 1908-09 by Austria's annexation of Bosnia and Herzegovina soon proved. The Congress of Berlin in June 1878 assigned control over the two provinces to Austro-Hungarian troops, though they formally remained part of the Ottoman empire. After the Young Turk revolution, Vienna decided to annex Bosnia and Herzegovina, fearing a further spread of revolutionary and national liberation sentiment in the Balkans and calculating that Russia, its chief rival, was too preoccupied domestically to resist. It sought a secret deal with the tsarist government, hoping the latter would consent to the annexation in return for a promise of support in the Straits issue. In the meantime, the tsar's diplomats were thirsting for some semblance of a diplomatic victory to offset the effects of the inglorious war with Japan and the 1905-07 revolution.

The deal was consummated at Buchlov by Izvolsky, the Russian Foreign Minister, and Aehrenthal, his Austrian counterpart, in September 1908. The tsar gave his consent to Austria's annexation of Bosnia and Herzegovina, while Austria-Hungary pledged her support in the issue of the Black Sea Straits, which Russia wanted opened for her navy. Some time later, the Russian Government obtained a similar pledge from Germany, though couched in vaguer terms and conditional on "compensation". The Italian Government, too, was prepared to back Russia in the Straits dispute, provided Russia consented to Italy's seizure of Tripolitania.

However, the outcome of the Straits problem depended much more on Britain and France. Izvolsky went to Paris and London to solicit support. The Austro-Hungarian Government, chafing over the delay, officially announced

[1] Ibid., pp. 226-27.

the annexation of Bosnia and Herzegovina on October 7, 1908. This was a body blow to the Young Turks and the national aspirations of the southern Slavs and, moreover, to Russia's aggressive diplomatic designs on the Straits.

The annexation of Bosnia and Herzegovina evoked vehement protests in Turkey and Serbia. The tsarist government also attempted to object, calling for an international conference to discuss the issue. Izvolsky's hope that France and Britain would back his claim in the Straits issue proved fruitless. The French were evasive, the British refused their support out of hand. Meanwhile, Germany threw her weight behind the Austro-Hungarians, and it was not mere diplomatic weight either. Conrad von Hötzendorf, Austria's Chief of the General Staff and an inveterate advocate of a preventive war against Serbia, decided that the hour had come for the Hapsburg empire to strike. He had received assurances of German military support from Moltke, Chief of the German General Staff. Moreover, the two staffs had agreed on several variants of joint action if the assault on Serbia would bring on a collision with Russia and, possibly, France.

The diplomatic crisis lasted several months. Then, in February 1909, through the good services of Germany, Austria-Hungary obtained Turkey's consent to the annexation in return for a financial compensation. Next, the Austro-Hungarian Government massed troops on the Serbian border. In the meantime, Germany told Russia in firm terms that she should honour the *fait accompli* and, moreover, get Serbia to state her consent. The German rulers were rattling their sabres. Kaiser Wilhelm declared menacingly that he would back Austria-Hungary to the hilt as his Nibelungian sense of loyalty required. Unprepared for war, the tsar's government yielded. Prime Minister Stolypin feared that a war would stimulate a fresh outburst of revolution in Russia and Foreign Minister Izvolsky had no choice but to resign.

Russia's stand was also undermined by the German-French agreement on Morocco concluded on February 9, 1909, at the height of the Bosnian crisis. For years, rivalry between French and German concerns over the ore mines in Lorraine and the Briey Basin, and the coal mines in the Saar and Ruhr had clouded relations between the two countries. At the beginning of the 20th century, the Moroccan crisis showed that colonial issues added to the Franco-

German antagonisms. The Algeciras conference dampened them somewhat, but failed to iron them out. While one German group, headed by the Mannesmann brothers, was determined to gain key economic positions in Morocco, another, headed by the Krupp and Thyssen monopolies, struck a deal with the French Schneider concern and accepted a share in a mixed mining syndicate. The German Government declared it had no more than an economic interest in Morocco and recognised France's "special political interests". The Moroccan deal ground the axe of the French financiers, for whom colonial expansion eclipsed the idea of revenge and who backed Rouvier's efforts for a rapprochement with Germany. German diplomacy made the most of this trend to weaken the Anglo-French Entente and the Russo-French alliance by deals with France on Morocco and other colonial issues.

The Bosnian crisis sharpened the Balkan contradictions, particularly those between Russia and Serbia, on the one hand, and Austria-Hungary and Germany, on the other. It bared the canker afflicting the Entente, but much more it revealed the depth of the contradictions between the Anglo-Franco-Russian imperialist alignment and that of Austria and Germany.

The existence of the Entente and the abortive German attempts to split it were evidence of far-reaching changes in the system of international relationships. The antagonism between Britain and France, the two veteran colonial powers, was relegated to the background. The contradiction between Britain and Russia in Asia Minor (particularly over the Straits problem), though extant, was no longer pertinent. The imperialist contradictions between Britain and Germany were more basic. The new world-wide economic crisis, which broke out in 1907, added gravity to the situation. The rulers of both countries sought salvation in a scrimmage for new concessions and new spheres of investment, in stepping up colonial expansion and, not least of all, in new government arms orders for ground and naval forces. The 1907 elections in Germany were highlighted by a hitherto unseen colonial psychosis (Hottentot elections) and raucous propaganda of *Weltpolitik,* aimed against Britain, Germany's chief rival, which, in turn, conducted a furious campaign against Germany.

The Anglo-German economic, political and colonial rivalry was made doubly perilous by the naval race, in which the industrialists and the associated financial groups had a vested interest.

The progress of Admiral Tirpitz's naval expansion programme greatly disturbed Britain. In response to Germany's challenge, Britain began building dreadnoughts, warships of a new type with considerable advantages in firing power and sailing speed. In 1905, Britain had 65 conventional battleships, while Germany had 26. The dreadnoughts were meant to increase Britain's lead and convince Germany in the futility of trying to wrest supremacy from the British navy. But Germany promptly responded by building dreadnoughts of her own and had as many as nine in 1908 against the 12 built by Britain. The scales were tilting somewhat, though Britannia still ruled the waves.

The British Government endeavoured to reach an understanding with Germany on naval arming restrictions with the proviso that the latter should reconcile herself to British superiority. This was first attempted at the international peace conference in The Hague in 1907, and again during the negotiations between Edward VII and Wilhelm II in 1908. The German Government turned down the British proposals on both occasions, being determined to build up its navy. "If all Britain wants to do is proffer us her hand with the admonition that we must limit our navy, it is an outright impertinence," Wilhelm wrote on the margin of a report submitted by Paul Wolff-Metternich, the German Ambassador to London, in the summer of 1908. He added: "On the same grounds France and Russia may later demand that we limit our land forces.... The bill [on naval construction.—A. Y.] will be carried out to the letter, whether the British like it or not. If they want war, let *them* start it. We are not afraid!"

On another report from Wolff-Metternich containing a fresh British proposal to halt naval arming, Wilhelm made the following inscription: "This sort of talk ... is improper and provocative. I must ask the Ambassador to put a stop to that kind of soundings in future.... What he ought to say to these gentlemen who object to our 'silly craving to attack', is 'go to hell, etc.' [obscene words follow.—A. Y.]. That would bring them to their senses.... Wolff-Metternich should have kicked these daydreamers in the behind; he is too soft."

These instructions, which indicated the mood of Germany's rulers, left the Berlin diplomats in no doubt as to how they should receive British overtures. While spurning Britain's initiative, Germany worked in a direction of her own, and to an entirely different purpose.

In April 1909, the British received Berlin's proposal of a naval convention obligating either party not to declare war on each other and observe a benevolent neutrality in the event of either party's military involvement against a third country or group of countries. It did not take London long to see through the German scheme. Under cover of the agreement, the Germans intended to reinforce their navy and, with Britain committed to neutrality, smash their European rivals, France and Russia. Then, they hoped, Britain might be compelled, for the first time in her history, to line up among the satellites of the German grouping.

Britain's proposals were, as a rule, animated by the wish to keep her naval supremacy. Germany's, on the other hand, pursued the aim of establishing her supremacy on the European continent, with Britain looking on as a neutral. The neutrality treaty offered by the Germans was, indeed, designed to isolate the co-signatory.

A similar proposal, made by Germany at the end of 1909, was supplied with the provision that the dimensions of naval building should be specified in advance for either party. As the price for British neutrality, the German Government promised somewhat to slow down the naval programme. British foreign policy planners concluded that the offer spelled much greater political advantages for Germany than for their country and turned it down.

Britain made up her mind to build two warships to every large warship built by Germany. The Germans responded by charging Britain of "surrounding Germany". The hue and cry was meant to justify the expansion of German arms, land and naval. Thus, the Anglo-German contradictions kept piling up.

The Franco-German deal and the tsar's setback in the 1909 crisis over Bosnia gave the German imperialists certain room for manoeuvre aimed at destroying the Entente. Eager to win time, build up its armed forces and carry through the reactionary Stolypin "reforms", the tsarist government dreaded a war with Germany and was willing to negotiate. Its effort to sidestep a conflict and come to terms with the

Kaiser was also closely associated with the insistent wish of the Russian bourgeoisie to block German expansion in Mesopotamia and, especially, in western and northern Iran. Sazonov, who replaced Izvolsky as foreign minister, steered the Russo-German conversations in Potsdam in November 1910 on to German penetration into Iran and the Baghdad railway project. German diplomacy, for its part, concentrated on political issues. It was willing to withdraw its support of Austria-Hungary's aggressive policy in the Balkans, provided Russia gave up her "intentions to support policies hostile to Germany in the event they emanated from Britain". This was an obvious attempt to pull Russia out of the Entente.

The negotiations moved from Potsdam to Petersburg and went on for months. British diplomacy tried to obstruct them, but a Russo-German agreement was finally hammered out on August 19, 1911. The tsar's government agreed to the Baghdad railway project and to foreign capital participating in the venture, on the stipulation that its own Khanakin-Teheran railway project would not be obstructed. This was a feather in the cap for Germany's expansionist policy. Yet the Germans failed where their main political aim was concerned, for Russia refused to pledge neutrality in the event of an Anglo-German war. The financial and economic hold Anglo-French capital had on Russia and the military and diplomatic mechanism which bound Russia to France and to a lesser degree to Britain, coupled with the economic and political contradictions between Russian and German imperialism—all this was stronger than the common dynastic interests of the Hohenzollerns and Romanovs. Yet the German rulers would not reconcile themselves to failure.

In 1911, as six years before, the German imperialists again picked Morocco as the bone of contention, because French capital was quickly making inroads there, while ousting its German rival. An uprising flared up in the spring of that year at Fez, the Moroccan capital. French troops moved in on the pretext of restoring law and order. The German Government, prompted by the aggressive Pan-Germanic Union and such financiers as Krupp, Thyssen and the Mannesmann monopoly with vested interests in Morocco, launched a strident press campaign for partitioning Morocco, then suddenly despatched a gunboat, the *Panther*, to Agadir, a Moroccan port. France interpreted the "*Panther*'s leap" as a challenge. The French nationalist press, egged on by the monopolies, raised an outcry. The monopolies behind the French Government were determined to drive the Germans out of Morocco, while some of the German monopolies, as the "*Panther*'s leap" demonstrated, intended to hang on and others (particularly banker L. Delbrück, member of the board of Krupps) intended to use Morocco as a bargaining point to be compensated with other colonies, notably the Congo. In the ensuing parleys the two sides showed inordinate pertinacity and fell back on mutual threats.

The new Moroccan crisis also strained relations between Germany and Britain, which was urging France to stand firm. In the event of a Franco-German war Britain would join in, said Edward Grey, Britain's Secretary of State for Foreign Affairs; if Russia were involved, he added, Austria would also be dragged in and the duel between France and Germany would develop into a full-scale European war.

But war was averted. Tsarist Russia was too weak still to give France a hand and promptly offered to mediate between her and Germany. The offer lashed the French Government into a fury. Poincaré recalls in his memoirs that Paris reminded Petersburg that Russia was committed to the Franco-Russian pact even over a colonial issue despite her defeat at the hands of the Japanese and despite her insufficient military and naval preparedness. However, there were strong financial groups in France, represented by Joseph Caillaux, who wanted to come to terms with Germany. In the meantime, neither Austria-Hungary nor Italy were inclined to give their German ally military support, each for her own reasons.

This was why the German policy-makers retreated when Lloyd George declared on July 21, 1911, that Britain would accept the challenge and fight by France's side. In November, France and Germany came to terms. The latter recognised the French protectorate over most of Morocco, and in return received a part of the French Congo.

Spain, too, was eager to get a slice of Morocco, but was no more than a "junior partner" of the big imperialist powers. The agreement concluded with France in 1904 gave her control over a narrow strip between Melilla and Ceuta. With the second Moroccan crisis resolved, France and Spain concluded a new agreement fixing the Spanish slice at 28,000 sq. km. and the French at 572,000 sq. km. An international zone, including the city of Tangier, totalling some 380 sq. km., was instituted on British insistence at the entrance to the Strait of Gibraltar.

The Agadir crisis, which had shown how acute the contradictions were between the German imperialists and the Anglo-French Entente, lifted the veil also on the sharp political fight among the powers over the guidelines of their future policy. In Germany the advocates of Tirpitz's naval construction programme, which envisaged three more dreadnoughts in the five years of 1912-17, fought the men who wanted a stronger land army for a continental war. The clash culminated in an explosive compromise, with the Reichstag discussing a fresh build-up of both army and navy. This was a triumph for all the aggressive trends nourished by the German militarists. In Britain advocates of increasing naval power and making closer contact with France and Russia by consolidating the Entente fought the party that wanted a rapprochement with Germany and curbs on naval arming in the hope of deploying the quickly growing German army against Russia, which had clashed with British imperialism in the Middle East.

British and German diplomacy made their last try at reaching an understanding early in February 1912. Lord Haldane, Britain's Secretary of State for War, went to Berlin where he suggested that the Germans scrap their new naval programme. He gave to understand that Britain would reciprocate by granting Germany "certain opportunities" in Africa. But the Germans thought this insufficient. They let Haldane see their new naval programme, not previously publicly announced, and said they would go through with it at all costs. Neither were they content with assurances of friendship and pressed for a formal declaration of British neutrality in the event of Germany's involvement in a war on the continent. What was at issue, Tirpitz said, was "Britain's renunciation of her ententes".

The Haldane mission was a dismal failure, to the general satisfaction of imperialist groups in all countries. For Tirpitz and the war party in Germany the triumph was complete. The advocates of arming in preparation for the imminent clash with the Germans won the day in Britain, for the immensity of the German naval construction programme was a secret no longer. The French financial group that clamoured for an accord with Germany through joint colonial ventures (Rouvier, Caillaux, Tardieu) lost influence as the government began fitting out the military and diplomatic mechanisms for a revanchist war. In Petersburg in autumn 1912 French Prime Minister Poincaré indicated that France would take action on Russia's side in any Austro-Russian conflict in the event of Germany intervening, compelling the latter to fight on two fronts. After the Russo-German agreement of 1911, whose terms were limited, the tsar also reinforced his position in the Entente; he was eager to delay a conflict with Germany, however, until his army should be fully restored and expanded.

Germany, as we see, did not succeed in smashing the Entente. On the contrary, Britain succeeded in strengthening it. In 1912, Britain concluded a secret naval convention with France, and the latter concluded one with Russia somewhat later. Without revealing anything in Parliament, and even without the knowledge of most of the cabinet, Grey exchanged letters with Cambon, French ambassador to London, in November 1912, reaffirming Britain's promise to honour the secret military conventions concluded by the staffs of the two countries in the event of France being involved in a war.

Early in 1912, General Joffre reported that all necessary preparations for a British landing were completed and that the British army could be engaged in the first big battle. Joffre thought a German advance across southern Belgium favourable to France, because the fighting would then be on foreign territory, in a theatre where the enemy had no fortifications.

Early in 1912 the French General Staff expected the war to break out that spring, possibly even earlier, for Germany would gain from the thaw and the muddy roads impeding mobilisation in Russia. The French also believed that Germany would seek a confrontation with Britain to put an end to the expensive naval rivalry.

The German General Staff, for its part, thought the French would look for a pretext to start a war because they considered themselves ready for it.

The German imperialists, too, thought they had an edge on land, if not on the sea, and intended to make the most of it in a favourable situation by actuating the Schlieffen-

Moltke strategic plan. To be sure, the German militarists close to the General Staff were immersed in a hot dispute with those closer to the navy, who were advising caution. Both represented the interests of the Junker and bourgeois imperialists, and both wanted a war to gain world supremacy. But one party thought that since the European continent would be the chief, and probably the sole, war theatre, it was essential before making the final decision to ascertain whether the land forces were ready, the mobilisation arrangements were superior to the enemy's, and the equipment and strategic deployment plans were adequate, while the other party thought the navy was the main weapon against Britain. There were grave doubts, roused by contradictions in the Triple Alliance and electrified by the increasing appetite of its members for colonial conquest. The militarists moved heaven and earth to hasten the conflict, because they feared Italy would drop out before long. But what they feared still more was the political decline, even fall, of the multinational Hapsburg empire, their only dependable ally.

For the Italian imperialists, who had their eyes on Tripolitania and Cyrenaica, the Moroccan crisis was a long awaited opportunity. These African provinces of the Osman empire had long attracted the Bank of Rome, which was closely connected with the Vatican, and other Italian financial and industrial groups. Capture of the two areas would, to the minds of the Italian imperialists, be a first step towards dominating the Mediterranean basin. The Tripolitanian question was also forcefully exploited in domestic policy. Home propaganda maintained that a war with Turkey would "weld the Italians", supplanting the class struggle with a "struggle of nations".

None of the European powers cared to contest Italy's plan. Germany feared Italy would refuse to renew the Triple Alliance Treaty. Austria-Hungary was delighted that Italy's ambitions had strayed from Albania and the Adriatic seaboard to Africa. France was pledged to support Italy under the secret 1902 treaty, and Russia had promised her backing under an agreement concluded in 1909 in Racconigi. Britain, too, whose relations with Germany were going from bad to worse, could ill afford to aggravate Italy. Tacit consent to Italy's seizure of Tripolitania had been given by the British Government in 1902. "What is amazing," the Russian naval attaché in Italy commented, "is that Italy went to war against Turkey with all Europe's consent."

Italy demanded (on September 28, 1911) that Turkey give up Tripoli and Cyrenaica and was naturally rebuffed. The Italian generals then mounted a swift assault, hoping that Turkey, unable to offer a strong resistance, would surrender. The Turkish army was weak, and in the early phases of the war Italy did succeed in capturing Tripoli and a few minor points along the coast. But in later stages, resisted bitterly by the local Arab population, the Italians made no headway and the war dragged out.

The Italian navy bombarded Beirut and the Dardanelles, and an Italian force landed on the Dodecanese islands. In the meantime, Turkey's mediation appeals to the other powers were ignored. She was totally abandoned.

A crisis in the Balkans and ferment at home compelled the Turks to accept defeat. A secret treaty was signed on October 15, 1912, and another one, made public on October 18, relinquished Turkey's rights to Tripoli and Cyrenaica.

Italy, which had at long last realised her long-time wish, turned Tripoli and Cyrenaica into a colony, Libya. Heavy losses were sustained by the Arabs, who continued to resist the Italian invaders for many years. Lenin wrote in 1912: "Despite the 'peace', the war will actually go on, for the Arab tribes in the heart of Africa, in areas far away from the coast, will refuse to submit. And for a long time to come they will be 'civilised' by bayonet, bullet, noose, fire and rape."[1] He described the Tripolitanian campaign as a typical colonial war waged by a "civilised" 20th-century state.

A new crisis broke out, this time in the Balkans, where deep-seated social and national contradictions combined with great-power rivalries.

The national liberation movement of the Balkan nations still languishing under Turkish rule (Macedonia, Albania, the islands in the Aegean Sea, etc.) gained momentum. Class contradictions there were coloured by national and religious antagonisms. In Macedonia, for example, the landowners were Muslim Turks, while the peasants were Christian Slavs. So the fight for freedom merged with a fight against medieval survivals, feudalism and absolutism. Lenin wrote: "To form united national states in the Balkans, shake

---

[1] Lenin, *Collected Works*, Vol. 18, pp. 337-38.

off the oppression of the local feudal rulers and completely liberate the Balkan peasants of all nationalities from the yoke of the landowners—such was the historic task confronting the Balkan peoples."[1] The best of the Balkan workers, who had a sound appreciation of their historic mission, fought for a consistently democratic, revolutionary solution of the national question. The interests of the people did not, however, determine foreign policy; it was shaped by the dynastic ambitions of the ruling monarchies, the intervention of the imperialist powers and the aspirations of the rising national bourgeoisie. In spring 1911, the governments of Serbia and Bulgaria thought a suitable time had come to settle the question of Macedonia and the other Turkish areas in Europe. When the Italo-Turkish war broke out, Serbia speeded up her negotiations of a military alliance with Bulgaria. Russian diplomacy took part behind the scenes. "Austria has torn off a chunk (Bosnia and Herzegovina) and Italy has torn off another (Tripoli); it is now our turn," wrote Lenin, exposing the arguments of the Russian nationalists. "The Triple Alliance (Germany, Austria and Italy) is weak at the moment," he continued, "for Italy has spent 800 million francs on the war against the Turks, and the 'interests' of Italy and Austria do not coincide in the Balkans. Italy wants to snatch another morsel—Albania—but Austria will not let her. Our nationalists, who count on this, are playing a reckless game of chance, relying on the strength and wealth of two powers in the Triple Entente (Britain and France) and on the fact that 'Europe' will not want a general war over the Straits or over the 'rounding off' of 'our' territories at the expense of Asiatic Turkey."[2] Indeed, taking advantage of the rifts in the Triple Alliance during the Italo-Turkish war, the tsarist government began to weave the meshes—not without French help—that ultimately united the Balkan countries in a politico-military bloc against Turkey as well as against Austria-Hungary. Unprepared as yet for a big war, the tsar's government did not wish Serbia and Bulgaria to get involved in a war with Turkey prematurely.

The Serbo-Bulgarian negotiations dragged on for nearly six months due to acute differences over how to divide Macedonia, which was to be delivered from Turkish rule

[1] Lenin, *Collected Works*, Vol. 19, p. 39.
[2] Ibid., Vol. 18, pp. 339, 340.

and to which Serbia and Bulgaria both laid claim. In the end, a treaty of alliance was concluded on March 13, 1912. Bulgaria and Serbia undertook to support each other if any great power attempted, if only temporarily, to annex any part of the Balkans. Serbia thus secured Bulgarian assistance against the aggressive Austro-Hungarians, while a secret instrument envisaged joint armed action against Turkey. The allies also reached an understanding on Macedonia, setting aside a "controversial zone" whose final fate was to be arbitrated by the Russian tsar. On May 12, 1912, the two countries also concluded a military convention specifying the troops to be put into the field by either party in the event of a conflict with Turkey or Austria-Hungary. Then Bulgaria signed a treaty of alliance with Greece, while Serbia concluded a verbal agreement to the same effect with Montenegro. A Balkan League evolved, whose main purpose was to banish the Turks from the Peninsula. Lenin wrote: "The weakness of the democratic classes in the present-day Balkan states (where the proletariat is small in number and the peasants are downtrodden, disunited and illiterate) has resulted in an economically and politically indispensable alliance becoming an alliance of Balkan monarchies."[1]

In summer and autumn 1912 relations between the Balkan allies and Turkey reached a breaking point. The two sides sent each other threatening notes. Russia and Austria-Hungary issued a declaration on behalf of the European powers to the effect that no violation of the *status quo* in the Balkans would be tolerated. But the warning had no effect.

On October 9 Montenegro started a war against Turkey, joined by Bulgaria and Serbia on October 17 and by Greece the next day. The superior strength of the Balkan allies was manifest from the first.

Serbian troops occupied the upper valley of the Vardar, the Sanjak of Novi-Pazar and the north of Albania, while the Greeks captured Salonika (outstripping the Bulgarian troops, who arrived a few hours later). The Bulgarian army advanced on Istanbul. Turkey still held the stronghold of Edirne (Adrianople), Janina and Shkodër (Scutari).

Turkish feudal rule in the Balkans collapsed. The social impact of this was described by Lenin as follows: "Although the alliance which has come into being in the Balkans is an alliance of monarchies and not of republics,

[1] Ibid., p. 368.

and although this alliance has come about through war and not through revolution, a great step has nevertheless been taken towards doing away with the survivals of medievalism throughout Eastern Europe", where, he noted, *"Russia alone remains the most backward today"*.[1] Assessment of the Balkan developments revealed two distinct political conceptions—the reactionary, bourgeois imperialist and nationalist, on the one hand, and the democratic, socialist and internationalist, on the other.

On November 7, 1912, Lenin wrote in the *Pravda*: "The bourgeoisie, even the liberal bourgeoisie, similar to our Cadets, shouts about the 'national' liberation of the 'Slavs'. Thereby it plainly misrepresents the meaning and historic significance of the events now taking place in the Balkans, and thus *hampers* the real liberation of the Balkan peoples. It thus *contributes* to the preservation of landlord privileges, political tyranny and national oppression in some measure or another.

"On the other hand, the worker democrats are the only ones to champion the real and complete liberation of the Balkan peoples. Nothing but economic and political liberation of the *peasants* of all the Balkan nationalities, carried through to the end, can eliminate all possibility of any sort of national oppression."[2]

Lenin's appraisal of the Balkan war of 1912 was built on the interests of the international working-class and socialist movement. It exposed the imperialist powers who, being rivals, were eager to step into the "vacuum" created by the Turkish defeat.

On November 3, 1912, the Turkish Government asked the great powers to mediate. An armistice was concluded by Turkey and Bulgaria early in December. In the meantime, each of the big European powers attempted to profit by the Balkan situation economically, politically and strategically. This meant, as Lenin put it then, that "the problem's centre of gravity has shifted from the theatre of operations to that of the squabbles and intrigues of the so-called Great Powers".[3] The scrimmage in the Balkans cast a sinister shadow on the overall international situation, presaging a world-wide conflagration.

---

[1] Lenin, *Collected Works*, Vol. 18, p. 369.
[2] Ibid., pp. 398-99.
[3] Ibid., Vol. 19, p. 39.

Soon, a conference of ambassadors of the great powers convened in London, while Turkey and the Balkan allies negotiated the peace terms. The imperialist powers exercised increasing pressure on the talks, and keen differences arose over some issues.

Austria-Hungary was displeased by Serbia's demand of an Adriatic port. Backed by Germany, she mobilised her troops and began massing forces on the Serbian border. Russia approved of Serbia's territorial claims, but counselled the Serbs to avoid an armed clash. France, meanwhile, gravitated towards a more aggressive line, hoping to use the Bulgarian and Serbian armies against the Austro-German bloc in the event of a big European war. Poincaré urged the tsarist government to support Serbia against Austria-Hungary more firmly, while the Paris stock exchange granted the tsarist government a fresh loan, earmarked exclusively for military purposes. Britain, for her part, fanned the antagonisms, hoping to profit subsequently by the role of arbiter. For all this, the powers had not dared to start a big war. Serbia was compelled to abandon her territorial plans on the Adriatic and console herself with a commercial exit to a free port in Albania.

Albania figured high up on the agenda at the London talks. By 1911-12, the national liberation movement swept the entire country. When the Balkan war broke out, the Balkan allies, and the great powers behind them, lost no time to pounce on Albania. Originally, the Balkan League planned to divide Albania between Montenegro, Serbia and Greece. Countering Serbia's claim for an outlet to the Adriatic, Austria-Hungary advocated an "independent" Albania, which it hoped to take under her protection. Italy and Germany backed the Austrian project on the assumption that Albania would be a barrier to Russian influence.

Heeding the Austro-Hungarian claim, on the one hand, and Serbia's, on the other, the powers decided on an autonomous Albania under the suzerainty of the sultan and the control of the European powers.

Shkodër was incorporated in Albania. Montenegro, whose troops were laying siege to Shkodër, refused to comply. Russia supported her. Austria-Hungary screamed abuse. Germany backed the Austrians, and Britain backed Russia. The Albanian question, particularly that of Shkodër, quickly expanded into a major international conflict. At long last Montenegro yielded and withdrew her troops.

Albania regained her statehood. She owed this to the people's struggle against the Turkish yoke and to the war fought against Turkey by the Balkan nations. But she did not, in effect, regain her independence. The foreign powers who put Prince William of Wied, a German, on the Albanian throne, interfered in her affairs.

At the peace negotiations deep-rooted differences came to light on other issues. Bulgaria wanted her borders moved east to include part of Eastern Thrace. Greece, which had occupied Salonika, wanted the Aegean islands and the southern part of Albania. Serbia annexed all Macedonia, including the "controversial zone" and the section earlier designated for Bulgaria, and had no intention of yielding. Bulgaria, in the meantime, refused to recognise the Serbian acquisitions and the transfer of Salonika to Greece.

The situation grew tenser still when a coup d'état in Turkey in January 1913 gave power to the warlike Young Turks, who renewed armed operations against Bulgaria. But soon the Turks suffered defeat again, and a peace treaty drafted under the pressure of the great powers was concluded by the Balkan League and Turkey on May 30, 1913, in London. Turkey retained control only of Istanbul and the adjacent straits zone bounded by a line running from Enos to Midia. The rest of European Turkey, save Albania (constituted as an independent state), was ceded to the members of the Balkan League. Only the fate of the islands in the Aegean Sea was left to be settled by the Great Powers.

The London treaty did not remove the contradictions between the imperialist powers. Those between the Balkan states were also unresolved. If anything, they had become more acute. The outcome of the Balkan war put the Austro-Hungarian bloc at a distinct disadvantage. Turkey, which the Germans had considered a possible ally against Russia, was defeated. Serbia, on the other hand, which had been the principal object of Austria-Hungary's ambitions, had grown stronger. Besides, the very existence of the Balkan League impaired the influence of the Austro-German imperialists on the peninsula, while buttressing that of the Entente powers.

So Austrian and German diplomacy set out to subvert the Balkan alliance. It made the most of the discontent in

Bulgaria over Serbia's acquisition of Macedonia, and endeavoured through tsar Ferdinand of Saxe-Coburg to precipitate a conflict between Bulgaria and the other members of the Balkan League.

Serbia, Montenegro and Greece concluded a secret military alliance against Bulgaria and were soon joined by Rumania. Russian efforts to avert a collision failed. Banking on her superior arms, Bulgaria made a surprise attack on her recent allies on June 29, 1913. However, the Serbian, Montenegrian and Greek troops stood firm, joined by the Rumanians and Turks.

Thus began a second Balkan war. Bulgaria was swiftly beaten. At a conference in Bucharest Bulgaria signed a peace treaty with Serbia, Greece and Rumania on August 10, 1913. A Bulgaro-Turkish peace was signed on September 29. Serbia gained possession of almost all the part of Macedonia previously seized from Turkey by Bulgaria, southern Macedonia and western Thrace went to Greece, southern Dobruja to Rumania and part of eastern Thrace, including Edirne (Adrianople), to Turkey.

Of the territory won in the first Balkan war, Bulgaria retained only a small tract of Macedonia and western Thrace. The Turko-Bulgarian border shifted west of the Enos-Midia line.

The Austro-German imperialists took advantage of the split in the Balkan League. Pro-German sentiment, coupled with revanchist tendencies, ran high in Bulgaria. Also, the German Government despatched a mission to Turkey. Its head, General Liman von Sanders, was soon put in command of Turkish troops stationed in Istanbul, then the capital of the empire. This indicated that Berlin was still intent on its "Baghdad policy" aimed at controlling the Osman empire and turning all Asia Minor into a zone of exclusive German monopoly influence.

The tsar's interests in the Balkans and Turkey, and especially in the Black Sea Straits, imperiled, he protested against the appointment of Liman von Sanders. A new Russo-German conflict began, but soon ended in a compromise. The German Government cancelled Liman's appointment as a corps commander and made him inspector of the Turkish army. The concession was largely a formality and the squabble between Germany and Russia continued.

The Balkan wars did not sluice off the highly inflammable imperialist antagonisms. On the contrary, the situation became more complicated and explosive, not only by reason of the Balkan relationships, but also of imperialist interests.

The arms race, galvanised by the militarists and the war industrial concerns, gained fresh impetus. The ruling classes used it as a means of improving business, but also as a tool against the labour and socialist movement, which worried them despite the ascendancy of reformism and opportunism. At the end of 1913, the bourgeois press, which noted instances of diplomatic animation, tended to create the impression that European governments were preoccupied with home affairs and viewed the coming year optimistically, thinking that if a conflict occurred, it could be localised by diplomatic means.

Parting with 1913, which had been highlighted by the Balkan war and fresh strife among the imperialists, most bourgeois papers said 1914 would witness a relaxation of tension. Lenin, however, predicted that the shift of attention to combating the labour and socialist movement was creating a grave peril to peace. As early as May 1913, he wrote: "The European bourgeoisie clings frantically to the militarists and reactionaries out of fear of the working-class movement. The insignificant number of petty-bourgeois democrats is not capable of a strong desire for peace and still less capable of bringing it about. Power is in the hands of the banks, the trusts and big capital in general. The one guarantee of peace is the organised, conscious movement of the working class."[1]

Immersed in the fight against their respective imperialist rivals and priming for a decisive clash, the ruling classes and governments of the big powers did their utmost to deter and divide the working class, banking chiefly on the support of the reformist and opportunist labour leaders. They sought a way out of their difficulties in speedy war preparations. The peoples of Europe were fast drifting towards a great tragedy.

1960-63

---

[1] Lenin, *Collected Works*, Vol. 19, p. 84.

THE "COLOURED BOOKS"

The voluminous Soviet and foreign collections of documents illustrating the origins of the First World War have discredited the much smaller collections, called "coloured books", issued by belligerent governments in order to prove their love of peace and the enemy's perfidy. Each of the governments involved in the armed collision of imperialist groupings occupied a specific place in the general picture and, accordingly, played a specific role. It was not as easy, therefore, as it may have seemed, to devise a simple and credible tale justifying the war.

The fairly extensive literature we now possess about propaganda techniques in the world war gives us a good idea of the general structure, even of some of the details, relating to the monopoly organisations formed for the sole purpose of conditioning millions of minds.

War propaganda was conducted with eminent skill in diverse directions and with every possible device. But it was all based on the particular conception developed by each government to fit its own purposes. Yet, since all the parties to the imperialist groupings had one purpose in common—that of rousing the people—all official concepts were permeated with the idea that the war was defensive and that it was brought on by the adversary. To bring home this idea—which was as necessary to bring home as it was difficult to substantiate—the governments issued collections of documents debated by the respective parliaments and instantly affecting the mood of the bourgeois press. The "war guilt" problem was not really first raised at Versailles, but in relation to the outbreak of the war, and swiftly became an issue of the class struggle.

This was pinpointed by Harold D. Lasswell, a U.S. investigator of war propaganda techniques. Here is what he said: "The Governments of Western Europe can never be perfectly certain that a class-conscious proletariat within the borders of their authority will rally to the clarion of war." Propaganda—which is a form of class struggle—was therefore so patterned as to rule out "ambiguity about whom the public is to hate".

"The war," Lasswell pointed out, "must not be due to a world system of conducting international affairs, nor to the stupidity or malevolence of all governing classes, but to the rapacity of the enemy.... If the propagandist is to mobilise the hate of the people, he must see to it that everything is circulated which establishes the sole responsibility of the enemy."[1]

1

Books of Lies, the sub-title of the Russian translation of the German *White Book*, could well be written across the cover of every other "coloured" book issued at the beginning of the war. This certainly includes those published by the Entente countries. "Coloured books" were media of political debate and tools of war propaganda, and if the German one differed in any essential respect from the similar products of other governments, this was purely for its somewhat contradictory arguments.

The *White Book* relating to the outbreak of the war which Chancellor Theobald von Bethmann-Hollweg submitted to the Reichstag on August 3, 1914, was completed at noon on August 2. This is a pertinent fact. In view of the extremely swift events, the military and political scheming of the German Government affected both the tenor and the choice of the documents.[2]

The memorandum and the documents in the *White Book* concern the July crisis—from June 28, the day the

---

[1] Lasswell, *Propaganda Technique in the World War*, London, 1927, p. 47.

[2] *Das Deutsche Weissbuch. Wie Russland Deutschland hinterging und den europäischen Krieg entfesselte*, Berlin, 1914.

Austrian Archduke was assassinated in Sarajevo, to August 1, the day of the French mobilisation. Within these chronological limits the material had to be presented as the military and political situation demanded.

Britain still pursued her dual approach to Germany. So the core of the German concept was that the Russian Government had embarked on aggression. To dovetail this with Austria's ultimatum to Serbia, sanctioned by Germany, the book aimed to prove that the German Government had viewed the Austro-Serbian crisis as a local conflict. "From the very beginning of the conflict," the German Government maintained in its *White Book*, "we held the view that the issue concerned none but Austria and should be resolved by Austria and Serbia. This is why we concentrated all our efforts on localising the war and prevailing on the other powers that Austria-Hungary was compelled to resort to arms by force of circumstances and the legitimate necessity of self-defence."

Glossing over the fact that Germany had supported, even guided the Austrian demarches after the assassination in Sarajevo, the *White Book* confined itself to the communication that Germany had accorded Austria-Hungary freedom of action in regard to Serbia and had stood aloof. Russia's intervention in the Austro-Serbian conflict was thus inferred as the decisive factor turning a conflict of no more than local significance into an all-European war.

Germany's attitude is presented from two points of view—first, unqualified but passive sanctioning of the Austro-Hungarian stand vis-à-vis Serbia and, second, persevering mediation attempts from the moment Russia intervened in the Austro-Serbian conflict. These two contentions were far removed from the truth, but mirrored the general political trend pursued by the German Government.

The German book contains none of the numerous messages exchanged by Berlin and Vienna during the prewar crisis. If at least one of these had been published, it would have knocked the political conception of the *White Book* into a cocked hat. The German Government had to conceal not only the fact of its active support of Austria-Hungary, but also some of the Austro-German tactical differences in connection with the threatening stance assumed by Britain between July 28 and 31. In view of the outbreak of war, the Germans wished to parade their noninvolvement, on the one hand, and their loyalty to commitments, on the other, thus underscoring the solidity of the Austro-German political alliance. The impression was to be created that Germany had become involved in the conflagration due to her passive attitude towards the reckless policy of Austria-Hungary.

The German Government kept up its posture to the end.

The demonstration of Austro-German firmness affected the general conception of the outbreak of war. Since the particulars in some of the documents would, if presented in full, reveal the true nature of the Austro-German relationship during the July crisis, the German Government preferred to mutilate, condense, amend, etc. Some of the documents relating to the efforts of mediation between Vienna and Petersburg, made at the close of July, could have helped the German Government to claim that Germany had done her utmost to avert the war imposed by Russia. But the idea of putting these documents into the *White Book* had to be abandoned. The war had begun and the least hint of friction between German and Austrian policy had to be avoided. What had to be stressed was not so much the defensive nature of Germany's own position as the distinctly aggressive nature of Russian policy.

The latter half of the issue was easier to compile, but all the same the documents had to be doctored. The desired result was achieved by expurgating and abridging the material relating to Russian policy. The tsar's telegram to Wilhelm, sent in the evening of July 29, suggesting that the Austro-Serbian conflict be submitted to The Hague tribunal, was simply left out, evidently because it may have indicated Russian readiness to make concessions.

Naturally, the Russian Government could at any time publish the telegram and expose the German version. It could also use it for anti-German propaganda. This is why German historians wrote subsequently that failure to publish the document had been a "tactically unwise" move.[1]

The main purpose of the *White Book* was to demonstrate the aggressiveness of the Russian Government. Wilhelm believed this essential, among other things, to win the backing of the German Social-Democrats. He thought his

---

[1] A. Bach, "Das erste deutsche Weissbuch", *Die Kriegsschuldfrage*, 1925, XI, S. 773.

purpose was best served by minimising the part France had played in precipitating the war. France was portrayed simply as a companion of Russia who followed her ally passively. The charge that France had provoked the war was withheld, because Germany was not yet at war with France when the *White Book* was being compiled (August 2). Besides, she was aware of the nature of Anglo-French relations.

Britain's conduct during the pre-war crisis, as mirrored in the German *White Book*, was given a peculiar slant. Britain was portrayed as a staunch champion of European peace. Documents testifying to the contrary were withheld (e.g., the German ambassador's telegram from London warning his government of Edward Grey's strongly anti-German sentiment). This was done for two reasons. First, to avoid irritating Britain, which could remain neutral, and, second, to accuse her of unheard-of perfidy if she should ultimately enter the war. An entirely incorrect impression was created of Anglo-German relations on the eve of the war. Thus, since Britain joined the war a few days later, the German Government provided documentary proof of its political incapacity. Later, in a new, considerably revised edition of the *White Book* it altered the pattern, but the original version of the *White Book* was borrowed by the British for their *Blue Book*, which appeared just two days later (on August 5, 1914), in order to justify Britain's entry into the war on the side of France and Russia against Germany. The British Government, after all, had ample experience in selecting and juggling diplomatic documents.

2

The *Blue Book* was designed to back up the speech delivered by Sir Edward Grey in the House of Commons on August 3, 1914, endeavouring to prove that Britain had no choice but to declare war on Germany.[1] "We shall publish papers as soon as we can regarding what took place last week when we were working for peace," said Grey

---

[1] *Great Britain and the European Crisis. Correspondence and Statements in Parliament, Together with an Introductory Narrative of Events*, London, 1914, pp. 123-24.

in this speech, "and when those papers are published I have no doubt that to every human being they will make it clear how strenuous and genuine and whole-hearted our efforts for peace were, and that they will enable people to form their own judgement as to what forces were at work which operated against peace."

Since the German Government had, in the hope of Britain remaining neutral, registered the conciliatory nature of Britain's policy, the British *Blue Book* had half its work done for it.

But Grey also had to justify the war against Germany by exclusively British interests, allegedly unassociated with any secret agreement or any "obligation of honour". The claim to Britain's being "free to decide" was the main guideline in selecting documents for the *Blue Book*. Need it be said that the approach employed in arguing Britain's case was deliberately false. France was said to have been compelled to defend herself against a German attack. Belgium's neutrality, guaranteed by the powers in 1839, was used as the decisive argument. "If her independence goes," Grey said in the Commons, "the independence of Holland will follow. I ask the House from the point of view of British interests, to consider what may be at stake."

In fact, however, the stakes had been made years before the war. Britain's policy-makers had known that in the event of a war on two fronts Germany would be sure to violate Belgian neutrality. Much more, in 1887, when Britain entered the Mediterranean Entente formed with Germany's covert support, she had been prepared to let Germany violate the neutrality of Belgium.[1]

In 1907, when the *Entente cordiale* was in the completion stage Britain's General Staff approached the Belgians concerning possible joint armed actions. In effect, therefore, Belgian neutrality had long since been a political fiction. Information at the disposal of the German Government during the first Moroccan crisis indicated that Britain had three alternate plans for shipping an expeditionary corps in the event of a Franco-German war: via Calais and Dunkirk, via Schleswig and Denmark and, lastly, via Belgium.[2] The last of these was considered the most prob-

---

[1] H. Lutz, *Lord Grey und der Weltkrieg*, Berlin, 1927, S. 257.
[2] GP, Bd. XXI, No. 6946.

able. The neutrality of Holland and Denmark to which Grey referred in his speech, had long been prejudiced, and by Britain not least of all.

The fiction of Belgian neutrality, which could be presented as a political fact in view of the special secrecy shrouding the Anglo-Belgian talks, was followed by an outright falsification of the crucial issue, that of Anglo-French relations. To prove that Britain was uninvolved in any political combinations, had no political or military commitments to live up to and had given France "no promise of anything more than diplomatic support", Grey resorted to what may, mildly speaking, be described as sleight-of-hand. Releasing the text of his unpublished letter to Cambon, French Ambassador in London, of November 22, 1912, which unofficially set out the principles of joint Anglo-French land and naval action, that is, commitments of a definite nature, Grey underscored that part of it which said Britain and France should discuss whether "to act together to prevent aggression and to preserve peace, and, if so, what measures they would be prepared to take in common". He left out the next sentence, which contained the principle of joint armed action against Germany. *If the measures would include armed action*, it said, *the General Staff plans should be taken into account without delay, and the government would decide to what extent they should be implemented.*[1]

Grey banked on the gullibility of his readers when he later wrote in his memoirs that inadvertently he had overlooked the sentence (which was a commitment in the full sense of the word) when Britain's entry into the war was being debated, because he was overwrought or, perhaps, thought it irrelevant.[2] Naturally, the reasons for the omission were entirely different. He affected simpleness in dealing with a matter he thought best hushed up. Speaking of the Anglo-French agreement of 1904, for example, both Grey[3] and Poincaré[4] refer but vaguely to its secret part as to something of secondary importance, although it con-

---

[1] B. v. Siebert, *Diplomatische Aktenstücke zur Geschichte der Ententepolitik der Vorkriegsjahre*, Berlin-Leipzig, 1921, S. 816.

[2] Grey, *Twenty-Five Years (1892-1916)*, Vol. II, London, 1926, p. 17.

[3] Ibid., Vol. I, p. 49.

[4] Poincaré, *Au service de la France, Neuf années de souvenirs*, v. 1, Paris, 1926, p. 107.

cerned Egypt and Morocco. In Poincaré's case the manoeuvre is camouflaged by good literary style, but in Grey's it is abused to absurdity. Affected simpleness fails when it is meant to vindicate previously carefully concealed facts that had come to public notice.

The other dodge, that of falsification and subterfuge, was more effective in Grey's speech of August 3 and in the *Blue Book*. Here are a few illustrations (not the most striking by far). The *Blue Book* contained the telegram despatched on July 24, 1914 by George Buchanan, British Ambassador to Petersburg, saying that in the opinion of the Russian Government, which had received the text of the Austrian ultimatum to Serbia, war was unavoidable. Buchanan gave his private opinion that no British declaration would contain "an unconditional engagement ... to support Russia and France by force of arms".

"Direct British interests in Serbia were nil," Buchanan said, "and a war on behalf of that country would never be sanctioned by British public opinion." This was the sentence that made the document worth publishing. The telegram also reported on the political agreements concluded during Poincaré's stay in Petersburg somewhat earlier, which had been revealed to Buchanan. In the light of how the British posture during the crisis was subsequently presented, the makers of British policy had no business knowing the content of the Franco-Russian talks concerning a plan of action which ultimately brought on the war. Otherwise British policy could at best be branded as dual. This is why a large passage of the telegram concerning the agreement reached during Poincaré's visit was circumspectly deleted. Also deleted was the sentence that gave reason to infer that if Britain had firmly rejected the aggressive implications of the tsar's policy at the beginning of the crisis, Russia would never have gone as far as it went.[1]

The object was to conceal the true nature of Britain's policy, a policy of deliberate waiting until the contradictions reached a point of no return, a policy of deliberate tacit support of France and Russia and, at once, of adroit provocation in relation to Germany. This is evident from what was done to Buchanan's telegram of July 25. It dealt

---

[1] BD, v. XI, No. 101.

with the obdurate representations of the Russian foreign minister, Sazonov, for Britain to dissipate Germany's confidence in her neutrality and forthwith publicly to join the Franco-Russian alliance. The version of the telegram made public by the British Government says the British Ambassador had replied that "England could play the role of mediator at Berlin and Vienna to better purpose as a friend". But the true sense of this pacifist formula is betrayed by the general content: after the French Government announced its unreserved determination to go with Russia, the British said it was necessary "to gain time".[1] Naturally, this had to be deleted. Britain's concern for peace is also illustrated by démarches taken in Petersburg angling for assurances that "Russia would not precipitate war by mobilising". What weight could such démarches have if they were made in reply to a Russian communication that mobilisation of 1,100,000 men had already begun?

The purpose was to create the impression that the British Government had tried to prevent the Russian mobilisation, which had a crucial bearing on subsequent events, and that it had not been warned of it by the Russian Government. Since the British commitments to France were being concealed from the public, everything hinting of France's unconditional resolve to back Russia in her conflict with Austria-Hungary over Serbia had also to be deleted. This was doubly true of France's blunt demand that Britain announce her readiness to honour commitments. "The French ambassador remarked," Buchanan noted in the telegram of July 25, "that the French Government would want to know at once whether our fleet was prepared to play the part assigned to it by Anglo-French Naval Convention. He could not believe that England would not stand by her two friends, who were acting as one in this matter."

This passage, too, was deleted, because British propaganda was endeavouring to show that Britain was stampeded into the war in behalf of her own interests, not by virtue of any extraneous commitments.

The British Government's propaganda aim of showing documentally that it had worked for peace entailed considerable effort: more than 100 of the 159 specially selected documents had to be falsified before publication.

---

[1] Ibid., No. 125.

Just as the *Blue Book* was put out to bear out documentally the conception formulated in Grey's speech in the Commons, so the *Orange Book* of the Russians, issued by the tsarist government on August 6,[1] was meant to substantiate the primitive conception presented by Sazonov in the State Duma. "Our enemies," Sazonov had declared, "are trying to blame us for the calamity they have loosened on Europe, but their false charges will mislead no one who has followed Russia's policies of the past years and past days."

Next, Sazonov resorted to the trick of blaming Austria-Hungary for the second Balkan war and glossing over Russia's part in precipitating the first. The same trick was employed in the *Orange Book*.

It was simple. The point was that the formal declaration of war—on France, as well as Russia—had come from the Germans. This made it easy to portray Germany as the chief "culprit of the war". The official version was that Austria-Hungary backed by Germany had attacked Serbia, expecting thereby to humiliate Russia, which had jointly with France and Britain done her utmost to achieve a peaceful solution of the conflict. Perfidious Germany, however, frustrated all peace overtures by Russia, her friends and her allies and, as Sazonov claimed, "for her own part, made empty assurances". Russia was therefore compelled, particularly by Austria's threatening posture, to mobilise her army and navy, while the tsar "had the grace to give his royal word to the German emperor that Russia would not resort to force".

Germany replied by declaring war. The conclusion of this artless government version was somewhat startling: Germany is the sole culprit of the war, because it had the temerity of putting greater credence in the mobilisation than in the "royal word".

These arguments delighted the bourgeois-landowner Duma. Now the official version of how the war broke out had to be backed up by documents. And since the latter did not bear out the government story, they had to be doctored.[2]

---

[1] *Oranzhevaya kniga. Sbornik diplomaticheskikh dokumentov*, Petersburg, 1914 (Russ ed.).

[2] C. v. Romberg, *Die Fälschungen des russischen Orangebuches*, Berlin, 1922.

Publication by Soviet Russia of the tsarist government's secret documents restored the picture of Russia's policies during the pre-war crisis, lifting the veil on the lie factory quartered in the tsar's foreign ministry, whose purpose it was to manufacture materials for political and military propaganda.[1]

It stands to reason that the documents connoting that "Germany did not aspire to a war at all costs"[2] had to be most thoroughly concealed. So were all clues likely to indicate the real reasons why the various German proposals for localising the Austro-Serbian conflict had been rejected. It was important in the political context to establish that "Germany's conduct of affairs was unquestionably aimed at dividing Russia and France, inveigling France into making representations in Petersburg and so compromising unity in our eyes, and in the event of a war putting the blame not on Germany ... but on Russia and France."[3]

The fact that the French Government, wishing to add tension, had deliberately delayed its reply to the German proposal for collective mediation, was naturally concealed. More deletion was necessary to hush up Izvolsky's revealing report. "I was struck," wrote Izvolsky to Petersburg, "to what extent the minister of justice [Bienvenu-Martin, who deputised for the foreign minister.—A. Y.] and his associates had grasped the situation and how firmly and calmly they were determined to accord us every support and to avoid the least difference with us."[4]

The documents were published after considerable doctoring to avoid all indications that the French Government had goaded Russia into battle with promises of support. The

---

[1] *Diplomaticheskaya perepiska s Berlinom za period 7 (20. VII-19. VII (1-VIII) 1914 (Krasny arkhiv*, 1922, t. 1); *Materialy po istorii franko-russkikh otnoshenii za 1910-1914. Sbornik sekretnykh diplomaticheskikh dokumentov byvsh. imp. rossiiskogo ministerstva inostrannykh del*, Moscow, 1922; *Mezhdunarodniye otnosheniya v epokhu imperializma*, ser. III, t. IV, V (Russ. ed.).

[2] "Sekretnaya telegramma rossiiskogo poverennogo v delakh v Parizhe Sevastopulo ot 25 (12) iyunya 1914, No. 186", *Materialy po istorii franko-russkikh otnoshenii*, p. 514; *Un livre noir. Diplomatie d'avant-guerre d'après les documents des archives russes, novembre 1910-juillet 1914*, v. II, p. 277; cf. *Oranzhevaya kniga*, No. 19.

[3] *Oranzhevaya kniga*, No. 35.

[4] Telegram of July 14 (27), 1914, No. 195, *Materialy po istorii franko-russkikh otnoshenii*, p. 520; *Livre noir*, v. II, p. 282.

French attitude had delighted Izvolsky, the Russian Ambassador to Paris, who thus reaped the harvest of long years in office. "It is my war," he declared later.

The part played by France had to be concealed because, for one thing, she was Russia's ally, but much more to justify Russia's own political and military behaviour. The chronological order of events had to be juggled, too, especially in regard to the general mobilisation. Officially, the mobilisation in Russia, which evoked a similar move on Germany's part, had followed the general mobilisation in Austria-Hungary and was therefore defensive. This had to be substantiated by documents. A very simple expedient was used. War preparations, Sazonov had cabled, "were made by us only after Austria mobilised eight corps". The last two words—"eight corps"—were deleted,[1] creating the impression that Russia had mobilised her troops in response to a general Austrian mobilisation. To prove its point and impress the petty-bourgeois and the worker, the tsarist government published a telegram indicating that "even Jaurès strongly condemned the Austrian stand, which may precipitate a universal war".[2] But it omitted all references to the anti-war demonstrations of French workers and to French Government measures to "convince" the French revolutionary workers that the war was defensive.[3]

How far the tsarist government went to dissipate suspicions about the actual behaviour of the French is illustrated by the following. "Last night," Izvolsky reported to Petersburg on August 1, "the Austrian ambassador called twice on Viviani [the French Premier.—A.Y.] ... and told him Austria had no intention of violating Serbia's territorial integrity and was prepared to discuss with the other powers her falling out with Serbia. *Today, before the appointed hour, the German ambassador called on Viviani, who expressed his surprise over the German's attitude of the day before, unjustified by Franco-German relations. When the ambassador said Germany was compelled to take vigorous measures in view of the general mobilisation of Russian land and naval forces, manifestly directed not only*

---

[1] *Oranzhevaya kniga*, No. 58.

[2] Ibid., No. 19.

[3] Cf. *Oranzhevaya kniga*, No. 55; *Materialy*, p. 519; *Livre noir*, v. II, p. 288.

against Austria but against Germany as well, Viviani replied that as far as he knew no naval mobilisation had taken place. This perplexed the ambassador. At the end of a long conversation, Baron Schoen renewed his demand for a declaration of French intentions and his threat to leave, and asked Viviani to receive him once more today at 6 p.m. Despite the casual nature of the German ambassador's démarche today, the French Government is perturbed by the extraordinary German military preparations on the French border, convinced that a full-scale mobilisation is under way behind the cloak of the so-called *Kriegszustand, putting the French army at a disadvantage. On the other hand, for political reasons concerning Italy and especially Britain, France cannot afford to mobilise before the Germans. French mobilisation must come as a reply to Germany's. The matter is being discussed this very moment by the Council of Ministers at the Palais de l'Elysée, and probably it will decide on a general mobilisation."*[1]

The foregoing italicised words were omitted in the *Orange Book*. The meaning was thus entirely distorted. This was just what the tsarist government wanted, whose version was promptly borrowed by the French.

By and large, the Entente governments did not passively accept each other's versions. They did not each independently publish and doctor the appropriate documentary material. They compared notes and eased the way for each other, and, moreover, established a system of mutual verification. This was not mere loyalty. It was important to produce their own versions of how the war broke out, but no less important to co-ordinate their versions with those of their allies, because any conflicting element could discredit them and their diplomacy.

In the archives of the tsarist foreign ministry we found the illuminating exchanges between the tsarist and British governments on co-ordinating certain falsifications. The British Government, which wanted to publish certain documents relating to Anglo-Russian relations in Persia on the eve of the war, sought Russian consent and informed Petersburg of the deletions it was intending to make. The tsarist government agreed and issued an order that the

---

[1] *Oranzhevaya kniga*, No. 73; *Materialy*, p. 253; *Livre noir*, v. II, p. 295.

British deletions should be taken into account in any Russian publication to avoid embarrassment for the Foreign Office.

4

This naturally complicated publication of the documents. The French Government therefore published its *Yellow Book*[1] after a considerable lapse of time. French officials ascribed the delay to the thoroughness and completeness of their publication. But it is more probable that it simply took them a long time to falsify documents and, furthermore, to produce documents that had never existed.

The intention was to prove that France had worked tirelessly for a peaceful settlement of the Austro-Serbian conflict, and that she had been compelled to do her duty by her ally, tsarist Russia, in face of the threat emanating from militarist Germany and Germany's attack on Russia.

To provide this version with a basis in history and to infer Germany's sole war guilt, the French *Yellow Book*, unlike the other "coloured books", which dealt only with events of the immediate pre-war period, opened with documents dating to early 1913. These were meant to demonstrate Germany's aggressiveness and long-time war preparations. If the French publication had opened with, say, the minutes of conferences held jointly by the French and Russian naval staffs, the political effect would have been entirely different. For this reason, the historical references were most thoroughly censored.

Besides withholding a number of important documents, the French Government resorted to other, more subtle, methods. A telegram dated July 30, 1914, for example, listed in the *Yellow Book* as No. 106, informs Grey of French and German war preparations in a manner showing that the French Government, "like Russia, is not responsible for the attack". The message was said to have been despatched by French Premier René Viviani through Paul Cambon, the French Ambassador in London. Yet it has now been ascertained that the document was no more than an

---

[1] *Le livre jaune. Documents diplomatiques français, relatifs à l'origine de la guerre, texte officiel complet*, Paris, 1915.

amalgam of two different documents. In addition, a number of omissions, alterations and outright falsifications were made, whose general political purpose may be illustrated by the following example. In enumerating the ostensibly belated and defensive measures of the French, which it called counter-measures, the document says *inter alia* that the railway stations were put under military control in France on "Tuesday, July 28", whereas the authentic documents said "on Sunday", indicating that the French railways were militarised as early as July 26.

True to the version devised by the tsarist government, the French policy-makers were hard put to it to falsify the chronology of the mobilisation. To prove the inevitability of the war, Poincaré informed the British Ambassador in Paris Bertie in the morning of August 1, 1914, that Russia had announced a general mobilisation in reply to the general mobilisation in Austria-Hungary. To substantiate this claim, the following manipulation was made with the telegram of the French ambassador in Vienna, despatched on July 31, 1914: after the ambassador's words, "a mobilisation applying to all men of 19 to 42 was decreed by the Austro-Hungarian Government" the words *"early this morning"* were added, while the rest of the text, embarrassing to the French Government, was simply deleted. The French Government stopped at nothing to attain its propaganda goal. Whenever the desired material was non-existent, it was simply forged. The brief telegram of the French ambassador in Petersburg, dated July 31, which read, "the order has been issued for the general mobilisation of the Russian army", was published as follows: *"Due to the general mobilisation in Austria and the secret mobilisation in Germany in the past six days, the order has been issued for the general mobilisation of the Russian army to avoid the risks of being outstripped: in fact, it took such military steps as Germany had already taken. For imperious strategic reasons the Russian Government could not, knowing that Germany was arming, delay the conversion of its partial mobilisation into a general mobilisation."*

All the italicised words did not occur in Maurice Paléologue's telegram, and it may be taken for granted that they were fabricated by the French Ministry of Foreign Affairs.

To disguise their imperialist aims, the governments of the Austro-German bloc were no less concerned (than those of the Entente) to support with documents their official version about the defensive nature of their stand. But unlike the Austro-German bloc, the Entente powers claimed to have championed lesser peoples. To make their point they produced the story of defending "little Serbia" and "little defenceless Belgium", assaulted by "Huns".

Lenin observed early in the war that "the national element is represented *only* by Serbia's war against Austria".[1] He stressed, however, that it "is an entirely secondary consideration and does not affect the general imperialist character of the war".[2]

The royal Serbian Government was, indeed, eager to corroborate the official versions engineered by the Entente governments.

On November 18, 1914, Serbia published a collection of documents, entitled the *Blue Book*, which was intended to bear out not only the peaceful aspirations of the Serbian Government, but also its innocence of the Sarajevo assassination. The methods of the Serbian publication differed from other "coloured books" only in the measure of its feigned naïveté. From the prolific correspondence between Petersburg and Belgrade, the Serbian Government saw fit to publish the minimum number of non-committal documents. The political accents were all so placed as to portray Serbia and tsarist Russia as conciliatory to the extreme. The question of the Sarajevo assassination, too, which was organised by the Black Hand, a secret society of officers, was naturally sidestepped.

In a modestly sized *Grey Book*,[3] the Belgian Government endeavoured to show France's formal readiness to observe Belgium's neutrality (No. 13), inferring thereby that Germany alone was responsible for violating international law.

The Austro-German group could not afford to ignore the Serbian and Belgian books. In 1915, the Austro-Hungarian

---

[1] Lenin, *Collected Works*, Vol. 21, p. 235.
[2] Ibid., p. 159.
[3] *Livre gris belge. Correspondance diplomatique ... relative à la guerre de 1914*, Berne, 1914.

Government came out with a *Red Book*,[1] a collection of documents bearing out the charges made in Austria's ultimatum to Serbia (particularly concerning the activities of the *Narodna odbrana*). The *Red Book* also endeavoured to prove that Austria had not prepared for war until the "Serbian mobilisation" (No. 39), that Russia had been the first to embark on general mobilisation (No. 42), and, briefly, that "Russia . . . attacked Germany".

The same means were used to attain different goals, and diametrically opposite contentions were backed by the same arguments.

In May 1915, when she entered the war against her former allies on the side of the Entente, Italy, too, attempted to substantiate her decision in a collection of diplomatic documents entitled the *Green Book*.[2] This small collection consisting of just 77 documents, was no less weighted than all the other "coloured books" of the two coalitions. If anything, it was even more one-sided. None but documents concerning Italy's relations with Austria-Hungary and Germany were selected. The choice was governed by the wish to prove, firstly, that by entering the war against Serbia without consulting Italy, Austria-Hungary had violated the terms of the Triple Alliance and, secondly, that Austria-Hungary and Germany were answerable to Italy for not giving her the territorial compensations she had asked for.

The Italian Government did not mention the documents showing that Italy had a secret neutrality treaty with France, concluded at the turn of the century when she was still a member of the Austro-Hungarian bloc. Furthermore, it also concealed its prolific correspondence with the Entente powers. A survey of its correspondence with the powers of the two military coalitions would have shown that Italy's rulers had played a devious diplomatic game amounting to territorial extortion under cover of neutrality. All in all, the *Green Book* was intended to disguise the programme of conquest pursued by the Italian imperial-

---

[1] *Österreichisch-ungarisches Rotbuch. Diplomatische Aktenstücke zur Vorgeschichte des Krieges 1914*, Wien, 1915.

[2] *Atti parlamentari. Legislativa XXIV—Camera dei deputati, No. XXXII (Documenti). Documenti diplomatici presentati al Parlamento Italiano dal Ministro degli affari esteri (Sonnino)*, Milano, 1915.

ists, for which the people of Italy had been dragged into a war on the side of the Entente.

The rulings classes in the belligerent countries hid their true imperialist goals behind a smokescreen of claims that the armed conflict was defensive. The secret diplomacy of the imperialist states had prepared the war methodically and continued its persistent efforts after it finally broke out in preparation for a redivision of the world. Lenin wrote back in 1916: "They [the bourgeois governments.—*A. Y.*] are enmeshed in a net of *secret treaties* with each other, with their allies, and against their allies. And the content of these treaties is not accidental, it was not determined merely by 'malice', but by the whole course and development of imperialist foreign policy."[1]

To reveal to the people that they had methodically prepared for war was the last thing the imperialists, their governments and their historians, wished to do. The true war aims were being concealed thoroughly. The people were led to believe that the war had been imposed from outside, that it was a defensive and holy war.

The imperialist legend was woven, and the Social-Democrats became its disseminators. The "coloured books", which consisted of specially selected and doctored material, were an attempt to substantiate the respective political myths. It was a criminal offence at the time to doubt the sacred nature of the war and ascribe it to the imperialist ambitions of the governing classes. The official conception of why and how the world war had broken out was turned into a compulsory article of faith, backed up by the social-democratic parties, who thus betrayed the cause of the labour and socialist movement and espoused nationalism and chauvinism.

Lenin and the Bolsheviks did a great service to history at the beginning of the war, when a nationalist frenzy gripped all the belligerent countries, by raising their voices boldly to expose the official versions of the various governments and the sophisms of the social-chauvinist parties.[2] "The entire economic and diplomatic history of the last few decades," wrote Lenin, "shows that both groups of belligerent nations were systematically preparing the

---

[1] Lenin, *Collected Works*, Vol. 23, p. 127.
[2] Ibid., Vol. 21, pp. 15-19.

very kind of war such as the present. The question of which group dealt the first military blow or first declared war is immaterial in any determination of the tactics of socialists. Both sides' phrases on the defence of the fatherland, resistance to enemy invasion, a war of defence, etc., are nothing but deception of the people."[1]

The "coloured books" were part of the grand fraud. No matter how many newly selected documents were produced, and no matter how adroitly these were embellished with arguments, none of them stood the test of time. History has shown that the various government versions were essentially specious, and thereby condemned all attempts of bourgeois historiography to modify them, to give them substance and to make them prevail. The European nations paid dearly for succumbing to the nationalist frenzy of 1914.

History proved thereby how profoundly Lenin understood the essence of things and how far ahead he saw when he exposed the falsehoods obscuring the imperialist nature of the conflict and blazed the trail in the fight against the war. May that be to the historian a reminder of his scientific, moral and political responsibility to his contemporaries.

1932

---

[1] Ibid., p. 159.

German civil and military representatives led by Matthias Erzberger emerged from Marshal Foch's railway coach in Compiègne at five in the morning on November 11, 1918, after signing an armistice containing the Allied terms of surrender. Six hours later the guns fell silent. The victor nations rejoiced that the First World War was over. In Germany, a revolution raged. The Kaiser had fled to Holland on the night of November 8 and his generals had scurried to hiding places.

For most people, the end of the war had come unexpectedly. When the guns began to boom in Europe in August 1914, nobody had any inkling how long the fighting would last. In Germany, it is true, the troops departing for the trenches were told they would soon come home. It was not a deliberate lie, rather a reasoned estimate. Germany's military leaders were convinced that events would follow the course charted in the Schlieffen-Moltke plan based on the idea of a swift war, with France subdued at one blow, then Russia, leaving Britain, the ruler of the waves, without mainland allies. German strategy was to avenge the debacle of German diplomacy, which had failed over the decades, ever since Bismarck's time, to isolate the adversaries from each other and thus avoid a war on two fronts. This objective had been impracticable: German militarism was not afforded the chance to crush its adversaries one by one. Besides, in the drive for world supremacy the German imperialists had antagonised all the major powers on all the continents. The rulers of the Entente, the other imperialist coalition which controlled vast economic and manpower resources, had been priming for a redivision of the world just as doggedly.

How could Germany win in the circumstances?

Six weeks after the war began it was clear that the Schlieffen-Moltke plan had foundered. However, mesmerised by its logic, certain of the superiority of German arms and proud of their own strategic wisdom, the German generals thought they could win a war of attrition if the swift war had failed. Two years went by. In 1916 the Germans were no closer to success. Bled white at Verdun, the German western armies had to stem powerful Anglo-French assaults on the Somme, and in the east a Russian breakthrough in Galicia imperiled the strategic situation of the Germans and their allies. German diplomacy was forced to go into action again, seeking to divide the Allies by various "peace" moves.

Although their original strategic plan had collapsed and the war had dragged out, it never occurred to the rulers of Germany that they had in effect lost. The more so since the German armies had captured vast territory in the east, west and south. Their faith in victory was fortified when Field-Marshal von Hindenburg was put in supreme command with Quartermaster-General Ludendorff as his chief-of-staff. Ludendorff, unquestionably one of the most eminent war adventurers of his time, was a cruel, persevering and imperious man, cold-blooded when scheming and hot-blooded in the fray, who later confessed that for him the war was a "wanton and delirious game", a game, we may add, in which millions of lives were sacrificed in the name of German imperialist world rule.

In September 1917 Ludendorff declared that Germany would not restrict herself to merely annexing territories already captured in the east and west. He wanted the Baltic states, Poland, a big slice of the Ukraine, Belgium, Holland and France, and "points of support across the ocean, in America and Africa, and naval bases within and without the limits of the colonial empire". He was determined on securing for Germany "economic and military conditions which will make possible another war without any doubt at all as to its outcome".

At the height of one war, as we see, the German command was working on plans for another! To be sure, these were not procreated by the ambitious mind of the Quartermaster-General. They had been nurtured by the German imperialists since the turn of the century, especially on the eve and at the beginning of the world war and, apart from the conquest of Europe, envisaged extensive colonial acquisitions in Asia, Africa and Oceania. In a nutshell, the imperialist and militarist leaders of Germany regarded the present and future as a continuously widening drive for world supremacy.

The success of German arms on the continent and the high seas was so substantial on the face of it, that the enemy was dismayed. The merciless German submarine war was anything but unsuccessful in its early stages, but failed to bring Britain to her knees. When the British navy began convoying the nation's merchant shipping, the submarines lost their sting. On the other hand, coupled with the provocative conduct of German diplomacy, it hastened the entry into the war of the United States.

The 1917 Socialist Revolution in Russia was a major setback for imperialism and repatterned the system of international relations. Germany's civil and military leaders did not, and could not, understand that a new era had begun. Blinded by their military successes, they hurried to exploit the predatory Brest peace to overrun vast territories in Russia and to transfer a large portion of their troops from east to west in the hope of crushing the Anglo-French forces.

The war was running out, but its outcome was still unclear. The German bloc was in control of vast territory in Europe—Belgium, part of France, part of northern Italy, the Balkan countries, and particularly large areas in the East: Poland, the Baltic states, the Ukraine and part of Russia. True, Germany had lost her colonies in Africa and the Pacific, but these did not weigh heavily on the scales. The showdown was fast approaching, with the balance seemingly tilting in favour of Germany. Yet her allies—Bulgaria and Turkey, and also Austria-Hungary— were beginning to lose faith, each looking for a way out of the impasse. Germany's rulers were still detailing how they would recast the map of the world, but they, too, were beginning to doubt the feasibility of their military and political schemes.

The German decision to launch a final desperate offensive matured in the winter of 1917-18. It did not stem from confidence in the power of the German armies and in early victory. On the contrary, the German generals had begun to realise that their war machine was losing muscle. It was badly depleted. Its losses were tremendous. The command had to comb the rear for reinforcements. The shortage of experienced officers was disastrous. The stockpile of strategic raw materials was shrinking, while new "ersatzes" could not fill the gaping breach. All this was disguised by loud talk. The people of Germany, her allies and, much more, the enemy, were not to suspect that German strength had waned and that the canker of defeat was already eroding the armed forces.

Final victory kept slipping out of Germany's grasp. The German command scrutinised the state of the army and the possibilities of reinforcing it. After weighing the pros and cons, it rejected the idea of going on the defensive. "Apart from the fact that our going over on the defensive would create an unfavourable impression among our allies," Ludendorff said later, "I feared that defensive battles, in which the enemy would have the advantage of concentrating his striking power in specific battlefields, would affect our troops more adversely than offensive operations. Offensives tax the soldier less than defence.... Offensives yield a tremendous moral uplift, which we could not afford to give up voluntarily. In defence, the weaknesses of our troops were sure to come to view in relief."

The die was cast. It was cast for an offensive, an offensive at all costs. "We had no other choice," wrote General von Kuhl in a book about the German campaign of 1918. The increasing economic difficulties coupled with manpower shortages, on the one hand, and the expanding strength of the Entente, particularly since the arrival of U.S. troops in Europe, on the other, forced the German command to mount a major offensive in the west, as well as the east. The German leaders calculated on paper that the U.S. army would not concentrate its forces in Europe until 1920 and that capture of the vast Russian territories would yield immediate advantages, both military and economic. Those were calculations of reckless adventurers, a frantic gamble. The German command overlooked an insoluble contradiction: conquest required immense material resources and manpower or, more precisely, just what the new offensive in the west required as well. Yet Ludendorff made up his mind to stake all he had on a victory prior to the landing of the main U.S. forces. "If the offensive had succeeded," he wrote later, "its strategic result would, in any case, have been very great."

The Anglo-French command knew that Ludendorff would try a fresh mammoth offensive in the spring of 1918, but nobody suspected that it would be the last major German drive. The military situation of the Allies was fairly grave. The British troops had not yet recovered from their reverses at Passchendaele, France was gripped by confusion and her armies were enmeshed in a reorganisation instituted by the bungling Pétain. All British and French hopes were therefore pinned on the United States.

An American mission headed by Col. Edward House, personal representative of President Wilson, had come to London at the close of 1917. Lloyd George told him his country was giving her last shirt to beat the Germans. He wanted the United States to provide the greatest possible number of men, trained as quickly as humanly possible and properly equipped. He also demanded that U.S. shipbuilding should be expanded to then unprecedented dimensions. Furthermore, he demanded food supplies. But what he asked for most was haste. He described the existing state of affairs in sombre tones, lest the Americans think they had all the time in the world to build up their army. It would be wrong to think, he said, that it was a matter of indifference whether U.S. troops came to Europe in 1918 or 1919. Any delay, he pointed out, could be fatal.

Colonel House, who was conversant with the military and political situation in Europe, did not have to be told twice. He informed the U.S. President in a secret message that "if this war is to be won, better team work between the Allies must be effected. . . . The Central Powers are not overmatched, because their resources are perfectly mobilised and under single control. The individual German soldier is perhaps not so good as the English, but the German military machine is superior to that of either England or France."

Very few people suspected that the United States was capable of swift action. General Pétain, for example, treated reports about the deployment of U.S. troops as "hypothetical data". He did not think it likely that U.S. troops would do any important fighting in 1918. Consequently, he reasoned, "the Franco-British troops must be handled with such prudence as to leave the slightest possible role to be played by chance". On January 24, 1918, in Compiègne he set out his strategic plan in no uncertain terms. According to official sources, "the French Supreme Commander made no secret of the fact that, to his mind, the Allied forces were not strong enough to launch an offensive in 1918. In his opinion shortages would be experienced until the contribution of the U.S. army became sufficiently great". This meant that Pétain underrated the strength of the Allies and overrated that of the enemy. Soon, Pétain sank into still greater pessimism. Clemenceau, the 76-year-old French Premier, was enraged over the "Hero of Verdun"; he told Poincaré that Pétain's pessimism irritated him and scoffed at Pétain's fear that the Germans might crush the British in a pitched battle and then make short work of the French.

Pétain, as we see, had a yellow streak in him already years ago.

The other Allied military leaders did not share Pétain's panic, but they, too, with the exception of Foch, were doubtful that an offensive could stagger the Germans in 1918. Weygand, Wilson and Cadorna, speaking for France, Britain and Italy, respectively, concluded at a conference in Versailles on January 21, 1918, that the expected arrival of U.S. troops would not that year tilt the scales against the Germans. They hoped that the flow of U.S. troops, guns, planes, tanks, etc., on the one hand, and the gradually failing resistance of the enemy, on the other, would reverse the balance of strength somewhere in 1919. This naturally affected the preparations for the 1918 campaign. Pétain pleaded for strictly defensive tactics, pending the arrival of U.S. troops. General Haig, on the other hand, called for an offensive in the spring of 1918, although he thought U.S. troops would still be far from Europe's shores then. These divergent views were evidence of divergent planning, or, more precisely, of a lack of planning. General Weygand observed anxiously on January 22, 1918, on the eve of the enemy offensive, that the Allies had no general plan for the 1918 coalition operations.

This, among other things, was an outgrowth of the differences obtaining between the military leaders of France and Britain. The French command complained that their country was shouldering the full burden of the war, with Britain suffering incomparably less. They complained, too, that the French troops were manning a bigger section of the front and called attention to too many British troops staying on the islands. They demanded that the British lines on the continent should be extended.

The German command concluded in spring 1918 that the situation was favourable for sledgehammer attacks in east and west, Ludendorff thought this would avert the disintegration of the German bloc and yield final victory.

On March 1, 1918, the German army captured Kiev, twelve days later it entered Odessa, Kharkov on April 8, the Crimea at the end of April and Rostov-on-Don at the beginning of May. Faced by disastrous oil shortages (for Rumanian oil could not meet the tremendous need), Ludendorff was poised to drive on to Baku. This diverted many dozen German divisions to the Eastern front— especially because Russians, Ukrainians and Byelorussians, and the Baltic nations as well, were disinclined to accept the German invaders and fought back bitterly.

On March 21, the German troops mounted an offensive on the Western front. They went off to a good start by virtue of their considerable numerical superiority: 197 against 167 British and French divisions. Though wearied by the drawn-out war, the German troops took heart. "The terrible physical suffering, the heavy moral pressure and the boundless exhaustion gradually became unendurable" —that was how General von Kuhl described the state of the German soldier on the eve of the attack. "One wish reigned in the whole army: better the most difficult offensive just to get out of the trenches and shell-holes!" The German soldiers went into battle with the belief that it was the final one, or, as they said, "the offensive to achieve peace".

Heavy fighting raged until April 4. The German successes were substantial. The troops rolled forward, capturing considerable booty and numerous prisoners.

This was much too grave a blow to cause no repercussions in the Allied camp. The German command was obviously determined to tear the front and cut off the British sector from the French. On March 26, the Entente decided to assign General Foch "to co-ordinate the operations of the British and French armies on the Western front". Effective U.S. assistance was more urgent than ever. Preparations in the United States were rapid, but the Anglo-French command thought them not rapid enough. General Robertson likened American aid to a fragile straw. Lloyd George was less melancholically inclined, but admitted later that the Americans had to be constantly goaded. On March 27, he appealed to the U.S. President to iron out whatever difficulties there were and hasten troop shipments to Europe. He pointed out bluntly that U.S. reinforcements were desperately needed.

The technical impediments were quickly eliminated. The British command was told that 150 more battalions could be shipped to Europe in three or four months, provided Britain cut her imports. Necessity proved the mother of invention.

The differences that had plagued the Allies were pushed to the background by the German offensive. The situation called for deeds, not words. The Americans were aware, Viscount Reading, special British envoy to the United States, observed, that speeches and propaganda would not stop the German militarists. They realised that if Germany was to be beaten, she must be beaten by force. Powerful reserves had to be marshalled to stem the German assault.

Few in the Allied camp knew that the German offensive, mounted with the last remaining strength, was liable to peter out at any moment. Even Marshal Foch exaggerated enemy striking power. He believed it would take at least 100 American divisions to gain numerical superiority and crush German resistance. This would mean an Allied strength of 4,000,000 men. Developments showed, however, that 55 per cent of this proved enough to turn the tide. When Germany was beaten in 1918, the U.S. expeditionary force had less than half the strength desired by Foch.

The German offensive in the west spurred the Americans to action. Ludendorff hoped, however, that he would succeed in exploiting the time factor.

No sooner the first battle ended than a new offensive was mounted on April 9 (five days later)—this time in Flanders on the Lys, lasting until the end of April. With almost double the strength of the British in the area, the German army advanced in triumph, but then ran into dogged resistance and ground to a stop. Ludendorff had his back to the wall. He ordered a fresh attack on the Aisne River on May 27. The German troops fought desperately, straining to reach Paris in a bid for final victory. On June 2 they were indeed close to the French capital, and even captured Chateau-Thierry. Ludendorff expected France to collapse.

"We are fighting, we are resisting, we shall conquer!" Clemenceau exclaimed in the Chamber of Deputies. "All is not lost! There are good signs. Take heart!"

He was right. The German offensive began petering out and was soon brought to a standstill. The commanders drove their men into a new offensive on the night of July 14, crossing the Marne. When news of this reached the German rulers they were jubilant, though they had never been closer to defeat.

Two days later General Foch's huge reserves were sent into action. The Germans recoiled, suffering fearful losses as the Allies seized the initiative. A fresh counter-offensive at Amiens on August 8, made the Germans roll back. The defeat was doubly painful because Ludendorff had no more resources, either economic or human, to turn the tables. "August 8," he wrote, "was the blackest day for the German army in the history of the world war."

Confusion reigned from then on. The spine of the German army was broken. German reserves were completely exhausted. The plan of deploying German and Austro-Hungarian troops from the east to the west was not fated to materialise. In the Ukraine a major rising flared up in August 1918. The hope that the Brest peace imposed on Soviet Russia would unlock the Ukrainian "granary" was in vain. German imperialist ambitions in Eastern Europe, which appeared to have been attained, faded into thin air, making Germany's military and political plight still more desperate. Seeing at last that the game was up, Ludendorff prepared to step down. Pale from horror, a ruined gambler, he could only mumble, "This is the end." Still, on August 14, 1918, the royal council attended by Ludendorff and Hindenburg decided that people need-ed to hear "inspiring speeches". A few days later, address-ing workers in Essen, Wilhelm declaimed that "the enemy had miscalculated" and that although the world hated Germany, "hate was the lot only of those who think them-selves defeated". Immersed in their hopeless gamble, the militarists continued a senseless resistance for nearly another three months. Posters in Berlin read, "German victory is certain. . . ."

The full impact of the August 8 counter-offensive was not at first appreciated. For months after the German war machine was virtually smashed, influential men in the Allied camp still thought that prolonging the war was a surer way to victory than a concerted assault. Pétain was still despondent, while General Wilson was weighing the chances of a decisive offensive in July 1919 or in 1920.

Evidently, it is hard to spot the moment when the tide of history turns. It takes a keen eye and an incisive brain to see through the blood-stained curtain of war and the welter of events. It takes will-power to assess the balance of strength and the material and moral resources, and to redirect the course of events. Tenacity, courage and deter-mination bring victory closer.

The blows delivered to the German army on the East-ern and Western fronts in 1918 were of much more than local importance. They hastened the German bloc to its doom.

Came autumn and Germany's allies were in a panic, says Erzberger. Some of them put out feelers for a separate peace. But things had gone too far. The decision lay with the armies rather than the diplomats. Taking the offensive at Salonika, General Franchet d'Esperey forced Bulgaria to her knees. After a full taste of trials for joining the German bloc, Turkey surrendered as well. Austria-Hungary fell to pieces and begged for peace.

A few days later imperialist Germany, too, surrendered. The German militarists realised that surrender was the only way to save their army from total defeat and to pre-vent devastating battles in Germany proper. On the orders of the German command, Erzberger went to Compiègne under a white flag on November 7, 1918, to plead for an armistice on any terms. Two days later Germany was engulfed in revolution and four days later the Soviet Republic declared null and void the Brest Treaty, an out-growth of German imperialist annexationist policy. Lenin's political strategy triumphed.

Never in history has one war been exactly like another. The Second World War differs from that of 1914-18. The tempo is different, and the scale. More important still, the peoples are propelled by other aims. The spectre of 1918 hovers over Germany again, but this time of more disastrous proportions. Fair retribution awaits fascism.

When the day of Hitler's final and complete defeat arrives, it will be unlike any defeat in the past. The collapse of Hitler's armies will seal the doom of Hitler's state. The surrender of 1918 will be eclipsed by the surrender of fascist Germany, a surrender just as inevitable as the coming of dawn after the darkness of night.

1942

Part Two

THE POLITICAL ZIGZAGS
OF THE WEIMAR REPUBLIC

THE OCTOBER REVOLUTION AND SOVIET-GERMAN RELATIONS

The Socialist Revolution in Russia wrought immense changes in international and inter-state relations. Chronologically, these changes first affected the relationships between the young Soviet state and Germany. Both in the general and particular contexts, the problem of Soviet-German relations had occupied Lenin and the Bolshevik Party even before the October Revolution and the birth of the Soviet state. First of all, it was an important component of the broader problem of Russia's revolutionary withdrawal from the imperialist war and then of the problem of the peaceful coexistence of states with different socio-economic systems.

But for the rulers of imperialist Germany the matter had an entirely different complexion. In the past, and today as well, German bourgeois historians have been digging deep into the problem of Germany's relations with East and West, though chiefly from the diplomatic or strategic angle. They were interested mostly in one thing: can war on two fronts be avoided, with each adversary crushed singly, in order to establish German dominion in Europe and then the rest of the world? Never did they look at the problem from the standpoint of peace for Germany and mankind. Even today this does not seem to concern them, though naturally they cannot sidestep the problem of Soviet-German relations. It is undeniably the central problem of European international and inter-state affairs, with peace depending to a very large degree on how it is solved.

The two world wars have shown that the time of

large-scale local conflicts is over. Soviet-German relations, therefore, have a strong bearing on the future of world peace. They are one of the most important and vital problems of our time, a study of which in the historical, as well as political plane, is highly instructive. It will help us establish what place history occupies as a science in moulding the political consciousness of social classes, to what extent it prompts the revision of one set of opinions, outdated or inept, and the development of another set which, having stood the test of time, proves its value to history, the strictest judge of all.

We shall see that modern West German historiography, consumed by hatred for the Soviet Union, is blind to the achievements of our time and to the possibilities for a positive Soviet-German solution, though such a solution is in the national interest of the German nation, of world peace, and the objective course of history. We shall also see that the reactionary West German historians have neither forgotten nor learned anything at all. History is not only a teacher; it is also a judge who metes out justice to those who make history and those who write it.

1

The Soviet state, undeniably, has been an international factor of the first magnitude since the day of its birth. The West German historians, however reactionary, admit it, but attempt to deny that this is objectively legitimate. Nobody can deny today that the ideas of socialism and peace, championed by the Communist Party, are universal. Even reactionary West German historians admit that the Russian revolution had deep international roots and a strong international influence. Georg von Rauch, a typical reactionary historian, delves into what he calls the mystic essence of Bolshevism rooted in the "dual nature of man as sinner and at once the likeness of God". "In any case," he writes in his *History of Bolshevik Russia*, "Bolshevism cannot be ascribed solely to the history of Russia and has struck root not only among the Russians or the other peoples of Eastern Europe or Eastern Asia."[1] Unwittingly,

---

[1] Georg von Rauch, *Geschichte des bolschewistischen Russland*, Wiesbaden, 1955, S. 581.

he confirms the deep devotion of the Russian people to Bolshevik ideas, on the one hand, and comes back, on the
other, to the old hope of stamping out communism and
destroying the socialist system by armed intervention. This
is, in effect, a modified restatement of the expectations and
plans of 1917-18, when the Kaiser was still in power. The
only difference is that Germany's rulers had not believed
at first that a Soviet worker-peasant state was possible in
Russia and, later, when it became a fact, were convinced
it would collapse under the blows of the counter-revolution.
The Entente thought the same. However, while the
Entente endeavoured to keep Russia in the war, the German rulers nurtured other plans. Seeing that victory on
two fronts had, by reason of attrition, become a mirage,
the Junkers and the imperialist bourgeoisie wanted a
separate peace with the Russian tsar. Though the war had
long since begun, they continued to consider the tsar a
potential ally, both as a partner in a possible deal behind
Britain's back and at the expense of her imperialist interests, and from the standpoint of common class and dynastic interests in the fight against the revolution maturing
in Russia and menacing the reactionary monarchy in
Germany.

Bourgeois and landowner Russia had gone through a
complex evolution in inter-state relations—from a reactionary alliance with Germany to a no less reactionary imperialist alliance with France and Britain—spurred by the
mounting economic and political contradictions between
Russian and German imperialism and the collision of Russian and German expansionist ambitions in the Middle and
Far East, which later spread to the Baltic states and Finland (for the German rulers) and to Galicia (for the Russian). Poland, whose partition had earlier propped up the
Russo-German alliance, became not only an object of contention, but a battlefield. Another important factor was
reflected in the effort of Anglo-French and German finance
capital to gain pre-eminence in the vast internal market of
Russia. This was something that added to Russia's economic and political dependence on Anglo-French capital.
All the same, the existence, even the growth, of imperialist
contradictions between Russia and Britain (particularly in
the Middle East and Persia), the dynastic bonds between
bourgeois-landowner Russia and Junker-bourgeois Germany

and, most of all, the common interest in joint action against the revolutionary working-class movement—all this made a rapprochement between old Russia and old Germany quite possible on imperialist and counter-revolutionary grounds.

Lenin proceeded from the history of the relations between the Hohenzollerns and the Russian empire of the Romanoffs when, during the war, he defined the possibility of "a turn ... from a Russo-British imperialist alliance against Germany to a no less imperialist Russo-German alliance against England".[1] He pointed out that, "whatever the outcome of the war", the German "bourgeoisie will, together with the Junkers, exert every effort to support the tsarist monarchy against a revolution in Russia".[2]

As we see, the Bolsheviks took into account the aggressiveness of German imperialism and weighed the possible twists that could either complicate or lighten the development of the revolutionary forces and, accordingly, the tactics and strategy of revolutionary action. In this context, the relations between imperialist Germany and imperialist Russia, and the international and military situation of each of the belligerents, were of the utmost importance. The Bolsheviks, the most consistent patriots and proletarian internationalists, viewed all these intricate factors not from great-power positions, but from the standpoint of a socialist revolution in Russia and the working-class movement in other countries, above all Germany.

German bourgeois historians of the First World War, the Weimar Republic and the subsequent period regard Russo-German relations as a part of the problem of politico-military alliances and look for a solution in the efforts of German diplomacy. This reflects the political interest and strategic designs of the ruling class. For one thing, Friedrich Meinecke, one of the stalwarts of German bourgeois 20th-century historiography, maintained that the negotiations of an alliance between Germany and Britain against Russia, and their failure, had been a turning point in German history and even in that of the world.[3] E. Bran-

---

[1] Lenin, *Collected Works*, Vol. 23, p. 178.
[2] Ibid., Vol. 21, pp. 27-28.
[3] Meinecke, *Geschichte des deutsch-englischen Bündnisproblems 1890-1901*, München-Berlin, 1927.

denburg,[1] H. Oncken[2] and other German historians had much the same methodological approach. Now that the papers of Friedrich von Holstein,[3] the top man in the German diplomacy of the post-Bismarckian period, have been found and published, West German historians are again examining the determinative role of diplomacy in the choice of allies, particularly the relationship to Britain, on the one hand, and Russia, on the other. It may be added that in Hitler's time the "geopolitical" school in historiography, raised to the status of an official doctrine, viewed Russo-German relations not only from the angle of politico-military alliances, but also from the angle of German colonial expansion in Eastern Europe.[4]

However, the problem of foreign policy, particularly that of Russo-German relations in the imperialist period, transcends such matters as the methods and aims of diplomacy. Neither has it anything in common with the notorious "geopolitical doctrine". It is not *diplomatic art* or a geographically preordained *political "destiny"* that concerns us most, but the highly complex question of class interests in inter-state and international relations.

The October Revolution bared the substance of the problem quite conclusively. It did so not only in theory, for the point was made long ago by Marxism, but also in the practice of political struggle during a crucial time in world history.

The October Revolution and Soviet power repatterned the country's social structure, extirpating the bourgeois-landowner state. The monopolies and banks closely associated with French, British, German and Belgian capital, the system of big landed estates, the old bureaucracy and the reactionary political organisations—from the arch-reactionary Union of the Russian People to the Constitutional Democrats, the petty-bourgeois Mensheviks and the Socialist-Revolutionary Party—collapsed. The Soviet worker-

---

[1] Brandenburg, *Von Bismarck zum Weltkriege*, Berlin, 1924.

[2] Oncken, *Das alte und das neue Mitteleuropa*, Gotha, 1917; *Das Deutsche Reich und die Vorgeschichte des Weltkrieges*, Bd. II, Leipzig, 1933.

[3] Holstein, *Die geheimen Papiere Friedrich von Holsteins*, Bd. I-IV, Göttingen-Berlin-Frankfurt a/M, 1957-63.

[4] Y. V. Tarle, " 'Vostochnoye prostranstvo' i fashistskaya geopolitika", *Works*, Vol. XI, Moscow, 1959, pp. 785-806 (Russ. ed.).

peasant state, a new social structure, a state of an entirely new type, came into being on the ruins of the old system. And the birth of a structurally new state gave birth to a new type of policy. It was most fortunate,[1] as Lenin put it, that the two imperialist coalitions were locked in battle when the October Revolution broke out in Russia. This does not mean, as reactionary historians would have us believe, that the Soviet state was and still is interested in a war between the Western powers, hoping to strike from it the sparks of socialist revolution. No, the international revolutionary movement bears no responsibility for imperialist wars. It opposes wars and works against them. The Twentieth Congress of the Communist Party of the Soviet Union proved that revolution can win in conditions quite unlike those of Russia in 1917, that is, when the people of Russia were tormented by a devastating war. The working class, the spokesman of the bulk of the nation, can seize power not only in war conditions and not necessarily by means of an armed uprising. This can be done also by peaceful means. Indeed, it was one of the chief aims of the October Revolution to extricate Russia from the imperialist war and show the peoples a *realistic* way of ending the war and establishing a *universal* democratic *peace.* The Decree on Peace drafted by Lenin was the first instrument in history to embody a realistic conception of democratic world peace responsive to the brightest hopes of the labouring portion of mankind, proposed by the Bolshevik Party at the height of the socialist revolution. This injects it with profound historical pathos and inexhaustible moral force, immortalising it in the ages.

Breaking once and for all with the class essence, the methods and aims of bourgeois-landowner Russia's foreign relations, Soviet policy gained *new class content* conforming with the peace-loving sentiment of the peoples, above all the working class. Its trend was new, too, both in relation to the foreign capitalist governments and the working class and the peoples.

The bourgeois press betrayed its incomprehension of the new, unprecedented methods of international intercourse, claiming that the Soviet Government had no "foreign, international policy".[2] Yet Lenin, who directed the

---

[1] Lenin, *Collected Works*, Vol. 27, p. 93.
[2] Ibid., p. 292.

foreign policy of the Soviet state, was also working out its *basic principles*. They were not formulated overnight, it is true, emerging gradually in the specific environment of the October Revolution, when the world was in the throes of the imperialist war, and when the workers in the capitalist countries were awakening to revolutionary action while the ruling classes launched an armed intervention to crush the socialist revolution. They emerged when the working class in Russia, equipped with Lenin's theory of the possibility of building socialism in one country, undertook the arduous mission of building socialism in a country encircled by hostile capitalist states at a time of armed intervention, with a *cordon sanitaire* and an economic blockade harrassing the world's first workers' and peasants' socialist state.

Lenin and the Soviet Government addressed their peace appeal to "All! All! All!". They believed that the labour movement in the main capitalist countries was strong enough to exert an effective, even decisive, influence on the policy of governments representing the interests of the ruling classes. Working for world peace on a democratic basis and compelled by the perversity of the Western powers to negotiate a separate peace with the Germans, Lenin and the Soviet people hoped that the workers in Germany would exert political pressure.

The October Revolution swept out the old Russo-German relations, replaced by Soviet-German relations with an entirely new class content. The problem now concerned the relationship of the Soviet state and imperialist Germany, on the one hand, and the relationship between Russia's working class, which had won political power, and the working class of Germany, ruled by capitalists. Relations with capitalist Germany followed the general principles of the peaceful coexistence of states with different socio-economic systems, worked out by Lenin, which the Soviet state has promoted throughout its history. Solidarity with the German working class followed the immutable principles of proletarian internationalism. When reactionary historians say that peaceful coexistence is a screen for proletarian internationalism, while the latter is the ideological justification and screen for "export of revolution", they only betray their ignorance and, still more, their desire to misrepresent the foreign policy of the Soviet state, its basic principles and guidelines. They endeavour to prove "export of revolution" from Russia to Germany, on the one hand, and conversely, "export of revolution" from Germany to Russia. Both contentions are false. And as a German proverb says, lies have short legs.

The principles of proletarian internationalism date to long before the October Revolution and long before Lenin worked out the concept of the peaceful coexistence of states with different socio-economic systems. Soviet foreign policy has always proceeded "not from the point of view of whether this or that imperialism is preferable, but exclusively from the point of view of the conditions which best make for the development and consolidation of the socialist revolution".[1] To sum up, Soviet foreign policy is not shaped by the traditional ties with capitalist states and certainly not by any economic or diplomatic dependence frequent in the inter-state relations of the capitalist world. The determinative factor is sovereign choice of the most favourable conditions for peaceful socialist construction.

On November 23, 1917, already after the Decree on Peace was issued, Lenin said: "We propose that the peace talks should be started immediately . . . with all countries, without exception."[2] The determination to settle matters by negotiation, to have peaceful relations with all countries, has been the basic motive of the Soviet state since its establishment. Not, naturally, isolated from other principles, such as, say, the principle of proletarian internationalism, for it was the combination of both that animated the October Revolution in its bid for peace, democracy and socialism. Lenin knew from his vast experience that only the international working class and socialist movement could be a true and dependable ally of the Soviet people in championing peace. But, for all his revolutionary optimism, he also knew that "revolution is not made to order; it results from an outburst of mass indignation".[3]

When the socialist revolution in Russia was imperiled by imperialist Germany, Lenin kept an eye on the development of the revolutionary working-class movement in Germany, on which he pinned considerable hope. He praised

---

[1] Lenin, *Collected Works*, Vol. 26, p. 445.
[2] Ibid., p. 315.
[3] Ibid., p. 345.

the labour movement in Germany and thought it highly important. This is rooted largely in the close ideological, political and, to some extent, organisational ties between the forward contingents of the socialist proletariat of Russia and Germany, and, moreover, in the mutual influence and assistance that prevailed in the common struggle against the reactionary and aggressive groups that governed the two countries. The traditional bonds of the Russian and German revolutionary movements dated back to the time of Marx and Engels and were especially strong early in the 20th century, on the eve of the first Russian revolution of 1905-07. All his life, Lenin had studied German history, the country's economic and political scene, German philosophy and science, Germany's culture and the lack of culture of her ruling classes. Most particularly, he studied the development, forms and ideology of the German labour movement—not as an onlooker, for an academic reason, but as a leader of the most consistently revolutionary wing of the world socialist movement. He admired such leaders as Singer, Bebel, Luxemburg and Liebknecht and denounced the revisionism of Bernstein, Legien, Parvus and, later, Kautsky, who did much damage to the German, and not only German, labour movement.

History willed that the German socialist movement should be a model for the socialist movement in Russia for a number of decades to a greater extent than for socialist parties in other countries.[1] In April 1914, shortly before the outbreak of the First World War, Lenin wrote on this score: "German Social-Democracy has many great services to its credit. Thanks to Marx's struggle against all the Hochbergs, Dührings, and Co., it possesses a strictly formulated theory.... It has a mass organisation, newspapers, trade unions, political associations—that same mass organisation which is so definitely building up in our country...."[2] He pointed out that the German socialist movement had distinguished itself despite the disgraceful conduct of the reformists and revisionists, and concluded: "We must not try to play down the *disease* which the German party is undoubtedly suffering from, and which reveals itself in phenomena of this kind; nor must we play it down with 'officially optimistic'

[1] Ibid., Vol. 21, p. 94.
[2] Ibid., Vol. 20, p. 257.

phrases. We must lay it bare, to the Russian workers, so that we may learn from the experience of the older movement, learn what should not be copied from it."[1] It will be recalled that the disease became still graver during the war, when social-chauvinism and centrism in the labour movement acted as allies of German imperialism. All the same, Lenin had deep faith in the revolutionary potential of the German working class. It was not a blind faith built on recollections of the fighting days of the German workers' movement, but confidence based on an analysis of the state-monopoly capitalism that appeared in Germany during the war, and of the changes in the economic situation and the political consciousness of the German working class and soldiers. When leaving Switzerland for Russia in April 1917, Lenin wrote in his parting letter to the Swiss workers: "The German proletariat is the most trustworthy, the most reliable ally of the Russian and the world proletarian revolution".[2]

Yet today reactionary historians say, of all things, that it was the German General Staff rather than the workers who had helped the socialist revolution in Russia. Literature has appeared in West Germany and elsewhere delving into Lenin's return to Russia from Switzerland via Germany and Sweden.[3] It is said that General Ludendorff had organised this route himself intimating that, first, Ludendorff and the General Staff engaged in "exporting revolution" or, more precisely, "transit of revolution" in order to lighten Germany's military plight and, second, that therefore the blame for the outbreak of the socialist revolution in Russia and its subsequent influence on Germany rests with Ludendorff and the General Staff. The authors would have us believe that if Lenin had reached Russia by some other route, world history would have followed a different course.

New historiographic zigzags have appeared alongside the general trend aimed at vindicating German militarism and at implanting the frenetic idea that revolution was "exported" from Germany to Russia, at loggerheads with the no less giddy though more widely circulated notion that revo-

---

[1] Lenin, *Collected Works*, Vol. 20, p. 258.
[2] Ibid., Vol. 23, p. 373.
[3] Werner Hahlweg, "Lenins Reise durch Deutschland im April 1917", *Vierteljahrshefte für Zeitgeschichte*, 1957, H. 4, S. 307 ff.

lution was "exported" from Russia to Germany. *Vierteljahr-shefte für Zeitgeschichte,* one of the leading West German journals in its field, invokes the evidence of German diplomatic documents, said to be available in London, to dismiss in all earnest Ludendorff's complicity in the outbreak of the socialist revolution in Russia, on the grounds that he had never personally met Lenin and had not even known his name.[1] But matters do not end there. The journal says with a straight face that the idea of "transit of revolution" via Germany to Russia came not from the sagacious German strategists, but from count Ulrich von Brockdorff-Rantzau, tabbed as a short-sighted diplomatist. The intimation is that Germany's rulers did not know what they were doing and that they cut the branch they were sitting on by negotiating with the leaders of revolutionary Russia.

The blast against the ludicrous idea of Ludendorff's blame for the October Revolution is meant to prove three things at once: first, naturally, that Ludendorff and the General Staff are free from all blame for the socialist revolution in Russia, which should clear them in the eyes of the West German arch-reactionaries; second, that Brockdorff-Rantzau was an abettor of the revolution who later promoted Soviet-German relations and, third, that all dealings with the Soviet Union and its leaders are undesirable because they open the door to "export of revolution" to Germany.

But this is not all. Two West German publications professing to be independent have published "sensational" excerpts from Wilhelmstrasse documents concerning the history of the October Revolution, patently falsified to discredit Lenin and the *Pravda.*[2] A closer look reveals that they resemble materials published by the Public Information Committee of the United States in Bern in 1919, which were proved to have been falsified by White émigré groups for Edgar Sisson, a U.S. agent, who had asked them to "document" the vicious inventions of *Rech,* a counter-revolutionary Russian Constitutional Democratic Party organ.[3] Lenin had retorted in the *Pravda* in 1917, proving the

---

[1] *Vierteljahrshefte für Zeitgeschichte,* 1957, H. 4, S. 307 ff.
[2] *Die Welt,* Nov. 7, 1957; *Die Zeit,* June 27, 1957.
[3] *Die deutsch-bolschewistische Verschwörung,* Hrsg. vom Committee on Public Information of United States of America, Bern, 1919.

dishonesty of the slanderers.[1] Yet, eager to discredit Lenin, West German reactionary writers have not hesitated to resuscitate the malicious, long since exposed lies.

2

If proof is needed of the vitality and realism of Lenin's foreign policy principles—proletarian internationalism, on the one hand, and the peaceful coexistence of states with different socio-economic systems, on the other—Soviet-German relations offer it amply. They were difficult and complex at most times, punctuated by the Brest peace whereby German imperialism attempted to enmesh the Soviet state; Rapallo, where the relations between Germany and the Soviet Union were normalised; a string of overt and covert deals between Germany's rulers and the Western imperialist powers to isolate the Soviet Union internationally; the 1939 Soviet-German treaty; the Great Patriotic War touched off by the treacherous nazi attack on the Soviet Union, marking a turning point not only in Soviet-German relations but also in world history.

While the war was still on, and later at the Potsdam conference, the Soviet Union championed the idea of rooting out German militarism and imperialism and, in the best national interest of the Germans, advocated the concept of a united, peace-loving, democratic Germany. At all times, in the most complex matters related to the future of the Soviet and German peoples, to that of Europe and the world, the Soviet Union took guidance in Lenin's principles born of the October Revolution.

These principles, like the Marxist-Leninist teaching, are no ossified formula. Realistic and dialectical in substance, they are embodied in reality in many different ways. Also, adequately geared to the tasks of socialist society in international affairs, they have nothing in common with the principles or, more precisely, the lack of principles, of bourgeois diplomacy, bred on the traditions of Talleyrand, Palmerston, Disraeli and Bismarck. These may indeed differ. For one thing, according to Alexander Herzen, Talleyrand proved that knavery did not mean brilliance, while Palmerston did not even try proving it, whereas Bismarck, who

---

[1] See Lenin, *Collected Works*, Vol. 25, p. 164.

fancied himself a skilled diplomatic juggler, had a knack of pretending honesty when the occasion required.

Lenin was aware not only of the historical tasks of the German working class, but also the national interests of the German nation, which German imperialism and militarism abused. But Germany's rulers interpreted the Soviet Government's appeal for peace as a sign of weakness and drafted strategic plans in East and West. True, they had to reckon with the revolutionary sentiment of the German workers, but expected to keep down the people long enough to impose piratic peace terms in the east and gain a military victory in the west before the revolutionary workers' movement in Germany got out of hand. However, strategy of aggression has no resemblance to strategy of revolution. Campaigning for peace, the Russian workers were championing the interests of the German nation, as well as their own, thus rendering the workers in Germany tremendous moral and political support.

Conversely, all news from Germany of revolutionary acts against war was welcomed in Russia as news of acts supporting the Russian working class. Fraternisation of German and Russian soldiers in the front lines was in the best tradition of proletarian internationalism and socialist mutual assistance. "Fraternisation," wrote Lenin, "is the revolutionary initiative of the *masses*, it is the awakening of the conscience, the mind, the courage of the oppressed classes; in other words, it is a rung in the ladder leading up to the socialist proletarian revolution."[1] Though the socio-economic preconditions for socialist revolution were on hand, it was yet unripe and the German imperialists were able to assail the young Soviet state with the full power of their "mailed fist".

With a heavy heart but conscious of its responsibility, the Soviet Government agreed to negotiate in Brest-Litovsk. This was when two distinct forces faced each other for the first time across the diplomatic table—the forces of revolution, socialism and peace on one side of it and the forces of imperialism, reaction and war on the other. It was also a clash of two strategic goals—the Soviet Government's to win time for the future victory of socialism and the German Government's to accomplish its piratic ambitions in the

---

[1] Lenin, *Collected Works*, Vol. 24, p. 318.

east and free its hands for a decisive military victory in the west. The Soviet goal was inspired by the interests of the people, of peace and of the socialist revolution, and that of the German Government—as borne out recently by pertinent documents—by the interests of the big German banks and monopolies and the Junkers (Karl Helfferich, Minister of the Interior, Rudolf Havenstein, President of the Reichsbank, Alfred Hugenberg, director of Krupp's, etc.).[1]

The world followed the diplomatic embroglio with bated breath. Many were the people who thought the aggressive German imperialism would overpower the Soviet revolution. Cowards, windbags, deserters, discovered themselves even in the Bolshevik Party. It took colossal will-power, exceptional lucidity of thought and deep devotion to principle to resist their "revolutionary" phrase-mongering, their provocations, and to cope with one of the most difficult problems of the time, which involved so many different factors.

A document in the Potsdam archive bears out how correctly Lenin assessed the correlation of forces within the ruling imperialist clique in Germany and, what is more, German expectations and designs. I am referring to the minutes of a conference in Bad Homburg on February 13, 1918, which discussed whether or not to resume armed operations after the Brest negotiations broke down.[2] As Lenin had anticipated, two distinct trends came into evidence there: the "moderate" represented by Foreign Secretary Richard von Kühlmann and Vice-Chancellor Friedrich von Payer, and the aggressive one represented by Hindenburg, Ludendorff and Wilhelm II. "We must act firmly and quickly," Hindenburg said. "The hostilities in the West will last a long time. We must free our forces for it. Therefore, the Russians have to be crushed. Their government must be overthrown." Payer endeavoured to prove that the Bolsheviks could not be overthrown because they had the people's support and warned that "sympathy for the Bolsheviks may also appear in our country". Ludendorff maintained: "We must end the war

---

[1] See W. G. Brjunin, "Die deutsche Regierung und der Friedensvorschlag der Sowjetregierung (Nov.-Dez. 1917)", *Zeitschrift für Geschichtswissenschaft*, 1957, H. 5, S. 962 ff.

[2] DZA Potsdam, Akten der Reichskanzlei, Bd. 2477, Bl. 77 ff. Taking part in the discussion were Wilhelm II, the Reichschancellor, Foreign Secretary Kühlmann, Vice-Chancellor Payer, Hindenburg, Ludendorff and Henning V. Holtzendorff.

by military means. For this we must have a free hand in the East. We are convinced that we can win in the East. We must have our hands free to do so."

The Kaiser argued in a similar vein, but added the following noteworthy argument. Some British quarters are of the opinion, he said, that "Britain must fight the Bolsheviks jointly with Germany". This bears out Lenin's belief, shared by the Soviet Government, that the Entente, or at least certain British quarters, were intent on embroiling the Soviet Republic with imperialist Germany.

The Bad Homburg conference decided on a military offensive, following which the Soviet Government was compelled to sign an "unfortunate peace"[1] on terms still harsher than those demanded in the first round of the Brest talks. Yet the minutes reveal how right Lenin had been in his calculations. The "moderates", as well as the militarists, were alarmed by the home situation, notably the strike movement in Germany. When Ludendorff declaimed, "We must march on Petersburg", the Chancellor parried, "We are risking a strike", and though Ludendorff retorted, "A strike is nothing", the conference was haunted by the thinly disguised fear that the October Revolution may galvanise the German workers into action.

This was where German imperialism dotted the i's as to its aggressive designs.

Later developments revealed how right Lenin had been in retorting to opponents of the "unfortunate peace" that, far from impeding the German revolution, the Brest peace would only expedite it.[2] At this critical hour, the fate of the socialist revolution hanging in the balance, Lenin and the Communist Party drew their strength from the revolutionary spirit and intelligence of the Russian workers and from the historical experience of the German people. Lenin compared the Brest peace with the peace of Tilsit, when Napoleon dismembered and humiliated Germany. "Nevertheless," Lenin noted, "the German people survived even *such* a peace, proved able to muster their forces, to rise and to win the right to liberty and independence."[3]

"At that time," he continued, "historical conditions were

---

[1] Lenin, *Collected Works*, Vol. 27, p. 51.
[2] Ibid., Vol. 27, pp. 479-82; Vol. 28, p. 102.
[3] Ibid., Vol. 27, p. 162.

such that this resurgence could be channelled only in the direction of a *bourgeois* state. At that time, more than a hundred years ago, history was made by handfuls of nobles and a sprinkling of bourgeois intellectuals, while the worker and peasant masses were somnolent and dormant. As a result history at that time could only crawl along at a terribly slow pace."[1]

The October Revolution, which roused the masses to active endeavour in the making of history, injected new powerful factors into the historical process and thereby accelerated the march of time, and not only in Russia. Lenin anticipated this. The German strategists did not. How could they perceive the purport and inevitability of the world-shaking events? Preoccupied with their reckless gamble in East and West, they were too busy estimating the amount of grain they could get in the East and ship to Germany, and the number of divisions that would become available for shipment to France once the East was forced to its knees. What they did not reckon with and failed to estimate was the energy of the revolutionary forces crystallising in Russia, where the October Revolution had already triumphed, and, much more, also in Germany, which would have her own November.

Though they had promised the German people "bread and peace", they gave them neither. Though eager to deploy their forces from the Eastern to the Western front, they were in effect bogged down on both and achieved what they wanted least of all—the spread of revolutionary sentiment among their soldiers in both East and West. Though they thought that by capturing territory with 34 per cent of the country's population, 54 per cent of its industry and 90 per cent of its coal they had vanquished the socialist revolution, in reality they were themselves tottering on the brink of defeat. The Brest peace, which exposed their voracity, was for them a fatal step closer to military collapse and a revolutionary explosion in Germany proper.

Subsequently, Hitler endeavoured to whitewash German policy in Brest in his *Mein Kampf*. But even reactionary German historians admit for the most part that Brest had been a diplomatic blunder and, moreover, a political and strategic setback at a time when the German rulers were

---

[1] Lenin, *Collected Works*, Vol. 27, p. 162.

first faced with the problem of dealing with the Soviet state.

Before drawing conclusions, one should refer to the topics modern German historians consider vital today. Historians in the German Democratic Republic, for example, devote their attention to the socio-economic, political and ideological circumstances prevailing in Germany at the time of the November revolution and delve into the influences of the October Revolution,[1] while reactionary writers in West Germany confine themselves to the "export of revolution" concept. Historians in the German Democratic Republic treat the events and problems implicit in the relations of the German and Soviet peoples as tokens of proletarian internationalism,[2] while the West German writers extol the rupture of relations with the Soviet state effected by the government of Friedrich Ebert and Philipp Scheidemann, the kaiser Socialists. Hermann Stegemann, the well-known reactionary historian, takes the matter farther still. He claims that the 1917-18 events wrote *finis* to the traditionally good relations between Russia and Germany and lays the blame on the October Revolution in Russia and the November revolution in Germany. To draw this conclusion he puts history on its head. Indeed, did these traditionally good relations between Junker-bourgeois Germany and bourgeois-landowner Russia prevent the war which the peoples of the two countries had to pay for by mutual destruction? Did not the revolutionary events of 1917-18 offer the peoples of Russia and Germany a splendid opportunity for restoring and consolidating the old traditions of proletarian internationalism and socialist mutual assistance, which would rule out a new Russo-German war? The fact is that Germany's ruling classes—the imperialist bourgeoisie and the Junkerdom, who had with the connivance of the Social-Democrats retained

---

[1] First and foremost, see *Revolutionäre Ereignisse und Probleme in Deutschland während der Periode der Grossen Sozialistischen Oktoberrevolution 1917/1918*, Berlin, 1957, ed. by Albert Schreiner; Klaus Mammach, *Vliyaniye Fevralskoi revolyutsii v Rossii i Velikoi Oktyabrskoi sotsialisticheskoi revolyutsii na rabochy klass Germanii*, Moscow, 1957 (Russ. ed.); a series of interesting articles on the subject in *Zeitschrift für Geschichtswissenschaft*, No. 5, 1957.

[2] See Albert Norden, *Mezhdu Berlinom i Moskvoi*, Moscow, 1957 (Russ. ed.); F. Klein, *Die diplomatischen Beziehungen Deutschlands zur Sowjetunion 1917-1932*, 2. Aufl., Berlin, 1953; G. Rosenfeld, "Die deutsch-sowjetischen Beziehungen bis 1925", *Deutsche Aussenpolitik*, 1957, H. 11, S. 995 ff.

their grip on the country—were determined to stick to their own line. As E. H. Carr indicates in his *Berlin-Moscow,* when the alliance of the General Staff and heavy industry came into strength "the policy of the new Germany depended on what they considered in their best interest".[1] Above all, they were eager to prevent any junction between the revolutionary forces of the Soviet and German peoples, to isolate these forces in Germany and to concentrate on crushing the German labour movement, not short of assassinating its leaders. They demonstrated thereby, to use Lenin's phrase, that " 'freedom' in the German republic, one of the freest and advanced republics of the world, is freedom to murder arrested leaders of the proletariat with impunity".[2]

Since the revolutionary labour movement was branded the root of all evil, it was natural for them to revive the old militarist conception of the "stab in the back" which the November revolution was alleged to have delivered to the German army. The political purpose of this reactionary tale was clear enough at the time of the Weimar Republic, when it was first circulated by the militarists to clear themselves of blame for Germany's defeat. Now the tale has been somewhat modified, and as such merits a closer look. Reactionary historians go out of their way to justify the refusal of the German Government of the time to accept aid from the Soviet Republic, even in terms of grain, on the one hand, and endeavour to prove, on the other, that the revolutionary menace emanating from the East compelled the German Government to surrender at Versailles. The modification, as we see, amounts to Germany's military defeat being blamed on Soviet Russia, whereas previously it was blamed on the German workers. Yet Lenin had warned that the Western powers were drawing up peace terms for Germany "completely devastating, far harsher than the Brest-Litovsk terms".[3] He had warned that the "anti-Bolshevik" policy which Germany had launched to appease the Western powers would not save Germany and, on the contrary, would plunge the country and her victors into a state of "chaos and confusion".[4]

---

[1] Carr, *Berlin-Moskau. Deutschland und Russland Zwischen den beiden Weltkriegen*, Stuttgart, 1954, S. 18.
[2] Lenin, *Collected Works*, Vol. 28, p. 463.
[3] Ibid., p. 159.
[4] Ibid., Vol. 33, p. 430.

The natural thing to ask is what Soviet Russia's attitude has been towards the predatory Versailles peace. West German historians give no answer to this question. However, a German proverb says no answer is also an answer. The historians in question are either evading an important historical issue bearing on the problem of Soviet-German relations, or supplanting it with others. Take Dietrich Geyer's "Wilson and Lenin", a paper that sets out to prove that the U.S. President approached international affairs from a "democratic" angle while Lenin viewed them from a "dictatorial" one.[1]

Whenever the Soviet anti-Versailles stand is, indeed, touched, the reactionary historians try to create the impression that Russian "Bolshevism" sought an alliance with German "nationalism", even militarism, in order to mount a joint assault on the Western powers. This version was first conceived by Lloyd George, then Britain's Prime Minister, who set it out in his famous Fontainebleau memorandum in 1919 to intimidate his Versailles partners.[2] Yet he described it not as an established fact but as a possibility. Today, reactionary writers are reviving it with the sole object of diverting attention from the established fact that the Soviet state and people rendered the German workers and the rest of the nation tremendous moral and political support in the struggle against the imperialist Versailles peace. At the black hour of Versailles and, later, during the occupation of the Ruhr, the Soviet people showed a deep understanding of German national interests and proved their good will even when Germany and the Soviet Union had no diplomatic relations. The German working class, for its part, launched an effective campaign under the watchword, "Hands off Soviet Russia!", inspired by its sense of proletarian solidarity and guided by the Communist Party.[3] The West German writers say nothing on this score. Historians in the German Democratic Republic, on the other hand, delve into this important aspect of the

---

[1] Geyer, "Wilson und Lenin", *Jahrbücher für Geschichte Osteuropas*, 1955, H. 3, S. 430 ff.

[2] K. F. Nowak, *Versailles*, Berlin, 1927, S. 145 ff.

[3] See Norden, op. cit.; interesting material is available in the collection of speeches at a conference on the "Hands off Soviet Russia" movement, held in Berlin under the auspices of the German-Soviet Friendship Society, June 6-7, 1957.

general problem of Soviet-German relations on the strength of extensive documentary material. It is commendable that German progressives do not lose sight of vitally important aspects of the general problem of Soviet-German relations.

West German historians, too, are going in for topical problems. In response to the political and ideological needs of the ruling element in West Germany, they concentrate their interests on later periods and invade the journalistic sphere as a medium for elucidating "modern history". The impartial approach in which old-time bourgeois historiography prided itself, claiming, as Leopold Ranke put it, to set out the facts "just as they happened", is flung overboard, especially in regard to the problem of Soviet-German relations. This is evidenced by the treatment of the Rapallo Treaty and the problem of the so-called Eastern and Western orientation of Germany's foreign policy during the inter-war period.

The Versailles system put Germany in a difficult position. So difficult, in fact, that for Germany, as Carr points out, already in 1919 "all the roads led eastwards".[1] Not only the people of Germany, but influential quarters of the ruling class as well, had a stake in closer relations with Soviet Russia, for they were looking for an escape from foreign isolation and wanted orders for their idle factories. Germany's rulers did not establish relations with Soviet Russia earlier for two reasons: firstly, because of the big forces (particularly the top section of the Social-Democrats) who had made "anti-Bolshevism" their political banner and, secondly, because of Entente pressure. Gustav Hilger, who was then councillor to the German Embassy in Moscow, tells in his memoirs that at the slightest sign of an improvement in Soviet-German relations the Western powers began weaving intrigues and sounding off so ferociously that the German rulers, especially those who wanted an excuse for it, shrank back in fear.[2] For all this, the two countries signed a treaty, known as the Treaty of Rapallo, at the Genoa Conference in April 1922. It provided for the resumption and normalisation of relations between Germany and Soviet Russia, and created a strong, though

---

[1] Carr, op. cit., S. 22.
[2] Hilger, *Wir und der Kreml. Deutsch-sowjetische Beziehungen 1918-1944*, Frankfurt a/M-Berlin, 1955, S. 55.

conflicting, reaction. Joseph Wirth observed aptly that "the Rapallo Treaty was hailed by the workers of the world as the first truly peaceful creation after the great catastrophe"[1], while Western leaders received it with dismay. *Temps*, the mouthpiece of the French imperialist bourgeoisie, went to the length of threatening a preventive war against Germany. Indicatively, most West German writers are campaigning against Rapallo.

Yet even its most inveterate opponents find nothing to take exception to in its text. What they cannot stomach is the "spirit of Rapallo", that is, the principles embodied in the treaty and in the objective outlook of the Soviet-German relations of the time—those of the peaceful coexistence of the Soviet Union and Germany, two major European powers with different socio-economic and political systems. If these principles had prevailed, European peace would have benefited considerably. The Western imperialist powers would then have been deprived of the chance of what Bismarck described as using Germany as a bloodhound against Russia. Peaceful coexistence in Soviet-German relations could change the whole political situation, allowing Germany to regain her place in international affairs and robbing the advocates of a crusade against the U.S.S.R. of a chance to start a new war. The Western powers were incensed. Now, too, a sizeable section of West German writers are attacking the "spirit of Rapallo" for the same reason. The journal *Die Gegenwart* describes the treaty as a "phantom" and a "sensational episode"[2], while the *Merkur*, which professes to be a German journal of European opinion, says Rapallo was a "mystery, a dream and a spectre".[3] It is argued that the Rapallo Treaty was concluded solely to scare the Western powers and that it was exploited not by Germany, but by Soviet Russia against Germany. It is further argued that Rapallo was a bluff and an instrument of political tactics. And some say Rapallo had all the makings of a Soviet-German military alliance.

All are wrong. Their aim is to discredit the spirit of Rapallo, one of the possible forms of the peaceful coexist-

[1] Wirth, *Reden während der Kanzlerschaft*, Berlin, 1925, S. 345. Also see F. Klein, "Joseph Wirth und Walter Rathenau", *Die Weltbühne*, Nov. 7, 1951, S. 1475 ff.

[2] *Die Gegenwart*, Nov. 5, 1955, S. 720 ff.

[3] *Merkur*, 1952, H. 9, S. 872.

ence of states with different socio-economic systems. What they fear most is for it to triumph today in the relations between the Federal Republic of Germany and the Soviet Union. They know perfectly well that the spirit of Rapallo is incompatible with, and would work against the militarism and revanchism now reviving in West Germany.

The cold-warriors, past masters at falsifying history, contend that the environment after the Second World War leaves no room for the revival of Rapallo, which they interpret as a disguised military alliance.

Yet there are people in West Germany who brand this as untrue. First, they say, Rapallo was never a mere tactical manoeuvre; second, it was never a secret military alliance and, third, nobody is suggesting to restore the letter of the Rapallo Treaty.

"Rapallo, not Tauroggen" is the title of an article by Dieter Posser,[1] author of a history of Soviet-German relations,[2] thus dissociating the Rapallo conception from the Tauroggen conception of the old Prusso-Russian military alliance.

There is also a third, and the oldest, trend in West German historiography: opponents and even some admirers of the "Rapallo spirit" weigh the problem from the standpoint of West Germany's succeeding to exploit the contradictions between the imperialist powers, on the one hand, and the Soviet Union, on the other. Some believe it could succeed, but most do not. One thing, however, is clear, West German historians and publicists are still enthralled by notions dating to the times of the Kaiser, of Weimar, and of the nazi reign. Capitalising on East-West contradictions is still viewed as a show of "political strength" and "statesmanship". What these people fail to grasp is that since the victory of the socialist revolution in Russia and, particularly, since the emergence of the world socialist community, the policy of provoking conflicts and preparing for war is at loggerheads not only with the vital interests of humankind, but also with the specific interests of countries and nations. What is needed in the present circumstances is to consolidate the principles of peaceful coexistence and carry through realistic constructive meas-

---

[1] See *Die Stimme der Gemeinde*, No. 4, 1954, S. 87.
[2] Posser, *Die deutsch-sowjetischen Beziehungen seit 1917*, Darmstadt.

ures to remove the danger of a war and create more favourable conditions for the settlement of concrete international issues.

Lately, West German historians have again focused their attention on the problem of Germany's foreign orientation between the two world wars. The "Locarno spirit" is again being opposed to the "spirit of Rapallo". A discussion has been sparked in West Germany about the worth of Gustav Stresemann's political legacy.[1] The debate has accentuated two indisputable facts: first, the published Stresemann documents were falsified, especially where they concerned the problem of Soviet-German relations and, second, the policy of balancing between East and West, that is, of manoeuvring between the Soviet Union and the Western powers, extolled by bourgeois historians as a Bismarckian feat, was really a screen for efforts to subvert the Rapallo policy.

The "spirit of Rapallo" was consistent with the principle of peaceful coexistence. But what was the "Locarno spirit"?

The "spirit of Locarno" cleared the path for Germany's inclusion in the Western imperialist bloc, for the Munich deal, and ultimately for the Second World War. True, it was a path that twisted and turned, one imperialist contradiction piling atop another, to be resolved, according to the well-laid plan, at the expense of the Soviet Union through the striking force of German militarism. This historical conception blossomed in the long run into a politico-strategic policy of "channeling" German aggression against the Soviet Union.

As we know, the scheme fell through. And mankind has shed too much blood to afford any recurrence of it in a new form. This is why its apologetics are a menace to European peace and security. Clearly, the peoples will gain from the conception of the peaceful coexistence of states with different social systems and the conception of proletarian internationalism. The impact of these Leninist principles, proclaimed at the time of the October Revolution, stems not only from their theoretical importance. Having

---

[1] See H. Gatzke, "Von Rapallo nach Berlin", *Vierteljahrshefte für Zeitgeschichte*, 1956, H. 1, S. 1 ff. Contains an exhaustive bibliography. The article is based on material from the Stresemann archive, now in the United States.

won the masses, they represent a formidable material force exercising an increasing influence on the destiny of mankind.

3

The new era ushered in by the October Revolution created a realistic possibility of preventing a new imperialist war. At the close of the 19th and the beginning of the 20th century, the international working-class movement was the only force that could bar the road to militarism and thwart the plans of war. However, due to the opportunist activity of Social-Democratic and trade union leaders, backed by a relatively small but politically influential so-called labour aristocracy and their betrayal of peace in the tragic August of 1914, the international working class was powerless to avert the imperialist war. Betrayed by the opportunist leadership, it was not united enough to begin determined mass anti-war actions and, besides, lacked the powerful bastion that the Union of Soviet Socialist Republics and the world system of socialist states later became. Their backing would make prevention of war and consolidation of peace a realistic undertaking.

Not until after the socialist revolution in Russia and the establishment of the Soviet state, with a socialist peace zone emerging on one-sixth of the earth's surface, did the struggle for peace and prevention of imperialist war acquire any tangible chance of success. And this chance doubled after the Soviet Union emerged from the capitalist encirclement and a powerful system of socialist states appeared alongside the existing system of capitalist countries, winning the sympathy of working people the world over and notably of the Asian and African peoples fighting for national independence against colonialism.

This world socialist system includes the German Democratic Republic. The G.D.R., the first worker-peasant state in German history, was founded after the Western powers chose to split Germany in pursuance of their economic, political and strategic aims and, defying the national interests of the German people, created the Federal Republic of Germany, which they promptly incorporated in the aggressive Atlantic pact. Two German states appeared thus in Central Europe with different socio-economic, political and ideological systems, which do not even maintain diplomatic relations with each other. These two Germanys have unequal populations, an unequal economic potential and divergent types of foreign economic relations. Yet, in the living dialectical process of historical development, especially if the energy of the masses becomes the creative motive force behind it, arithmetical summations, however important they may be, will hardly reflect the vast potentialities brought into motion by the progressive forces, and the prospects they create. The tragedy of the German nation is rooted in its failure to prevent the revival of monopolies and militarism in West Germany. Its good fortune, on the other hand, is rooted in the fact that despite twelve years of nazism, which destroyed Germany's finest sons and exploited racialism, nationalism and aggressive militarism to bedrug the nation, there survived political forces who rallied the working class and the people of East Germany to salvage the nation's honour and open vistas brighter than the Germans ever knew before. These are being moulded by the conscious efforts of people who have understood the pernicious role of German militarism and imperialism. There is at the back of this situation also the new correlation of world forces, an outgrowth of the Soviet victory over Hitler Germany, and also the vast store of experience accumulated in the field of Soviet-German relations since the October Revolution.

The German working class shoulders a tremendous historical responsibility, both national and international. Establishment of a united, peace-loving, democratic republic will be its important contribution to the solution of the general problem of security in the European continent. This is the reason why, as Walter Ulbricht noted rightly, "the historical significance of the German Democratic Republic lies in the fact that it is performing a great and important role in Germany's national revival and development into a peace-loving, democratic state".[1] The proposal for a confederation of the two existing German states, which could be the first step towards a solution of the German problem,[2] is historically justified and realistic, and consistent with

---

[1] *Neues Deutschland*, Aug. 9, 1957.
[2] Ibid.

the national interests of the German people and of European peace. This is why it is backed by the Soviet Union. By ignoring it and seeking atomic arms within the aggressive Atlantic bloc framework, the rulers of West Germany betray their lack of desire to settle the German question peacefully. Having embarked on their unilateral course in the NATO framework, they ignore all Soviet offers to adjust relations in line with the principles of peaceful coexistence, deliberately scorning the past lessons of Soviet-German relations.

Yet these lessons have not been lost on the German working class. The German Democratic Republic created by the German workers and in their historical interest, has built up fraternal co-operation and close economic and political ties with the U.S.S.R. There is every legitimate reason to say that the problem of relations between the Soviet Union and the German Democratic Republic has been settled once and for all. *The solution embodies the Marxist-Leninist principles of proletarian internationalism.* European peace would benefit greatly if the German Federal Republic were to abandon its revenge-seeking policy in favour of a policy of peaceful coexistence with the Soviet Union and all the other members of the community of socialist states in Europe. Then Mars, god of war who so often laid Europe waste, would never dare trample her fields again.

Rapprochement of the two German states in the framework of a confederation would bring about a détente not only in Europe but throughout the world. Relations between the G.D.R. and the Soviet Union are making splendid headway on the basis of socialist internationalism and testify to the enormous changes wrought after the Second World War when the German Democratic Republic started building socialism and became an important factor stabilising peace in Central Europe. If the Federal Republic were to pattern its policy on the peaceful coexistence principle, a new phase would open in the history of the European nations, paving the way to fruitful exchanges of material and cultural values created by the genius of the Soviet and German peoples, and this in the interests of the world as a whole.

1957

THE VERSAILLES THESIS AND ITS REVISION

(Historical Documents as Tools of Political Struggle)

In the fight for a world-wide democratic peace the socialist revolution which wrenched Russia out of the system of imperialist states was keyed on exposing the secret diplomacy and the secret treaties whereby the ruling classes had paved the way for the imperialist world war and were plotting an imperialist peace.

In March 1917, drafting the peace programme of the future Soviet Government, Lenin postulated the need for publishing forthwith "*all* these treaties in order to hold up to public shame the predatory aims of the tsarist monarchy and of *all* the bourgeois governments without exception".[1] When the October Revolution triumphed, this programme was instantly set in motion. That the secret treaties would be published was announced on the third day of the proletarian dictatorship. Secret diplomatic correspondence directly related to a very recent past was being made public for the first time in history. And for the first time, too, there was so unusual a publisher to do it as sailor Nikolai Grigoryevich Markin, who, witnesses attest, was highly conversant with a machine-gun and proved no less adept with another weapon of the socialist revolution: the publication of documents. His seven *Collections of Secret Documents* (Petrograd, 1917-18) exercised an influence on the international affairs of the end of 1917 and the beginning of 1918 matched only by the impression they

---

[1] Lenin, *Collected Works*, Vol. 23, p. 338.

made on the masses.[1] None will deny the significance of these, albeit technically imperfect, publications as a genuinely democratic action furthering a foreign policy of peace.

Their revolutionary class background is a self-evident fact. "The struggle revolved round the exposure of secret archives," wrote A. Rosenberg, a German historian, "and it was a bitter, ferocious fight involving all kinds of people, because both sides knew that the issue was one of war or peace, of a democratic or maximalist [Soviet.—*A. Y.*] republic. The force of example exerted on subsequent movements aiming to crush the existing system was very strong."[2] Elsewhere Rosenberg wrote: "Publishing secret archives while the documents in them still have a bearing on contemporary life is something new.... This revolutionary form of action had a revolutionary purpose."[3]

The Soviet publications did indeed pursue a revolutionary purpose. They denuded the contours and certain specific traits of imperialist policy and the methods of secret diplomacy used in preparing the world war. In this sense they proved a powerful weapon of peace.

But the impact of the first and the subsequent publications was augmented by the fact that they exposed not only the preparations for the First World War, but also the negotiations, agreements and secret deals during the war which, formulating the terms of the future imperialist redivision of the world, became the core of the Versailles system. The political impact of these documents increased greatly, especially since they set a precedent, for, save for the crudely falsified "coloured books" published for specific propaganda purposes, diplomatic documents were not usually made available for publication for a number of decades.

The imperialist governments wished to clear themselves of blame in matters related to the origin of the world war and none of their publications contains materials concerning the wartime wrangling over the future peace terms or,

---

[1] See B. Shtein, "K istorii vneshnei politiki SSSR", *Mirovoye Khozyaistvo i Mirovaya Politika* No. 10, 1930, pp. 67-68.

[2] Rosenberg, "Erschliessung der Geheimarchive", *Neue Zürcher Zeitung*, Dec. 23, 1928.

[3] Rosenberg, "Die neue französische Urkundenveröffentlichungen", *Vossische Zeitung*, July 24, 1929.

briefly, over the post-war system whose built-in contradictions paved the way for fresh intensive war preparations. But inasmuch as the Soviet precedent prompted the publication of a fresh batch of material, its scientific import, too, can hardly be overrated.

1

At every political and diplomatic zigzag in Weimar Germany's relations with the victors, the "war guilt" question cropped up unavoidably as an object of official discussion between the German leaders and their "Western" counterparts. The debate was impelled by the new political conditions resulting from Germany's defeat and served new political purposes in the devious struggle over the Versailles system.

Originally, war guilt was only a propaganda issue. But the Soviet publications of secret political documents baring the content of secret agreements redividing the world, forced the imperialist governments to change their methods, the new approach being epitomised by Wilson's famous 14 points, by appeals to repeal secret treaties and military alliances, to uphold the self-determination of nations, etc.

In view of the Soviet exposures and the arrogant posture of the German imperialists at the Brest-Litovsk negotiations, the Entente thought it wise to shift from the "war guilt" question to the theme of a "fair peace". But as soon as the victorious Entente began dictating its peace terms to defeated Germany the question of "war guilt" reappeared. Here the German people, who had hoped for a "fair peace", saw for themselves that the peace terms hinged much more on material things than on the pacific pronouncements of the U.S. President.

Yet Wilsonism was the guideline in the foreign policy orientation of the German Social-Democratic Government which, hating revolution, went out of its way to breed and sustain bourgeois pacifist illusions among the people. The Social-Democrats endeavoured to convince the people that Germany will get the desired Wilsonian "fair peace" if the demands of the Entente are unquestioningly fulfilled.

Then came the day when the elated victors began sharing the booty. The secret agreements concluded by the imperialist powers during the war were now due to come into force. The victors sat down to staking their excessive claims, while the war-weary and impoverished masses overburdened by heavy taxes were told: "The Germans will pay." The "fair peace" formula was twisted to mean that the degree of "fairness" would be proportional to the degree of Germany's guilt in starting the war. The German Social-Democrats accepted this interpretation without a murmur, and also the arguments of the overbearing Entente.

This propaganda was continuous from the day of the Compiègne armistice, becoming even more strident as the Paris conference of the victor-countries worked on the basic principles of the peace treaty.

Concurrently, the Entente made the most of the situation in Germany. The "independent socialist" Kurt Eisner, who headed the government of Bavaria, hoped for clemency. To demonstrate his rupture with the policy of the old militarist Germany and of the Social-Democrats of the Wilhelmian school like Friedrich Ebert, Philipp Scheidemann and Gustav Noske—all three members of the Berlin government—Eisner published certain diplomatic documents of the former royal Bavarian government, pillorying Wilhelm II and his political advisers as the main culprits of the world war. "I have shown everybody who can read and who is honest," Eisner declared, "how the criminal gang staged this world war like they would a stage play; the war did not break out—it was fabricated." Elsewhere he wrote that "the handful of people responsible for the war are not Germany; the guilty handful is not the fatherland".[1]

While exculpating the Entente politicians, notably Edward Grey, Eisner denounced the Kaiser government, "guilty of the war and the war policy which brought the German nation to the brink of the abyss". He believed that publishing documents damnatory to the Kaiser government

---

[1] Eisner, *Unterdrücktes aus dem Weltkrieg*, München-Wien-Zürich, 1919, S. 58 ff.; P. Dirr, *Auswärtige Politik Kurt Eisners und der bayerischen Revolution*, Leipzig-München, 1922; Dirr, *Kriegsschuldfrage und Bayerische Dokumente, Eine Abrechnung*, München-Berlin, 1924; Rosenberg, "Erschliessung der Geheimarchive", *Neue Zürcher Zeitung*, December 23, 1928.

would help the peace conference "proceed in a spirit of mutual trust". Since the goal was set, the method was made to fit it: the documents were taken out of context and abounded in deletions. But the reaction they evoked was staggering. The monarchists branded Eisner a traitor and falsifier, while the insurgent masses demanded the publication of all the secret German archives, the exposure of all imperialist politics.

Karl Kautsky asked the Social-Democratic government for permission to publish documents pertaining to the origin of the world war.[1] It was farthest from Kautsky's mind to take a swing at imperialism. He held essentially the same view as Kurt Eisner, with the sole difference that he was more cautious and kept a weather eye on Ebert and Scheidemann. His purpose, he said, was to prove to "a suspicious world that the new regime has completely broken with the old". But this appeared too risky to the Ebert-Scheidemann Government. It set the condition that Kautsky would not publish "separate documents the moment he found them, as Eisner had done"; Quarck, a Right Social-Democrat, was even attached to Kautsky for a time to oversee his actions.

Kautsky planned to begin publishing his collection before the peace negotiations began. He believed it would prove that "the German Government conducting ... the negotiations has nothing in common with the government that declared the war". But the Social-Democratic government ordered him to postpone the publication, which was ready for the printer, and Kautsky, as he later admitted, complied and "kept my silence ... not for legal, but for purely political reasons". Doubtlessly for the same reasons he consented to his collection being screened and altered by Professor Walter Schücking and Count Max Montgelas, appointed for this purpose by the government after the Versailles Treaty was already signed.

In a book written while he was compiling his collections, Kautsky touched—for unquestionably the same political

---

[1] *Die deutschen Dokumente zum Kriegsausbruch 1914. Vollstandige Sammlung der von Karl Kautsky zusammengestellten amtlichen Aktenstücke mit einigen Ergänzungen.* Im Auftrage des Auswärtigen Amtes nach gemeinsamer Durchsicht mit Karl Kautsky herausgegeben von Graf Max Montgelas und Prof. Walter Schücking, Bd. I-IV, Charlottenburg, 1919.

reasons—on the personalities responsible for the war. We say "touched" because a deep study and class analysis were conspicuously absent. "It is not Marxism," he said, "when the blame is anonymously put on capitalism in order to discourage a search for the culprits." Kautsky, for his part, preferred to twist the matter in a way more convenient for the Social-Democrats. He concentrated on "a search for the culprits" and thus diverted attention from the guilt borne by capitalism. "The word 'imperialism'," he said, "does not bring us closer to the solution."[1] This could not but affect the choice of documents and their arrangement. A similar approach is seen in the Austrian publication made on the instructions of Otto Bauer, then State Secretary.[2]

The basic political conception that prompted the publication of the German documents also affected the chronological limits of the material. Since the origin of the war was identified with the war guilt of individuals, the war motive became the main determinative factor. Hence the over-emphasis on the pre-war crisis and hence the Sarajevo assassination as the opening subject of the collection, which distorted the historical perspective. Some other opening date would probably have led to other judgements and conclusions. A wider chronological framework might have revealed the welter of international contradictions in the imperialist era. Kautsky sidestepped it all, probably not for failing to understand the true essence of imperialism, but for considerations of a political order.

Kautsky's collection saw the light of day after the Entente powers had already handed down their verdict and the full weight of the war guilt was placed on Germany, justifying the reparations. Prior to the formal Allied decision to demand contributions in the guise of reparations, the German Government approached them through Switzerland, suggesting that a neutral commission should study the question of "war guilt".[3] The reply was as brief as it

---

[1] Kautsky, *Wie der Weltkrieg entstand. Dargestellt nach dem Aktenmaterial des Deutschen Auswärtigen Amtes*, Berlin, 1919, S. 14-15.
[2] *Diplomatische Aktenstücke zur Vorgeschichte des Krieges 1914. Ergänzungen und Nachträge zum österreichisch-ungarischen Rotbuch*, Wien, 1919; Cf., R. Gooss, *Das Wiener Kabinett und die Entstehung des Weltkrieges*, Wien, 1919. Another collection appeared in Austria by A. Pribran, *Die politischen Geheimverträge Österreich-Ungarns 1879-1914*, Wien-Leipzig, 1920.
[3] Note of November 29, 1918.

was categorical: German responsibility has been established beyond any doubt. In fact, while discussing reparations, the Allies had appointed a "commission to determine responsibility for the outbreak of the war".[1] At Paris, reparations were an object of bitter struggle between France, Britain and the United States, creating a near-crisis in March 1919. By this time the commission had completed its study and submitted a report.

To be sure, the U.S. members refused to endorse some of the sections of the report. Their abstention was in line with the political stand of the United States on reparations. The U.S. Government insisted on the letter and spirit of its note of November 5, 1918, which said "compensation will be made by Germany for all damage done to the civilian population of the Allies and to their property by the aggression of Germany by land, by sea, and from the air". Britain and France, on the other hand, wanted full reimbursement of *war* costs which, by the way, created a new area of dispute, because each of the parties wanted to secure its share of the future reparations. Finally, a compromise was reached. British diplomats, who had reached an understanding with their French counterparts, clothed their claims in terms acceptable to the doctrinaire approach of the U.S. spokesmen,[2] who were ultimately isolated and gradually lost the backing even of influential political groups in their own country.

The U.S. representatives believed that the United States should be the arbiter between Germany and the Entente countries and steer their relations in the direction that suited it most, even in the event of the reparations problem developing prejudicially to U.S. interests. What the U.S. rulers were really most concerned about was to get back their loans.

The skirmish over reparations bared the reverse side of the Wilson doctrine: the politically isolated American delegation, compelled to compromise and, in effect, to abandon their original stand, backtracked even farther than the British diplomats had wanted and compensated their political concession with a discourse on German guilt and

---

[1] It consisted of 15 members from different countries: Lansing, Tardieu, James Brown Scott, Politis, and others.

[2] B. M. Baruch, *The Making of the Reparation and Economic Sections of the Treaty*, New York-London, 1920, p. 31.

obligations. The moral pillars of the Versailles edifice were thus put up and the U.S. principle of a "fair peace" could celebrate a victory.[1] Yet the Wilsonian orientation of the German Government connoted something entirely different. The governing bourgeois groups fell out among themselves as to the tactics of countermanding the terms of the Entente. There was friction between the government and the delegation it sent to Versailles, headed by Count Ulrich von Brockdorff-Rantzau. Matthias Erzberger, leader of the Catholic Centre, thought it inadvisable to argue against the peace terms. He believed that a complete and unconditional surrender would mitigate Germany's lot and avert an invasion and partition of Germany, and that it would be unwise to discuss matters in the context of Germany's war guilt. The Social-Democrats were inclined to agree with him and sent pertinent instructions to the delegation at Versailles. But the political battle there was already under way, and precisely over the war guilt. Having obtained advance unofficial information about the findings of the War Guilt Commission, the German delegation made public its opinion.[2] The main points were set out by Brockdorff-Rantzau in his speech at the Paris conference. "We are told," he said, "that we must admit to being the sole culprits of the war. If I made this admission, it would be a lie. Far be it from us to deny all responsibility for what led up to the war and for it being fought the way it was. The behaviour of the former German Government at the peace conferences in The Hague, its course of action and its evasions during the twelve tragic days of July may be responsible for the fact that Germany alone, whose people were convinced in the defensive nature of the war, is being blamed for its outbreak.... The Russian mobilisation robbed the statesmen of any chance to save the situation."[3]

The outcome of the discussion was a foregone conclu-

---

[1] Subsequently, the United States did not endorse the Versailles Treaty. The peace concluded by the U.S. and Germany had no article laying down Germany's sole war guilt.

[2] *Das deutsche Weissbuch über die Schuld am Kriege,* Charlottenburg, 1919, S. 15 ff. The authors of the memorandum were Hans Delbrück, Mendelssohn-Bartholdy, Count Max Montgelas and Max Weber. The political background of the last named and the conditions in which the memorandum was written are described by Marianne Weber in *Max Weber. Ein Lebensbild*, Tübingen, 1926, S. 665-70.

[3] K. F. Nowak, *Versailles*, Berlin, 1927, S. 261.

sion. In 1919 the victor-countries declared Germany not only the main, but the *sole* culprit. The German delegation was told the issue it had raised was not subject to discussion. Brockdorff-Rantzau resigned, and his successor signed the Versailles Treaty.

The governments of France, U.S.A., Britain and Italy set out, first, to repugn Lenin's thesis that *all* the imperialist governments, the *whole* imperialist system, were equally to blame and, second, to justify the reparations exacted from Germany, whose limits were at first not even specified. The culprit pays, the culprit compensates all losses and expenditures[1]—this was how the matter was put in Article 231 of the Versailles Treaty. The economic implications of this thesis became a sufficiently strong reason, therefore, for the war guilt question to serve for the victor-countries, especially France, as an article of faith. When the rulers of Weimar Germany, their government, diplomacy and press, described the "war guilt" question (*Kriegsschuldfrage*) as the "war guilt" lie (*Kriegsschuldlüge*), they did so not because of any special reverence for Clio, the Muse of history.

The political battle continued. The reparations had not been specified, the size of the payments had not been defined, the Anglo-French contradictions that broke to the surface had a bearing on reparations. This made the wrangle over the Versailles thesis more acute. Both sides knew its real political significance. "Indeed," wrote Poincaré, "if the Central powers had not been the ones to cause the war, why should they have been sentenced to pay the damages? It follows necessarily and justly that if responsibility is shared, the damages should also be shared."[2]

The matter became more urgent still and, so to say, materially clear by the spring of 1921, when the British Government, alarmed and irritated by the negotiations between the French Government and the French industrialists, on the one hand, and major German industrial

---

[1] "One of the Allies," wrote Bernard M. Baruch later, "went even further and made claim for loss and damage resulting from the fact that the armistice was concluded so unexpectedly that the termination of hostilities involved it in financial losses" (Baruch, op. cit., p. 20).

[2] Alfred von Wegerer, *Die Widerlegung der Versailler Kriegsschuldthese*, Berlin, 1928, S. 111-12 f.

interests, on the other, suddenly put the full weight of its support behind the most extreme French demands. The German counter-proposals at the London conference early in March 1921 were rejected out of hand. Germany was told in no uncertain terms that if she did not comply with the fixed reparations, which were in effect ruinous, Duisburg and Düsseldorf would be occupied. The ultimatum was accompanied by Lloyd George's angry tirade that "for the Allies, German responsibility for the war is fundamental. It is the basis upon which the structure of the Treaty has been erected, and if that acknowledgement is repudiated or abandoned, the Treaty is destroyed. . . . We wish, therefore, once and for all to make it quite clear that German responsibility for the war must be treated by the Allies as a *chose jugée*."[1] Aristide Briand spoke essentially to the same purpose in August 1921.

2

The war guilt question thus developed into an instrument of political practice and, notably, of pressure on Germany. In Germany, too, the various bourgeois groups were entangled in a controversy over the advisability of referring to the Versailles thesis in relation to questions of a more specific political character. The pacifist and bourgeois-democratic camp, represented among others by Count Johann-Heinrich von Bernstorff, a member of the so-called Democratic Party, ex-Ambassador to the United States and subsequently German delegate to the preparatory disarmament committee, advised against raising the "war guilt" issue in practical politics and favoured directly political arguments. But the bourgeois element which was in the saddle held the opposite view, making the Versailles thesis a powerful political tool in their fight against the Versailles system as a whole. The machinery of state, the universities, the press and the schools were drawn into the battle. A special bureau financed by the German Foreign Ministry was instituted as an ideological headquarters and co-ordinating centre. Alfred von Wegerer, a former colonel in the Kaiser's army, who headed the bureau, set out to lay "the

---

[1] *Times*, March 4, 1921.

necessary moral foundations for a revision of the Versailles Treaty".[1]

The German Foreign Ministry decided to publish documents from its archive. The early volumes appeared in 1922, when the reparations issue was most acute and new political and economic pressure was being brought to bear on Germany. This time the shoe was on the other foot. After the 1870-71 war it had been the French Government which published diplomatic documents pertaining to events preceding the war and challenged Germany to publish her own secret archives. After the 1914-18 war it was the German Government which, having begun to publish diplomatic documents on the origin of the war, challenged the Entente to follow suit.[2]

The political goals naturally coloured the key aspects of the collection, the chronological range and the arrangement of the documents. The publication was not chronological, but by subjects. Besides, many of the documents were abridged, with passages from them presented in different sections of the same or even of different volumes.

This met with serious criticism abroad and from certain German researchers.[3] Friedrich Thimme, who did all the spadework and editing, said that the topical principle of arranging the material was prompted by political motives in the broad sense of the word.[4] It was political motives, too, that set the chronological limits and the main breakdown of the volumes. These do not go back to the pre-war crisis of 1914, but, in a way, lead up to it (it was covered by Kautsky's publication) in order to explain and at once justify the stand of the German Government during the crisis. "The documents," writes Wegerer, "furnish incontrovertible proof that Germany was not a 'criminal state' ... and that the policy of the German Reich in the past forty years has been at least as peaceful and at least as morally justified as the policy of the Serbs, Russians, French and British."[5]

---

[1] Wegerer, op. cit., S. 10.

[2] See Rathenau's speech on June 13, 1922 and Stresemann's on December 16, 1923 (*Archiv für Politik und Geschichte* No. 1, 1924).

[3] Cf. E. Brandenburg, *Von Bismarck zum Weltkriege*, Berlin, 1924, S. VIII.

[4] F. Thimme, "Die Aktenpublikation des auswärtigen Amtes", *Preussische Jahrbücher* No. 7, 1929.

[5] Die *Kriegsschuldfrage*, No. 12, 1926.

The publishers denied the guilt of individuals and described the international political situation which divided the world into two hostile groupings and caused a military explosion.

The fundamental methodological aspects of this conception go no deeper than issues of a politico-diplomatic order. It is assumed that immanent in these issues are forces forming the various large-scale political combinations which, by virtue of different conditions, became centres of attraction for all the other, less prominent political formations.[1] Not the profound contradictions of imperialism but the "big politics of the European cabinets"—words used as the title of the publication—were presented as the moving spirit of European history leading up to the world war. In this respect, the title mirrors the methodological pattern of the whole publication.

It is understandable, therefore, that the publication was devoted to Foreign Ministry material only and that no use was made of documents illustrating the volatile colonial policy of the German imperialists. The colonial problem is dealt with solely in relation to the basic lines of European policy and the balance of forces in the political realm of Europe. These forces acquire something of a self-sufficient complexion and are portrayed as having their own intrinsic regularity and their own definite orientation by reason of being conditioned by the system of alliances and secret diplomacy.

It was this concept of motive forces that lay behind the chronological starting point, because, in the circumstances, it was important to elucidate the reshuffle of international strength culminating in the combination that entered the world war, that is, the Austro-German alliance. The publication had to offset yet another political factor: French propaganda, which exploited as evidence of the original German guilt the establishment of the Austro-German alliance in 1879, which ostensibly pointed to an offensive policy and generally branded Bismarck's attitude as a ceaseless craving for hegemony in the European concert, even

---

[1] This conception is seen still more clearly in the condensed edition of the big German publication: *Die auswärtige Politik des Deutschen Reiches 1871-1914*, Bd. I-IV, Berlin, 1928.

for world rule.[1] The publishers indicate that this was one of the reasons why they published the first series of documents (six volumes) related to the Bismarckian epoch and opening with the founding of the German empire. It is clear, too, that the decision to shift the opening date of the collection to 1871 was prompted by a desire to produce material that would compare favourably in illustrating German occupation policy after the Frankfurt Peace and the French occupation regime after Versailles. At the time the publication was begun it was politically desirable to stress that Germany withdrew from the occupied French departments *before* the stipulated date.

Acting on the conception that the system of political alliances was determinative, all German policy, including the policy of balancing and of alliances, is presented in the publication as a projection of the elements laid down by Bismarck: protection of German interests and maintenance of the *status quo*. Yet it shows that the policy of the Wilhelmian period was inept in the sense that it failed to prevent and, later, dissolve the "encirclement of Germany". In the final count, as most commentators agree,[2] the documents were meant to show that if the question of responsibility should be raised at all in relation to German statesmen, Wilhelm at their head, it is their responsibility to the German people that should be raised, first, for it was they who reaped the storm they had sown. The Versailles thesis was countered with the declaration that any action, even though dangerous and ambiguous, was subordinated to the ultimate purpose of preserving peace. Wherever a document could be interpreted to imply that the political method used was at loggerheads with the above purpose, the publishers supplied voluble footnotes, usually weighed in both the historical and political sense.

The publishers admit that they often disregarded the marginal notes made in the Kaiser's hand on some of the documents, because they did not think these notes had influenced the subsequent conduct of affairs by the Foreign Ministry. These evasions, too, evoked much criticism. The

---

[1] *Die Grosse Politik der Europäischen Kabinette, 1871-1914,* Bd. I, S. VIII. The publication consisted in all of 40 volumes (54 parts).
[2] Thimme, "Rückblick und Ausblick" (*Archiv für Politik und Geschichte* No. 1, 1924).

publishers, however, had to reckon with the influential old politicians and diplomats of the Kaiser school and with the Rightist nationalist groups.

What needs mentioning is that protests against the publication of secret documents of so recent a past were made by the monarchist elements. These feared that the publication would discredit the leaders of the old monarchist regime. "This sort of publication," wrote an old diplomat of the Wilhelmian school, "is, *meo voto*, premature. The time is not ripe, because even the most objective historian, to say nothing of journalists, etc., still lacks, and cannot but lack, a far-sighted opinion. We are contestants in a most bitter struggle, internal and international, between the new regime and the old victorious alliance of the enemies of defeated Germany.... The policy of the decades since the founding of the German empire and the defeat of France is still in evidence and keeps entering the lists at every point.... The discussion will be envenomed by a coming to grips over contemporary issues. I ask myself about the present publication: *cui bono*? For purely academic purposes? As a politician I cannot recognise the publication as a goal in itself. The political goal (to which the documents also owe their existence) stands higher. When documents are published in relation to our epoch (for we are completely in the shadow of the past four decades), the political goal has to be reckoned with."[1]

But soon the displeasure of the Rightist element evaporated, giving place to satisfaction. At the other pole, the publication evoked certain critical remarks from bourgeois pacifist and Social-Democratic quarters, chiefly because the publishers had left out a number of typically Wilhelmian resolutions which, in their opinion, would discredit the German Kaiser. Retorting to his critics, Thimme referred to a similar omission by Ed. Bernstein in the collection of the correspondence of Marx and Engels. Anybody in the least conversant with Bernstein's ruses will recognise how injudicious it is to excuse oneself on such grounds.

In other respects, the criticisms in the German press did

---

[1] This letter by an unknown author is quoted by Thimme in "Die Aktenpublikation des Auswärtigen Amtes und ihre Gegner" (*Archiv für Politik und Geschichte* No. 5-6, 1924).

not go beyond complaints about deletions in the published texts and failure to publish others.

Yet the French nationalists made this the object of their most bitter attacks. Rightist French periodicals called the German publication a propaganda hoax, and serious accusations were flung at the publishers. The campaign was headed by Emile Bourgeois,[1] a Sorbonne professor, co-author of the war guilt report submitted to the French Senate[2] in 1919 and co-publisher of the French documents related to the origins of the Franco-Prussian war. He charged that even the title of the German publication, *The Big Politics of the European Cabinets,* was deliberately slanted, the editors aiming to accentuate the peaceable German policy against the setting of aggressive political schemes nurtured by her adversaries. He spotted a number of deliberate omissions and accused the German publishers of maliciously suppressing documents of prime importance, concluding with the demand that the Germans publish "all the despatches of the German General Staff and its military attachés".

The German publishers pointed out that some despatches found in the archive of the German Foreign Ministry had been published by them and declared themselves ready to publish the documents of the German war ministry if the French Government publishes a similar collection.[3]

The Franco-German embroglio reflected the tension in the political relations of the two countries. Another indication of this strain is evident in Friedrich Thimme's satisfaction over the resignation of Poincaré which, he said, showed that "people seeking to benefit from legal chicanery and distortion are beginning to lose their footing even in France".[4]

The political purport of his derision is underscored by France's failure in the Ruhr shortly before, and by the then still pending London conference of 1924, which adopted

[1] Bourgeois, "Les Archives d'Etat et l'Enquête sur les origines de la guerre mondiale", *Revue Historique* No. 155.

[2] Bourgeois et Pagès, *Rapport pour la Commission d'Enquête sur les faits de la guerre*, Paris, 1919.

[3] Thimme, "Französische Kritiken zur deutschen Aktenpublikation", *Europäische Gespräche* No. 8-9, 1927.

[4] Thimme, "Die Aktenpublikation des Auswärtigen Amtes und ihre Gegner", *Archiv für Politik und Geschichte* No. 5-6, 1924.

the Dawes Plan, compelling France to abandon her suggested coercive solution of the reparations issue.

The subsequent phase in Franco-German relations was also mirrored in the controversy. M. Lhéritier, for example, who exposed omissions concerning the part played by Greece in the pre-war period, regretted that the German publication was not undertaken after the "consequences of Locarno" could have affected its make-up.[1] This statement was clearly a veiled suggestion that absence of French aggressive designs should be brought out in the German studies of the origins of the world war. After retorting on the specific points,[2] the Germans suggested caustically that France publish her own documents in the "Locarno spirit".[3] Now that Britain was made arbiter in Franco-German relations, France and Germany endeavoured to settle certain political and financial issues on their own. In the circumstances, the German proposal was an obvious plea that the prospective French publication should not be anti-German.

This exchange of opinion was no more than a reflection of the big press discussion concerning the war guilt, conducted with animation in connection with Germany's admission to the League of Nations, later picked up by French and German political leaders in their speeches, and foundering like the German attempt at a rapprochement with France.

"Germany's admission to the League of Nations and the new phase in German-French relations that came into sight at Locarno and Thoiry," wrote the *Kölnische Zeitung,* a paper close to Wilhelmstrasse, in an article entitled "New Spirits—Old Spectres", "gave reason to hope that the Versailles verdict of guilt would be overruled".[4]

It did not take long for these hopes of revision to prove illusory. The Reichstag decision backed by the German bourgeois parties to appeal to the League of Nations and the International Tribunal for a final adjustment of the

---

[1] Lhéritier, "Les documents diplomatiques allemandes sur les origines de la guerre", *Revue d'Histoire de la guerre mondiale* No. 6, 1926.

[2] Mendelssohn-Bartholdy, "Kleine Missverständnisse über eine grosse Publikation", *Europäische Gespräche* No. 7, 1926.

[3] Thimme, "Französische Kritiken zur deutschen Aktenpublikation", *Europäische Gespräche* No. 8-9, 1927.

[4] *Kölnische Zeitung*, Oct. 3, 1926.

"war guilt" issue[1] was as sterile as the earlier hope that the League of Nations would prevail on its members to publish materials concerning the origin of the war and initiate an international committee of experts to make an "impartial study and settle the German 'war guilt' problem".[2]

Soon, after the trend aimed at scuttling the Thoiry policy took the upper hand in French politics, Poincaré made it clear in response to Stresemann's revisionist speech that his cabinet would oppose all such tendencies in German policy and the German press.[3] The zigzags in Franco-German relations reflected in the Locarno and Thoiry policies did not live up to the expectations of the resurgent German imperialism. The French Government, which changed nothing but its methods, rejected the German demand of revising the terms of the Versailles Treaty.

At the time of this Franco-German "rapprochement", Émile Bourgeois understandably opposed Aulard's plan of translating into French the German publication, which he considered crude political propaganda.[4] He thought it foolish to produce for the French public what he himself termed an instrument of propaganda grinding the axe of the Germans, the enemies of France, which would, at the very least, plant dangerous seeds of doubt in a matter which a good Frenchman ought not discuss at all.

If the French translation did finally appear[5] despite these objections, this was not due to Aulard's failing to see Bourgeois's point or opposing the Versailles verdict. The two were really of the same mind, but their approach differed. Aulard rearranged the material in chronological order. This was not a purely academic exercise. He meant thereby to bring into relief the glaring omissions. This, he hoped, would discredit Germany's decision of opening her archives and at once expose the true nature of her policy. To drive home his point, he gave the French translation a new title, "The Foreign Policy of Germany, 1870-1914".

[1] *Berliner Lokalanzeiger* Nov, 23, 1926.
[2] *Berliner Tageblatt*, Nov. 19, 1925.
[3] Official Havas communication dated Oct. 4, 1926.
[4] *Revue Historique* No. 5-6, 1927.
[5] It began appearing (in 1927) under the title, *La Politique Exterieure de l'Allemagne 1870-1914. Documents officiels publiés par le Ministère Allemand des Affaires Etrangères*, Avant-propos de A. Aulard, Paris.

Shortly, the Foreign Policy Institute in Hamburg issued an abridged version of the big German publication under what was virtually the same title, "The Foreign Policy of the German Reich, 1871-1914."[1] This collection was also arranged chronologically. The editors, Albrecht Mendelssohn-Bartholdy and Friedrich Thimme, put the main emphasis in their general conception on Anglo-German relations in the context of the more general problem of the origin of politico-military groupings in Europe, to which they attributed the source of the world war. This was vital for the Weimar Republic, considering that its inclusion in the Western bloc and, hence, its orientation in foreign policy became a point of major interest not only among the dominant classes, but the public at large.

Earlier, Thimme publicly attacked Aulard's French version of the original German publication,[2] pointing out, among other things, that the French Government was keeping the secrets of its diplomatic and military archives well guarded, reluctant apparently to make revelations in an issue as vital and topical as the origin, establishment and activities of the Entente.

A Soviet publication of documents related to the history of Russo-French relations,[3] acclaimed as highly valuable by all quarters, was nonetheless sneered at by the French, who said it had been put out "with the aim of anti-tsarist propaganda".[4]

In Germany, the Foreign Ministry proposed to publish the diplomatic correspondence of Izvolsky,[5] the Russian Ambassador to Paris, with the obvious political purpose, as pointed out by Herman Kantorowicz,[6] of exposing French

[1] *Die auswärtige Politik des Deutschen Reiches. 1871-1914.* Unter Leitung von Albrecht Mendelssohn-Bartholdy und Friedrich Thimme herausgegeben vom Institut für auswärtige Politik in Hamburg, Bd. I-IV, Berlin, 1928. Contained new documents relating to the history of Anglo-German relations.

[2] Thimme, "Französische Kritiken zur deutschen Aktenpublikation", *Europäische Gespräche* No. 9, 1927.

[3] *Materialy po istorii franko-russkikh otnoshenii za 1910-1914 gody*, Moscow, 1922 (Russ. ed.).

[4] C. Bloch, "Les documents officiels sur les origines de la guerre", *Revue d'Histoire de la guerre mondiale* No. 3, 1929.

[5] *Der Diplomatische Schriftwechsel Iswolskis 1911-1914... Im Auftrage des Deutschen auswärtigen Amtes*, Hrsg. von Friedrich Stieve, Bd. I-IV, 2 Aufl. Berlin, 1925.

[6] H. Kantorowicz, *Der Geist der englischen Politik und das Gespenst der Einkreisung Deutschlands*, Berlin, 1929, S. 456.

policy, particularly Poincaré's. Lastly, the publication of the diplomatic correspondence of Count Benckendorff,[1] the Russian Ambassador in London, was intended to corroborate the policy of "encirclement" pursued methodically by the Entente against Germany. (Benckendorff's correspondence, chiefly copies of the documents, was stolen by B. von Siebert, a secretary of the Russian Embassy, and subsequently given or sold to Germany.)

3

Publication of Austrian documents made the Germans change their line in the "war guilt" issue, all the more so since it almost coincided with the 1930 Hague ruling on Young's reparations plan, which, in effect, relieved Austria of reparation payments.

This coincidence indicated that the reparations issue was being isolated from the "war guilt" issue. But since the original point of view on Germany's war guilt had gained currency by then, it obstructed and at once facilitated the spread of the political ideas implicit in the German collection of documents. "Together with our kindred Austria," wrote the *Berliner Tageblatt,* mouthpiece of the German liberal bourgeoisie, "we rejoice that she has achieved successes by her clever policy, prompted exclusively by her need; but we are compelled to oppose certain conclusions about the war guilt that may be drawn against us from the lifting of reparations in Austria's case. The impression may arise that the only remaining payer of reparations is also the only culprit."[2]

The arguments that could dissipate this notion were rooted in the political conception shaped by the documentary testimony of the Austrian publication.

The nine-volume collection[3] appeared unexpectedly and

---

[1] B. v. Siebert, *Diplomatische Aktenstücke zur Geschichte der Ententepolitik der Vorkriegsjahre,* Berlin-Leipzig, 1921. In this edition the material is arranged by subjects. In another, revised, edition the material is chronological: B. v. Siebert, *Graf von Benckendorffs diplomatischer Schriftwechsel,* Bd. I-III, Berlin-Leipzig, 1928.

[2] *Berliner Tageblatt,* April 1, 1930.

[3] *Österreichs-Ungarns Aussenpolitik von der Bosnischen Krise 1908 bis zum Kriegsausbruch 1914. Diplomatische Aktenstücke des öster-*

created a sensation in the European press. It was compiled in total secrecy, because the states constituted in the territory of former Austria-Hungary, who were then allies of France, had priority access to diplomatic archives and could have taken advantage of it. "They will do so beyond doubt," wrote one of the editors of the Austrian publication, "and will select and arrange the material in a way that will establish Austria's responsibility for the outbreak of the war on the strength of her own documents."[1]

This was why the Austrians published the collection. It was meant to avert this menace and present their case. The editors stuffed more than 11,000 documents, just 3,000 less than the number included in the 40 volumes of the German publication covering a period of 43 years. It was a technical feat for a nine-volume collection covering some six or seven pre-war years. Such quantity was meant to create an impression of the utmost thoroughness.[2] Yet the editors did not shrink from abridging documents wherever they thought it would buttress the basic principles of their publication.

The bulk of the documents naturally referred to Balkan problems. Naturally, too, the collection opened with papers casting light on the shadier aspects of the Bosnian crisis.

The period is highlighted by fresh Russian activity in the Balkans (after the Far-Eastern setbacks), the revolutionary turmoil in Turkey and, as a consequence, by stepped up political activity on the part of the Balkan states. The latter aspect is given the most space and forms a substantial portion of the broad documentary canvas of the first three Austrian volumes.

The impression is conveyed that in 1908, when poised to seize Bosnia and Herzegovina, Austrian policy-makers were

---

reichisch-ungarischen Ministerium des Äussern, Ausgewählt von Ludwig Bittner, Alfred Francis Pribram, Heinrich Srbik und Hans Übersberger, Wien-Leipzig, 1930.

[1] Ludwig Bittner, as quoted in an article by E. Glaise von Horstenau, "Das Österreichische Aktenwerk über die Vorgeschichte des Weltkrieges", Die Kriegsschuldfrage No. 1, 1930.

[2] However, a number of key documents, such as the minutes of the Council of Ministers for March 29, 1909, concerning mobilisation against Serbia and Montenegro, were omitted. Cf., Conrad v. Hötzendorf, Aus meiner Dienstzeit 1906-1918, Bd. I, Wien, 1921, S. 162.

chiefly concerned with liberating Novi Pazar Sanjak: if Austria-Hungary did go to the length of annexing Bosnia and Herzegovina, this was done to counteract the Serbian aggressive trend. It is true, the editors did not conceal documents revealing that plans of partitioning Serbia had been drafted in Vienna as early as in the summer of 1908. But they are engulfed by others to persuade the reader that Hapsburg policy was guided by the sole idea of safe-guarding the territorial integrity of Austria-Hungary, which had no intention whatsoever of conquering foreign land.

The editors endeavour to show that the Bosnian problem had been fully settled by Vienna and Petersburg when the sudden crisis was precipitated by an unexpected covert British intervention. This side of the matter is illustrated quite exhaustively, stressing that the first, let alone all the other, Austro-Hungarian action on the Balkan stage was prompted by factors unrelated in any direct way to Austro-Russian and Austro-Serbian relations. Vienna's Balkan policy is fitted thus into the broader context of Anglo-German contradictions elsewhere in the world.

A responsive reader was expected to come to the conclusion that Austria's interests were prejudiced by the intricate combinations imposed on her by her alliance with Germany. This is usually illustrated by the utterances of Austro-Hungarian Foreign Minister Aehrenthal, who formulated the idea that Austria-Hungary had gradually to forge her alliance with Germany into a relationship based on "reason" in order to be able to establish friendlier relations with Britain and France. In place of Nibelungian loyalty, on which the Austro-German alliance was based, he implied, mutual safeguards against a possible Russian attack would have been quite sufficient.

Depending on the angle of approach, this basic notion related to the main theme of the publication, that is, to the Austro-German alliance, becomes the ganglion of different political appraisals.

Inasmuch as Aehrenthal's successor, Count Leopold Berchtold, had no opportunity to put into effect this ostensibly politically desirable and historically far-sighted conception, the policy of the Austro-Hungarian monarchy is depicted as being under pressure of extraneous forces of far greater influence and with far greater operational scope.

Even so, the published documents produce a striking picture of Austro-Hungarian political planning against Serbia—plans of "taming" or partitioning that country. This, too, however, is garnished with the official conception that no other way existed to ensure the territorial integrity of the multinational state.

Apologists of Hapsburg policy suggested that Austria-Hungary's policy in the Serbian issue, particulary during the July 1914 crisis, was fashioned, if not justified, by the necessity of safeguarding the state. In any case, the Austro-Hungarian scheme envisaged an inevitable Balkan —and *exclusively* Balkan—war. This brings to light a discrepancy between the appraisal of the Austro-German alliance and the possibility of a European war. The documents stress certain Austro-German contradictions over a number of political and economic problems, especially in the Balkans.

Naturally, German bourgeois historians tackled this question of Austro-German contradictions with a will, for it was an area providing prodigious arguments in favour of the claim that Germany had not caused the war and had been drawn into it. The question of German responsibility was supplanted by that of the expediency of Germany's alliance with Austria—a problem of vital importance at a time when political discussion centred on annexation (*Anschluss*) of Austria. When broached in 1929 and 1930, the German plan was acidly opposed by France with a plan for a Danube federation.

The problem of Austro-German relations was thus patterned to suit political practice. E. Fischer, general secretary of the Reichstag committee studying the origins of the war, wrote:

"Austria-Hungary, contending with the 19th-century spirit of nationalism, saw herself threatened from all sides. At last, in face of these dangers and threats of attack, she decided to strike first, thinking that this will save her. It was right and wrong: her fate was tragic. The question is whether Lesser Germany (*Kleindeutschland*) united by Berlin should have conducted the struggle ... together with her."

This gave expression to a politico-historical conception that pervades with various modifications all the pertinent utterances of the German bourgeois and Social-Democratic press.[1] A historical issue thus suggested a solution for the problem of Austro-German relations: the national question that plagued the Hapsburg empire no longer exists for modern Austria.

And this is supposed to lead to the notion that a favourable situation had come for Austria's inclusion in Germany.

The German bourgeois press won an unexpected ally in the former Hungarian Foreign Minister, G. Gratz.[2] To prove Hungary's innocence, Gratz published documents that were meant to show that Count Tisza had objected to an armed Austro-Hungarian move as vehemently as British Minister John Morley had objected to British armed action by resigning in protest to the policy of Grey and Asquith.[3] Referring to mutual Austrian and Hungarian rebukes as to who had done more to bring about the war, Gratz set out to demonstrate that both sides were guided solely by "the interest of the third side—the monarchy". Gratz maintained that Tisza, who had originally objected to war but later became its advocate, was a tragic victim of circumstances (being assassinated in protest to the war).

The purpose of Gratz's historical excursus will be clear if we recall that he was, and remained, one of the most eminent legitimists. For all this, his version was open to a variety of interpretations. The bourgeois press in Vienna and Budapest totally denied the responsibility of Austria and Hungary. The Social Democrats, who sidestepped the problem of the war's imperialist nature, pinned the war

---

[1] E. Fischer, "Das Verhängnis der Nibelungentreue", *Vossische Zeitung*, Dec. 12, 1929; W. Schaer, "Von der Bosnischen Krise bis Sarajevo", *Kölnische Zeitung*, Dec. 1, 1929; F. Thimme, "Österreich-Ungarns Vorkriegsdokumente", *Berliner Tageblatt*, Dec. 10, 13, 1929; H. v. Hindenburg, "Eine Anmerkung zu den Österreichischen Vorkriegs-akten", *Berliner Tageblatt*, Apr. 1, 1930; F. Stieve, "Bundesgenosse Österreich-Ungarn", *Hamburger Fremdenblatt*, March 5, 1930; E. Käbisch, "England und die Annexionskrise 1908/09", *Berliner Monatshefte für internationale Aufklärung* No. 10, 1930; A. Rosenberg, "Zur Vorge-schichte des Weltkrieges", *Die Gesellschaft* No. 1, 1931.

[2] Gratz, "Tiszas Haltung bei Ausbruch des Weltkrieges", *Pester Lloyd*, Dec. 28, 1928; "Graf Tisza und das Ultimatum an Serbien", *Kölnische Zeitung*, March 30, 1929; "Die Kriegsschuldlüge gegen Ungarn", *Deutsche Allgemeine Zeitung*, March 30, 1929. Another document to the same effect, giving an identical interpretation to Tisza's conduct, appeared in *Pester Lloyd*, July 9, 1929.

[3] Morley, *Memorandum on Resignation*, London, 1928.

guilt on the Hapsburg monarchy conveniently late, while the monarchists argued that Austria had been compelled to act against Serbia in self-defence.

The exposures made by Stanojveić[1] and Jovanović[2] relating to the wrangle between the various political groupings in monarchist Yugoslavia laid bare many of the threads linking the Sarajevo assassination with the Black Hand, a Serbian secret society.

The Austrian collection (Nos. 2911, 2921, 2928, 2966, 3041, 3264 and 3270) revealed that since November 1911 Vienna was well informed about this secret society, its political role and methods, and its moving spirit and organiser, chief of Serbian counter-espionage, Colonel Dragutin Dimitrijević (Apis). However, in its ultimatum to Serbia in 1914, the Austro-Hungarian Government made no mention of the Black Hand and chiefly attacked Narodna Odbrana, a legal organisation. Yet in drawing up their ultimatum, Austrian officials must have been aware that reports on the Black Hand were available in the Foreign Ministry archives. It is far more likely that the writers of the Austrian ultimatum did not mention the Black Hand because they knew enough about it and about its dual relationship with the leading Serbian political groups, and the strife beneath the surface, which burst into the open in spring 1917 when the political clique known as the White Hand rigged up a trial in Salonika and executed Dimitrijević.

It was politically undesirable to mention the Black Hand in 1914, for it could give the Serbian Government a chance to disclaim responsibility for the doings of a society it was persecuting (for not all the facts of the assassination could have been known by the Austrian Government). All the greater was the impact of the historical documents stressing that the Hapsburg monarchy had been compelled to act firmly because it knew of Belgrade's aggressive designs.

---

[1] Stanojveić, *Die Ermordung des Erzherzogs Franz-Ferdinand. Ein Beitrag zur Entstehungsgeschichte des Weltkrieges.* Aus dem serbischen Manuskript übertragen und herausgegeben von Hermann Wendel, Frankfurt a/M, 1923.

[2] For a German translation of Jovanović's article, which originally appeared in a Belgrade collection, see *Kriegsschuldfrage* No. 2, 1925. Other articles on the subject are by M. Boghitschewitsch, Wegerer, Lutz, etc., in the same journal, 1924 and later.

The revelations by Stanojveić were doubtless meant to vindicate the Serbian Government, showing that the charges in the Austrian ultimatum had been groundless and that the Narodna Odbrana, an organisation close to the Serbian Government, had no relation to the assassination, committed by a secret organisation hostile to the government.

But a former Serbian minister, Jovanović, threw a monkey-wrench into the works by declaring publicly that the assassination of the Austrian Archduke had been organised by the Black Hand with the knowledge of the Belgrade government and, particularly, the Serbian Prime Minister Nikola Pašić. After an embarrassed silence, the latter issued an emphatic denial, because according to the Yugoslav envoy in London the Jovanović story had created a stir in Britain, where the royal Yugoslav Government was then putting out feelers for a loan. A campaign was also launched in the German press. Belgrade had to complain to the British Government about the press campaign in Britain and later lodged a similar complaint in Berlin concerning articles appearing in Germany, in particular about the alleged complicity of Yugoslav King Alexander in the Sarajevo assassination.[1]

In face of the campaign, the Yugoslav Government announced[2] that it would put out a *Blue Book* to counter German attempts at "shifting the responsibility for the greatest bloodbath in history of Serbia". The book did not appear for a long time, however, and a Serbian journalist[3] close to the government said no heretofore unknown facts, let alone exposures, should be expected, advising the royal Yugoslav Government to publish documents from 1878 to 1914.

His advice was sound. A collection of documents compiled by M. Boghitschewitsch had appeared in Germany in 1928 covering the period from 1903 to 1914.[4] The Yugoslav Government which according to Boghitschewitsch

---

[1] *Deutsche Allgemeine Zeitung*, July 24, 1926.
[2] Wegerer, "Wo bleibt das Serbische Blaubuch?", *Kriegsschuldfrage* No. 4, 1929.
[3] F. Kulundschitsch, "Hat Serbien Österreich gewarnt?", *Berliner Tageblatt*, April 17, 1929.
[4] Boghitschewitsch, *Die auswärtige Politik Serbiens, 1903-1914*, Bd. I-III, Berlin, 1928-31.

"treated so-called national interests mostly as the private interests of various individuals and cliques in power",[1] hastened to announce through Avala, the official news agency, that Boghitschewitsch, who had been in the Serbian diplomatic service in Berlin before the war, had been dismissed because of dealings with the enemy.[2]

Boghitschewitsch's slanted publication was intended to corroborate the tale he told in all his other writings that Serbia had primed for war ceaselessly over the years with the assistance of tsarist Russia, and had deliberately provoked it. The bulk of the material referred to 1908-14, when Serbian foreign policy was most active. By his arrangement of the material the compiler endeavoured to underscore two distinct lines, which intertwined and finally led to a world war. The first was the Serbian policy against Austria-Hungary, especially virulent after the Bosnian crisis (when it was thought that end justified any, even the most provocative and reckless, means), and then the guiding line of Russian policy supported by France, Britain and Italy, now restraining and now goading Serbia to action against Austria-Hungary. Speaking of the policy of Austria-Hungary and Germany vis-à-vis Serbia, Boghitschewitsch thought both had erred by underrating the perils of Serbian policy and overrating their chances of safeguarding peace.[3]

Besides Serbian diplomatic material, Boghitschewitsch included material elucidating the Balkan policy of tsarist Russia. He also used documents from Soviet archives. After a scrutiny of the authentic documents we discovered that in some cases the compiler joined passages from different texts, while deleting or abridging relevant data.[4] No picture of Serbian foreign policy will be complete, therefore, until documents kept in Belgrade are finally published.

---

[1] Boghitschewitsch, "Mord und Justizmord", *Süddeutsche Monatshefte* No. 5, 1929, S. 1.

[2] H. v. Hindenburg, "Wann erscheint das Serbische Blaubuch?", *Berliner Tageblatt*, March 12, 1929.

[3] Boghitschewitsch, *Die auswärtige Politik Serbiens, 1903-1914*, Bd. II, S. 7.

[4] Of many documents Boghitschewitsch published only excerpts,

4

For years the victor governments showed no inclination
to publish their secret documents. The tradition to guard
diplomatic secrets over decades was still in force. Besides,
they were in no need of publishing their documents. The
origins of the war had been defined in the Versailles and
other post-war treaties, and all they needed was to keep the
Versailles system intact. When the German Government
pointed out to London, Paris and Rome in 1925 (on the eve
of the signing of the Locarno pact which placed Germany
into the system of Western capitalist powers in order to
isolate the Soviet Union) the incompatibility of the Versailles thesis of German war guilt with the Locarno spirit,
it heard an almost identically worded reply: the question
of war guilt had no relation whatsoever to the signing of
the Locarno pact, all the more so since the pact itself should
be regarded in the context of the Versailles instruments.
The British answer alone sounded somewhat milder, or
more evasive, because Britain was more eager for Germany
to sign the anti-Soviet Locarno pact, dragging her into the
orbit of British policy. This evasiveness came into still
bolder relief in a speech by Ramsay MacDonald to a German
audience, rousing the displeasure of the German official
press.[1]

A few years before, prompted by earlier (Soviet, German
and Austrian) publications denuding Britain's role in the
war preparations, MacDonald ventured at last to mark the
"pacific era" of his government with a promise to publish
pre-war British documents. The apologist tenor of the projected publication, an eleven-volume collection encom-
passing 1898 to 1914,[2] was so obvious that the Conservative
government which succeeded Labour, endorsed it.

Sidestepping the wartime period of 1914-18, the British
publishers focused their attention on the time when Germany began pushing her big naval programme and the conflict in Fashoda reversed Anglo-French relations and paved
the way for the Entente. The curious thing was that
the first volume to come off the presses was the eleventh,

---

[1] H. Schnee, "Widerlegung oder Schweigen", *Deutsche Allgemeine Zeitung*, Nov. 21, 1928.
[2] *British Documents on the Origins of the War, 1898-1914*, ed. by G. P. Gooch and H. Temperley, V. 1-11, London, 1927-36.

that is, the last, which concerned the so-called pre-war crisis of 1914, the Sarajevo assassination and Britain's entry into the war. Sir Wycliffe Headlam-Morley, historical adviser to the Foreign Office, who was in charge of the volume, said in the introduction he had chosen the opening date by analogy with Kautsky's publication, describing the meeting in Schloss Konopischt (Konopiště) of Wilhelm and Admiral Tirpitz with Archduke Franz-Ferdinand and the subsequent events.

The choice of the opening date and the introduction were doubtless intended to underscore the secret deal between Austria and Germany and their provocative stance before the Sarajevo assassination. If the volume had opened with documents relating to the Anglo-French "gentlemen's agreement" or the Anglo-Russian naval convention, the impression would naturally have been the reverse of what the compilers of the British publication wanted. Anglo-German relations of the time would have revealed the true sense of the Anglo-Russian confrontation in Persia, which the compiler accentuated to show that at the time of the 1914 crisis London had seen no trace of tension in Anglo-German relations and that the adverse course of events took it by surprise.

The apologetic tendency of the publication comes into evidence also in the choice of documents and the notes and footnotes of the publishers, as well as in the arrangement and the general conception. Like all other bourgeois collections, the British one deals with foreign policy only in the immediate sense, ignoring British colonial policy. But even within these limits, the selected documents dealt with questions of "big policy" only. Besides official reports, the publishers used the private correspondence of top-level British diplomats and statesmen wherever the individuals concerned consented.

Before going into the volume, even the official reports had to be cleared by the Foreign Office and the government of the country concerned. The documents or marginal notes of Edward VII, too, needed a special approval of King George V. In brief, there was a distinct element of censorship, with even the specially selected and approved documents often being abridged or merely paraphrased.[1]

---

[1] E.g., Grey's telegram to Buchanan of July 24, 1914, in volume 11.

The many notes and inscriptions made on documents by various officials and office-holders, often in the nature of a directive, were not reproduced at all.

The editor of volume 11 endeavoured in his notes, quite hopelessly, to whitewash the falsified *Blue Book* with unconvincing references to technical difficulties. In effect, this was part of the general effort of vindicating Grey and the policy of British imperialism, as evidenced by the arrangement of the material. Volume 11 followed the chronological principle, while in all the preceding volumes the material is grouped by subjects within certain chronological brackets. Historical matter is thus used as a diplomatic apologia. This fusion of historical and political is also perceptible in the memoirs of Edward Grey which came off the presses, possibly deliberately, at or near the time the British publication began,[1] and is also evident in the general conception of the publication.[2]

The basic thesis was imperialist Britain's unfaltering love of peace. It explained nothing, but performed a useful propaganda service. Its object was to substantiate the more topical tasks and measures defined when the publication was being prepared for print in a secret memorandum of general British policy principles in relation to the Locarno policy.[3]

In its analysis of the general European situation, which precedes and substantiates the suggested political judgements the memorandum specifies the basic European problems from the standpoint of British imperialist interests. In so uncertain a situation, it says, sound British policy can pursue nothing but British interest. The path was too dark, it adds, to consider others or to make any deviations. The main task was to remove the danger to Britain of any one power or coalition of powers, dominating the Channel or any of the North Sea ports, which could eventually facilitate an attack on Britain. This strategic point of departure is then expanded into a broad programme on the continent,

---

[1] Grey, *Twenty-Five Years (1892-1916)*, V. I-II, London, 1925-26.

[2] See survey of G. P. Gooch's reports in Berlin in February 1929, "Die Entstehung der Triple Entente", *Die Kriegsschuldfrage* No. 6, 1929.

[3] The reference is to Austen Chamberlain's memorandum of February 20, 1925, first published in the Paris edition of the *Chicago Tribune* on March 6, 1925, and later reproduced in full in *Europäische Gespräche* No. 9, 1925.

aimed at realigning forces and repatterning the system of international relations created by the post-war treaties and, among others, the Dawes Plan. The problem of guarantees assumed a new political complexion. The point at issue was a system of relationships in which British policy would predominate. Britain's top political leaders maintained that isolation meant peril, vulnerability and impotence. It was doubtful, they said, that Germany would have started the war in 1914 if she had known for certain that Britain would come to France's assistance.

As we see, the problem of deliberate "isolation" reappeared in British policy, sparkling a discussion and political wrangle between groups of British imperialists. This was where Grey's memoirs entered the picture, advocating succession in British diplomacy, the principle of a relatively "free hand" and a political equilibrium in Europe, ensuring British naval supremacy. These are ideas substantiated in the British collection of documents. But if Grey could evade such facts as the Anglo-French naval convention of 1912, the collection, for its part, had to illustrate all events that had come to public knowledge. It was all a matter of the angle of approach.

The Germans published documents seized in 1914 in Belgium, lifting the veil on how little the general staffs of Britain and France made of Belgian neutrality. Britain was compelled to publish the documents in question, revealing that negotiations inconsistent with the neutrality principle had proceeded since the beginning of 1906. One of the arguments of British propaganda was thus discredited.

To save the situation, the British editors were forced to explain that Grey had known nothing of the Anglo-Belgian parleys and that these concerned solely a possible German attack on Belgium and were therefore of a purely defensive nature. The explanation was well received in France. *Temps* devoted a special article to the matter,[1] while a mouthpiece of the German Foreign Ministry responded with a diametrically opposite appraisal.[2]

The French official response to the British publication was indicative in more ways than one; it stressed the

---

[1] *Temps*, Aug. 9, 1928.
[2] *Kölnische Zeitung*, Aug. 14, 1930.

Anglo-German contradictions more than anything else,[1] whereas the British indicated that it was the Franco-German contradictions that had brought on the war. The controversy had a certain political colouring in view of the Anglo-French rivalry for priority influence on the Weimar Republic.

The British documents provided considerable background to the problem of Anglo-German naval rivalry, a problem still topical in view of the post-war political realities.

British imperialism with its doctrine of naval supremacy had at the price of a war frustrated the German plan of building a first-class navy, but was harrassed, and painfully so, by the United States' demand for "freedom of the seas" and naval parity.

In view of the Anglo-American rivalry, naval superiority became a problem of great political significance. The compilation of documents by Washington concerning the Anglo-American conflict precipitated in 1916 by the British naval blockade, was received in London as an anti-British act timed to prejudice the tense naval talks under way then. It took a British diplomatic démarche for the U.S. Government to hold up their publication until after the political visit to Washington of the Labour Prime Minister.

But as soon as the 1930 London naval conference closed, opening a new chapter in Anglo-American rivalry on the seas, the Washington collection saw the light of day,[2] and Britain countered with a special volume of its own, containing materials related to the little-known Anglo-American pre-war talks on the vital issue of "limiting naval armaments".

Thus, the subject-matter of the various collections of diplomatic material was predicated by the daily political realities and intertwined with them. This is true to an even greater extent of the interpretation of the published material.

---

[1] E.g., see *Temps*, May 9, 1930.
[2] See *Frankfurter Zeitung*, Dec. 24, 1930. The reference is to one of the supplementary volumes of the official U.S. publication, *Papers Relating to the Foreign Relations of the United States*, Washington.

5

After so many collections had thrown light on France's part in preparing the world war 1914-18, the French Government had no choice but to put out a collection of its own. Only documents dating to before 1852 were open to researchers at the time, with a decision having been passed to unseal archives referring to the reign of Napoleon III. Authentic diplomatic documents of the Third Republic, meanwhile, were under lock and seal.[1] Nothing but *Yellow Books*[2] were put out, specially compiled for specific political purposes, including slender booklets on Balkan problem, Morocco, the 1900-02 Franco-Italian negotiations and the Franco-Russian alliance, all of them almost unnoticed. The feeble campaign launched in 1920 by French syndicalist and pacifist groups urging the belligerent countries to publish their diplomatic archives was obscured by the victory cries of the French imperialists and, in effect, had little or no influence on the government. Poincaré's version of the origins of the world war was elevated to a dogma and the Versailles postulate of Germany's exclusive guilt became a political axiom.

The Soviet collection on Franco-Russian relations in 1910-14, published in French in Paris by René Marchand in early 1922 therefore created a sensation.[3] The government had to answer embarrassing questions in the Chamber of Deputies. A political discussion ensued. The Soviet collection attracted public attention instantly and was closely studied in Western Europe and the United States. The French leaders were confused by the unexpected exposures. Poincaré, whose name was implicated, charged that the documents were false. Then he announced that Izvolsky, the Russian Ambassador in Paris, whose published reports seemed so convincing, was untrustworthy because he attributed to Poincaré his own political plans. Subsequently, Poincaré wrote ten volumes of memoirs in

---

[1] An exception was made for the authors of *Rapport pour la Commission d'Enquête sur les faits de la guerre*, published in Paris in 1919.

[2] The first of the *Yellow Books* appeared in 1860, followed over the years by several hundred, mostly on colonial matters.

[3] *Un livre noir. Diplomatie d'avant-guerre d'après les documents des archives russes, novembre 1910-juillet 1914*, v. I-III, Paris, 1922-34.

an endeavour to justify his policy in the service of imperialist France.[1]

All the same, under pressure of the facts, which became
widely known and were used in France by his political
adversaries from the pacifist camp,[2] Poincaré was con-
strained, when questioned by a journalist,[3] to go back on
some of the assertions he had previously attempted to
defend. Taking advantage of the way the questions were
worded, Poincaré avoided the subject of Britain and France
and grew voluble about the role of tsarist Russia, and
ended up by placing much of the war guilt on Austria-
Hungary, thus partly cancelling his own previous charges
against Germany. "It is true," he wrote, "that in 1927 I
did not want to express myself as severely as before concerning the German empire for two reasons: firstly,
because it seemed expedient after Germany subscribed to the
Dawes Plan to practice the policy of rapprochement and,
secondly, because studies of the origins of the war revealed
that the guilt of Austria-Hungary, without lifting that of
Germany, was chronologically first and consequently
greater."[4]

This priority of political motives in assessing historical
matters came into evidence, too, when Poincaré, then in
power, eased a decision through the cabinet to publish
diplomatic documents concerning French foreign policy
between 1871 and 1914. This stalled the publication
of wartime documents planned by the Herriot cabinet
in 1925, the first six volumes of which had been compiled
by officials of the Foreign Ministry and were ready for
print.

---

[1] Poincaré, *Au service de la France. Neuf années de souvenirs,*
t. I-X, Paris, 1926-33.

[2] A. Fabre-Luce, *La victoire,* Paris, 1924; G. Demartial, *L'évangile
du Quai d'Orsay. La guerre de 1914,* Paris, 1926; G. Demartial, *La
mobilisation des consciences,* 2 éd., Paris, 1927, etc. Georges Demartial
was stripped of his order of the Legion of Honour for his views, which
diverged from the official stand on Germany's sole war guilt.

[3] *Les responsabilités de la guerre. Quatorze questions par René
Gerin. Quatorze réponses par Raymond Poincaré,* Paris, 1930.

[4] It may be interesting to note that the German press instantly
reacted to the forced change in Poincaré's attitude while the French
press passed over it in silence, confining itself to the remark that
Poincaré's answers "allayed the conscience of every Frenchman not
inclined to look for faults in himself that really belong to the neighbour".

The French policy-makers, as we see, decided to issue their own documentary apologia.[1] The publication was entrusted[2] to a 54-man commission, including such veteran retired diplomats as Maurice Paléologue, Jules Cambon and Maurice Bompard and such prominent figures still active in French politics as Henri Fromageot and Victor de Lacroix, and the influential Philippe Berthelot, said to differ from his chief, Aristide Briand, who knew nothing and understood everything in that he knew everything and understood nothing. The decorum created by the group of "immortals" accentuated the political weight of the commission, in which there were also historians, such as Émile Bourgeois, Alfred Baudrillart, head of the Paris Catholic Institute, and others.

The principles of the French editors differed from those of the German. The French collection was more academic in appearance, strictly chronological, containing a bare minimum of editorial notes and no commentaries. However, the general idea was basically the same. The policy of alliances and anti-alliances was presented as the core of European diplomacy, while French colonial policy was totally ignored.

The chronological arrangement was an indication that the French publication was a reply to the German. The first to appear was volume one of the third series, relating to the few months after the conclusion of the Franco-German agreement on Morocco and the Congo (November 4, 1911). For the French the choice of the opening date was certainly a good one: it was a time when tension in Franco-German relations, pregnant with the menace of an armed collision, gave way to agreement.

Besides, the commission was thus able to present its own view of a period earlier illustrated from an entirely different standpoint in the Soviet publication of Izvolsky's correspondence. The indicative thing was, however, that this particular period was poorly documented—a sign that the compilers did not wish to say more than was already known to the public from the Soviet collection. Far more

---

[1] Volume 1 of the third series of *Documents diplomatiques français (1871-1914)* appeared in Paris in 1929.
[2] The appropriate decree signed by Poincaré and Briand was issued on January 21, 1928.

startling was the documentation of Franco-Russian relations, all the more significant because it was related chronologically to the time immediately preceding the Balkan alliance, spearheaded against Turkey, but also against Austria-Hungary. The publishers took pains to underscore the difference between the policies of France and Russia, with the former depicted as restraining the aggressiveness and "whimsicality" of the tsarist regime, above all in the Balkans.

It was clear, judging even from volume one, that a shift had occurred in the question of who and what brought on the world war. The French collection contained a few diplomatic reports testifying to the peaceful sentiments of the German people, even the German Kaiser—a fact received with deep satisfaction and much publicity by the German bourgeois press.

Accents were also laid on other points of history, evoking a lively public response. The topical question of Anglo-German relations was presented, on the one hand, in association with the general problem of consolidating the Anglo-French Entente as an alignment which had enabled France to protect herself against German pretentions, and, on the other, with the question of Italy's wavering between the Triple Alliance and the Triple Entente. The exposure of Italy's pre-war policy, of her disloyalty to commitments, her dogged aggressiveness, which plunged Europe into countless political complications and conflicts—all this reflected the deepening of the Franco-Italian contradictions highlighting the European political scene at the close of the twenties and in the early thirties. It was not surprising at all that, reporting the French revelations of Italian policy at the turn of the century, a German paper representing the Foreign Ministry said:

"This retrospective glance appears most fittingly at this time when certain elements in Germany are thinking of putting their stakes on the Italian card."[1] With Germany's rulers casting about for new foreign policy guidelines, this was a warning people were inclined to heed.

It would be an error to assume, however, that the French publication, though it included certain testimony "favourable" to Germany, abandoned the anti-German

---

[1] *Kölnische Zeitung*, Dec. 28, 1930.

orientation. On the contrary, volume one of the first series ending with the "1875 war alarm" was largely devoted to German plans of an anti-French preventive war thwarted by vigilant French policy and the diplomatic pressure of Russia and Britain. The French, as it were, flung a pack of fresh evidence on the table, pillorying Bismarckian Germany and refuting the arguments of German bourgeois historians of the Weimar period.

By and large, it may be said of the first three French volumes that the shadings were so chalked in as to make specific points of Prussian, Italian and British policy stand out in relief, while the role of French policy was obscured. But it was impossible to maintain this line throughout. The next volume (volume two of the third series), relating to February-May 1912, delved into such matters as the Haldane mission and the talks on Belgian neutrality. Here the French commission departed from its avowed principle of selecting documents in keeping with historical authenticity. One set of documents was completely removed from the text and presented instead in an editorial note. The note indicated that the French General Staff had been planning to violate Belgium's neutrality back in 1912. Poincaré had worked assiduously to make the plan possible and, among other things, sought British acquiescence. Britain, he wrote on March 28, 1912, should not assume commitments of neutrality in relation to France and Germany even if it would appear that France was the attacking side.

This shows that despite the objective chronological principle, the French editors, like those of Germany and other capitalist countries, concealed certain important documents. They admitted, moreover, that some of the documents published were abridged. This left ample room for speculation as to what was left out, though it was easy to guess what had prompted the deletions. We are willing to believe that the commission had examined the private correspondence of contemporary French statesmen and diplomats. After all, it included a number of prominent French diplomats who were involved in this correspondence. But we mistrust the claim that this private correspondence contained nothing of political interest.

One of the members of the French commission, seeking to assure the reader that no documents related to French policy in 1871-1914 would be withheld, said that concealing documents which the Bolshevik government, in control of the "old Russian archives", was able to publish at any moment, was senseless. He said this automatically created mutual control.[1] When in the winter of 1931 Poincaré predicted publicly that the big Soviet collection related to the history of the world war would contain "many very paradoxical inventions" this only bore out the fact that the Soviet publication, *International Relations in the Imperialist Epoch*, was dreaded as a continuation of the earlier Soviet publications, which exposed imperialist policy.

That the official French concept of war guilt had changed was soon evident from an article by Sorbonne professors Camille Bloch and Pierre Renouvin in the organ of the French Foreign Ministry.[2] Arousing the interest of the European bourgeois press, the article maintained that though the victors once thought the old Kaiser government bore the sole guilt, they did not presume the moral resposibility of all Germany. The victors, the article said, had been intent on establishing the formal fact of the German attack in August 1914 as a *legal* point postulating compensation for losses sustained. The usual interpretation of Article 231 of the Versailles Treaty, it added, was historically groundless, being an unfortunate consequence of an inaccuracy in the official German translation of the Versailles papers.

It may be worth noting, however, that the German press denied credence to these assertions.[3] The ensuing discussion revealed that they echoed behind-the-scenes probes and negotiations which may now safely be said to have taken place on the reparations issue soon after the Franco-American agreement on the terms of the one-year moratorium. The French side gave to understand that it was willing to make concessions on secondary issues and, among other things, discount the Versailles ruling of Germany's unilateral war guilt, provided the latter declared formally that she would abandon all efforts to revise the material basis of the Versailles Treaty and the subsequent agree-

---

[1] L. Eisenmann, "Die französische Aktenpublikation", *Europäische Gespräche* No. 10, 1929.
[2] *Temps,* Nov. 15, 1931.
[3] See *Germania,* Nov. 24, 1931; *Vossische Zeitung,* Dec. 12, 1931; *Kölnische Zeitung,* Dec. 13, 1931; *Deutsche Allgemeine Zeitung,* Dec. 15, 1931.

ments. The attempt at partially "absolving" Germany was no more than a feeler. The utterances on this score of the Archbishop of York on January 31, 1932, made on the opening of the disarmament conference, were still more revealing. The Archbishop demanded in the name of Christian forgiveness and brotherhood that the Western powers cease their strife, give up the Versailles ruling on Germany's war guilt and pave the way to unity in order to settle the common problems troubling the capitalist world. The Rightist press in France was outraged and the conservative element in Britain even more so. The *Times* mounted a fierce attack, seconded by Austen Chamberlain. "It does no service to morality, it is not the enforcement of Christian faith, but a denial of Christian morals, to say that all nations were equally guilty," he said. "There must be a moral opinion of the world which can be brought to bear upon the transgressor and keep him back from his transgression.... But to confuse the innocent with the guilty ... is to destroy the basis of international morality.... The strength of the League of Nations lies in its power to ... determine ... the responsibility and the guilt of any nation which prefers war."[1]

The importance Chamberlain attached to Article 16 of the League of Nations Covenant at the negotiations concerning Germany's entry, which envisages use of the territory of League members for passage of troops against states qualified by the League as attackers, sheds light on the political implications of his utterances concerning war guilt.

The explanations which the Archbishop of York offered his numerous indignant opponents showed that his point of view did not conflict with that of Austen Chamberlain.

Not only was Germany's war guilt for the preceding war reiterated, but the point was made that Germany was to pledge support of the new war prepared by the imperialist powers and comply with Article 16 of the League of Nations Covenant, which British diplomacy intended using for definite, far-reaching aims—those of making Germany join the anti-Soviet bloc of Western powers.

As German imperialism gradually recovered and its revisionist ambitions increased, documents were often used

---

[1] *Times*, Feb. 13, 1932.

as a tool of political struggle. B. Schwertfeger, a former
colonel in the German army, wrote in his book, *World War
of Documents*, in 1929, that "we Germans are now compelled to wage a real world war against ... the Versailles
Treaty".[1] But already there were entirely new aims crystallising behind these words in view of the prospect of a new
war.

The political war, fought with historical documents,
continued unabated.

The attempt made by means of a Christian formula at
the Geneva disarmament conference, a theatre of struggle
for the realignment of imperialist forces, to absolve German imperialism was prompted by obviously political
motives. Plato, Archbishop of York remarked later, looked
to the future when war between Greek cities would be
regarded as a civil war.[1] This was meant as a warning to
the ruling classes in the capitalist countries, victors and
losers alike, calling on them to rally to the fight against
the Soviet Union and the world working-class movement.

1932

[1] Schwertfeger, *Der Weltkriege der Dokumente*, Berlin, 1929.
[1] *Berliner Monatshefte* No. 4, 1932.

In the Swiss spa of Locarno on October 16, 1925, four West European powers—Britain, France, Italy and Germany—initialed a pact guaranteeing the borders established at Versailles between France and Belgium, on the one hand, and Germany, on the other.

French and Polish efforts to obtain similar guarantees for the frontier between Germany and Poland were unsuccessful. On November 27, 1925, the Reichstag ratified the Locarno Pact with 291 against 174 votes with 3 abstentions. On December 1 it was also ratified in London and the bourgeois press told the world triumphantly the "Locarno spirit" would henceforth prevail.

British diplomacy put the pact down as a success in buttressing Britain's influence within the West European system of states aimed at isolating the Soviet Union. In a secret memorandum to the cabinet (soon published) Austen Chamberlain, the Foreign Secretary, defined the building of a system of mutual guarantees as a first step towards an anti-Soviet military bloc in Western Europe under the League of Nations. Far from being a factor of stability, Chamberlain wrote, Russia was a dangerous factor of insecurity. It was therefore essential, he added, to formulate a policy of guarantees in relation to Russia, even against Russia. Germany was cast in a special role in this made-in-London policy.

The Dawes reparations plan drawn up under Wall Street and City auspices flung open the sluice-gate to large U.S. and British loans to Germany. Anybody living in Berlin or any other large German city could see the rapid effect the Anglo-American shot in the arm was having on capitalist enterprise and the country's general economic state. The revolutionary eruptions of the working class that shook Germany in 1923 were crushed by the Reichswehr. The unheard-of inflation, the mark slipping to one-billionth of its previous worth, wage-earners hurrying to spend their weekly wages before they depreciated to nothing, a wave of suicides across the country while profiteers lined their pockets, faded into the past.

Capitalist economy entered a phase of relative stability. The monopolies grew stronger and sought ways of extending their influence. The imperialist groups in Germany were busy mending their economic and political fences. And the workers, too, after the 1923 defeat, were rallying for new economic and political battles. The Communist Party was redeploying its ranks and collecting experience of class struggle in the new conditions. The Social-Democrats worked assiduously to tighten their hold on the workers and the petty bourgeoisie. Professing republicanism and allegiance to the bourgeois Weimar constitution,[1] they proclaimed their readiness to co-operate with the Left-bourgeois Democratic Party and the reactionary wing of the Catholic Centre Party, and even the monopoly-capital German People's Party.

Nobody was more zealous than the Social-Democrats in singing the praises of the Dawes Plan, which they considered a heal-all for the ills of the class struggle and the post-war economic adversities. Neither was anybody more zealous in extolling the policy of conciliation with the Western capitalist powers, the policy of "Western" orientation. Even the monopoly groups that had devised the policy were more moderate and anxious to avoid a final commitment, seeking to capitalise on the contradictions between the capitalist countries and the Soviet Union with the ultimate objective of accumulating economic, political and, later, military power, undermining the pillars of the Versailles Treaty and then entering the lists again for a "place in the sun".

The Treaty of Rapallo concluded with the Soviet Union

---

[1] See further, "Dissolution of the Prussian State. The Militarist Tradition".

in 1922 evoked an outburst of fury among the Western powers, doubly so since German diplomacy and part of the German press harped on the country's readiness to stick to its new "Eastern" orientation. True, there were influential objectors to the Rapallo policy among the rulers of Germany, especially since the "Eastern" trend—that is, commercial, political and diplomatic rapprochement with the Soviet Union—was in the interest of the German working class. Dismayed voices rang out among the Western imperialists who suspected a secret German-Soviet military alliance, a suspicion that the reactionary element and the Reichswehr leadership seized upon to wrest concessions from the victor-countries. While the exponents of the Rapallo spirit among the German industrialists (Otto Wolff, Walther Rathenau, etc.), diplomatists (Freiherr Maltzan, Count Brockdorff-Rantzau, etc.) and bourgeois intellectuals (Prof. Otto Hoetzsch, etc.) invoked the time-hallowed Bismarckian tradition of good neighbour relations with Russia, its opponents, particularly those connected or eager to be connected with the international monopolies, endeavoured to chart and formalise a "Western" orientation. They hoped this would conciliate the Western imperialist powers and invigorate the capitalist system in Germany. The German bourgeoisie, its government and press, were inclined to take advantage of the international differences that kept flaring up among the Western imperialist partners—the United States, Britain, France and Italy. The big German banks and monopolies looked for a way of establishing or expanding contacts with former partners in Britain and the United States. Some industrialists looked for contact with the French monopolies and hoped the French Government would support them. This was true, among others, of the Ruhr magnates and of Konrad Adenauer, then Oberburgomaster of Cologne and a covert proponent of a separatist Rhine policy.

The French occupation of the Ruhr, ordered by Premier Raymond Poincaré to promote French imperialist supremacy in Europe, was a blow to the German advocates of a separate understanding with France. Lacking a prop in the East in the shape of the Rapallo Treaty with the Soviet Union, Germany, they saw, would not weather a clash with France. In the meantime, British diplomacy decided to wait and see. The United States followed suit. They did not step in until it was clear that both sides—Germany and France—had exhausted their strength and that the international crisis in the Ruhr would precipitate a crisis of the capitalist system in Germany. The Dawes Plan helped stabilise German capitalism, shore up the monopolies and militarist forces who, having adapted themselves to the post-Versailles realities, were out to restore their power and improve Germany's strategic position. Their prime concern was to see the occupation troops of the victor-countries abandon Germany.[1] However, under the Versailles Treaty the evacuation was conditional on Germany's fulfilment of her disarmament commitments. Therefore, they set out on a dual path of, first, concealing militarism by giving it a new form, and, second, undermining the Versailles provisions hampering the rebirth of German imperialism, militarism and revanchism. The Locarno Treaty offered the German rulers considerable opportunities in both directions. However, Germany's entry into the concert of Western capitalist powers was walked by many zigzags and tied in the internal contradictions that beset the West.

1

When the spadework for the Locarno Treaty was almost done, the German Government demanded that the victors withdraw their occupation troops from the Cologne zone. Domestically, this would win the government the backing of a political front ranging from the rightist National Party to the Social-Democrats, for the evacuation would show the benefits of the "Western" orientation and of the "spirit of Locarno".

On September 26, 1925, the German ambassadors informed the governments of France, Belgium, Britain and Italy of Germany's consent to a conference in Locarno, and submitted a note stating that so long as the occupation of a large part of Germany continued no confidence could be mustered for peaceful development, on which implementation of the proposed international agreements depended.

---

[1] The First Zone (Cologne) had an area of 64,000 sq. km. and a population of 2,500,000, and under Versailles terms was to be evacuated in 1925, the Second Zone (6,400 sq. km., population 1,200,000) in 1930, and the Third Zone (19,000 sq. km., population 3,000,000) in 1935.

Each of the allies promptly replied to this timid demand made in a "spirit of loyalty".

The British Government declared three days later that the date of the evacuation depended wholly on Germany's fulfilling her disarmament commitments. The replies of Belgium and France were almost identical. But the similarity of language did not carry with it any similarity of attitude. A backstage diplomatic scuffle ensued.

The agreement signed in Locarno said nothing of any evacuation of the occupied zones. But the conferees discussed the matter at length during their motor trips through the idyllic Swiss countryside. Stresemann insisted on evacuation, pointing out that he had to placate the political parties and German public opinion. Austen Chamberlain, the moving spirit of the Locarno talks, was inclined to satisfy Stresemann and help him bring Germany into the Western system. Aristide Briand, the consummate orator, endeavoured to talk Britain out of making concessions. Finally it was decided to submit the matter to the Council of Ambassadors of the principal victor-countries which would establish whether or not Germany had fulfilled her disarmament commitments. Spadework for the council's session began on both banks of the Rhine as soon as the conference in Locarno ended.

Though France still insisted that Germany comply with her commitments to the letter before its demand is honoured, the German bourgeois press listed a set of new demands, of which the Cologne evacuation was only one. Among the other demands were a change of status for the Saargebiet (autonomy), reduction of foreign troop strength in the occupied areas to equal the strength of German pre-war garrisons, change of status along the Rhine and, among other things, a curtailment of the powers of the Allied High Commission, dissolution of the Allied military tribunals, a stop to French propaganda of separatist ideas in the Rhine area, non-interference in Rhine shipping and release of Germans sent to prison by the Allied military tribunals.

On November 7, 1925, the Council of Ambassadors began deliberations on the report of Marshal Foch's Versailles military control commission. It was understood before even the council convened that no serious differences over disarmament existed "in principle" between the Allies and

184

Germany. What the Versailles commission thought had to be done was (1) restrict the powers of General von Seeckt, commander of the Reichswehr, (2) terminate military training conducted by ex-officers' sports clubs, (3) demilitarise the police, whose strength should be kept down to 150,000 men, and a few lesser matters.

The Ambassadors' Council endorsed Foch's report. The German ambassador in Paris was asked to state his government's attitude to these demands. Britain gave to understand unofficially that its troops would evacuate Cologne zone by December 1, 1925, if the Germans complied.

Berlin's reply was swift. It said Germany would comply. The only unexpected thing about it was its verbosity.

The Versailles commission, it is true, thought the German reply not explicit enough. But it was the Council of Ambassadors that had the final say. On November 14 it pronounced Germany's reply as satisfactory. This haste was prompted by concern in London and Paris over the extra-diplomatic methods of pressure exerted by the German nationalists, who had scheduled a demonstration against the Locarno Treaty on November 15. The demonstration was obviously rigged and demagogical. The Ambassadors' Council could either stand firm or relieve the position of the German West-oriented cabinet. It picked the latter course, promising that the Cologne zone would be cleared of Allied troops by December 1.

The "Locarno spirit" thus supplanted the Versailles tradition with the token provision, however, that Germany's disarmament would be discussed at a later date.

This time the German militarists hastened to acquiesce. That they had scored a substantial victory was clear, for the problem of occupation had been divorced from that of disarmament. Aristide Briand, chairman of the Ambassadors' Council, handed the German envoy a note on November 16, acknowledging that Germany had in substance fulfilled Art. 429 of the Versailles Treaty and announcing the evacuation of the Cologne zone. The note described this as the beginning of a "new era" in international relations.

By December 1, 1925, the British occupation force abandoned Cologne, giving a start to the evacuation of the first zone.

Briand, meanwhile, informed the German ambassador

of the modifications decided on by the Council in other zones of occupation. The official notification was couched in terms that were soon to become known as "Locarno language". Lauding the "spirit of goodwill and trust" that prevailed after Germany joined the major West European capitalist powers under the Locarno Pact, the Ambassadors' Council and later the Inter-Allied Commission, announced that the Western powers would repattern the occupation regime. They declared their consent, among other things, for the German Government to appoint a commissioner to the occupied Rhineland and said they would maintain contact with him. They also promised to reduce the strength of the occupation armies, revise the police regulations, etc. However, within ten days of the Rhineland announcement, the German Government protested against France's reinforcing her occupation troops in Trier and Jülich. In Mainz and Koblenz, too, the occupation troops were strengthened. At the end of November it was learned that the Allies intended to keep 79,000 men in the still occupied areas. The German Government insisted on not more than 42,000, the strength of the pre-war German garrison. German diplomacy pleaded the "Locarno spirit" and referred to promises it had received from Britain.

Reduction of the occupation force had been demanded by the German Government at the negotiations in Locarno. France, however, had consented only grudgingly and vaguely. When the German diplomats named the ceiling figure of 42,000 men, Briand objected. The powers initialled the Locarno Pact, leaving the matter of occupation strength hanging in the air. Negotiations reopened when the Locarno Treaty was being signed in London, where Stresemann suggested as a compromise that the Rhine occupation army consist of 60,000 men. Briand sidestepped nimbly by claiming that he could not assume any commitments before discussing the matter with the French generals. Not surprisingly, the latter found the German offer "impracticable". The German diplomats countered by declaring the French stand incompatible with the assurances furnished in the note of the Ambassadors' Council on December 16, 1925. The French promise to reduce the occupation army to nearly "normal strength" had then been interpreted to mean a reduction to the size of the pre-war German garrisons.

The Reichstag foreign affairs committee passed a resolution protesting the French stand, while the German Government took fresh diplomatic action. The German ambassadors in London, Paris and Brussels protested against the strength of armies in the second and third occupation zones (60,000 French, 8,000 British and 7,000 Belgian men), invoking Article 429 of the Versailles Treaty and the "spirit of Locarno". For Britain, by the way, the reference to the "Locarno spirit" was more convincing than that to the Versailles Treaty. London made it plain that treaty articles were irrelevant, but that the Dawes Plan and the Locarno agreement made it highly desirable for Germany to get what she demanded. But British diplomats said they could not shrug off France's firm attitude. French diplomats, for their part, declared that the final decision rested with the Ambassadors' Council, stressing, however, that the Military Control Commission in Berlin had reported to Marshal Foch, chairman of the Versailles Commission, that "German disarmament has not been completed". But the French effort to block a reduction in occupation strength failed. Talks between Chamberlain and Briand culminated in a decision to set it at 60,000 men and leave the question of a further reduction open until Germany's entry into the League of Nations. This was a typical British compromise. The French demands were not entirely rejected, while Germany was given a chance to renew hers. *Deutsche diplomatisch-politische Korrespondenz*, the official bulletin of the German foreign ministry, pointed out at the end of January 1926:

"The ultimate purpose of the Locarno Treaty has not yet been attained; nor will it be attained by reducing the occupation troops to 50 thousand or less men." In this matter, too, Britain did not miss the opportunity of exerting pressure by dangling before Germany the probable advantages to her of joining the League of Nations. Since Article 16 of the League Covenant provided for the passage of foreign troops across the territory of member-countries against states said to be aggressive, the British architects of the Locarno system aspired, by means of an insignificant compromise in the matter of the Rhine occupation, to embroiling Germany in their political course against the Soviet Union.

The Locarno plan envisaged Germany's admission to the League of Nations as an equal power with a seat on the League Council. So the rulers of Germany began rehearsing their great-power stance long before joining the League. They gave to understand that Germany intended to assume responsibility, of all things, over all German-speaking peoples and ethnic groups, wherever these may be. The official terms in which the claim was couched referred to the Reich's responsibility for the singleness of the German national culture. What this implied in practice, however, was a revival of the old political traditions and aspirations of the Pan-Germanic ideology, slightly adjusted to fit the post-Versailles realities. The revival was in evidence in Germany and Austria, where Pan-Germanic plans and organisations cultivated since the end of the 19th century had struck deep root and survived the collapse and dissolution of the Hapsburg empire. The ruling element in France and Italy were definitely alarmed. When Austria's ex-Chancellor Dr. Seipel, a prelate known as scholar and historian of the early Christian period, spoke publicly in Berlin of the grandeur of German cultural unity, which, he said, made up for the violated unity of German statehood, the press in Paris and Rome wondered if Germany and Austria were planning amalgamation.

As German imperialism gradually recovered its economic and political positions, helped by the influx of American and British capital under the Dawes Plan, encouraged particularly by the Locarno talks concerning recognition of Germany as a great power, Pan-Germanic sentiment invaded not only foreign policy propaganda, but also affected some of the practical diplomatic steps. The German posture in matters of foreign policy became more abrupt and forward, but was usually swiftly recast and made more evasive when it ran into resistance. This is borne out by the conflict between Germany and Italy after their joining the Locarno system.

According to the Saint-Germain Treaty concluded by the Western powers with Austria, Tyrol was divided, the northern part remaining Austrian and the southern going to Italy. "The non-Italian population in the new Italian territory ought to be told," Tommaso Tittoni said in parliament, "that it is farthest from our minds to oppress or assimilate them, that their language and cultural institutions will get every consideration and that their administrators will have all the rights provided for by our liberal democratic legislation."

Yet Mussolini's fascist government opted for a policy of Italianisation. Fascist centralism and its attributes supplanted self-administration. Fascist trade unions were formed, a fascist national militia instituted, and the Italian language made obligatory. A decree was issued requiring Italianisation of German names and surnames. The Austrian and German press protested. Italy retaliated with demonstrations. As usual, publicists appealed to history. The German and Austrian press recalled the era of the migration of peoples. The Italian fascist press referred to the fact that traditionally Italian territory only recently peopled by groups "speaking a different language" had been restored to its rightful owner. But it gave priority to combating any revival of Pan-Germanic ambitions. "Any attempt at uniting the 80,000,000 Germans," wrote an Italian newspaper, "would be politically dangerous and intolerable."

The German bourgeois press called for a boycott of Italy, of tourist travel in that country and of trade with it. A society was promptly formed in Bavaria to promote the boycott. It was an empty threat, though it infuriated Mussolini, who declared that Italy would retaliate "by a threefold boycott and threefold repressions". The caustic speech of Held, the Bavarian Minister-President, was countered with an interpellation in the Italian chamber by Roberto Farinacci, secretary-general of the fascist party. In a belligerent speech on February 5, 1926, Mussolini said Italy's policy would not be modified. "Italy," he declared, "will never remove her flag from the Brenner Pass and will carry it farther still if necessary."

This was the culmination point of the Italo-German conflict, received as a statement of the true intentions of "young, proud, fascist Italy". In tone and content it was a challenge to Germany. Austria, which the Italian dictator threatened most, instantly reverted to a conciliatory tone. The Vienna press voiced concern for "genuinely friendly relations" with Italy. The German press, even the nationalist papers, followed suit. It ascribed the sharpness of Mussolini's speech, which transcended the bounds of diplomatic tact, to the exigencies of fascist home policy, going out of its way to stress that Germany could not care less for the Brenner Pass.

Speaking in Reichstag on February 9, 1926, Stresemann outlined the official policy of his government. Referring to the drastic measures of the Italian fascists, he said: "German public opinion spoke passionately against them in view of our cultural bonds with the population of South Tyrol. Exaggerations and inaccurate reports poured oil on the fire. The government interfered only to the extent of warning the press and pointed to the harm done by excessive agitation."

This was an obvious diplomatic retreat. What was more, Stresemann disavowed the Bavarian Society for boycotting Italy and declared that boycott appeals had no relation to official policy. He wanted Germany admitted to the League of Nations, despite one of its members, Italy, treating Germany so curtly. This is why he sounded off in milder terms than the bourgeois and Social-Democratic press.

But fascist Italy meant to consolidate her diplomatic victory. On February 10, Mussolini replied to Stresemann in the Italian Senate. He was less belligerent now, but what he said reaffirmed the Italian stand on an issue which, the Duce said, was not open to discussion. The speech was of interest in only one respect: it lifted the curtain on backstage Italo-German talks over the Locarno Treaty. Evidently, Italy wanted guarantees for her northern frontier in anticipation of German annexationist ambitions. But German diplomacy reminded Italy that Austria, not Germany, bordered on the Brenner Pass. Thus, retaining a free hand, the German Government appeased the Pan-Germanists who, adapting themselves to the new conditions, had found shelter in almost all the parties of the Weimar Republic. Their propaganda of Austria's "right of self-determination" revealed a revival of annexationist sentiment among the German imperialists, who used ethnographic and historical arguments in their discourses about the borders of states having to coincide with the language borders.

The old contradictions, which no amount of pacifist talk could overcome and which were generating new dangers to world peace, blossomed forth again against the Locarno backdrop. The official British press, the principal herald of the "Locarno spirit", commented with deliberate restraint on the Italo-German conflict and voiced the belief that the clash reflected more profound differences in other spheres. The Right-wing press in France, on the other hand, was candidly elated, interpreting Mussolini's attitude as an awareness of the dangers of Pan-Germanism and as a warning that Germany, once admitted to the League of Nations, would seek Austria's annexation and, later, a revision of the Brenner frontier. The Italian press responded by inferring on the community of Franco-Italian interests and went to the length of assuming that French diplomacy had had a hand in kindling the Italo-German conflict.

The very possibility of a conflict so soon after the conclusion of the Locarno Pact and on the eve of Germany's admission to the League of Nations, like the general climate generated by the conflict, were highly symptomatic.

3

Even so specifically a European issue as the Italo-German conflict created by the fascists wanting to Italianise South Tyrol and by the revisionist ambitions of the German Government, was unavoidably coloured by the power struggle for a redistribution of colonial possessions. The British press, for one thing, conjectured that the diplomatic Rome-Berlin scuffle over South Tyrol was motivated by something more, that is, by Italy's wish to obtain certain colonial mandates before Germany's demands were satisfied. The German nationalist press, we may add, gave credence to this report and stepped up its anti-Italian campaign, maintaining that the "spirit of Locarno" would collapse unless Germany were given first choice of the colonial mandates.

Yet the Versailles Treaty, Article 119, said:

"Germany renounces in favour of the Principal Allied and Associated Powers all her rights and titles to her overseas possessions."

In the 1914-18 war Germany lost 2,953,000 sq. km. of territory—all she had acquired since embarking on her colonial policy. But soon, when the reparations issue reached a stalemate in 1921, certain sections of the German bourgeoisie suggested that the question of reparations could be settled at the expense of the colonial peoples. However, the idea was not fated to materialise at the time of the French occupation of the Ruhr. So it was not until Anglo-American capital worked out the Dawes reparations plan and a coming to terms loomed in Locarno that the German bourgeoisie again raised the question. By the end of 1924 the German Government was on the offensive. In a memorandum to the Council of the League of Nations it pointed out that Article 22 of the Covenant stipulated that peoples incapable of governing themselves would be placed under trusteeship of the foremost nations. Barred from colonial activity by her defeat, the memorandum said, Germany expected the League to call on her at a suitable time to participate in the system of mandates. During behind-the-scenes negotiations German diplomacy again angled for colonial mandates. *Weltwirtschaft*, an influential and well-informed journal, stated: "Although the question of a colonial mandate for Germany was only lightly touched upon during the Locarno talks, the reply, though hypothetical, was affirmative. Whether it will be followed by the granting of a mandate depends not only on the consent of the powers concerned, but also on what Germany decides."[1]

The principal bourgeois parties (National Party, People's Party, Economic Party, the Centre, etc.) campaigned for the return of Germany's colonies. The colonialists maintained that fulfilment of the Dawes Plan depended on greater German exports, which, however, were restricted by customs barriers, industrialisation of other countries, etc. The accent, therefore, had to be on the home market, which could be expanded through acquisition of colonies. General Schlee-Pascha, author of an article entitled "Does Germany Need Colonies?", said recovery of colonies was essential for economic headway and for the further development of the German nation. "If consumption of colonial goods, which makes us dependent on alien colonial peoples, is not decisive enough," he wrote, "the role of various

---

[1] A. v. Rechenberg, "Der Erwerb deutschen Kolonialbesitzes in seiner Bedeutung für Deutschland und die Weltwirtschaft", *Weltwirtschaft* No. 12, 1925, S. 226.

raw materials essential for our industry is certainly decisive. . . . The German colonies would not meet our demand
for primary materials ... but the raw materials received
from the colonies could regulate prices on the world
market."[1]

During the Locarno conference, the German bourgeois
press harped on the return of Togo and Cameroon. It hinted by way of a feeler that Stresemann had obtained assurances to this effect from Britain. The British press responded by suggesting that if the question of a colonial
mandate for Germany ever arose, it would concern a
French, rather than British mandate. This irritated the
French Government, precipitating a debate in the Chamber
of Deputies on December 19, 1925. In no circumstances,
France made clear, would she give Germany any of the
colonial mandates she had acquired in Africa. If London
expected France to restore to Germany the French part of
her former colonies in Africa, Paris said, it was deeply
mistaken. It was also made clear that if Britain ever set
an "example of generosity", France would not follow suit.
On the strength of Article 119 of the Versailles Treaty,
Leon-Perrier, Minister for Colonies, pointed out, France
would relinquish none of her colonies.

This was a cold shower for the hotheads in Germany.
Besides, it complicated British backstage diplomacy, which
employed cautious, non-committal reconnaissance, hints,
dodges, bargains and parleys concerning the German colonial demands to induce Berlin to climb on the Western
band wagon, entirely isolating the Soviet Union. It may be
safely assumed that after its pleas for colonial mandates
were turned down, German diplomacy confined itself to the
benefits it expected to reap from joining the League of
Nations.

At a conference in Berlin early in January 1926, the
Imperial Colonial Society suggested that the government
play its hand to the end, that is, delay entry into the League
of Nations until its claims should be honoured: 1) repeal forthwith all regulations requiring liquidation of German property in the colonies and abolish all rules restricting German immigration, settlement, commerce and pro-

---

[1] Gen. Schlee-Pascha, "Braucht Deutschland Kolonien?", *Weltpolitik
und Weltwirtschaft*, München, 1925, Bd. I, H. 10, S. 369.

duction, and 2) grant Germany mandates for Cameroon and Togo.

This was not all. Should these demands, on which Germany's entry into the League would be made conditional, be turned down and Germany still be compelled to join the League, a detailed directive was drawn up for German spokesmen in Geneva envisaging 1) maintenance of the system of mandates so long as Germany had no hope of recovering her colonial possessions, 2) measures preventing any formal incorporation of former German colonies in the possessions of the victor-powers, 3) Germany's economic equality, that is, provision of favourable conditions for German capital and goods in all, notably the former German, colonies.

As the day of Germany's admission to the League approached, her colonial programme expanded.[1] The increasing demands caused jealous anxiety among the Italian imperialists whose appetite for colonies was not sated at the Paris peace conference in 1919. They began peddling their own demands. Fascism stiffened its approach. Not surprisingly, therefore, the British official press interpreted the South Tyrolian conflict as a sign of Italo-German antagonisms in other spheres, above all over colonies. In any case, the conflict showed that the "Locarno spirit" had failed to remove tension, irritation and mistrust in Europe. The circumstances of Germany's admission to the League of Nations only accentuated this impression.

4

Germany's efforts to join the League are tied up with Anglo-French rivalry. They reflect British efforts to enlist Germany in the system of Western capitalist countries with the purpose of isolating the Soviet Union.

Germany first asked to be admitted to the League of Nations at the peace conference in Versailles. Her request was turned down. At the London conference in 1924, however, the question of Germany's admission was brought up again, with British diplomacy dangling certain prospects before the German delegation.

---

[1] See further, "The Colonial Designs of the German Imperialists".

On September 23, 1924, German President Friedrich Ebert decided to seek the earliest possible admission to the League. Six days later, Germany officially notified the countries represented on the League Council that she had demands "with a decisive bearing on Germany's collaboration in the great cause undertaken by the League of Nations". These were: 1) a permanent seat on the League Council and equal representation in the Secretariat and other League bodies, 2) a qualification to Article 16 of the Covenant obliging League members to act against any state branded as the attacking side, 3) a qualification to Article 1 of the Covenant guaranteeing observance of international commitments (the German Government pointed out that the article should not be interpreted to mean that Germany accepted "the moral guilt of the German people" for the outbreak of the war of 1914-18), and 4) participation in the system of colonial mandates.

The Council took cognisance of Germany's wish to be a member of the League Council, but rejected the German qualifications, especially the one concerning Article 16, on the grounds that only the League of Nations as a whole was competent to deal with the matter.

The German Government then approached Sir Eric Drummond, Secretary-General of the League, in a note dated December 12, 1924, arguing that it could not comply with Article 16 because it had been compelled to disarm under the terms of the Versailles Treaty. Drummond took three months to reply. His answer did not come until negotiations of the guarantee pact had made sufficient headway. On March 14, 1925, the League Council pointed out to the German Government in a note that participation in armed operations undertaken by the League in pursuance of the Covenant was necessarily different from country to country, depending on their military status. The reassuring vagueness of the wording touched off a new diplomatic round. British diplomacy, however, had to exert considerable effort to, firstly, pressure France into complying with Germany's entry into the League and, secondly, find a formula enabling Germany to join the League without spelling out the terms of Germany's participation in any active effort of isolating the Soviet Union.

After a drawn-out backstage struggle the formula was finally found. It was set forth by the French Government in the following terms: the Allies are convinced that the status of a member of the League of Nations would, on Germany's entry into the League, furnish her with the best means of working for her *desiderata*, as was the case with other states; Germany's entry into the League is the only dependable basis for mutual guarantees and European concord. The German Government was urged to hasten the negotiations. When the guarantees were initialled at Locarno it was understood that they would not enter into force until Germany became a member of the League of Nations.

On February 3, 1926, Reichstag's foreign affairs commission voted 18 to 8 for Germany's entry into the League. The British press welcomed this as a feather in the cap of Britain's diplomacy. On February 10, Aschmann, the German Consul-General in Geneva, tendered Secretary-General Drummond his country's application signed by Stresemann. The League Assembly and its Council were scheduled to deal with it at the beginning of March. Then came news which threw a monkey-wrench into the diplomatic machinery. Poland, followed by Spain and Brazil, were learned to be contemplating to demand permanent seats on the League Council along with Germany. The British press was perplexed, even irritated. At the beginning of February, prior to Germany's official application, word leaked to the press that the question of expanding the Council had been brought up in Paris when Briand conversed with Hoesch, the German Ambassador. Thereupon, the French official press began suggesting a permanent seat on the Council for Poland, a participant in the Locarno conference, for Spain, a representative of the "neutral" states and, finally, for a representative of the Americas, meaning Brazil. It appeared that in this French diplomacy had the support of the United States, which was outside the League but interested in reducing Britain's influence.

The first British reaction was firm. London maintained that in the existing circumstances permanent seats on the League Council should belong to Britain, France, Italy, Japan, Germany and nobody else. Delighted over Germany's departure from her "Rapallo line" and, as a corollary, her firmer "Western" orientation, and her joining the League of Nations after signing the Locarno Pact, the British bourgeois press was somewhat perturbed by possible complications in the League, which was to a great extent an instrument of Britain's foreign policy. The Anglo-French diplomatic scuffle continued. If anything, it became more acute. Aware of this, the German Government bargained with some assurance. German press commentaries noted the revisionist claims Berlin was slowly but surely pushing to the fore. The French press understood it well. It exploited the German imperialist ambitions not only against Germany, but also, and mostly, against Britain. The Foreign Office mouthpiece responded on February 11 with an article by its diplomatic correspondent, who pointed the finger at the culprit of the inescapable difficulties: France, the principal organiser of the big diplomatic coalition of "Latin and Slav countries", bent on reducing Britain's weight inside and outside the League of Nations. The British cabinet avoided stating its position. In Paris, Austen Chamberlain sidestepped assurances to Briand and the Polish ambassador. But the London press wrote about the "impending crisis in the League of Nations", instantly attracting public attention. It was clear to everybody concerned that if Germany did not join the League or if conditions complicating her admission would arise due to internal differences, the far-reaching British plans in relation to the Locarno Pact would collapse whole or in part. The pact was designed as the cornerstone of British policy in Europe and since the purpose of this policy was to use Germany, her geographic location, economic potential and eastward ambitions, the question of Germany's place and role in the system of West European capitalist states had to be reckoned with.

Another important factor was the balance of internal forces in Germany. The German Communist Party, backed by the foremost sections of the working class, was firmly opposed to Germany's embarking on an anti-Soviet course. The Social Democrats, the Centre Party, the Democratic Party and a big section of the People's Party, on the other hand, favoured the "Western" Locarno orientation and, therefore, Germany's entry into the League of Nations. But in the People's Party, the principal monopoly capital party, and still more strongly in the National Party, were elements who banked on the mounting economic potential of German capital. Yearning for a rapid rebirth of German militarism and jockeying for a better bargaining position in negotiations with the Western powers, they were delighted that this kindled nationalism and revanchism. This was the time, moreover, when the Italo-German conflict flared up over the Brenner Pass, and Italy's stand in regard to Germany's admission to the League of Nations was therefore more than doubtful. In spite of this or, more precisely, for this very reason, the German Government gave to understand that it was not dropping its demand for a permanent seat on the League Council and, what was more, objected to any further expansion of the Council.

March 10 was named as the date when Germany would be accepted into the League with the appropriate fanfare, but even the top League administrators, optimists *ex professio*, were obviously apprehensive. The Council convened on February 12 to appoint the day for the assembly, but was immersed in a stormy discussion of the new claims to a permanent seat. Germany's admission was, in a way, relegated to the background, giving place to the new problem—that of expanding the Council. The controversy created an atmosphere of uncertainty. Britain gave Germany clandestine support, while France candidly backed Poland and its plea for a permanent seat, noting that since Germany wished her eastern frontiers revised, an equilibrium in the Council was logical and vital. Soon the number of claimants to a permanent seat was augmented by Czechoslovakia and Belgium, and Italy's conduct over South Tyrol added fuel to the fire. The situation was described as serious. Even the German nationalist press was alarmed and called on the government to take diplomatic action in order to avoid failure.

The closed Council sitting on February 12 adopted the agenda for the assembly, envisaging the possibility of expanding the Council. France stuck doggedly to her course. The French programme soon leaked out: a) raising the number of permanent Council members from 4 to 7 (Germany, Spain and Poland) or 8 (Belgium) and b) granting three non-permanent seats to Latin American countries, one to a Scandinavian country and one to an Asian state. Britain, the French press observed, was unlikely to back this plan. The extreme conservative press in Britain, however, dissipated the French doubts. In the meantime, British officials refused to commit themselves. By mid-February signs of a change appeared in Britain towards Spain and Poland. For Germany this meant that the Council would not be conducive to her pressing her demands. A deep impression was created by the sensational report in the liberal *Manchester Guardian* that secret talks between France and Britain concerning a permanent seat for Poland dated as far back as Locarno. This was followed by a communication that if the Council is expanded prior to Germany's admission to the League, the German Government would take back its application. Eric Drummond hastened to Berlin. On the day of his arrival, word reached the German capital that Spain would vote against Germany's admission if she was not given a permanent seat on the Council. In a Franco-German "friendly exchange of opinion" on February 17, Briand set out the French position in no uncertain terms. France, he said, would press for the admission of Poland to the League Council and for a possible further expansion of that body. Britain, which was negotiating with the dominions and had to reckon with their views, persisted in her uncertain stand. To top this, the question of colonial mandates for Italy, with distinct hints at Cameroon, an object of German ambition, cropped up in view of the opening of the League's mandates committee.

"The Locarno honeymoon is over," commented an influential Italian newspaper.

The communist proposal to withdraw Germany's application to the League of Nations, made at the Reichstag foreign affairs committee on February 18, was voted down. The government was instructed to demand a) a permanent seat on the League of Nations Council; b) that no other power be admitted to the Council, and c) that Germany get the seat at the coming March session concurrently with her admission to the League.

Other plans appeared. Poland, it was said, would get a permanent or temporary seat at the autumn session. This was a feeler for compromise solutions. Yet Poland stuck to her guns and France gave her all-out support. Italy followed France's lead. In reply to Stresemann's speech and the Reichstag declaration, the official press of the two countries stressed that no promises had been made at Locarno, that Germany alone would get a permanent seat on the League Council. Furthermore, Brazil declared that the question of Germany's admission to the League could not be settled until after the expansion of the Council and Spain campaigned in the same vein.

On February 23, the German cabinet empowered Chancellor Luther and Stresemann to go to Geneva. There they learned of the welter of different plans. France continued to insist on permanent seats for Poland, Brazil and Spain. Britain, despite her non-committal attitude, was inclined to give a permanent seat to Spain and a temporary one to Poland. Italy demanded a permanent seat for Poland. Spain, Poland and Brazil were blowing their own trumpets, with Czechoslovakia backing Poland's claim with an eye to a permanent seat for herself. China demanded a permanent seat. Uruguay opposed Spain and suggested a temporary seat for Brazil. Japan objected to any further expansion of the Council, but her stand was not firm. Sweden alone backed Germany's claims.

The German bourgeois press was obviously ruffled. It endeavoured to reason Germany's case one day just to fall back on threats the next.

By the beginning of March the clouds over Geneva grew more ominous still. A scuffle was in progress within the British cabinet, but the Foreign Office was obviously inclined to bend to French insistence. Paris made it clear that if Germany balked, France would vote against her. Faced by this diplomatic disharmony, the German Government went on the defensive and cast about frantically for support. On March 2, Luther spoke in Hamburg's town hall. He said Germany did not intend to build her policy on a choice between East and West. In the same breath he issued assurances of loyalty to the League of Nations. In effect, he betrayed fear over the future of the Locarno agreements. On the following day, Briand told the Chamber of Deputies that the French Government would stand firm. British diplomacy kept up its search for a compromise, suggesting an unofficial sitting of the League Council to look for a solution and to conduct private parleys with the German delegation. Its compromise plan was to give Germany a permanent seat on the Council at the first sitting, and at the second, with Germany taking part, a temporary seat to Poland. Germany rejected the idea. The nationalist press spoke of a new "encirclement of Germany". Clearly, said Lloyd George, Britain's ex-Prime Minister, on the eve of the League session there is a conspiracy aimed at neutralising Germany's voice in the Council.

In Geneva a certain amount of confusion followed the

fall of Briand in March. The government crisis in France created the opportunity of putting the matter off until September. The idea of a postponement was subsequently adopted, but under pressure of circumstances of a different order.

Throughout March 7 lively negotiations proceeded between the various delegations in Geneva, but no understanding was reached when the Assembly opened on March 8. The opening address by the chairman, Costa of Portugal, about "the Locarno spirit that had brought Germany here" and about the "fraternal spirit that linked all nations" was common-or-official rhetoric. No headway was made. France and her allies were willing to grant Germany a permanent seat provided the Council was expanded. Berlin made no secret of the fact that the German delegation had gone to Geneva without a clear-cut programme. Yet it insisted that the suggested compromise was unacceptable. The negotiations between Stresemann and the French delegation on March 10 proved fruitless. Spain and Brazil spread word of their determination to vote against Germany. So did the Italian delegation. The ending of the government crisis in France reinforced the champions of an expanded council. In the circumstances, the decision of the League's political committee with Austen Chamberlain in the chair to admit Germany to the League passed almost unnoticed.

If Briand's return to Geneva had any repercussions, these were to strengthen the hand of Poland, an ally of France. This was the result of a compromise between France and Britain, both compelled now to exert pressure on those whose irreconcilable stand previously strengthened their own hand. The new plan was to remove from the Council Czechoslovakia or Sweden, Belgium or Uruguay, and give the thus vacated seat to Poland. On March 15, Sweden's foreign minister told the German delegation of his country's readiness to withdraw and make room for Poland. Czechoslovakia, too, succumbing to pressure, announced her readiness to step down in Poland's favour. Brazil, however, declared firmly that she would vote against Germany if a permanent seat was not made available to her. This disrupted the proceedings once more. Obviously, the Brazilian announcement had been plotted by a skilled hand and was made at the very hour when the situation appeared to be clearing and Briand spoke of an understanding between the German and French delegations. The last glimmer of hope faded. All efforts to adjust the confusing issue by diplomatic intrigue collapsed. The principal signatories of the Locarno Pact had no choice but to register this fact, which they did in a sweet-and-sour declaration issued on March 16, expressing the hope that the obstacles would be surmounted at the next session of the League in September. A sitting of the League took place the following day, at which the Brazilian delegate made his explanations, followed by Chamberlain and Briand. Thus the session ended, and the coming into force of the Locarno agreements had to be postponed.

5

This object lesson of the "Locarno spirit" prompted the German Government to enter into negotiations with the Soviet Union concerning a treaty of neutrality. Later, seeking to vindicate this in the eyes of the Western powers, the German press revealed that the Soviet-German talks had begun in December 1924. The first report in the *Times* of London[1] of the imminent conclusion of a Soviet-German treaty created dismay among the West European rulers. Top German statesmen explained that they needed a political treaty with the Soviet Union to balance Germany's westward move at Locarno. "Close relations with Russia, which could involve us in dangerous conflicts, are out of the question," wrote Theodor Wolff, a well-informed and influential publicist. "On the other hand, it is just as impossible for us to accept Articles 16 and 17 of the League of Nations Covenant, which may compel us to act against Russia by affording freedom of passage across our territory and participating in an economic boycott."[2] The French press, sliding back to the Rapallo times, spoke again of a Russo-German bloc against the Versailles Treaty. No longer did it bother to conceal that the Locarno Treaty had been meant to drive a wedge between Germany and the Soviet Union and that if a Soviet-German agreement gets in the way, the Locarno instruments should be scrapped. Seeking

---

[1] *Times*, April 13, 1926.
[2] *Berliner Tageblatt*, April 18, 1926.

to placate France and Britain, a section of the German press, obviously inspired by the government, produced its own interpretation of the parleys with the Soviet Union. The treaty was said to imply limited neutrality, leaving Germany a free hand if the Soviet Union attacked any other state.[1] British diplomacy attempted to foil or hold up the Soviet-German talks, by promising Germany a permanent seat on the League Council at the next session and leaving Poland out in the cold. But this could no longer satisfy the German Government. The official press replied with irritation that Germany had been deceived in Locarno, where France and Britain secretly promised Poland a seat on the Council. "The Soviet-German negotiations show," said the *Deutsche Allgemeine Zeitung*, organ of the Foreign Ministry, "that Germany is again able to pursue an independent policy. At Locarno Germany was still dominated by British initiative, Britain using her as an instrument to attain British aims, whereas the negotiations with Russia are an indication that Germany is determined and able to pursue a policy that may, at first glance, appear to contradict the interests of the Western powers."[2]

On April 24, 1926, in Berlin the Soviet Union and Germany signed a neutrality treaty consisting of four articles and two notes. The document pointed out that the treaty concluded in Rapallo was still the basis for Soviet-German relations. "Both governments," said a note of the German Government and the Soviet reply, "proceeded from the view that agreement on all political and economic matters concerning the two countries will greatly contribute to universal peace." Article 2, which established the principle of neutrality, was the core of the treaty. "If despite its peaceable behaviour one of the contracting parties is attacked by a third power or group of powers, the other contracting party shall observe neutrality throughout the duration of the conflict."

The neutrality commitment was indeed limited and did not hinder Germany's entry into the League of Nations, whose Covenant required sanctions against the "attacking side" whether or not it was a League member. However, the big question was who would define the "attacking side".

---

[1] *Kölnische Zeitung*, April 15, 1926.
[2] *Deutsche Allgemeine Zeitung*, April 18, 1926.

In the event of complications, the League of Nations could under pressure declare the Soviet Union to be the attacking side and demand that its members apply military and economic sanctions. Germany would then have to be an instrument of alien political aims. To avoid this the German Government made the following statement:

"If ... at any time there arise among League members aspirations which in contradiction to the basic policy of peace are aimed unilaterally against the U.S.S.R., the German Government shall work energetically against such aspirations."

It added: "It should be borne in mind that the question of whether or not the U.S.S.R. is the attacking side could be settled in the obligatory sense for Germany solely with its consent and that therefore any charge against the U.S.S.R. by other powers which Germany may consider unjustified shall not oblige Germany to participate in measures taken on the strength of Article 16."

As we see, Germany undertook not only to oppose within the framework of the League of Nations any anti-Soviet bloc or any acts aimed against the Soviet Union, but also to qualify her participation in applying sanctions against the Soviet Union. The signatories of the Berlin treaty agreed, both in peacetime and in a conflict with a third power, to stay out of coalitions initiating an economic or financial boycott of one of the sides. As for disputes between Germany and the Soviet Union, the treaty provided for conciliatory machinery or arbitration.

The treaty was important for the Soviet Union, for it blunted the Locarno agreement of the West European capitalist countries, and the effects of Germany's induction into the League of Nations. The treaty suited not only the purpose of ensuring the security of the Soviet Union, but also international security, because its objective was to prevent war. Hence, it was equally important for Germany.

The French Rightist press expressed its annoyance above all over the fact that Germany's international position on the eve of her admission to the League had grown stronger.[1] Britain and France feared that the treaty could become a stepping-stone to a Soviet-German alliance. Lloyd

---

[1] *Temps*, April 26, 1926.

George suggested rectifying the mistakes of the League's March session, chiefly by affording Germany a clear passage into the Geneva organisation.

This point of view prevailed. Britain sought to extend her political influence over Europe, to weaken France and isolate the Soviet Union. In this set-up Germany was to be a counter-weight to France and a staging area for an offensive against the Soviet Union. But with the relative stabilisation of capitalism, Germany, which had earlier begun to turn from an object of the Entente policy into a subject of independent policy, started to work for her own goals. By a series of intricate diplomatic manoeuvres, she endeavoured to exploit the contradictions among the victor-powers, but most of all those between the Soviet Union and the principal capitalist states. In this context, the Soviet-German neutrality treaty, a projection of the "Rapallo policy", and Germany's entry into the League of Nations, a projection of the "Locarno policy", are part of Germany's political game with East and West.

1926

Germany is priming for elections. The Reichstag's four-year term does not expire until December 7, 1928, but the government coalition has agreed to hold the elections earlier.

The crisis of the governing bloc of Right parties was not precipitated by any parliamentary offensive of the opposition, but by an explosion in the coalition itself. In a way, it was unexpected. The apparent reason for it was a wrangle over an insignificant detail in the educational bill concerning mixed Catholic and Evangelical schools in Hessen and Baden.

Far be it from us to attach more than the due significance to this break-up of the coalition. It is the bloc of Right bourgeois and Junker parties that has fallen to pieces, not the bloc of the ruling classes of Germany. An examination of the political power pattern reveals two basic trends, externally conflicting ones but essentially convergent. On the one hand, we are witnessing the break-up of a Right government coalition, which has decided to dissolve the Reichstag and hold new elections. On the other, there is a distinct consolidation of monopoly capital, which has gained a stronger grip on the state machine than it ever had and is now endeavouring to gain still more influence among more sections of the bourgeoisie and the intermediate social strata in order to direct this complex economic, political and governmental machinery against the working class and its vanguard, the Communist Party.

These latest trends reveal why a new organisation, the League of Renovation, has been established. Its official purpose is to eliminate internal friction between the German state (Reich) and the independent constituent lands (Länder). The point at issue is to strengthen the German Reich and to eliminate the various technical, administrative, juridical and particularist impediments preventing monopoly capital from steering the state through the shoals of internal and external difficulties on to the arena of imperialist policy. Monopoly-financed propaganda is trying to prove that despite the stabilisation of the capitalist system, despite the firming up of the currency and despite good foreign commerce, Germany is endangered from within and without.

"In the hour of danger," says the inaugural proclamation of the League, "there can be no other slogan but that of strengthening the state. The imperial government must have decision-making powers in relation to all the general important questions. Apart from foreign policy, law and military affairs, it is concerned with finance and all other determinative economic issues. Such an empire must have the power that once built the old empire and that should now serve the common cause."

The League of Renovation has set out to unite the various groups of the German ruling classes. Its membership consists of prominent agrarians, bankers, businessmen and, to an overpowering degree, of representatives of corporation industry. Heading this new organisation, which has wasted no time establishing contacts with the imperial and Prussian governments, is Dr. Luther, ex-Reichschancellor, intimately connected with German heavy industry. This gives us reason to assume that the League is, so to say, a reserve organisation of the German bourgeoisie and Junkerdom under the general leadership of monopoly capital, out to secure closer links with the state for effective expansion in foreign markets and consolidation of all Right forces in an offensive on the working class.

The cry for "national unity" and combating "frictions" is being fashioned into an ideological battering ram to crush the independent and concerted actions of the working class. But the new League is not confining itself to organising a united bourgeois and Junker front and to subordinating the state to monopoly capital. Its other purpose is to split the workers organisationally and draw some sections of them, together with the petty bourgeoisie, into the orbit of its own political and ideological influence; hence the blandishments showered these days on the Social-Democrats. "If combating the inflation and firming up the mark required extraordinary measures and emergency laws," wrote the *Deutsche Allgemeine Zeitung,* mouthpiece of heavy industry, in its issue of January 10, 1928, "and if in the past years of internal instability and grave crises, Germany has had to resort to unusual measures, now it is highly desirable to secure the necessary development in possibly normal ways. Certainly, one element of this—therein lies our political sagacity and also our hope—is that the Social-Democrats have to be prevailed upon to co-operate. There can be no two-thirds majority in the Reichstag without the Social-Democrats, and no changes in the constitution are conceivable without such a two-thirds majority. It is absolutely essential that the party which, compared to other parties, embraces the greatest number of workers, should participate actively and joyfully in patterning the new state."

The invitation to the Social-Democrats is accompanied by disguised threats of extra-parliamentary reprisals. Parliamentary forms are staked against the co-operation of the Social-Democrats, and it is more than likely that certain Social-Democrats (such as Noske) will swallow the bait. As for the Social-Democrats as a whole, they are hardly likely to accept the idea in the foreseeable future. For one thing, it is unpropitious at the moment because of the election campaign. It should be borne in mind, however, that in May 1927 at a congress of the Social-Democratic Party Hilferding called for a close-knit German state (*Einheitsstaat*), which indicated a readiness to enter a coalition government.

One thing is certain: having set its sights on imperialist policy, the League will make the most of the manoeuvres the bourgeoisie and certain of its groups, and the Junkers as well, are compelled to undertake to extend and buttress their political influence in the election campaign and, what is more important, at a time when Germany's ruling classes are headed for grave economic and political difficulties.

The new organisation masterminded by corporation capital was founded shortly before the break-up of the government coalition. By gaining ascendancy in the League, the People's Party, which is a party of industrialists, has in a way secured its rear when instigating the rupture of the government coalition. What we should remember is that the crisis has, for a setting, a bitter class struggle in the steel and coal industries, highlighted by a wave of powerful strikes and lock-outs.

The government bloc exploded over an educational bill. This was where tempers flared and a fight ensued between the Catholic Centre Party (supported by the Bavarian People's Party and the German National Party) and the German People's Party. The curious fact is that the press connected with the German People's Party, backed by that of the Democratic Party, is trying to create the impression that the wrangle over the educational bill was an important action to stem aggressive clericalism. But that is an obvious overstatement. The People's Party opposed the demand of a secular school, that is, the final separation of school from church, which came from the Left, just as strongly as it opposed the Centre. It was reluctant to abolish the ideological influence on the rising generation of religious education, because—and this was said in so many words—a secular school is bound ultimately to "proletarise" the mind, something described as intolerable.

Since the opposition (the Social-Democrats and the Democratic Party) did not for tactical reasons press hard enough for the secularisation of schools, the People's Party benefited from the fact that the main fire was directed rightwards, against the so-called clericalisation of schools and, more correctly, for perpetuating the existing state of affairs in which the two dominant churches, the Catholic and Evangelical, possess a sufficiently strong hold on education.

The Weimar constitution has done little to change the school. Confessional (that is, Catholic or Evangelical) schools predominate in Prussia and Württemberg, and so-called simultaneous (that is, mixed) schools in Hessen, Baden, Saxony and Thuringia. In Bavaria, there operates a concordat concluded with the Roman Curia in January 1925.

The difference between the two dominant types of school is by no means fundamental. The People's Party opposition to the pretensions of the Catholic Centre backed by Bavarian reactionaries and the German National Party, which want to convert simultaneous schools into homogeneous confessional schools, is not, therefore, any outstanding act of anti-clericalism or any revival of liberal tradition, as the capitalist press connected with the People's Party would have us believe. The remarkable thing is that the press of the Left-bourgeois Democratic Party appears to hold the same view. It is more than evident that it hopes to profit by the break-up of the Right bloc and to win a toehold in a grand coalition that may result. It is therefore prepared to consign to oblivion its own plans of completely liberating schools from religious influence in order to back what is essentially a reactionary posture of the People's Party.

While the Catholic Centre Party campaigns for a fixed term in which simultaneous schools are to be converted into confessional ones, the People's Party is merely insisting on the *status quo,* nothing more. But inasmuch as the opposition has gone out of its way to obscure its own demands, the perspective has been pulled out of shape. By the logic of events, the People's Party became the initiator of a fight against the aggressive tendencies of reactionary Catholic and Protestant clericalism represented jointly by the Centre Party, the German National Party and the Bavarian People's Party.

The arguments of the German People's Party are essentially centred on two points, each addressed to the opposed social groups. Clericalisation, it says, would be very expensive; according to different estimates it would cost from 250 to 600 million marks, with the cost for Prussia alone amounting to between 60 and 200 million marks. Sums of this magnitude were sure to impress those sections of the petty bourgeoisie and the backward section of the working class who, still enthralled by the church, continue to support the Centre and the Right German parties. By shocking them, the People's Party hopes to win more of the electorate to its side. Further, the People's Party, that mouthpiece of monopoly capital, uses the press to create the impression that it was prepared to compromise with the Catholic Centre, which is portrayed as intractable. By so doing, the People's Party is seeking to vindicate itself of responsibility for the break-up of the Right government coalition.

The support rendered to the Centre Party by the nationalists is the price they are paying for inclusion of the

National Party in an eventual Right bloc government. Besides, the reactionary bill envisaging the clericalisation of Protestant as well as Catholic schools agrees with the general line and social nature of this monarchist party in the republican government. The failure of the educational bill was a painful blow to the Centre Party, which was compelled on February 8-12 to associate it with the fate of the government coalition. The threats it made left no impression. Having provoked the crisis, the People's Party acted. It came out not only against the Centre, but also against the nationalists.

The political situation created by a secondary issue was a peculiar one. It was not brought on by any deep-going contradictions in the bourgeois camp, but merely by tactical considerations of the People's Party. Yet the very fact that such devious tactical manoeuvres were needed is symptomatic in view of the realignment of socio-political forces in modern Germany. The processes within the Centre Party, by the way, are also highly illuminating, for in view of its specific social heterogeneity, the variety of its basic composition and voting reserve, it reflects the general social processes under way in the country, where imperialism is making a comeback.

The Catholic bourgeoisie has made the most of its well-geared and ramified machinery to retain its hold on large sections of the petty bourgeoisie and even on certain groups of the industrial proletariat. But the candid class policy of German capital, the experiences of the struggle of recent years, have gradually drawn the lines between classes also within the Centre Party, organised on the confessional principle.

The brunt of the hardships occasioned by the Franco-German conflict of 1923 has fallen on the workers of the Ruhr, who are mostly Catholics. Then the German industrialists managed to repeal the eight-hour working day. They were just as intent as their Protestant brethren on stepping up the exploitation of the working class and on shifting the burdens of the Dawes Plan on the proletariat. Tycoons such as Klöckner complemented their posts of leadership in the Centre Party with similarly high posts in the Steel Trust and the Coal Syndicate and, needless to say, never confused their political line: it was the coal and steel policy that dominated the party, not vice versa. In any case, such political issues as repeal of the eight-hour working day, capitalist rationalisation of production and the offensive on the workers brought about a cleavage not along religious and party lines, but exclusively on class lines.

The class struggle, which is sifting and polarising the Centre Party following, has inevitably produced repercussions in political affairs. As far back as September 1926, at an international conference of Catholic workers' unions, Yoos, a spokesman of the Centre Party, said that the attitude of the Catholic workers to the workers' socialist movement is gradually changing.

The offensive of the bourgeoisie, the policies of the government bloc which the Centre Party helped to hammer out, are inciting even those backward sections of the German proletariat on whom Catholic capital could always rely in the past. Labour Minister Brauns, of the Centre Party, has proved beyond doubt by his social policies and the system of compulsory arbitration in labour-management conflicts that his general line is aimed against the workers. The true role of the working-class flank in the bourgeois politics of the Centre Party is gradually sinking in among members of the Catholic trade unions, who voted for the Centre. Attacking Centre policies in the bourgeois bloc, *Der Deutsche,* organ of the Catholic trade unions, wrote: "What is considered politically necessary is not the workers, but their votes. By reason of these votes we get friendly smiles and blandishments, while things are really quite different inside. . . . The time when the workers were satisfied with fetching gestures is over. . . . No longer is it enough that the leadership is not aimed against the workers. The workers want to participate in the leadership."

By joining the government coalition, the Rightist core of the Centre Party, which represents big industrial capital, has joined hands with the most reactionary section of the bourgeoisie and the agrarians. By pursuing this policy behind the backs of the Catholic workers, and, moreover, to their detriment, the Centre Party ran into resistance in its own ranks. And this resistance became tangible indeed when all attempts to squash it proved unsuccessful. The struggle between the workers' flank and the big capitalist element in the Centre Party flared up when the Right-wing leaders joined the same bloc as the reactionary monarchist German National Party without notifying the appropriate party bodies and in so doing flaunted the prescribed procedures and faced the party with a *fait accompli*.

The crisis in the Centre Party was preceded by an exchange of messages between the party leader, Reichschancellor Wilhelm Marx, and one of the leaders of the Catholic trade unions, Imbusch. It concerned further political planning. The party crisis, which reflects the general aggravation of the class struggle in Germany, was epitomised by Marx's statement that "the Centre is neither monarchist nor republican; it is a constitutional party". With the elections near, this meant that the capitalist wing of the party was prepared to co-operate with the nationalists and, in doing so, use the Catholic workers and the petty bourgeoisie in the interest of its class policy. Under pressure of the Catholic workers, Stegerwald, and notably Imbusch, came out with sharp public criticism of their representative in the government. Imbusch pointed out, among other things, that Wilhelm Marx's policy was "anti-social", that is, anti-proletarian and coloured by class interests. The struggle fast became acute, then subsided when Marx enlisted the support of the greater part of the party functionaries and Reichstag members, who, led by Guerard, chairman of the parliamentary faction, began to dampen passions by the usual method of compromise.

At the end of January 1928, the leadership attempted to create the impression that the party had passed the crisis stage and regained unity. To do so, Marx paid lip service to the "rebels", declaring that the party's allegiance to the republic was not open to question. He gave to understand that any future coalition with the nationalists was ruled out, peppering his speech with phrases to the effect that the Centre was determined to follow a "social policy", duly recorded in the final resolution.

The concession was naturally forced. Politically, it was a manoeuvre to avoid losing the votes of Catholic workers, who threatened to nominate their own candidates in the coming election. Marx and his group made verbal concessions which enabled them to retain control over the party and thereby continue the former political line.

The stand of ex-Reichschancellor Joseph Wirth attracted considerable attention against the setting of sharpening class antagonisms. When the Right coalition was formed, Wirth opposed it, particularly the home policy of Reichs-chancellor Marx. But this did not prevent him from pub-lishing a message, "Where are you going, friend Imbusch?", in which he pointed out that socialist sentiments are liable to smash the Centre Party from within and warned Im-busch: "So far the process is being retarded by extraneous circumstances of a technical order, but I doubt that the brakes will hold for long."

This accentuates the fact that workers still ideologically and politically enthralled by Catholicism and the Catholic bourgeoisie are going Left. Wirth's sudden expostulations embarrassed the functionaries of the Social-Democratic Party so greatly that *Vorwärts* was compelled to devote a special article to the matter, titled, "Where are you going, Joseph Wirth?".

The magnitude of these internal frictions in the Centre Party should not, however, be overestimated. They amount to ordinary inner-party manoeuvres of the Catholic leader-ship, generated by the "break-up" of the government coali-tion and, consequently, by an aggravation of inner-political contradictions. The People's Party has taken note of the discredit brought on the Right-bourgeois bloc by the latter's stand in the intensifying class struggle, and has decided, in view of the imminent elections, to exploit the current situation and win the votes of those going Left, chiefly the petty bourgeoisie, by a shrewd tactical dodge and an ap-parent revival of liberal traditions, hoping that this will strengthen its band in the future cabinet. The internal scuffle in the Centre Party facilitated its manoeuvre. The relatively secondary question of educational policy on which the government coalition foundered was very convenient ground, because it hinged on interests of an ideological complexion.

The *Rote Fahne* in its issue of December 20, 1927, in-dicated that the German People's Party is gravitating towards an alliance with the Social-Democratic leadership, while the Right flank, the big bourgeoisie and the agrarians contiguous with the National Party, is still figuring on an out-and-out dictatorship and building up reserve power for this purpose in such paramilitary organisations as the Stahlhelm. We might add that the Leftward shift of the People's Party does not rule out support, whenever needed, by reactionary nationalist organisations. All this should be borne in mind when assessing the stance assumed by Marx, the leader of the People's Party, and of Foreign Minister Stresemann, who has demanded from the Reichstag rostrum that the Western powers evacuate their troops from the Rhine zone. The diplomatic duel between Stresemann and Briand is really being impelled by the coming elections in both France and Germany.

Stresemann's strong language is a deliberate use of nationalist terminology, for all that the National Party has been doing in the government was chiefly aimed at promoting the predatory interests of the agrarians. Take minister Schiele's report at the National Party congress in Königsberg, September 1927, where he urged government support of the agrarians. The National Party is making the most of its participation in the cabinet. In doing so, it seeks the backing of the Centre, hoping that this will sway the outcome of the coming Reichstag elections. The Nationalists cannot do without outside help, because local elections have revealed—as an outgrowth of the drop in prestige of the Rightist coalition, notably its nationalist wing—that it is losing votes and, consequently, seats. Hence all these election manoeuvres of the National Party, designed to recover lost ground and win it a place in the future cabinet.

Since foreign policy is the concern of the People's Party, its principal rival in the elections, the National Party is intent on exploiting the general discontent over the Locarno policy, Germany's entry into the League of Nations and its attempted rapprochement with France. But here it is running into rebuttals by the People's Party, particularly Stresemann. While making a big show of their monarchist sentiment and, at once, outwardly stressing their loyalty to the republican government, of which they are a part, the Nationalists are trying hard to adapt themselves to the existing state of things, to be pliable and yet preserve by means of nationalist slogans what they could easily lose. There are two distinct, seemingly conflicting, trends in their policy: on the one hand, they are concerned with buttressing the militant reserves of monarchist reaction, notably the Stahlhelm, and, on the other, they are endeavouring to penetrate into the workers' quarters and gain supporters there. We have seen the same thing happen during the 1924 election, when the attempt failed. This time the effort is more concentrated. "If the German National Party wants to achieve its aim," says a circular issued by its leaders, "and if it wants to come out of the coming elections stronger than before, it must look for new adherents where it can still find them, profiting from the gigantic reserves of the German working class."

While the parties of the government coalition were quarrelling among themselves about the culprit of the crisis—a matter of no more than purely propaganda importance—Field-Marshal Hindenburg took advantage of his prerogatives as President of the Republic to carry out what amounted to a blunt political intervention: he sent a message to Reichschancellor Marx, pointing out that Germany needs an operative government to pass certain legislation and added that the fate of the educational bill should not be linked with the question of dissolving the Reichstag.

Hindenburg's intervention was made in the interest of the National Party, which was eager to drag out its participation in government and ease through certain legislation, such as the "aid to agriculture" bill, designed, of course, to benefit the big landowners. Not surprisingly, it went out of its way to keep the Centre Party in the cabinet. It declared publicly that it would do its utmost to "remove the difficulties obstructing unity in relation to the educational bill". But the retort of the People's Party amounted to a rejection of any concessions, compelling the other parties of the Right-bourgeois bloc to admit that the government coalition was falling to pieces.

It was agreed in the ensuing party parleys that the Reichstag was not to be dissolved at once, so that the government would retain its powers to carry out Hindenburg's programme. The Democratic Party and the Social-Democrats were also involved in these negotiations. Instead of organising a united proletarian front at this time of strikes and lock-outs in Middle Germany, the Social-Democratic leadership entered into parliamentary negotiations with the coalition parties concerning the President's reactionary programme, and on the following, rather peculiar, excuse: the longer the Right bloc stays in power, the better for the workers.

Evidently, this attitude envisages further alienation of the petty bourgeoisie from bourgeois parties and is expected to win petty-bourgeois votes. Small wonder that the Social-Democratic press stressed so assiduously that it would back legislation (e.g., aid to pensioners) favoured chiefly by the petty bourgeoisie, while expressing discontent over certain items in Hindenburg's programme prejudicious to the interests of the workers.

One thing is certain: having been assured that elections would soon take place, the Social-Democrats have ceased all fundamental opposition to the bourgeois bloc and agreed to make no so-called agitational demands, that is, in effect, not to oppose the bourgeoisie's main demand that they approve the budget. Here is how leader Hermann Müller formulated this attitude in the Reichstag:

"We have expressed our readiness, though we are not going to vote for the budget, to refrain from creating any special difficulties, because we want the budget, most of which has already been discussed, to be passed before the new election."

As we see, the bourgeois government bloc, that collapsed because of manoeuvres by the political alignment of monopoly capital, is being artificially supported from outside, by the intervention of the President, the chief of the nationalists, on the one hand, and by the loyal opposition of the Democratic Party and Social-Democracy, on the other. To facilitate the People's Party stand on the educational issue, the Social-Democrats have gone to the length of abandoning their own demand of a secular school, although this was put down in a resolution passed by the latest party congress in Kiel. This disregard of their own resolution and the obsequious attitude in relation to the People's Party stems from the general trend of the Kiel congress— collaboration with the bourgeoisie. Participation in a coalition government politically, coupled with "economic democracy", which is uppermost in the policy of the Social-Democrats, affects their stand in all specific matters of current policy as well. They have to manoeuvre to resolve these issues before the coming Reichstag election in order to make the most of the radicalisation of the masses and win petty-bourgeois votes, and yet not burn the bridges leading to a future coalition with bourgeois parties.

The Landtag and community elections have shown that, though the Social-Democrats have managed to retain their hold and even gain ground in some of the areas, they were defeated in others (e.g., in Hessen), while the Communist Party polled considerably more votes. Yet to gain admission to the future coalition cabinet as a strong party, the Social-Democrats hope to win more than 30 seats.

Their gravitation Rightwards prompts the Social-Democrats to intensify their offensive against the Communist Party and draw the workers' attention from economic battles against the bourgeoisie to battles at the polls.

The election campaign which has gone off to a start shows clearly what ideological and political stock the Social-Democrats intend to use. Let us look at Carl Severing's programme article, "Our Tasks", in the February 19, 1928, issue of *Vorwärts*, which says preconditions have to be created for increasing German exports and sustaining the economic upswing of 1927. This definition of Social-Democratic policy lies at the root of reformist tactics towards the trade unions and in the working-class battle against industrialists and the capitalist state.

The attitude of the Socialist-Democrats during the latest class collisions in Middle Germany which flared up when the government coalition announced its failure, is a striking illustration of this fact. Besides, the break-up of the bourgeois coalition is eclipsed by the emergence of a united bourgeois front, which asserted itself during the latest class conflicts in the Middle-German steel industry. The conflict, which began over the workers' demand of a 15-pfennig increase of their hourly wage, developed into a major collision when the All-German Union of Steel Industrialists threatened a lock-out if no agreement was reached by February 22.

To get an idea of what this lock-out could mean, let us recall that the Steel Union has a membership of 4,474 and that the workers employed at their factories number 815,000. The Union represents such giant enterprises as AEG, Siemens-Schuckert, Borsig, Schwartzkopff, etc. *Vorwärts* reacted with the phrase, "The decision is either madness or bluff",[1] while the Council of the Metalworkers' Union de-

---

[1] *Vorwärts*, February 8, 1928.

clared: "The lock-out will injure the German economy and the industrialists will have to bear the responsibility for it. The trade union is following the industrialists' intentions calm in the knowledge that its wage demands are fair and that they accord with the interests of the nation's economy."

But the threat of a lock-out drew closer, while a mediation board of the labour ministry ruled a 5-pfennig hourly rise for skilled workers. Both parties rejected this ruling, and it was proclaimed not obligatory.

At first the trade union described the 5-pfennig rise as insignificant and unsatisfactory, but thought better of it and hastened to accept the ruling, thus protecting the government's prestige. The circumstances were favourable for the workers, but their reformist leaders evaded a show-down, though they threatened to exploit the industrialists' attitude and promised to fight all down the line by means of a general solidarity strike. More battles between the German workers and the employers are therefore to be expected.

What appears to be a crisis of the bourgeois bloc is really a realignment of forces in the bourgeois parties, a realignment which the People's Party, a party of monopoly capital, is trying to use for its own ends, namely, to build bridges to the Left by reviving "liberal" and seemingly anti-clerical traditions in secondary matters while maintaining its bonds with the Rightist parties of the ruling class. It has the support of the Social-Democrats, who are trying to dampen the class struggle and win admission to a "grand coalition" government.

In the circumstances, the German Communist Party has a broad field for action.

While petty-bourgeois discontent over the government of agrarian and monopoly capital is prompting a realignment, the gravitation of the masses towards the Social-Democrats and the appearance of a crop of small and local parties, the swing Leftward of the workers has added visibly to the influence of the Communist Party at the expense of the Social-Democrats and, partly, the Centre Party. If the Social-Democrats have gained any votes, they are petty-bourgeois votes, while the growth of the Communist Party speaks of a consolidation of working-class strength and of the success of united front tactics. The elections in

Altona, Hamburg, Königsberg and elsewhere, where the Communist Party following increased considerably, have been an important trial of strength for the communist political line.

"What are the lessons we should draw?" asked the *Rote Fahne* after these elections. "We must follow our united front tactics still more consistently and systematically; we must make our ties with the masses still stronger."[1]

Germany is preparing for the Reichstag elections. Whatever their outcome, the German workers are facing heavy economic and political battles.

1928

---

[1] *Rote Fahne*, Oct. 11, 1927.

REALIGNMENT OF FORCES AND THE FASCIST OFFENSIVE

(1930 Elections)

The Reichstag elections on September 14, 1930 are a milestone in the history of the Weimar Republic, and not only because their outcome revealed the crisis of bourgeois parliamentarism even to its staunchest supporters. The change in the correlation of seats won by the political parties is incomprehensible, unless we analyse the deep-going socio-political changes indicated by the election results, which presage grave political developments and violent class explosions. The outcome of the Reichstag election confused those who are accustomed to dealing exclusively in terms of parliamentary combinations and are blind to the realignment and struggle of class forces behind the shifts in the system of political parties—a realignment that has been under way since the November revolution of 1918.

Eager to mitigate the impression created by the election, the Social-Democratic press has joined the papers supporting the Brüning government in claiming that the radicalisation of the masses is no more than transient. The purpose of this is to tranquilise the stock exchange, which reacted to the elections with a drop in German papers, notably those released under the Dawes and Young plans, to reassure the foreign, especially U.S., interests which have been plying Germany with now markedly shrinking loans, and to set at ease those sections of the German bourgeoisie who had hastened to transfer their capital abroad and remove themselves to Holland and Switzerland. The propaganda is also naturally designed to minimise in the eyes of the people the acute polarisation of class forces, unavoidable and typical in face of the world-wide economic crisis.

Though the Young Plan somewhat reduced the reparations imposed by the Dawes Plan, it has failed to mitigate Germany's economic and financial plight, while adding to the contradictions of German capitalism, especially because it was put into operation during the burgeoning crisis. With her balance of payments almost invariably passive, Germany has so far been paying her reparation annuities solely out of foreign, primarily American, loans. To transfer annuities regularly in future under the Young Plan out of domestic resources, she will have to boost exports by about 5,000 million marks, meaning that German capitalists have to sell their merchandise at prices even lower than the extremely low prices prevailing in the crisis-afflicted markets of today.

On the other hand, the competitive capacity of German capitalism depends on the organisation of production. The acute competition generated by the crisis faces the German bourgeoisie with the problem of accumulating capital and, consequently, maintaining the rate of profit. To accomplish this, it has to force up the productivity of labour, while reducing wages. The aim is clear: to shift the heavy burden of the Young Plan and the profound economic crisis on to the working people.

In a memorandum on November 23, 1928, issued to substantiate the revision of the Dawes Plan, the German Government pointed out "that a final accommodation of the reparations problem is possible ... provided the living standard of the people of Germany is not reduced". This was empty talk with but demagogical purport. On accepting the Young Plan, the bourgeoisie mounted a determined offensive on the living standard of the workers, while the government launched a financial reform designed to cover the 1,000-million mark deficit. The emergency bill enacted by the Brüning government under §48 of the Constitution (published end of July 1930) provided for obligatory contributions by employees and civil servants, retrenchment of some items of the estimates, a tax on unmarried citizens totaling 110 million marks and a 5 per cent increase of the income tax.

This accounted for but 400 million marks, with the remainder to be raised by reducing the expenditure stipulated by social legislation. Seasonal workers, for example, were in effect totally deprived of unemployment relief, the time of previous employment essential for qualifying for relief being considerably lengthened, and a reduction was planned in unemployment relief for the higher paid workers, while young workers were for the most part effectively cut off. The whole system was so patterned as to deprive the majority of unemployed of any assistance, which was moreover considerably reduced. And the blow struck at medical insurance was more drastic still.

The government lowered taxes on big capital, shifting some of the tax burden on the people (tax on beer, tobacco, and the like) and envisaging new taxes amounting to some 526 million marks. Import of cheap frozen beef was banned and duties on all other farm products were raised to protect the interest of the big and medium farmers.

An assault was mounted on workers' wages. "In the first ten months of 1929 the income of the German workers was 85 per cent of the living minimum," wrote statistician Robert Kuczynski, adding: "At no time in 1929 did the worker's weekly wage suffice to feed and clothe his family. The worker's income was 15 per cent below the living wage."

As time went on, Brüning's offensive, backed by the Social-Democrats, added to the workers' troubles. Calculations based on the set of measures taken after adoption of the Young Plan (wage reductions, higher indirect taxes, climbing food prices caused by the steep rise of customs duties on farm products, deductions for social insurance, etc.) reveal that real wages dropped by about 20 to 30 per cent.

The deteriorating crisis means more unemployed. The mounting unemployment affects greater segments of working people, pulling the rug from under the feet of the petty bourgeoisie. The agrarian crisis, in the meantime, brings into motion the mass of farm labourers and small peasants.

Germany, gripped in the vice of the Versailles system and depressed by the Young Plan, is the focus of the basic post-war contradictions. The class struggle was extremely acute. May-day battles, endless demonstrations of the revolutionary workers, a powerful and persistent tide of strikes and stronger trade union opposition, on the one hand, and the unfolding of fascism and police terror, on the other, coupled with a general capitalist offensive supported by the Social-Democrats on the workers' standard of living, low though it is, and the outcome of the communal elections and of those to the Saxony Landtag—cumulatively, all these things highlighted the situation on the eve of the portentous elections of September 14..

Just like the American reformists, and not only reformists, construed "prosperity" as something immanent in U.S. capitalism, so too the German bourgeoisie, let alone the German reformists, tried at first to present the crisis in the United States as something purely local, something that might even enliven Germany's economic scene. The latter point of view was fatuously based on the slight and transient improvement of the money market in Europe after European capital participating in New York stock exchange operations flowed back to the continent. The facts soon shattered these illusions. The U.S. crisis spread throughout the capitalist world, adding greatly to the economic crisis in Germany, connected by a thousand threads with U.S. capitalism.

German policy-makers admitted this connection between Germany's dire economic straits and the world capitalist crisis. The Berlin Economic Institute, which published its report at the height of the election campaign, saw no sign of a possible improvement. On the contrary, referring to sinister symptoms of a further drop, it predicted that unemployment would continue to spread, estimating that the jobless figure would climb to 3,500,000 by the end of December 1930. Considering the apologetic posture of the Institute and its specific computation methods, it is safe to say that the figure will be surpassed, and quite considerably at that.

The Institute described the situation as a "deep depression", whereas all the facts show that German capitalism plunged into a crisis in the latter half of 1929. There is every economic indication that the crisis is growing still more acute, that unemployment is swelling, that it is spreading structurally and affecting more segments of workers, making the position of the petty bourgeoisie still more precarious. The agrarian crisis is afflicting farm labourers and small peasants. Higher taxes, an unprecedented rise in customs duties in the interest of big farmers, reduction and for some categories even full repeal of social insurance, and the drop in wages by 15 to 20 per cent—all this adds to the gravity of the crisis, with monopoly capital endeavouring to restore its bloc with the big landowners and shift the burden of both crisis and reparations on the general public. The economic crisis has developed into a political one, as evidenced by the social changes and political realignments after the September 14 elections and by the general course adopted by monopoly capital, the governing force in modern Germany.

Though it is backed by the Social-Democrats, monopoly capital has not abandoned its project of a fascist dictatorship and is buttressing its military organisations of the Stahlhelm type. Calling on the Social-Democrats to take part in the government, monopoly capital expected their help in revising the Weimar Constitution and implanting fascism by legal means. By participating in the grand coalition, the Social-Democrats could stay in power until the minimum programme of German capital was realised. In the meantime, monopoly capital mobilised the social forces and consolidated its more immediate guidance and influence by fascist dictatorial methods. The enforcement of §48 of the Constitution, the efforts to extend the powers of the President, the enactment of emergency laws depriving German workers of their gains—this, coupled with the high tide of revolutionary sentiment among workers, meant that Germany approached the elections amid bitter class contradictions (as one industrialist, a member of the People's Party, put it, Germany was entering a stage of dictatorship —Right or Left).

The capitalist makers of policy take a sober view of the impending class battle, at least from their class standpoint. "Confidence in the state has been dangerously shaken and the prevailing economic plight and unemployment will assume ugly forms in winter," said the Imperial Union of German Industry in its election appeal. The Union suggested consolidating all social forces and political parties of the governing classes for joint struggle against "collectivist experiments". It called for an "effective government ready to make reforms" which would "safeguard and maintain private enterprise". This government, its appeal said, should abandon the "incorrect economic and financial policy" and tackle what the appeal called social reforms and what really implied social reaction by coercive means.

The appeal is not a mere assessment of the situation in Germany on the eve of the elections; it is a demand by monopoly capital of an economic and political programme for an offensive on the working class.

However, the economic crisis did much more than deepen the basic class contradiction of capitalist society, that between the bourgeoisie and the workers. It also bared contradictions within the bourgeois camp. The agrarian crisis had hurt the interests of the East German landowners and the *kulak* element in North Germany. It gave fresh impetus to their campaign for higher rents. In the political sense, it spurred to action the Landbund, which prevailed on the government to set higher customs duties on food imports and carry through an independent policy over the head of the old National Party, the traditional spokesman of the big agrarians. But whereas the big landowners in East Germany wanted higher duties, the peasants in the South and especially in West Germany, which is chiefly cattle-breeding country, wanted lower prices for fodder.

In view of the acute class struggle and the revolutionary activity of the workers, the old capitalist parties were compelled to back the landowners and, helped by the Social-Democrats, enacted the appropriate legislation. Yet some German industrialists opposed the landowners' attempts to lay their hands on more surplus value by raising the price of food products. For one thing, the Imperial Union of German Industry objected to the higher food tariffs, while the influential industrialists of the Rhine and Westphalia helped the agrarians get what they asked for.

This is evidence that the economic crisis sharpened contradictions not only between the workers and the governing classes, but also between the various groups and organisations of the latter. The antagonism was most acute between the heavy and the manufacturing industries, and also between the steel and chemical industries. The chemical industry went to the length of founding a political party of its own. At the same time, the realignment caused by the crisis revealed the incompatibility of the policies of old bourgeois parties and some of the class associations of German capitalism. This came to the surface when the political groups representing the economic interests of the German bourgeoisie and landowners in the old Reichstag attempted to form a bloc. The People's Party, the veteran monopoly capital party of Weimar Germany, suggested a united front of bourgeois parties in the election campaign and in carrying through a common line in the new Reichstag. With certain monopoly groups supporting the fascist movement, this plan revealed that the old parties feared defeat. It was designed to ensure their future in the context of a common leadership for all the capitalist political groups. But the contradictions surfaced in the very first attempt to put the plan into practice.

The Economic Party and the Conservative People's Party, which had branched away from the National People's Party, both with deep social roots among the reactionary segment of the middle and petty bourgeoisie, turned down the mediation proposal of the People's Party leadership. Not until after an agreement was reached in direct parleys was the initiator of the plan, the German People's Party, invited to join the political bloc. When the election campaign began, this bourgeois-agrarian bloc was finally consummated on the seeming basis of the common aim of "consolidating and continuing Hindenburg's reform programme in finance, the social sphere, the economy and the state".

The three-party bloc announced its allegiance to the reactionary Brüning programme effected under the emergency provisions of §48. According to the bloc, the Brüning programme was consistent with "the most urgent needs of home policy to promote the German economy, notably agriculture, to save the German East ... to restore the prestige of the state".

After the bloc was formed, the conservative landowner party set out to buttress its political position by negotiating with the political groups of German *kulaks,* while the industrialists' party entered into negotiations with the State Party, a new political entity.

Since the Centre Party (backed by the Bavarian People's Party, a sister group) is the leading party in Brüning's cabinet, these political manoeuvres before the elections were a desperate monopoly capital attempt to assume control of all the old political alignments of the German governing classes. The "Hindenburg programme" was to have been the common ground for this union, and the fact that the government had begun putting the programme into effect seemed to be an earnest of success. However, the first obstacle arose when the agrarian party gave to understand that it would enter no bloc as a subordinate member, and another arose when the industrial interests came to grips with each other: the German State Party refused to join any bloc sponsoring the Hindenburg programme, although the programme was being carried through by its founders and representatives in the government. This apparent conflict between words and deeds, so common among bourgeois parties, was rooted in the role played by the new party on the German political scene.

The Democratic Party, which had been the nucleus of the new party and came forward during the November 1918 revolution as a champion of bourgeois democracy, polled more than five million votes in the January 1919 elections at the expense of the bourgeois parties of the Wilhelmian epoch, and captured 75 seats. But as the realignment of the bourgeois political groups progressed, the influence of the Democratic Party kept dropping. In the last Reichstag it had only 25 seats and there was every indication that it would wither the most in the heat of the class struggle. This was all the more probable, because by participating in Brüning's government it had in fact forfeited all its salient original features. Even its name, Democratic Party, was incongruous against the setting of the fascist offensive. So the crumbling party entered the lists under a new name, that of State Party.

It was founded by Dietrich, who was Brüning's finance minister, Höpker-Aschoff, the Prussian Finance Minister, and Eugen Fischer, member of countless boards. But its social weight came more from such figures as Bosch, agent of Farbenindustrie, banker Melchior, involved in financial operations under the Young Plan, and Artur Mahraun, leader of the Young German Order, a semi-fascist organisation subsidised by the chemical industry.

That the outdated Democratic Party was converted into the new State Party by merging with the Young German Order corroborates the fact that the old bourgeois parties are at a crossroads, that they cannot discharge their former functions and are trying to meet the situation by "rejuvenating" or turning fascist. I say "rejuvenating" because the September 14 elections showed that the post-war youth are extraordinarily active on the political scene, and I say "turning fascist" because fascism is the only thing that can keep the capitalists in the saddle, for to cope with the acute class struggle they are rejecting bourgeois parliamentary democracy.

If the State Party refused to join the bloc of Right bourgeois parties, this was not because its programme differed in any of the essentials from the Hindenburg programme. It was colourless and vague. The concept of "social capitalism" which it coined is, in effect, the same old system of capitalist relationships which all the political parties from National-Socialists to Social-Democrats would be eager to safeguard. It is only the tactical relationships with the latter that draw the line of demarcation. The State Party's refusal to formally join the Hindenburg programme bloc (that it is in Brüning's government makes it a partner all the same) is rooted in the contradictions between individual groups of big German capital and in the two trends operative in the common struggle for domination.

The fact is that some monopoly groups, chiefly of the chemical industry, represented in the State Party, want to retain their independent political position vis-à-vis heavy industry, strongly represented in the People's Party. But that is not all. Though it agreed to all the points of the programme pushed by the three-party bloc, the State Party refused to sign it on the ground that it was associated with Hindenburg's name. So the scheme of a bloc of all the major bourgeois parliamentary parties foundered.

From the standpoint of capitalist class interests and the objective trends of the political realignment, this failure afforded freedom for subsequent manoeuvre. The German bourgeoisie is not yet ready to burn the bridges linking it with the Social-Democrats. "In the hard times ahead," said an influential paper, "these bridges will still serve a useful purpose."

The Catholic Centre Party, the most complex and interesting phenomenon on Germany's political scene, reflects the general processes of modern German socio-political life in view of its motley composition and voting potential. This big party, which draws its strength not only from the Catholic Church, but also from mass organisations of different kinds, has kept considerable segments of the petty bourgeoisie and the industrial workers under its direct and stable control. But the determinative role in the Party is played by the wing consisting of industrial tycoons and representatives of big monopolies.

Some three years ago, the methodical bourgeois offensive against the working class, conducted with the connivance of the Centre Party, caused unrest among Catholic workers.[1] The leaders of the workers' wing in the party were compelled under public pressure to oppose the party leadership and demand adherence to a "social policy". Subsequent events showed that the Centre Party leaders surmounted the "Left" trends of the Catholic trade unions and other organisations mirroring the mood of the workers and set a reactionary course in the interest of big capital. The Centre picked Brüning, who as Reichschancellor dissolved the Reichstag and mounted a capital assault on the workers under the emergency provisions of §48. It also charged Stegerwald to mount an offensive on the workers' interests in his capacity of labour minister.

The short space of time since the crisis in the party showed clearly the purpose of its political line. Time showed also what means it employed to consolidate: Stegerwald, grown "rebellious" under the Catholic workers' pressure, was given a chance to enter the government, and betrayal of the workers' demands served as the brake the Centre leaders had clamoured for. The betrayal only accentuated the sharpness of the contradictions: as the September 14 elections showed, the Communist Party made gains in some of the bigger working-class areas at the expense of the party of Catholic reaction. The organ of the Catholic unions, which a mere two or three years before charged the party leadership with deceiving the Catholic workers, came out in vigorous defence of Stegerwald's policy, backing Brüning's dictatorial moves and garnishing the dish with anti-Semitic demagogy that equalled the Jew-baiting tactics of the Hitlerites. This change of face is typical of the class polarisation under way in Germany.

Brüning and the other Centre Party leaders dissolved the Reichstag in the hope that the Right bourgeois bloc would gain strength and form a government capable of carrying through the capitalist offensive without the aid of Social-Democrats. The latter lost no time in agitating against the Brüning cabinet, but as the elections approached became increasingly importunate in offering their services, betraying the fact that their blasts at Brüning had been a smokescreen. Brüning, meanwhile, knew from the previous

---

[1] See earlier chapter, "Break-up of the Government Coalition in 1928".

Reichstag that the Social-Democrats, rather than the nationalists, were saving the day for the government by their
abstentions in parliament. Shortly before the elections,
Social-Democrat Braun, head of the Prussian Government,
offered Brüning "the assistance of Social-Democracy" in
just so many words, proposing "positive co-operation".
Severing made an identical offer and devoted his election
speech on the radio to demonstrating the need for co-
operation with the ruling element for the sake of "nation-
wide solidarity", the "supreme obligation and virtue" of all
classes.

Old Kautsky, too, in an article on the eve of the elections, argued on theoretical grounds that agreement with
the bourgeois parties was essential, his exposition being of
the same low standard as his latest theoretical constructions.
Agreement is essential, he averred, because "National-
Socialists and Communists alike are pursuing the same aim
of ruin and plunder". Shabby talk. Kautsky called for
agreement with the "old parties" of the bourgeoisie because,
he argued, "the notion that the propertied classes alone
are interested in normal production is a mistaken one".
The old renegade deliberately closed his eyes to the fact
that the "old parties", having lost influence, were seeking
salvation not in bourgeois democracy, but in supporting the
reactionary, aggressive policies of German imperialism.

Vorwärts, the central organ of the Social-Democratic
Party, wrote on the day of the elections in an article entitled "Long Live Social-Democracy":

"In the old Reichstag the Social-Democrats followed a
policy of reconciliation and are prepared to do the same
in the new Reichstag. . . . If the middle-of-the-way parties
want to return to untroubled constitutional development
after the elections, which is the soundest thing for the
economy, Social-Democracy is ready to come to their aid."

However, the Social-Democrats did not confine themselves to forthright overtures and warned German capitalism of lurking dangers. If the Social-Democrats are not
invited to co-operate, *Vorwärts* said, the results could be
disastrous, "presaging a battle whose dimensions are as
hard to foresee as it is hard to estimate its effect on the
economy".

The Social-Democrats thus showed greater solicitude for
the fate of the capitalist economy than its own captains.

It was a sight for the gods, but made no impression on the political Olympus of the German monopolies. Brüning answered that they would have to accept the whole of his programme or nothing. Though after the elections the Social-Democrats let it be known that they would condone his entire reactionary programme carried forward under §48, they were left out in the cold.

Monopoly capital followed a different political tack with the ultimate object of installing a fascist dictatorship. "What is on the Order of the Day?" asked the *Deutsche Allgemeine Zeitung*, mouthpiece of the heavy industries associated with the People's Party. And here is the answer it gave, the most exhaustive and firm to date: "No new compromises and no endless talk about coalitions, which cause nothing but indignation among the broad, not even national-socialist, circles and are sure to whip up still more hatred (if this is at all possible) of everything to do with parliament. What we need are firm and effective reforms. The lesson of the elections, the elections of national protest ... can only be the following: effect reforms not only against the Social-Democrats, who have shown conclusively their opposition to these reforms and are now in dread of the Communists, but reforms against parties generally and against parliament."

In the context of class relations, this formula implies that the overhead expenses borne by German capitalism for the existence of Social-Democracy are now, in view of the world economic crisis and acute competitive struggle in the markets, considered too extravagant. Though they have not yet entirely ruptured relations with the Social-Democrats, the monopolies have mounted the attack, leaning on the new political force they have themselves nurtured—the fascist National-Socialist Party.

The attack is proceeding simultaneously on the economic and political fronts. Shortly before the elections, the steel tycoons announced mass dismissals of factory and office workers. Even the Left bourgeois press discerned a political element in this move.

"The methods of hyper-democracy and schematic parliamentarism are being rejected more and more," wrote the *Bergwerkszeitung*, organ of the German mining industry, after the elections. "The broadest segments of the population (first and foremost the bourgeoisie) wish not parliamentary tactics but action; they want not parliamentary impotence, but unqualified clarity, and this even of the hard variety. They have served notice that they want to know nothing of complex deliberation, of 'problems', and the like. What they want is a train of thought and the kind of slogans that are absolutely simple and, precisely for this reason, will enable them to see the underlying causes. The elections were prompted by the economic problem. The present Reichstag will confront the question whether socialist or capitalist thought is to prevail in Germany."

In accordance with this unambiguous approach to the destiny of German capitalism, the *Bergwerkszeitung*, which accuses the bourgeoisie of placidity and defensive tactics, draws a very definite conclusion:

"The industrialists have no choice but to apply their greatly enhanced political dynamism ... which must be manifested above all in the advancement of a strong personality."

If we recall the expressive definition of the mine-owners' newspaper, "politics is a craving for power", little doubt is left as to the methods the big monopoly capital organisations expect to use in their economic and political offensive on the workers, and what political force they intend to back. It is national-socialism, which disguises its nefarious aims behind adroit demagogy about "nationalism" and "socialism". However, the realignment of *political* forces reflected in the outcome of the September 14 elections also implies a realignment of *class* forces, facing the leaders of the German bourgeoisie with complex political and tactical problems of great weight both at home and internationally.

2

The sharpening of class and political contradictions drew more segments of the population into the election battle. The air was charged with trouble. Of the five million who entered the political fray for the first time, over two million had just come of voting age and nearly three million had formerly been passive. The number of voters soared relatively higher in areas with a predominantly working-class population. In some places (notably Thuringia) all 100 per cent of the voters came to the polls. According to surveys made in towns with a chiefly petty-bourgeois population (e.g., Wiesbaden), women voted mostly for the old bourgeois parties or the Social-Democrats. Berlin election statistics bears this out even more conclusively. Communists, however, gained a relatively larger number of male votes.

The elections revealed that the traditional German bourgeois parties have lost the trust of the voters, that the bloc of parties in the Brüning government, or supporting it, has suffered a smashing defeat. If political strength were measured exclusively by the number of votes and seats won in parliament, it would be safe to say that Brüning's bloc is far weaker in the new parliament than it was in the one it dissolved. The elections also betoken a decline for the old party of landholders and some industrialists, the German National Party, which lost almost two million votes. Even though most of its loss went to such *kulak* and petty-bourgeois groups as the Conservative People's Party, the Peasant Union, etc., the drop in their influence is still considerable. Besides, the decline of the old National Party and the appearance of small independent groups is not to be taken lightly. Stresemann's People's Party, the principal party of German monopoly capital, also lost half its voters, polling a mere 4.5 per cent of the total vote, and as little as 1.5 per cent in such constituencies as Oppeln, a working-class district. A similar lot befell the Democratic Party. Its shift fascist-wards and its merger with the Young German Order under the name of State Party did not improve matters.

A study of the figures reflecting the influence wielded by these three bourgeois parties indicates that the petty bourgeoisie is quickly losing confidence in the National and the People's parties. After the November revolution, the Democratic Party served as a barrier which reined in the electors abandoning the old capitalist parties. But not any longer. The September elections showed that the barrier has been torn down by the realignment of political strength, with the D.P. barely polling 1,300,000 votes. Subsequent developments spoke of a progressive break-up: the "Democrats" abandoned the Young German Order to its own ends and, as was only to be expected, went back to their old fold as a faction of the People's Party, spelling the end of the State Party.

The defeat of the three bourgeois stalwarts will appear all the more crushing if we recall the unprecedented animation of the election campaign and the more than two million young voters politically raised in post-war Weimar Germany who plunged with a will into the battle. The appearance of the numerous small and local parties (the Deutsches Landvolk, Sächsisches Landvolk, Landbund, Deutsche Bauernpartei, etc.) is itself evidence of acute contradictions within the various strata of the ruling classes and evidence, too, that segments of the reactionary petty bourgeoisie and the *kulaks* have abandoned the old parties and are trying to create their own political bodies on the basis of the still extant particularist traditions in order to protect their purely local interests.

The relative stability of the Economic Party, which polled nearly 1,300,000 votes, is evidence of the same thing, though it lost some 85,000. To be sure, any loss of votes in the past election, in which the number of voters was far greater than in the previous one, is a revealing factor. The only old bourgeois party to register a gain (of about 400,000 votes) was the Catholic Centre Party, but relative to the general accretion of voters it also fell below the mark, for it polled 11.9 per cent of the total vote in the 1928 election, and this time 11.7 per cent.

A study of the figures in the breakdown by constituencies reveals portentous changes in the class structure within the Centre Party. Though it made gains in a number of areas with a considerable farmer population, chiefly in South-West Germany where it is organisationally linked with the Bavarian People's Party, the Centre lost much of its influence in some areas with a predominantly working-class population. The modest gain in votes there lags far behind the increased political response of the masses and the increase in voters, and does not, therefore, reflect the prevailing state of the Centre Party. Figures showing the percentage of votes polled in relation to the total voters as compared with the same figures for 1928 are therefore far more indicative. Despite the small gain of votes in such working-class areas as Oppeln, Düsseldorf-West, etc., the Catholic Centre there lost 3, 5, 7 and even more per cent of the total votes. This is a sign of flux among Catholic workers, which the Centre endeavours to keep under tight control through the system of Christian trade unions. Yet some of the Catholic workers are abandoning it in favour of the Communist Party, as may be inferred from the Communist gains in the working-class areas of West Germany, which exceed the losses sustained there by the Social-Democrats.

Their few months of dubious opposition in parliament did not suffice to absolve the Social-Democrats from the blame they incurred by their 21 months of political concubinage to the reactionary bourgeois parties, while their social demagogy of the election period, which was coupled with undisguised overtures for further collaboration, failed to convince the masses of any essential distinction between a Müller and a Brüning cabinet. It was the Social-Democrats who made their début in the coalition government with a decision to build a battleship, and they too who resolved the class conflicts in Hamburg, the Ruhr and elsewhere by instituting obligatory mediation in the interest of the employers. They were the ones to raise the question of reducing unemployment relief, they who assaulted social insurance and they who paved the way for a tax on every person—all measures that will weigh heavily on wage-earners.

Furthermore, their vote in the Reichstag saved the day for Brüning and it was they who declared publicly on the eve of the elections that they were willing to go on co-operating. It was they, in brief, who were prepared to place the full weight of the economic crisis and the war contributions under the Young Plan on the workers' shoulders. For all these moves, they lost 600,000 votes and, considering that the total vote climbed nearly 14 per cent and that some of the former followers of the Democratic and other bourgeois parties voted for them this time, their losses among the workers are probably in excess of the one-million mark.

In no constituency have the Social-Democrats held their own. The insignificant nominal gains in Leipzig, Württemberg, Baden and Hessen-Darmstadt do not count, considering the much greater number of voters there than in 1928. In effect, the Social-Democrats there lost ground by respectively 10.1, 9.5, 10.7 and 1.6 per cent. Their losses in the big industrial centres were still greater. If the 5 million new voters are taken into account, the Social-Democrats registered a drop of 28.2 per cent in Berlin, 25.5 in Frankfurt-on-Oder, 28.1 in Breslau, 25.4 in Oppeln, 31 in Westpha-lia-South, 29.9 in Düsseldorf-East and 30.6 in Düsseldorf-West. The loss was also considerable in the agrarian areas, say, East Prussia (31 per cent), where the National-Socialists made a marked advance. As we see, the Social-Democrats thought they made some gains at the expense of bourgeois groups, lost much of their influence precisely among the workers, and it is safe to say that large sections of the working class went over to the side of the Communist Party.

Just two parties—the Communist and National-Socialist —were successful in the September 14 elections. Surveying the returns, the Social-Democratic leadership, which usually calls the Communist Party a party of the lumpenproleta-riat, admitted that "among workers of many industrial areas the C.P.G. is no weaker and even stronger (in six constituencies)" than the old Social-Democratic Party. "We should have the courage," it added ruefully, "to admit this unpleasant fact without embellishments." The "unpleasant fact" is that the September elections indicated in all the industrial centres that the working class is shifting *en masse* from the Social-Democrats to the Communist Party.

The social basis of the S.D.P. has shrunk and is now absorbing increasingly more petty-bourgeois elements, while communist influence on the working class is con-tinuing to grow. The Communist Party has registered substantial increases in all constituencies, especially in areas with a predominantly working-class population, where the realignment of class forces came into evidence most tangibly. In many areas the Communists are far ahead of the Social-Democrats. In Oppeln, for example, the Com-munist vote totalled 111,000, and that of the Social-Democrats 62,700, in Merseburg 205 and 160 thousand, in Düsseldorf-West 176 and 119 thousand, and in Düsseldorf-East 321 and 169,5 thousand, respectively. To some extent, though far from sufficiently, the Com-munists have also registered gains in the country's farming areas among labourers and some sections of peasants. In industrial areas their influence on the workers has soared, exceeding that of Social-Democrats in some places and in some even the combined influence of Social-Democrats and National-Socialists. The returns in the workers' quarters of Berlin are highly revealing, for there the Social-Democrats and National-Socialists combined polled less votes than the Communist Party. The overall returns for Berlin show that every third vote was Communist and that no party polled as much as the Communist Party (738,986).

The Communist programme of national and social emancipation, which outlines the way for combating German and international capitalism, the revolutionary way for combating the Versailles Treaty and the Young Plan, won a total of 4,600,000 votes.

With the National-Socialists gaining more followers, the steep rise in Communist Party influence means that the polarisation of class forces has become more rapid.

The unprecedented success of the National-Socialists (who made a nearly 700 per cent gain since the last elections) is a complex thing. Large sections of the petty bourgeoisie, farm labourers, some of the farmers and the backward part of the workers who had previously voted for the old bourgeois and Junker parties or had been politically inactive, ranged themselves behind the nazis. So did a considerable number of young people (chiefly white-collar workers) who went to the polling booths for the first time in their lives.

These social segments were activated by the economic crisis, the burdensome terms of the Young Plan imposed on Germany by the victor-powers and shifted by the German bourgeoisie on to the people. The voting was a protest, indicating that the masses could no longer bear the existing state of affairs. But although the majority of those who cast their vote for the National-Socialists thus expressed their opposition to prevailing conditions, their hopes and aspirations are vague and varied—as varied, in fact, as their social background. The fascist victory stemmed from the facile nazi social and nationalist demagogy and the generous financial backing of the monopolies.

The German capitalists are fostering a new political agency to use the mounting social discontent for their own ends and establish a frankly fascist dictatorship to contain the working class and its vanguard, the Communist Party.

"Increasing the workday by another half-hour would act as a miracle," wrote the *Deutsche Allgemeine Zeitung* soon after the election. But the path to this miracle is to be cleared by smashing the revolutionary movement, by violence, in face of the rising militancy and preparedness of the workers and the growing influence of the Communist Party. This was exactly what the nazi battalions were for, who had managed to marshal 6,500,000 votes by playing on nationalist and anti-plutocratic sentiments. The international stock market was uneasy; it had good reason to interpret the nazi victory, on the one hand, and that of the Communists, on the other, as the effect of extreme strain in class contradictions, and reacted by pressing down German papers. But the far-fetched nazi demagogy which paid off so surprisingly in the elections, put the nazi chieftains in a quandary, and also troubled certain bourgeois quarters.

"The National-Socialists," wrote the *Deutsche Allgemeine Zeitung,* "are captives of their own agitation. It would be better for them to have entered the Reichstag in lesser numbers. With 50 or 60 seats they could depart more easily from their line, at least in economic matters. With 107 seats they will have to stick to their programme in all respects, because numbers oblige." This was one way of telling the nazi movement that it better abandon its demagogy in economic and social matters, and show its true face.

The break-away from Hitler of the "revolutionary" Strasser group in Berlin is indicative: a small group of nazis realised that their leaders had sold themselves to those whom they professed to be fighting. But the top bourgeoisie was troubled by an entirely different thing: the aim was to help Hitler abandon all his quasi-socialist talk and act as a political weapon of capitalist reaction with the least possible loss of influence among the people. "Many voted for the National-Socialists," wrote the *Deutsche Allgemeine Zeitung,* "because they were sure their socialism should not be taken too tragically. Indeed, if the National-Socialists come to power, the socialist aspect will quickly be jettisoned." The mouthpiece of heavy industry is afraid Hitler and his associates will not cope with the opposition quickly enough. "The Social-Democrats," it said, "have at least run aground with their socialisation; but the National-Socialists are only beginning. They haven't even paid for their tuition."

It appears that Hitler and his clique, procreated to fight the working class, are expected to furnish guarantees that they will cope with the deceived masses and carry through the capitalist offensive against the workers.

"Those who want a hand in this programme," wrote the *Bergwerkszeitung* after the elections, "should be invited. . . .

This applies equally to the party which scored the biggest success in the last elections, which will therefore, according to parliamentary procedure, be inducted into the new government and which has already declared its consent. The latest elections showed that national-socialism recruits its forces not from socialism, but from the bourgeoisie. The sooner national-socialism is politically enlisted to assume responsibility, the greater will be the chances of keeping it . . . within politically tolerable bounds. If, on the other hand, no responsibility is placed on it . . . it will sooner or later gain still greater success, and will hardly be able to assume political responsibilities without a grave upheaval, for then the party will, at least externally, have to become a revolutionary party, whereas now it can still adopt a conservative ideological stance."

Hitler went through the motions of rejecting the offered opportunity. Responding to the feelers put out by Alfred Hugenberg's nationalists on forming a joint faction in the Reichstag, he said pompously that his "social revolution" party would have nothing to do with Hugenberg's party of "social reaction". It was the only thing he could say a few days after the elections. The nazi struggle for power was still in its initial stage and he could not afford to go back on the election demagoguery so soon.

Yet influential bourgeois groups feared that nazi demagoguery might go too far and the cost of the fascist coup might prove too heavy. Charles F. Speare, editor of *Consolidated Press Association* closely acquainted with top financial and industrial quarters in Berlin, who observed the elections in Germany, noted in one of his reports that industrialists had helped the National-Socialists to power, though the flames they had kindled may turn the tables.

The bourgeoisie, and not in Germany alone, was dismayed mostly because it understood the implications of the big success scored in the elections by the German Communist Party. The Berlin bankers, Speare wrote, received telegrams indicating that banking circles in New York, London and Paris were of the impression that the Communists had won a smashing victory, polling 1,300,000 more votes than in 1928. But the National-Socialists were antagonistic to the Communist Party, he added, and Hitler presented no threat to either capital or property.

240

This is something the German Government hastened to tell the world. Even Hindenburg referred to the police and Reichswehr as dependable keepers of the law. Hitler, too, declared at the Leipzig trial of Reichswehr officers who had organised nazi cells in the army, that he had no thoughts of an armed coup and that his militant programme was designed to win the "hearts of the German nation". Should Hitler have said that by his fascist third Reich he meant the kingdom of God he would have surprised no one, because he was an executor of the wishes of the most bellicose and influential group of German capitalists, who would not venture on an armed, frankly fascist coup until all conditions—and notably international conditions—were favourable. Until then, nazism is to consolidate its forces and conquer the state machinery from within. The nazis endeavoured to win the army, and after the elections asked for the posts not of foreign or finance minister (undesirable because they augur discredit in the eyes of the masses) but posts which will enable them to assume control over the army and police. Already, they are in the Right bourgeois government of Thuringia, have joined the government of Braunschweig after the elections and are out to get top posts in the government of Saxony together with their political allies from the old Rightist parties.

Here is the tactics Hitler has mapped out for the foreseeable future:

1) inducting National-Socialists into the state machine;
2) gaining a firmer hold on the army and police;
3) carrying on the "method of coercion" by building up the armed party units and thus paving the way to power;
4) forming broad "supra-party" organisations to embrace millions of electors.

While waiting until the German bourgeoisie considers propitious an open fascist coup, the National-Socialists intend to broaden their influence organisationally in the machinery of state and among the misguided masses, and at the same time conduct an all-out campaign against the revolutionary working-class organisations.

So far the Social-Democrats have not come round to the idea of a united front with the Communist Party against the increasing fascist peril, and this in spite of demands from their rank and file. Their efforts to preserve the grand coalition with the bourgeois parties in Prussia are, in effect, grinding the axe of the reactionary Brüning government. On returning to the Reichstag after their defeat in the elections, they—who promised their electorate to depose the Brüning cabinet—saved it at the crucial hour and, what is more, sanctioned all the measures Brüning had carried through on an emergency basis under §48. The key to their conduct will be found in their backstage negotiations with top bourgeois quarters, as a result of which Karl Severing, the "strong man" of the S.D.P., was appointed to the post of Prussian minister of interior.

But the class struggle has burst out of parliamentary bounds. It is fought at factories, involving millions of workers. The mammoth strike of Berlin's metalworkers serves notice that revolutionary activity is on the upgrade. The reformist trade union leadership had no choice but to head the strike so broadly supported by the people, but no doubt its purpose was to behead it. This reformist policy is tied up with the general political line expressed in the reformists' support of Brüning and of the set of measures he instituted to shift the ills of the crisis and the weight of the Young Plan on to the workers.

The differentiation of class forces and the deepening of the contradictions of German capitalism were accelerated by the economic crisis. In October 1930, German industry operated just 53.4 per cent of capacity. Unemployment climbed accordingly. A disastrous crisis of government finances broke out, exacerbating the industrial and agrarian crises. Brüning's emergency directive at the close of July 1930, designed to cover the 1,000 million mark budget deficit at the expense of the people, the unemployed included, was a temporary remedy. After the elections the crisis deepened, one of the reasons being the outflow of capital from Germany to the extent of 1,500 million marks, while the payment of reparations consumes about 240 million marks monthly. Since the "gold clause" of the Dawes Plan was waived in the Young Plan, the reparations have in effect risen 20 per cent due to the rising price of gold. Lower world commodity prices are compelling Germany to increase the volume of her exports in order to meet the reparation payments. Furthermore, the foreign debt, which will soon reach the 27,000 million mark, is still growing because part of the German bourgeoisie prefers to export its capital, shipped back to Germany through foreign middlemen with the object of getting a bigger interest—an operation costing Germany much more than 1,000 million marks annually at present. Two thousand million marks in reparations and 1,000 million marks in interest on foreign loans—that is the annual debt which the German bourgeoisie is determined to cover by stepping up the exploitation of workers.

The industrial and agrarian crisis, coupled with the financial crisis and the substantial budget deficit, is goading the German bourgeoisie to attack the vital interests of the working class. On December 1, 1930, the Brüning government promulgated a new emergency law in accordance with §48. Issued to cover the deficit, this law provided for a further 6 per cent salary cut for government employees, stoppage of social relief to young unemployed and a reduction of social insurance for various categories of unemployed, invalids, etc. The law also provided for higher taxes and placed more of the burden of social insurance on the workers.

The campaign for lower retail prices yielded negligible results. The wage cut, higher taxes, notably the personal tax, and the steep reduction of social relief all meant a wage drop of 17 per cent against the 1929 average. By supporting Brüning's harsh financial programme, the Social-Democrats subscribed to the wage cut for government and city employees, and also to the item in the plan which says the existing wage scale creates "insufferably high expenses for the German economy". Viewed from this angle, the manoeuvres of the reformist trade unions to block strikes and get the workers back into the factories are part of the general social-democratic policy of supporting Brüning's government and refusing to co-operate with the Communist Party for workers' interests and united action against the fascist peril. Small wonder that Otto Braun appealed for readiness to back an "unpopular policy".

None know better than the bourgeoisie that the Communist Party is the only force that rallies the working class for revolutionary struggle against capitalism and fascism. Though it does not reject the services of Social-Democracy, which is losing its hold on the masses, the bourgeoisie is banking on fascism which, among other things, has acquitted itself creditably in the eyes of the capitalists as a strike-breaker during the walk-out of Berlin's metalworkers.

As the class struggle grows fiercer and the "unpopular policy" of the Right-wing Social-Democratic leadership gets more unpopular, still more workers will turn their backs on the S.D.P. In the meantime, bourgeois papers are wondering how long the nazis will succeed in befogging the masses with their demagogy. "Possibly," said the *Kölnische Volkszeitung*, "the national-socialist wave will still mount, but it is no less possible that it will break up against the communist shore."

The fight for influence among the masses is now the most vital and the most pressing problem of the German communist movement. Nazism is the chief enemy of the German workers, and of the nation as a whole.

1930-31

Part Three

THE THIRD REICH:
AGGRESSION AND DOWNFALL

1

In the old university town of Freiburg near Germany's south-western frontier at a colonial congress in June 1935 the audience heard the speech of Bavarian *Statthalter* Franz Xaver von Epp, a typical German militarist and active member of the old fascist guard. Once more, Germany's colonial claims resounded in the world. At about the same time, at another extreme point, the city of Königsberg in Germany's north-east, there gathered the annual convention of the People's League of Overseas Germans, a nazi organisation headed by Rudolf Hess, Alfred Rosenberg and Joseph Goebbels.

The League's main purpose is to promote the grasping ambitions of the German imperialists in Europe. So the coincidence in time of the two gatherings may have been unintentional. Yet it is indicative, while the venues of the two seem to symbolise the directions in which fascist Germany is laying her plans. While plotting its eastward drive—capture of the Baltic states and war against the Soviet Union—Hitler Germany is not giving up its designs in the opposite direction. On top of this, it is nurturing plans for large-scale colonial acquisitions.

"Speech is silver, silence and action is gold," writes Manfred Sell in a book agitating for a nazi colonial policy.[1] There he is right. For a number of tactical considerations nazi Germany is reluctant at this juncture to lay the accent

---

[1] Sell, *Die neue deutsche Kolonialpolitik*, München, 1933.

too strongly on her colonial ambitions. At any rate, the latest congress in Freiburg got relatively little publicity in the press: German diplomacy was preoccupied talking with Britain on naval issues and, understandably, the nazi papers avoided complicating matters with colonial claims which, in the final analysis, were aimed chiefly at Britain. The efforts to revive German naval power are being indicated by the wish to buttress positions in the Baltic, implying eastward expansion. But it is more than clear that the new naval arming is only the initial phase in a more general revival. Nazi Germany, which is building up immense striking power, has much more far-reaching intentions than a drive eastward. It has other objectives, and the drive for colonies interrupted by the setback in the 1914-18 war is not the least of them. The nazis are priming for a redivision of the world.

Decades ago, on April 24, 1884, the first chancellor, Prince von Bismarck, announced that the German Government would protect the colonial concerns of Lüderitz in South-West Africa, giving a formal start to German colonial policy, riding on the crest of the quickly growing German capitalism which had later than others entered the club of colonial powers and was therefore more vociferous in its demands for a place in the sun.

At the close of the 19th century the world was already shared out among the bigger imperialist powers, and Germany received the least lucrative of the possessions, whose economic, political and strategic worth was reduced by their being scattered. This created difficulties as regards their exploitation, defence of communication lines and conflicts with rival colonial powers. Needing immense governmental subsidies, covered naturally out of the taxpayer's pocket, the colonies entailed considerable financial and political outlays in the first stage which, it may be said, dragged out substantially. And this instead of the expected limitless economic advantages.

But as German imperialism expanded, its colonial appetites grew too, until Bernhard Bülow, the Foreign Minister, one day enunciated in the Reichstag the general problem of redividing the world. This clearly weighed and openly defined idea of an inevitable struggle for redivision was backed up by a naval policy envisaging a huge fleet alongside the expanding land forces.

By the end of the 19th century, sucked into the vortex of colonial policy fraught with conflicts and wars, the German Government made no bones about backing the colonial movement. At first it was pioneered by a few political maniacs, colonial adventurers and Hamburg tycoons. Its ideological leaders were missionaries and doctors of theology. Literature appeared in the late 1870s advocating colonial conquests on grounds ranging from the theological and "ethical" to the economic and strategic, widely employed to this day with only slight variations in German colonial propaganda. The nazis have picked them up wholesale, admittedly with certan modifications.

The nazi plan of conquest as set out in a series of official documents and statements, matches in scope and scale the programme of redivision nursed by the leaders of German imperialism during the First World War, although the two are not identical. Yet the old programme was so extensive that its colonial section, for example, is still being judiciously concealed by official quarters.[1] It has become public knowledge, however, that detailed plans submitted by the Colonial Society to the government in 1916 advocated seizure of coaling stations, cable posts and communication lines in various parts of the globe and envisaged the need for occupying a large colonial hinterland at each of these points. In particular, the German imperialists nursed the idea of a vast colonial empire in Africa with a large and independent army that would, if necessary, wage its own wars without help from the metropolitan country.

Although the transition of German imperialism from its "continental" policy to *Weltpolitik* was tied up with the acquisition of strategic positions in the Far East, its principal colonial interests were throughout its history centred on Africa. This does not go to say that other spheres of exploitation commanded less attention. In some fifteen years it made considerable inroads into certain parts of China, the Pacific basin and, economically, into South America, notably Brazil and most of all—both politically and economically—into Asia Minor. But at all times its

---

[1] See F. Fischer, *Griff nach der Weltmacht,* Düsseldorf, 1961, a well documented investigation showing the vast plans of German conquest in 1914-18. It devotes considerable space to the colonial programme.

fight for influence in Africa was particularly intensive. The uprisings there were put down brutally, yet the German colonialists pleaded that their imperialist rivals—Britain and France—employed similar methods, methods of total annihilation, in similiar circumstances.[1]

In the quarter-century of its rule over African colonies, German imperialism managed to exterminate several tribes, and particularly, as we know, the big Herero tribe. But despite rapid rates of economic exploitation, Germany made relatively little headway. Trade statistics show that her colonies, five times as large in area as the metropolitan country, played a minimal role in the German economy, expanding in the fifteen years before the world war of 1914-18 from 46,600,000 marks to a mere 319,170,000 marks. The part played by the African colonies in foreign trade, let alone economic development, as we see, was only a minor one. Capital invested in various colonial enterprises aggregated a relatively modest 505 million marks in 1912. In spite of this, or perhaps precisely because of it, the German imperialists fought on with extraordinary tenacity for their economic and political positions on the African continent. Although, as we have shown, the overall scale of German interests there was both relatively and physically negligible, the rate of economic development held out promise. For example, plantations expanded from 11,000 hectares in 1896 to as much as 179,000 in 1913. The capital invested in colonial enterprises increased nearly ninefold in the same period. The railways expanded most rapidly, growing in a matter of twenty years, between 1894 and 1914, from 14 to 4,176 kilometres. Trade, too, despite its insignificant volume, registered a staggering rate of growth. German emigration, however, fell far short of the expectations nursed by the makers of German colonial policy. At the crest and during the recessions of the migration wave, emigrants from Germany avoided the colonies, which were climatically unattractive, and streamed chiefly to the United States and, shortly before the war, to Brazil.

Cumulatively, all these factors spurred the German imperialists to securing still higher rates of monopoly exploitation, export of capital, expansion of markets, sources of

---

[1] T. Seitz, "Die deutschen Kolonien", *Zehn Jahre Versailles 1919-1929*, Bd. II, Hrsg. H. Schnee, Berlin, 1929, S. 50.

raw materials and, last but not least, strategic points. What is more, they worked assiduously to acquire new colonies. It was not surprising in the circumstances that Africa, an object of rivalry between Germany, Britain and France, was a frequent source of acute conflicts laden with the seeds of a major war. This was due to the fact, Lenin pointed out, that this group, chiefly Anglo-French, was confronted by "another group of capitalists, an even more rapacious, even more predatory one, a group who came to the capitalist banqueting table when all the seats were occupied, but who introduced into the struggle new methods for developing capitalist production, improved techniques, and superior organisation, which turned the old capitalism, the capitalism of the free-competition age, into the capitalism of giant trusts, syndicates, and cartels".[1]

Germany's colonial possessions, which aggregated 2,900,000 sq. km. populated by 12,300,000 people, were far short of what the German imperialists would have liked to possess. They controlled Togoland, Cameroon, so-called German South-West Africa, German East Africa (Tanganyika), Wilhelm Land, Bismarck Archipelago, the Solomon Islands, Samoa, Palau, a part of New Guinea, Kiaochow and the Caroline, Marshall and Mariana islands. They augmented their influence in Asia Minor through the Baghdad railway concession, stretching their tentacles to Persia and India and trying to win influence in many other colonial and semi-colonial countries, such as Siam, Liberia, Egypt and Morocco. But they wanted much more than that and cast about for new places to export their capital, for new markets to sell their goods and for sources of raw materials which would be all their own.

But the war and the Versailles Peace ended their plans. What is more, they lost the colonies they had, which were promptly shared out among the victor-countries on the strength of League of Nations mandates, with Western Togoland, a part of Cameroon and most of German East Africa (Tanganyika) going to Britain, excluding Ruanda and Urundi which went to Belgium. France gained control over Eastern Togoland, the German possessions in South-West Africa were turned over to the Union of South Africa, New Zealand gained Samoa and Australia—the German part

---

[1] Lenin, *Collected Works*, Vol. 24, p. 403.

of New Guinea, while the Caroline, Marshall and Mariana islands were claimed by Japan.

Though it lost all its colonial possessions, German imperialism survived and began growing muscle for a new redivision of the colonial world.

2

The phasing of the post-1918 colonial movement in Germany coincided very nearly with the phasing of German imperialism's recovery from its disastrous defeat. The German bourgeoisie took its cue from domestic circumstances or the international situation in now withholding and now pressing its colonial claims. This was due to the need for disguising its long-term designs, concealing the political purport of its economic measures, diverting the attention of its adversaries in colonial policy matters or, reversely, advancing exaggerated demands in order to obtain small concessions.

Internal political considerations, too, had a part in this tactics. For example, the German Government was in too great a dread of the workers' wrath in the early years after the war to extend support to the colonial movement organised by interested bourgeois quarters. The colonial groups knew, of course, that in the early stages of the Versailles system the German bourgeoisie was too busy fighting for survival against the rising revolutionary movement to think of any colonial acquisitions. Therefore, they confined themselves to reorganisation, busied themselves with consolidating leadership and used only some colonial slogans retailored to suit the prevailing situation.

The moving spirits of the German Colonial Society consisted of the executives of various export firms, scientists, retired officials of the colonial administration and admirals jobless after their navies were sunk—all of them members of the different bourgeois political parties. Having lost even those of its adherents who had stuck to it faithfully through the preceding 36 years since its foundation, the Colonial Society endeavoured to establish a system of "daughter" organisations. A body embracing the various "colonial leagues and leagues interested in colonies" was founded in 1921. A society of veterans of colonial wars was set up in

1922, and in the autumn of that year there came into being an imperial colonial association comprising the aforesaid organisations in addition to a women's league, a league of colonial soldiers, a colonial economic committee, a colonial union of German nationalists, a women's Red Cross league for Germans residing in colonies, and a society for German settlement and travel. These were joined by commercial firms, transport companies and industrial concerns, which, in effect, subsidised colonial propaganda. An integrated and highly ramified system of organisations came into being, dominated by the German Colonial Society.

Wielding an influence over numerous like-minded bourgeois bodies, the Society launched a propaganda campaign against the colonial provisions of the Versailles Treaty. All its other aims and purposes, as officially formulated, were in essence also focused on this goal. The victorious Entente justified Germany's dispossession of her colonies with the claim that throughout her history she had proved totally incapable of conducting an "enlightened colonial policy". Imitating the German bourgeois historians and journalists who used the much abused war guilt question as an instrument of propaganda for revising the Versailles Treaty and setting the stage for a new imperialist war, the Colonial Society exploited the press and other media to campaign at home and abroad against what it called the "colonial lie". Its purpose was to vindicate the colonial activities of pre-war German imperialism. To be sure, its propaganda made negligible headway at first among the people in Germany proper, let alone abroad.

From time to time, leaders of the victorious Entente spoke of formalising the annexation of former German colonies juridically under League of Nations control. It was against these hints of a full and formal annexation that the German Colonial Society fired its broadsides through the press every time the symptoms appeared. It operated as the organiser of German "public opinion" to spur the government into action: diplomatic interventions and categorical protests. If prior to the signing of the Versailles instruments, it had objected to the system of mandates, terming it a concealed form of dispossessing Germany of her colonies, now the Society became a dedicated champion of that system.

In the early stages, German Colonial Society propaganda was centred chiefly on using the mandate system for its own ends. Before the system was formalised and the colonial mandates were shared out in the name of the League of Nations, interested quarters wanted the German Government to press more vigorously in the international organisation for at least some sort of mandate. But the government was powerless. It could do no more than announce that it was reserving the right to regain the colonies "until a not too distant future." The sponsors of the propaganda campaign, too, did not really hope for positive results. All they wanted was to show that, though defeated, the German bourgeoisie was unbowed and gathering strength, waiting for a suitable moment to renew its claim to a "place in the sun".

The capitalist quarters behind the German Colonial Society were apprehensive of any British or French attempt to convert mandates into total annexation. When word was received that France was poised to annex Togo and Cameroon, the Society organised a protest in the Reichstag, which issued a formal demand that the system of mandates be fully honoured.

Among other things, the Society extended aid and comfort to German subjects residing in mandated territories and to German capital intending to launch out into colonial business.

But by and large, the question of colonial acquisition was platonic in the early post-war period, a period of acute revolutionary crisis when Germany was gripped by inflation, when her economy was on the brink of total collapse and the bourgeoisie was eager to come to terms with the victor-countries at any price in order to stem the rising revolutionary tide. Against this setting, the colonial problem played a most insignificant or, at least, obscure role. This affected the tactics of the leaders of the colonial movement. They appealed to the principles of Wilsonism, tactically consistent with the prevailing balance of strength and the position of the German bourgeoisie, whose militarist and naval fangs had been filed down considerably in the war. The tactical slogan of the day was: revise the colonial provisions through the good services of the League of Nations.

To be sure, even then certain bourgeois quarters endeavoured to take the initial and, so to speak, timid steps of an organisational and economic order. While waiting for better times, Germany set out to renew her commercial ties with other countries, and her negotiations with them concerning trade and navigation reflected a distinct interest in colonial affairs.

The German press connected with the colonial group hailed the new agreement between the Hamburg-America Line, one of the biggest German shipping companies, and its United States counterparts as the first significant post-war blow delivered to the maritime policies of Britain, the principal rival on the colonial scene. But more indicative still was the attempt by Hugo Stinnes, the industrial king of inflation-time Germany, to organise a special commercial concern in association with certain industrial and colonial quarters in the Netherlands with the aim of penetrating into East Africa. Less influential industrial groups were hatching plans of exploiting African colonies in conjunction with French and Belgian capital. To top this, certain German capitalist quarters enlisted American backing in organising regular communications between Hamburg and Africa. These and other facts reported in the French colonial press show that certain attempts were made to come to terms with U.S. capitalists in combating Anglo-Franco-Belgian influence. The French press reported that these German-American quarters were subsidising certain Negro organisations with an eye to winning their support for future colonial undertakings. There also were reports to the effect that U.S. missionaries, who had stepped up their activities in the Belgian Congo, were acting as German agents. True, all these reports, some of them quite amusing, may have been invented by the new colonial bosses. Though it could scarcely dent the armour of the new proprietors, a former colonial administrator and subsequently one of the leading lights of the Colonial Society, one Hans Zache, threatened to keep secret, until Germany got back her colonies, a drug developed by German researchers to treat the sleeping sickness then ravaging Africa. "Warnings" of that sort troubled no one, and if we mention them here it is only to show how impotent the German bourgeoisie was at the time.

In 1923, at a most critical and dangerous juncture for the bourgeoisie, when a new revolutionary outburst seemed to be ripening, colonial demands were heard no more, only to be redoubled after Germany, like the rest of the capitalist world, entered a period of relative stability. The previously platonic, purely perfunctory demands were then gradually supplanted by economic penetration and practical efforts to regain influence in the colonial world. Towards the end of the year, German firms were again active in East Africa. A British colonel Franklin reported early in 1925 that at least ten large German exporters were doing a thriving business in former German East Africa, seeking to resume connections severed by the war, particularly in areas which they had previously monopolised, notably Tanganyika.

Along the coast, especially, German firms re-established commercial ties with the old Indian companies, mostly in the food trade. Made-in-Germany hardware began to appear on the African market, forcing out British imports, which dropped as much as 40 per cent in a matter of twelve months. No headway was made in Zanzibar, but the spadework done there by German businessmen, their agents and middlemen, began to worry British administrators. Imports to Kenya and Uganda were on the upgrade in the first three months of 1925. Britain controlled but 40 per cent of the trade, and her share did not seem to be rising. Yet Germany's 5 per cent (really quite insignificant in volume) showed an upward trend (to 7 and more per cent). In any case, Germany was second to Britain (exporting chiefly metalware and cotton goods).

According to official British figures for 1925, Germany was the third biggest importer to Tanganyika. But if merchandise (of German origin) shipped in from Holland were also counted, Germany would probably share second place with India (about 17 per cent of total imports) behind Britain (39 per cent).

Statistics for the years of relative capitalist stability show that Germany was economically active wherever she could operate on safe juridical ground. In 1927 she moved up from the previous year's fourth place to rank third among importers to Tanganyika. The British press was alarmed, moreover, that she had risen to second place for metalware, showing a decided tendency to overtake Britain. Germany's economic penetration into South-East Africa, another of her former colonies, was also perceptible; whereas total imports there doubled in the latter twenties, Germany's share more than tripled.

German attempts to regain a foothold in colonies she had lost to France and Belgium were less successful, though the new administrators were worried. For Germans access to these colonies was either restricted or totally banned, as in the case of French Cameroon and Togo. Yet, despite the ban, the German share in their commercial turnover was ten per cent and showing an upward trend, although France was determined to block the inflow of German goods and capital.

The methods employed then, shortly after the conclusion of the Versailles Treaty, may be illustrated by the following episode: the French authorities would not allow a German cargo vessel to enter Togo ports, announcing that any ship flying the German flag would be considered a pirate and treated accordingly. When a vessel flying the Norwegian flag steamed in it was also turned back because chartered by a German firm.

But the old German firms soon adapted themselves to the new exigencies. Where they were not allowed to recover lost positions, they looked for alternative ways, producing goods under foreign trade marks, and the like. The business reports of certain colonial firms contain interesting material to that effect.

The German Togo Society, for example, told its shareholders "with deep pain" that it was "standing over the grave of many years of faithful colonial activity". But things looked up. The German Government made available considerable subsidies in partial compensation for the Society's forefeited property. Promptly, the latter amalgamated with "daughter" companies and shifted its business to Colombia. Its Colombian endeavours, however, though reportedly lucrative, did not diminish its craving for Togo. The same is true of the German planters formerly active in Cameroon, notably the Oliwe Pflanzungs-Gesellschaft which resumed business in 1925. The bulk of the former German property in Cameroon was put up for sale in London and thus retrieved by Germans, notably A. Borsig, a large German monopoly firm. Colonial activity yielded dividends described in official accounts as "living up to expectations", and soon German capital spread from Cameroon to Togo.

The German East Africa Society, one of the biggest German firms, adapted itself rapidly to the new state of affairs. On learning that Germany would lose her colonies, it looked for resources to carry on in the then mandated territory. Backed by a number of Rhine banks, it demanded compensation from the German Government for property lost in Africa. Given redress, though the sum was smaller than it had asked for, it succeeded in enlisting certain British capital and spread out from Tanganyika and British East Africa to the Portuguese East African colonies. When an opportunity appeared in 1926 to acquire large coffee plantations (notably in Tanganyika), the concern issued new shares and soon founded a daughter enterprise. But though it had absorbed British capital, the Society was directly connected with the Darmstadt Bank.

The annual reports of Otavi Minen-und Eisenbahn Gesellschaft reveal that its business was on the upgrade, for its rights were recognised by the administration of the South African Dominion.

Yet, even in the best post-war years, German colonial activity was impeded by capital shortages. Top German colonial quarters tried to whet the interest of the banks. Also they looked for various forms of collaboration with foreign, above all American, capital. The New York-based European Shares Incorporated, among others, was backed by German banks. "Daughter" enterprises of big concession societies connected with German colonial quarters, were yet another form of collaboration, notably in the Portuguese colonies of Angola and Mozambique.

Angola was a coveted colony. Twice under secret agreements concluded before the 1914-18 war Britain and Germany proposed to wrest it from Portugal. There were hints after the war, too, during the Anglo-German negotiations over Locarno and the League of Nations, that Angola may, in one way or another, become a German domain. The German bourgeois press discussed the prospect quite candidly. But though the British stand was one of restraint, the undisguised German agitation put Portugal on her guard and she began to resist attempts at buttressing the German economic position in Angola. To get into the colony was difficult, particularly because control over it was, in effect, in U.S. hands, those of Sinclair Oil. Yet Germany managed to get a firm enough foothold there. The Bank of Angola, connected with leading German commercial and farming enterprises and coal-mining companies, though formally Dutch, was, the French press said, largely controlled by German interests. But Germany had many other irons in the fire—Mozambique, Spanish Guinea, Fernando Poo, etc. Having bought back much of its former property in the British part of Togo and Cameroon, and in Tanganyika, German capital set out methodically to expand relations with these mandated territories; a special company, Deutscher Afrikadienst, was launched for that express purpose. Reports of the Ostasiatischer Verein indicate also that German capital was recovering in the Far East, notably China, although clearly it had no illusions about repossessing Kiaochow and knew it was hopeless to join the imperialist scuffle over China.

To sum up, in the late twenties when German capitalism was doing relatively well and had achieved a partial stabilisation and when the German bourgeoisie was beginning to gather strength for an imperialist policy, Germany's colonial aspirations soared.

Militarily weak, lacking a strong army and, more important, a navy, the German bourgeoisie could not hope to carry through an aggressive colonial policy. German imperialism was not yet economically, politically and militarily ready to fight for a redivision of the world, particularly the colonial world. It made the most of all available opportunities, however, to gain a firm economic foothold in the colonies and cast about for means and methods of expanding and strengthening its positions. Schacht's colonial plan was a cogent step in that direction. Its point of departure was that Germany could not expect to regain her colonies, at least in the foreseeable future, or to conduct an independent colonial policy. Schacht pointed out that Germany's colonial interests were so far purely economic and suggested forming an international colonial society through which German capital could participate in exploiting the former German possessions. He even attempted direct negotiations on this score with top banking groups in the United States. But his plan misfired, because the mandate holders were not inclined to relinquish to Germany a "place in the sun" in colonies which they controlled. In Germany, too, the plan was bitterly attacked, because the agrarians and those of the bourgeoisie who had no stake overseas were unwilling to see the country reverting to large-scale colonial activity, while the supporters of the colonial revival would not accept the plan, because it confined itself to economic aims and laid no accent on the importance of thereby reviving German imperialism.

In the meantime, with German imperialism gradually recovering, all colonial plans assumed an increasingly political complexion. Beginning in 1924, the turning point in the history of German post-war capitalism, the colonial issue gained ever greater prominence in the bourgeois press. On the 40th anniversary of Germany's emerging on the colonial scene, the press launched an intensive campaign for repossessing the former German colonies.

When the Imperial Colonial Union sent the League of Nations a telegram asking for the return of Germany's colonies in April 1924, the meaningless demonstration was ignored by almost everybody. But gradually German colonial claims began overspilling into official inter-governmental negotiations. The colonial groups became more active. In the Reichstag elections, particularly, they endeavoured to promote their supporters. During the Dawes Plan negotiations they exerted pressure on the government, demanding that it raise the question of colonies through official channels. It was obvious, however, that the demand was intended as a bargaining point. The policy-makers knew that German imperialism was just beginning to recover and that the first step was to clear Germany of occupation troops. The German Government did, indeed, express its sympathy for the plan to regain the colonies, but did not feel it could afford to raise the issue in official talks.

After the Dawes Plan was adopted, German colonial propaganda was stepped up. Colonies alone, it said, could supply Germany with cheap raw materials which, in turn, would pave the way to greater exports—the only way of fulfilling the Dawes Plan commitments. This was the main argument in favour of a colonial policy and a convention of German bankers expressed itself to the same effect.

Not until British efforts to win Germany for the "Locarno policy" became obvious did the colonial issue become an object of official negotiation. The German Government gave to understand in backstage talks that it was expecting concessions from Britain with respect to Togoland and Cameroon. There were intimations in the press that British diplomacy was inclined to delude the German collocutor with promises of colonial rewards. True, it did not assume any direct commitments. Then, pressure by pertinent

British groups robbed it quickly of its power of speech and it confined itself to platonic expressions of sympathy.

After Germany joined the League of Nations a German delegate appeared in the committee handling the distribution of colonial mandates. This made plain that, having mended its economic and political fences, the German bourgeoisie was determined to resume its colonial ways. The German Colonial Society, which had dragged out an inconspicuous existence in the first few years after the war, broke into the political limelight. When rumours spread that Britain intended to incorporate priorly German East Africa into her colonial empire, the Society organised a protest by German political parties, from the National to the Democratic, in an attempt to form a united front of reviving German imperialism. A colonial programme was spelled out in 1928, published over the signatures of the colonial organisations, the various employers' unions and the top German monopolists. The common immediate goal being to reinstate Germany in the club of colonial powers, the programme had what was a tactically defensive aspect and an offensive one. It expressed opposition to the mandate-holding powers annexing the former German colonies and dragged out of the dust-bin all the old arguments in favour of Germany possessing colonies: over-population and the consequent drive for territory, and the need to have her own raw materials and a source of food supplies. Lastly, the programme declared more or less clearly for the first time since the war what the German bourgeoisie thought equality really meant: a redivision of the colonial world.

As German imperialism grew muscle, the influence of the opponents of colonial acquisition dwindled. The motives for a German colonial policy may have differed in the various sectors of the German bourgeoisie, but all of them stressed that it was necessary. Not the real or imagined arguments invoked by the various quarters are of interest to us, however, but the tactical lines deriving from different assessments of the immediate and more long-term prospects of German imperialism. There were those, it is true, who drew attention to the insignificant place the former German colonies had held in the country's overall economic development and, anticipating considerable political perils, spoke out against acquiring colonies. They pointed

out, among other things, that the national liberation movement burgeoning in the colonial countries could create new,
unforeseeable complications with the undesirable effect
for the bourgeoisie of encouraging the workers' revolutionary movement in Germany proper. These views, some
disguised and others not, by pacifist verbiage, were fairly
widespread among people who, on the one hand, feared
the political risk and, on the other, pressed by the petty
bourgeoisie, balked at the financial and economic outlays
involved.

The more influential bourgeois groups, particularly those
connected with the Rhine industries, thought it wise, for
the time being, to labour for colonial mandates, but not to
lose sight of the ultimate political aim—that of acquiring
full possession of colonies. The extreme Right, meanwhile,
thought all compromise unbecoming and insisted that on
prestige grounds Germany should reject mandates entirely. There ultra-Nationalists, once the nucleus of the Pan-
Germanic movement, thought that if Germany accepted
colonial mandates it would thereby extend *de facto* recognition to the "plunder" of the victor-powers. They advocated economic penetration and all but declared publicly
that war was the only means for Germany to reinstate
herself as a colonial power.

But the quarters with an immediate stake in colonial
expansion, strange as this may seem at first glance, were
more cautious: they recommended a policy of the least political risk with the greatest economic pay-off. They knew
politics cost money and refused to pay with their dividends
for the strident nationalist propaganda and ultra-patriotic
slogans demanding the *immediate* return to Germany of
all that was taken from her. These groups, connected with
the Hamburg and Bremen export firms, were, in a certain
sense, more restrained. Shared by certain other industrial
and commercial groups, this restraint stemmed mostly from
tactical considerations. Better to wait for a more opportune
moment, they reckoned, before making the first big
plunge into independent colonial politics, lest a premature
move upsets the apple-cart and spoils opportunities bound
to arise one day. Furthermore, cautious politicians realised
that it was more profitable for the German bourgeoisie to
expand economic relations in various directions than to tie
itself down to some colonial mandate.

To sum up, the growth of German imperialism whetted colonial appetites and the question of acquiring colonies turned from a simple propaganda device into a basic political slogan of the German bourgeoisie, which speculated more and more over the strategic and tactical means that could put Germany back among the imperialist colonial powers.

Naturally, various colonial plans were gradually tied in with the general foreign policy conceptions of German imperialism. The contradictory development of German imperialism was evident, among other things, in that propaganda and actual efforts to regain colonies were redoubled rather than reduced as Germany's economic condition deteriorated during the economic crisis (1929-33) and economic expansion in the colonies hit serious snags (statistics shows a considerable decline in German trade with the colonial world during that period).

The breakdown of the Dawes Plan was used as an excuse for new demands. Although the matter was never brought up at official diplomatic talks, it was raised time and again in negotiations with influential semi-official quarters as, for example, the conferences of economic and financial experts doing the spadework for the Young Plan. Schacht, a fairly influential personality in the banking and industrial world, put forward new demands. He made payment of reparations conditional on Germany's getting "her own colonial sources of raw materials, which may be created and developed by German means of production, German capital and with German responsibility". His programme was turned down, it is true, and the German Government was compelled to accept the Young Plan irrespective of Schacht's conditions.

At the time of the world crisis, German colonial plans assumed the complexion of a purely political issue pushed vigorously by interested parties, especially the German Colonial Society. By that time, nearly all the bourgeois political groups supported a colonial drive. There were garrulous Reichstag debates in the nature of political demonstrations. With the German bourgeoisie turning nazi and ultra-nationalist, revenge-seeking instincts were cultivated among the petty-bourgeois mass. The influence of the National-Socialist Party kept mounting and the old bourgeois parties, desperately striving to retain their grip, hastened to climb on the nationalist band wagon and drum up the demagoguery which the nazis were thriving on.

The colonial issue acquired sizeable though not altogether top-priority proportions. Von Papen's government of cold fascisation endeavoured to sluice off the colonial clamour. Papen was immersed at the time in clandestine talks with France and Britain on plans against the Soviet Union and did not dare raise the question of Germany's former colonies officially. But he assured the bourgeoisie at home that the time was approaching when the government would take the initiative and demand an "accommodation". Symptomatically, the colonial question, fast nearing a show-down, was associated to a certain extent with the question of relations with the Soviet Union. The renascent German imperialism, waging a fierce preventive war on the working class and extending support to the nazi party, a party of extreme reaction, militarism and war, insisted more stridently on redividing the world. As the National-Socialists, who put the matter in the most brutal form, grew stronger, the official spokesmen of the colonial movement began to seek contacts with Hitler, the resultant negotiations culminating in an agreement on joint political efforts and propaganda for the return of German colonies. The nazis gave fresh momentum to the colonial scheme, ranging very far afield even in this sphere. Colonies became one of the practical aims of German imperialism.

3

The world-wide economic crisis drew a line through one of the main rulings of the Versailles Treaty—that of reparations. The "equality for Germany" slogan on the fascist banners betokened the imperialists' determination to remove all obstacles to the revival of German land and naval power. Coming from the imperialist bourgeoisie, the slogan of opposition to Versailles was nothing but ideological priming for a new armed redivision of the world. The nazi government promptly put down colonies as a key objective of its foreign policy.

Before gaining power the nazi party declared itself the east-oriented force, the anti-Soviet war party, and now had its work cut out in the question of colonies. In his

Mein Kampf, Hitler said that the territorial boundaries of the future Germany would differ substantially from pre-war. He pointed out that he would not limit his task to merely reconstituting Germany within her old-time frontiers. This signified that he construed the question of colonial possessions somewhat differently to what was expected of him by the leaders of the German colonial and political groups in the preceding period. Their aim was to retrieve what Germany had lost in the First World War, whereas Hitler proclaimed a total break with pre-war colonial and commercial policies. He promised a policy of "conquering new territory", and made plain what he meant: "When we speak of new territory in Europe today we must principally think of Russia and the border states subject to her."

This scheme of an eastward drive, this plan of making the Baltic countries an outpost of German influence, this ambition to convert the Ukraine into a colony, were a dominant feature of the nazis' foreign policy and military conception. By the way, it was the subject of talks between the National-Socialist Party and the top German colonial organisations long before the nazis came to power. The colonialists feared that the overemphatic accent on eastward aspirations would eclipse, or at least obscure, the colonial issue, the object of their untiring economic and political efforts. The nazi press was quick to reassure them, however, that the nazi party did not counterpose "eastern" to colonial policy.

This was true. In *Mein Kampf* Hitler did, indeed, define the drive into Eastern Europe as the preponderant task, but did not thereby rule out a struggle for African or other colonies. Vindicating its war preparations by the problem of overpopulation, German imperialism made plain its aspirations of conquest in all directions. "We demand countries and land (colonies) to feed our people and to settle our excess population," said the programme of the German National-Socialist Party. In a special statement in 1931, Hitler pointed out that his party would work "for the return of the main German colonies". He said: "We do not deny the importance overseas colonies may have for re-settling and for supplying our economy with colonial products and raw materials. On no account are we rejecting possible colonial acquisitions in the future, since this would serve the above aims." But he went on to say again that the tasks in Europe held top priority. Subsequently, the question of colonies was elucidated at greater length in the general concept of a redivision of the world and, first and foremost, a war against the Soviet Union. The nazis pointed to two possible ways of resolving the "territorial question".

One way, the main one, was colonisation of the East, "eastern policy", which the nazis defined as "extension of state territory beyond the present eastern imperial frontiers". This implied a policy of conquest, annexation of new land and then colonial enslavement of the Ukraine and the vast Russian expanses.

The other way was overseas colonial policy. Aiming his main blow at the East, at the Soviet Union, Hitler warned against the notion of colonies being the panacea of all economic and political ills assiduously maintained for propaganda purposes by colonial quarters. Falling back on historical experience, nazi literature noted that from the standpoint of population, colonies would not provide the desired outlet: just 5,000 whites lived in German East Africa before the war and as little as 7,000 fifteen years after it, and it was not likely that the figure would swell to any appreciable extent through German immigration. Hence, it could not be expected that colonial immigration would absorb millions, or even hundreds of thousands, of Germans. At best their number would run into several tens of thousands. The bulk of the "overspill" population, the nazis said, would colonise the still-to-be-conquered East of Europe.

This did not mean that the nazis, even in their early years, had no thought of building a colonial empire. They were demanding colonies from the first, arguing that colonies were economically and politically desirable. If no Germans could be exported to colonies, at least German goods could, they said, and if Germany needed raw materials (rubber, cotton, hides, and the like) to boost her exports, the colonies could be an adequate source of such materials. Last but not least, they added, if Germans needed foodstuffs, the colonies could supply cocoa, rice, maize, bananas, tea, tobacco, coffee, beef, etc. All these arguments resembled those of the traditional bourgeois political parties and societies with a stake in colonial policy. But the nazis clothed them in terms more likely to appeal to broader groups hit by the economic crisis.

A party of revenge and war, the nazis stressed vigorously

that Germany needed more, much more, arms on land and sea before she could pursue a colonial policy. Rebuilding a powerful ground army is unquestionably a major act not only in the imperialist struggle for supremacy in Europe, but also in the fight for a new universal imperialist redivision of the world. More directly still is the latter tied up with the nazis' efforts to rebuild a first-class navy.

"Communications between the metropolitan country and overseas possessions is the lifeline of all colonial policy," wrote Manfred Sell, a fascist proponent of colonialism. "If communications are temporarily cut, nothing but naval power will restore them. Naval power is a necessary precondition of colonial policy."

However, this fascist outlook was not an ordinary revival or reproduction of Admiral Tirpitz's old politico-strategic designs. Tirpitz, who created the German navy, thought Germany had to be a first-class naval power before she could take precedence over her British rival. He maintained that to hold her own against British imperialism, Germany had to abandon her aggressive designs in Eastern Europe for quite a considerable period. The nazis have an entirely different view and scorn the old Wilhelmian policy of naval arming. They think the high rate of naval construction under Admiral Tirpitz entirely insufficient. Hitler's naval programme, framed after the 1935 Anglo-German agreement, is modelled to obviate the factors that, in effect, resulted in the virtual inactivity of the German navy during the First World War. Rebuilding its navy, German imperialism intends to regain the colonies it lost in the world war. But that is far down the list of targets it has set itself: what it wants are new territories which were then only objects of its colonial claims.

Doubtless, a further build-up of army and navy will whet the appetite of nazi Germany, though its programme of colonial conquest has always—from the beginning—been anything but modest. True, the nazis did not detail it, and not just because they did not wish to annoy the British imperialists. They were too preoccupied elaborating, and beating the drums of, their European and especially anti-Soviet plans. Yet the nazi press never tired of saying that the mandate desired by influential German colonial quarters would be altogether insufficient, because the demand of a mandate limited the aims and objectives of colonial policy. "German colonial policy has gone bankrupt," Sell says. "Its bearers, the traditionally colonial groups, notably the German Colonial Society, hoped to secure a colonial revision of the Versailles Treaty by a peaceful exchange of opinion. All hopes were pinned on the League of Nations."

Nazi Germany has turned its back on the League. It scoffs at the very idea of a peaceful accommodation. "German colonial expectations connected with the League of Nations," writes Manfred Sell, "are a silly pipedream, just as silly, indeed, as the hope of Germany getting a colonial mandate. No mandates are free, and none will ever be free." He reiterates the thesis already advanced by the ultra-aggressive element: a mandate will not satisfy Germany, for it may be taken to mean her formal recognition of the post-war division of the colonial world, whereas the nazis are nursing plans of a redivision.

German fascism attaches immense political importance to its colonial plans. The nazis think their propaganda of nationalist and militarist ideas, their propaganda of reinforcing the politico-military potential of German imperialism, will benefit. But fanning nationalist sentiment at home and furthering the propaganda of war and revenge, is not all. The nazis think that once they build up a strong army and navy, they will exploit their colonial claims as bargaining points in talks with other countries, blackmailing possible friends and unavoidable enemies in the capitalist camp. The nazi press believes that this approach, based on the growing German militarism, offers promising prospects. The purposes of the nazis' colonial plans, to which they attach increasing political weight, are thus broader than they were in the preceding period, although for obvious tactical reasons official quarters are avoiding any stresses in public statements. First Germany has to become a major militarist power that could speak out as loud as it pleased and compel attention. "This task," Sell says, "is not one of today or tomorrow. It calls for time. But ... a definite moment has to be fixed—the moment when we begin to carry it out. Time is favouring the mandate-holders. Germany should not procrastinate, for delay is not going to make the conditions more favourable."

Indeed, the day it came to power, the nazi party instantly began to follow the policy of ground, air and naval arming, scrapping the military provisions of the Versailles Treaty and setting the stage for a new redivision of the world, particularly the colonial world.

The first year of the nazi dictatorship did not witness any build-up in colonial propaganda. On the contrary. In the first few months after coming to power, the nazi government was almost totally isolated on the world scene and, hoping to build contacts with Britain, toned down the colonial demands. Moreover, it was troubled by the zeal of the colonial quarters. While training all its propaganda guns on the idea of seizing new territory in Eastern Europe, especially the Soviet Union, the nazi press was almost totally silent about the question of colonies. In the early period certain influential bourgeois groups and the political headquarters of the nazi dictatorship scrimmaged behind the scenes over Germany's short-term stand on colonies.

A controversy ensued and even burst to the surface, reaching—in greatly euphemised form, of course—the columns of the fascist and bourgeois press. Those nazis who were, for socio-demagogic purposes, portraying German plans of conquest in Eastern and South-Eastern Europe as something of a boon for the German peasants, the *Bauernschaft*, ostensibly prostrated by land shortages and needing extensive territorial acquisitions, endeavoured to object to colonial propaganda. They did not hesitate to employ anti-imperialist formulas to blame "reactionary circles" for inspiring colonial propaganda, which they rejected, saying that "Germany's destiny is in the East, doubly important to us because Germany is the heart of Europe".

They doubtlessly feared that pronounced German interest in Africa and elsewhere may prejudice the *Drang nach Osten* policy and the anti-Soviet designs. Symptomatically, however, these quarters knew better than to volunteer any categorical judgements concerning nazi foreign and colonial policy. In the final analysis, they pointed out, the matter will be dealt with by the government in conformance with the general interest and the international situation.

Yet the view that colonial plans should not be played up did not find favour among the leading nazis. Hitler told a *Sunday Express* correspondent a few days after the takeover that he was farthest from the thought of rejecting in advance the possibility of claiming colonies. To

Daily Mail correspondent Ward Price, Hitler hinted in 1933 that Germany might, in view of her overspill population, raise the question of colonies, which he hoped would be settled by "peaceful negotiations". Quite early in its reign (1933), the nazi government even attempted to speak out officially concerning colonies in a memorandum submitted by Alfred Hugenberg to a world economic conference in London. The candidly anti-Soviet tenor of Hugenberg's memorandum was firmly denounced by the Soviet Government. The nazi colonial ambitions raised a storm of protest in the French and British press. As a result, the fascist government was compelled to disavow, somewhat ungracefully, Hugenberg's clumsy manoeuvre.

But it did not take long for the nazis to renew their talk about colonies in more definite terms, and in early 1934 there began a fresh vociferous colonial campaign in the nazi press, delving into the aims and methods of fascist colonial policy.

Taking advantage of the 50th anniversary of Bismarck's début on the colonial arena, the German Colonial League gave extensive publicity to the fascist colonial programme. It averred that the nazis had no intention of abandoning the colonial question and that the basic drive eastward did not stand in the way of the German imperialist colonial designs. "No rejection at all!" was the slogan mouthed by Bavarian Statthalter Franz von Epp, who strove to galvanise the political campaign for a colonial policy.

The campaign did, indeed, go off to a rapid start, joined instantly by the old colonial organisations, infused by the nazis with fresh strength, new propagandistic zeal and new political sharpness. A colonial exhibition was held in Cologne in the summer of 1934. The old-time ideologists of German imperialism returned to the stage alongside the newly-fledged nazi functionaries. Among them was long-forgotten Paul Rohrbach, who had vigorously advocated seizures of land in Eastern Europe before and during the 1914-18 war, calling at once for the destruction of Britain's colonial and naval power. In fascist Germany Rohrbach found fertile soil for his old idea that German imperialist ambitions in Eastern Europe in no way precluded the plan for redividing the colonial world. That was the basic point in all official German propaganda under the watchword, "Blood and Land", first formulated by Darré, a fascist

270

ideologist. *Deutsche Bergwerkszeitung,* mouthpiece of German monopoly capital, wrote on March 25, 1935: "We are a 'nation without territory' and are therefore determined to colonise the German east first, but also to press for territory elsewhere in the world."

4

The German fascists know perfectly well that they will not get back their old colonies or acquire new ones in the foreseeable future. Since redivision of the colonial world is, however, a prominent item in their political and ideological programme, they know they have to accomplish two things. To begin with, they are bent on gaining economic influence in the former German colonies, for the headway made there by German capital over the years was largely cancelled out by the economic crisis. German exports fell disastrously and were insignificant by 1932. In 1930, they amounted to 11 per cent of the total imports into French Cameroon and two years later dropped to a mere 5.9 per cent, rising a little in 1933 to 6.4 per cent. In the Congo under French mandate German imports and exports shrank almost to nil. In 1933, German trade there amounted to the trifling sum of 10,000,000 francs, lower even than the 1932 figure. A similarly steep drop was also officially registered in relation to other colonies. Imports from the former German colonies dropped from 20,300,000 marks in 1929 to 5,300,000 in 1932, with exports shrinking accordingly from 19,400,000 marks to 2,200,000. True, 1933 witnessed a small rise (imports amounting to 9,100,000 and exports to 3,600,000 marks). Naturally, there was no question in those years of any export of capital from Germany for investment in the former German colonies.

The decline of Germany's economic influence in her former colonies, a decline even against ten years before, dismayed the bourgeoisie. The press connected with the banking world and the stock market wrote at length about the "patriotic" need, and advantage too, of German trade and investment in the mandated territories. Dwelling on the economic resources of these territories, the nazi press argued that they could meet German needs in many foods and raw materials. A new press campaign began. The nazis appealed to the political sentiments and commercial instincts of those who could be enlisted in exploiting the lost colonies and, much more, recommended with pedantic pragmatism how to gain the maximum profit with the minimum outlay.

The press is printing detailed lists of what should be exported to the colonies, and counsels on how to penetrate from there into colonies belonging to other states, notably Portuguese Angola. Practical advice is given as to effective commercial advertising. More, this commercial advertising is combined with political propaganda. While buttressing their economic position, the nazis are conducting extensive political agitation in the colonies in preparation for a general redivision of the colonial world.

The French colonial authorities are perturbed. The nazis are soliciting the support of Germans living in the former German colonies and, spurning their own racial theories, also of native organisations formed under their auspices. The Deutscher Togobund is one such organisation consisting entirely of Africans. The French press reports that German agents have even succeeded in prevailing on some of the tribal chiefs to petition the League of Nations, requesting that they be put again under German rule. When a German consulate was opened in Dar-es-Salaam, an African demonstration filed past the German swastika-adorned black-white-red flag. The German press, oblivious of past reprisals, is pleased. Priming for all-out penetration into colonial domains, the nazi organisations are eager to build up a local following. No mention is made of this in the press for understandable reasons; only meagre, accidental reports indicate that nazi organisations have stepped up their work even in remote colonial areas. The main accent is on Africa. There the nazis have ambitious designs.

To gain added political influence among the local population, the nazis are using the old but effective missionary organisations. In early 1935, for example, ceremonies were held in Cologne at which two aircraft, *Peter* and *Paul*, were consecrated for German missionary service in Africa and New Guinea.

Summing up, we see that German fascism has in no way abandoned the fight for colonies. On the contrary, it has plunged into the fray, especially after Schacht, nazi Germany's economic dictator, backed by the monopoly press, declared Germany's desperate need in colonies.

The German Government alternately stresses and relaxes its colonial claims, depending on the international situation and its manoeuvres to exploit the existing contradictions between states. In a way, the seeming inconsistencies in the mouthings of individual nazi chiefs is due to these manoeuvres. Soon after Hitler told a *Daily Mail* correspondent, for example, that colonial possessions are a luxury in the existing circumstances, his deputy Rudolf Hess interpreted this as having meant a luxury only for states that have abundant colonies, whereas for Germany they are a prime necessity.

Germany's colonial claims were more frenzied than ever at the beginning of 1935. The outcome of the Saar plebiscite touched off a new eruption of annexationist sentiment, and after the Anglo-French negotiations in London in February the intensified propaganda of German colonial plans was a kind of build-up for separate talks with Britain which the nazis were angling for with the backing of certain influential British imperialist quarters.

At the Berlin talks with Sir John Simon, then British Foreign Secretary, Hitler was reported by the well-informed Italian press to have said that in addition to a "free hand" in the East, to arming, and the like, he wanted back Germany's former colonies in East Africa, particularly Tanganyika and part of the Congo. The Italian press also reported that Hitler had made it plain to Simon that Germany wanted back the colonies that had been turned over to Japan. To be sure, judging by the nazi press, the colonial claims of the German imperialists go very far afield.

For the present, the nazis demand back from Britain, France and Belgium the colonies that once belonged to Germany. But they have an eye on the Portuguese colonies, too, and it is quite possible that a deal is contemplated with Britain to divide up Angola. The nazi press is also raising the question of Australian and New Zealand mandated territories once in German possession.

Besides, nazi writers point out that Japan, "whose vital rights the new German colonial policy certainly honours, will have to appreciate the fact that German demands of her colonies are prompted by no less vital subsistence problems". In short, the German press is saying in so many words that since the uneven distribution of colonies among the big capitalist states had brought on a world war, the way to avert a new war was to satisfy the German claims, that is, give Germany such colonial territory as she had not previously possessed.

For understandable reasons, the demands are couched in relatively restrained terms, but are highly indicative and fall in with the general tendencies pursued by the German imperialists in their bid for a redivision of the world.

The nazis hope to benefit by the contradictions prevailing between other imperialist states. In a survey of the immediate goals of German foreign policy on May 21, 1935, Hitler endeavoured to drive a deep political wedge between Britain and France—who had registered coinciding views at their London conference—and to blow up the diplomatic front that came into being at the conference in Stresa. Hence his declaration that German naval rearmament was in no way connected with German colonial claims. Hitler wanted to set at rest the minds of Britain's rulers, adding that a colonial agreement was practicable between his country and Britain. Naturally, it would be oriented not only against the Soviet Union, but also against France.

"German colonial policy," Sell wrote, "will impede the further colonial expansion of France. Thereby, first and foremost, German policy serves the ends of Britain." Portraying German diplomacy as Britain's valuable ally, the nazis hint that Britain should, for "services" rendered, help Germany get back the new mandated territories of British dominions.

Certainly, the nazis also expect to profit by other imperialist contradictions, namely, the U.S. antagonisms vis-à-vis Britain and the struggle between Italy and France. Further German colonial claims will no doubt be directed against the interests of France, but also those of Britain. But *fascist Germany's basic designs are associated with a war against the Soviet Union*. Among other things, Germany expects to get certain compensations in the Far East if the Japanese imperialists go to war against the U.S.S.R. In any case, it is clear that the nazis have hitched their colonial plans to the question of an anti-Soviet war. "It stands to reason," wrote the *Kölnische Zeitung* on January 12, 1934, "that we shall not get our former colonies back in the immediate future. The wheel of history never turns in reverse. The German nation is not likely to satisfy its colonial demands without great political upheavals."

This is meant to say that German fascism has made up its mind to turn "the wheel of history" to a world war and obtain satisfaction for its colonial grievances and, moreover, make a general bid for world supremacy.

What the nazis are indeed priming for is a war to redivide the world. Seizures in Eastern and South-Eastern Europe will not block colonial seizures in other parts of the globe. Given a large navy, a huge army and a powerful economico-military potential, colonial acquisitions would facilitate expansion eastward in Europe. On the other hand, conquest in Eastern Europe, against the Soviet Union, may give impetus to the fight against the big Western capitalist powers, notably to expedite colonial conquest. "German commercial policies, territorial acquisition in the East and German colonial policy complement each other," says Sell. "Clever and skilful German policy will secure formidable economic and political advantages in Eastern Europe and, possibly, will even win allies for its colonial plans, provided, of course, nothing restrains us in questions related to our 'eastern policy'. The colonial issue has gained influence on the historic mission of the Germans in Central and Eastern Europe."

It is quite true that the German imperialist colonial policy cannot be dissociated from the policy of expansion in Eastern and South-Eastern Europe. Renascent German imperialism and the nazi party it has brought into being are determined to recarve the world. Colonial claims are still at this point kept in the background. But the question of redividing the colonial world is sure to be put on the agenda in the most acute form at a subsequent date.

The British imperialists expect Germany to drive eastward. But Hitler's plans of conquest reach out to all the four winds. The nazi claim to world supremacy will keep pace with the growing German war potential. And when German fascism will bluntly demand a redivision of the colonial world, a grave threat will confront Britain, which is permitting German naval rearmament. This will bring nearer the outbreak of the world war for which the main war architect, German fascism, is preparing so assiduously.

1935

18*

From the day the fascist revolt erupted against the Spanish Republican government, all Europe, its peoples and governments, knew that its outcome would have repercussions far beyond the frontiers of that country. The man in the street gave his sympathy to the Spanish people and their lawful Republican government locked in mortal combat with fascism and reaction, for democratic freedom and peace. International reaction, on the other hand, and notably the fascist governments in Europe, ranged themselves behind the Spanish rebels, giving them aid and succor before even the mutiny began.

The civil war front became, as it were, a watershed between the progressive forces of the world and international reaction. The longer the war continues, the more savage it becomes, the more overt and active becomes the aid to the rebels by fascist Germany, Italy and Portugal, and by reactionary elements in other European countries, the clearer it becomes that its outcome depends on how the architects of a new war manage to muster their strength.

1

Spain was a non-belligerent in the imperialist world war of 1914-18. Yet long before that war the Triple Alliance (Germany, Austria-Hungary and Italy) and the Entente (Britain, France and Russia) took pains to win influence over Spain and drag her into their respective orbits.

Spain was still weighed down by various feudal appurt-enances and had not yet passed the stage of bourgeois-democratic revolution. Her economic development was therefore extremely slow, with the result that her influence and prestige on the international scene kept declining in the imperialist epoch. At the close of the 19th century, Spain's rulers, unable to enter the lists with the imperial-ist powers for a place in the sun, were bent at any price to retain their grip on the colonial possessions they had acquired in preceding centuries. They tried to profit by the new international contradictions to buttress their position and, if possible, obtain territorial accretions. But economi-cally backward and politically feeble monarchist Spain had to align, even subordinate, her plans and aspirations in one way or another to the policy of the big imperialist powers, which, furthering their own economic and politico-strategic aims, fought for greater influence on Spain's foreign policy.

It will be recalled that in 1870 a conflict over the can-didature to the Spanish throne served as the *casus belli* for the Franco-Prussian war. Bismarck wanted a Hohen-zollern, Prince Leopold, to rule Spain in pursuance of the aims of bourgeois-Junker Prussia, weakening hostile France by creating a menace on her Pyrenean frontier. Somewhat later, at the height of the scrimmage for the final division of the world, the German empire sought to impose its influence on Spain by drawing her into the sphere of the newly formed militarist alignment, the Triple Alliance, and, dreading the mounting influence of France in the Mediterranean, Spain joined the bloc in 1887.

This move was unquestionably prompted by British diplomacy. By virtue of her economic role and enormous navy in the Mediterranean, and her first-class strategic positions which included a stronghold (Gibraltar) on the Iberian Peninsula, Great Britain wielded preponderant influence on the foreign policy of Spain.

While no particularly acute economic and political con-tradictions yet affected Anglo-German relations, there were sharp British collisions with tsarist Russia and France. So, seeking a temporary improvement of relations with Germany, the British imperialists compelled Spain to follow a similar course, while Britain reinforced her Mediterranean positions by coming to terms with two of Germany's allies—Austria-Hungary and Italy (forming the so-called Mediterranean Entente in 1887).

Spain thought France, bent on acquisitions in Africa, her greatest rival in colonial matters, for Germany was then still a marginal entity and only making her first timid steps. In this, too, Spain was following Britain's tack, albeit with some deviations and zigzags, for Britain considered France a formidable competitor in the acute fight for influence in Indo-China and, even more so, in the final carve-up of colonial Africa.

At the close of the 19th century, however, seeing the fierce imperialist clashes over colonies, Spain realised she would get nowhere if she relied on the Triple Alliance. She realised, too, that she might even become the object of imperialist conflicts.

In 1898, Spain was attacked by the United States, which had just embarked on a policy of outright imperialist conquest. She lost Cuba and the Philippines. What sank in at that time was the high price she had had to pay for her friendship with the German imperialists. Germany seized on the opportunities offered by the Spanish-American war and, bent on expansion in the Far East (after capturing Kiaochow in 1897), endeavoured to grab the Philippine Islands, then Spanish. Failing due to U.S. resistance (an acute conflict brewed over possession of the main harbour in the Philippines in 1898), she reconciled herself with the seizure in the Pacific of the Carolines, then also a Spanish possession. True, this acquisition was camouflaged by a "legitimate" political deal (1899).

The polarisation in international politics resulting in the appearance of a new alignment, the Entente, counterweighing the Triple Alliance, naturally affected Spain. The powers were keenly aware of her weight as a sphere of investment and, much more, as a politico-strategic factor in the Mediterranean and the Atlantic Ocean. Anglo-French rivalry in the Mediterranean and in Africa was still fairly keen, though less so than previously. The two powers were determined to combat German ambitions, and each sought Spain's help. In 1902 France and Spain came to terms: Spain was promised possession of Northern Morocco, provided Tangier was neutralised, upsetting the plans of the German imperialists who meant to use Spain in their projected clash with France and as a jumping-board for their expansion in the Atlantic and Mediterranean.

The growth of German imperialism, its economic and political expansion and the rapid progress of its naval programme, compelled Britain to reappraise her policy and seek closer relations with France (in 1904). The rapprochement was based, as we know, on a division of spheres of influence in the whole area of Anglo-French colonial rivalry. Among other things, France was given a free hand in Morocco. But the British did not want a big power next door to Gibraltar and insisted that the northern part of Morocco go to Spain.

Wilhelm spluttered threats in retaliation at Tangier (in 1905), testing the strength of the Franco-British agreement. Besides, Germany wanted to draw Spain into her sphere of influence. Soon after the first Moroccan crisis (1905), which created a danger of war in Europe, Germany attempted to prevail on Spain to give her the Balearic Islands. This would put her in virtual control of communication lines connecting the British Isles via Gibraltar and the Suez Canal with India, and France with her African possessions, even if her further efforts to gain more influence in Morocco should fail. Furthermore, Germany could then maintain pressure on Spain, exposed to a flanking attack.

The lax political ties between Italy and the other members of the Triple Alliance spurred Germany to action in consolidating her grip on North-West Africa and the extreme south-west of Europe.

The second Moroccan crisis erupted in 1911 when France sent her troops to Fèz and Germany countered by despatching the gunboat *Panther* to Agadir. Berlin endeavoured, but failed, to embroil Spain against France. The Agadir crisis, which pushed Europe to the brink of a war, culminated in a compromise.

Needless to say, this did not dampen German efforts to gain a firmer foothold in Spain. But with direct negotiations yielding little or no results, Germany evidently decided to utilise her Italian ally, who was negotiating a broad agreement with Spain. Word of the probable Italo-Spanish deal alarmed the Entente.

The Italian imperialists had just defeated Turkey and captured Tripolitania (1911-12) and itched for fresh seizures. The young Italian imperialism, "done out of its share", took advantage of the tension between the two imperialist alignments to buttress its position in the Mediterranean. Seeking a tighter grip on the area, it took a stand against France, accusing her of trying to upset the equilibrium, with the French rulers getting the impression that Italy was gravitating more than ever towards the Triple Alliance and performing blindly the bidding of Berlin. The vigour displayed by Italian diplomacy and the backstage German promptings persuaded the Entente that Spain had to be tied to its apron-strings economically and politically.

The tug-of-war for influence in Spain was won by the Entente. When war broke out in 1914, Spain remained neutral, ensuring the safety of the French frontier along the Pyrenees. The German plan of straddling the communication lines connecting Britain and France with their colonial possessions fell through, too. It must also have swayed Italy to some extent to abandon her German ally—for Italy bordered on the sea—and to join the Entente after months of negotiation over compensations. The promises made to Italy concerned chiefly the eastern part of the Mediterranean. The importance of dominating the western part was clear to the Entente and the German leaders. Germany tried to prod Italy into action precisely with promises of expansion in the western Mediterranean. But in face of the obvious superiority of Anglo-French naval forces such promises were easier made than kept.

Matters may have looked differently if the German imperialists had managed to keep Spanish neutrality less partial in respect to France. It was not for lack of trying, however, especially during the war, that they did not succeed. More German political influence in Spain would in many respects have changed the strategic situation in Western Europe.

Germany's defeat in 1918 temporarily interrupted her Spanish overtures, but as German imperialism gradually recovered, it resumed them in the post-war environment. German fascism, the political vehicle of the most reactionary and aggressive section of German imperialism, was working strenuously to convert Spain into a seedbed of war.

German efforts to tighten the grip on Spain became particularly insistent after the nazis seized power. Throughout the post-World War I period Germany's economic ties with Spain were fairly modest. Spain was more closely linked with France, and also with British capital. The German plans of penetrating Spain, enlivened by Hitler's coming to power, were centred chiefly on politico-strategic aims prompted by the intensive war preparations for a new redivision of the world.

Naturally, the German imperialists are disguising their plans, as well as their methods of penetrating into Spain and North Africa. Yet scraps of information percolating into the press now and then give a more or less accurate idea of nazi designs.

In 1934, the press observed nazi attempts to penetrate into Morocco, the Spanish colony of Ifni and the strategic Canary Islands. Typically, the nazis are putting every chance of economic penetration to strategic use. German firms contracted to supply port equipment for Las Palmas, the main harbour on the Canary Islands, insisted on the right to supervise installation and endeavoured to inundate the port with German specialists. Germany also sought permission to operate an air base in Ifni, a wedge into the southern section of French Morocco. But a firm French démarche persuaded Spain to withhold consent. Checked by the French intervention, the German air company, Lufthansa, managed all the same to gain a grip on the strategically important communication lines in North-West Africa through the Spanish air company which has, in effect, fallen under Lufthansa control.

Soon after coming to power, the nazis planted secret agents in North Africa and the adjoining islands, notably the Canaries, to contact local tribal chiefs and supply them with arms, setting the stage for acts of diversion in the event of a German war against France. With the help of the local chiefs, the fascists expect at least to wreck the regular ties between France and her colonial empire in the African mainland, a vast store of human and material resources. The German missionary service, which is building a fairly ramified system of organisations, is working in the same direction. This is borne out by British press reports of nazi subversion in Spain and Morocco.

The *Manchester Guardian* quoted secret fascist papers in its possession revealing centres (Stützpunkte) and branches (Ortsgruppen) of a nazi network in Ceuta, Tetuán and elsewhere. Just as in Spain, the fascist agents in Morocco have a so-called port service, the usual signboard for an agency of the Gestapo. Its function is to smuggle in nazi propaganda, conduct political and economic reconnaissance and military espionage. To prepare the ground for political penetration into North Africa, the nazis employ slogans of liberation, fanning anti-British and anti-French feeling among the local population. Secret nazi papers obtained and published by the British press indicate that Hitler aims to penetrate into the Arab East. The *Manchester Guardian* reports evidence of close links between the clandestine nazi agencies abroad and the official German diplomatists. Various overt and covert agencies are especially active in Morocco, for, says the British press, fascist attention is riveted on that country. Since the 1914-18 war, notes a secret nazi document quoted in the British press, Britain, France and the United States blocked Germany's paths to East and West, but here in Morocco Germany can open a new door to the Moslem world of North Africa and the East.

Morocco may indeed be the place that German fascism fancies as a "door" to Africa, where it wants good positions in anticipation of a redivision of the colonial world. Spain is a totally different thing: for the nazis it is a convenient political staging area for a war in Europe. In any case, nazi subversion in Spain began long before General Franco's fascist revolt.

Official diplomatic and unofficial nazi agencies knew of the revolt well in advance, because they had helped to prepare it. German agents in Spain made the most of their diplomatic immunity to weave the pattern of the fascist conspiracy. And General Sanjurjo, a leading Spanish fascist who masterminded the plan for the armed rising, lived in Berlin for some time, where he was in continuous contact with top nazi party people. The latter helped him considerably, with the Spanish military attaché in Berlin acting as the middleman between the German authorities and the Spanish conspirators. Shortly before the rising, Juan March

Ordinas, a prominent Madrid banker who had amassed his vast fortune through smuggling, visited Hamburg, where he negotiated secretly with nazi leaders. The parleys centred on organisational aspects of the projected mutiny and also on the question of nazi subsidies. General Franco, who took over when General Sanjurjo was killed in an air crash at Lisbon airport, collected the subsidies precisely through a Hamburg bank. It is also reported that negotiations with General Franco, then still in Morocco, were attended by Schleher, head of the Brown House in Paris and a known fascist agent.

When the mutiny erupted in Spain, the German Government despatched two naval squadrons into Spanish waters ostensibly to protect German lives and property: one to patrol Spain's northern shore while the other cruised between Barcelona and Moroccan ports. The nazi press raised a hue and cry about the notorious "hand of Moscow" as a smokescreen for the German intervention. To vindicate their interference, the nazis endeavoured to provoke the Republican government. As a counter-measure the Spanish Government announced that it would assume full responsibility for the lives and property of foreigners resident in areas unoccupied by the Falangists. Ignoring this guarantee, the German Government despatched more warships.

The naval force was more than a demonstration. It intervened in the civil war and comforted the rebels. Its aid came in different forms. German vessels screened rebel forces from bombardment by the Spanish fleet loyal to the republic and escorted rebel units shipped from Morocco, the main base of the fascist revolt. Moreover, German ships acted as spotters for rebel guns shelling republican vessels, reconnoitred republican naval movements and supplied various other information useful to the fascist generals. Never would the rebels have succeeded in deploying forces from Morocco to Spain without German naval help, for the Spanish navy was for the most part loyal to the government.

3

Clearly, the sudden bodyblow delivered to European peace by the arrival of German naval forces in the Bay of Biscay and the Mediterranean, coupled with undisguised

help to the rebels with arms, munitions, planes and instructors, is prompted by preponderantly politico-strategic
aims. The fierce fascist propaganda assault on the Soviet
Union is added proof of this. The Nuremberg convention
of the nazi party in 1936 devoted much of its time to the
Spanish situation. The nazi claim that the Spanish civil
war is the revenge Jews are taking for the policies of King
Ferdinand and Queen Isabella, who reigned in the 15th
century, is meant for gullible fools and the sort of men
gathered at the Nuremberg convention. Everything the German fascists have done, secretly before the rebellion and
almost overtly after it broke out, shows that the nazis are
bent on using the civil war as a vehicle for definitive
political plans.

The nazis want a new beachhead for the war they are
planning in Europe. If the "leap" of Kaiser Wilhelm's
Panther in 1911 gave expression to certain German political and colonial ambitions of that time, then the leap of
the fascist *Leopard* and the other German naval vessels to
the Spanish shore and Morocco now, a quarter of a century
later, is a token of the nazis' intention to secure a redivision of the colonial world and seize important politico-
strategic positions. Another purpose is to test the
effectiveness of the new German arms.

German armed forces have thrust themselves into the
extreme south-west of the European continent, straddling
key communication lines between the Atlantic and
Mediterranean, in a radically changed situation.

Early in the 20th century, facing a rapid build-up of
German naval strength, especially that of dreadnoughts,
the British Admiralty was compelled to concentrate the
bulk of its forces in the North Sea, with France delegated
to guard Mediterranean communications. The outcome of
the 1914-18 war and the sinking of the German navy off
Scapa Flow enabled the British to reconcentrate in the
Mediterranean nearly half of their naval strength. The
first few years after the war were highlighted by rivalry
between Britain and France not only in Europe, but on
other continents washed by the Mediterranean Sea. In this
scuffle with France, Britain had a certain amount of Italian support. But the rapid growth of Italian ground, sea
and, notably, air strength after Mussolini came to power
changed the balance in the area. Fired by colonial ambi-

tions, the Italian fascists started a war against Ethiopia. Italian imperialism, protected in Europe by its agreement with France (of January 7, 1935), thus began to move into a section of East Africa which British imperialism had for some decades considered highly important for the security of its lifelines from Egypt to India. But the unambiguous British threat implied by the naval build-up in the Mediterranean yielded no tangible result for the first time in the imperialist epoch. The Italian fascists, who exploited the disunity of the capitalist states that have a stake in keeping the peace, felt strong enough to stand their ground. The British imperialists, on the other hand, did not dare, for a number of reasons, to carry their threat into effect.

One of the reasons was the radical change in the politico-strategic balance in the Mediterranean occasioned by the presence there of a strong Italian air force, deeply involved in the war against Ethiopia. In addition, as noted by the European press, it imperiled the British fleet stationed in the Mediterranean.

Malta, a key British naval base, lost its original importance due to the Italian air force build-up. Located in the middle of the Mediterranean, Malta is far from the other British bases in East and West and too close to the Italian air bases. Yet Hoare's inspection of British Mediterranean strongholds and what he said after his voyage show that the British Admiralty has not the slightest intention of abandoning so important a support base, despite its being within striking distance of the Italian bomber force. Britain is now shoring up Malta's anti-aircraft defences and reinforcing her other Mediterranean bases. She is also buttressing her positions in the area by coming to terms with Greece and Yugoslavia, and other countries. Firming up strategic points in the eastern part of the Mediterranean, where the menace of Italian expansion is greatest, Britain has a first-class fortress and naval base in Gibraltar at the entrance to the Mediterranean—a base whose fate depends on the Mediterranean power balance.

In the context of any future war, therefore, the intervention of Italian and German fascism in the armed revolt against the Spanish people may have grave political and strategic repercussions. Back in the twenties, when Italian fascism was still priming for its expansionist policy, Mussolini nursed plans of penetrating into the western as well as the eastern part of the Mediterranean. Between 1923 and 1926 he endeavoured several times to prevail on Primo de Rivera, the Spanish dictator, to give Italy a naval base at some strategically located point, notably the Balearic Islands. In those days Italy's designs were essentially anti-French. If the fascists had gained a hold in the strategic triangle formed by the Balearic Islands, Cartagena and Ceuta—and that was, indeed, its aim—France would have been in a tight spot, for communications with her African possessions would be exposed even in peacetime, let alone wartime, to Italian control. So France naturally saw to it that the Italian plan should fall through. As a result of a strong French diplomatic intervention, Primo de Rivera concluded with Italy merely a treaty on arbitration in August 1926.

This Italo-Spanish treaty was a kind of starting point for the Italian démarche concerning Tangier which showed that the Italian imperialists, though deeply involved in the eastern section of the Mediterranean, were equally concerned about the western section. In 1923 Italy had not been invited to the conference of Britain, France and Spain renewing the status of Tangier—and this despite her wish to attend. In 1927 and 1928 the Italian fascists demonstrated their naval power and succeeded at negotiations in Paris with British support to press home the issue: Italy was given a share in administering the international zone, and a say in several other matters related to Tangier.

After Primo de Rivera's downfall a certain change occurred in Spanish foreign policy. Spain drifted away from Italy and established closer relations with France. The Italian Government kept a wary watch. During and especially after the war in Ethiopia, it renewed its interest in Tangier. The *Azione Coloniale*, mouthpiece of the fascist colonial ministry, again discussed the future of that international zone. Rossi, head of the Italian diplomatic mission in Tangier and simultaneously member of the international administration, gave overt help to the Spanish rebels. He removed from police posts those Spanish officials who remained loyal to the Spanish Government, replacing them with Italian fascists, who are giving comfort in many ways to General Franco's agents. It is also very probable that Rossi was the moving spirit behind Franco's "ultimatum" demanding the withdrawal of Spanish Republican warships from Tangier, from where these could have threatened communications between Morocco and Spain and thus hindered rebel generals from moving their troops. Yet he turned Tangier into a transit base for Italian equipment going to the rebels. In Spanish Morocco, reported the *News Chronicle*, Italy has every intention of digging in. Tetuán has become a base for Italian planes. It is run by Italian officers. Italy is where she wants to be, and this without a single incident.

Italian imperialism made plain its political designs by sending warships into Spanish waters. A large Italian force is concentrated in Palermo. The fortified island of Pantelleria, halfway between Sicily and the northern shore of Africa, has become a major strategic naval base. The support rendered to the Spanish rebels by the Italian fascists, who are sending them planes, fliers, army equipment, etc., is an indication that Italy means to attain her designs in the western Mediterranean and relies heavily on opportunities presented by the Spanish civil war. In effect, Italy has occupied Majorca, the most important of the Balearic Islands, administered now by the Italian military command. The European press reported long ago that Italy wants the Balearic Islands as the price for her support of the Spanish rebels. This is a menace to Gibraltar, a key British base. In the changed politico-strategic climate of recent years seizure of the Balearic Islands (whatever the form) may have far-reaching consequences and, not surprisingly, French political quarters are perturbed.

4

The Italian fascists have been working hand in hand with the German nazis from the beginning. Unquestionably, says the *Times*, the Italians and Germans have a formal treaty or, in any case, an agreement for joint action. German and Italian warships streamed into Spanish waters almost simultaneously. The German and Italian pressure on the Spanish Government was simultaneous, with demands and protests, and outright threats, being showered on Madrid without rhyme or reason. The political campaign against the lawful Spanish Government in the German and Italian press was also timed to coincide. Voices resounded simultaneously in Germany and Italy in favour of recognising the rebel government in Burgos. Lastly, though the anti-Soviet smear campaign was initiated by the nazis, the Italian press soon joined in. This political tie-up between the Italian and German fascists in behalf of the Spanish rebels was formalised during the stay in Berlin of the Italian propaganda minister, Count Alfieri.

Italo-German political collaboration naturally conditioned the methods of the intervention and the concrete aims pursued by the imperialists of the two countries. Information has leaked into the foreign press about negotiations between the interventionists, on the one hand, and the Spanish rebels, on the other. Reports have it that the Italian fascists want a foothold on the Balearic Islands, while Hitler wants the Canaries, where, as noted, German agents are highly active. It is a safe guess that, depending on the further train of events, the interventionists will raise the price. Fascists, who are spoiling for a war to secure a new division of the world, intend to take advantage of the Spanish fighting, which they are stoking with fuel, to lay their hands on points adjoining the chief arteries connecting Britain and France with their colonial empires in Africa. In any case, both fascist powers are obviously seeking to exploit the situation and gain support bases that would weigh heavily in their favour in the event of a European war.

Formally compelled to accede to the international agreement on non-intervention in Spanish affairs, neither the nazis nor the Italians have abandoned their political line. They have decided to use Portugal as their headquarters and a dependable rearward area for the Spanish rebels. The press in Europe is of the opinion that Salazar's fascist dictatorship wants nothing better than for democracy in Spain to be squashed, because it hopes a rebel victory will buttress its own reactionary regime.

But fascist designs go still farther afield. A fascist dictatorship in Spain would naturally give Italy and Germany preponderant influence in the Iberian Peninsula creating new perils for the important British communication lines and naval bases but, much more, an immediate threat to France proper. France would find herself in a far more crowded position in the event of a war than in 1914-18. A fascist Spain also means that fascist reaction in France, now repulsed, will rear its head and try to assume the offensive against the working class and the democratic gains of the French people. Hitler and his clique are quite obviously expecting the extreme reactionary element to gain the upper hand in France, betray the national interests and come to terms with nazi Germany.

When plotting the armed fascist revolt in Spain, the nazis clearly expected that the country would become, first, a jumping board for German colonial ambitions and, second, a political and, if need be, strategic theatre in a future war. If the nazis succeeded in spreading to France the political methods they are using in Spain, their projected military aggression in Europe would be much easier to get off the ground. The nazi press is making no secret of these designs, tied in with plans of splitting the United Front in France.

The civil war which erupted in Spain with the connivance of the German and Italian fascists has a direct bearing on the general international situation. A Falangist victory would mark a fresh step forward by the fascist aggressors towards a major war.

The fascist intervention in Spain is part of the aggressive plan nursed by the architects of a new war, part of their effort to create a new political and military threat to European peace. The Franco rebels would never have made their bid without nazi and Italian aid, for they would then be doomed to fail. But for German and Italian help the insurrection of a handful of feudal and church reactionaries and the financial oligarchy would have been put down long ago by the lawful government of democratic Spain, which has the support of the masses. That the technical potential of the government armed forces, which include the bulk of the air force and navy, was counterweighed by a considerable technical edge of the rebels, is due entirely to German and Italian aid: modern planes, tanks, heavy guns, etc.

The fascist intervention and the conversion of Spanish Morocco into a rebel supply base is a gross violation of international treaties. Yet it is continuing despite the non-intervention agreement of August 1936, and offers fresh evidence of the contempt in which the aggressor states hold international commitments.

The Italo-German intervention is a graphic lesson of what concession and conciliation by capitalist countries that have no stake—at least at present—in a war can lead to. The non-intervention agreement is a product of the hesitant and unstable foreign policy of the French Government. The idea for a non-intervention committee, it is true, came from British diplomats. And Léon Blum, head of the French Government, seized on the idea. It was decided that he, a Socialist leader, was better cast as an advocate of non-intervention than British Prime Minister Baldwin, the Conservative leader. British policy had a dual motive: first, a deep-going aversion for the democratic forces of Spain, especially the United Front, and, second, a reluctance to complicate the "big game" with Hitler Germany aimed at channelling German expansion eastward against the U.S.S.R.

French reactionaries were elated by the stand of the French Government. Encouraged by the fascist insurrection in Spain, they dreamed of starting a civil war in their own country. The fascists in France, though they style themselves "nationalists", are quite willing to help create a new base of German aggression against France at France's back door, across the Pyrenees. Portugal, for its part, evidently had the blessing of the top British bourgeoisie, without which it would never have dared to serve as a gateway for the intervention of the big fascist states in Spanish domestic affairs.

The Soviet Union denounced the fascist interventionists and also unmasked those who thought they could intervene, or abet the rebels, behind a screen of non-interference. It has put its signature under the non-intervention agreement, though it regards neutrality as incorrect in respect to the lawful Spanish Government. It did so in the interest of peace and on the insistent request of the French Government, hoping it could work through the Non-Intervention Committee to end, or at least greatly restrict, the scale of the Italo-German intervention in Spain. Clearly, Franco's fascist revolt would be quickly put down if military aid to it were cut off. When it turned out, however, that the non-intervention agreement was merely a screen for fascist aid to the rebels, the Soviet Union firmly demanded that it be invalidated.[1]

Spaniards fighting against the Franco rebels are championing not only their own democratic rights, their own freedom and independence, but also European peace against forces that are hatching a new war for an imperialist redivision of the world. The heroic Spanish people are writing a fine chapter into the peoples' fight against fascism, for peace and security in Europe, with the blood they shed in battles against the rebels and the joint intervention of the fascist powers, Germany and Italy.

1936

---

[1] Seeing that the non-intervention agreement, brazenly violated by Hitler Germany and fascist Italy, had become a travesty, the Soviet spokesman on the committee, Ambassador Ivan Maisky, announced that the Soviet government could not consider itself committed. The U.S.S.R. began to supply the Spanish Republic with arms, munitions, etc.

Of some red-letter days in man's history the peoples may be legitimately proud. They reinforce faith in man's reason, lighting the way to progress, affirmation of lofty human values, to a better future. But there are occasions that serve as a reminder of profound danger, such as that to which the peoples are exposed when aggressive imperialist forces bent on expansionist designs fling Europe and the world into the vortex of war, death and destruction.

When German imperialism mounted its assault on Poland on September 1, 1939, starting a second world war, it was sure of its strength and the impotence of its adversaries. Hitler was confident that on seizing the initiative he would with a few lightning thrusts rapidly crush each of his foes in turn and establish his dominance over Europe and the world.

Giving priority to anti-communism, Hitler made no secret of his intention to make war against the Soviet Union, and prepared for it. But his frenzied anti-communism had yet another purpose: as he once admitted, he hoped the "bogey of Bolshevism" would help him convince the Western capitalist powers that "a nazi Germany is the last bulwark against the Red flood". To convince them of this was, he said, the "only way to come through the danger period, get rid of Versailles and re-arm".[1]

Indeed, between the two wars the West, notably the U.S. and British monopolies, took pains to revive German

---

[1] Kurt G. W. Ludecke, *I Knew Hitler. The Story of a Nazi Who Escaped the Blood Purge*, New York, 1938, p. 468.

imperialism and militarism, which they intended to employ against the Soviet Union. The revival was so rapid, however, that on establishing a fascist dictatorship German monopoly capital could launch expansion in many directions.[1] Its tentacles stretched to countries in Central, Southeast and Southwest Europe, to the Middle East (Turkey, Iran, Iraq, Egypt and Palestine), to South Africa and the British and French colonies, especially those that it once ruled. Soon German economic and political influences became noticeable in Latin America, which the United States and Britain, competing against each other, had come to regard as their exclusive domain.

Hitler's growing economic, political and territorial claims in and outside Europe, the phenomenal growth of German militarism, its unbridled propaganda of racism, revanchism and aggression, and the Berlin-Rome-Tokyo axis in which the nazis played the leading part, served notice that Germany had again become a menace to world peace.

With war blazing in the Far East, where the Japanese militarists had pounced on China, and another war incubating in Europe by reason of the aggressive militarist policy of nazi Germany, the peace-loving nations were still hoping that a new world eruption could be prevented. The experience of the 1914-18 war which began in the Balkans, and the aggressive aspirations of the militarist powers, who wanted a redivision of the world, made plain that peace was indivisible, that an aggressive war in one part of Europe was almost sure to spread to the whole continent and a continental war was almost sure to spread to the whole of the world. The lessons of history showed that the fascist conception of minor or localised wars was a fraud calculated to disguise the intention of disuniting the adversaries and finishing them off one by one.

Acting on past experience and deeply conscious of the prevailing situation, the Soviet Union felt that its mutual assistance pacts with France and Czechoslovakia were insufficient. It worked with dedication for a system of collective security that could bridle Hitler, avert a war and firm up peace. All peoples, big and small, European and non-European, would benefit therefrom.

---

[1] See earlier chapter, "The Colonial Designs of the German Imperialists".

This was why Hitler marshalled his diplomacy, first, to consolidate the bloc of aggressive powers and, second, frustrate the collective security project. The first objective was served by the frankly anti-Soviet so-called anti-Comintern pact concluded on November 25, 1936, also aimed, in effect, against Britain, France and the United States, while the second was to be attained by diplomatic manoeuvres designed to isolate and weaken the world's first socialist state. The two were closely linked, for by proclaiming themselves champions of anti-communism, the German imperialists hoped to profit from the financial and political support of the Western powers, to wrest concessions from them and then, with solid positions in Europe, to strike out in the direction that augured the quickest success.

The Western powers, meanwhile, hoped to make the Soviet position untenable by imposing on the U.S.S.R. a war on two fronts—against Hitler Germany and militarist Japan. Their wish was so great that it seemed to justify the German plan. Indeed, Italy's aggression against Ethiopia, the Japanese assault against China and the Italo-German intervention against Republican Spain revealed that the Western powers, far from checking the aggressors, seemed inclined towards the very contrary. What was more, learning that Hitler intended to seize Austria and Czechoslovakia, Lord Halifax, the British Foreign Secretary, assured him that he and other members of the cabinet "were fully aware" of Germany's role and that Germany could "rightly be regarded as a bulwark of the West against Bolshevism". Knowing the aggressive intentions of German imperialism, Halifax hastened to agree that "the world is not static" and suggested directing the "available energies toward a common goal".[1]

We may ask, what "common goal"? When Hitler formulated his claim to colonies, Halifax advised him to steer German expansion in an entirely different direction: Central and Eastern Europe, notably Austria, Czechoslovakia and Danzig (Gdansk).

At the beginning of March 1938, Sir Neville Henderson, British Ambassador in Berlin, assured Hitler, that he, the

---

[1] *Documents and Materials Relating to the Eve of the Second World War*, Vol. 1, pp. 19, 20, 25.

Führer, could wish for no better partner in London than Sir Neville Chamberlain, British Prime Minister, who "heeding nothing, unmasked such international phrases as collective security and the like",[1] and, moreover, made plain that his government did not object to Austria's annexation by Hitler Germany.

Hitler replied that what he had in mind was "a union of Europe without Russia",[2] while nazi emissaries were dispensing similar talk in negotiations with the rulers of France.[3]

On March 11, 1938, German troops overran Austria. The United States, Britain and France recognised the seizure. The Soviet Union alone condemned it in strong terms and warned the world of its consequences to world peace. "It may be too late tomorrow," the warning ran, "but today is not yet too late if all the States, and the Great Powers in particular, take a firm and unambiguous stand in regard to the problem of the collective salvation of peace."[4]

The Western powers, meanwhile, kept goading Hitler to capture Czechoslovakia, which had a mutual assistance pact with the Soviet Union.

The tragic story of how the West abandoned Czechoslovakia to the mercies of German imperialism on the pretext of "appeasing" it, is all too well known. When Czechoslovak representatives were shown into the conference hall at Munich on the night of September 30, 1938, where the four powers—Germany, Italy, Britain and France—had been in session, a witness recalls, the "atmosphere was oppressive; it was as though sentence was being pronounced".

That sentence had been drawn up behind closed doors. When Hitler said it was high time to partition Czechoslovakia and was backed by Mussolini, Chamberlain replied that be did not think anybody needed to wait any longer. French Premier Daladier declared: "I have been of this opinion long ago, though there is a treaty of alliance between France and Czechoslovakia".

[1] Ibid., p. 58.
[2] Ibid., p. 59.
[3] *Documents on German Foreign Policy. 1918-1945*, Series D, Vol. 1, No. 22, pp. 41-45.
[4] *Documents and Materials Relating to the Eve of the Second World War*, Vol. 1, p. 91.

The top United States monopolists had a hand in the matter too. In December 1937, Dieckhoff, Hitler's envoy in the U.S.A., reported to Berlin that German expansion in the East would meet with no objections in Washington because quarters shaping U.S. policy in Europe favoured the idea of such expansion. U.S. Ambassador to Britain, Joseph Kennedy, connected with Morgan, Baruch and Hearst, expressed the view that to settle her economic problems, Germany should be given a free hand in the East and Southeast.

Convinced that their judgement was infallible, goaded by their anti-communism, the rulers of Britain and France, with U.S. monopolists backing them, struck a deal with the nazis. Meanwhile, Western propaganda put the blame for the consequences of Munich on the Soviet Union, though authentic documents prove that the U.S.S.R. had urged all quarters to organise collective resistance and assured Czechoslovakia through diplomatic and military channels that it would honour its obligations. In mid-May 1938 the Soviet Union informed President Eduard Beneš that it was prepared to assist Czechoslovakia even if France went back on her commitments, provided Czechoslovakia decided to defend herself and requested such assistance.[1] But Beneš and the Czechoslovak Government first pretended to be still choosing between resistance and surrender, then frankly picked the latter.

Imperialists were elated. The self-enamoured Neville Chamberlain declared on returning from Munich that peace had been made secure "for a generation". By this he meant peace in the West at the price of a Soviet-German war in the East. William Bullitt, prominent in U.S. diplomacy, said: "By leaving Russia to her fate, England and France will be diverting the threat of Germany from their own lands."[2]

Developments showed that the Munich deal was not merely a Western illusion, but a criminal transaction.

True, for some time the Western powers were sure that "expansion eastwards renders a clash between Germany

---

[1] *Noviye dokumenty po istorii Myunkhena*, Moscow, 1958, Nos. 6, 7, 14, 20, 24, 26, 38, 50, 53 (Russ. ed.).
[2] Harold L. Ickes, *The Secret Diary*, Vol. 2, New York, 1954, p. 519.

and Russia some day or other highly probable".[1] That, after all, was the rockbottom motive for all their designs. However, in April 1939 Hitler reshuffled the cards. Seeing that the strategic and political situation of Britain and France had deteriorated considerably since Munich, he concluded that the first blow would be more profitably directed at the Western powers rather than the Soviet Union, with an attack on Poland as a "preliminary".[2]

Having swallowed Czechoslovakia, Germany was in no hurry to attack the Soviet Union and was stepping up her military and ideological preparations for an attack on the West. Spurred to action, Britain and France entered into negotiations with the Soviet Union (April 15, 1939), but what they proposed was clearly designed to obtain unilateral Soviet commitments of all-out aid, while sidestepping reciprocal guarantees. If Hitler Germany were to attack the Soviet Union, the latter would be left to fend for herself. British and French designs were all the more suspicious, because the two powers adamantly rejected the Soviet suggestion of guarantees to the Baltic republics. This meant that they were pointing out to Hitler that his aggression should be eastward, endeavoring to use their Moscow parleys as a means of influencing Germany and striking a deal with the nazis, rather than reaching effective agreement with the U.S.S.R. to combat aggression and war. This became doubly clear when the military missions of the Soviet Union, Britain and France opened negotiations in Moscow on August 12, 1939.[3]

When the Soviet Union, which had initiated these talks, suggested a military convention, as well as a political agreement, the British and French military missions evaded a discussion of how to coordinate the strategic effort and suggested instead to work out the "common goals" and "general principles" of military co-operation. Furthermore, it turned out in the course of the negotiations that the British and French military missions, which, by the way, consisted of minor personages, had no preliminary military plan of *joint* operations, while the British mission

---

[1] *Documents on British Foreign Policy. 1919-1939,* Third Series, Vol. IV, No. 195, p. 214.

[2] *Nyurnbergsky protsess. Sbornik materialov,* Vol. II, 3rd Russ. ed., Moscow, 1955, p. 697.

[3] *International Affairs* Nos. 2, 3, Moscow, 1959.

was not even empowered to undersign a military convention.

Marshal Kliment Voroshilov asked: "How do the missions or the general staffs of France and Britain envisage Soviet participation in a war against the aggressor if he attacks France and Britain, if he attacks Poland or Rumania, or Poland and Rumania at once, and if he attacks Turkey? Briefly, how do the British and French missions envisage our joint operations against the aggressor or bloc of aggressors if they mount actions against one of the negotiating parties or the countries I have just mentioned?"

General Doumenc, of France, replied:

"As concerns the countries you have mentioned, we think defending their territory is their own business. But we must be ready to come to their assistance when they request such assistance."

Marshal Voroshilov: "If they fail to ask for help before it is too late, they will have put up their hands, they will have surrendered."

General Doumenc, lamely: "This would be extremely unpleasant."[1]

The Western powers had no other suggestions. Again and again they referred to the stand of the reactionary governments of Poland and Rumania which, at their urging and betraying the interests of their countries, rejected the very idea of Soviet aid. An impasse ensued in the negotiations, making them pointless. On August 21, the head of the Soviet delegation observed that "the responsibility for dragging out the military negotiations, and for interrupting these negotiations, naturally lies with the French and British sides".[2]

The Soviet surmise was correct. Documents bear out the fact that Britain and France negotiated with the Soviet Union in order to conceal from public view their backstage parleys with Hitler Germany and to exert pressure on the latter and make it more amenable.

At first, Hitler was deeply perturbed by the prospect of a pact between the Soviet Union and other powers. But Dirksen, the German Ambassador to London, briefed by British official quarters, hastened to allay his fears. "The

---

[1] *International Affairs* No. 2, 1959.
[2] Ibid., No. 3.

object of the military mission," he cabled Berlin on August 1, 1939, "is more to ascertain the fighting value of the Soviet Army than to make operational arrangements.[1] He confirmed that the British military mission came to Moscow for reconnaissance. In a way, it was a smokescreen, nothing more.

Published documents indicate that at the height of their talks with the U.S.S.R. the Western powers were seeking an agreement with Hitler. On Berlin's initiative, their negotiations with Germany[2] were resumed on June 7 and proceeded through various channels until the day Hitler assaulted Poland. Through Swedish middlemen, the industrialists Wenner, Gren-Axe and Dahlerus, Hitler kept raising his terms: colonies in Africa one day and oil-bearing territory in the Middle East the next.[3] Naturally, Britain was not inclined to meet these nazi demands. Instead, it suggested that Germany still her hunger at the expense of the Soviet Union and China, with the proviso that British and German spheres of influence were strictly defined. Reactionary U.S. quarters took a similar stand (e.g., Arthur Vandenberg, Hamilton Fish, and others).

Horace Wilson told Wohltat, who represented Göhring, that a pact with Germany "would enable Britain to rid herself of her commitments vis-à-vis Poland",[4] that is, abandon Poland to the nazis, provided the latter directed their aggression east and southeast. On July 29, Charles Roden Buxton, a Labour Party spokesmen, called on Kordt, counsellor at the German Embassy, and again spoke of a broad Anglo-German agreement on the following terms:

"1) Germany promises not to interfere in British Empire affairs.

"2) Great Britain promises fully to respect the German spheres of interest in Eastern and Southeastern Europe. A consequence of this would be that Great Britain would renounce the guarantees she gave to certain States in the

---

[1] *Documents and Materials Relating to the Eve of the Second World War*, Vol. 2, p. 103.

[2] *Documents on British Foreign Policy. 1919-1939*, Third Series, Vol. VI, No. 9, p. 13.

[3] Ibid., pp. 736-38, 756-57.

[4] *Documents and Materials Relating to the Eve of the Second World War,* Vol. 2, p. 71.

German sphere of interest. Great Britain further promises to influence France to break her alliance with the Soviet Union and to give up her ties in Southeastern Europe.

"3) Great Britain promises to give up the present negotiations for a pact with the Soviet Union."[1]

After this far-reaching scheme was approved by both Wilson and Chamberlain, the negotiations proceeded along official channels. A few days later, on August 3, 1939, Wilson explained to Dirksen that the projected Anglo-German agreement "would completely absolve the British Government from the commitments to which it was now pledged by the guarantees to Poland, Turkey, etc."[2]

Wilson demanded that the Anglo-German negotiations should be secret. Dirksen saw Lord Halifax, Foreign Secretary, who also assured him that "the British side would go very far to reach an adjustment with Germany".[3]

Dirksen went to Berlin. The British Government hoped he would bring back Hitler's consent. But it was farthest from Hitler's mind to abandon his claims. To him the British proposals were fresh evidence of weakness and an indication that "in the event of a German-Polish war England would *not* join in on Poland's behalf".[4]

Western rulers, as we see, had no intention of coming to terms with the Soviet Union. They wanted a broad politico-military agreement with Hitler Germany, channelling nazi aggression to Eastern and Southeastern Europe.

At the height of the talks in May 1939, Japan attacked the Mongolian People's Republic, a friend of the Soviet Union, with the obvious aim of breaking through to the Soviet border at Lake Baikal. The United States and other Western powers were planning a Pacific conference, an "eastern Munich", with China suffering the fate of Czechoslovakia and Japanese aggression being channelled against the U.S.S.R.

The Soviet Union saw through this scheme. There was for it a danger of war against a united imperialist front in East and West. It worked on for a collective security system that would avert or at least delay the outbreak of

[1] *Documents and Materials Relating to the Eve of the Second World War*, Vol. 2, pp. 110-11.
[2] Ibid., p. 118.
[3] Ibid., p. 128.
[4] Ibid., p. 191.

a war. And seeing that the Western powers wanted no such system, Moscow sought an effective equal agreement for joint resistance to fascist aggression. It worked on for collective security after Hitler Germany put out feelers in May 1939 to ascertain the Soviet stand. Soon it was clear, however, that the West wanted an agreement not with the U.S.S.R., but with Hitler Germany against the U.S.S.R.

Later, Hitler Germany offered the Soviet Union a non-aggression pact. The nazis knew the dangers of a war against the powerful Soviet Union, and hoped to bring the Western powers to their knees swiftly before tackling a strong adversary, while fearing that a war against a strong adversary would exhaust their resources, which would prevent them from reaching their aims in the West.

In that tense and critical August 1939, the Soviet Union had to make a choice: either continue the hopeless negotiations with the Western powers, thus helping them indirectly to strike a secret deal with Hitler, or accept the German proposal. In the first instance, it would expose itself to an imperialist attack in unfavourable circumstances, and in the second instance it would frustrate the plan of world reaction to embroil it in a war with Germany and Japan, which it would have to fight in complete international isolation. Besides, a non-aggression pact with Germany meant a gain in time that could be used to reinforce Soviet defences against any future Hitler aggression. To escape the trap set by the imperialist powers, the Soviet Union decided to accept the German proposal.

In the meantime, the nazis, who had in March made up their minds to attack Poland, continued their war preparations. Hitler and his coadjutors were sure Poland would be abandoned by Paris and London. While promising the rulers of landlord Poland that in the event of a war against the U.S.S.R. they would be rewarded with territory in the Soviet Ukraine, the Hitler clique primed for an assault on that country with the object of destroying it as an independent state. Blinded by class hatred for the Soviet Union, Józef Beck and Ignacy Mościcki chose collaboration with Hitler. Leon Noël, former French Ambassador to Warsaw, wrote that Beck rendered valuable services to the nazis. Poland lost no opportunity to back German manoeuvres against the League of Nations, collective security and multilateral mutual assistance pacts.[1] Time and again, the Soviet Government warned of the deadly peril faced by Poland from German imperialism. But in vain.

After working for years to isolate the Soviet Union, Beck saw Poland totally isolated at the most critical hour in her history. This was the price his country paid for the lack of political common sense displayed by the ruling class, which did not understand to the end of its days that it had been anti-communism that caused Poland's national catastrophe. Ten days before signing the non-aggression pact with the Soviet Union, Hitler informed Mussolini on August 13 that his attack on Poland would come off in a matter of days. Yet as late as August 20 the Polish Government told London that it would not deal with the Soviet Union on any terms. Not until August 25, with the nazis obviously provoking a conflict against Poland, did Britain sign a mutual assistance treaty with Warsaw. However, for Britain it was an instrument for a new "Munich", this time at Poland's expense. Talks to appease Hitler continued until the nazis mounted their aggression and thus put the Western imperialist powers among their military adversaries, something the West had wanted the least.

The diplomatic prehistory of the Second World War shows that Britain and France had made concession after concession to Hitler, goading him eastwards. They expected thus to contain nazi aggression against themselves and channel it against the Soviet Union. This was why they rejected the collective security idea, then best fitted to frustrate fascist aggression and deliver the world from the conflagration into which it was plunged by the nazis, their allies and satellites. On seeing the collective security idea collapse, Hitler first assaulted the West—the powers that had done the most to eliminate collective security—then, after overrunning nearly all Western Europe and absorbing its economic potential, invaded the Soviet Union. That day the tide of the war changed, spelling the doom of Hitler's armies and the Third Reich.

1959

---

[1] Noël, *L'agression allemande contre la Pologne,* Paris, 1946, p. 167.

September 25, 1942

A battle is in progress that will determine the future of our country and, therefore, that of the world. Hardly anybody outside our country expected the German army to run into such unexampled resistance, least of all the German command. Early in August, nazi propaganda said the stronghold on the Volga would fall in a matter of days. By the end of August, it whipped up such utter confidence in victory that crowds of Germans gathered beneath loudspeakers in Berlin streets, awaiting the announcement of the capture of Stalingrad and—for the nth time—of the final defeat of the Red Army. But in the past few days nazi propaganda has changed its tune. Germans are told about "Russian fanaticism" and "intransigence". Explanations are sought for the German failure to end the war on the Volga at one stroke.

Meanwhile, the Anglo-Saxon press is drawing comparisons between Stalingrad and Verdun. That, I hold, is artificial and incorrect. French tenacity and morale at Verdun are not open to question. But we should consider not only subjective fighting qualities, but also the objective situation. At Verdun, the French were defending a first-class European fortress. They knew that the allied Russian army on the Eastern front was drawing away a considerable German force from the Western front and from Verdun. The situation now is different. Making the most of the opportunity of warring on one front only, the German command is deploying troops and air strength from the Western theatre, even from Northern Africa, and engaging them against Stalingrad, which is anything but a fortress. Yet the defenders of the Volga city are standing firm. Our losses are great. But by fighting for every centimetre of ground we have worn down many a nazi division. German propaganda is no longer as strident. In early August, the Berlin press said that after taking Sevastopol the remaining battles would be child's play. On September 11 the German radio admitted that taking Stalingrad is a task far more complicated than taking Sevastopol.

The nazi army is still on the offensive, though casualties are heavy. I wonder about the mood of the German population? Goebbels has admitted that many Germans ask: "How long until victory?" Mündler, editor of *Das Reich*, is evasive. "German soldiers in the East," he writes, "do not look at the calendar." Goebbels's answer is more to the point. "The drawn-out war," he says, "will take its toll in lives and tension."

On the eve of the fourth year of war, on the eve of the second winter campaign in Russia, the headman of the nazi lie factory can promise the Germans nothing save more blood, more losses, more strain.

Hitler, it appears, is looking for fresh reserves. All over Europe he is gathering whatever he can. He has rounded up Poles, Frenchmen and the Dutch, and inducted them forcibly into his army. But he is having difficulties. When with a flourish of the pen he incorporated Alsace-Lorraine in the Third Reich the population, in dismay, kept its silence. A few days ago, London reports, the German authorities announced an obligatory registration, expecting to pick out reinforcements for the depleted German army. Many people made up their minds to flee. Some succeeded, others were caught and shot. The population is seething.

Having rechristened Luxemburgians as Germans, Hitler ordered their induction into the German army. But a big surprise was in store for him. Inspired by the Soviet resistance, the population refused to comply. A general strike flared up—the first wartime general strike in a nazi-occupied European country. The infuriated nazis announced a state of siege. The Gestapo went on a rampage. But the fact remains that the peoples of Europe are rising against the nazis, readying themselves to strike at the German armies from the rear if and when a second front opens in Europe. In that sense, the general strike in little Luxemburg speaks volumes and is tied up with what is happening in France.

The foreign press and radio lead one to the conclusion that the French nation is waiting, waiting tensely. France, that beautiful and unhappy country, is paying a heavy price for the incapacity of her leaders. But the Frenchman is banishing his illusions. He is absolving himself of his errors with a rising hatred of invaders and traitors. He has become grim and is, evidently, readying for battle. "Many think," writes Björk, the *Stockholms Tidningen* correspondent just back from Vichy, "that in France a time of grave internal convulsions is drawing near. There are rumours of disorders in Paris, Lyons, Marseilles and other cities. An insurrection may flare up if the fortunes of war change and the grip of the occupationists loosens."

The occupation regime and the new pressure to which Hitler is putting the European peoples are generating resistance. The nations are encouraged by the example of the Red Army. They are waiting for support from across the Channel. But how long must they wait?

December 8, 1942

Rommel's army has suffered a defeat in Egypt. The efficiently organised Anglo-American landing in Northern Africa radically changed the situation in the Mediterranean. But the gigantic battle at Stalingrad, on the Volga bank, is still the decisive factor. It is now clear that the strategic and political plans of the fascist coalition for 1942 will fail. The time factor works in our favour. One of the indirect but important symptoms of the emerging situation is that, according to many signs, the prestige of the Italo-German coalition in the neutral countries has begun to drop.

Few are the European countries whose neutrality the German army has spared. There was a time when Hitler handed out promises to observe their neutrality. That was his way of eliminating them from the struggle against aggression, making it so much easier for him to swallow them one by one. In all of them he planted his agents. In some he formed fascist organisations, a "fifth column" backing his aggressive designs. In others he employed the method of broad economic penetration, designed to yield the same result. But by and large German imperialism exploited these methods in combination. Everywhere, Hitler gave priority to the slogan of "combating Bolshevism", winning the allegiance of the extreme reactionaries. He expected to use some states as "allies", and to occupy others. He hoped that the remainder, which have so far escaped the flames of war, will fall sooner or later.

Early in November nazi pressure on the neutral states increased perceptibly. Some days ago the *Völkischer Beobachter* demanded again that neutrals make "sacrifices". The SS mouthpiece, *Das schwarze Korps*, was even more explicit. "The national-socialist and fascist system will be installed in your countries whether you like it or not," it snarled at the Swedes and other European neutrals.

The nazi rulers are displeased that the press in the neutral countries expresses its own opinions about current developments and does not reproduce the claims of German propaganda, particularly about the "crushing defeat" of the Red Army. In eary November, Dietrich, head of the nazi press, mounted from Berlin an offensive on the press of neutral states, demanding that it obey German orders. He styled this as "ideological neutrality". But his attack was repulsed and its objective exposed. "Dietrich thinks," wrote the Swedish *Dagens Nyheter,* "that the newspapers in neutral countries are obliged to preach the religion of a new Europe, and if they cannot, then at least not speak against the German 'new order'. But the nazi demand of ideological neutrality is firmly rejected in the neutral countries."

Despite the watertight nazi censorship, word is leaking out to the foreign press about Hitler's policies in occupied countries, about the brutal regime in Poland and in the captured territories of the Soviet Union. Our own press is reporting facts that lift the veil on what is going on behind the signboard of a "new order" in Europe.

Hitler Germany is spending vast sums to make her propaganda in neutral countries more effective. In Sweden, for example, nazi agents distribute handbills, photographs and literature to depict the welfare in nazi Germany and the invaded countries. But bloody deeds belie honeyed words. According to foreign observers, the sympathy of the

Swedish public is with the Norwegians, gripped by the "new order" but refusing to bend to Terboven, Hitler's emissary, and his puppet Quisling. At public meetings voices resound in solidarity with Norway, which is fighting for its freedom. Mass organisations, such as trade unions, etc., are not alone in making monthly contributions to the Aid Fund for Norway; so are certain stock companies, savings banks, etc.

These facts, too, are an indication of Hitler's dropping prestige. "We have no reason to lose our self-control," writes the Swedish *Göteborgs Handels-och Sjöfarts-Tidning,* "because we understand the alarm created among Germans by the changing tide of the war. The time of big German victories is over."

The German and Italian fascists are having difficulties in their relations with the neutral states. Where once they needed merely to stamp their foot, they now have to reckon with a mounting determination to safeguard neutrality and independence.

January 26, 1943

A few days ago nazi propaganda was still silent about the German defeat at Stalingrad. Evidently, Berlin and its allies hoped that the disaster could be remedied, in which case silence would appear wise. But for how long can one hush up an event that the whole world is talking about? Word of the defeat has percolated past the barriers put up by nazi censors, and Hitler had no choice but to speak up. It was clear that Berlin and Rome were dismayed.

According to the Berlin correspondent of *Svenska Dagbladet,* "people are saying quite openly in Berlin that the current winter campaign in the U.S.S.R. is the most difficult and fateful so far experienced by Germany. It is constantly stressed that the giant defensive battles in the East are claiming the maximum of effort and sacrifice."

Only recently, the German press and Hitler promised that the Red Army would be crushed in 1942. Now, the nazi mouthpiece, *Völkischer Beobachter,* writes:

"The German army is compelled to fight a second winter campaign on the Eastern front against a most serious adversary intent on crushing the German army."

20*

The fascist paper, which only recently painted lurid pictures of Soviet defeat, speaks of the need "to win the battle on the Eastern front at any cost, for otherwise the Third Reich will be destroyed once and for all".

A new tune!

Hysterical voices resound Rome. Understandably so. The Italian colonial empire has collapsed. Divisions have gone to eternal rest in the cold earth of the Don steppes. Yet Rome seems more inclined to speak of the German setback. Appelius, an Italian commentator, says: "We admit the Russian successes at Stalingrad. We admit the desperate plight of the German troops fighting in that area. We admit that their situation is dramatic. The Russians are fighting with extraordinary ferocity and strength."

But that is not all.

"The situation on the Russian front," says Appelius, "is most grave, and not only because the Russians have flung vast reserve forces into the battle, but also because the axis powers cannot use more than the designated number of divisions in the winter campaign. The Russian pressure is truly frightening."

In its official reports the German command endeavours to keep up a good front. The Red Army has crashed through the nazi defences along a big stretch, advancing as much as 400 kilometres. Yet the German command maintains that things are shaping out as it had planned all along. It speaks of "elastic defence".

The Red Army crushed a huge enemy force, took more than 200,000 prisoners, seized 13,000 guns and many other weapons. Was that, too, part of the nazi plan?

May 12-14, 1943

Reports have dribbled into the foreign press about certain backstage diplomatic moves. The nazi ship is not sinking yet, but certain quarters in the nazi vassal states are sniffing for possible avenues of escape. In mid-February, in an article in *Giornale d'Italia*, Gayda, the Duce's literary armourer, said Italy intended to keep on fighting, but that, in principle, it did not reject the possibility of peace with Britain and the United States.

Earlier still, at the end of January, the British conservative *Daily Mail* pointed cautiously to symptoms that in the near future Germany would undertake a fresh, more determined peace offensive. A well-informed paper! Or perhaps a paper with foresight. During the Roosevelt-Churchill talks in Casablanca, rumours of German peace feelers were discussed in the foreign press most extensively.

Newsweek said in January it thought that influential quarters in Berlin are either already feeling out the Allies, or propose to try. It is assumed, wrote *Newsweek*, that some members of the German high command have realised that Hitler is doomed. It is expected, therefore, the journal said, that they will try to split the allied nations by offering "peace" terms to either Britain and the United States or to the Soviet Union. Early in February, when the German press, reacting to nazi defeats on the Soviet-German front, especially the surrender of the 6th Army at Stalingrad, was beating the drums of "total mobilisation", Goebbels wrote an article in *Das Reich* which foreign observers describe as a peace overture. *La France* wrote on this score:

"Unquestionably, the nazis will feel out the situation through various channels. Whether they use Stockholm, Berne, Madrid, Lisbon, Rome or Helsinki, there is no shortage in middlemen."

In late April foreign papers reported the speech of Spanish foreign minister General Jordana, who offerred Spain's "good services" in arranging peace talks between Germany and the Western powers—Britain and the United States. Hull and Eden rejected the offer, stressing that the United Nations are determined to secure the unconditional surrender of the Italo-German coalition and its satellites. The nazis had no choice but to announce that they had known nothing beforehand of Jordana's offer. A month earlier the Swedish fascist-controlled *Dagposten* hinted that peace between Germany and, of all things, the Soviet Union was a distinct possibility.

The purpose of the nazi "peace" feelers could not be more obvious. It appears that certain influential quarters in Hitler Germany expect that adroit moves could create a situation in which, as once before, they would deal with their adversaries one by one. Even a compromise peace would yield the nazis considerable advantages. They would then escape responsibility for their villainy. They would retain the wealth they plundered in Europe. They would have a chance to prepare for new wars of aggression. So they are hoping that one of their adversaries will betray the others, who have joined hands on the basis of common interest to fight the nazi plague.

I recall that on November 11, 1941 (the 23rd anniversary of the German surrender at Compiègne in 1918), when the nazi army was at the approaches to Moscow, Schmidt, a spokesman of the German foreign ministry, declared in an official statement: "When the history of the war will one day be written it will not contain the words: Germany sent out peace feelers. It will speak only of German victory."

No, the history of the war will be written in entirely different terms. It is obvious, even at this early stage, that it will contain, as does that of the First World War, many pages about the "peace" moves of the German imperialists. It is clear that nothing but the complete defeat of the nazis and the unconditional surrender of Hitler Germany can bring peace to the long-suffering peoples of Europe.

July 20, 1943

Today, our *Red Star* received the first number of a truly unusual newspaper, *Freies Deutschland* (of July 19, 1943). For those who have read the brown (or, more precisely, yellow) nazi press, which evokes disgust, the new paper will be like a breath of fresh air: at long last one can read the truth in German, too, written for Germans by Germans. Before the war I saw a few numbers of the underground *Rote Fahne*. Printed in close but clear type on a quarter sheet of thin paper, the German Communist Party paper was exciting, being the voice of the finest men of the German working class, the clarion call of fighters raised on the traditions of revolutionary struggle.

Freies Deutschland is different. It is something new in the anti-fascist movement of Germans, and nobody can tell how it will develop. We must go by the facts: a conference of German P.O.W.s, officers and privates, took place in Moscow on July 12-13 jointly with anti-fascist public leaders, trade unionists and Reichstag deputies residing in the U.S.S.R. Delegates from all P.O.W. camps were present. After a two-day debate, the conference elected the Free Germany National Committee with Erich Weinert, the poet, as president and Major Karl Hetz and Lieutenant Heinrich von Einsiedel as vice-presidents.

On its front page *Freies Deutschland* carries the Manifesto of the National Committee, addressed to the German army and the people of Germany. Here are its guidelines, which, presumably, will win a place in the history of the anti-fascist struggle:

"The facts indicate inexorably that *the war is lost*. At the cost of enormous casualties and privations Germany can protract the war for some time.

"*Forming a truly national German government is a pressing task*. This government, and no other, will win the trust of the people and their former adversaries. It alone can bring about peace.... This government can be formed only through a struggle of liberation by all sections of the German people. It will lean on fighting groups that will unite to overthrow Hitler.

"*Our aim is a free Germany*.

"This means: *A strong democratic government*;

"*Complete repeal of all laws based on national or racial hatred*;

"*Restoration and extension of the political rights and social gains of the people*;

"*Freedom of economy, trade and the crafts*;

"*Immediate release of victims of nazi terror and material compensation for their adversities*;

"*Just and merciless trial of war criminals, of those who started the war*.

"*Forward Germans, fight for a free Germany.*"

That is the programme of Free Germany. The future will show what support it will muster. Today, the 33 signatures beneath the Manifesto reveal that the programme has brought together people from different walks of life, with different political views and convictions. Among them are veteran leaders of the Communist Party of Germany, political friends of Ernst Thälmann, such outstanding figures of the German and international labour movement as Wilhelm Pieck, Walter Ulbricht and Wilhelm Florin, the Reichstag deputies. Hitler took their seats from them forcibly, but who will deny that they retain the powers given them by the German people. In addition to Erich Weinert, other prominent poets and writers entered the National Committee, championing free speech and creative thought: Willi Bredel and Friedrich Wolf (authors of "Professor Mamlock", that splendid anti-fascist film).

What strikes the eye is that the Manifesto is also signed by professional officers and soldiers of the German army: Major Heinrich Homann, formerly of the 100th Jäger Division, Erich Kühn, formerly a Berlin worker and later private of the 368th infantry regiment, and many others.

The newspaper *Freies Deutschland* and the newly founded National Committee may be the beginning of a new stage in the history of the German anti-fascist liberation movement. It is still far to the end goal. What will it be like, this free Germany?

September 20, 1943

A new important document appeared in the *Pravda* today, entitled Appeal to German Generals and Officers, to the People and the Army, adopted at the inaugural meeting of the League of German Officers, held near Moscow on September 11 and 12. The meeting was attended by over 100 delegates from five officers' P.O.W. camps and by members of the Free Germany National Committee. In their appeal, the generals and officers who survived the defeat of the 6th Army at Stalingrad say that "the National-Socialist regime cannot embark on the only road that leads to peace". They urge "a declaration of war on that destructive regime". The appeal ends on the following note: "Demand the immediate resignation of Hitler and his government! Long live a free, peaceful and independent Germany!" Under it stand 95 signatures, including those of Artillery General von Seydlitz, Lieutenant-General Edler von Daniels, Major-General Korfes, and others.

Who do these men count on for support? Of themselves they write: "In Germany we have been buried alive, but we have come alive."

Are there elements in Hitler's war machine who have retained the faculty of independent thought and can act against the regime? That is the big question. And can these elements comprehend that the only way to act is in concert, on a wide front embracing all active democratic forces? The important thing now is that the League of German Officers has decided to join hands with the Free Germany movement.

October 16-18, 1943

The shock wave of the Soviet offensive has rolled across Europe, rousing the spirit of resistance. Even in places where the popular forces seemed to be drowsing, people have rallied. Take the reports reaching us from Denmark. When Hitler invaded that country in April 1940, the Danish government issued orders to let in the nazi troops unhindered, hoping thereby to earn their goodwill.

At first, Hitler pretended kindness. It appears he was not inclined at first to put Danish nazis at the helm, one of the reasons being that the nazi group there has not the least influence (in the elections to parliament in March 1942 as much as 98 per cent of the votes were cast against them). So Hitler decided to preserve the appearance of Danish "independence". This yielded certain advantages: he did not have to use up personnel and funds for administering the country, for a military government. Besides, for propaganda purposes, Denmark could be a model of submission for other, more reluctant nations incarcerated in the "European fortress".

This summer, when Germany's military and political situation deteriorated, especially after the battle of Kursk, the German command stepped up pressure. It demanded from Denmark more food deliveries and intimated that the officers of the small Danish army could be useful to the German war machine. Ending the pretense of "non-interference" in Denmark's internal affairs, German envoy Best demanded that Copenhagen revise service rules to enable Danish officers to enter into German employ. Scavenius, the Danish Prime Minister, Best's obsequious helpmate, had a hard time in prevailing on his government to make certain concessions. But the result came as a shock to the Berlin rulers and their Danish executors: only five men of the Danish officer corps enlisted in the German army. As a result, many Danish officers were shipped to German concentration camps.

313

This was only a beginning. Formerly, Danes retaliated to the occupation by cold-shouldering the invaders. Now there is reason to believe that these taciturn, peaceful people have gone over to more active forms of resistance. They have begun blowing German ships, derailing military trains, setting fire to German army barracks and killing nazi servicemen. The upswing in resistance was particularly marked in recent months, after Germany's military prestige plummeted. Torgni Segerstedt, a Swedish journalist writing for the English *Evening Standard*, describes the political mood in Denmark in the following terms: the Danes are realists and have no illusions about their southern neighbour. They know that if their factories keep on working for Germans, the Allies may bomb them out of existence. And if Danes blow them up, they have the satisfaction of knowing that they did what the Allies would have done. Moreover, for them it is a national humiliation to do nothing to help themselves. They have no wish to be the tame canaries of a gang of killers.

Returning from Berlin on August 28, Best demanded that the Scavenius government proclaim a state of emergency, set up German censorship and surrender Danish patriots to the German military courts. What he demanded, in effect, was the introduction in Denmark of all the attributes of the blood-stained Hitler regime. Scavenius's government turned down the demands. It had no other choice, for the people would have rebelled. General Hanneken, commander of German forces in Denmark, instantly proclaimed a state of seige. Best mourned: "My conciliatory policy has foundered." He blamed the Scavenius government for its unwillingness to co-operate. But that was a staged comedy in which all players were cast in their specific roles. Berlin had known in advance what it would do: it sent in a force of at least 50,000, with tank and artillery support.

Hanneken instituted a reign of terror. At first he disarmed the Danish army, then attempted to seize the navy, but failed. The ships' commanders received a secret order from the Danish admiralty, "Manoeuvre No. 3", and either scuttled their vessels or sailed to Swedish ports. Fresh reprisals followed. The German command set out to squash Danish resistance by its usual brutal methods.

When the nazis occupied Denmark and Norway in the

spring of 1940, they thought they had secured cover for Germany's northern flank. Only recently, German Vice-Admiral Braun noted in the journal *Kriegsmarine* that Germany had by conquering the two countries ensured for herself predominant political influence in Scandinavia and, moreover, immense strategic advantages. Its supremacy in Denmark and Norway, he said, enabled her to exert continuous pressure on the British Isles and the northern areas of the Soviet Union, and gave her control over sea routes from Britain to the U.S.S.R. But that is now changed. Put on the defensive, the German invaders are aiming to establish total control over Denmark and to exterminate all people likely to go against them.

A few days ago the German occupation authorities announced the formal lifting of the state of siege in Denmark. They are trying to tell the world that all is well in the Danish kingdom. But they have so far failed to muster people willing to form a government. Reports have come to hand that an underground liberation committee has been formed. The nazi reign of terror continues, indicating that a good stock of inflammable sentiment has accumulated on the northern flank of the "European fortress", ready to burst aflame when the Allied troops open a second front in Europe. But when will that be?

October 25, 1943

Reports are at hand that Anglo-American troops have force-crossed the Volturno, captured Vinchiaturo and Campobasso and are approaching the central part of Italy. However, the German army still controls two-thirds of the country.

Fighting the advancing Allied armies, the German command is perturbed by the state of affairs in the rear, where the people are also offering resistance, especially in the big industrial centres of northern Italy. The assassination of Ricci, the fascist chieftain, in Milan is evidence that the German invaders are not coping with the situation and cannot ensure the safety of their puppets. According to available evidence, the German military authorities are uncertain and disturbed even in Rome. They behave as though each of the seven hills on which Rome is built is a Mount Vesuvius emitting hot lava. After Mussolini's flight, with the Badoglio government declaring war on Germany, the resistance of Italians in nazi-occupied provinces has doubled.

Now, the German command has instituted a savage occupation regime to keep its "ally" in line. German troops have been moved in—no, not from the Eastern front, of course—from Austria and the south of France. Field-marshals Rommel in northern Italy and Kesselring in central Italy have become military dictators. Gauleiter Hofer, known for his brutality during the nazi *Anschluss* of Austria, has been appointed military administrator of the three northern provinces. German troops have begun disarming Italian army units, but not always successfully: many Italian officers and soldiers resist or go off to the mountains, where they form guerrilla units.

Rolling northward, the German troops leave a trail of blood. Foreign war correspondents report that in Naples the nazis blew up steel plants and a chemical works employing some 4,000 workers. Many were killed by a nazi time-bomb concealed in the general post office building. Demolition gangs follow a plan, causing monstrous destruction along the line of retreat. Reuter correspondent reported from Naples that demolition gangs set fire to houses along the shoreline road.

Wherever Italian patriots take action against the occupationists, the German military authorities are particularly ferocious. A nazi order posted in towns and villages reads: "For every killed German we shall shoot 100 Italians."

This is not an empty threat. In Naples, the population resisted the German order for 30,000 Italians to report for forced labour. Failing to get more than 150 people, the German authorities took revenge. People were shot indiscriminately, and their property was plundered. The Neapolitans took rifles and knives and attacked the German troops. The nazi force created carnage. I have the text of an official German war report. Here is how it describes the nazi counter-action in Naples: "German task forces crushed the rising without mercy. Our tanks raced through the streets and destroyed seats of resistance one after another. Sappers destroyed the port facilities. Naples paid dearly for its disobedience."

That is the German version. But word has come, too,

that the outraged Neapolitans drove the nazi invaders out of their city.

Now the German command is on the rampage in Rome. It has requisitioned the capital's food supplies. The people are starving. German patrols detain Italians of conscription age for shipment to northern Italy, where they will do forced labour. In the outskirts of Rome the German authorities have set up several concentration camps, where tens of thousands of Italian soldiers are interned. According to foreign reports the German authorities have evacuated forcibly the population along the coast from Ostia to Nettuno and in-shore to Velletri. They sifted evacuees for labourers, whom they shipped off to build fortifications on the peninsula. The battalions of forcibly mobilised Italians are put under the command of German officers and labelled "new Italian labour army". Having politically resuscitated the Duce and put him at the head of a puppet government, Hitler has ordered him to form a new Italian army. But Mussolini is powerless, even in nazi-occupied areas. The mobilisation order had therefore to be issued by the Germans. Rommel's latest instruction reads:

"Every Italian can choose: he may either join the first-line German troops or be used in auxiliary units."

But the people are determined to avoid either choice. Foreign papers report that in the north the German authorities are concealing from the population that the Badoglio government has declared war on Germany. They are afraid, it appears, that on learning this, Italians in nazi-occupied areas will redouble resistance.

It is still hard to say how quickly events will unreel. This will depend largely on the Allied military operations.

December 9, 1943

News of top importance: leaders of the Big Three, U.S.S.R., U.S.A. and Great Britain, the principal members of the anti-Hitler coalition, held a conference in the Iranian capital. On December 1 they signed a joint declaration, saying: "We have concerted our plans for the destruction of the German forces. . . . No power on earth can prevent our destroying the German armies by land, their U-boats by sea, and their war plants from the air. Our attack will be relentless and increasing."

After the trials that fell to the lot of our country, which has fought single-handed for eighteen months against the nazi war machine powered by the vast economic potential of Germany and nazi-occupied Western Europe, this sounds like a death sentence to fascism and militarism. The Declaration is imbued with optimism, grown so much stronger after the battles on the Volga and at Kursk. Now the same spirit will grip countries languishing under nazi tyranny. Let us hope it materialises into active military operations by our Allies.

My historian's memory retains numerous examples of coalition wars. Some serve as a reminder that often political differences arising during the war weaken the concerted effort or even dissolve a coalition before the common aim, the enemy's defeat, is attained. Other examples reveal how difficult it is for members of the coalition to co-ordinate their strategic plans and how much more difficult to carry them into effect. In some cases, coalition members confined themselves merely to agreeing military operations of a more or less limited nature. In Teheran, the Declaration says, the Big Three leaders "have reached complete agreement as to the scope and timing of the operations which will be undertaken from the East, West and South". This broad agreement on strategic matters of immense scale is unprecedented in the history of coalition wars. If it is properly observed, it will usher in a new round of major military operations against Hitler Germany, the common enemy.

Few can assess events swiftly, correctly and lucidly. Historical experience does not offer the key to possible variations. Yet in the present situation the importance of the military agreements reached at Teheran is obviously immense. Despite this—or, perhaps, because of it—voices have resounded in the United States and Britain seeking to undermine faith in the Teheran decisions. In a way, it is a comfort for Hitler, who has striven throughout the war to divide the members of the anti-nazi coalition, to sow mistrust and hostility and impair or altogether frustrate their joint military efforts.

German fascist propaganda is going out of its way to belittle, even deny, the military impact of the Teheran conference. Semmler, one of Goebbels's aides, said on December 6 that Berlin attaches little or no significance to the event and that the "German front in the East is, and will be, firm". Otto Kriegk, another Goebbels's aide, declared that the "decisions of the Teheran Conference are bluff". The *Berliner Börsenzeitung*, close to the General Staff, writes: "The Conference in Teheran is an indication of the disastrous failure of the military policy of our adversaries; they do not know where to mount an offensive." Today, Berlin Radio said: "The issues raised in the three-power declaration evoked smiles here in Berlin. The talk of a second front amused our people." It is hard to say of what there is more in this utterance—obtuse self-assurance or frenzied fear.

June 7, 1944

The second front in Europe is now reality. At dawn yesterday British, American and Canadian troops landed in excellent style in Normandy, crushed German resistance swiftly and dug in. Last night, Soviet correspondents were invited to a press-conference at the premises of the British military mission in the U.S.S.R. in a Moscow sidestreet, given by Lieutenant-General Brocas Burrows, head of the British mission, and Major-General John Dean, head of the United States mission.

Lieutenant-General Burrows showed on a map the intentions of the Anglo-American command, pointing out that according to available information the operation was proceeding smoothly in accordance with the general plan and the specific assignments to all service arms engaged in the expedition. In his communication, brief and to the point, the General referred to just the military aspect and the situation on the day of the landing. He observed with restraint that the Normandy operation had necessitated thorough preparations. He seemed to think that this was enough to forestall the question of why the crossing was not made earlier, since an agreement had been reached in June 1942 at the Anglo-Soviet negotiations in London and the Soviet-American negotiations in Washington to open the second front in Europe in 1942.

None of us seemed to want to put the question directly. Those who followed the British and American press in the past two years could not help seeing that the second front problem was not just military, but also political in complexion. Throughout the two years there has been overt and covert conflict among the top leaders. Some future historian will relate the story of that complex tug-o'-war in its various stages. It will be an interesting and an instructive tale.

In any case, the long-awaited second front in Europe is an event of the first magnitude. Much still depends on what strategic and political aims the United States and Britain will pursue in Europe. And Berlin knows it. What will the reaction be, military or political?

June 26, 1944

Nearly three weeks have gone by since the Allies opened the second front in Europe. It is clearer than ever now that Hitler is banking chiefly on differences between the Soviet Union and the Allies. After the myth of the nazi "European fortress" evaporated into thin air, one would expect the German political strategists to try and produce some new method of averting a total military defeat. But judging by the general tenor of German propaganda beamed abroad, Berlin has invented nothing after the Normandy landing. More desperately than before, they are clinging to their old line of fanning differences and mistrust between members of the anti-nazi coalition, notably the Anglo-Saxon countries and the Soviet Union. On June 9, three days after the landing, Helmut Jaksch, a Goebbels's operative, asked sarcastically:

"If Allied troops are trying to make headway in the West while quiet reigns in the East, where is the coordination proclaimed in Teheran?"

A few days later the Red Army delivered its reply. It was conclusive, definite and devastating. The Goebbels lie factories did not at first appreciate its implications. Four days ago, on the third anniversary of the nazi attack on the Soviet Union and on the eve of the powerful Soviet thrust at Vitebsk, *Bremer Nachrichten* was still mumbling from habit that "by relinquishing part of the vast conquered territory in Russia, Germany acted on conclusions drawn level-headedly from the course of military operations". Fascist propaganda was still peddling its old story of an "elastic defence". But a few days later the tale collapsed. Now a new formula has been contrived: "straightening the front according to plan". The liberation of Cherbourg was followed closely by the liberation of Vitebsk, Orsha and Mogilev in the East. The swiftness of the Soviet operation, begun on June 23, its scale and force, altered entirely the military situation in Europe in a matter of days. It is still too early to say what the probable effects of it will be. One thing is clear: crashing through the deep zone of first-class German fortifications, encircling and wiping out a large German force, intensifying the drive and rapidly advancing westwards, the Red Army has foiled nazi plans for the summer of 1944. The June events in both European theatres have at last brought home to the German command what it only recently denied: that the armed forces of the anti-Hitler coalition are superior.

July 4, 1944

At Kursk last year Hitler lost the initiative for good. It is now safe to say that the Red Army and Anglo-American operations are quickly bringing closer Germany's *total defeat*. Goebbels is beating the drums for a supertotal mobilisation. Short of manpower, nazi strategists are now banking on two factors only—space and time.

This means that they want to continue resisting as *long* as possible and as *far away* as possible from Germany's vital centres. A *Dagens Nyheter* correspondent reports from Berlin that "German military reviews on June 29 say Germany would, for the time being, assume the defensive both in west and east.... Berlin says France is big enough for Germany to fight a defensive war and not expose to danger vitally important German zones."

The Berlin correspondent of the Japanese *Yomiuri-Shimbun* reported on June 29:

"The military situation is becoming tenser in view of the rate at which the Red Army has been advancing in the past five days.... One German military expert says Field-Marshal Model can withdraw into Poland and still have 200,000 sq. km. of territory behind him.... German military quarters point out, however, that the situation will become still tenser in summer."

German "military quarters" ought to know, because they are well briefed on the situation in the Soviet-German theatre. The Red Army has liberated Polotsk and is poised to liberate all Soviet Lithuania. Its powerful thrusts westward have stunned the nazi command, who now have to decide how they will cover the approaches to East Prussia.

July 28, 1944

Colonel Stauffenberg's abortive attempt on Hitler's life eight days ago and the generals' plot were like a flash of lightning in the "power crisis". Judging by information and misinformation appearing in the foreign press, the plotters were spurred to action by their conviction that the war is lost. Like Ludendorff in 1918, they hoped to salvage what they could: save the army from total collapse and prevent Germany proper from becoming a theatre of operations. Like Ludendorff, who realised at the eleventh hour that Kaiser Wilhelm had to be sacrificed, they, too, realised that Hitler and his clique had to be disposed of. In both cases it appeared to diminish the generals' own culpability for what they did earlier.

According to an official nazi version, the plotters were chiefly generals dismissed from active service. Yet they are being blamed for the latest German defeats. "The critical situation in the central sector of the Eastern front," a nazi commentator writes, "was created largely by the ring of conspirators." By standing his generals to the wall and shooting them, Hitler says he is removing the last remaining obstacle to victory. Yet the generals conspired because they think Hitler is responsible for the defeats.

Himmler's carnage is to help the nazis gird for a war of attrition. Hitler is making convulsive efforts to put off the catastrophe. Those, at least, are the implications of Hitler's latest extra-total mobilisation, which Dittmar, a commentator, describes as an "improvisation". He, too, it appears, is not sure it will work, but knows that Hitler's "intuition" can offer nothing more at this point. The drowning man catches at straw. Goebbels has been put at the head of the new extra-total conscripts and Himmler has been given extra-total powers in the rear.

At a conference of East front commanders, Hitler spoke

of the dangers looming in Poland and East Prussia. "Our gravest concern," wrote Dittmar, "is in the East," where, he added, "a terrible threat has arisen at the gate to Germany."

Developments indicate that, firstly, Hitler, the proponent of lightning war, has become an advocate of a war of attrition, and, second, that a crisis is brewing among the German generals and, possible, in other high spheres. When everything is said and done this is a result of stinging nazi defeats and of strategic and political errors.

August 8, 1944

Through the near-impregnable nazi smokescreen, on the strength of certain indications, especially the German press and radio, I see the revival of the militarist legend devised in 1918 about "a stab in the back" by defeated generals, touched up to suit the present situation. Recently, Hitler said that German victory was assured because, unlike the First World War, German troops were not exposed to a "stab in the back". Yet on August 4 he admitted that he cannot be entirely certain of the outcome because he is "not sure that total security, deep faith and close co-operation prevail in the rear". He is placing the blame for his defeats on the July 20 conspirators.

A few days ago Hitler and his entourage told the world that the conspiracy, however serious its consequences might have been, lacked deep roots. Now, even Fritzsche, one of Goebbels's closest associates, confesses that "the originally detected three or so plotters had outside support in preparing their scheme. The group turned out to be bigger than was thought."

In addition to Beck, other prominent generals and officers participated, who by reason of their official posts obtained an accurate idea of the true military situation. One of them was General Fellgiebel, chief of technical communications, who handled all secret reports from war theatres. Colonel Hansen, chief of a Supreme Command department, Artillery General Wagner and Major-General Stieff, associated with the Supreme Command, had access to information about manpower and material resources. Colonel von Freytag-Loringhoven, chief of another department, was fully briefed on the scale of the active resistance in occupied areas and the extent of damage inflicted by the many millions of resisting foreign workers forcibly shipped into Germany. Many names have been written into the list of defendants subject to execution by Hitler's improvised "court of honour". But the number of officers involved in the conspiracy is far greater than that in the list. There were also plotters among the civil administration, and a few of the industrialists who once subsidised Hitler and his clique. One of these is Goerdeler, who was well enough informed about the dwindling economic reserves.

What were the political aims of the plot? Where do the threads lead to in Germany and possibly abroad?

The answers to these questions would cast more light on the situation, at least in general terms, or, possibly, in terms of the war's political history.

What are Hitler and his clique counting on? The *Reichsleiters* and *Gauleiters* urgently summoned to a conference appear to be the force that Hitler is marshalling to delay the hour of collapse. Speer, the armaments minister, said he is re-arming the German forces. He said the "secret weapon" (V-1, a guided missile) developed in Germany is a "strategic factor" certain to frustrate the Allies in Western Europe. The country must "hang on", he said, until it becomes available. Goebbels said salvation would come from the latest, extra-total mobilisation of which he has taken charge. Himmler promised to sustain the "purge" with the usual ferocity. In the nazi jargon this is styled as "flushing the remaining grains of sand out of the war machine". Cumulatively, says the *Hackenkreuzbanner*, this means, "we are determined to win time". That was indeed the keynote of the urgent conference at which Hitler said he feared nothing save "a stab in the back". What he is really afraid of is new defeats and the approaching breakdown of the German army.

August 30, 1944

Ten days ago the nazi *Flensburger Nachrichten* wrote: "The war has entered an extremely serious phase. In the East, Soviet troops have reached the Vistula and are threatening Germany proper somewhat north of there."

In the interim Germany's military and political situation has deteriorated. While the nazis concentrated on the northern and central sectors of the Soviet-German front, the Red Army struck in the south.

Soviet troops drove to the bank of the Danube, touching off political repercussions. The eruption of the crisis long brewing in Rumania toppled the Antonescu dictatorship. The newly formed Sanatescu government broke with Hitler Germany and announced its wish to fight on the side of the Allies. Transocean, the nazi newsagency, commented sulkily that this was "a fact of secondary importance", indicating, however, that confusion reigned in Berlin and that Hitler Germany was no longer able to head off the break-up of her bloc of satellites.

The fate of the German divisions in Rumania is sealed. They have been pounded and mauled by the Red Army.

Reuter correspondent Dennis Martin reports that nazi divisions quartered in Yugoslavia have come under heavy pressure in their confrontation with Tito's liberation army.

Paris is free! These few words speak volumes. Allied troops have crossed the Marne and are driving on. Forces landed in southern France are advancing eastward. Soon they will reach northern Italy, creating new difficulties for Kesselring's troops. Other Allied units, heading north, are expected any day to reach Germany's south-west frontier.

October 23, 1944

The outcome of the Anglo-Soviet talks in Moscow on October 9 through 18 eclipsed all other international events. Held after Churchill's and Roosevelt's negotiations in Quebec, where they formulated decisions concerning the West European theatre, the Moscow parleys, the *Times* observed, are of "vital significance for the further consolidation of allied policy both in the military and the political fields".

The fact that Washington approved and appointed an observer, Averell Harriman, the U.S. envoy in Moscow, is fresh evidence of the wartime friendship of the three great powers, the Soviet Union, Britain and the United States, which the Moscow talks cemented. The Anglo-Soviet communique said a "free and intimate exchange of views" took place on "many political questions of common interest". But that is not all: the talks yielded results on joint strategy, the ultimate goal of which is the quickest possible defeat of the common enemy, Hitler Germany. The long and strenuous Moscow conference was imbued with the spirit of Teheran, whose decisions, time has shown, have borne good fruit.

The best evidence of how successful the Moscow parleys were is the new fear that grips the nazis. A spokesman of the German foreign ministry admitted sombrely on October 21 that "the curt formulas of the Moscow communique conceal a far-reaching allied plan aimed at crushing Germany".

The Red Army registered fresh victories: jointly with Marshal Tito's troops it liberated Belgrade; it has mounted an attack on Budapest; it breached a 250 km. stretch of enemy lines in the Carpathians, is completing mopping-up operations in the Baltic area and driving through East Prussia. In the meantime, the Allied troops have captured Aachen. The strategic situation is making the German command cringe in anticipation of co-ordinated assaults against the heart of Hitler Germany.

November 30, 1944

Even at an arduous time it is often useful to look back and see how much has been done. It is a year tomorrow since the announcement that the leaders of the Big Three conferred in Teheran. In these twelve months the Red Army has won victories of the first magnitude. It has cleared the land from Dnepropetrovsk to Belgrade, to Warsaw and to Tilsit. The Allied armies crossed the Apennine Peninsula from south to north, and their landing in Western Europe (which they could no longer delay) created a new war theatre, advancing from the Channel to the upper reaches of the Rhine.

Our Army has driven the invader not only out of Soviet territory, but also out of Rumania, Finland, Bulgaria, most of Hungary, most of Poland, Yugoslavia, a part of Czechoslovakia and Norway. It has entered East Prussia and is poised to strike at South Germany and Austria. In the meantime, Anglo-American troops have liberated much of

Italy, almost all of France and Belgium, and a considerable part of the Netherlands. They have crossed into West Germany and are about to thrust at the Rhineland and Ruhr.

However long the road has been for the Red Army and the armies of our Allies, it should not be measured in kilometres alone. The turning of the tide is decisive and it is quite clear now that Hitler's final defeat is not far distant. Hitler has lost his European allies and vassals, excepting Hungary. Plagued by insoluble problems, chiefly economic, military and political, by the shortage of reserves and possibly by a power crisis, he confronts a powerful coalition of democratic powers whose strength is continuing to increase. In the vice-like grip of the two fronts, Hitler Germany is still resisting, and frenziedly, but it is the desperate stand of someone doomed to die.

On October 25, 1944, the *Völkischer Beobachter* said "the situation is doubtlessly grave, very grave.... The danger hanging over East Prussia and Germany is as grave as ever."

The German press has struck a note of despair. In his latest appeal, Hitler admitted that the sledgehammer blows of the Red Army "have disrupted the fronts" and that the Anglo-American offensive has worsened the situation for Germany. Hitler Germany now knows the impact and significance of the military decisions taken at Teheran.

January 2, 1945

I have the texts of two of Hitler's New Year's appeals to Germans—one made in 1944 and the other a few days ago. Last year Hitler maintained that German troops were a dependable shield far advanced in the East, and that nothing, therefore, could imperil the *Vaterland* from that direction. He also said the German army south of Rome would not give ground and would keep its grip on Italy. Lastly, he declared that the German army was in full control of the Balkans and would repulse any attempt at invading the "European fortress" in the West.

His claims have been dashed. Summing up 1944, Hitler admitted yesterday that "one disaster literally followed another". Top army spokesmen said just about the same thing. General Guderian, chief of the General Staff, said: "Last year our foes succeeded in reaching the borders of Germany." Grossadmiral Dönitz, who once promised to bring the Allies to their knees by a merciless submarine war, declared: "Behind us is a difficult and fatal year. For Germany it was a year of serious defeats." Göring, who once said his air armada would crush all foes and let no enemy bomb drop on German soil, was cautious to say nothing of the past, for the destruction wreaked on German cities is eloquent evidence of the overwhelming superiority of the Allied air strength. He confined himself to vowing loyalty to his *Führer*; possibly because he was, according to Hans Fritzsche, "one of the many Germans conscious of their responsibility, knowing that they are gazing down into the abyss".

The *Führer*, too, gazed into the abyss. Admitting "terrible defeats", he blames them on the former rulers of Rumania, Bulgaria and his other satellites, as well as the generals who conspired against him and were executed. He entreats Germans to "trust their National-Socialist leaders", to trust him, his policy and his "intuitive strategy". He pleads with them to "fight fanatically to the finish". But the "crises and not a few defeats", he is compelled to admit, are not making the Germans any more hopeful. Hitler can promise them nothing, so lashes out at them: he tells them in no uncertain terms he will "wring the neck of anyone who tries evading" battle. He tells them he can work wonders, and Goebbels hastens to declare him a miracle-maker. Nazi propaganda claims, by the way, that the offensive in the West by Rundstedt is just such a "German miracle".

January 9, 1945

It is now patently clear that the Rundstedt offensive in Belgium and Alsace pursued major political, not only strategic, aims. When it was still progressing successfully, the *Völkischer Beobachter* observed that "in this battle the issue does not hinge on towns and rivers, not even on the fate of divisions and armies, but most of all on who will lay down the law in the West European theatre in the weeks to come". The paper said that having lost the ability "to lay down the law" after its defeat at Stalingrad, the nazi command is determined to regain it and avert the storming of the "German fortress" surrounded on three sides by the Red Army and its Anglo-American Allies.

To begin with, the Germans expected to wrest the initiative from the Allies, hoping this would have considerable *political* repercussions. The theatre chosen for the offensive is clear evidence of political aims: breaking into territory held by the U.S. 1st Army, the nazis hoped to drive on into territory held by the British in Belgium. Strategically, the thrust was aimed at Liège; its political aims were much more far-reaching. In the past few days, Rundstedt has been straining to get to Strasbourg, and hoped the impetus would carry him to Paris.

Hitler hopes the offensive will create confusion and dissent in the Allied camp. That is the only hope he has left. Roosevelt called attention to this in his latest message to the Congress. "The wedge that the Germans attempted to drive in Western Europe," he wrote, "was less dangerous in actual terms of winning the war than the wedges which they are continually attempting to drive between ourselves and our Allies. Every little rumour which is intended to weaken our faith in our Allies is like an actual enemy agent in our midst, seeking to sabotage our war effort."

A timely reminder!

The made-in-Germany label is easily discernible on propaganda products of the Goebbels lie factories and the backstage "peace" manoeuvres of the Ribbentrop diplomats. But now and then similar products see the light of day where Hitler could not conceivably have any adepts. Take the influential *Army and Navy Journal* appearing in the United States. Its latest issue says it was Red Army inactivity that made the German offensive in Belgium possible. It endeavours to create the impression that Rundstedt's offensive is prosecuted by troops deployed from the Soviet-German front. On the contrary, to recapture Budapest the nazi command is shifting to Hungary troops from the West, notably Holland. But the U.S. armchair strategists are blind to this fact. "If nothing is done to take Budapest," they write, "Hitler could send reinforcements to Rundstedt and delay our invasion into Germany." Some quarters in the United States are obviously out to sow doubt and mistrust of the Red Army in the Allied camp.

Truth-seeking men will not tolerate it. Patrick Lacey, a British observer, takes issue with the *Army and Navy Journal*. It is obviously out of touch with the facts, he says, and overlooks Soviet operations in Czechoslovakia and Hungary, where the Red Army is in the midst of a winter offensive as big, if not bigger, than the Allied operations in the West. The Red Army has cut off the city of Budapest, one of the key German fortresses in Europe. Throughout the war, the Russian front diverted the maximum German forces and even now, after three and a half years of war, the Soviet Army is holding down much more than half the German divisions.

The U.S. journal turned a deaf ear to these facts. The Red Army offensive in Hungary, it said, has a "special purpose". It is hard put to conceal its displeasure over Red Army successes. The nazis are allergic to them, too. So Patrick Lacey asks: "Who are these men that criticise the Russians?" This is not rhetoric. Especially if we recall which forces in the United States have a stake in sowing mistrust of the Soviet Union.

February 17, 1945

The documents of a new Allied conference were published a few days ago. Rumours of the three-power meeting first appeared in the press in autumn last year. After the re-election of President Roosevelt they became more insistent. The foreign press speculated about the probable venue. Some named London or Paris, others named Fairbanks in Alaska or Teheran. Still others hinted of a point in the Mediterranean. A State Department spokesman said to correspondents he would not reveal the venue, because the place might still be used. It turned out that the conference took place on February 4-11 in our own Crimea.

All of us looked forward to the conference with hope and trust. The enemy, too, waited, but with fear. Before the Teheran Conference Hitler still reckoned that if he failed to win the war, he could at least avoid losing it.

On the eve of the Crimea Conference the nazis were too deflated to brag. In deadly terror they followed all reports. This time they voiced no doubts about the likelihood of a meeting. A spokesman of Ribbentrop's ministry said, in his opinion the main purpose of the conference was "not military, but political: to salvage the Anglo-American-Soviet coalition". None of the partners, he said, had any faith in it any more. This was wishful thinking, which lifted the veil on the nazis' hope that differences over specific issues would grow into a profound rift that the nazis could exploit to save themselves or to delay the hour of doom.

During the months before the Crimea Conference, certain sections of the Allied press did, indeed, pursue a controversy over various issues, chiefly economical and political. They discussed the problem of oil, maritime communications and post-war civil aviation. A sharp dispute erupted over Poland, the former nazi satellites and, last but not least, the future of Germany. Nazi propaganda took this as a sign of insurmountable differences. The Japanese press was of the same opinion. The *Mainichi Shimbun*, for example, maintained on January 23, 1945, that the absence of solutions for some issues ruled out an early three-power conference.

Shortly before the Crimea Conference, Goebbels wrote in *Das Reich* that agreement among the Allies, especially between the Soviet Union and the Anglo-Saxon countries, was impossible. A fresh campaign followed against the "Bolshevik menace". Regrettably, it won followers elsewhere. Reactionary publications in the United States, Britain and other countries went out of their way to poison the atmosphere and were sceptical about parleys succeeding to resolve the basic problems of the war and the future peace.

The Yalta resolutions should be viewed, therefore, as a victory over those who had hoped the Allies would fail to come to terms.

Judging by published documents, the problem of crushing Germany militarily held top priority. We know nothing of the details. They are down in the operational plans of the Red Army and the Anglo-American Allies. We know, however, that the plans have been co-ordinated, envisaging powerful drives from east, west, north and south to bring the end of the war nearer.

Germany will be defeated. It is time to think of her future. This is important not only for Germany, but for the future peace. The Crimea Conference worked out a general plan of how to bring about Hitler's unconditional surrender. Certain people in Britain, the United States and elsewhere object. The Vatican calls for "reconciliation". The Catholic press in Britain, and certain other quarters, are following the same line. The journal, *The Nineteenth Century and After*, thinks a militarist Germany could be a useful tool of anti-Soviet policy. Prominent U.S. isolationists, notably Senator Wheeler, think so too. Dorothy Thompson, the well-known columnist, pleads that the nazis should be spared. The principle of unconditional surrender must be scrapped, she writes, and negotiations with Germany should precede an armistice. But the Crimea Conference ignored Hitler's advocates. Unconditional surrender remains the ultimate war aim.

The terms will be made known after German armed resistance is finally crushed. Much depends on the military situation at the hour of surrender. If German troops resist to the end, it may be scattered army formations without centralised control that will capitulate. General Dittmar, the nazi commentator, invented a term indicating the futility of resistance by encircled armies, namely, "wandering kettles". These vagabond "kettles" are not likely to resist for long, presaging disintegration of the German military machine and its final extirpation.

The main war criminals will propably try to escape to a neutral country, perhaps elsewhere. At the Moscow Foreign Ministers' Conference the Allied powers agreed that retribution would be meted out wherever they may try to hide, "even on the edge of the world".

Goebbels said: "We'll sooner die than surrender." Almost right for once. Hitler and his clique will escape neither surrender nor death. The Yalta Conference reaffirmed that retribution will be swift and fair, applying also to the top militarists. *Mitgefangen—mitgehangen*, says a German proverb. The Big Three leaders have made the only possible decision: the nazi army will be disarmed to the last man, the German armed forces disbanded, German arms destroyed, the German war industry wound up or placed under control. This will spell the end of Prusso-German militarism.

The Yalta programme is designed to plug up all loopholes that the German imperialists could one day use to revive their power. Germany will be occupied—not partially as after the First World War. There are to be three large occupation zones. Roosevelt announced that the eastern zone will be occupied by the Red Army, the north-western by British troops and the south-western, plus a corridor to Bremen, by the U.S. Army. France could have a zone too if she wants one.

What is unclear is the question of Berlin, the German capital. That, too, will surely be settled no matter what army enters the city first. Evidently, it will be occupied by troops of states represented on the Allied Control Council, consisting of the commanders-in-chief of the principal powers of the anti-Hitler coalition, whose seat will be in Berlin.

Nothing was said in the published Yalta decisions about the territorial issues. Yet the foreign press is speculating on the subject in lively fashion. Two points are clear: Austria is to be reconstituted as an independent state and Poland "must receive substantial accessions of territory in the north and west".

The published Declaration on Liberated Europe makes a deep impression. It plots the path that will "enable the liberated peoples to destroy the last vestiges of nazism and fascism, and to create democratic institutions of their own choice".

The road to the complete and final defeat of German militarism, embodied by the Hitler state, has been hard and tortuous. The road traversed by the Soviet armies from the bank of the Volga to the Oder has, unquestionably, had a strong bearing in more ways than one on the success of the Crimea Conference. Despite the wiles of Hitler diplomacy and the ascendancy of reactionary elements in Britain, the United States and other countries, the anti-Hitler coalition has not fallen to pieces. The war is entering its final stage. He who drew the sword, shall perish by the sword!

February 28, 1945

Having captured nearly all East Prussia and the vital war-industrial centres of Silesia, the Red Army is pounding the heart of Germany. In the West, American and Canadian troops have breached the Siegfried Line and are poised to assault the Rhine-Westphalian area. If nothing unforeseen of a political order happens, the nazi army and the Hitler state face imminent defeat. The nazi clique knows it. Its propaganda can no longer hush up the facts.

Only a few weeks ago General Dittmar extolled the German troops cut off at Königsberg, Breslau, Poznan, etc. A week later, on February 24, Hitler dropped Poznan from this list in his message to the *Gauleiters* of cities encircled by Soviet troops, for it had been liberated. Neither did he mention the group encircled at Schneidemühl for the same reason. He promised no aid to the *Gauleiters* of Breslau and Königsberg, whom he entreated to have "trust in the future" and resist to the end.

What happened to German troops in Budapest, Poznan and other cities shows what the outcome will be of desperate and senseless resistance. The fate of Hitler Germany is sealed. It is hardly possible that Hitler, the German command and the other nazi chiefs are unaware of what the blows from east, west, north and south projected at Yalta spell for their country. They dread what Rudolf Semmler, one of Goebbels's aides, described as "a synchronised general offensive from east and west". Offensive operations have begun at both ends. In his latest war report, "The Battle in East and West", on February 27, General Dittmar told Germans to be prepared for more defeats. It is reliably learned that operations in east and west have shattered morale behind the lines, especially in areas adjoining the battlefields, and only few German provinces are now at some distance from the front. According to the Swedish *Aftonbladet*, the population of Saxony is in an uproar because *Volkssturm* battalions are being deployed to the lines. Women demonstrated in Cottbus, where they are said to have chanted: "What good are old men? If the *Führer* wants to fight, let him fight." The foreign press reports that desertions are widespread, especially from the *Volkssturm*.

Yet Hitler published a new appeal, saying the fight must go on "with the utmost fanaticism and fierce tenacity". Defying common sense, Hitler wants the nation to believe what he no longer believes: "A historic change will come about before the year is out." What he avers is that Germany will win. Clearly, as an English paper put it, his promise is not worth a rotten potato. Clearly, too, Hitler Germany is continuing resistance with the madness of despair to delay the final hour.

What is Berlin hoping to achieve? Sven Hedin, the Swedish pro-nazi now in the final phase of senility, once said Germany would win the war unless she lost it. Today, with Germany plummeting to her doom, this is a total anachronism. After Yalta Hitler should have realised there was no hope of a "compromise peace", much less victory. There is reason to believe the nazi clique is hoping against hope. On February 24 Hitler assembled *Reichsleiters, Gauleiters* and other nazi chiefs to orient them as to what the official announcement described as "continuing resistance". It seems they are planning an underground nazi army, banking on aid from old and new friends and influential supporters in the Allied and neutral countries. Wilfred von Ofen, a nazi commentator, declared in a radio broadcast on February 23 that "we need to resist", for political differences may erupt among the Allies.

March 13, 1945

The latest developments indicate that the military and political decisions taken at the Crimea Conference, published a month ago, are now being put into effect. Soviet troops have reached the approaches to Danzig and Stettin. They have captured Küstrin and are closer to Berlin. Anglo-American troops have crossed the Rhine at several points and set up beachheads on its east bank. A mere 500 kilometres lie between the Red Army advancing westward and the Allied troops advancing east. "I have the impression," Hitler said in his latest appeal to the German armies, "that fate has turned against us."

The latest appeal differed from previous ones in many ways. The *Yorkshire Post* said it was a study in criminal psychology. Hitler made no promises. He demanded: "resist, keep resisting until you wear out the enemy." Yet German troops have learned that, far from subsiding, Allied assaults are becoming more devastating. German commanders are taking stock of their last surviving reserves, while the new propaganda outcry over the *Volkssturm* indicates that manpower is running out.

Hitler's appeal is not even propaganda. It is a hysterical plea to delay defeat, to postpone surrender. It betrays the animal fear that gripped the Führer when he realised the Red Army and the Allies would carry their cause to a triumphant finish.

March 26, 1945

Things are moving fast. One wonders what the Berlin clique and its generals are banking on? After the Yalta Conference they could hardly have retained any illusions. Their propaganda machine had to condition the nation to withstanding the joint offensive. Nazi generals, too, had to prepare. They endeavoured to frustrate, or at least impede, the military plan worked out in Yalta. This was the purpose of their abortive attack at Lake Balaton along a line covering those provinces of the Third Reich, Austria and Western Czechoslovakia where the German war industries are sheltered. After losing Upper Silesia, with the Ruhr menaced by the Allies, those are areas of prime importance for Hitler. However, the nazi offensive broke down. General Dittmar hastened to elucidate on March 23: "It would be a fallacy to assume that the area is of secondary importance. The road upriver along the Danube leads from Budapest to Bratislava and Vienna. Doubtless, the Red Army is quite capable of a big offensive there sooner or later."

The Red Army struck earlier than the nazis anticipated. Moreover, it supplemented the drive from around Budapest with an operation in which it encircled and annihilated a large enemy force at Oppeln. The nazis are stunned and have stopped prattling about the "salvation" that army groups encircled by the Red Army at other points spell for Germany. These encircled groups did not head off new blows at Hitler Germany; nor did they escape annihilation. The East Prussian group is being methodically destroyed. Dittmar, who no doubt reflects the sentiment of the nazi command, is speculating darkly about what will follow. He looks into the future and arrives at the conclusion that "the Red Army offensive is proceeding, as it were, in several stages".

With the main nazi forces pinned down in the East, the

Anglo-American armies have crossed the Rhine. Not only have the nazis lost a powerful water barrier, the locale of so much tradition and hope, but also a number of major industrial centres, the core of the German war potential. Paralysis of the Ruhr is imminent. "It is clear," Hitler said a few days ago, "that the situation there calls for urgent radical solutions." But what solutions can Hitler offer? The substitution of Kesselring for Rundstedt has changed nothing. Kesselring has nothing except his understrength 15 divisions to counterweigh Marshal Montgomery. *Transocean,* the nazi newsagency, says the Anglo-American divisions in the past few days "were in a favourable position, particularly since their operations became synchronised with the Soviet operations".

This synchronisation based on joint planning at Yalta is inspiring deep fear in Germany. Official nazi propaganda media cannot help betraying it. U.S. commentator Lewis wonders how much longer Hitler will be allowed to lead the Germans from one defeat to the next.

What is the dastardly nazi clique—Hitler, Himmler, Bormann, Goebbels and Göhring—counting on? Probably a "political crisis". After the Grimea Conference they ought to know better. Yet they are clinging to this vain hope. That is the only possible explanation for their new, despairing acts of secret diplomacy. Take von Hesse's "peace feeler" mission to Stockholm—an attempt at sowing suspicion among the Allies, poisoning the political atmosphere and impeding the Allied strategic and operational plans.

Yet these endeavours are failing dismally. As for their purpose, it was reaffirmed the other day by Goebbels. "We are determined," he said, "to begin all over again."

That is why the Soviet Union is determined, for its part, to crush Hitler Germany and wipe fascism off the face of the earth.

April 10, 1945

The Red Army has captured Königsberg. It is fighting in the streets of Vienna. Soviet and foreign observers say this is of cardinal strategic importance.

The victory at Königsberg, an important seat of nazi resistance on the Baltic, culminates the operation against the East Prussian army group. Elliott of the *New York Herald Tribune* notes, also, that the Red Army drive from Lake Balaton to Vienna was one of the biggest military feats of the war. Once Vienna falls, the Red Army will have entered an internal German fortress. *Associated Press* commentator Mackenzie notes, too, that no other current event can eclipse the battle for Vienna because it checkmates Hitler's intention of making his last stand in the Alps.

The *political* impact is also very great. Eastern Prussia, historically the citadel of Prusso-German reaction and aggressive eastern policy, is lost to German militarism forever. The Soviet troops fighting in Vienna have delivered a lethal blow to German imperialist domination in Central Europe. Vienna is the sixth European capital to be liberated by the Red Army. According to reports, Austrians are not fleeing with the German troops. What is more, they are resisting the nazis by slow work, frustrating nazi attempts to ship out plant and refusing to join the *Volkssturm*. The official Soviet statement that the U.S.S.R. "will help abolish the regime of the German nazi occupation forces and restore in Austria democratic institutions" has evidently met with a favourable response in Austria and other countries. It made plain that the Red Army has no intention of acquiring Austrian territory or changing the social system. Soviet policy is based on the letter and spirit of the Allied declaration on Austria's independence.

Hitler Germany spread the insidious rumour that the Soviet Union will go back on that declaration and, regrettably, certain Western quarters accepted the legend, though it is so obviously designed to sow mistrust among the Allies.

This and similar facts show that the nazis are casting about for political means to replace the military capability they no longer command. Hitler has mobilised and engaged every bit of manpower he could. German reserves have run dry. Now, the nazis are deploying to the Eastern front their "special units", the *Walküre*, and the *Gneisenau* battalions. *Transocean* describes them as fire-brigades assigned to "eliminate sudden dangers". Such "fire-brigades" are an admission that the hopes pinned on the *Volkssturm* are dashed. Nothing on earth, neither the *Volkssturm* nor the *Walküre* or *Gneisenau* units, nor the ferocious resistance of the regular German troops shifted from the Western to the Eastern front, can ward off the sledgehammer blows of the Red Army and avert Germany's rapidly approaching collapse.

Developments on the Western front bear this out, too, although they differ visibly from what is happening on the Soviet-German front. The *Times* of London on April 7 took note of the "striking accompaniment in the east, where the Germans still fight as organised armies, to the victory and pursuit in the West".

Their rulers are trying to conceal from the German people the disastrous defeats in the East and the evidence of collapsing resistance in the West. They are trying to create the impression that on all fronts—east, south, and west—German troops are still equally capable of resisting. On April 7 the nazi information bureau claimed that the perimeter defence of the German Reich is highlighted by stubborn resistance at all points. On the following day, *Transocean* admitted that "the situation on the Western front keeps changing every hour and minute", while the spokesman of the German command in the West said this state of affairs would continue until "the single line of the front is restored". He admitted thereby that the Germans no longer have a single line against the Allies in the West, adding: "The Allies have not yet succeeded in smashing the big German troop concentrations."

It is impossible to smash anything non-existent, such as any big German troop concentrations in the West. Neither do the nazis have any reserves they could use there. The *Manchester Guardian* reports that units are formed hastily of men with no military training. These inferior troops are sent to the lines wherever any exist. Almost none exist, however, and the nazi command cannot create any even if it tried, for the simple reason that it lacks the requisite troops. A prominent official of the German foreign ministry captured by the Americans testified that "the menace from the East was considered graver than that from the West, and most of the troops were used there".

A German spokesman claims that "the commander of German armed forces in the West has no illusions about the situation". Today, to use Churchill's expression, after the Red Army has torn the guts out of the German monster, this sounds like a macabre joke by a man condemned to the hangman's noose. Yet it is no joking matter.

The Germans know that the end is near, very near. "A new offensive is under way in the East," said Hans Fritzsche, "so this is no time for talk." He urges Germans to form Werwolf groups and fight on underground. German banks and industrialists are overtly and covertly shipping out capital, papers, valuables, patents, and the like. Plans have long been in existence in Germany, said U.S. Deputy Secretary of State Holmes, to preserve the industrial and military power of German imperialism after the defeat. Von Papen was in charge of these plans in 1943. In autumn 1944 German industrialists began exporting capital and sending their top specialists to safer places. In November 1943 an I.G. Farben spokesman told certain foreign industrialists that his concern would endeavour to retain its position after the war in Germany and abroad.

According to Reuter, well-informed London quarters have learned that German financiers and industrialists were busy throughout the war devising plans for restoring their power in the event the Third Reich collapses. Here are some of the elements of the plan: complaints to courts of law in various countries that German property was "unlawfully" seized by the Allies; proxies to establish German control over patents in other countries; encouraging German specialists to seek employment with foreign enterprises and research institutes in order to widen the spy network in the industries of the Allied countries; propaganda and other measures to create political dissent among the Allies.

April 26, 1945

We have made it! The Red Army has invested Berlin and is fighting in its streets and squares. The world is following the fierce battle with bated breath. Nazi troops are still desperately resisting. The nazi command is flinging into the battle all available forces. The big city with its many suburbs, its barrack-like buildings, its straight streets, large squares and numerous canals has been turned into a fortress. Goebbels, who is Berlin's *Verteidigungskommissar*, told inhabitants that "formidable defences have been raised in the capital in the past weeks. Fortifications stretch from the outskirts to the centre of the city. Several thousand tank barriers, barricades, bottlenecks and earthworks have been erected round Berlin. The capital is ready to defend itself."

Goebbels said this on April 22, or exactly three years and ten months after Hitler read in Berlin the order to invade the Soviet Union. Justice has triumphed. Hitler's Third Reich is breaking up. The resistance to Soviet troops is agony, the agony of a dying monster that has still to be helped to its death.

"The torch that was lit in Berlin has come back to the city of its origin," writes the *New York Times* of April 23. "The great conflagration which it spread across more than two thousand miles of Europe, and finally to the whole world, is now sweeping through the capital from which it started. And the ragged remnants of the once proud armies that marched out of it to strut through many lands, to murder, rape and loot, are now buried under the falling walls of their own doomed capital."

The Berlin armies have nowhere to retreat. Surrounded by Soviet troops, they are doomed. The German radio announced a few days ago that Germans are prepared to resist bitterly—in their south Bavarian redoubt and in Norway. But that can alter nothing. Now the nazis say Berlin will resist to the end. On their way out they want to turn Berlin into rubble. Beneath this rubble will be buried the German imperialist plan of world power. Never again must an attempt be allowed to carry out German imperialist designs.

Berlin, May 3, 1945

Nazi Germany is in her death throes! Even the towns and villages of the north-eastern regions that escaped the devastation of war and somehow survived, stand abandoned, desolate, showing no signs of life. On the town-halls hang large white sheets, denoting surrender. But the Stettin-Berlin *Autobahn* and all adjoining roads are crowded.

In the mid-thirties, soon after the nazis seized power, the Todt organisation used the pretext of combating unemployment to build strategic motor-roads carefully drawn into the maps of the prospective aggression. The men who had calculatingly fostered Hitler and those who had worshipped him blindly, could scarcely have anticipated that one day they would have to blow up bridges along those roads to deny their use to Soviet troops driving inexorably towards Berlin after having been pressed back to Moscow, Leningrad and the Volga earlier in the war.

Where are the people of these numerous towns? What are they thinking, what hopes have they? Turn off the *Autobahn* along one of the many highways and country roads; you will see a gaudy stream of tens of thousands of Germans—men, women and children, carrying their belongings. The nazi authorities are said to have first planned to evacuate the population of the eastern provinces to the West. But moving 30 million people while unintermittent battles were fought all round was impracticable. Another misdeed, another crime of the nazis—this time against their own people. In fact, the nazis helped to evacuate only the local authorities, the top officials, the wealthy families, and the families of *Wehrmacht* and other officers. As a result, the bulk of the population, frightened out of their wits by Goebbels's tales of "Bolshevik atrocities", driven by a long-cultivated mass discipline and chiefly by their terror and their fear of retribution for nazi crimes on Soviet soil, is trekking blindly westward, or southward, or northward. Accustomed to obedience but now abandoned to their own ends, they have lost control over their actions, and over their wits to boot. Fear and confusion have seized them and driven them to flight. The most fanatical and hard-headed nazi officials ordered them one minute to dig trenches round every village and fight for every house, and the next minute to pack and flee. Panic is contagious. Many trekked off with the nazi troops, some fell behind and walked into battle areas where tanks and artillery were at work. Their senseless death inspired terror among the survivors. But the German command is blind to this. By refusing to surrender, continuing the stubborn and useless resistance, it is deliberately sacrificing its soldiers and the civilian population, deceived once more and driven to despair.

For the first time, Germans have learned the hardships of war on their own soil. Never since the Napoleonic wars were battles fought on German land. In the past 80 years, Prussia and Germany were involved in five wars, but never on home soil. Throughout this Hitler-engineered war, too, they let themselves be persuaded that, having seized vast "living space", the German army would achieve its aims in battles fought far from the borders of Germany proper. Yet the war is ending in a crushing defeat, not in a victory securing a thousand years of the Third Reich. The population knows by now that Berlin was pounded. The German capital surrendered yesterday to the Soviet Army after a senseless resistance.

Vast crowds of people are wandering about in a state of shock, some in search of shelter, others on the way back to their hastily abandoned homes. Their eyes are empty. No one can tell what is going on in their minds, belaboured for so long by venomous propaganda, a blend of nationalism, militarism, demagogy and anti-Semitism, a vicious ideology known as "national-socialism". None but the Communists and trade unionists who survived miraculously underground know what has to be done. They offer their services to the Soviet military authorities in restoring democratic order.

I have seen crowds of German "refugees" meeting on their way groups of Poles, Frenchmen and Italians released from concentration camps or forced labour at war plants or Junker estates, carrying their national flags as they march to the East where deliverance had come from. The Germans let them pass in silence, lowering their eyes, pretending not to see them. This exodus in different directions, this migration of numerous people of whom only yesterday some were conscious of belonging to the "master nation" while others were reduced to slavery—those are the first tangible signs of the disintegration of the nazi-patterned society and the beginning of the end of the nazi state.

One has to see Berlin to realise the extent of the disaster inflicted on Germany by fascism.

The German capital lies in ruins. Sunk into total darkness at night, Berlin is like the crater of a huge volcano in which lava has congealed in most bizarre and grotesque shapes. The city is dead. Here and there, fires still burn. The biggest of these, somewhere near the Reichstag, is the landmark we use to get our bearings. Only the flames remind us that this is a city, not a nightmare. In daylight, Berlin is just as unrecognisable, and much uglier. Its straight streets and its squares are impassable: shell-holes, bomb craters, piles of rubble torn out of the houses and flung to earth, block all traffic. A yellow dust hangs over the ruins and contaminates the air. In the destroyed residence of Adolf Hitler, the Imperial Chancellory, there is foul desolation. The same is true of Wilhelmstrasse, the street of Ribbentrop's ministry and other government buildings, including that of the General Staff.

Where is Hitler, the Reichschancellor, Führer of the German people and Supreme Commander of the armed forces of the German Reich? He is said to have committed suicide. His body is said to have been burned; the bodies of a few of his doubles have been found, too.

Where is Goebbels, Berlin's *Verteidigungskommissar*? He has also committed suicide.

Göhring, Bormann, Himmler, Jodl and Keitel—those have fled ingloriously.

The curtain is going down on the greatest crime of the century.

Berlin, May 5, 1945

This noon the nazi garrison, which surrendered earlier and was disarmed, was led out of the cellars of the Reichstag. In those cellars twelve years ago nazi provocateurs started a fire which they conceived as a declaration of war on communism and a pretext for clamping down on the democratic forces and traditions of the German nation.

How myopic were those who said then that the Reichstag fire was no more than an abortive episode in the nazis' fight against communism. No, the Reichstag fire was only a preliminary for the torchbearers dreaming of setting fire to Europe, to the whole world. One had to possess a profound understanding of history and, more, a sense of responsibility for the future, to accuse one's accusers publicly, as Georgi Dimitrov did when in Gestapo hands. The only way Hitler Germany could assert herself was through incendiarism, through war crimes and crimes against humanity.

Three days ago the German capital surrendered. The remnants of the warmakers sought refuge in cellars to save their lives. Under the nazi dictatorship, the Reichstag played no practical role and its huge old building was not even restored after the fire. Yet the fire had made it a symbol of fascist policy. So the Soviet flag planted on its dome has become a symbol of victory over the sinister forces of reaction, fascism and aggressive war.

The battle for Berlin was a hard one. Not only the German commanders and officers, but the soldiers as well, resisted bitterly to the last, although they must have known that resistance was senseless. What were they hoping for? Were they enthralled by the slogans Goebbels pasted on all walls: *Berlin bleibt treu, Berlin bleibt deutsch,* even *Berlin siegt*? Or did they think the reinforcements they were promised from the Western front would really arrive? They could hardly have believed that the *Volkssturm* would be effective, consisting as it did of 14-year-old Berlin boys hastily put into outsize mouse-grey uniforms. By and large, one must admit that the reflex of unquestioning obedience and Prusso-German military discipline cultivated over the centuries and multiplied by fear of retribution, pervaded all levels of the nazi army.

What did the nazi rulers and the German command count on? The rapid Soviet advance, enveloping and breaching the Berlin defences, the advance of the Allied armies across Germany, it would seem, should have brought home to them that they lost the war and that after inflicting unthinkable suffering on the peoples of Europe, and on their own people, their defeat is complete and final. Yet by continuing to resist they clung to life in cowardly despair. What was the last hope of Hitler, who, captured German generals say, did not shoot himself until the afternoon of April 30, when Soviet troops were already nearing his underground den? What is the last hope of his successor, Grossadmiral Dönitz, who has not laid down arms somewhere in Schleswig despite Berlin's surrender three days ago?

One day the world will learn, and the historian comprehend, what happened among the nazi rulers in these spring days of Germany's defeat. But even today, monitored radio broadcasts and dispatches lift the veil somewhat on the politico-strategic hopes of the nazis, possibly also of Dönitz. It is evident that something of a political battle has begun in the Allied press and radio over a long since accepted and agreed question—that of Germany's unconditional surrender. In the interest of the future peace, Franklin Roosevelt defined this war aim in 1943 at the Quebec Conference. The three-power conferences in Teheran and Yalta formulated and reaffirmed it. But it appears that Roosevelt's sudden death has roused to action his political opponents in the United States and Britain. By demanding a new foreign policy, especially in relation to the Soviet Union, these quarters have evidently given Hitler and his clique cause to hope that the anti-nazi coalition would break up. In any case, judging by the nazi press and radio, the hope that the differences would become insuperable have developed into the belief that disintegration is inevitable.

The situation is strange indeed. The nearer the Red Army and the Anglo-American troops are bringing the hour of unconditional surrender, the more vehemently certain quarters in the United States, Britain and the neutral countries press their political arguments against unconditional surrender. Roughly, their arguments are: the demand for unconditional surrender is robbing the German people and the German army of all prospects, embittering them, and thereby prolonging the war and causing needless sacrifice on both sides. If the Western powers lifted the demand, the German rulers could enter into negotiations. Abandoning the demand of unconditional surrender is therefore sensible policy in the interests of humanity.

But the premises and the inference are equally false. True, Hitler and his political and military clique have frightened Germans into believing that their fate is linked with the fate of the nazi army and state. One cannot help admitting that by unbridled nationalist propaganda and just as unbridled terror, the nazis have attained this purpose. But that is precisely the reason why other facts are immeasurably more important. After all, the 6th Army at Stalingrad and the armies at Budapest and elsewhere, and finally the German troops in Berlin, surrendered not because enticing prospects were offered to them. On the contrary, they surrendered totally and unconditionally because no such enticing prospects existed, because they had no other choice. The demand for unconditional surrender is not inspired by any craving for revenge. It is prompted by the wish of putting Hitler Germany in a position where every German, whether serviceman or civilian, should see clearly that the nazi state, that nazism and militarism, must and will be destroyed in the interest of all peoples, including the German. This alone will offer the German nation a new historical perspective. And that is the only sensible and genuinely humane policy as viewed in terms of the future.

But it is just what the German rulers evidently wished, and still hope, to evade before going off the stage. Some of them probably expect the question of Germany's future to create differences in the anti-Hitler coalition and others possibly nurse the idea that a separate peace with Britain and America is still practicable, provided the fight against the Soviet Union continues.

Deplorably, one cannot say that their expectations are totally groundless. Somewhere at the end of April, I think it was on the 26th, the *Daily Mirror* correspondent in San Francisco reported with undeniable joy that influential quarters in Britain and the United States are initiating moves to re-create a strong post-war Germany as a bulwark against the Soviet Union. Nor is this the only report of that kind. Reports dating to the end of April say that Count Bernadotte, president of the Swedish Red Cross, has acted as middleman between some nazi quarters and representatives of the British and American ruling circles.

Hitler is no more, but his generals survive. Perhaps the delay of the general surrender is due to their attempting the same thing via other channels. One can never tell.

Berlin, May 9, 1945

The world has waited for this day. Now it has come— the day of victory, the day of hope. The concentrated will of our people and the peoples of the anti-Hitler coalition was stronger than the diplomatic intrigues of the nazi generals and admirals who had cast about desperately for underhand deals with Western quarters.

Yesterday, the Berlin population came out into the streets decked out with Allied flags, hazily conscious that something was about to happen in this semi-demolished

347

capital of the demolished nazi Reich. At about noon, there arrived at Tempelhof airfield Air Marshal Sir Arthur W. Tedder, representing Supreme Allied Commander in Europe, General Dwight D. Eisenhower, and General Carl Spaatz, head of U.S. Strategic Air Force in Europe. They were met on behalf of the Soviet Command by Generals V. D. Sokolovsky, N. E. Berzarin, S. I. Rudenko, F. E. Bokov, and others. For some reason, no representative of the French army arrived.

Soon another plane landed, out of which emerged Field-Marshal Keitel, Admiral Friedeburg and Air Colonel-General Stumpff, accompanied by their aides. Holding his Marshal's baton before him, Keitel walked in the van of his party, eyes unconsciously squinting right, where the Allied Commanders were being met ceremoniously to the strains of a military band. Keitel's companions looked like a band of would-be suicides.

In the afternoon, General Delattre de Tassigny, Commander-in-Chief of French forces, arrived in a special plane. Late in the evening, sowewhere round midnight, after tiring but joyful hours of waiting, the instrument of surrender was signed at a ceremony in Karlshorst's former school of war engineers.

Obsessed by the ambition of conquering Europe and the world, Hitler once said: "Though we may fail to conquer, we shall destroy half the world. Never shall we surrender."

His apocalyptic prophesies did not live up to the hopes of German imperialism and militarism, those of politicians and ideologists. Having indeed demolished half the world, aggressive German militarism created disaster for Germany, but did not escape surrender, unconditional surrender. Hitler was right in one respect only: 1945 was no repetition of 1918. The fact alone that the historic signing of the surrender instrument took place this time not in Compiègne or elsewhere outside Germany, but in her capital, Berlin, speaks of the extent of the disaster visited on German imperialism and militarism, on their fascist executors and their ideology of war and aggression. The surrender of Kaiser Germany in 1918 was signed not by General Ludendorff but by Reichstag Deputy Erzberger with the Western powers alone. This time the unconditional instrument of surrender was signed in Berlin by Field-Marshal Keitel and other representatives of German militarism. The decisive contribution to the victory was made by the Soviet Union, and this is of historic significance not just militarily, but also in the political sense. All peoples championing the idea of national freedom, of peace and democracy, have a stake in the victory.

When Marshal of the Soviet Union G. K. Zhukov, who was in the chair, ordered the German delegation to be shown in, a hush fell over the hall. On entering, Keitel raised his baton but probably instantly realised how fatuous his gesture was, the last gesture of nazi militarism, smashed in battle, condemned by history and subject to total eradication.

Keitel was obviously nervous (his eyeglass slipped several times) but still trying to play a part, if only for himself. He asked to speak before signing the instrument of surrender. What could he say, this war criminal, at the moment when history was ringing down the curtain on the bloody tragedy fascism had inflicted on humanity? Did he wish to vindicate the villainy of German imperialism, reviving a nazi version of the old militarist legend about the "encirclement of Germany" and the need for a "preventive war"? Or did he perhaps want to revive the old militarist legend of a "stab in the back" received by the German army? Or did he wish to call for revenge as he stood beneath the flag of surrender, so that Germans at some favourable time should again hoist the militarist standard and begin preparing a new war?

The speech was not fated to be made, for history had handed down its verdict. On presenting their credentials, Keitel, Friedeburg and Stumpff approached the table in turn and put their signatures under the surrender instrument.

"We, the undersigned," the instrument read, "acting by authority of the German High Command, hereby surrender unconditionally to the Supreme Commander, Allied Expeditionary Force, and simultaneously to the Soviet High Command, all forces on land, sea and in the air who are at this date under German control."

The concluding clause provided that if the German side did not observe all stipulations, "punitive or other actions as they deem appropriate" would be applied.

"Punitive actions". Signing their names beneath these

words, the German militarists as much as admitted that their conduct had been criminal.

It had been criminal from the beginning. The soldiers, officers and generals of the Soviet Army are witness thereto, for it was they who faced the brunt of the assault of the nazi war machine, they who withstood it, and who broke its spine. General V. I. Chuikov is here, in this hall; his troops marched from the banks of the Volga to the Spree. Everybody is here, at least in spirit, everybody who made Hitler Germany surrender. This modest-sized hall seems to hold all the immense heroic and painful efforts made by the Soviet people and all the other peoples, big and small, who fought the nazi tyranny. It holds all the soldiers, all the partisans—those still alive, and those who fell for the cause; Communists and non-Communists, the whole big army of Resistance fighters, heterogeneous, multilingual but united by their craving to defeat fascism. Millions of people are here—men and women, living and shot and killed, from all the concentration camps that pockmark the body of Europe; also the children asphyxiated in the gas-chambers, cremated in the furnaces of Majdanek and Auschwitz and shot in the towns and villages captured by nazis. All who fought, all who struggled, who gave their lives that the will of the nations should prevail —all of them have done their bit, a precious bit, to compel the militarists of the nazi Reich to come to this hall, to admit defeat, and exit. At last, after so many years, the air has begun to clear of the stench spread by nazism.

From now on the task of extirpating German militarism and fascism is a political and moral one. Everybody wants it accomplished—the peoples that fell prey to German imperialist aggression and the progressive democratic forces of the German nation who languished for years, and were methodically destroyed, in nazi death camps or fought Hitler tooth and nail underground or abroad. The future of the German people and largely that of Europe, too, depends on how thoroughly this task is fulfilled.

We rejoice today over the victory, but tomorrow we shall have to give thought to the shape of the post-war peace. Opinions may differ, but one thing is certain: there is no room in a peaceful Europe for German militarism.

Part Four

MILITARISM AGAIN. PEACEFUL COEXISTENCE OR NUCLEAR DISASTER?

DISSOLUTION OF THE PRUSSIAN STATE. THE MILITARIST TRADITION

History has seen many complex, seemingly fateful modifications which, it turned out, had much less bearing on events than originally thought. This is not due to the historian's error, nor to any misjudgement of contemporaries—provided, of course, that the general assessment of the event is commensurable with the fundamental conflicting trends that brought it about, some of them presaging a new course in history and others a restoration of old forces, albeit in forms differing from the old.

The dissolution of a state is sure to be viewed by historian and contemporary alike as the result of some military, social or political upheaval, and at once as a major event bound to affect the future. But before our very eyes the Prussian state, a symbol of the militarist tradition in the heart of Europe, folded up and none could say what influences this would exert on the future of the militarists.

Seen from the formal angle, the Council of the Foreign Ministers of the big four anti-Hitler powers (the U.S.S.R., the U.S.A., Britain and France) convened in Moscow in 1947 to endorse the law promulgated by the Allied Control Council on February 25, 1947, dissolving the Prussian state. The law was preceded, as we know, by the defeat of the nazi state in the Second World War and the unconditional surrender of Germany, of which Prussia was the most important component. The Prussian state, the law read, long a bearer of militarism and reaction, has ceased to exist, and, by endorsement of the anti-Hitler powers, it also ceased to exist formally, being wiped off the political map.

What impact could this exert on modern history? Was it a symbolic act of transient importance or did it ring in a new era in Germany, whose destiny, as the two world wars have shown, has a strong bearing on the fate of Europe? In political and sociological terms, the question is whether or not the end of the Prussian state will also be the end in our time of the Prussian tradition?

For over 700 years since its inception, the Prussian state has mostly been militaristic. Its home, as well as foreign, policy was always made to serve the interests of war. And seeing that in the last three-quarters of a century it was the political spine of the German empire, its dissolution should, one would think, have far-reaching consequences for the political reconstruction of post-war Germany. And none are more conscious of this than the reactionaries, who have a stake in maintaining the militarist pillars, having long since brought into the world the concept that war is the only vital source assuring first Prussian, and then also German, unity. They laboured perseveringly to inculcate the notion that *Eisen-und-Blut* (iron and blood) alone, war or continuous war preparedness, could secure and sustain the unity of the German nation. Bismarck fathered this concept and Hitler repatterned it somewhat, applying it to aims aggressive to the extreme. It was by the Prussian militarist tradition that he endeavoured to justify his monstrous imperialist programme.

The influence of the Bismarckian concept was so prolonged, so considerable and profound, that German reaction wants to revive it, now that the war is over, to prop up its political and ideological designs. Weakened by the crushing defeat, it is casting about for supporters in the camp of international reaction, and has grounds enough to win them. Some English and American newspapers said the formal demise of the Prussian state meant little or nothing, while others lamented it deeply. The *Times* of London focussed on the virtues of the Prussian character— the diligence, thrift, piety and reverence for law and order

—giving cause to assume that certain quarters wish this false portrait to spare the Prussian character from total and final discredit.

1

The Prussian state dates back to the remote Middle Ages when the Brandenburg Mark, constituted as the eastern outpost (on Slav land known as Brenabor) of the German empire, was still one of the more than 1,700 fiefs of the Holy Roman Empire.

Brandenburg, named the Northern Mark, was as first a modest-sized military unit on the Elbe, from which countless raids originated on the neighbouring Slav tribes. In due course the Slavs were either driven off or exterminated, the Brandenburg Mark acquiring new possessions, reaching as far as the Oder and then across it to the east.

At first the raids were led by dukes, who in the 12th century took the title of Markgrafen of Brandenburg. They were of the Haus of Anhalt, later of the Bavarian house and later still of the house of Luxemburg, followed early in the 15th century by the scions of the decrepit Swabian house of Hohenzollern, giving rise to the dynasty that ruled first Brandenburg, then Prussia, and finally Germany until 1918.

When the Hohenzollerns installed themselves in Brandenburg there already was in the east a Prussian state strongly resembling Brandenburg in type and character— a state of Teutonic knights who, defeated in a crusade against Syria, made a try at capturing the Austrian province of Burgenland, but, defeated once more, marched away to the Baltic shore at the north-eastern tip of Europe. There they settled after a series of devastating wars against the Borussi, an ethnically Lithuanian people, reducing the prosperous countryside to a desert by the end of the 13th century, either annihilating or enslaving the inhabitants, and then soliciting colonists to repopulate it. Karl Marx, who made a close study of the forcible Germanisation of Slav lands, wrote:

"The foreign invaders drove deep into the country, felled the forests, dried the swamps, *stamped out the free-*

dom and fetishism of the indigenous population, and founded castles, towns, monasteries, signorias and bishoprics after the German pattern. Wherever the people were not killed off, *they were reduced to slavery.*"[1]

That was how the Prussian state originated, that was how it expanded—born of violence, thriving on violence and, like the Brandenburg Mark, espousing violence as the means and purpose of its existence.

At the beginning of the 16th century, Albrecht of Brandenburg, a Hohenzollern, was elected Grand Master of the Teutonic Order. Adopting the teaching of Luther and secularising the state, he declared the territory a duchy and a hereditary Hohenzollern possession. Teutonic knights became owners of large tracts of land, growing subsequently into the Junkerdom.

In the 17th century, when Albrecht's male line of succession ended, the Elector of Brandenburg extended his power over the Prussian duchy and in 1701 raised it to the status of a kingdom, crowning himself King of Prussia.

This was how, out of Brandenburg and Teutonic Prussia, erected on the land of Slav and Lithuanian tribes, there came into being a Prussian state.

Until the end of the 18th century, the Prussian kingdom was territorially divided by a corridor of Polish land.

A military state of colonisers, Prussia was ruled by robber barons who appropriated the wealth and fields of conquered peoples and who at the end of the 18th century seized the traditionally Polish territory forming the corridor between their possessions—Gdansk, Torun (Thorn) and Poznan—and at the beginning of the 19th century annexed a considerable part of Saxony and land on both banks of the Rhine, making Prussia one of the most powerful states in Central Europe.

This was when the Prussian character was moulded, creating peril for its neighbours to east and west. The bearers of the aggressive Prussian spirit were the Junkers, owners of great estates, a class of men who were as obtuse as they were greedy and thirsting for conquest, and who

---

[1] Marx, *Severniye i vostochniye gosudarstva Yevropy do serediny XIV veka.* In: Arkhiv Marksa i Engelsa, Vol. V, Moscow, 1938, pp. 342-43.—*Ed.*

clung jealously to their feudal privileges. From their forebears, the Teutonic knights, they inherited the notion that brute force was the source of right and that force should be used to consolidate power and expand. They fostered an exclusive military caste, crude and arrogant, whose ideas were imprinted on the country's entire political life.

Time went by, history posed new, progressive problems in culture and social relations, but Prussia kept her specific traits. If the Junkers could, they would conserve the Prussian state in perpetuity, keeping it reactionary and militaristic.

Mirabeau observed once that war was Prussia's national industry. Berenhorst, who was war chronicler for Frederick II, the Prussian king, thought Prussia was not a state in the ordinary sense. He called it an army camp. Vittorio Alfieri, the Italian tragic dramatist, who travelled in Prussia in 1770, wrote that Berlin, the Prussian capital, was a "disgustingly big barracks and Prussia with its thousands of mercenaries a giant army prison". This was also true of the earlier period and of later times as well.

Frederick II, idol of the German militarists, was the incarnation of "Prussianism", as well as "enlightened absolutism". It was he who, faithful to the philosophy of his forebears, built an army of mercenaries which, to use the phrase of Gerhard von Scharnhorst, one of the few progressive early 19th-century generals, was composed partly of forcibly recruited serfs and for the most part "of vagabonds, drunkards, thieves, cut-throats and various other scum from all over Germany". It was an army so big that to feed it continuous raids were made into foreign lands. Frederick II was the one who instituted the hidebound military principle that "a soldier must fear his officer more than the enemy". It was he who designed the bureaucratic police which, wrote Lessing, turned Prussia into a country of slaves. It was he, too, who thought the Prussian aristocracy was "endowed with so many virtues that it must be guarded and revered". And it was he who never missed an opportunity to grab land from his neighbours, German though some of them were.

Frederick II was never squeamish about the choice of means; perfidy was for him a favourite political tool. He rejoiced at fooling an adversary. On the margin of a report he wrote: "The British are stupid, the Dutch are simpletons. Let's take advantage of it and fool them both." Poised to invade Wroclaw, he made sure of diverting the attention of all those who were likely to hinder him. "Be the most adroit charlatan in the world," he wrote to his foreign minister. "Then I shall be the happiest soldier of fortune and our names shall never be forgotten." Quite true, the Prussian militarists and Germany's imperialists did not forget him. They worshipped Old Fritz. The old Prussian aims and methods were refashioned, but their influence on the succeeding generations of Prusso-German militarists did not wane until the big crash came in 1945.

The descendants of the Teutonic knights and the Prussian militarists figured prominently in the rise of the German empire. When the gale of the great bourgeois revolution swept out the feudal order in France at the close of the 18th century, Germany was still politically divided. It was more a geographic than political entity. There were more than 300 feudal domains on its territory —kingdoms, archduchies, duchies, principalities, archbishoprics, bishoprics, free cities and other states—some of which, Heinrich Heine observed, were so small they could be carried away on the sole of one's boot. Napoleon reshuffled these states, big and small, to suit his best advantage. But after the crushing defeat of the Prussian army at Jena in 1806 there incubated in the German mind in the midst of burgeoning capitalist relations the idea of national unity. Yet the people was still too weak to sweep away the feudal order and the dynastic partitions, while Prussia, the strongest of the German states, was totally preoccupied in sating the Junkerdom and its dynastic interests.

The ideas of the French bourgeois revolution made a strong impression on the people. Gripped by fear, King Friedrich-Wilhelm III promised them a constitution. But that was a hoax: he could not and would not in any way impair the preponderance of the Prussian Junkers. Engels wrote later that he was "one of the biggest dolts that ever adorned a throne. Born to be a sergeant-major and check the buttons on his soldiers, a cool libertine and at once a preacher of morality, incapable of speaking other than in the indefinite mood, surpassed in the art of writing orders only by his own son, he had two sentiments only—fear and a sergeant-major's arrogance."[1]

Fear was what he felt of Napoleon and, after Napoleon's collapse, of the Russian tsar, who stage-managed the policies of the reactionary Holy Alliance. His sergeant-major's arrogance, however, knew no bounds with respect to his subjects and the minor German states.

After the Congress of Vienna in 1815 the German states were reshuffled once more. Just 39 remained, with Prussia, the biggest, growing with the Austrian empire into the main citadel of reaction in Central Europe. After the Prussian government issued the edict abolishing serfdom in 1807, there followed so many other laws, edicts and government directives, that the Junkerdom once more emerged the victor. Feudalism retained many of its privileges, including corvée and other duties. By speculation and profiteering, multiplying their wealth rapidly by selling the old feudal duties, the Junkers adopted the capitalist methods of exploitation and, taking advantage of the ruin and impoverishment of the peasants, quickly affirmed their priority in agriculture and the Prussian state. Thus began the long process of capitalist development in Prussian farming, leaving for over a hundred years an imprint not only on the economic, but also the political scene of Germany.

The Junker remained the dominant power in Prussia, while the military caste he had spawned continued to set the tune in politics. Nothing changed in the Prussian kingdom even after the bourgeoisie came into being and, unsatisfied with *Sturm und Drang* in the realm of just abstract ideas, laid claim to political rights to promote its interests.

Alexander Herzen, the Russian man of letters, who visited Prussia shortly before the 1848 revolution, wrote ruefully in his diary:

"Humanism is being implanted in Prussia ... with the sergeant-major's whip and a philistine concept of economy. Prussia is heartless."

The 1848 revolution failed to bring about German unity on a democratic basis. The democratic elements were not

---

[1] Engels, *Deutsche Zustände*, Brief II (Marx/Engels, *Werke*, Bd. 2, Berlin, 1962, S. 572-73).—*Ed.*

yet strong enough to undertake Germany's unification on their own. They were forceful enough, however, and the German bourgeoisie, in dread of the revolution, turned coat and joined the absolutist counter-revolution.

2

This was when Bismarck first appeared on the political scene. His manners and convictions were such that he soon earned the nickname of Wild Junker even from his neighbours, landowners themselves. Learning of the revolution in Berlin, he engineered a Prussian Vendée, arming his peasants with the intention of restoring the Prussian king's autocratic power—autocratic, that is, insofar as it coincided with the Junkers' will.

Even the king was cowed by Bismarck's outspokenly reactionary stand. But Bismarck was undaunted. The revolution was crushed, Prussia's reactionaries celebrated a victory. The idea of unity that sprang from the depth of the people, remained no more than an idea. But soon Bismarck took it up. When he was appointed Minister-President of Prussia (1862), he said:

"Germany has eyes not for Prussia's liberalism, but for her might. Great issues are not settled by speeches and parliamentary resolutions, but by blood and iron." Elsewhere, he declared: "No parliament will ever settle the German question; it will be diplomacy and the sword."

In 1864, as he began carrying out his plans, he said: "Ultimately, questions of state law are settled with the bayonet."

To extend Prussian rule to all Germany, Bismarck snatched at the idea of unity, in which the bourgeoisie had a vested interest. When the hour came he tackled the matter in the usual Prussian manner, by war. Prussian diplomacy got busy, acting on the simplest of principles: adversaries are easier beaten one by one. At first, war was waged on Denmark, then on Austria. Few people understood Bismarck's aims. Many Junkers who acclaimed his methods refused to accept his plans. The German bourgeoisie, on the other hand, was enthusiastic over both the plans and the methods. Espousing the policies of Junker Prussia, it quickly cast off the remnants of its liberal ideas.

The more penetrating contemporaries, however, saw through Bismarck's policy.

"Bismarck has come out into the open," wrote Alexander Herzen. "He means to turn Germany into an empire of Prussians; the shreds of the torn-up constitution will be used as wads."

"Bask in your grandeur," he said sarcastically to the Germans, "and pray for the future Emperor of the Prussians, but remember that the hand which crushed kingdoms will also sternly and ruthlessly crush any ungrateful attempt you may make." Herzen knew that Prussian preponderance in Germany stood for reaction, that growth of Prussian militarism continuously created the danger of a war in Europe. Alluding to the needle-pointed rifle of the Prussian soldier, he wrote: "Everybody knows that Europe, patched together with Prussian needles, is poorly patched and will fall apart."

The war against France completed Germany's unification along Prusso-militarist lines. Prussia defeated France. She annexed the old French provinces of Alsace and Lorraine. She received huge indemnities, most of which were spent on more arming. But the victory was also over the German states whose rulers offered the Prussian king the crown of Germany.

The military victory over France, coupled with the political victory over the German states, infused Prussian militarism with defiance. The victories went to its head. Prussia was gripped by a nationalist fever; its passion infected all Germany. Saltykov-Shchedrin, the Russian writer who visited the Prussian capital at that time, observed that Bismarck's policy of Prussianising Germany was distasteful to many Germans. "For half of Germany at least," he wrote, "Berlin is not only unattractive, but positively repellent. It has taken from everybody, and given nothing. Worse still, it has placed the Berlin soldier everywhere, with the corresponding number of officers."

Prussia's military caste, proud beyond reason, evoked not fear, but disgust. Saltykov-Shchedrin, for one, could not suppress his distaste. "When I pass a Berlin officer," he wrote, "I am invariably perplexed. By his bearing and manner, his puffed out chest and clean-shaven chin he seems to say: I am a hero. I should feel far more comfortable, I am sure, if instead he said: I am a robber and shall now skin you alive."

Saltykov-Shchedrin knew that behind the screen of unity, the Prussian militarists were gradually tightening their hold on all Germany to promote their aggressive plans. He knew Berlin was the seat of Prussian militarism, that Berlin was where the plans were being framed that put peace in peril.

"The essence of present-day Berlin, its universal importance," he wrote, "is concentrated this very minute in the building dominating Königsplatz known as Supreme Headquarters."

Quite true. The Prussian General Staff played a far bigger role in matters of both foreign and home policy than any other in any country. Saltykov-Shchedrin left the Prussian capital, now the capital of all Germany, with a sense of dismay.

Other contemporaries, too, spotted what Saltykov-Shchedrin portrayed so incisively. After his travels in Germany, Gleb Uspensky, another distinguished Russian writer, wrote:

"The moment you cross the frontier you come to Berlin where reigns a militarist spirit my compatriots would not suspect could exist. . . . Sabre, spur, helmet, moustache and two fingers raised in salute above the smug visage of the conqueror screwed into a tight collar: you run into him at every step. Saluting, changing guards, drilling—seemingly touched in the head—then marching on proudly. . . . What is worst, he is deeply convinced that what he is doing is right."

3

Prussianism as a socio-political force and Prussia as a state gained a dominant place in Germany. Created by Prusso-militarist reaction, the German state was really Greater Prussia or, as Engels said scathingly, a "German empire of the Prussian nation". Prussia held the commanding political heights, the Prussian King was also the German Kaiser, the Prussian Minister-President usually also the Reichschancellor and Minister of Foreign Affairs. Occupying 65 per cent of Germany's area, accounting for over 61 per cent of her population, with two-thirds of the cultivated land and an equally big share in industry, and fielding two-thirds of the armed forces, Prussia was the most influential of the states of the German empire. She controlled in the Bundesrat, the representative body of all the states of the empire, 17 out of 61 votes, and was naturally dominant. When she was outvoted on some minor issue in 1880, the Minister-President, who was also Reichschancellor, compelled the "recalcitrants" to bend to Prussia's will and guarantee that an unfavourable vote would never recur.

While Prussia dominated Germany, the Junkers and the big bourgeoisie dominated Prussia. Not just because they controlled the country's agriculture and industry, but because for decades they succeeded in retaining the old Prussian election procedures. While the all-German system was based on universal male suffrage, voters in elections to the Prussian *Landtag* cast their ballots in three classes, depending on the taxes they paid. The voting was by acclamation, the country was divided into an antiquated maze of constituencies, and, as a rule, the authorities, aided by the police, saw to it that just a third of the electorate came to the polls. As a result, the Conservative Party, polling, say, a mere 17 per cent of the votes, held more than half the seats, while the Social-Democrats who polled 24 per cent despite the triple grading, seated just seven deputies in the *Landtag*, which was two-thirds Junker, capitalist and bureaucratic. The Prussian reactionaries fell back on the *Landtag* when assaulting the all-German *Reichstag*, elected in a somewhat more democratic manner Marx rightly described the political system in Prussianised Germany as a "police-guarded military despotism, embellished with parliamentary forms, alloyed with a feudal admixture, already influenced by the bourgeoisie and bureaucratically carpentered".[1]

At the beginning of the 20th century the Prussian-bred German imperialism brandished its "mailed fist" at all Europe. Later, in line with the militarist Prussian tradition, General Ludendorff, the typical militarist, devised the doctrine of "total war". In the Weimar Republic this tradition was maintained by the *Reichswehr*, whose founder,

---

[1] Marx, *Selected Works* in two volumes. Volume II, Moscow, 1963, p. 33.

General von Seeckt, said: "The army is the state." To some extent, German fascism, too, germinated on Prussianised soil.

But the rapid growth of the German monopolies, their frank expansionism, gave Prussianised Germany's aggressive policy a new dimension. The capitalist press called Germany a "world power", the Kaiser devised a "world policy", the German banks itched to play a "world role", and German merchants clamoured for "world trade". To them, the continental scale began to look provincial. The old Prussian concepts were used for a new purpose. All reactionary ideas were promptly exploited. The war cult was revived, and so was the cult of brute strength and of relentless will-power.

While a war was brewing in Europe, the German army fought in the colonies. In one of its colonial wars it exterminated the trustful and peaceable African Herero tribe almost to a man.

Far-sighted contemporaries who followed the early political development of Prussianised Germany, saw through the designs of this war-made and war-like state. N. Mikhailovsky, the prominent Russian publicist, wrote in 1871:

"Europe will see blood, will hear groans and gunfire. The Prussian progressists are so carried away by their success that they are planning an alliance with Austria against the Slav world. Moltke, a British newspaper reports, has a plan ready for invading the British Isles. What is ahead? It seems certain that 'Prussian civilisation' will impose itself on the world in the coming decades. But the collapse of that civilisation is a matter of time.... The question hinges on how and when Bismarck's ambitions will run aground. Possibly, its destruction will be accomplished by a coalition of European states."

At the end of 1918 Bismarck's cause did indeed collapse. A coalition of European and non-European states inflicted a crushing defeat on Prussianised Germany. A revolution erupted, sweeping away the German dynasty. Kaiser Wilhelm II, forced to abandon the German throne, hoped to remain King of Prussia, but was soon compelled to flee to Holland.

The Prussian dynasty was deposed, but the generals remained. They were the focal point of Prussian and all other German reaction. Retiring to the background at first, they later became more active. Their avowed purpose was to gain power and suppress the people. The November revolution of 1918 had not deprived them of their economic strength: since the Junkers were as much the masters of their huge estates as the capitalist monopolies were of the industries, they had a firm grip on Germany's political life, using their resources to block her democratic reconstruction. But they did make some concessions.

When the monarchist regime was flushed out, the question arose of the basic principles of a new constitution. Among others, there was the question of Prussia's role in the German state. In early January 1919, Hugo Preuss, home minister and a leading light in the liberal Progressive Party, submitted a draft of the future "imperial constitution". A foe of federalism, Preuss maintained that "incontestably, the new German republic must be constituted as a united popular state on the basis of the right to self-determination".

He held that neither the monarchist nor the federalist principles were "the prime and decisive factors in the political life of the German nation", arguing that "the very existence of the German people as a historically given political entity" was a more accurate definition.

"Neither a Prussian nor a Bavarian nation exists," Preuss wrote, "just as there is no nation of the principalities of Lippe or Reuss; what exists is the German nation, which must corporify the political form of its life in a democratic German republic."

Preuss thought Prussia's existence and hegemony were incompatible with his principle of a "united people's state" (*einheitlicher Volksstaat*). He also drafted a project for a new territorial arrangement. He believed bourgeois democracy would thrive best in Germany if Prussia were divided among the other German *Länder*. This would restrict, if not do away with, the Prussian state. But he evaded the question of extirpating the economic and social foundation on which Prussia originated and grew.

His project was vehemently attacked by all quarters. The Prussian reactionaries, the south-German particularists and the Social-Democrats, who came to the defence of the ruling classes and tried to head off the assault on the political rudiments of the German empire, joined hands to defeat the Preuss project. And they succeeded. At the end of January 1919, his back to the wall, Preuss announced that the scheme was impracticable. A thoroughly revised draft of the constitution was submitted to the National Assembly in Weimar on February 21, 1919. A wild controversy erupted over what name to give the German state. Some wanted Union (*Bund*), some the United States of Germany, while Preuss argued that both were particularist and meant a step backward in German history. The National Assembly, however, went dead against German Republic and adopted *Reich* (empire) on the grounds that the latter accorded with the long-time tradition of the German people who had always yearned for national unity. This was a concession to the reactionaries, who had since the Middle Ages given the idea of an empire top priority.

A still more ferocious scuffle broke out over the relationship between *Reich* and *Länder*. Again, Preuss suggested, though much less categorically, destroying Prussia's hegemony. "The purpose of the constitution," he said, "is to create a German Germany, free from either Austrian or Prussian hegemony, a Germany with a German central authority over all the member states (*Gliederstaaten*)."

There were strong objections for different reasons and from different quarters. Spahn, a leader of the Catholic Centre Party, opposed Prussian hegemony which, he said, was founded on military superiority, the Prussian bureaucratic system and the dynastic union of Prussia and Germany. The fall of the Hohenzollerns, he said, had undermined Prussian preponderance. But he did not infer from this that Prussia should be abolished as a state. What he wanted was a bigger role for the other *Länder*. He was moved by particularist ambition to suggest that Germany take advantage of Prussia's decline and reconstitute herself along federalist lines. The Agrarians and monopoly capital defended the Prussian state tooth and nail. Delbrück, a prominent member of the People's Party, argued that Germany could not survive without a strong Prussia. Heinze, who made no secret of his reactionary views, said abolition of the Prussian monarchy precluded any concentration of military strength in Prussian hands and urged the Prussian military system to be extended to all Germany. He loathed the republican system and wanted Prussia preserved.

"We cannot afford to atomise Prussia," he said, "for we shall then destroy the only pillar of our *Reich*. We refuse to partition Prussia."

Stresemann, too, a political leader of the German monopoly bourgeoisie, spoke to the same effect. He endeavoured to justify his plea by contending that Prussia had ostensibly ceased to be the citadel of German reaction.

The Weimar constitution preserved Prussia as one of the states of the German Reich. But its main failing was that some of its articles went against the interests of democratic growth, notably Article 48, which allowed extraordinary powers to the President and set the stage for the Hitler dictatorship.

All the same, in German history the Weimar constitution was an advance to a bourgeois-democratic order. It assured rights that people in Germany, let alone Prussia, never had before. It assured parties, trade unions and other public organisations the right of free activity, proclaimed freedom of the press, of assembly, etc. The *Länder* were granted a certain amount of autonomy and the opportunity to set up democratic structures within the framework of a united German state.

During the Weimar period Prussia's formal and politico-administrative status was somewhat modified. No longer did it have a crowned head, whom it shared with Germany. Its Minister-President was not at once Reichschancellor and the German Foreign Minister was not a member of the Prussian Cabinet. The political face of the Prussian cabinet differed from that of the all-German cabinet, consisting mostly of parties of the so-called Weimar coalition (Social-Democratic Party, Democratic Party and Catholic Centre), while the all-German cabinets had ministers from the People's Party, representing Big Business, and the Nationalists, representing the reactionary bourgeoisie and Junker imperialism.

Some Germans claim that since then Prussia's role changed. Once the citadel of Junker reaction, they argued, it became a democratic citadel. They said to prove their point that after the 1918 November revolution reaction had removed itself to Bavaria, that it was in Bavaria where the semi-legal armed fascist organisations sprang up first and Bavaria where Hitler began laying the foundations for his coup.

Incontestably, Bavaria is a close match to Prussia as a bastion of reaction and a source of feudalist and separatist tendencies. In his *Success*, Lion Feuchtwanger produced a striking picture of Bavaria becoming a shelter for German reaction by reason of its social, economic and ideological backwardness. After a frankly reactionary government took over, many German militarists, General Ludendorff among them, moved to Bavaria. Shortly, they threw their weight behind the Hitler movement, playing it with funds, leaders and political experience. But it is strange to deduce therefrom that Prussia turned into a home of democracy. It is true that the democratic movement in Prussia expanded, especially in the key industrial regions—Berlin and the Rhine-Westphalian area. But this was not due to any especially favourable factors. The Prussian police, though controlled by Social-Democrats, fired on workers' demonstrations with no more compunction than the reactionary governments in Thuringia and Bavaria. The Prussian Government did nothing to restrict the economic might of the Junkers and tycoons in industry and finance, the pillars of rule in Prussia and the rest of Germany. Their economic strength gave the reactionary forces leave to cultivate Prussian traditions in the army, in politics and social relations. They adapted themselves to the new times, and resorted to unheard-of demagogy.

It was in this political and ideological climate that Oswald Spengler produced his book, *Preussentum und Sozialismus*, and Hitler named his party National-Socialist.

Eager to consolidate the all-German reaction and fearing resistance by some of the *Länder*, the imperial government began "rooting out" the vestiges of independence that they still retained. Friction increased between the two central governments—the imperial and the Prussian—over certain administrative measures. Advocates of reforming the relationship between the Reich and Prussia howled about the duplication of government functions and about other inconveniences stemming from the existence in the German system of such a large state as Prussia. To reorganise the relationship, Bund zur Erneuerung des Reichs was founded in 1928, with Hans Luther, a prominent Big Business spokesman, ex-Chancellor and later Reichsbank president, at its head. Also a special committee was established under Social-Democrat Arnold Brecht which worked out the following plan:

1) to incorporate the central administration of the Prussian Government in the administration of the imperial government;

2) to incorporate the regional and local institutions of the Prussian Government in the corresponding institutions of the imperial government;

3) to dissolve Prussia as a *Land* and autonomous entity;

4) to constitute new territorial units in its stead, making new *Länder* out of the 13 Prussian provinces, Berlin included.

The suggestion was to divide Prussia into a number of *Länder* with the same status as the other German lands—Bavaria, Saxony, etc. But it was vehemently opposed, notably by the reactionary Bavarian representatives. Though long a rival of Prussia, Bavaria, in the persons of its reactionary rulers, wanted Prussia preserved. Firstly, they feared that Bavaria would be next. Secondly, they considered Prussia's existence a vindication for their particularist ambitions. And above all else, they feared that Prussia's reorganisation would invigorate the democratic movement throughout the country.

In the meantime, though the interests of the ruling classes were the same, rifts had appeared between them: the Junkers east of the Elbe wanted new privileges, and the industrial tycoons from Prussia's western regions also wanted privileges. Yet both feared the workers' and socialist movement developing throughout Germany, chiefly in Prussia's industrial regions.

The project for Prussia's reorganisation finally reached the *Reichstag*. The ruling classes were unalarmed. They knew that the imperial government, like the Prussian, would not dare assault the foundation of their economic and political dominance. Reichschancellor Brüning, busy clearing the way for a fascist dictatorship, would not allow any discussion of the project in parliament. He applied the notorious Article 48 of the Weimar constitution to mock the constitution by dissolving the *Reichstag*. His successor,

Franz von Papen, gave the Prussian reform project an unexpected twist. At his suggestion, Field-Marshal von Hindenburg, the old Prussian monarchist who was President of
the Weimar Republic, issued an order retiring all Prussian
ministers. Their functions were turned over to the Reichschancellor and his commissars.

Prussia was thus relieved of her constitutional rights by
an inveterate Prussian militarist. After considerable argument, the conflict was put before the Supreme Court, which
reinstated the Prussian Government.

Headed by Social-Democrat Otto Braun, the Prussian cabinet fought desperately for its existence, but being neither
righteous nor massive, the fight was a losing one. The Social-
Democrats dreaded the workers, who could have helped
them prevail, more than they feared the semi-fascist imperial government. In the meantime, the Prussianists gravitated to the reactionary imperial government, which they
urged to assist the nazis, the most reactionary imperialist
party. Hitler took over and lost no time setting up controls
over the Prussian bodies of state. The political efforts made
by the Social-Democrats to win support in Prussia in
combating nazi reaction were in vain.

Determined to win over the bearers of the old Prussian
militarist tradition, Hitler made no move to destroy the
Prussian state. He held a gala celebration in Potsdam and
promptly turned Prussia fascist like the rest of Germany,
putting Hermann Göring at the head of the Prussian cabinet. The Prussian government differed from the imperial
only in that Hitler and the foreign minister were not members of it. Hitler integrated the Prussian state in the nazi
Third Reich and introduced super-centralisation geared to
the interests of the more aggressive segment of big monopoly capital, priming for an all-out war.

5

The defeat suffered by Hitler Germany is unequalled in
the annals of war. The nazi army and state, embodying
the most reactionary and aggressive features of Prusso-
German imperialism and militarism, were crushed. After the
war, the Big Three gathered in Cecilienhof Palace at Potsdam to agree on how to deal with Germany and work out

the principles for reorganising her economic and political life along new, democratic lines.

The Potsdam Conference decided on disarming and demilitarising Germany. Her economy would be decentralised, abolishing cartels, syndicates, trusts and other monopoly associations prominent in preparing the war. It decided also to dismantle, or put under control, such German industries as could be converted to military production.

The remnants of nazism and all nazi organisations were to be rooted out. Nazis who were more than nominal members of Hitler's party and all other elements opposed to allied aims were to be removed from public office and from responsible posts in important private enterprises.

The most important, truly historic decision taken at Potsdam was to eradicate Prusso-German militarism and its economic, socio-political and ideological pillars. Scheduled for full dissolution were all German ground, sea and air forces, all special military and paramilitary formations established by the Hitler regime and all the clubs and societies (*Vereine*) that for decades cultivated the military tradition. The German General Staff, too, the brain of Prusso-German militarism and always prominent in political affairs, was to be disbanded. The economic principles formulated in Potsdam indicated that the German war potential would be eliminated and the economy reconstructed along new, democratic lines.

The economic disarmament plan applied to the entire country, which was to be treated as a single economic entity.

A mere two years have passed since the Potsdam Conference, but it is clear that its decisions are not being carried out anywhere, except in East Germany. There, the nation's democratic forces, awakened to active socio-political life, have rallied round the Socialist Unity Party, the united working-class party, and tackled the deep-going structural reforms geared to the Potsdam principles. Worked out in common by the great powers of the anti-Hitler coalition, these principles accord with the historical tasks and interests of the German nation in face of the adversities to which it was exposed by militarism, imperialism and fascism.

It is the national mission to remove from power all these forces. The agrarian reform and the nationalisation of big industry in East Germany have been of overwhelming, one might say determinative, importance in this respect. Transfer of land once owned by the Junkers to the land-hungry *Bauer* ushered in a new phase in German history. The Junker class, which spawned the military caste and the spirit of conquest, piracy and oppression, has been deprived there of its economic power. The monopolies and big industrialists who, like the Junkers, supported the nazi dictatorship, have also been uprooted. Important measures have been taken to democratise socio-political life. In sum, a large part of Prussia and Germany will no longer follow the old, militarist course. Foundations have been laid there in accordance with Potsdam for new, democratic development.

The dissolution of the Prussian state, citadel of aggressive traditions, has opened possibilities for reconstructing Germany on a democratic groundwork. A line is drawn beneath Prussia's history, which could spell the end of militarism throughout Germany, turning that country into a united, peace-loving democratic state disavowing aggressive and revenge-seeking ideas and moving to economic and cultural progress.

This could be so; then the history of Germany and Europe would follow a new trend. However, in West Germany the trend is in the other direction, departing completely from the agreed Potsdam principles.

These are the accents: not elimination of monopoly rule but recovery of monopoly power; not obliteration of militarist influences but promotion and reorganisation of militarism; not total denazification but a scheme designed to safeguard the old nazi cadres; not democratisation but reaction in a new, clerical guise.

It is folly to assume, therefore, that dissolution of the Prussian state could, *ipso facto*, imply extirpation of militarist traditions. Though modified, the roots of aggression once located in Prussia are now imbedded in the monopolies and the system of West German militarism. Nursed back to life by the Western powers, militarism is entrenching itself in West Germany, refusing to depart from the arena of history.

In the circumstances, the dissolution of the Prussian state is no more than a symbol of the historical opportunity offered by the Potsdam decisions of solving the German problem in an anti-militarist spirit, treating it as a problem of the democratic growth of the German nation. But a symbol is not reality, an opportunity is not realisation. The dissolution of the Prussian state will leave no mark in history, unless the militarist system, enemy of German democracy and a tool of aggression and revenge whatever guise it may assume, is rooted out in West as well as East Germany.

1947

1

Gone is the time when bourgeois historiography could pride itself in knowing the way history unfolded. The most advanced source investigation techniques cannot help it any more. After the bourgeoisie had asserted its predominance and the revolutionary class, conscious of its mission of emancipating mankind from capitalist oppression, stepped on the scene, an irremediable crisis surfaced in reactionary historiography. "It was thenceforth no longer a question, whether this theorem or that was true," Marx wrote, "but whether it was useful to capital or harmful, expedient or inexpedient, politically dangerous or not. In place of disinterested inquirers, there were hired prize-fighters; in place of genuine scientific research, the bad conscience and the evil intent of apologetic."[1]

In the early 1870s, when capitalism was just entering the imperialist stage, Edward A. Freeman, a typical exponent of British liberal historiography, wrote: "History is past politics and ... politics is present history."[2] This notion, which, in effect, denies that history is a science of the laws governing society, reducing it to a political tool, is the alpha and omega of contemporary reactionary historiography.

Historians of the imperialist epoch are mainly intent on justifying the policies of the ruling classes. In Germany there prevailed the Pan-Germanic concept, which treated

---

[1] Marx, *Capital*, Vol. I, Moscow, 1965, p. 15.
[2] Freeman, *The Methods of Historical Study*, London, 1886, p. 44.

imperialist Germany as the "heart of Europe" and Germans as the race chosen to rule Europe and the world.[1] It extolled militarism and reaction, imperialist aggression and war, and was carried to its most misanthropic extreme by the nazi historians of the Hitler period.

In Britain, John Seeley pieced together the late 19th-century imperialist conception set out in his book, *The Expansion of England*,[2] still the bible of British colonial expansionism. His other book, *The Growth of British Policy*,[3] is an apologia of Britain's aggressive aims and specific imperialist methods in the drive for world power.

A. Mahan was an early imperialist ideologist in the United States, whose ideas expressed in his *Influence of Sea-Power upon History*[4] are still popular in certain U.S. quarters as an exposition of the historical mission borne by the United States, said to be destined to rule the waves and play top dog throughout the world.

There were disparities between Seeley's and Mahan's conceptions. The former placed Britain in the fore as the guiding political force of the Anglo-Saxon framework, while Mahan gave preference to the United States. The same tendency was prevalent in later imperialist policies and in historiography.

Apart from racism and the idea of world power, Seeley and Mahan, the troubadours of British and American imperialism, advanced the reactionary idea that the people should not be allowed to influence foreign policy on the plea of historical necessity and political expediency. Hence the apologia of secret diplomacy which lent itself so generously to shady backstage deals in the interests of expansion and aggression. Not surprisingly, Joseph Chamberlain and Cecil Rhodes extolled the "Anglo-Saxon" racism and

---

[1] E.g., *Alldeutsche Blätter*, 1894-1919; E. Hasse, *Deutsche Politik*, Bd. I-II, München, 1905-08; D. Frymann, *Wenn ich der Kaiser wäre*, Leipzig, 1914; H. Oncken, *Das alte und das neue Mitteleuropa. Historisch-politische Betrachtungen über deutsche Bündnispolitik im Zeitalter Bismarcks und im Zeitalter des Weltkrieges*, Gotha, 1917; H. Class, *Gegen den Strom*, Stuttgart, 1928; E. Jäckh, *Deutschland als Herz Europas*, Berlin, 1929; L. Werner, *Der Alldeutsche Verband 1890-1918*, Berlin, 1935.

[2] Seeley, *The Expansion of England*, London, 1921.

[3] Seeley, *The Growth of British Policy*, Cambridge, 1922.

[4] Mahan, *The Influence of Sea-Power upon History, 1660-1783*, London, 1890.

apologetics of colonial aggrandisement preached by John Seeley, while Theodore Roosevelt, a typical aggressive American imperialist, declared himself a disciple of Mahan and hailed the latter's view of the navy in the fight for world power.

Between the two world wars the top role in Anglo-American historiography was played by professional historians such as Charles Austin Beard, Sidney Bradshaw Fay, George Peabody Gooch and Harold Temperley, each reflecting and formulating the political interests and views of the governing classes, and some even connected with the State Department or Foreign Office.

However, during the Second World War and after it they withdrew to the background. The monopolists themselves, and their political protégés, elbowed their way to prominence in Anglo-American historiography. This unprecedented development was admitted by the official Bulletin of the Business Historical Society, which said: "It is exciting to think that before our very eyes the gulf between the scholar and the businessman is narrowing and close co-operation between them is developing."[1]

Post-war co-operation between U.S. historiography and the Pentagon has been remarkably close. The intimate link between military leaders and scholars in the United States is described by U.S. publicists as "self-evident and profound". The *Business Historical Society Bulletin* holds, for one thing, that any truthful account of U.S. monopoly expansionism would undermine State Department efforts. And since the efforts of the State Department and Pentagon alike are concentrated of late on restoring the power of the German monopolies and rebuilding revenge-seeking armies commanded by ex-nazi generals, reactionary U.S. historians are going out of their way to whitewash German militarism, and strive to spread their ideological influence to other countries. West Germany, naturally, ranks highest in their favours, for it is viewed by U.S. imperialism as its closest ally, and reactionary British as well as West German historians chime in with them in their interpretation of modern and current German history.

---

[1] Business Historical Society Bulletin, Boston, v. XXII, No. 1, February 1948.

While the Second World War was still raging and the peoples of the Soviet Union and the other freedom-loving nations were locked in battle with Hitler imperialism, the U.S. monopolists were planning how they would secure world power.

The Wall Street community viewed the German monopolists as its most dangerous rivals and was bent on crushing German economic power, driving Germany off the world market and thereby expanding its own might. In autumn 1944 Henry Morgenthau Jr., then Secretary of the Treasury and a prominent Wall Street figure, framed for President Roosevelt a plan of destroying German industry, reducing the country to an agrarian colony. At war's end, Morgenthau wrote a book, *Germany Is Our Problem,* in which he endeavoured to substantiate his scheme.[1]

What he wanted was to dismantle Germany—not just the Hitler state but German statehood, and not just the war-industrial machine but the German economy. "My own programme for ending the menace of German aggression," Morgenthau wrote, "consists, in its simplest terms, of depriving Germany of all heavy industries." To give substance to his political plans, Morgenthau begins by dispelling what he calls misconceptions widespread in the United States. He observes sarcastically that U.S. historiography tends to depict early 19th-century Germany as "a land of fairy tales where Prince Albert and Prince Ernest collected botanical specimens in the woods or played their little pianoforte duets in shabby castles, where the peasant fattened his Christmas goose in neatly tended farmyards, where most of the kings and princes of Europe found their remarkably plain wives".[2]

Morgenthau debunks these sentimental tales and calls attention to an entirely different, he thinks much more cogent, aspect of the case, namely, that "for centuries Europe also recruited its mercenaries from these picturesque villages". He avers that since the German states were purveyors of mercenaries they were basically aggressive, a trait, he claims, that is historically, even biologically,

---

[1] Morgenthau, *Germany Is Our Problem*, New York-London, 1945.
[2] Ibid., p. 102.

inherent in the German nation. He goes on to contend that its people were the prime movers of all the wars ever fought by Germany, including the two world conflagrations of the first half of the 20th century. Morgenthau describes the Junkerdom, whose warmongering he mentions only in passing, not as a specific social force, but as part of the nation, and makes no mention at all of the other reactionary class, the German financial tycoons, who inspired and organised the armed aggressions. He places the blame for the war squarely on the German people, especially the German proletariat, inferring that since German industry worked chiefly to meet the needs of war, the German workers were one of the main motive forces of German aggression.

This perversion of history has a dual purpose. First, by arguing that the "will to war" and "distaste for democracy" are intrinsic German traits, Morgenthau wishes to discredit the democratic forces in Germany or even entirely to deny their existence. Second, he wishes to whitewash German finance capital, which is long connected with U.S. finance capital by countless threads.

Obviously, the historical excursus of the Secretary of the Treasury was politically biased. Morgenthau advocated Germany's agrarianisation, the dispersal and extirpation of the German proletariat by a forcible conversion of workers into farmers. But that was not all. He also advocated Germany's partition. His account of the emergence of German statehood and national unity is a distortion of the fact. So is his inference therefrom that unity had been the motive force of German aggression.

"Two Germanys would be easier to deal with than one," he writes, "because in the odd arithmetic of international politics it is not true that two halves are equal to the whole. They are substantially less."[1]

While the guns were still booming, he was busy justifying the political scheme of Germany's division.

A similar programme was suggested during the war by Lord Vansittart. A permanent under-secretary of state for foreign affairs before the war and then chief diplomatic adviser to the foreign secretary, he had at one time been

---

[1] Morgenthau, *Germany Is Our Problem*, New York-London, 1945, p. 155.

prominent in making British foreign policy. His conception of history filled several volumes and a number of articles.[1] Vansittart clothed his reactionary and impracticable idea of destroying the German nation and its statehood in doubtful paradoxes. "In point of fact *no* history is to the point when nations have outgrown it," he wrote among other things, and added: "What makes German history to the point is that Germans have actually deteriorated."[2]

Did he mean that militarism had played an excessively prominent part in German history? But why did he say nothing of the social forces that effectuate aggressive militarism? Who has a stake in supporting and consolidating these forces? Lastly, what was the soil on which German militarism flowered to such dangerous dimensions?

Here is Vansittart's answer to all these questions. Capitalism, he says, may be the cause of other evils, but not of this one, while socialism perhaps will help against other evils, but not against this one. The culprit of this evil is a definite factor—the nation.

What Vansittart was after was, first, to vindicate the ruling classes of imperialist Germany, the bearers of militarism, the Junkers and monopolists, and, second, to discredit socialism, the guarantee of prosperity and peace for all. Third, he wished the German nation to be condemned, as though the whole nation can be blamed for wars aimed at enslaving other nations. Vansittart averred that the causes of both the First and Second World Wars were not rooted in any economic system. For him these were rooted in the tyrannical cravings of the German soul. He also contended that the German socialist movement was militarist right from the start. Nor was his monstrous charge levelled specifically at such Right-wing Social-Democrats as Scheidemann and Noske. He meant Frederick Engels and August Bebel, those two great Germans. It will be easily seen that he had to do some nimble juggling with historical facts to substantiate his invention.

Fearing that after the defeat of the German war machine, the Germans would embark on broad national democratic development, Vansittart advocated not destruction of

<hr>

[1] Vansittart, *Lessons of My Life*, London, 1944; *Bones of Contention*, New York, 1945; *Events and Shadows. A Policy for the Remnants of a Century*, London, 1947.

[2] Vansittart, *Lessons of My Life*, p. 32.

German imperialism, but of the German state, supplanted by years of Anglo-American occupation. Projecting this course to the time when the Federal Republic of Germany was established in the west and the German Democratic Republic in the east, Vansittart crowned his historical concept with the following political conclusion: Our only hope, he said, is Adenauer.[1]

3

Soon after the war, when the political situation changed drastically, new variations appeared of the old arguments. The United States and Britain abandoned their plans of scuttling German industry and agrarianising the country, In view of the new situation wrought in Europe by the Soviet victory—the emergence of the world system of socialist countries and the growth of democratic forces in Germany herself—the Western powers split Germany and began resuscitating militarism and reaction. They trampled underfoot the Potsdam decision of establishing a united, independent, peace-loving and democratic Germany. Wall Street and the City set out to rebuild the economic and military potential in West Germany and to turn it into a staging area and arsenal.

Their previous ideas about Germany's future were refashioned to suit the new political tasks, with even prominent industrialists and financiers joining the fray. Heads and agents of various U.S. monopolies visited Europe, notably West Germany, and published the results of their investigations and their thoughts about the purposes and methods of U.S. expansion, and the histories of countries that had aroused their specific interest. Lewis H. Brown, chairman of the board of Johns-Manville Corporation, wrote *A Report on Germany*, studied closely by Wall Street, the State Department and the Pentagon. Brown opened the book with an analysis of the "Origin of the Present Situation" and, plunging into the thickets of history, declared stoutly that he was dealing with the issues concerned not as a historian, but as a businessman.

Wrote he: "My approach to this problem has been from the standpoint of an industrialist's attempt to analyse the

---

[1] *Daily Sketch*, Sept. 1, 1953.

problem of a bankrupt company and to determine the simple common-sense fundamentals necessary to get the wheels of production turning, and the company on a profitable basis as soon as possible."[1]

Prompted by this aim, Brown relates in a special section devoted to Germany's development the story of that "company's" bankruptcy. Before treating the patient, he says, the doctor must know the case history of his complaint.

According to this case history, Germany had been visited before by times such as those which followed the collapse of Hitler's war machine. He pointed to the Thirty Years' War (1618-48), after which, Brown contended, the people of Germany were immersed in militarism and "became willing to pay any price for a powerful army".

Casting himself in the role of historian, the U.S. industrialist revives the legend that militarism was long a distinctive feature of the German people. Brown endeavours to prove that the Junkerdom and the financial tycoons, the governing classes in Germany, were blameless for the first and second world wars. Who, then, bore the guilt for starting them? To begin with, Brown says, it was fear, the fear the French had of the increasing German population at the turn of the century, when a heavy industry began to grow in Germany. Under the effects of this fear, France hastened to conclude an alliance with Russia. And, Brown avers, "this in turn led to the Triple Alliance of Germany, Austria-Hungary and Italy".

Any intelligent schoolboy will tell Brown, however, that the Franco-Russian alliance concluded in 1891-93 could not have served as the motive for the Triple Alliance concluded in 1882 and was itself motivated by the latter. This is scarcely a deliberate falsification on Brown's part, however, and smacks much more of crass ignorance. But it is a gross falsification to maintain, as Brown does, that the First World War was triggered not by contradictions between German and British imperialism, but merely by a conflict between Russia and Germany which, for some unearthly reason, "would likewise draw in the West". Brown is clearly regretful: how much better if Germany and Russia went it alone, bleeding each other in an endless round of butchery.

---

[1] Brown, *A Report on Germany*, New York, 1947, p. IX.

With dodges such as these Brown seeks to whitewash the German militarists in the Second World War. He says Hitler accepted the support of monopolists, Junkers and militarists for a short time only. He claims they were willing "to serve as a ladder for him", expecting to use Hitler for their own ends, but "Hitler, once in power, promptly kicked the ladder aside".

The implications are simple: "The traditional militarists of feudal origin and the industrialists of recent origin, long in alliance under the Kaiser" were during the Second World War merely innocent lambs who had "played into Hitler's hands".

Then Brown eulogises his German counterparts as "men of brains and skill" and thinks this justifies their return to power in Germany, being "among the world's greatest human assets". Then, falsifying history once again, Brown attributes the victory over nazi Germany solely to the armed forces of the United States. Silent about the historic role of the Soviet Army, which performed its heroic mission and liberated the European peoples from nazi tyranny, he declares that Berlin collapsed "before the terrific driving power of America's motorised columns".

Brown voices the hope that the lesson of history will not be lost and the times of the Thirty Years' War when, he claims, the Germans became steeped in militarism, will be remembered. True, Brown admits that Germans do not want to be drawn into a third world war, to supply cannon-fodder to the United States or participate in a new aggression against the Soviet Union.

As historian, he holds that these sentiments of the German people stem from what he calls a *Hoffnungslosigkeit* complex, a sense of futility, while as a man of affairs who has taken up social medicine in order to put things "on a profitable basis", he suggests a truly novel remedy against peace sentiments. "The prescription," he says, "must call for a combination of ingredients based on a realistic understanding of the patient's nature—a door of hope left open and a kick in the pants to propel him through."

No comment necessary!

Brown endeavours to prove that the German people's further history is inconceivable unless the big German industrialists "appointed by Uncle Sam" are put in power. He confesses that U.S. imperialism has no ideas in its arsenal that could capture the "souls of nations". For this reason, pleading the lessons of past history, Brown maintains that the Germans can be made to "take orders and like it—particularly if the fist of government is behind" them. Pleading the expedience of expansion and of a big stick U.S. policy in Germany, Brown says he does not expect enemies of the American way of life to agree with him. That is probably the only thing in Brown's book that need not be denied.

4

Current American and British historiography is going out of its way to whitewash the German generals, particularly the General Staff. A closer look will reveal that this is motivated, even in the historical context, by purely practical aims: the United States, *U.S. News and World Report* admits, is eager to test the idea of the German General Staff.[1] Yet it should be obvious without any verification that this "idea", like German militarism, failed ignominiously in both the First and Second World wars.

The Soviet Army exploded the notion of German invincibility, smashing the reputation carefully built up by the German General Staff. The moral assessment of it was succinctly formulated in the particular statement of the Soviet member of the Nuremberg Tribunal. The General Staff, he said, was the embodiment of the most typical traits of aggressive Prusso-German militarism. He showed on the strength of documents that it was a criminal organisation and that, as such, it should be destroyed.

But the Western members of the Tribunal chose to rehabilitate German militarism. They backed the agreed version set out at the trial by witnesses Field-Marshals Walther Brauchitsch, Erich Manstein, Albert Kesselring, and others. Having evaded trial themselves, these men declared that Hitler had fought a "preventive", not an aggressive, war, that the role of the General Staff and Wehrmacht Command had been no more than "technical" and that, moreover, by opposing Hitler's policy and strategy they were not an aggressive force but a deterrent.

---

[1] *U.S. News and World Report*, Feb. 10, 1950.

Since the new U.S. pretenders to world power set their sights on reviving the German armed forces, certain reactionary U.S. historians, and some in Britain too, began probing to what extent the experience of the German General Staff could be applied in a new world war. This was tied in with the idea of reorganising the U.S. command and the entire system of U.S. militarism. One of the projects for this reorganisation was drawn up by the former Hitler general, Heinz Guderian. "Centralisation of power in professional military hands," wrote *U.S. News and World Report* of February 10, 1950, "is at the heart of the Guderian plan. There would be no layers of civilian authority between the military and the President."

Reactionary American and British historians are concentrating their efforts on two things: first, they want to absolve German militarism of blame for war crimes and, second, to demonstrate that the German generals, particularly the General Staff, are not to blame for the crushing German defeat. The campaign of whitewashing war criminals has gone on for years in the U.S. and Britain, as well as in West Germany. Some U.S. historians magnify not only the German militarists, but even Hitler. Writing in *New York Times Magazine* (Sept. 4, 1949), Trevor-Roper, a professor of history, dug into such "historical sources" as Hitler's own *Mein Kampf*, Hitler's correspondence with Mussolini, Goebbels's diaries, Hermann Rauschning's notes and similar writings, to produce eulogies comparable to the worst models of Goebbels's propaganda.

While the war was still on, U.S. historians made an inglorious try to demonstrate that the German General Staff was a corporation of top-rate specialists who could not care less for nazi policy and were not, therefore, responsible for any war crimes. Numerous books and articles were written on this score. The war over, the same line continued. J.F.C. Fuller, the British war historian and theorist, declared in his book, *The Second World War. 1939-1945*, that the idea behind Hitler's strategic plan was essentially correct. It was just that error upon error was made in carrying it through. The reference to Hitler's "errors" is designed to vindicate the German aggression against the Soviet Union and belittle the decisive part played by the Soviet Army in smashing the nazi war machine.

B. H. Liddell Hart thinks along the same lines. The Soviet

reader knows his book, *The Real War 1914-1918,* which, though it contains no few controversial statements, is nonetheless of definite interest. In the capitalist countries he is rated rather highly as historian and ideologist, which makes it doubly regrettable that he, too, came out in behalf of Hitler's generals, as in his *The Other Side of the Hill,* based on biased accounts tendered by the top men of the reactionary German corps of generals: Hans von Seeckt, Werner von Blomberg, Werner Fritsch, Walther von Brauchitsch, Franz Halder, Günther von Kluge, Heinz Guderian, Gerd von Rundstedt, Erich von Manstein and Erwin Rommel.

Liddell Hart holds that the role of the German General Staff changed considerably since the days of the Kaiser. It had not wielded much influence over Hitler, he says, and was more inclined to impede than encourage his aggressive plans. Seeking to absolve German militarism of criminal guilt, he goes on to say that "the German Army in the field on the whole observed the rules of war better than it did in 1914-18". Since this claim is at odds with the universally known facts, Liddell Hart cautiously adds the reservation: "at any rate in fighting its western opponents". He writes off the monstrous crimes committed by the nazis against the peoples of the Soviet Union, Poland, Czechoslovakia and Yugoslavia, and the peoples of Western Europe as well. Yet he describes the organisational skills of the nazi generals as a prime historical factor. He says that during the war they acted with the precision of "mathematically calculating professionals" and that they were "the best-finished product of their profession anywhere".

One might wonder after hearing this how Hitler Germany had come to lose the war. What were the reasons for the Soviet victory? Liddell Hart thinks that "what saved Russia above all was not her modern progress, but her backwardness". Referring to sundry despatches issued by Kleist-Schmenzin and other nazi generals, he contends that the Soviet Union was saved by the cold and by impassible roads. But he qualifies as the main reason the psychological situation wrought "on the other side of the hill" by the conflict between "Hitler's strategic intuition" and the "school of generals".

The conclusions Liddell Hart reckons to draw by reviving the notion of German invincibility is that the German generals are unbeatable, provided they show a "deeper understanding" and confine themselves to carrying forward their immediate professional duties under the guidance of the forces that intend to pursue a "war policy" and "grand strategy" on a world-wide scale. These conclusions are prompted by ambitious political designs envisaging the revival of German militarism and its use in the interest of the aggressive Atlantic bloc.

5

Clearly, reactionary American and British historiography is helping to revive the revenge-seeking militarist ideology in West Germany.[1] Soon after the nazi defeat, monopoly and militarist quarters began, under the wing of the Anglo-American occupation authorities, to whitewash their past historically and politically. In historiography this was done at first through "reassessment" and recapitulation of those chapters of history that witnessed two crushing defeats inflicted on Germany in the lifetime of one generation. Self-seeking West German quarters, hand in glove with their American and British patrons, pulled out from oblivion distorted versions of history, which they modified to suit the new political climate and their own new aggressive revenge-seeking aims.

This was something in which German historians have more than enough experience. At the time of the First World War, capitalists and Junkers alike delighted in the writings of Count Ernst zu Reventlow,[2] who made it his life's work to demonstrate that upon embarking on her *Weltpolitik* Germany displayed a crass lack of acumen by failing to pepper her policy with more powerful means of persuasion, such as a big army and strong navy. His was a call for a still more aggressive *Weltpolitik* than that of the Kaiser. Not surprisingly, Reventlow subsequently joined the nazi party.

After the First World War, German historians produced several legends tailored for the propaganda of revenge

---

[1] See further, "German Imperialist Ideology and the Realities of Our Time".

[2] Reventlow, *Deutschlands auswärtige Politik. 1888-1914*, Berlin, 1918.

and for the political priming of a new war. Then followed version upon version to promote the revival of imperialism and militarism and the military, political and ideological preparations for a new aggressive war.

At first, the historians endeavoured to prove that the German Government was no more guilty of starting the war than the governments of other European states. This tale was backed in part by U.S. historians, since it sidestepped the question of U.S. imperialism. Then came the tale that German imperialism was entirely without fault in the question of "war guilt". Reactionary quarters in the United States and Britain were at the time financing the revival of German militarism and, naturally, were more than eager to support anything that vindicated German imperialism. The story was revived, too, that Germany had been compelled to go to war purely to block the pernicious policy of "encirclement", the main responsibility for which rested with British imperialism.

British and U.S. historians, meanwhile, brought forth a tale about the constant desire of the rulers of their two countries to remove the antagonisms and differences with Germany. That was part of the Anglo-American effort of coming to terms with Germany and channelling her aggression eastward, against the Soviet Union. The "war guilt" controversy came to a point where the rulers of Germany, Britain and the United States came to the compromise of mutual vindication. Indicatively, a new version came into being, pronouncing Russia, along with the Balkan nations and the Slavs of Austria-Hungary, who fought for their national liberation, the main culprits of the First World War. This was backed in both Britain and the United States.[1]

After Hitler began his war against the Western powers (1939), German historiography promptly discarded the mask. It declared for all the world to hear that it considered the Second World War a historical continuation of the First.

In sum, the nationalist school of German historians served faithfully the purposes of revenge and aggression. And wherever this dovetailed with the interests of the British

---

[1] See G. P. Gooch, *Studies in Modern History*, London, 1931; S. B. Fay, *The Origins of the World War*, Vols. I, II, New York, 1928.

and U.S. rulers, the latter did not hesitate to back them.

After the Second World War, too, when West Germany was first an occupation zone, then an ally of Anglo-American imperialism, writings whitewashing the German monopolists and militarists were even more vigorously supported. Old and untrue versions of history were galvanised and new ones fabricated to promote the aggressive policies of United States imperialism in Europe.

The discussion of Germany's war guilt and her culpability for war crimes died down. Writing in the *Annals of the American Academy of Political and Social Sciences* in 1949, William Abenstein offers the following candid explanation:

"The discussion of German guilt for the crimes committed ... during 1933-45 seems lately to have lost the sense of practicality and urgency.... The Russian issue dominates our thinking to such an extent that problems relating to past wars are no longer held to be important enough to distract our attention from the one key problem."

Spurred by the exigencies of the cold war, U.S. ruling quarters concentrated their propaganda efforts on evading the question of guilt for the Second World War and on producing plausible motives for the political vindication and moral rehabilitation of German imperialism and militarism. Historical or philosophical works appearing in West Germany that minimise the responsibility borne for the war by German imperialism and militarism, while condemning Hitler's barbarity, were received with open arms.

Karl Jaspers in *The Question of German Guilt*[1] said many a thing of delight to U.S. reactionaries, among them that the German nation ostensibly has no tradition of struggle for national liberation. For U.S. imperialism this is a vital matter, because its policy of partitioning Germany is opposed by the progressive section of the German people. This is why, responding to Jaspers's contention, the *Annals of the American Academy of Political and Social Sciences* draws the following deduction:

"Germany (apart from Japan) is the only major country which has never known a successful revolutionary experience of a popular libertarian kind."

---

[1] Jaspers, *Die Schuldfrage. Ein Beitrag zur deutschen Frage*, Zürich, 1946.

But it is not all that simple! What about the fight for liberation in the Napoleonic era, the revolution of 1848 and its democratic *motifs,* and the revolutionary struggles of the German workers during the Western occupation of the Ruhr? And what about the programme for national and social emancipation put forward by the advanced section of the German working class at the time of Hitler's advent to power?

U.S. finance capital prefers to gloss over these facts in arguing the case of the reactionary course in West Germany. Should it be surprising then that Karl Jaspers's book, translated into English, attracted the attention of reactionary U.S. and British publicists?

Interest was also aroused in the United States by Friedrich Meinecke's book, *The German Catastrophe,*[1] translated into English by U.S. historian Sidney Fay, an admirer of the foreign policy and diplomacy of German imperialism. Meinecke, who published his book in West Germany soon after the war, arrived ruefully at the conclusion that "the craving to be a world power turned out to be a false idol". He acknowledged that German imperialism's attempts to gain world power were futile and recognised the claim to power in Europe staked out by the United States. He did not mind U.S. dominance over Germany, and twisted the facts in piecing together a scheme of his own, hitching Germany's future to the U.S. imperialist chariot and endeavouring to justify the partition of Germany by contending that it was Bismarck and not the Germans who wanted a united Germany. He objected to the idea of a single Germany as a united democratic state and urged a return to the Germany of "Goethe's times", when the country was splintered but when, he averred, lofty spiritual values were the foundation for West European universalism. He idealised the cultural life of the Germans then, and pleaded: "Let us follow their example. We can regain strength only as a member of the future federation voluntarily created out of the states of Central and Western Europe."

By propagating this idea of a West European federation, he pretended to counter Bismarck's legacies with a thesis contrary to the progressive historical tradition of the German

---

[1] Meinecke, *Die deutsche Katastrophe. Betrachtungen und Erinnerungen.* 3. Aufl., Wiesbaden, 1947.

nation. Pleading for a "European community", Meinecke tried to prove that the German people could escape a new catastrophe by abandoning the fight for their national interests and submitting to West European integration.

His conception was acclaimed by the reactionary U.S. press. The *New York Herald Tribune* of January 29, 1950, for example, extolled it as a good try at reappraising German history, hoping that German youth raised in the sombre environment of the 1945 defeat would, as Meinecke evidently expected, revert to the old German traditions. Yet these old traditions of particularism and hidebound West European universalism have nothing in common with the progressive democratic traditions that reactionaries have tried to choke so many times.

It was not the war guilt and the war crimes that bothered German historiography so much as the question of responsibility for the crushing military defeat and the disaster that overcame the nazi state. Many a writer in West Germany tried to pinpoint the reasons for the "catastrophe". Whatever their worth from the factual and documentary angle, the political views and tendencies they reflected were highly indicative.

Take Ludwig Heilbrunn's book, *The Kaiser Empire, the Republic and Nazi Rule*, which attempted to justify the policy opposing the Potsdam plan of a united, peace-loving, democratic Germany. To make his point, he said Hitler's fascist rule was the result of Germany's long historical road. "The blame," he everred, "goes back to the past, to the times of Bismarck."[1]

Eduard Hemmerle, still more candid, urged a "review of the general historical picture" in order to grasp the causes and effects "not only of the political and military, but also of the spiritual disaster".[2] Unlike most of the other apologists of German militarism, he did not blame the "disaster" on mistakes made by Hitler and his coadjutants, but on the general spiritual make-up of Germany since the conception of the German Reich.

This pushed to the forefront the question of Bismarck's

---

[1] Heilbrunn, *Kaiserreich, Republik, Naziherrschaft. Ein Rückblick auf die deutsche Politik. 1870-1945*, Hamburg, 1947; also, see Hegeler, *Die deutsche Tragödie und ihre geschichtlichen Ursachen*, Celle, 1947.

[2] Hemmerle, *Deutsche Geschichte von Bismarcks Entlassung bis zum Ende Hitlers*, München, 1948.

role in German history, sparking a discussion on whether the Iron Chancellor was a proponent or adversary of conquest, thinking Germany sufficiently "saturated". The political overtones are easy enough to discern.

Firstly, by obscuring the catastrophic results of Hitler's blood-stained dictatorship and aggressive imperialism, German reactionary historians are, in effect, vindicating Hitler. Secondly, by pretending to speak out against Bismarck, the old-time idol of bourgeois and Junker reaction, they appear to denigrate the idea of national unity and German statehood, setting their sights on atomising and federalising the German structure and on West Germany's inclusion for revenge-seeking purposes in the Western bloc.

Hemmerle's historical concept leaves no doubt on that score. Under the guise of anti-Bismarckism, Hemmerle ran down the idea of German unification while hailing the "federalist" principle promoted by the Anglo-American occupation authorities. Under the guise of "anti-nationalism" he spoke out for a "cosmopolitan world of Western culture, with which Germany should share its principles". And under the guise of "anti-materialism" he pleaded for a crusade against the economic and political ideals of German progressives, notably the workers. He also endeavoured to substantiate his views by the distinctly reactionary idea of a religious revival, geared to the interests of the nascent system of political clericalism.

Indicatively, Admiral Canaris, head of military intelligence from 1934 and co-plotter in the anti-Hitler conspiracy of July 20, 1944, for which he was executed, is described as a "religiously-minded fighter against Hitler"[1] and a "world citizen" who conceived Germany's salvation through close ties with the Western powers.

Soon after war's end, financiers and generals forged to the fore as historians. According to the conservative *Daily Mail*, their essays and memoirs sold like "hot cakes". True, they were baked of sub-standard historical material and stuffed with the venom of revenge-seeking, aggressive, even neo-fascist, ideas. But that is precisely why the reactionary British and American press accorded them so much publicity.

Among the earliest of these neophyte writers, who under-

---

[1] K. H Abshagen, *Canaris. Patriot und Weltbürger*, Stuttgart, 1950.

took to revise German history, was Hjalmer Schacht, a minister in Hitler's government and the "financial genius of the Third Reich" tried by the Nuremberg Tribunal. Too many apologias have been written for causes whose culprits act as their own perjurers, defenders and judges rolled into one. Among them, Schacht's historico-political exercise ranks second to none. His book, *Settling Scores with Hitler*,[1] is not a mere self-vindication; it is a brazen-faced attempt to settle scores with the progressive democratic forces in Germany, magnify the role of the German financiers and justify their post-war orientation on U.S. imperialism.

It is grossly dishonest to place modern German history on its head and claim that all blame for Hitler's advent to power and the Hitler dictatorship devolves entirely on the people of Germany, "nobody else", and that the German monopolists and financiers were the sole bearers of democracy in the country. One must be a barefaced liar and demagogue to write that the Deutsche Bank was the citadel of German democracy, and certainly sure of impunity to claim that he himself was apostle and champion of democracy, he, Hjalmar Schacht, a defendant in Nuremberg, ex-member of the nazi government, in which he had allegedly acted "deliberately as an opponent". How much a Jesuit to maintain that by running the finances of Hitler's war machine he made sure it would not be turned to aggressive purposes!

Schacht wants us to believe that the nazi army and state collapsed not under the pounding of the Soviet Army and the rest of the anti-Hitler coalition, but chiefly due to his own efforts of "foiling" Hitler's penchant for "injustice and violence".

Recalling the old First World War "war guilt" debate, Schacht says: "The question of guilt cannot be raised this time. It cannot be raised without accusing both sides." He hints that any new war guilt discussion would destroy the "sense of community" between German and Anglo-American monopolists, adding: "I, for one, want to help the reconciliation."

The reactionary press in Britain and the United States hailed his offer. It described Schacht as the German Talleyrand, probably intending this to sound as a tribute to

---

[1] Schacht, *Abrechnung mit Hitler*, Hamburg-Stuttgart, 1948.

his historical and political acumen. To give historical plausibility to what the West would gain by supporting German imperialism, Schacht revives the Pan-Germanic Union's jingoist legend that "after the fall of Rome, Germany became the heart of Western culture". Then he asks: "Can this culture live without a heart?"

And the former nazi minister goes on to produce one more legend, designed to justify the eagerness with which the West-German monopolists seek the backing and friendship of the U.S. rulers. He repeats the shopworn nazi claim that the Second World War was a continuation of the First, and writes: "The German people suffered a similar disaster once before, during the fratricidal Thirty Years' War. When the butchery ended, 300 years ago, Germany was as devastated as now." Then, producing no historical proofs thereof—for they are non-existent—Schacht maintains in so many words that the German people recovered after the Thirty Years' War, because they accepted the "spiritual guidance of the New, rather than the Old World". Now, Schacht says, the nation should follow the same course.

The "scores" that Schacht "settles" with Hitler concern the latter's failure to accomplish the expansionist plans of the German capitalists. Despite the defeat, and much more because of it, he says, these plans can and must be brought to fruition, because, he vows, they have profound historical and economic roots. The German imperialist plans of conquest in Europe and the colonies Schacht justifies with the old Pan-Germanic and fascist "theory", to wit: "The German nation has outgrown the living space which history assigned it."

Schacht admits that he needs the nazi concept of the origin of the First World War to justify his idea of a third war of revenge. "If it was impossible to feed the Germans off their own land before 1914, it is doubly impossible now," he says. He is against any democratic agrarian reform. He thinks it is the duty of the German monopolists to back large-scale landownership, and, more important still, to prepare for a new war for *Lebensraum,* this time jointly with the Western powers, notably the United States.

In effect, as we see, the newly fledged German Talleyrand, sporting the garb of an anti-Hitler historian, encourages the idea of German imperialist revenge. While "settling scores" with Hitler, Schacht wants historians to rehabilitate the German monopolists, declaring that "those whose profession is to deal with money, cannot be popular very long". He thinks it is essential, therefore, for German history books to put alongside the names of the top Prusso-German militarists those of Deutsche Bank director Georg Siemens, Disconto-Gesellschaft director David Hansemann and other prominent backers of German aggression in whose footsteps followed Schacht himself, Pferdmenges and other financiers.

The endeavours to rehabilitate German militarism were no less vigorous in historical researches and in memoirs. The most thorough was Walter Görlitz in his *German General Staff*,[1] a detailed history of that institution, which played the top role in preparing and guiding all the aggressive wars fought over three centuries (1657-1945) by Prussia, then by Prussianised and finally Hitlerised Germany. Here and there Görlitz puts down authentic facts. For one thing, he describes the Stalingrad Battle as having "largely foreshadowed the bankruptcy of Hitlerite strategy, based on illusions and prestige".

But it is farthest from his mind to expose the General Staff. On the contrary, he does his utmost to restore its prestige and prove that the defeat of Hitler Germany was not a defeat for the military ideology built up over the centuries by aggressive German militarism. He strives to prove that after Hitler's advent the General Staff fought against war and opposes to Hitler and his strategy, the German corps of generals, the General Staff and its strategy. His main purpose is to discredit the verdict of the Nuremberg War Crimes Tribunal. While pronouncing the principle of "objectivism", protesting against history being made prosecutor or judge, he acts in effect as an advocate of the German General Staff, the corps of generals and the militarist system.

The curious thing is that, at first, the response to the book by the more reactionary quarters in West Germany, the United States and Britain, was no more than lukewarm. To them its apologia was too timid, too closely veiled, bearing little resemblance to their own, now outspoken

---

[1] Görlitz, *Der deutsche Generalstab. Geschichte und Gestalt 1657-1945*, Frankfurt a/M, 1950.

methods of whitewashing the German militarists and, more important still, their ideology of "European integration" and supranational Atlantic collaboration. Writings like Schacht's are more to their liking. And Colonel-General Franz Halder, Chief of Hitler's General Staff, came in for the greatest plaudits. A total failure as wartime strategist, Halder has turned historian.[1] In an introduction to the book, *Hitler as Soldier*, he maintains that his historical concept is aimed at debunking Hitler's reputation as military strategist. But actually Halder has a totally different purpose: to uplift his own reputation and that of the German generals of Hitler's time.

As Halder sees it, nazi strategy failed because Hitler was campaign commander (*Feldherr*), a role Halder claims to be historically outdated, objectively inept and contrary to the nature of modern warfare. "For a *Feldherr,* that is a general in the old sense," Halder writes, "no place exists any more in a modern war." He does not pull any punches in discrediting his former *Führer,* mocking his cowardice and indecisiveness, ridiculing his reckless irresponsibility and his delusions of grandeur. But the main point he endeavours to make is that the failure of Hitler's strategy does not mean failure of the strategy of the German General Staff. He singles out as the main, even the sole, cause of the defeat the fact that Hitler concentrated in his hands all military as well as political power and could thus, claiming "supreme political considerations", oppose the arguments of "military specialists" embodying the experience and reason of the German corps of generals.

Yet it is evident from Halder's own account that these "arguments" differed little from Hitler's own "high politics". Halder thinks Hitler was right to attack the Soviet Union, but blames him for failing to prepare for it. He thinks Hitler was right to try and capture Moscow in 1941 and Stalingrad in 1942, but blames him for ignoring the "desperate appeals of the army *Oberkommando* to concentrate all reserves". He says nothing of the role played by the German militarists in preparing the nazi aggression and tries to prove that the main reason for Hitler's downfall was that the generals had no say in the strategic solutions. To hear him hold forth, it was anything but the

[1] Halder, *Hitler als Feldherr*, München, 1949.

crushing and decisive blows of the Soviet Armed Forces, of which he makes no mention, that defeated the German armies. Failing to make the ends meet, he promptly appeals to God as the arbiter who always sides with the German *Generalität*. Thus, seeking to rehabilitate militarism, Halder "settles" his own "scores" with Hitler.

He is not the only one. Sensing the support of the trans-Atlantic power, the German militarists regained their poise and became an important tool of the West German revenge policy. Reactionary historians went so far as to pronounce German militarism pacifistic. This "point" is carried to absurdity by H. Laternser in *A Defence of the German Soldiers*: "Where do you find the least trace of the German 'militarism' that is said to have been the forerunner and maker of Hitler's aggressive plans? . . . The officers in those days were moved by the spirit of peace and humanity, to ensure defence in the event of an enemy attack. . . . If unanimity existed at all among the military leaders, it certainly did not apply to framing plans of aggression, but . . . solely to rejecting such plans of the head of state."[1]

While aiming to restore the prestige of German militarism, reactionary historians and writers of memoirs also serve as purveyors of militarist ideas used extensively by the U.S. imperialists for their own ends. West German militarist literature has gained a wide circulation and considerable influence in the United States and Britain.

6

To say that current reactionary historiography, inspired in its main trends by the big monopolists, militarists and their political protégés, distorts just some of the aspects of the case in sprucing up the image of German imperialism, is an understatement. It treats the problems of German history as part of a far broader historical conception, geared to definite political aims.

Take George Kennan's concept, as presented in his cycle of lectures at Chicago University and, later, in his book, *American Diplomacy. 1900-1950*.[2] The writer is a

---

[1] Laternser, *Verteidigung deutscher Soldaten*, Bonn, 1950.
[2] Kennan, *American Diplomacy. 1900-1950*, Chicago, 1951.

political figure close to the State Department and associated with the U.S. finance oligarchy. The fig leaf of objectivism is not for him. He makes no bones about admitting that his wish to probe history "stems from no abstract interest in history for history's sake. It stems from a preoccupation with the problems of foreign policy we have before us today."

That was indeed the angle from which Kennan approached German history—as the history of one of the principal theatres of U.S. West European policy. He admits that total subordination of this and other theatres (the Far Eastern and Latin American) to U.S. influence is a stepping stone, the principal one, to U.S. world leadership. He treats the German problem as part of the general European problem, and qualifies its solution in the latter half of the 20th century as the key challenge to the United States.

His conception is fairly simple and frank, based on the old "balance of power" idea which once did duty as a screen for the British policy of fomenting antagonisms on the European mainland in order to leave Britain's hands free in the colonial domains.

"The absence of a major war on the Continent during the century before 1914," writes Kennan, "had rested on a balance of power which presupposed the existence of France, Germany, Austria-Hungary, and Russia as dominant elements—and all of this flanked by an England.... In this complicated structure lay concealed not only the peace of Europe but also the security of the United States."

He overlooks all the wars fought in Europe after Napoleon and evidently attaches little significance to the wars in the fire of which Germany was forged into a *Reich*, which, therefore, could not have counted in the "power balance" before it was constituted. Furthermore, should we accept Kennan's concept, it is clear all the same that the constitution of Germany was bound to have altered the "power balance" that prevailed after the conclusion of the Napoleonic wars. Also, Kennan's "power balance" idea ignores the many bloody wars for the division and redivision of colonies and semi-colonies.

It will be recalled that the birth of imperialism was heralded by the predatory U.S. war against Spain, loosened with the object of enthralling Cuba and capturing the Philippines. Yet Kennan excuses the capture of the Philippine Islands by pleading the same case of peace and "power balance".

He says about the Philippines that "the alternative to our taking them would probably have been a tussle between England and Germany over their possession". Retailoring the old British theory, Kennan endeavours to prove that even in the late 19th, let alone the 20th century, the United States safeguarded peace and stability in international affairs.

Knowing his conception, one is scarcely surprised to find that Kennan holds the "world crisis" that erupted in 1914 and has continued to this day to be of purely European origin. He thinks the First World War was caused partly by the "still unsolved problems of the breakup of the old Turkish Empire" and partly by the "restlessness of subject peoples in the Danubian basin", which robbed Austria-Hungary of her *"elan vital"*. In sum, Kennan names the national liberation movement of subject peoples, primarily Slavs, as the main cause of the war. This is no novelty in reactionary U.S. historiography. He mentions a few other causes of the war, among which "the rivalry between Germany and England" is listed last. Referring to the war guilt, he compiles a long scale of responsibility, so utterly groundless that he himself feels obliged to describe it as a "rather fuzzy pattern". On this scale, he writes, "the Austrians and the Russians [are] no doubt in first place, the Germans with less but certainly with a goodly share, and no one with none at all". In this, indeed rather fuzzy, pattern, only one thing is clear: the writer places U.S. imperialism far apart from the European, even from world history, and makes it appear that the United States had no relation whatsoever to the outbreak of the war. He looks for the causes of the *world* war not in the *world* system of states and not in *world* antagonisms, but solely in the interlacement of *local* conflicts which, he maintains, upset the balance in the European continent.

Neither is this a novel idea. Beard, Fay and many other American historians held the same view. They skimmed over the surface of diplomatic history, carefully avoided the question of the profound economic and class motives of imperialist world-scale wars, and contended that U.S. imperialism had no part at all in the outbreak of the First

World War and that its involvement expedited the end of the war. Kennan does not deny that at the time of the war Germany was a "militaristic and anti-democratic country", but thinks that in the light of later developments this was of no consequence, an advantage rather than a fault.

The October Revolution in Russia evokes from Kennan an outburst of blind hate. He cannot reconcile himself to the fact that by the time the Versailles Treaty was signed, the limits of the region where Western leaders, especially those of the United States, could "restore genuine health and peace to Western civilisation ... had been grievously and tragically narrowed". On the other hand, he follows the example of nazi writers and says the Second World War was a direct continuation of the First.

"These wars," he argues, "were fought at the price ... of the destruction of the balance of forces on the Continent—at the price of rendering Western Europe dangerously, perhaps fatefully, vulnerable to Soviet power."

Not only does he endeavour thereby to exonerate the aggressive German imperialism; he supports the nazi propaganda that cloaked Hitler's predatory aim of conquering and subjugating the peoples under the slogan of "combating communism". Also, he obscures the role of the U.S. monopolies, which had by backing and financing the German monopolists and Hitler helped to bring on the Second World War and, primarily, the German imperialist attack on the Soviet Union. Kennan claims that he "personally can find no evidence that any substantial body of responsible opinion in any of the Western countries really wished for war at all at that time—even one between Russia and Germany".

He feels free, it appears, to ignore the facts that reveal the sense and purpose of the Munich policy pursued by the Western capitalist powers at that time. He thus evades an analysis of the basic trends in U.S. policy during the Munich period, particularly the line followed backstage by the influential U.S. monopolies. It appears, in fact, that Kennan would like nothing better than to write off the whole period after the First World War and the October Revolution in Russia, and to begin all over again. In the context of the present U.S. imperialist interests in Europe, this would mean restoring "a vigorous Germany ... able to play a part again in the balancing-off of Russian power". What he wants, obviously, is a militarist state in the heart of the continent.

However, though eager to provide historical excuses for the revival of German militarism, Kennan thought fit to warn that America should have "provided itself right then and there with something in the way of an armed establishment, so that our word would carry some weight and be listened to in the councils of the powers". What he was driving at were U.S. war bases, not in West Germany only. More generally, it meant that, steeping current in past history, Kennan devised a conception to justify the expansionist designs of the U.S. rulers, designs that also envisage the revival of the German militarism.

Kennan's concept is one of the most striking and typical examples of the political pragmatism of contemporary bourgeois historiography. Ideologically sterile, as the cold war revealed clearly, it chose to revert to the old, shopworn theories, ideas and conceptions, adapting them to its aggressive political aims. Among others, it is trying to revive the old theory of cyclicity, a modernised and much simplified version of which is now peddled to counterweigh the idea of the progressive historical process. Kennan's aim of turning back the clock forty years in German and European history and thus justifying the U.S. imperialist plans, is indeed but a variant of this notion of cyclicity. The cycles are applied to different geographic and historical areas but, inevitably, they all end up in attempts to substantiate the U.S. bid for world power or to rehabilitate German imperialism and, in all cases, to contribute to the cold war ideology.

In sum, the reactionary theories of the cold war period are produced by the financiers and industrialists and their ideologists, by politicians dabbling in history and historians dabbling in politics. U.S. historian Donald Mitchell posed in *Current History* as an expert on the military aspects of the Atlantic Pact, and newspaper strategist Hanson Baldwin as war historian in *Atlantic Monthly*, while Kennan, recently a politician and diplomatist, devoted himself not only to the history of U.S. diplomacy, but to German history as well, fitting it into the cyclical conception of the 20th century.

Professor Frederick H. Cramer, too, followed the cyclical

approach to link the two world wars, but went a step farther, spotting a historical parallel in the antique world. In an article, "The Decline and Fall of Western Europe",[1] he drew a parallel between the economic and political growth of Western Europe since the outbreak of the First World War and the growth of the Greco-Roman civilisation. In both cases, he says, "civil wars and prolonged emaciation of the body politic" were the cause of decline. But speaking of our times, he singles out the historical role of Germany. His point of departure is that the existence of the German Reich was one of the most substantial factors of the West European civilisation. On the other hand, he says, the independence fought for by the European nations was like a "cancer".

He contrasted the liberation struggles with the "ideas of West European community", the loss of which, he held, could have the same repercussions as the collapse of the single Greco-Roman civilisation. The other important reason for the "decline and fall of Western Europe" is identified by Cramer as the disintegration of the system of international relations forged at the end of the 19th century, when "Great Britain, Russia, Germany, Austria-Hungary, and France were the joint rulers of the world".

As he sees it, "the end of an era of unprecedented European power and prestige is at hand". He believes the time has come "to intone a *de profundis* at the tomb of the old and powerful Europe which died in the past third of a century" and to celebrate the capture of world power by the United States. Yet his concept is evidence of nothing but the extreme shortsightedness of those with whom the wish is father to reality.

In modern history the German problem has always been among the most important, acute and complicated, reflecting on the destiny of other nations, and in the new period of German history is an object of bitter ideological struggle between the forces of aggression, on the one hand, and the progressive forces, with a stake in peace, on the other. In the circumstances, reactionary historiography which strives to whitewash German imperialism and militarism is a component of the cold war, aimed against all peace-loving peoples, the German included.

---

[1] *Current History*, No. 87, 1948.

Progressive historians in all countries, and in Germany too, are leaving no stone unturned to expose the militarist and revanchist conceptions for what they really are. Historians of the German Democratic Republic are making a valuable contribution. So are some of the West German historians, those who oppose the attempts at rehabilitating German militarism, imperialism and Hitlerism.

But one need not be a historian to see that the cold war ideology and the efforts to reinstate German militarism are at odds with the peaceful aspirations and interests of the peoples. After all the peoples in Europe and elsewhere have gone through in the Second World War, the effort to comprehend the role in history of German militarism is a pressing task. The history of German imperialism and militarism needs to be thoroughly examined in order to establish its roots, and then to extract them. This task, we hold, is more than just scientific and political; it is also moral. It will not, if accomplished, bring about the decline and fall of Europe. Far from it. It will help reinforce the peace and thus give impulse to Europe's regeneration.

1953

For several weeks in the summer of 1959 public attention was focused on the shore of Lake of Geneva, where in the Palace of Nations and the residences of the foreign ministers of the Soviet Union, the United States, Britain and France, intricate talks proceeded over problems whose solution would write *finis* at last to the consequences of the Second World War. The main topic was a peace treaty with Germany and normalisation of the situation in West Berlin.

The conference of the foreign ministers of the principal member-countries of the anti-Hitler coalition was also attended by the foreign minister of the German Democratic Republic and a representative of the Federal Republic of Germany.[1]

None will deny that the question of a peace treaty and that of West Berlin constitute a historical anomaly at this time. Modern history knows of no other case when changes wrought by a war were not formally recorded in a peace treaty so many years after the hostilities. The Franco-Prussian war of 1870-71 was formally terminated a few months after it ended, while the occupation of French departments by German troops continued for somewhat longer than two years. Even the Versailles Treaty imposed on Germany by the Western powers was concluded about six months after the shooting stopped and the somewhat longer

---

[1] F.R.G. Foreign Minister von Brentano came to Geneva, but demonstratively refused to appear in the Palace of Nations.

occupation of the Rhine area by Western troops was discontinued earlier than originally planned.

The present situation, however, is more than unprecedented; it is highly explosive. The absence of a peace treaty with Germany for so many years and the survival of the occupation regime in West Berlin are in no way conducive to stabilising international relations. Quite the reverse. They preclude normal contacts and stoke up tension in Germany, Europe and throughout the world—something none but the cold war architects find agreeable.

The realities are as follows: two independent and sovereign states have emerged in post-war Germany, each with its own socio-economic and political system, while the still occupied city of West Berlin remains a front-line city against the German Democratic Republic, in the territory of which it is situated. The two German states have different ways: the German Democratic Republic, where the Potsdam decisions have been put into practice, has torn down the economic, political and ideological pillars of militarism, whereas the Federal Republic chose to revive militarism, which is becoming more of a peril to the world each day because it craves to lay its hands on nuclear weapons and rockets.

To end the anomaly, the two German states must first normalise relations. This would speed up the conclusion of a peace treaty which, conversely, would help promote normal relations.

The various provisions in the draft treaty submitted by the Soviet Union may be debated one way or another; so may the question of how much time it will take to end the occupation regime in West Berlin. The one thing that is beyond debate is the immense importance of the Soviet initiative, geared to the compulsive urgency of resolving the German problem by peaceful means. This, in effect, is something the Western powers, too, are bound to recognise; how else to explain the fact that they consented to holding the Geneva conference?

Despite the efforts of the cold warriors to the contrary, world opinion has shown a profound interest in the Soviet initiative and a deep appreciation of the problems raised. The strident campaign drummed up by the reactionary press in West Germany, the United States and elsewhere, naming the peace move a "challenge", "threat" and "ultimatum", fell far short of its aim of torpedoing the idea of a foreign ministers' conference and obstructing attempts at resolving the controversial points by negotiation.

Yet the necessity of East-West talks has sunk in everywhere, in all continents, and become so forceful that even the opponents cannot but reckon with it. In the meantime, the political cold war concept has so obviously revealed its weakness that even John Foster Dulles, its chief proponent, realised in the latter period of his life that some of its major aspects need to be revised.

We could be blamed for over-optimism if we suggested that the revision had begun in Geneva and yielded palpable results. Yet it is undeniable that an appreciation of the need for revision to fit the wide-ranging changes in the world balance is beginning to make headway, and the Geneva conference is one of the signs thereof.

But the friends of militarism and the revenge-seeking policy pursued by West Germany are busy consolidating forces. After Dulles's departure, Chancellor Adenauer came into the open with claims to succeed him as top ideologist and promoter of the cold war in the North-Atlantic alignment and is branding as "betrayal of the free world" any departure by any of the Western powers from "positions of strength" to positions of reason.

When British Prime Minister Harold Macmillan professed his readiness to negotiate with the U.S.S.R. in a bid to resolve some of the controversial questions, Adenauer made undisguised crude attacks on British policy, comparable only to the attacks on the "perfidious Albion" once made by Wilhelm II and Hitler.

The outcome of the Geneva conference, too, where some progress was made in the teeth of opposition by Adenauer and von Brentano, evoked bitter resentment in Bonn.

The British press was compelled to point out that Adenauer's pretensions to leadership fall far short of his actual place in the Western world, even in West Germany. The *Scotsman*, of June 24, 1959, noted rightly that in his own country, even in his own party, Adenaur's tough stand is not universally supported. Although in the main his position was backed by the leaders of some Western states, they had had to consent to the Geneva conference, the idea of resolving controversial issues by East-West negotiations gaining its first big victory.

The facts revealed, however, that the cold warriors would not lay down their arms. At first, they went to uncommon lengths to block the conference, thinking that this would preclude an easing of international tension. And when they saw that the Geneva conference would take place all the same, they exerted themselves to minimise its effects.

On the day the conference opened, the lie factories told the world that the ministers would go home before ever starting, due to procedural differences (about the seating of the two German delegations, that of the G.D.R. and F.R.G.). However, it did not take long for the controversy, an artificial hurdle, to peter out. The matter was settled despite the men who wished the conference torpedoed.

There were people on the technical staff, too, who made a point of creating obstructions rather than assuring favourable conditions for the parleys. They tried to hinder the G.D.R. delegation from arriving at the conference in time, and did so with refined courtesy. There was one thing they had overlooked: the four powers had agreed beforehand that the two German states would participate in the talks on equal terms. Hence, the conference could not begin until the G.D.R. delegation arrived.

As the talks got off to a start, in the early stage, and later too, in the conference hall and outside it, efforts were made to distract the parties from the main topics, block the deliberations, create a blind alley and discredit the idea of negotiations. Yet their attempts evoked an opposite reaction: Geneva became a Mecca, a centre of attraction, for many hundreds of delegations, for thousands of petitions, urging prompt conclusion of the German peace treaty and an agreed solution for West Berlin.

Throughout the conference, Geneva was a cockpit of contention between those who wanted the conference to succeed and those who wanted it to fail. The Western powers and their press strove to create the impression that the negotiations would break down and that the gulf between the Soviet and G.D.R. stand, on the one hand, and that of the West, on the other, could not be bridged, blaming this on Soviet "intransigence" and "inflexibility". But that was putting the proverbial boot on the wrong foot.

When the talks opened the Western powers hastened to counter the Soviet project of a settlement with their own "package deal", which, it turned out at close range, ignored the historical fact that two independent and sovereign states existed in Germany and envisaged four-power interference in the domestic affairs of the German nation. The much advertised "package deal" was so patently unrealistic that even its sponsors relegated all its elements save those concerning the status of West Berlin to the background. The proposals on the West Berlin issue, meanwhile, boiled down to perpetuating the city's occupation regime. In effect, they sidestepped the solutions put forward as the principal subject of the talks.

Furthermore, time and again the Western powers declared they would break off the talks if the Soviet Union did not abandon one or another of its proposals. The foreign press reported that the West Germans were anxious to provoke a breakdown. It reported also that towards the end of the first phase of the negotiations State Secretary Christian Herter had ordered a plane to stand by and take him home in the event the Soviet delegation refused to withdraw its proposals.

Pressure of this kind is no novelty in the history of diplomacy. Back in 1878 it was used by Prime Minister Disraeli at the Berlin Congress against the aged Chancellor Gorchakov. Disraeli announced then that his locomotive had been stoked up. Yet much has changed. What could make an impression then is now treated as an anachronism.

Despite the difficulties created by certain Western quarters, the Soviet delegation worked perseveringly for an agreed decision on the German peace treaty and the abolition, within set limits of time, of the occupation regime in West Berlin. In particular, it recommended converting West Berlin, situated in the heart of the German Democratic Republic, into a free city retaining the social system and free communications with both East and West under the control of the four powers—the United States, the U.S.S.R., Britain and France.

The Soviet Union is anxious to end the dangerous historical anomaly in Central Europe in the best interests of the peaceful development of all, especially the German, peoples.

In the long run the Western powers, though hostile to the Soviet proposal of concluding a peace with Germany, were compelled to admit the benefits of negotiating. True, they went no farther. But the Soviet Union, and the world's peace-loving forces are determined to work on, in order to end the present anomaly.

The Soviet Government pointed out that a treaty with the two existing German states would be the most realistic and effective approach, unless Germany is reunified by confederation. The sole purpose in drafting the peace treaty, it said, was to write *finis* to the Second World War, buttress peace and security in the centre of Europe, thus relieving the tensions in one of the most sensitive areas of international relations.

The Soviet delegation proved in every way that it was anxious to find a solution acceptable to all the parties represented in Geneva. It made new constructive suggestions as the work of the conference went on, seeking to untie the knots. It elucidated its position and was always ready, provided the basic principles were upheld, to look into any proposal earnestly, whomsoever it came from.

Take the Soviet proposals concerning West Berlin. Seeing that the Western powers were not ready yet to end the occupation regime in West Berlin, and meeting their wishes more than halfway, the Soviet delegation suggested a temporary status. The head of the Soviet delegation, A. A. Gromyko, proposed that the agreement should cover the following points: reduction of troops in West Berlin to a token force, cessation of subversive activities and hostile propaganda from West Berlin against the German Democratic Republic and other socialist countries, and non-stationing in West Berlin of atomic and rocket weapons.

Western spokesmen expressed apprehensions over the question of access to West Berlin. So, with the approval of the G.D.R. Government, the U.S.S.R. gave assurances that during the time of the temporary agreement West Berlin communications with the outside world would remain unaltered.

To be sure, the temporary status should not be perpetuated. According to the Soviet proposal, its operation would be limited to a definite agreed term.

There is an intrinsic connection between the temporary agreement on West Berlin and the question of negotiations between the two German states. During the operation of the agreement, an all-German committee or some other mixed body could work out measures promoting contacts between the F.R.G. and G.D.R. and examine matters related to the peace treaty and Germany's unification. If the efforts of the all-German committee or direct negotiations between the F.R.G. and G.D.R. in any other mutually acceptable form within the specified term provided the opportunity for concluding a peace treaty with Germany, the question of West Berlin would be automatically resolved. If, on the other hand, the G.D.R. and F.R.G. would, due to Bonn's blunt rejection of a rapprochement, fail to reach agreement, the nations represented in Geneva could re-examine the status of West Berlin.

This, in general terms, was the purport of the Soviet proposal, Soviet goodwill preventing the Geneva conference from foundering.

True, there is ample evidence that the West wanted to confine the talks to a temporary agreement on West Berlin and evade the question of G.D.R.-F.R.G. negotiations. Yet the exchanges concerning the latter, too, had not been entirely fruitless. In effect, the Western powers recognised the need for talks between the two German states concerning preparations for, and the conclusion of, the peace treaty, as well as for concrete steps towards unification and extension of contacts. It may be added that talks of that kind are conceivable only as between two sovereign states without outside control or patronage by any or all of the four powers.

During the intermission in the Geneva negotiations, initiated by the Western powers, newspapers in the West described the parleys as senseless and futile. The *Washington Post*, for example, predicted on June 20, 1959, that "the whole world will be depressed by the outcome". Adherents of the cold war painted a pessimistic picture, betraying their secret hopes.

Indeed, it would have been a miracle if in the existing climate of East-West alienation and hostility the parties to the talks had come to terms in a few days or weeks on the most acute and relevant problems left unsettled after war's end. Over the years, they have become so much more complicated, so much more sedimentation has accumulated, that all in all they present what may be described as the Gordian knot of contemporary European relations. Should the Western powers have accepted the Soviet proposals for a peace treaty with Germany, that Gordian knot, which also covered the West Berlin problem, would have been untied by common effort.

In 1919, the Western powers imposed on Germany the Versailles Treaty. The Soviet Union bears no responsibility for this instrument, which raised no barriers to the revival of German militarism. Anxious to draw the line beneath the Second World War, the Soviet Union came out with the proposal of a treaty positing not a militarist but a peaceful development of Germany in conformance with the interest of all peoples, the German included. There is nothing dictatorial about the Soviet project, and the fact that foreign ministers came to Geneva to discuss the matter is in itself highly significant. Earnest attempts were made at the conference to bring about a convergence of views on some of the key international problems. The work tackled in earnest, frank exchanges highlighting the proceedings, the opponents of negotiating could do nothing to stop it.

What was of cardinal importance was the presence of representatives from the G.D.R. and F.R.G., who participated in the discussions freely, without any trace of *diktat* by any of the others. This was in tune with the realities. That the G.D.R. was represented by Lothar Bolz, its Foreign Minister, while von Brentano, Foreign Minister of the F.R.G., preferred to operate backstage and Grewe, a former nazi, came to the conference instead, made no difference. It was a tragicomic thing, illustrating the state of affairs in West Germany, showing in any case that Bonn pretensions to the sole representation of Germany were groundless.

The conference offered the Germans a realistic opportunity of resolving the all-German problem. If the chance went by the board, the blame falls first and foremost on the F.R.G. rulers, who are obstructing reunification and the peace treaty.

The exhaustive discussion cleared up many of the aspects involved, producing a conclusive picture of the various attitudes and bringing the positions closer together on some issues. This is highly valuable and clears the path for further studies and settlements. It would be foolish, of course, to overlook the many considerable differences that still remain, especially on such key matters as the peace

410

treaty and direct F.R.G.-G.D.R. negotiations. These differences should spur the states represented in Geneva to fresh efforts in the search for mutually acceptable solutions.

It became obvious towards the end of the conference that certain Western quarters would continue obstructing any accommodation of the German problem. What they would like most is to charge the Soviet Union with wanting, as a "long-term task" to preserve the split in Germany. But making this charge, to use State Secretary Herter's expression, is seeing things inside out. Speaking of a "long-term task", in the present circumstances nothing would encourage progress towards a united, peaceful, democratic Germany more than a peace treaty and an all-German committee established on equal principles.

The Soviet Union has always opposed partitioning Germany. But now, by virtue of past historical experience, it holds that the unification problem was, is and will be an internal German affair. Interference by foreign powers—recall the attempts by Napoleon III in the 19th century and those of Poincaré in the 20th—is sure to misfire.

It should be borne in mind, on the other hand, that in the past German unity did not remove the danger of a universal war. On the contrary, the Kaiser Germany that precipitated the First World War and the Hitler Germany that precipitated the Second were united Germanys. They were not split in any way, and, striving to conquer and partition other lands, inflicted on the world untold suffering.

It is not, therefore, the existence of two independent states on German soil that presents a threat to world peace, but the revival of aggressive German militarism, again rearing its head in West Germany.

This does not go to say that the present state of affairs in Germany—the two Germanys—should go on forever. No, out of respect for the basic interests of the German nation, the Soviet Union is in favour of a rapprochement, of an all-German committee or some similar body. It holds that this would be the first realistic step towards resolving Germany's reunification problem by Germans and none but the Germans.

The Western powers, in the meantime, have offered no constructive plan for resolving the matter, because they treat the international problem of a peace settlement with Germany and the common problem of German reunification solely as an element of the aggressive politico-military NATO designs. At no time, the *Stockholms Tidningen* observed rightly during the Geneva Conference, did the Western powers suggest a unified Germany independent from both the Atlantic Pact and the Warsaw Treaty, for that would have upset all their economic, political and military plans. "For after all is said and done," it wrote, "West Germany is one of the mainstays of the North Atlantic Pact and the six-nation alliance."

Most active in their efforts to scuttle a peace settlement are those F.R.G. politicians who, having failed—for succeed they could not!—to head off a conference and then to frustrate its work, feel that it is still possible to nullify its success. Revanchist rallies were held in West Berlin and a number of West German cities, where Adenauer, Strauss and other spokesmen of the Bonn Government fulminated against the Geneva parleys, giving to understand that they do not conceive German unification as anything but a militarist absorption of the German Democratic Republic. Many were the revenge-seeking threats that resounded also against Poland, Czechoslovakia and other socialist countries.

West Berlin Oberburgomaster Willy Brandt, too, exerted himself to torpedo the conference. He demanded that the occupation regime in West Berlin be reinforced, that hostile propaganda against the G.D.R. and the other socialist countries be stepped up, and that control be extended over the G.D.R. territory between West Berlin and West Germany. If anyone still wants proof of the dangers emanating from West Berlin, Herr Brandt's utterances furnish it in ample quantity.

But Adenauer and the other cold warriors did not reckon with world opinion, which wants the negotiations to continue. Some of the bigger bourgeois papers, for one thing, were prompted by this public sentiment, veering off from their previous course, to warn the various governments against doing the will of cold war architects such as Adenauer. "Adenauer's well-known opposition," wrote the *New York Post* on June 25, 1959, "may serve his own political ends; it does not necessarily serve the ends of the West." The paper opposed "obsequious reverence for a nation that brought so much horror to the 20th century," and concluded:

"What we must insist on is that every path toward a European settlement be explored, as often and as persistently as possible, on every level."

The Conference of Foreign Ministers in Geneva epitomised what everyone following international developments has come to realise by now: not the political climate only, but the balance of forces and the situation as a whole are such that negotiations should be the sole method of regulating controversial questions.

The Geneva Conference has proved that agreement concerning a peace treaty and a solution, on this basis, for the West Berlin problem, would draw a line beneath the Second World War. It proved, too, that this is practicable if, naturally, there is a will. To lack this will is to support the revenge-seeking militarists in West Germany and keep alive the danger of a sudden explosion.

It was in anticipation of this danger, anxious to avert it, that the German Democratic Republic, backed by the other members of the Warsaw Treaty Organisation, took a series of defensive steps on August 13, 1961, to reinforce the frontiers in Berlin and all along the strip adjoining the eastern border of the Federal Republic of Germany. This was a forced move. If a peace treaty had been signed as a result of the Geneva talks, thus resolving the problem of West Berlin, or if the Western powers, above all the F.R.G., showed the slightest inclination to remove the historical anomaly in the heart of Europe, the German Democratic Republic may not have had to reinforce her western frontiers. The prospect of a peaceful accommodation would, after all, have presaged an ultimate convergence of the two German states towards confederation or some other form acceptable to the two states with their different socio-economic system. But that was the very prospect that frightened the wits out of the militarists in West Germany.

After the Geneva Conference ended, they set out to torpedo all chances of a peaceful settlement. It was farthest from their minds to explore possible routes of rapprochement with the G.D.R. They could not care less about framing constructive proposals facilitating a peaceful accommodation.

Quite the reverse. They made a big show of ignoring *all* G.D.R. proposals, without even examining them, and worked up a new wave of revanchism in the hope that

413

their cold war policy in Europe would generate extreme tension in the rest of the world, enabling them, with NATO backing, to operate with impunity. This is why the defensive measures taken by the G.D.R. on August 13, 1961, came to them as a move upsetting their plans. Earlier, they had hoped for an X-Day when some tense international emergency would enable them to send large groups of men across the open West Berlin border to stage a putsch that could be a pretext for a militarist annexation of the G.D.R. This dangerous plan, nursed by them for nearly a decade, was squashed overnight and nothing on earth can revive it.

The reaction to the defensive moves was one of shock, preceded by confusion. Hans Zehrer, editor-in-chief of *Die Welt*, the biggest West German paper, of the Springer empire, wrote: "The question is what's going to happen?" The warlike neofascist element represented by the *Deutsche Soldatenzeitung* and *Nation Europa* set up a howl. "March on Berlin before August 13 ends!", they exhorted, and: "Incorporate West Berlin in the Federal Republic!"

Those were exhortations which, if followed, would push Europe instantly over the brink of war. Seeing that Bonn could not in any practical way thwart the G.D.R. measures, the ultras lashed out, charging it with indecision. But their most scathing attacks were against NATO and, especially, against the United States. M. Freund, historian and publicist, virtually ground his teeth. "It is too late to do anything now," he wrote a few days later. "On Sunday, August 13, before sunrise it was still possible. Never again must the West miss the bus on mornings like that."[1] This sounded like a threat, which the ultras couched in still more definite terms as follows:

"If the West betrays Berlin, Germany may turn her back on the West."[2]

The West German rulers made no move to block the campaign launched by the ultras against the G.D.R. and even the Western partners of the F.R.G. There were two reasons why they welcomed it. First, it obscured the failure of their policy vis-à-vis the German Democratic Republic and, second, it gave them grounds for additional pressure on the Western powers in their bid for nuclear weapons.

---

[1] *Frankfurter Allgemeine Zeitung*, Aug. 19, 1961.
[2] *Deutsche Soldatenzeitung*, Sept. 1, 1961.

Their diplomats lost no time officially to classify nuclear weapons for the Bundeswehr as the top priority. This is the centre point of all West German policy and ideology.

By eliminating the open frontier in Berlin, a survival of the occupation regime established by the anti-Hitler coalition after the military collapse of the Third Reich, the G.D.R. firmed up its sovereignty and, at once, international security. Nobody can tell what would have resulted if the revenge-seekers massed in West Berlin had slunk past the Brandenburger Tor to stage an armed provocation in the G.D.R. capital at, say, the height of the Caribbean crisis, with the world a hair's breadth away from war. The firm action has reduced that sort of danger, though it will not be entirely dissipated until the German problem is settled in a peaceful way. When the Caribbean crisis was over, the Western press reported that millions of Europeans had been very uneasy, fearing that events in the Caribbean would, due to the unsettled state of the German problem, precipitate a situation of the utmost danger.

After the defensive G.D.R. measures in Berlin on August 13, certain political quarters in the West contended that the question of a peace treaty was thereby struck off the agenda, betraying their yearning to sidestep a solution of the principal question of our time posited by the post-war pattern of European relations. The August 13 measures certainly altered the general pattern. But they did not remove the anomaly prejudicing European relations and jeopardising the peaceful coexistence of states with different socio-economic systems. The Soviet draft of a peace treaty with the two German states, and the settlement on its basis of the West Berlin problem, was no tactical manoeuvre to justify measures strengthening the G.D.R. frontier. It was prompted by the sole aim of reinforcing security in the heart of Europe at one of the nerve centres of world politics.

A German peace treaty even at this late hour, nearly twenty years after the Second World War ended, would infuse international affairs with the stability so essential in our atomic age. Flowing from the pattern existing in Europe as a result of the Second World War, the treaty would injure none of its signatories. On the contrary, it would yield incalculable advantages to all, not only its signatories. By formalising the long-existing frontiers it would squash the unjustified pretensions of the West German revenge-seekers and thereby remove a cockpit of tension in the centre of Europe as a possible cause of nuclear disaster inevitably involving the whole world, as well as of local armed collisions between the two German states.

Also, a peace treaty would imply acceptance of the peaceful coexistence principle by the two German states, offering a realistic prospect for their convergence in the common national interest. In that event West Berlin, which throughout the post-war period has been—and remains—a NATO war base, a "front-line city" contaminating the political atmosphere in Europe, could become a seat of international contacts, contributing to a better international climate.

Incontestably, a peace settlement would also present other favourable possibilities. The Federal Republic, which has isolated itself from the East European states by its revenge-seeking policies, could normalise relations with them through mutual recognition and economic reciprocity. The Western capitalist states, too, would, on normalising their relations with the G.D.R.—already recognised *de facto* and *de jure* by many European, Asian and African countries —develop advantageous relationships.

Removal of the historical irregularity in the centre of Europe would also expedite a general détente, ending the cold war. This, in turn, would create the preconditions for the withdrawal of foreign troops both from the F.R.G. and the G.D.R. It would eventually enable the two German states to withdraw simultaneously from the respective military alignments and clear the ground for a nuclear-free zone in their territories.

That, indeed, would be the outlook in the latter half of the 20th century for war-torn Europe, which would for once in many centuries become an area of peace. Can mankind afford to turn down this enticing and, moreover, realistic perspective?

It is only natural, I might conclude, that it was the Soviet Union and the other socialist countries in Europe which initiated the question of a *peaceful* settlement in Germany.

When the cold war policy sponsored by the extreme reactionary and aggressive Western forces proved ineffectual and President Kennedy realised that negotiations on an equal footing were the only alternative to a nuclear war, the problem of a peaceful German accommodation was promptly made the object of Soviet-American exchanges. Parleys that began in New York in September 1961 were continued in Moscow, Geneva and Washington. The talks concerned the key aspects of a peaceful settlement, notably normalisation in West Berlin and formalisation of the existing German frontiers and, by this token, respect for the political sovereignty of the German Democratic Republic. The non-arming with nuclear weapons of the two German states and the possibility of a non-aggression pact between NATO and the Warsaw Treaty Organisation were other prominent topics of discussion. In a nutshell, the ice appeared to have been broken and the climate, poisoned by the cold war, seemed to be improving.

Words, however, are measured by deeds, and deeds by their results. Western opinion has shifted, and the shift seems to favour negotiations. The press has made a spate of constructive suggestions concerning a peaceful accommodation of the German problem and the ways of relieving international tensions. Each of them merited deep thought and study, but too many influential groups in the United States and, especially, West Germany saw to it that the ice of cold war should not thaw in the warm breeze, that it should pile up and block peaceful coexistence. To discredit peaceful coexistence, *Die Aussenpolitik,* an influential West German journal, tried to demonstrate that it was a form of cold war promoted by the Soviet Union. In that case, why do the Western exponents of cold war refuse so stubbornly to take advantage of it?

Whatever the case may be, Western reactionary quarters did their utmost to impede, even to torpedo, the normal course of the Soviet-American talks which could in the long run bring about an accommodation in the centre of Europe. Signs of convergence on some of the specific issues were at hand. At the end of November 1961, for example, President Kennedy, who is not to be denied breadth of vision and a sense of reality, so essential in our rapidly changing world, showed a distinct interest in an international body that would ensure free access to West Berlin. While the F.R.G. resisted every U.S. diplomatic move that meant progress towards an acceptable solution, the G.D.R. gave ample evidence of its willingness to meet the U.S. halfway wherever its suggestions contained a constructive, mutually acceptable element. Berlin announced that the G.D.R. consented to an international body to arbiter controversies, so long as it did not arrogate administrative functions and any right to interfere in the internal affairs of the German Democratic Republic. This being inalienably part of the sovereignty of any state, the proviso was more than reasonable. As for the consent to international arbitration, it was incontestably a demonstration of goodwill.

When it became clear, however, that the U.S. negotiators want to invest the body with functions prejudicious to the sovereignty of the G.D.R., the matter was shelved.

In the meantime, the Western powers endeavoured to injure G.D.R. sovereignty still more gravely by suggesting that all Berlin, including Democratic Berlin, should be subject to the status, with the *Commandants* of the four powers—U.S.A., U.S.S.R., Britain and France—exercising their prerogatives over the entire city. The inter-Allied *Komendatura* in Berlin, a body of the occupation regime, was dissolved in 1948. Besides, the discontinuance of the *Komendatura* of the Soviet garrison in Berlin (Aug. 22, 1962) upset the Western scheme of using the Soviet Union to impair G.D.R. sovereignty, and, of all places, in its capital. The objective is not to extend the occupation status to Democratic Berlin, but to lift the occupation, a legacy of the war, in West Berlin.

The Soviet-American exchanges continued, but every time a glimmer of hope appeared on some issue, quarters seeking to trip up the talks exerted fresh pressure on the American side. True, in the course of the exchanges U.S. diplomacy briefed the NATO Council and a special working group in Washington consisting of U.S., British, French and West German representatives. Dramatic collisions occurred behind the scenes. While the British position was in general outline the same as that of the United States, the Bonn-Paris axis was obviously anxious to torpedo the difficult Soviet-American negotiations. On May 15, 1962, General de Gaulle, the French President, publicly described the German problem as a "square circle" and spoke out emphatically in favour of retaining West Berlin's occupation status. Bonn was still more negative. F.R.G. ministers and other political figures made frequent trips to the United States in an effort of exerting pressure and, if possible, frustrating U.S. contacts with the U.S.S.R. Casualties were unavoidable. Ambassador Grewe's endeavours in Washington were so importunate and tactless that he was told to resign. At the other pole, Bonn's Ambassador to Moscow, Kroll, who was fairly realistic in the reports to his government and searched for a way of improving relations between his country and the Soviet Union, was also recalled.

Chancellor Adenauer, who fancied himself chief apostle of the cold war, was busy hotting up the climate. At the beginning of 1962 he renewed his campaign against Soviet-American exchanges. By so doing, he in effect admitted that his idea of resolving the German problem did not hinge on peaceful negotiations but on militarism and revenge. In April, he was instrumental in leaking to the public the U.S. plan for a German accommodation, exposing it to attacks by the reactionary press, which took advantage of this deliberately contrived opportunity to parade its "independence" and to attack exchanges of opinion concerning a peaceful German solution.

On May 8, 1962, the 17th anniversary of Germany's surrender, Adenauer in Berlin announced for all to hear that he objected to the American, as well as the Soviet proposals. Briefly, his stand was the following: no peaceful settlement and no negotiations. What was more, on October 9, 1962, Bonn issued a threat to governments which, impatient with its negative stand, expressed their readiness to conclude a separate peace treaty with the German Democratic Republic.

There is one thing about these threats: West German reactionaries hold that despite the inevitable end of the "Adenauer era" they are still standing their "watch on the Rhine", whose purpose in the present conditions is to continue the policy of cold war and revenge. But that is neither positive nor realistic, and therefore without a future.

Viewed from this angle, the programme of regulating relations between the two German states formulated by Walter Ulbricht at the 6th Congress of the Socialist Unity Party in Berlin, January 1963, certainly merits a closer look. It envisages an accommodation on approximately the following lines:

1. Respect for the existence of the other German state and its political and social system. A solemn undertaking to refrain from the use of force in any form.

2. Respect for the frontiers of the other German state. A solemn undertaking to refrain from all attempts to violate or alter these frontiers. Finalisation and formalisation of the existing German outer frontiers.

3. A solemn undertaking to refrain from nuclear arms tests, from owning, manufacturing or acquiring nuclear weapons, and to reject any right of disposal of nuclear weapons.

4. Discontinuance of arming by both German states, based on commitments not to increase expenses for military purposes. Subsequently, an understanding on disarmament in both states.

The programme also envisages the rejection of all discrimination and unequal treatment of citizens of the two German states at home and abroad, resumption of normal cultural and sports contacts between the two states, and a trade agreement between the governments of the G.D.R. and F.R.G. in order to extend and develop economic ties and trading between them.

Once a German peace treaty is concluded, the co-operation of the two states would gain a firmer foundation.[1]

The G.D.R. Government announced that it expected counter-proposals from the Federal Republic and was prepared to discuss them. But the Bonn government chooses to ignore the G.D.R. offer. It continues along its course—the dangerous militarist revenge-seeking course with an accent on obtaining nuclear weapons for the Bundeswehr.

All the same, under the impact of the setbacks suffered by the policy of aggression and revenge, new ideas are surfacing in West Germany. Certain forces—still far from gaining ascendancy—are advocating a reasonable and therefore realistic policy, based on the necessity of recognising the existence of the two German states, and of an understanding between them. The others, though exponents of revanchism, believe it desirable "to jettison some of the ballast" and thus gain a "free hand".

Neither of these tendencies is yet determinative. But each mirrors the people's ferment, indicating a desire for a realistic way out of the anomaly in the centre of Europe.

---

[1] *Protokoll der Verhandlungen des VI Parteitages der Sozialistischen Einheitspartei Deutschlands*, Bd. I, Berlin, 1963, S. 61-62.

The two German states are a fact. And many people in West Germany realise that removing this fact by war is impossible. "A war will burn us to cinders," said the West German historian and publicist, Golo Mann. "The right and the wrong as well."

However, the Bonn rulers are clinging to their revenge-seeking policy and hoping to resolve the issue through nuclear arming. But if war is an unrealistic approach, then the tactical manoeuvres of the German revenge-seekers against the G.D.R. are equally unrealistic.

The problem of a peaceful accommodation in Germany is moving towards a solution. That is necessary and inevitable. History is irreversible, and usually it follows a zigzag path. No matter how high the barriers erected by those who think themselves all-powerful, the collective reason of millions of people is clearly aware of the choice of our time: peaceful coexistence or nuclear disaster. This is why the anomaly in the heart of Europe has to be extirpated. That, as we see it, is the writing on the wall, conditioned by our sense of duty to future generations.

1959-63

The bitter experience of two devastating world-wide wars twice in this century, both started in Europe, has been varied, conclusive and instructive. It has prompted the peoples to rise in defence of peace. The peoples want no war. The peace movement impelled by the danger of a nuclear war embraces vast numbers in all countries.

The aggressive element in the imperialist camp is trying to stamp out, or at least inhibit, that movement. Reactionaries are exerting themselves to prevail on the people that war, war against the Soviet Union and other peace-loving states, is inevitable. No longer is this an apologia of war in general, in the spirit of Count Helmuth von Moltke or Friedrich von Bernhardi, the old Prusso-German militarists, or in that of Winston Churchill, who said between the two wars that "the story of the human race is War".[1] What we are faced with now are the exertions of ultra-reactionaries in the United States and West Germany to impress on the peoples that peaceful coexistence between states with different socio-economic systems is impossible.

Needless to say, this political conception is as foolish as it is reckless. And it is losing ground rapidly among people even in those European countries which, being involved in the aggressive Atlantic bloc, have long been exposed to vigorous indoctrination.

Propaganda of military blocs as an inescapable factor of modern history is carried on under different disguises. The

---

[1] Churchill, *The Aftermath*, New York, 1929, p. 479.

main accent is laid on the notion that policy from "positions of strength", that revival of German militarism and invigoration of existing military blocs, is the only possible way of delivering the West European states from the threat of a new, devastating war.

Yet the history of international relations provides ample evidence that, firstly, the initiative in creating a military bloc usually emanates from states gripped by aggressive aspirations, and, secondly, that imperialist war blocs, far from consolidating peaceful relations, tend to generate international tension and ultimately bring on a major collision which, in one way or another, involves all European countries, big and small.

The mortal danger implicit in military blocs came to light most forcefully at the time in European history when the old "free" pre-monopoly capitalism entered into its higher, imperialist, stage. Scaling-up reaction all down the line was imperialism's catchword from its inception. That was when the wrestling match began in real earnest between the principal capitalist powers, between the burgeoning monopolies—and not only for markets and sources of raw material, but also for spheres of investment, for new colonial possessions. That the economic and territorial division of the world was completed did not relieve the international strain. On the contrary, tension increased, because due to the uneven development of capitalism there arose a still more acute, still more ominous struggle for a redivision of the world, undermining the peaceful relations of the then existing system of states. This was the environment in which military blocs of the old type, which emerged after the Franco-Prussian war and, essentially, had a common dynastic interest, were transformed into military blocs of an imperialist complexion.

At the turn of the 20th century at least three major imperialist powers—Germany, the United States and Britain—were fired by the newly conceived idea of world power. It was no abstract idea nursed by sociologists, philosophers or demagogues. No, in various forms, at different periods, it was a tool of universalist pretensions by the rulers of those three powers. It assumed the shape of far-reaching political plans and, highly aggressive in substance, became the foundation on which the respective forces endeavoured to build up military blocs for promoting their designs.

As far back as 1885, Lord Randolph Churchill told the German Ambassador in London that Britain and Germany were ideally fitted to govern the world jointly.[1] Time and again, Germany, Britain and the United States nourished schemes for a political compact, even a military bloc, expressing the world power aspiration of their rulers. But the presence of imperialist contradictions, especially between Germany, on the one hand, and Britain and the U.S.A., on the other, frustrated these designs, with raucous phrases lingering behind as a rudiment about "the common destiny of the Anglo-Saxon and Teutonic races" and the "common interests of Western civilisation". The very same language is now used by the Atlantic bloc ideologists to camouflage efforts of strengthening German militarism in the Western imperialist system.

The wealth of experience paid for dearly in blood by the peoples in two world wars provides conclusive evidence that German militarism played the more aggressive role in the system of imperialist blocs.

The aggressive bloc formed in preparation for the Second World War emerged under conditions that differed profoundly from those preceding the First World War. Similarly, the Atlantic bloc policy, of which West Germany is a participant, is pursued in conditions that differ from those on the eve of the Second World War.

At that time, the bloc-making initiative came from German imperialism. Now, it comes from the aggressive elements of U.S. imperialism. By integrating German militarism into the NATO system, they have only multiplied the aggressive aspirations of the imperialist bloc. This underscores the identity of the functions which aggressive military blocs perform in modern history as instruments of war.

1

Thus, the first European power to begin hammering out military blocs after the Franco-Prussian war was the German Reich.

Bismarck, first Reichschancellor and the moving spirit of the policy of blocs, "confessed" that he was constantly

---

[1] GP, Bd. IV, No. 788.

tormented by the "nightmare of coalitions".[1] But his confession should be taken, as the Romans said, *cum grano salis* (with a grain of salt). In reality, anxious to form a coalition, Bismarck was striving to put fear of coalitions, of the danger of war, into the Germans, to preclude resistance on their part to his programme of invigorating militarism. His initial efforts were aimed at a politico-military line-up with tsarist Russia, and then with the Hapsburg empire. There came about the Alliance of Three Emperors, a military and diplomatic alignment based on the reactionary monarchist interests of the East-European powers. By virtue of his rapprochement with Russia, and then by virtue of the Alliance of Three Emperors, Bismarck endeavoured to keep France internationally isolated. Next, the "nightmare of coalitions" cultivated in Germany was used by the militarists to justify a real coalition in 1879. That was the Austro-German alliance, a bloc which in 1882, after it was joined by Italy, matured into the Triple Alliance. The Austro-German bloc was the main axis in German policy throughout the preparatory period preceding the First World War until Germany's military defeat and the collapse of the German coalition in 1918. True, the nature of the alliance underwent considerable changes in that period.

The text of the Austro-German Alliance Treaty, which heralded the emergence of military blocs in Europe, merits a closer examination. The Treaty envisaged military operations by its signatories exclusively if either one of them is "attacked by Russia" or "by any other power" supported by Russia. In the text, the military bloc was named an "alliance of peace and mutual defence". Subsequently, Bismarck grudgingly admitted that, though concluded with a defensive purpose, the bloc also had a "military (*kriegerischen*) aim".[2] What was more, Bismarck and the other organisers of the bloc did not stint high-flown language to promise each other solemnly that they would "never, in no direction, wish to impart any aggressive tendency to their purely defensive agreement". The architects of this alignment of the Central European powers decided to keep the treaty a secret in order "to avoid all false interpreta-

[1] Bismarck, *Gedanken und Erinnerungen*, Bd. II, Stuttgart-Berlin, 1922, S. 260.
[2] Ibid., S. 283.

tions".[1] To mislead Russia, the country against which the treaty was aimed more than any other, the German Government informed Alexander II that Germany and Austria-Hungary had signed an agreement on maintaining universal peace. What is more, Russia was offered to join the agreement[2] on the assumption that Alexander II would reject it by reason of the mounting antagonisms in the Balkans between Russia and Austria-Hungary.

The treaty of alliance concluded between Germany, Austria-Hungary and Italy on May 20, 1882, introduced new aspects presaging a drive for colonies.[3]

Like the dual (Austro-German) alliance, the Triple Alliance (Austro-Germano-Italian) was cloaked in verbiage about the eagerness of its signatories to "enhance the guarantees of universal peace". At the same time, just as in the case of the Alliance of Three Emperors, it laid emphasis on reactionary *motifs* of an ideological nature, namely, the desire "to reinforce the monarchist principle and secure thereby the immunity of the social and political system" in states party to the Triple Alliance. In substance, the Austro-German alliance and the parallel Triple Alliance represented a military bloc aimed against France and Russia. However, after the Austro-German alliance was concluded, the old Alliance of Three Emperors, embracing Germany, Russia and Austria-Hungary, was revived. In the mid-eighties, after the antagonisms between Russia and Austria-Hungary in the Balkans became so acute that the Alliance of Three Emperors fell to pieces, Germany concluded with

---

[1] A. F. Pribram, *Die politischen Geheimverträge Österreichs-Ungarns 1879-1914*, Bd. I, Wien, 1920, S. 6-9.

[2] S. S. Tatishchev, *Imperator Aleksandr II, yego zhizn i tsarstvovaniye*, t. II, St. Petersburg, 1903, pp. 696-97 (Russ. ed.).

[3] The treaty's Article 2 read: "In the event of Italy being attacked by France on any pretext whatsoever, without any direct challenge on her own part, the other two contracting parties shall be obliged to render aid and co-operation with all their forces to the attacked side." Yet in the then existing conditions any collision between France and Italy could only come about over Northern Africa. If such a colonial collision would generate a direct clash between France and Italy, Article 2 envisaged the involvement not only of Germany, but also of Austria-Hungary against France. A similar commitment devolved on Italy if Germany should be attacked "without provocation" by France. On the other hand, just as under the 1879 treaty, Austria-Hungary was not to take sides against France in the event of the latter's collision with Germany. See GP, Bd. III, No. 571.

Russia a secret "treaty of reassurance" and at once encouraged the establishment of the Mediterranean Entente by Austria-Hungary, Britain and Italy.

Bismarck Germany's diplomacy was as interested in seeing contradictions grow between Russia and Britain as the diplomacy of tsarist Russia was interested in conflicts between Germany and France, and French diplomacy in collisions between Germany and Russia. Each of the European states acted on the dictates of its own economic, political and military interests, promoting them by various diplomatic combinations and politico-military blocs. In the final analysis, all German diplomatic efforts to prevent the other European powers from forming a military bloc, ended in failure. The most that Bismarck managed to accomplish—and this by means of complex diplomatic juggling —was to delay to some extent the political and military convergence of tsarist Russia and France. Each of these powers was intent on its own interests, which clashed both with German and British interests. Each of them feared that Britain would, in one way or another, align herself with the Triple Alliance.[1] Furthermore, two of the signatories of the Triple Alliance, namely Austria-Hungary and Italy, were immersed in conflict: the former with Russia and the latter with France. Last but not least, economic and political contradictions increased between Russia and Germany. The ruling classes in France were at loggerheads: while one segment of the bourgeoisie, with a stake in colonial undertakings, flirted with Bismarck Germany, another section, dreaming of revenge, flirted with Russia and sought its support against Germany. These zigzags on the international scene were evidence of an instability caused by the transition of the old capitalism to its new stage, imperialism, and especially by the mounting struggle for dividing the colonial world. This was the time when the Alliance of Three Emperors and the Russo-German alliance fell to pieces, while the Triple Alliance, created under the aegis of the German Reich, took strength, making the soil fertile for an opposite military bloc: an alliance between tsarist Russia and France.

Quite soon the bloc was formed, but not at once and not

[1] *Documents diplomatiques français (1871-1914)*, 1e série, t. VIII, doc. 427.

along the lines of the Central European bloc. The idea came off the ground when the foreign ministers of Russia and France exchanged letters.[1] A secret alliance followed in the form of a military convention framed by the general staffs and endorsed in December 1893.[2] The main purpose of the convention was to create a situation in which Germany would have to "fight in east and west at the same time".

Like the treaties concluded by Germany, the documents concerning the Franco-Russian alliance were kept in deep secrecy. Not only the French parliament and its various committees, but even most of the members of the French and Russian governments knew nothing of the contents of the military convention, which became the basic guideline for the governments and general staffs of tsarist Russia and France.

The political impact of the documents was very great. After a German bloc had emerged in Europe, the appearance of a Franco-Russian alliance implied the emergence of a second European military bloc. Reflecting on that period, when capitalism had not yet entered the imperialist stage, Lenin used the example of military blocs to show the deep-going transformations under way at that time in the system of European states. Comparing the time when Europe split into two military blocs (in the early nineties) with the time of the imperialist world war that broke out in 1914, he described the situations in specific historically-grounded terms: "Everything depends on the *system* of political relations before the war and during the war," he wrote. Assessing this system in the pre-imperialist period, Lenin noted: "Caesarism in France + tsarism in Russia against *non-imperialist* Germany in 1891—that was the historical situation in 1891."[3] Elsewhere, reflecting again on the changes in the system of states, Lenin wrote: "1891. The colonial policy of France and Germany was *insignificant*. Italy, Japan, the United States *had no* colonies *at all*. . . . In Western Europe a system had come into being . . . a *system* of states, on the whole constitutional and national.

---

[1] V. N. Lamsdorf, *Dnevnik 1891-1892*, Moscow-Leningrad, 1934, pp. 171, 177-79 (Russ. ed.).

[2] Ibid., pp. 388-89.

[3] Lenin, *Collected Works*, Vol. 35, p. 264.

Side by side with them was powerful, unshaken, pre-revolutionary tsarism, which had plundered and oppressed everyone for hundreds of years, which crushed the revolutions of 1849 and 1863."[1]

Certainly, Lenin knew that Bismarck Germany was a militarist state. But he appraised events in concrete fashion, historically, from the broad standpoint of general tendencies and the interests of socialism and democracy. That is why he came to the conclusion that any war in 1891, the time when the Franco-Russian alliance was concluded, *"on the part of France and Russia ...* would have been a reactionary war".[2] If General Boulanger, the proponent of French *revanchism*, and Alexander III, the pillar of Russian reaction, had begun a war against Germany it would, Lenin held, be for Germany "a peculiar variety of *national* war".[3] In the general assessment, Lenin considered it fundamentally important to pinpoint three things: firstly, that the imperialist system had not yet taken final shape, particularly in Germany, and that therefore Germany could not yet wage an imperialist war; secondly, that the socialist movement in Germany stood in the van of the international labour movement, and, thirdly, that "there was no revolutionary Russia then either; that is very important".[4]

At the beginning of the 20th century, when imperialism was fully formed and an imperialist war was on, the general international situation and the system of states changed. "Tsarism has been undermined by 1905, while Germany is waging a war to dominate the world," wrote Lenin, arriving at the important conclusion that "to identify, even to compare the international situations of 1891 and 1914, is the height of unhistoricalness".[5]

When pre-monopoly capitalism completed its passage to imperialism, the Triple Alliance and the Franco-Russian alliance became equally aggressive imperialist war blocs. The Entente (specifically as a politico-military bloc of Britain, France and Russia) was a progeny and an instrument of imperialism, like the opposite Triple Alliance, concluded earlier under the aegis of German militarism.

---

[1] Ibid., p. 273.
[2] Ibid., p. 268.
[3] Ibid., p. 251.
[4] Ibid., p. 268.
[5] Ibid., p. 274.

It goes without saying that the general, fairly long process of Europe's division into two hostile alignments entailed the gravest of consequences for all the other European powers as well, and subsequently for the world as a whole. To begin with, it gave impulse to an arms race that heavily burdened the budgets of states, that is, ultimately, the peoples in each of the countries party to either military bloc. At the end of 1905 Henry Campbell-Bannerman, then Britain's Prime Minister, said: "A policy of huge armaments keeps alive and stimulates and feeds the belief that force is the best if not the only solution of international differences."[1] The following figures will give us an idea about the dimensions of the arms race: the peacetime armed forces of the Entente powers (Russia, France, Britain, Belgium, Serbia and Montenegro), on the one hand, and those of the Austro-German bloc, on the other, totalled more than four million men at the beginning of 1914, with nearly 21 million men under arms towards the end of that year.

That was how the European continent was transformed into a vast military camp, a field of universal slaughter.

2

Hardly anyone could foresee in November 1918, when militarist Germany lay prostrate and signed the instrument of surrender in Compiègne Forest that in a mere two decades militarism would again be ascendant in Germany, that it would start a new war in Europe and, what is more, that it would compel France to sign a surrender in the same Compiègne. After four years of world war which exacted a heavy toll in lives the European nations thought peace would be lasting and stable.

Never in history were the circumstances as favourable in this respect as after the 1914-18 war. In the east of Europe, Russia, previously a tsarist monarchy and the citadel of Russian and international reaction, had become a powerful democratic state of a new type—a Soviet state that devoted all its efforts in foreign policy to the struggle

---

[1] J. A. Spender, *The Life of the Right Hon. Sir Henry Campbell-Bannerman*, G.C.B., Vol. II, London, 1923, p. 208.

for universal peace. The same hope of peace inspired the peoples in other countries, Germany included. The nations knew that the crushing defeat suffered by German militarism had made it far easier for them now to combat the danger of a new war. Merging with the endeavours of the Soviet state, the efforts of the peoples would unquestionably have yielded the best of results. The general historical task was to prevent any revival of aggressive German militarism, prevent the establishment of military blocs as a preparatory step to war, and create a new enduring system of international relations on a peaceful, democratic basis. If this task fell woefully short of the mark, the blame lies on the influential reactionary forces in Germany, in other West European countries, and also in the United States, who were nursing plans of a new conflagration.

In Britain, the United States and even in France the rulers were inclined to preserve the backbone of the German army with the intention of using it at some future date against the democratic and socialist movement in Germany proper, and also against the Soviet state, the tireless and consistent champion of peace in Europe. The Versailles Treaty limited the German army to 100,000 men, but it did not impair the economic and political basis of German militarism. Small wonder then that a few months after Versailles, as the Nuremberg Tribunal determined, the governing element in Germany began by a thousand artful dodges to violate the Treaty's military provisions.[1]

The post-Versailles system was created without the participation of Soviet Russia. What is more, it was directed against that country. From the first, it created a climate in which the more aggressive, more inveterate exponents of militarism, such as Max Hoffmann and Erich Ludendorff could aspire to restoring the whole militarist establishment. They reckoned on a secret, or perhaps even open, military bloc of Germany and other West European powers, enabling Germany to mount a new *Drang nach Osten*. Although such a military bloc did not materialise, the economic, financial and political support of the Western

---

[1] See *Trial of the Major War Criminals Before the International Military Tribunal. Nuremberg, November 14, 1945-October 1, 1946*, Vol. XIV, Nuremberg, 1948, Doc. D-854, GB-460.

powers paved the way for a rapid revival of aggressive militarism in Germany.

Less than 15 years after the collapse of the Triple Alliance and the end of the First World War, German imperialism had recovered its power and could set to building a new military bloc in preparation for a second world war.

Unlike the period before the First World War, when the emergence and consolidation of military blocs took years, even decades, the preparatory process for the Second World War went along at a much faster pace. Fascism, too, had the effect of speeding preparations. This was encouraged by Western policies, which rejected the idea of collective security in Europe. If a security system, tirelessly advocated by the Soviet Union, had been instituted, Hitler Germany, fascist Italy and militarist Japan could not have effected their aggressive plans. They could not have co-ordinated their actions, nor created a military bloc which imperiled the peoples of Europe, Asia, Africa and the rest of the world.

The creation of a military bloc of aggression on the eve of the Second World War is usually traced to the Ciano-Hitler negotiations at Berchtesgaden, October 20-25, 1936. In effect, however, agreed political, and later military, actions by the future signatories of the military bloc began much earlier. In 1933, after Japan (March 27) and then Hitler Germany (October 19) withdrew from the League of Nations, these two powers began the diplomatic and ideological spadework for a new bloc. The idea was, as Hitler put it, to hammer out a "syndicate of discontented powers". Yet its accomplishment had to wait until Germany, which universally rejected the military restrictions of the Versailles Treaty, stepped up her earlier course towards rapid remilitarisation. In March 1935, Germany announced that it would build up her army to a strength of 500,000 men. It was also busy building up an air force. At the end of 1934 Hitler began in secret to build a submarine fleet. Having informed the British military attaché about this he had his violation of Versailles legalised in 1935 and, what is more, concluded an official agreement with Britain on questions of naval armament.

All disguises shorn, the nazi government declared that it would not "turn Germany's national arming into a means of warlike offensive policy and would use the Wehrmacht exclusively for defensive purposes and, therefore, for maintaining peace". Exactly a year after the announcement that Germany would build up her army to 500,000 men, Wehrmacht units entered the Rhineland and, remilitarising the area, lined the French frontier. The guarantees that Britain had given France at Locarno were, naturally, so much scrap paper.

That was when nazi diplomacy tackled the job of creating the Italo-German military bloc. Even Galeazzo Ciano, foreign minister of fascist Italy, observed that the strident Hitler propaganda "against communism" begun in September 1936, was a mere screen for this bloc, based on a division of spheres of influence and aggression. Germany obtained Italy's recognition of her "right" to dominating Austria and to colonial claims aimed, first and foremost, against Britain, after it promised the Duce to consider the Mediterranean an "Italian lake" and to recognise the Italian "empire" in Eastern Africa. Later, Hitler demanded that Mussolini, who had relinquished his interest in Austria, should consent to more intimate politico-military co-operation. As Mussolini put it, it was not only a question of "solidarity of regimes", but of the general policy "towards east and west and towards south and north".[1]

That was the underlying purport and, indeed, the true essence of Hitler's anti-communist policy. The conquest of Ethiopia showed that the anti-communist cloak could benefit an aggressor even in the African backwoods. There was all the more reason, therefore, to expect success behind such a screen for aggressive acts in Europe. The formula was simple to the extreme: condoned, even encouraged, by reactionaries in Western Europe and the United States, a shock force was built up in the shape of an aggressive military bloc capable of operating in several directions at once. As the Wehrmacht grew, under cover of anti-communism aggressive initiatives in Europe shifted clearly to Hitler Germany. And on having seized the initiative, Hitler did not let it out of his grasp even in relation to other aggressive powers. Not only did he work out a programme of further operations; he imposed it on his Italian partner. When Ciano came to Berchtesgaden, a protocol was ready awaiting his signature as a basis for the new military bloc.

---

[1] Ciano, *Les archives secrètes du comte Ciano, 1936-1942*, Paris, 1948, p. 44.

Also, a communique had been drawn up in which anti-communist verbiage was to disguise the true aggressive nature of the Italo-German deal.

The agreement envisaged Germany's recognition of Italy's conquest of Ethiopia and established a general line of conduct by Germany and Italy in all questions of international politics, particularly concerning matters of joint operations in Spain. The two aggressive powers came to terms about their behaviour in the London non-intervention committee, which they aimed to use (not without the help of its Western members) in supporting Franco and his rebel fascist army. It also provided for a build-up of the German and Italian air forces. Lastly, it specified the respective spheres of influence in the Balkans and the Danube states. The two aggressive powers also worked out intricate tactics aimed at undermining the League of Nations if that body should become an obstacle to their military adventures. The decision was that Italy should remain in the League and apply "acts of sabotage benefiting joint aims".[1]

This laid the groundwork for a new aggressive military bloc, which Mussolini christened the Berlin-Rome axis. In November 1936, speaking in Milan, Italy's dictator elucidated the political orientation of the newly created "axis". "It is necessary," he said, "in the first place to make a clean sweep of all illusions. . . . One of these illusions has been dashed to the ground already—the illusion of disarmament. . . . Another illusion we reject is that which passes under the name of collective security. . . . Yet another commonplace to be rejected is that of indivisible peace."[2]

Thus, a co-founder of the "axis" admitted in public that the newly established military bloc was aimed against disarmament, against the basic principles of collective security and against universal peace. What Mussolini did not say was that the signatories had decided under cover of "anti-Bolshevism" to go over "to the attack" against the Western powers, France and Britain. In secret parleys with his Italian partner, Hitler spoke heatedly of far-reaching plans to crush the British empire, which, he said, was "governed by incapable people". In their public appear-

---

[1] Ciano, *Les archives secrètes du comte Ciano 1936-1942*, Paris, 1948, p. 51.
[2] Maxwell Macartney and Paul Cremona, *Italy's Foreign and Colonial Policy, 1914-1937*, London, 1938, p. 247.

ances, however, the founders of the fascist alignment preferred to accentuate their "anti-communism" and to advertise the "axis" as an instrument of "co-operation and peace".[1]

The Berlin-Rome axis was a stepping stone to a bigger military bloc. In Berchtesgaden, the German side informed Ciano "in absolute confidence" that two important protocols were soon to be signed by Germany and Japan—one of these, which was to be made public, would proclaim the conclusion of an "anti-Bolshevik alliance", while the other, a secret instrument, would contain an article on favourable neutrality by either side in the event that the other party mounts aggressive operations. Hirota, Japan's Foreign Minister and later Premier, declared that this military alignment was essential "to contain Europe and create a strong foundation for imperialist policy in the Far East". Each of the parties expected considerable advantages from this co-ordination of aggressive actions in the different theatres of world politics.

On November 25, 1936, the Japanese-German bloc was formally instituted through an agreement on "defensive co-operation against the Communist International". A pact was made public to the effect that the parties to it have undertaken to exchange information on the activities of the Communist International and to establish close co-operation. The pact invited third countries to adopt "preventive measures" against the Comintern in the spirit of the Japanese-German agreement or to join that agreement. Also made public was a supplementary protocol, saying that "the competent authorities ... will within the framework of the existing laws take severe measures against those who at home or abroad are engaged directly or indirectly in the service of the Communist International or promote its subversive activities". A permanent Japanese-German committee was set up to devise measures "against the Comintern".[2]

This was the outer shell of still another military bloc which came to be known as the Berlin-Tokyo axis. Yet handing the text of the "Anti-Comintern Pact" to the Western powers, nazi diplomats tried to create the impres-

---

[1] Ciano, op. cit., pp. 53-56.
[2] *Documents on International Affairs, 1936*, London, 1937, pp. 297-99.

sion that the Pact was purposed solely to combat "Comintern propaganda". Particularly, in their talks with William E. Dodd, U.S. Ambassador in Berlin, they repeated time and again that "they greatly disliked propaganda". "Of course," Dood observed at the time, "they dislike any but their own."[1]

To be sure, world opinion was aware even then that the published Pact was no more than a propagandist ruse, covering up a secret agreement. Now that agreement is public knowledge. It envisaged, firstly, that in the event of one of its signatories embarking on war against the Soviet Union the other signatory would adopt a position favourable to the first, with both parties consulting on "what measures to take to safeguard their common interests". Secondly, the secret agreement provided that neither signatory should conclude any political accords with the Soviet Union conflicting with the spirit of the Pact.[2]

In any case, before the Anti-Comintern Pact was signed, the Japanese journal *Bungei-shunju* lifted the curtain on the political and strategic plans that were being worked out backstage. "The agreement is important," the journal said, "because it enables Japan and Germany to form a military alliance ... with an extraordinarily broad sphere of application; though it is aimed exclusively against the Soviet Union, it may at once be turned against other countries."

The foreign press, even its reactionary element, gave to understand that it considers the Anti-Comintern Pact a screen for broader aggressive designs. The *New York Herald Tribune*, for example, held that the architects of the Pact overestimated the credulity of world opinion. The *New York Times* thought that Germany and Japan were trying to assure the world that they were defending all countries against the Comintern, but other countries did not believe it. The *Economist* drew attention to the fact that under guise of combating communism, Germany and Japan arrogated the right to "severe measures" and to interfering in the domestic affairs of other states. " 'Severe measures' implies military activities," the journal wrote. "Persons 'at home

---

[1] Dodd, *Ambassador Dodd's Diary 1933-1938*, London, 1941, p. 366.
[2] *Documents on German Foreign Policy 1918-1945*. From the Archives of the German Foreign Ministry, Series D, Vol. I, Doc. 463.

or abroad' can easily be accused, 'within the framework of the existing laws' of Germany or Japan, of being engaged 'indirectly' in Comintern service, or of promoting its activities.... It is insistently reported that Czechoslovakia is to be soon treated by Germany as another Spain."[1] The *Times* of London was certain that the German-Japanese agreement was much more than a simple declaration against communism.

In sum, the British and American press was aware of the fact that the slogans of combating communism were no more than an ideological smokescreen designed to conceal the aggressive substance of the military bloc.

Contemporary American historians cannot but admit that the Anti-Comintern Pact was a grave peril which subverted world peace.[2] They admit, too, that the rapid revival of German militarism stimulated arming in the other countries aligned with the nazis.

Germany could never have restored her heavy industry in such short order without the powerful aid of the United States. U.S. banks and trusts poured billions of dollars into the German economy after the First World War. The leading U.S. monopolies established close relations with German heavy industry, which were military in purport, as well as commercial. The direct and extensive U.S. financial support was a precondition for Hitler aggression.

German militarism played first fiddle in the pre-war arms race. In 1933, Hitler Germany spent 3,000 million marks on armaments, whereas on the eve of the war, in 1938, its military spending added up to 27,000 million. "The expenditure of effort in preparing war under fascism," wrote Jürgen Kuczynski, a prominent German economist, "differed but little from the expenditure of effort in waging the war."[3]

After concluding the Anti-Comintern Pact, Japan's military expenditures increased greatly as well. In 1936 they amounted to 1,059 million yen, mounting to 1,500 million yen the year after the conclusion of the Pact, exceeding 60 per cent of the state budget. Italy's arms spending, too,

---

[1] *Economist*, November 28, 1936.
[2] Ch. C. Tansill, *Back Door to War. The Roosevelt Foreign Policy 1933-1941*, Chicago, 1952, p. 320.
[3] Kuczynski, *Die Geschichte der Lage der Arbeiter unter dem Kapitalismus*, Bd. 6, Berlin, 1964, S. 134.

increased from 10,500 million liras in 1934/35 to 27,700 million in 1939/40.[1] But the Anti-Comintern Pact had other, still graver consequences: a few months after it was concluded, the Japanese militarists mounted an assault against China, and a few months later still Hitler Germany began her military, diplomatic and propaganda offensive in preparation for the invasion of Austria. Those were the first results issuing from the Berlin-Rome-Tokyo alignment under cover of the Anti-Comintern Pact.

Next, Italy acceded to the Anti-Comintern Pact. And there, too, the initiative was German. On October 20, 1937, Hitler Germany made a formal proposal to Italy to join the Pact, and the Italian Government was handed for signing the text of a protocol drawn up in Berlin. Then, Ribbentrop came to Rome and demanded out of hand that the Italian ally of the Berlin-Rome axis sign the protocol at once. Mussolini and Ciano wanted to know the content of the supplementary secret agreements between Japan and Germany, but were told that no secret agreements existed. We know now that this was a lie. To be sure, Ciano refused to believe his German allies.[2]

To raise the stakes and obtain certain colonial and political compensations, Italy's fascist rulers tried to resist. But in the end, after considerable pressure and various blandishments, nazi Germany dragged Italy into her military bloc. The protocol to this effect was signed on November 6, 1937.[3]

The tripartite military bloc of Japan, Italy and Germany was thus formalised.

The initiators of the new military coalition insisted that it had none but peaceful purposes. But within a few days, Ciano bragged that the three-power alignment was the "world's strongest" and that the Anti-Comintern Pact was "but a first step towards an internal strengthening and outer expansion of this coalition". Indeed, the Berlin-Rome-Tokyo axis proved a springboard for expansion and a universal holocaust.

Austria's invasion by German troops brought the world a

---

[1] A. M. Alexeyev, *Voyenniye finansy kapitalisticheskikh gosudarstv*, Moscow, 1952, p. 36 (Russ. ed.).

[2] *Documents on German Foreign Policy 1918-1945*. From the Archives of the German Foreign Ministry, Series D, Vol. I, Doc. 10.

[3] Ibid., Doc. 17.

considerable step closer to war. The Western powers did not block the aggressive act; on the contrary, they prodded German militarism into making it. Next came the seizure of Czechoslovakia, after Britain and France, with the U.S. a silent partner, struck a deal with Hitler at that country's expense. Western policy helped to consolidate the fascist military bloc. Formalising this, Germany and Italy signed a new politico-military alliance treaty on May 22, 1939. The treaty stipulated that in the event of an armed conflict both signatories would forthwith come to each other's assistance "with all their ground, naval and air strength".[1]

In just a few years after German militarism helped by the West financially and politically, had flung off the trammels inhibiting its growth and formed a tripartite aggressive bloc, an imminent danger of a new world war appeared. The bloc rapidly established a military and diplomatic mechanism, whereby it started the war. First it fought the Western states whose economic and political support it had enjoyed in all the preceding stages of its war preparations. No political failure in history was more ignominious than that suffered by the Western powers: a mere twenty years after bringing German militarism to its knees, they had to pay heavily for their post-war policy designed to revive German militarism and to direct its aggression eastward against the Soviet Union. The results are all too well known: the conflagration engulfed the whole world and Europe was drenched in blood.

3

No other politico-military realignment in the system of capitalist states was as rapid, as significant and as dangerous to mankind as the one that followed the Second World War. The deep wounds of war inflicted by nazi imperialism and other aggressors had not yet healed, the history-making results of the war had not yet been recorded in a peace treaty, when the United States and Britain, aiming to eliminate the anti-Hitler coalition, began building a new politico-military bloc, the North Atlantic Treaty Organisa-

---

[1] *Jahrbuch für Auswärtige Politik*, 1940, S. 167.

tion, aimed against the Soviet Union, the chief member of the coalition of freedom-loving nations.[1]

The rate at which NATO was organised is unprecedented in history. It took at least a quarter of a century for the Triple Alliance and the Entente to materialise, and about six years to form the politico-military fascist bloc. The NATO plan was formulated and carried into effect in a matter of three years, with direct negotiations between its members lasting something less than a year.[2] "Where time is running out is Germany," John Foster Dulles, moving spirit and ideologist of NATO and the cold war policy, said later. "There is no good solution of the problem of Germany unless Germany ... is brought into the framework of the West as an integral part of the West."[3] Field-Marshal Bernard Montgomery said in reference to NATO that "speed was necessary too, since Russian Communism was beginning to spread westwards".[4]

None of this meant, of course, that NATO's organisers had it all their own way. Having set out to erect a large politico-military bloc against the Soviet Union and the other countries of the world socialist system that emerged after the war, and to inhibit the communist, national liberation and anti-imperialist movements, reactionaries in the United States, Britain and other capitalist states struggled through several stages and experimented with several variants. Not only did they look for new forms and methods. Their changes and manoeuvres were evidence of the difficulties that beset them.

Treating Western Europe as a vast preserve of economic and human resources, and as an important strategic springboard, U.S. imperialism created NATO, hoping through it

---

[1] See *Atlantic Alliance. NATO's Role in the Free World. A Report by a Chatham House Study Group*, London-New York, 1952; B. T. Moore, *NATO and the Future of Europe*, New York, 1958; *NATO. 1949-1959. The First Ten Years*, Washington, 1959; F. W. Mulley, *The Politics of Western Defence*, London, 1962; B. M. Khalosha, *Severoatlantichesky bloc*, Moscow, 1960 (Russ. ed.); G. M. Sverdlov, *London i Bonn. Angliisky imperializm i politika perevooruzheniya F.R.G. (1955-1963)*, Moscow, 1963 (Russ. ed.).

[2] The NATO Pact was signed in Washington on April 4, 1949, by the United States, Britain, France, Italy, Canada, Iceland, Belgium, Denmark, Norway, Holland, Luxemburg and Portugal.

[3] Dulles, *War or Peace*, New York, 1957, p. 220.

[4] Montgomery, *Memoirs*, London, 1958, p. 506.

to achieve power that no other country had ever possessed. This power was to be epitomised by the atomic bomb, whose development U.S. imperialism had demonstrated back in 1945. The senselessly brutal explosions at Hiroshima and Nagasaki heralded not the ending of the Second World War and the collapse of the last member of the fascist bloc (for that collapse was imminent); it heralded the birth of a new pretender to world power. "The atomic bomb," General Maxwell D. Taylor wrote later, "offered air power a new weapon with tremendously increased destructiveness and encouraged once more the belief that an ultimate weapon was in the hands of our Air Force which would allow the United States to impose a sort of Pax Americana on the world."[1] This Pax Americana was, however, no more than a short-lived illusion.

In October 1949 the world learned that despite the estimates of the Western capitalist powers the Soviet Union had once and for all broken the atomic monopoly of the United States. The historical impact of this cannot be overrated. The end to the U.S. atomic monopoly was tantamount potentially to the ending of U.S. pretensions to world power.

In view of the correlation of forces between the socialist and capitalist systems, the atomic era in the latter half of the 20th century could have been one of peaceful development, of development in which mankind that had suffered the terrors of the Second World War had so great a stake. Regrettably, the imperialists, who refused to give up their aggressive plans, who nursed their historical and political illusions, did not draw the due realistic conclusions even when the more far-sighted of them realised that a "decisive change has taken place in the relation of world forces".

More than that, they decided to plunge forward with consistency and determination, and "yet with caution", stepping up the cold war and starting a new round of atomic and conventional arming. This was an act of political lunacy spurred by the hope that the policies of cold war and "rolling back communism" would succeed.

"American rearmament," Hans J. Morgenthau wrote, "should have had unquestioned priority, with the rearmament of Western Europe and of Western Germany following

---

[1] Taylor, *The Uncertain Trumpet*, New York, 1960, p. 12.

in that order."[1] Atomic arms were to be within the NATO framework still a U.S. monopoly, while the other NATO members, along with the United States, were to bear the burdens of the conventional arms race.

The point of departure in the subsequent course of events, centred on reviving German militarism and inducting it into the NATO system, was Germany's split, effected as a dramatic culmination to negotiations between the imperialist Western powers and influential quarters in West Germany. In that sense, apart from the collapse of the U.S. atomic monopoly, the establishment of the Federal Republic of Germany, on the one hand, and later of the German Democratic Republic, on the other, became the key events which, within the limits of our subject, determined since the autumn of 1949 the subsequent developments in present-day Europe. One more important event of that time was the framing by NATO (in November 1949) of the tentative variant of the strategic "shield and sword" doctrine. Somewhat later, when this variant was accepted by the NATO members as a common doctrine, it became clear that the ground armies of Western Europe, the tactical air force and the navies were to be the "shield", while the nuclear-armed U.S. strategic bomber force was to be the "sword", that is, the main shock force. What this meant was that the West European powers accepted military dependence on the United States, and, moreover, undertook the burdens stemming from participation in the arms race.

Only naturally, this was bound to create friction within each of the NATO member countries and between these countries and the United States. Bonn was able to capitalise on these frictions and differences to sell to the United States the idea of a revived German militarism effectively usable in the context of the "shield and sword" doctrine. However, the NATO members were at the time still suspicious of this scheme. In the summer of 1949, when the ratification of the NATO pact was being debated in France's National Assembly, Robert Schuman, the French foreign minister, promised that Germany would not be admitted into the Atlantic Pact, that Germany had no army and could not have one, that it had no arms and would not get them. When Winston Churchill, then Conservative leader, told the House of Commons

---

[1] Morgenthau, *American Foreign Policy*, London, 1952, p. 181.

in March 1950 that West Germany should be given a chance to join the armaments system of the West European countries, Bevin, foreign minister of the Labour government, described the ex-Prime Minister's proposal as "terrible" and said that the United States, as well as Britain and France, was opposed to rearming Germany. But those were just words. In September 1950, John J. McCloy, U.S. High Commissioner in Germany, declared publicly: "In some manner, in some form, the Germans should be enabled, if they want to, to defend their own country.... If that sounds like rearmament, then it's rearmament."[1]

The British and French governments, it is true, still resisted West German remilitarisation, but their objections were timid, inconsistent and uncoordinated. Influential U.S. quarters were busy behind the scenes, working in close contact with Bonn. Chancellor Konrad Adenauer declared at the end of August 1950 that the Federal Republic would be glad to make available an armed contingent for a West European army if such were established. The U.S. government and generals were sold on the idea of West German remilitarisation and exerted so much pressure that Britain and France began to back down, doubly so as their stand in the diplomatic tussle had been neither firm nor definite from the beginning. Early in 1951, giving way to pressure from Washington and Bonn, the two countries consented for a large West German contingent to be integrated in the "European army". This was a triumph for those who had a stake in reviving German militarism, for, a year later, the NATO Council meeting in Lisbon endorsed the project of a European Defence Community and adopted a number of other decisions aimed at reinforcing the NATO military system in Western Europe.

However, the rate of growth imposed by U.S. imperialism was far beyond the financial and economic means, and the general political mood, of the West European states. As a result, the rate dropped; in the circumstances, the willingness and ardour of the Bonn militarists rapidly won the support of the top NATO leaders and the Pentagon. On May 26, 1952, shortly before the European Defence Community was formed, the United States, Britain, France and

[1] James P. Warburg, *Germany, Key to Peace*, Cambridge, 1953, p. 141.

the Federal Republic signed a joint treaty formally repeal-
ing the occupation regime in West Germany, though the
Western powers retained the right to maintain troops in
her territory. True, the idea of the European Defence Community, which had originated in France under certain U.S.
prompting, brought about an acute controversy among the
NATO countries. The British Government refused to enter
the Community on the grounds that Britain belonged to the
Commonwealth and because it wanted to retain the role
of arbiter in Western Europe; the French Government, on
the other hand, though formally an initiator of the idea,
encountered strong resistance from the National Assembly.
These external and domestic differences, though they
delayed West German remilitarisation, gave Bonn wide
scope for manoeuvre.

At the end of 1953 and early in 1954, signs appeared in
the world of a certain relaxation, particularly in connection
with the cease-fires in Korea and, somewhat later, in Viet-
nam. In August 1953, after the world learned that the Soviet
Union had the hydrogen bomb, it became clear that all the
aggressive political and military designs nursed by the U.S.
imperialists and NATO, related to the cold war and the
policy of "rolling back", were losing ground no less than
the "shield and sword" concept. Good prospects appeared
for a search of ways and means to end the cold war, to
relieve international tensions and, consequently, transform
the aggressive NATO bloc into a genuinely defensive organisation in the context of universal collective security.
During the last five months of 1953, the Soviet government
issued a call for a foreign ministers' conference on five
different occasions to examine measures for relieving tension and, particularly, to study the German question, whose
solution is intimately linked with European security. At the
beginning of 1954, the Soviet Union drafted a treaty for a
system of collective security, but this proposal, too, was
turned down by the Western powers.

Seeing that the NATO authorities, bent on justifying the
inclusion in their system of the militarist forces brought
back to life in West Germany, had issued assurances that
this would work effectively to prevent a new German aggression (since NATO was a purely defensive organisation),
the Soviet Union announced on March 31, 1954, that it
would be willing to discuss its possible entry into that

organisation. However, the Western powers rejected the Soviet proposal, which could have created most favourable opportunities for normalising international relations in Europe and the rest of the world. That was the time, in fact, when the United States and NATO were engrossed in drawing up a new programme "from positions of strength" and a new doctrine of "massive retaliation". They overrated the first ever hydrogen bomb test over Bikini Atoll on March 1, 1954, thinking that possession of the new super-weapon gave them back the initiative. The "rolling back communism" idea appeared to gain fresh impulse. Julian Lider, a Polish publicist, noted in his study of NATO history that this prompted two decisions: that Western military planning should envisage the use of nuclear weapons, and that West Germany should be integrated in NATO.

Acting on its "massive retaliation" doctrine, NATO geared its plans to its U.S. contingents being equipped with tactical nuclear weapons and to the U.S. nuclear-armed strategic air force. The situation was complicated by the fact that considerable NATO forces were stationed in the proximity of the eastern frontiers of the F.R.G. But the United States retained its nuclear monopoly, which disgruntled other members of the bloc. Although people in the Federal Republic knew perfectly well that in the event of an atomic war Germany would be devastated, Bonn fell into line with U.S. policy. The Bonn militarists had excellent bargaining power in view of the importance attached to the German striking force. Not surprisingly, British military quarters noted, West German self-confidence increased. Fired by their revanchist aspirations the militarists waited for the right hour to present their strategic and political demands.

4

That hour came soon enough. On October 21, 1954, agreements were signed in Paris opening the door for the remilitarisation of the Federal Republic (allowing for a force of over 500,000 men, including 12 motorised divisions) and Bonn's admission to NATO. On May 8, 1955, which was the tenth anniversary of Hitler Germany's unconditional surrender, the German militarists were officially admitted to that military bloc, culminating the process of Western realignment. The day the F.R.G. entered NATO the division of Germany became final.

Since that day German miltarism has been working in four directions:

first, to complete arming within the fixed limits in the shortest possible time (at the end of 1956 the Bundeswehr had 67,000 men under arms, and more than 400,000 by mid-1964; the 12 motorised divisions are activated and the ground has been laid for a build-up to two million men). The German divisions, observers hold, are better trained and better armed (also with means for delivering nuclear warheads) than any other NATO national contingent;

second, to obtain high posts in NATO for F.R.G. officers, giving them a say in political, strategic and operational decision-making. In this respect, too, German militarism has gained considerable ground, especially in the past few years;[1]

third, to use for rearming its favourable economic situation and politico-financial pressure on other NATO countries. In the light of past experience, the German militarists preferred to shift the economic burden of war preparation on others, leaving for themselves the role of "integrator" of armaments.[2] In 1963, Bonn's military spending topped DM 18,000 million. Yet in percentage terms this was much less than the military expenditure of the United States, and even of Britain and France. By placing military orders abroad, Bonn stimulates the arms race and gains an additional instrument of pressure. At the same time, enforcing the principle of specialisation in military production, the German monopolies operating hand in hand with the militarists are trying to lay their hands on aircraft manufacture and, chiefly, manufacture of rockets. That is an area in which they operate in close contact with the big U.S. monopolies.

Last but not least, since its admission to NATO, German

---

[1] German militarism is represented in the NATO Headquarters in Europe, the Allied Command in Northern Europe, the Allied Command in Central Europe, the Allied Command of Ground Forces in Central Europe, the Allied Command of Ground Forces in Schleswig-Holstein, in the Joint Danish-German Command, the Air Force Command in Central Europe and the Naval Command in Central Europe.

[2] L. G. Istyagin, *F.R.G. i NATO*, Moscow, 1963, pp. 31-48 (Russ. ed.).

militarism has pressed doggedly for access to atomic weapons. Before entering NATO and in the first few years after entering it, Adenauer, Strauss and other Bonn leaders vowed that they did not want atomic arms. But their assurances were worth as little as the earlier assurances that they did not want to remilitarise. The manoeuvres they employed were nothing if not ingenious. At the beginning of May 1957, speaking before the NATO Council in Bad Godesberg, Adenauer backed Dulles, who pressed for the endorsement of nuclear strategy and reinforcement of the nuclear "sword". But when some of the NATO members, fearing the "deterrent power" of the nuclear "sword", called rather for a stronger conventional "shield", none supported their demand more enthusiastically than the West German militarists. They knew it meant that the Bundeswehr would be expanded, putting it in a better position to demand nuclear weapons at some later date.

The launching in the Soviet Union of the world's first earth satellite (October 4, 1957) precipitated a crisis of strategy in the United States and NATO.[1] Adenauer was the only one who pretended that nothing had changed. The German militarists clung to their basic line—revenge-seeking claims and efforts to gain access to nuclear arms. Washington cast about for a way out of the crisis, while the German strategists in Bonn and NATO laid the accent on aggressive political solutions. Soviet proposals to discontinue the nuclear arms tests and conclude a universal non-aggression pact were turned down. So was the Polish proposal of an atom-free zone in Central Europe (the Rapacki plan). Bonn, meanwhile, backed the various NATO solutions that, as Lider pointed out rightly, "were designed to galvanise the 'shield and sword' concept by complementing the theory of total nuclear war with a theory of limited nuclear war in Europe".[2]

The MC-70 plan framed in the spring of 1958 provided for an increase in "shield" divisions over a five-year term and envisaged tactical nuclear arms for them. The German militarists were more than willing to help work out and implement the plan. The Bundeswehr's atomic arming

---

[1] See W. Rostow, *The United States in the World Arena*, New York, 1960, p 366.
[2] Lider, op. cit., p. 161.

project whose existence had earlier been vehemently denied, was pulled out of the secret War Ministry files and presented to the Bundestag, which hastily approved it. Strauss, Minister of Defence and a zealous advocate of nuclear arms for the Bundeswehr, thus won a free hand, and although he lost his post due to the scandalous *Spiegel* affair, his successor Hassel picked up where he left off. Under the MC-70 plan the Bundeswehr would get rockets, the nuclear warheads for which are stored in U.S.-controlled depots.

But the German militarists want more. They welcome NATO's aggressive formulas for the Bundeswehr and endeavour to impose on NATO formulas promoting their own revenge-seeking aims. In August 1960, a "generals' memorandum" said that "the commanders' responsibility for their soldiers compels them in the existing circumstances to demand atomic weapons". Also, it made demands on NATO and the F.R.G. Government. What the generals wanted was a stronger NATO, a stronger "shield" (that is, nuclear weapons for West European troops, including the Bundeswehr) and universal conscription in the F.R.G.

When the U.S. militarists tried to end the crisis of NATO's strategic doctrine by advancing the idea of "limited wars", with specially designated forces acting as the "sword", while the atomic power would be the "shield", the German militarists hastily voiced their support. The makers of the "limited wars" doctrine knew, of course, that their conception was unrealistic and dangerous. In 1958, the Soviet Union warned that a limited war could easily spread, like fire in a strong wind. All talk about "minor" or "local" wars was a naive illusion and all intentions to restrict the military operations either gross deception or self-deception. Men in responsible offices could not afford to forget the past: the chain of events that led up to the Second World War had also consisted of "minor" and "local" wars and of seizures of foreign territories.[1] However, the German militarists did their utmost to steer the U.S. concept in a direction fitting their aggressive aims. To begin with, they wanted a green light for a "limited war" in Central Europe, aiming to absorb the German Democratic Republic. Second, they were enthralled by the related conception of "gradual intimidation", since, as the ex-nazi general Speidel, commander

---

[1] *Pravda*, July 20, 1958.

448

of NATO ground forces in Central Europe, put it, conventional troops could be used without immediate resort to a total atomic war.[1] Third, and the "generals' memorandum" said so clearly, the "intimidation" concept implied nuclear weapons for troops participating in the "limited war".

At the same time, the German militarists lost no opportunities to exert political pressure on the United States. Backed by the increasing weight of the German monopolies in the Common Market and in neocolonialist expansion, they worked with some success of greater political influence in NATO. Political and diplomatic channels and the press were used to exert pressure on the United States, impressing on Washington that the post-war period of dependence on the United States was over and that the "contribution" which the Federal Republic could make to NATO was sorely needed, especially at critical times in its internal development and the general international situation. That was why the German militarists so zealously applauded the project of making NATO a "fourth nuclear power". It was first formulated by Lauris Norstad in December 1959; he suggested that 300 Polaris launchers and nuclear warheads be made available to the NATO command. Bonn was delighted. Adenauer, Strauss and von Brentano made no secret of their feelings: they gave to understand that the plan would go a long way in meeting their nuclear aspirations. But the Norstad project ran into vigorous French and British opposition. Britain and France considered it a threat to their own nuclear capability, present or future. Besides, they were aware that it would fortify German militarism in the NATO system. So it collapsed. Instead, the Kennedy-Macmillan parleys in December 1962 produced a multilateral nuclear force project.

In the meantime, the Federal Republic and France, both committed to NATO, formed a new military bloc based on a convergence of West German and French monopolies seeking to harmonise their differing interests in the fight for ascendancy in the Common Market and for favourable conditions in which to pursue neocolonialist expansion. Formalised by a treaty on January 22, 1963, the Bonn-Paris "axis" also had important political and military aspects, making it still more difficult to resolve the German ques-

---

[1] See *Wehr und Wirtschaft*, September 1960.

tion; it was designed to obstruct a German peace treaty and an accommodation on its basis in West Berlin. Also, it gave the German militarists fresh hope for obtaining nuclear arms through co-operation with France, the new atomic power. Besides, the Bonn-Paris "axis" afforded the F.R.G. an opportunity of pressuring the United States in matters of NATO and general policy, to which it attached special weight in connection with nuclear arming as an instrument of revenge.

At the end of 1963 the German militarists worked out "a new front-line defence strategy", envisaging the use of tactical nuclear weapons at all stages of an armed conflict in contrast to the U.S. doctrine providing for "conventional" arms in the first 30 days of any European armed clash. Referring to "reliable" NATO sources, *Die Welt* reported: "The new German conception envisages use of atomic 'combat weapons'. It is based on the use of long-range tactical nuclear weapons. The preconditions are that all designated units should 'go into action' from staging areas in the eastern part of the Federal Republic."[1]

This "front-line strategy" is no mere project any longer. Set out in detail to an American audience by Bonn Defence Minister von Hassel, it was accompanied by demands for a multilateral nuclear force within the NATO framework and reaffirmed the "deterrence theory".

"The North Atlantic Alliance," Hassel said, "must be able to use nuclear weapons when they would not be an act of despair but a military and political expediency."[2]

A few years after entering NATO the German militarists feel free to impose their aggressive aims on that organisation, presaging a possible nuclear disaster for Germany.

So the search for a realistic solution is the most urgent task of our time. There are many ways of dissipating the nuclear threat. The best is to conclude the peace treaty, finalising the changes in Europe and writing *finis* to the Second World War. A general and complete disarmament treaty with, of course, strict international control, is another important step in the same direction. Other contributory acts could be an understanding restricting the number of missiles and defensive nuclear weapons in Soviet and U.S.

---

[1] *Die Welt*, October 30, 1963.
[2] *Foreign Affairs* No. 1, 1964.

territory until they are done away with altogether in the final phase of disarmament, coupled with a withdrawal of troops from foreign territories, reduction of the armed forces of states, non-proliferation of nuclear weapons, measures against sudden attack, a non-aggression pact between the NATO powers and members of the Warsaw Treaty Organisation, and, last but not least, an atom-free zone in Central Europe. After the Moscow partial test ban treaty, the Soviet-American agreement on the non-orbiting of objects with nuclear or other means of mass annihilation and, lastly, the agreed reduction by the United States, the Soviet Union and Britain of the manufacture of fissionable materials for military purposes, an agreement freezing nuclear arms followed by the establishment of an atom-free zone in Central Europe would go a long way to relieve international tension.

The men who want nuclear weapons for the Bundeswehr say an atom-free zone would not secure German safety, because nuclear missiles ring the frontiers of the two German states. That is a lame argument, one prompted by aggressive militarist aspirations. Concerned over the future of the German nation, the German Democratic Republic has worked out an effective programme that could prevent another world war from erupting on German soil. What the G.D.R. suggested is known as the German peace doctrine based on recognition of the existing situation and on a normalisation of relations between the two German states. It envisages an undertaking by the two German states to refrain from manufacturing, acquiring or using nuclear weapons, from endeavouring in any form, directly or indirectly, through third countries or groups of countries, singly or in alliance with other states, to acquire access to, or to station nuclear weapons in any shape or form in their territory, and to prevent any third country or groups of countries from stationing nuclear weapons in Germany. This should go hand in hand with a considerable cut in military budgets and other measures conducive to a détente in Europe and the rest of the world.[1] For the first time, the German

[1] See "Erklärung des Vorsitzenden des Staatsrates der D.D.R., Walter Ulbricht, vor der Volkskammer am 1. September 1964 aus Anlass des 25. Jahrestages des Ausbruchs des zweiten Weltkrieges und des 50. Jahrestages des Ausbruchs des ersten Weltkrieges." (*Neues Deutschland*, September 2, 1964).

militarist doctrine is counterweighed by a German peace doctrine, which, moreover, is anything but utopian—a truly realistic doctrine geared to the world balance and the nuclear peril.

An atom-free zone in Central Europe would encourage the establishment of similar zones in Scandinavia and the Balkans. With Austria and Switzerland neutral, the nuclear disengagement would then in fact stretch from the northernmost point of Europe to the shore of the Mediterranean and, since the African states have also evinced eagerness to make their continent a vast atom-free zone, the result would be highly beneficial. Far-reaching changes would come about in international relations. Briefly, the idea of a nuclear-free zone in Europe is one of the most promising in current history, and it is practicable too, since a sense of urgency has gripped the general public in all capitalist states. None but the American and West German ultras want a renewal of the cold war.

Some Western groups say that by promoting the idea of an international détente, the Soviet Union is trying to exploit the differences in NATO, weakening it. That differences exist there stems from the general crisis of imperialist policy. They should be neither over- nor underrated. No aggressive bloc can be devoid of cracks. Yet blocs existed, and sometimes for decades. It is folly to think, therefore, that differences in NATO, acute though they may be, could bring about its collapse. Neither should the existence of NATO obstruct the search for ways of eliminating the war danger. The German militarists, aspiring to a big role in the NATO bloc, want to head off the search, but with opposite socio-economic systems existing in the world the only way to remove the danger of an armed conflict in Central Europe—one that in present conditions may develop into a world-wide nuclear disaster—is to affirm the principles of peaceful coexistence. Then, German militarists could not use military blocs for their warlike purpose.

1964

GERMAN IMPERIALIST IDEOLOGY
AND THE REALITIES OF OUR TIME

T he great epochs of flux create profound problems. Long-established notions fall to the ground. Irrational thinking collapses, and Reason probes deeper into the dialectics of nature and of society, repatterning man's knowledge and outlook. This was true during the transition from feudalism to capitalism, the Renaissance when Nikolaus Copernicus, Giordano Bruno and Galileo Galilei, giants of learning, spirit and character, penetrated the secrets of the Universe and challenged Catholicism, which rested on age-old tradition and the powerful Inquisition, exposing the laws of the motion of our planet. It was true of the time of the early revolutionary workers' assaults on the bastions of capitalism in Western Europe when Marx and Engels, the fathers of materialistic dialectics, defined the laws of the class struggle in the successive socio-economic formations and pinpointed the inevitability of the advance from capitalism to communism, a new formation, a classless society. It holds true today, too, in the epoch highlighted by the great discoveries of Lenin, who exposed the features and laws of imperialism, blazing new trails in communist theory and in its practical revolutionary realisation. After the Second World War scientific communism, a creative generalisation of all man's experience, is dominant in a large part of the globe. It has won the minds of the foremost workers and intellectuals in the capitalist world, where people are prompted to seek relief from imperialist dominance and its inescapable satellites: militarism, colonialism and the threat of new aggressions. Imperialism is still pregnant with the danger of a new world war which, in our nuclear age, would be the most destructive in history.

The only realistic way to eliminate the war danger is for the imperialist powers to halt the cold war, abandon the policy from "positions of strength" in favour of one from positions of reason and recognise the principle of the peaceful coexistence of states with different social and political systems. Even since the world split in two—the socialist and the capitalist worlds—this principle, worked out and substantiated by Lenin, has carried a universal message.

However, a special situation has arisen in Germany, imposing on the German people special national tasks with a bearing on the fate of Europe, even of the world. Objectively, this situation stems from the existence of two independent German states, each with its own social and political system. Socialism, democracy and peace won in one of them, the German Democratic Republic. In the other, the Federal Republic of Germany, imperialism and militarism are dominant and, spurred by an ideology of revenge, seek to spread their ideas to all spheres, befuddling the masses. Having brought about the split of Germany and incorporated her Western part into the NATO system, the aggressive forces present a grave danger to Europe, for, dreaming of restoring the German Reich within its 1937, or even 1871, frontiers, they nurse designs of forcibly absorbing the German Democratic Republic and taking revenge on Poland, Czechoslovakia and the Soviet Union. Their immediate aim is to win dominance in NATO and gain access to nuclear arms. That is why in the centre of Europe the ideological struggle of the two systems over the fateful choice—either peaceful coexistence or nuclear war—is truly crucial.

It would be untrue to say that the apologists of German militarism are blind to the objective implications and the role ideology will play in resolving the problem. That is why they distort the problem to suit their ends. Theodor Litt, a West German ideologist, says all the issues of our time hinge on "how our epoch understands itself".[1] Bent on justifying their course and their ambition of arming the

---

[1] Litt, "Wie versteht unser Zeitalter sich selbst?", *Schicksalsfragen der Gegenwart*, Bd. I, Tübingen, 1957, S. 9 ff.

Bundeswehr with nuclear weapons, Bonn ideologists seek the answer in the "nuclear age" concept. That is why, now that man's destiny really hangs in the balance, the new forms and specific trends in the imperialist ideology revived in West Germany—as compared with the old forms and their historically pernicious role—have to be comprehended by all people, not just the progressive democratic forces, for everybody on earth has a stake in removing the threat of a third world war, a nuclear disaster.

1

Looking back on the history of German politico-historical thought one will easily see how vigorously its most eminent exponents advanced the idea of a "German mission". Not German humanism, acclaimed as a contribution to man's culture and not the attainments of the German philosophers, Johann Herder and Immanuel Kant, but different variations of the "German mission" advanced in changing historical conditions, variations that sometimes collided, were brought forward, and all had an inevitable feature—that of justifying ideologically and ethically the reactionary policy and expansionist aspirations of German militarism and imperialism.

At the source of this tradition stood the "German school of history" of Leopold Ranke. Though his historico-critical method and general use of archive documents created the illusion of scientific impartiality, his philosophico-historical concept with its deceptive appearance of realism and historicity, gave him leave to describe the Prusso-German state as the embodiment of "divine thought".[1] His idea of deifying the state rested on an old tradition which even the great Hegel failed to shake off. Concentrating his studies on the ideas of the principal political leaders, which he described as a materialisation of the historical process, Ranke thought that objectively this process, to use the expression of his more liberal disciple Friedrich Meinecke, substantiated the view that "the policy of might is an organic and vital function of the state".[2]

---

[1] Ranke, *Sämtliche Werke*, Bd. 49/50, Leipzig, 1887, S. 329, 339.
[2] Meinecke, *Die Idee der Staatsräson in der neueren Geschichte*, München, 1925, S. 429.

This reactionary view applied specifically to the Prusso-German state led, on the one hand, to a flat denial of the people's sovereignty, of democracy and even of liberalism, qualified as hostile to the "German essence". On the other hand, it led to no less flat an assertion of the primacy of foreign policy.

Defining the state as the demiurge of the historical process, Ranke endowed it with an all but mystical content, viewing its external functions as primary and determinative. He held that the system of European states was the key to the historical process—an idea that could be scientifically fruitful if given a progressive meaning. Ranke, however, and his disciples, filled it with reactionary venom, building it round the idea of an equilibrium of "great powers".[1] Not only did they impart to it a Europocentric narrowness (only to be expected in the early half of the 19th century), but also created the conception which was used as the ideological basis and historical justification of militarist Prussia's domination over Germany and then of militarist Germany's efforts to gain control over Europe. Falling later on the fertile soil of the German militarists' hegemonic ambitions that found expression in the Bismarckian system of politico-military alliances, the power balance idea won many followers among contemporary bourgeois and Junker historians and publicists.

At the end of the 19th century, Ranke's school degenerated into the simplistic nationalist doctrine of Heinrich von Treitschke, whom Lenin branded as a police-minded official historian.[2] Scorning the elementary rules of science, Treitschke saturated his shallow ideas with a candidly aggressive purport, delighting the band of reactionaries and champions of the "German mission". Among them was the Pan-Germanic Union founded by industrialists and colonial tycoons to propagate expansionism, which was happy to reinforce its ideological arsenal from that murky source.[3]

---

[1] Ranke, "Die grossen Mächte", *Historische Zeitschrift,* Berlin, 1833.

[2] See Lenin, *Collected Works,* Vol. 13, p. 23.

[3] H. v. Treitschke, *Deutsche Geschichte im 19. Jahrhundert,* Bd. 1-5, Leipzig, 1904-20; *Bundesstaat und Einheitsstaat,* 1864; *Frankreichs Staatsleben und der Bonapartismus,* 1861 ff; *Das konstitutionelle Königstum in Deutschland,* Berlin, 1869 ff; *Der Sozialismus und seine Gönner,* Berlin, 1875; *Der Sozialismus und Meuchelmord,* Berlin, 1878; *Ausgewählte Schriften,* Bd. I-II, Leipzig, 1907; *Historische und politische*

Soon, however, the "German mission" was so broadly conceived that the European continent seemed too narrow for it. A new content geared to the aggressive aspirations of the burgeoning imperialism was injected into the old nationalist idea. In 1895, anticipating the growth of these aspirations and, as it were, proclaiming them in the context of the now firmly entrenched idea of a "German mission", publicists in Germany declared, "What is essential to become somebody is to conquer something somewhere in the world."

A year later the following words, far more specific and far more meaningful, appeared in black and white in Friedrich Naumann's *National-Social Catechism:* "What is national? It is the German people's desire to spread their influence to the ends of the world." The author of this new interpretation of the "German mission" subsequently became the author also of the broad imperialist conceptions of a *Mitteleuropa.*[1]

So, the cry, "We want a place in the sun!", was a plagiarism when it resounded from the Reichstag rostrum at the turn of the 20th century. However, his contemporaries, to use Naumann's phrase, responded to it as if it were a formula for the "great invasion into world history". Subsequent studies showed[2] how great was the role of publicists in making public opinion when the financiers, industrial kings and colonialists, the new "men of power", pushed with Admiral Alfred von Tirpitz for naval armament as an instrument of *Weltpolitik*. They expected the navy to help them wrest the trident of Neptune out of Britain's hands, thereby undermining the latter's world power. Naumann, one of the first to sense the spirit of the times and, moreover, to fit the old traditional ideas to the new era, wrote in 1900: "If there is anything unconditional in world history it is the future world war, that is, the war of those who

---

Aufsätze, Leipzig, 1911; *Die Politik*, Vorlesungen gehalten an der Universität zu Berlin, Leipzig, 1911.

[1] Naumann, "Was heisst christlich-sozial?", *Sammlung von Aufsätzen*, Bd. I-II, Leipzig, 1894-96; *Soziale Briefe an reiche Leute*, Göttingen, 1895; *National-sozialer Katechismus*, Berlin, 1899; *Weltpolitik und Sozialreform*, Berlin, 1897; *Mitteleuropa*, Berlin, 1915; also see T. Heuss, *Friedrich Naumann*, Tübingen, 1949; G. Theodor, *Friedrich Naumann oder der Prophet des Profits*, Berlin, 1957.

[2] E. Kehr, *Schlachtflottenbau und Parteipolitik. 1894-1901,* Berlin, 1930.

want to deliver themselves from Britain." Thus, the idea of the "German mission" with its Prusso-German, and later continental, garb of the Bismarck era, was viewed in the imperialist epoch as all but providential and historically preconditioned, because the geopolitical, central location of Germany and the system of politico-military great-power alliances on the European continent could not be included in the general conception of *Weltpolitik*.

For all the diversity of views and problems raised in the historical and philosophico-historical studies in German bourgeois historiography, the neo-Ranke school, as the main trend, embodies all the general ideological aspirations of German imperialism in its various stages of growth. Brought together by their common belief in the primacy of foreign policy and the reactionary tradition of "German historicism", exponents of the neo-Ranke school retain their specific individual inflections and arguments in assessing the historical perspective and the correlation of methods and objectives whereby they expect to consummate the "German mission" despite the ever-changing "balance of power". Max Lenz, who borrowed Ranke's title for his own historico-political essay, *The Great Powers,* endeavoured to prove at the turn of the century that the balance may be restored by spreading the "German mission" beyond "continental" limits and, albeit historically late, taking part in the division of the world not merely by activating capital, but by military means. To restore the balance on a new world-wide basis in the interest of the "German mission", Lenz averred, the might of the nation should be committed against the Great Powers who had upset the equilibrium: "We can order them; we hold the scales in our hands."

This appeal to militarism was complemented by Delbrück, an influential historian of the Wilhelmian era, who appealed to marinism: according to Tirpitz's politico-strategic conception dreadnoughts on the high seas rather than a continental army would equilibrate the world power balance. But whereas Delbrück thought it essential to make the maximum use of diplomatic channels until a time when Britain, "ruler of the waves", considered it too risky to come into a preventive collision with the new naval rival, Otto Hintze, like all neo-Ranke historians, fired by a *Streben nach Macht* (itch for power), formulated the task thus: "We want to complement the balance of land by balance on the seas." Ludwig Dehio commented, and rightly so, that this was "Tirpitz's formula letter for letter!"[1]

As the notions of imperialist *Weltpolitik* gained fresh prominence and the correlation of forces changed, the neo-Ranke "balance of power" conception acquired new range: from Meinecke's attempts to attribute to the "German mission" a world-wide significance and assert the superiority of German philosophy, history and statehood (he described Hegel, Ranke and Bismarck as the "three great liberators of the state") to a candid apologia of German militarism, the system of political military alliances and the ideas of an "old and new *Mitteleuropa*", as we see in Hermann Oncken.[2] But despite the externally diverse aspects, there crystallised a few determinative features which bared the functional purport of the general concept: firstly, substantiation of the Prusso-German state's leading role in history and modernity; secondly, historical substantiation in the new twentieth century of the "German mission" as opposed to the "cultural monopoly" of the Anglo-Saxon countries and the "Russo-Muscovite world"; thirdly, appeal to militarism as the force assuring Prussia's accession to the status of German empire and of the latter to the status of a "great power" in Europe; fourthly, substantiation of the German hegemonic idea not only in Europe but the world as a whole.

As Walter Vogel, the German historian, later recorded, "shortly before 1914 the German concept boiled down to the following thesis: Germany's historic mission is to translate the European balance into a world balance".[3]

In effect, it inferred the historical inevitability and necessity of German imperialism's world domination. History was thus reduced to the role of handmaiden for imperialist aspirations. In 1912, the neo-Ranke school had all but coalesced with the frankly aggressive Pan-Germanic camp: Delbrück maintained in *Preussische Jahrbücher*, an influential organ of conservative politico-historical thought, that Germany's

---

[1] Dehio, *Deutschland und die Weltpolitik im 20. Jahrhundert*, München, 1955, S. 54.

[2] Oncken, *Das alte und das neue Mitteleuropa. Historisch-politische Betrachtungen über deutsche Bündnispolitik im Zeitalter Bismarcks und im Zeitalter des Weltkrieges*, Gotha, 1917.

[3] Vogel, *Das neue Europa und seine historisch-geographischen Grundlagen*, Bonn-Leipzig, 1921, S. 51.

"world mission" made it imperative "to participate in world rule".[1] Paul Rohrbach, one of the best known publicists of his day, endeavoured to demonstrate in his book, the *German Idea in the World*, that in the historical sense the purpose of forming a German Reich was to assert its supremacy in the world and that to accomplish the "German idea" the guns would have to speak.[2] Last but not least, General Bernhardi caused a sensation with his book, the title of which, *Germany and the Future War,*[3] revealed its bias and, moreover, the purposive imperialist conception of "German historicism". Dissecting the history of the neo-Ranke school, the main and determinative school of German bourgeois historiography, one arrives at the conclusion that the war of 1914-18, vindicated and ideologically prepared beforehand, inflicted on it a terrible blow. Gripped by nationalist fever, it eulogised the war as a "German war", a war prompted less by economic rivalry, which torpedoed the old "balance of power" system, and much more by the craving of the young German "heroism" to assert its superior ethics over the dispirited British "shopkeepers" and other historically decadent adversaries who had no right at all to a historical existence and future. The "ideas of 1914" advanced at that time were aggressive ideas which, upsetting the original tale about the war being defensive, described it as the supreme historical necessity, the destiny and calling of the "German spirit, German culture and German statehood" to challenge the powers of the hostile camp.[4]

The German school of history candidly declared its allegiance to militarism (Statement of 93, under which about 4,000 German intellectuals signed their names). But it went farther. Reiterating its ideological alliance with monopoly capital, it devoted itself to framing far-reaching annexationist plans. The professorial memorandum submitted to the government was only one of many such documents. In sum, all of them aspired to a *Mitteleuropa.*

The German school of history put itself entirely at the

---

[1] *Preussische Jahrbücher,* Bd. 149, Berlin, 1912.

[2] Rohrbach, *Der deutsche Gedanke in der Welt,* Düsseldorf-Leipzig, 1912, S. 191.

[3] F. v. Bernhardi, *Deutschland und der nächste Krieg,* Stuttgart-Berlin, 1912.

[4] F. Fischer, *Griff nach der Weltmacht,* Düsseldorf, 1962, S. 178 ff.

service of imperialist war. Annexationist plans were substantiated not only in the traditional concept of a "German mission", but in various other no less irrational ideas borrowed from the Pan-Germanists, close to the later concepts of *Herrenvolk* and *Lebensraum*. The differences in politico-historical assessments were tactical rather than fundamental: arguing the advantages of either a "peace by negotiation" or "peace through violence", in both cases in the historical context of a future war.

But the idea of world power, no matter how substantiated in philosophico-historical or politico-ethical terms and no matter how strongly backed by the old ideas of militarism and preventive war or the new ideas of colonialism and marinism with its "theory of risk", proved stillborn and unrealistic. German bourgeois historiography parading as a superior embodiment of the national consciousness, betrayed its limitations by failing to understand even in the final stage of the war that it was on the brink of bankruptcy: in the spring of 1917, after the February Revolution in Russia, Friedrich Meinecke, a historian of the liberal school, assisted in drawing up a petition demanding the annexation of the Baltic states.[1] Yet it was in the confrontation with the October Revolution in Russia that it proved itself totally bankrupt.

2

At the dawn of the new epoch, when on one-sixth of the earth's surface history changed its course, the system of states that came into being in Europe at the close of the 19th century fell apart. The collapse of the Russian empire was followed by that of the Austro-Hungarian and then the German empire, which surrendered and accepted the terms of the Versailles Treaty.

The October Revolution in Russia opened up new unexplored opportunities for transforming society along socialist lines and gave a powerful impulse to the workers' revolutionary movement in Western Europe. German militarism, which had shortly before seemed unassailable at home and abroad, was badly undermined by the defeat

---

[1] Fischer, op. cit., S. 202.

and the November Revolution of 1918. This was no mere military and political defeat; it was a defeat for German's hegemonic aspirations, for its historical illusions and the equally unrealistic ideas of the old Ranke. The variants of the idealist "power balance", each seeking to substantiate the necessity or inevitability of changing the balance in favour of the "German essence", were all debunked by history. The traditional views, concepts and categories lost lustre, especially after revolutionary Marxist thought demonstrated irrevocably its ability to comprehend the times and look ahead.

The most prominent German thinkers, who saw that the ideology of Prussianism, monarchism and Pan-Germanism was stillborn, did not at first know how to begin adapting to the new conditions. Max Weber, head of the Heidelberg school and one of the most distinguished of the conservative brand of liberals, wrote in the winter of 1918 that "at present our image has suffered considerable damage, such damage, in fact, as no other nation suffered in similar circumstances. As after 1648 [when the Thirty Years' War ended and the Peace of Westphalia was concluded—*A.Y.*), and as after 1807 [that is, after the defeat at Austerlitz and the establishment of Napoleonic rule over Germany—*A.Y.*], we are now having to begin all over again. That is how the facts stack up. . . . Naturally, our urge to be truthful prompts us to say that Germany has forfeited her role as a power determining world politics."

These lines, written before the Versailles Treaty was signed, were unfortunately mistrustful of the German working class, which in that stormy period was eager to restore Germany's national image, though by different means than the German militarists. The German workers were bent on removing the imperialists from power and on remodelling the country socially along democratic lines. Since *Weltpolitik* was the main and determinative idea of the long since finalised ideology of world power,[1] the politico-military defeat of the German imperialists was thought to show that

---

[1] C. Bornhak, *Die Kriegsschuld. Deutschlands Weltpolitik von 1890-1914*, Berlin, 1929; B. v. Bülow, *Denkwürdigkeiten*, Bd. 1-4, Berlin, 1930-31; A. H. Cartellieri, *Deutschland in der Weltpolitik seit dem Frankfurter Frieden*, Jena, 1923; O. Hammann, *Deutsche Weltpolitik von 1890-1912*, Berlin, 1925; J. Hashagen, *Umrisse der Weltpolitik*, Bd. I, Leipzig-Berlin, 1918.

Germany had been flung back to the times of the Peace of Westphalia or the Napoleonic period. Hence the reflections on "having to begin all over again".

Depressed by events of great immensity, the German school of history concentrated above all, to use Meinecke's words, on "buttressing the narrow dam that still separated us from Bolshevism".[1] The task was defined as preventing or delaying the surge of revolution in Germany. By and large, however, bourgeois historians were in a state of extreme confusion. The prestige of the neo-Ranke school, like that of German militarism, was shaken. The gods on the Mount Olympus of the German school of history were in eclipse.

The bourgeois historians were robbed of their philosophy. Yet in this foggy state there appeared a philosophy resuscitating the old components in new forms and combinations, producing a still more reactionary concoction: the *Lebensphilosophie* (Georg Simmel, Ludwig Klages, Hermann Keyserling, Richard Müller-Freienfels, etc.)[2] inordinately irrational, coupled with the Nietzschean irrationalism of Oswald Spengler and his sublime, perverted pseudo-historical aesthetic cult of the "heroic personality" and his disdain, varnished with a thick coating of demagogy, of the masses, the true makers of history. The *Lebensphilosophie* had its source in Nietzsche, Wilhelm Dilthey and Edmund Husserl.[3] It worked to consolidate all reactionary, particularly historical, thought. "What we want," Spengler declared, "everybody must want."[4] Treating world history not as the history of peoples but of states, and treating the history of states as the history of wars, Spengler—despite his unique phraseology—simply followed in the footsteps of Treitschke, Bernhardi and other ideologists of the traditional Prusso-German militarism. Like his predecessors, Spengler maintained that war generally is the eternal form and supreme value of man's existence; he defined the waging of

---

[1] Meinecke, *Strassburg-Freiburg-Berlin, 1901-1919. Erinnerungen*, Stuttgart, 1949, S. 260.

[2] G. Mende und W. Heise, "Die Lebensphilosophie", *Die deutsche bürgerliche Philosophie seit 1917*, Berlin, 1958, S. 32 ff.

[3] Dilthey, *Einleitung in die Geisteswissenschaften*, Bd. I, Leipzig-Berlin, 1933; Husserl, *Logische Untersuchungen*, Halle, 1900 f.; Husserl, *Ideen zu einer reinen Phänomenologie*, Halle, 1913.

[4] Spengler, *Preussentum und Sozialismus,* München, 1924, S. 22.

wars as the purpose and mission of the state.[1] Here is how he formulated his general conception: "Since life has for us become an external political, social and economic life, all others must either adapt themselves to our political, social and economic ideal or perish. This notion, which is becoming clearer, I have called modern socialism. . . . But it belongs *only* to us; there is no antique, Chinese or Russian socialism in that sense."[2] He postulated "Prussian" or national German "socialism" as a new form of imperialist expansion and world power.

Specifically, Spengler's idea of "Prussian socialism" copied not the Prusso-German state-capitalist pattern of Bismarckian times but the German state-monopoly capitalism of the 1914-18 war. The attempt Spengler made in his quasi-scientific morphology of social and cultural development to show the "decline of the West" expressed his disappointment over the collapse of German imperialism, but also the counter-revolutionary intention of saving the "eternal and unrepeatable values" of the West from the destructive powers of "Eastern communism" through "Prussian socialism", the synonym of imperialism and militarism.[3]

Thus, at the height of the ideological crisis gripping German imperialism after its defeat, Spengler's reactionary concept became a fashionable panacea, not because it contained undercurrents of irrationalism and elements of scepticism, but rather because it treated the "West" as a single organism, the seat of supreme, supra-historical cultural values, orienting it on struggle against "Eastern communism". Spengler's conception appealed to the ruling classes because, among other things, it juggled with the concepts of international socialism and "imperialists international" and cast discredit on the workers' revolutionary movement, counterweighing it with "Prussian socialism" as something morphologically impregnated with Prusso-German realities. A tool of virile anti-communism, Spengler's philosophy was, therefore, to no small extent a prototype for German fascism. This was by no means evidence of Spengler's foresight, but rather of the wretched eclecticism and extreme pugnacity of the ideological concoction that became part of Hitler's national-socialism.

---

[1] Spengler, *Preussentum und Sozialismus,* München, 1924, S. 53.
[2] Ibid., S. 22-23.
[3] Spengler, *Der Untergang des Abendlandes,* Bd. 1-2, München, 1922.

What is striking, however, is that alongside Spengler's unhistorical conception the ideology of Germany's ruling quarters contained a conservatively liberal academic historicism shed of all demagogy, which opposed Spenglerism, and not because Spengler's anti-communism was unacceptable, but because, as Ernst Troeltsch, prominent historian and sociologist, said in 1922, Spengler's was an "immoral . . . cynical conception of individualism based on violence".[1] Those were new words, denouncing for the first time some of the candidly militaristic ideas and seeking to replace them with "an idea of natural right and humanity". It was a time, indeed, when Germany could revise her place in the new system of states and strike a blow for peace, for an eclipse of German militarism could make it easier for the democratic forces to find relief from the stranglehold imposed on the country by the Versailles Treaty.

The young Soviet state, which issued the historic Decree on Peace, condemned the Versailles decisions. It took some years, however, before the German rulers realised that they had to find a way out of the blind alley. The Treaty of Rapallo, epitomising the Leninist principles of peaceful coexistence, helped the Weimar Republic to emerge from its state of international isolation.[2]

Faced by these major events, which evidenced the enormous changes taking place in the world system of states and opened the way for peaceful democratic growth, the German school of history failed to do what it always considered its *forte*—to comprehend the present in historical terms. The latent possibilities of the Rapallo Treaty were obviously underrated. Otto Hoetzsch, who was not, in effect, associated with the neo-Ranke school, was among the historians a happy exception—an active and convinced advocate of the Rapallo policy.[3] A conservative and nationalist, he and some of his friends and disciples defended it historically from the standpoint of Bismarck's "eastern" orientation.

---

[1] Troeltsch, *Deutscher Geist und Westeuropa. Gesammelte kulturphilosophische Aufsätze und Reden*, Tübingen, 1925, S. 23.

[2] See earlier, "Great October Revolution and the Problem of Soviet-German Relations"; also *Rapallsky dogovor i problema mirnogo sosushchestvovaniya*. Materials of the symposium on the 40th anniversary of the Rapallo Treaty (April 25-28, 1962), Moscow, 1963 (Russ. ed.).

[3] In 1935 Hoetzsch was banished from Berlin University by the nazi authorities.

This writer, who visited the Weimar Republic frequently at that time and called at its universities and research institutions, studying its historiography, saw how bourgeois historians gradually realised that they had to revise their ideas. However, in most cases this was not sparked by any real wish to break with the past, their own included, but rather by a desire to preserve the basic principles, the methods and notions, and merely adapt them to the new situation. One got the impression that they sought to evade all deep-going self-criticism, that they refused to admit failure or, at least, to admit their setbacks in comprehending the paths of history that had brought Germany defeat and the Versailles Treaty; one got the impression that the historians were stumped, that they were incapable of producing ideas that would open up broader horizons for the German nation. Indeed, this was farthest from their minds. The sociological method of Max Weber, head of the Heidelberg school, who replaced the objective laws of history with "ideally typical notions", was still highly influential, not only among bourgeois historians but also among Social-Democrats, who viewed it as a sufficiently adroit and virile counterweight to Marxism. Eduard Meyer, one of the most eminent scholars of the antique world after Theodor Mommsen, kept saying in his lectures at Berlin University that capitalism was everlasting and its basic features cyclical. Hans Rothfels (then a young *Privatdozent*, later a professor who left Hitler Germany for the United States and is now a leading figure in West German historiography) read a course on the war guilt, a topic that was then the object of political struggle not only in Germany itself, but also in its relations with the Western imperialist powers. Basing himself on the old Ranke objectivism. Rothfels fell back on various idealist categories to lead up to the notion that the Versailles Treaty placing the sole responsibility for the war on Germany was unjustified. He also argued against Lenin's theory and that of Rosa Luxemburg about imperialism and imperialism's responsibility for the world war, for no longer at that time could Lenin's theory of imperialism be ignored.

The war guilt problem was tied in with the problem of the origin and outbreak of the war. However, this latter was viewed solely from the diplomatic angle. The accent on diplomatic questions enabled historians to revert to the "power balance" conception, and doubly so because after the downfall of the hegemonic idea of "world balance" they could go back to the old Ranke notion of a European balance of power. After the French imperialists endeavoured to consolidate their ascendancy in Europe by invading the Ruhr and erecting a system of military alliances, historical studies of the period of the Napoleonic wars and similar historical parallels appeared relevant: the traditional idea of German nationalism was being given impulse for a new upsurge. However, reminiscences of the power balance in Europe sidetracked historians from the main problem of current German history—the problem of imperialism and militarism. One would think that after the militarists had suffered defeat and were morally discredited, and that after the dictates of Versailles had reduced their forces and possibilities, historians could, addressing a broad democratic segment of the nation, produce a decisive scientifically grounded denunciation of militarism. But they did not.

The reader today will hardly believe the immense impression created among the academic and political circles in Weimar Germany by *The Idea of State Reason in Modern History,* a book by Friedrich Meinecke.[1] To begin with, it was the first book to criticise the German school of history. "It was a profound deficiency of the German school of history," Meinecke wrote, "that it dressed up and idealised the policy of strength by means of a theory which described it as a token of lofty morality." However, Meinecke did not develop his attack on the German school into an attack on German militarism. He thought his self-criticism would invigorate historical thinking and extend its scope to a point approaching the pattern dominant in Western bourgeois-democratic historiography.

Yet Meinecke would not accept all the aspects of Western "natural law thinking". He held it to be divorced from the actual life of the state, while the stability of German historicism was rooted in its recognition of "the wisdom of the state". In this way, keeping well within the traditional limits of the idealist philosophy of history, the path was cleared for a merger of such elements of the German school of history and of Western (chiefly British) ideas which,

---

[1] Meinecke, *Die Idee der Staatsräson in der neueren Geschichte,* München-Berlin, 1924.

Meinecke thought, could stand the test and become a common basis for further historical and political exercises. This dualistic principle, he observed, would offer "an opportunity for theoretical and practical mutual understanding with the West".[1]

As we see, under the flag of German liberalism and the artificially galvanised traditions of German humanism an attempt was made to substantiate philosophically, historically, methodologically and sociologically the ideology of anti-socialism and anti-communism, although the form adopted was not yet frankly aggressive and brutal. Few, however, could elevate their views to the sublime heights of general and abstract categories of a world-wide or at least Europocentric complexion.

Although Meinecke's philosophico-historic conception did not attack the ideas of German imperialism and militarism, with which the German school of history was closely associated, and although his conception anticipated and embodied the new political tendency of certain sections in the ruling camp (Stresemann's Locarno policy), Meinecke's new ideas were severely criticised by many prominent bourgeois historians. German historicism, which regained its vigour in the environment of relative capitalist stabilisation, would not suffer any criticism, even if it emanated from its own ranks. Gerhard Ritter, whose politico-historical ideas had also flowered on neo-Ranke soil, declared that he saw too many profound "contradictions between the Western natural law and German idealistic ways of thinking ... to believe in the possibility of their 'synthesis' ".[2]

One got the impression that Meinecke's fairly numerous opponents were out to consolidate themselves in the old bastions, because they laid the stress on reviving the traditional militarism in order to revise the Versailles system and prepare for revenge, rather than search for spiritual unity and unilateral agreement with the West. But to achieve this aim, the international situation had to be favourable. Acting on the old Ranke idea about the primacy

---

[1] Meinecke, op. cit., S. 502.
[2] *Neue Jahrbücher für Wissenschaft und Jugendbindung,* 1925, No. 1, S. 114. Concerning this polemics and the problem in general see Berthold, "... grosshungern und gehorchen". *Zur Entstehung und politischen Funktion der Geschichtsideologie des westdeutschen Imperialismus,* Berlin, 1960.

of foreign policy, Weimar Germany historians centred their investigations, reflections and discussions on the "Eastern" and "Western" orientations in the history of the German Reich. To an observer it could appear that the German school of history was breaking up into at least two hostile camps. But despite the acute polemics it was faithful to itself, to its imperialist ideas and ideals. "Who would dare censure the German people and its leaders," Meinecke wrote, "for their proud self-awareness and for their pretensions to world recognition and to a share of world wealth? *This self-awareness has not been eradicated by defeat, and the pretensions are still valid*, although now they have to be achieved in entirely new forms rather than those typical of the old power politics."[1] Ritter, on the other hand, who was convinced that "the national will for action has to be maintained in defiance of all the winds of fate",[2] nursed the same historical aims but thought them attainable only on a distinctly revanchist course, through a more decisive break with the "1918 Democrats" who reckoned that Germany would "by abandoning its 'imperialist' policy of strength earn the moral sympathy of the whole world".[3] This was a head-on attack on the foremost section of the working class and those groups of German intellectuals who had through past and present experience acquired a profound understanding of the historical danger implicit in militarism.

The German school of history refused to abandon the "policy of strength" doctrine. In its search for a personification of true "state reason" it extolled Bismarck. But not Bismarck alone. Ritter, for one, was also inspired by Luther who, he said, "promoted the self-awareness of the German's metaphysical essence",[4] and by Friedrich II[5] as well, and finally by old Hindenburg.

In its polemics against Meinecke's liberalism as the ideological pillar for a spiritual convergence and political agreement with the Western powers, the traditional school

---

[1] Meinecke, *Geschichte des deutsch-englischen Bündnisproblems 1890 bis 1901*, München-Berlin, 1927, S. 268 (italics mine.—*A.Y.*).

[2] Ritter, *Stein. Eine politische Biographie*, Bd. II, Stuttgart-Berlin, 1931, S. 67.

[3] Ritter, *Friedrich der Grosse*, Heidelberg, 1954, S. 267.

[4] Ritter, *Luther—Gestalt und Symbol*, München, 1925, S. 153.

[5] Ritter, *Friedrich der Grosse*, Heidelberg, 1954, S. 256.

avoided criticising the concept of "demonism" as an irrational force that, being part of life, may gain control over history and, consequently, leave an impression on "state reason".[1] This conception, which surfaced from the depth of reactionary romanticism, became one of the basic concepts in the various endeavours to comprehend fascism.

In sum, various trends of the Weimar school of history reverted in substance, though perhaps in a different form, to the old conceptions, modified somewhat to fit the new historical environment. And none of these conceptions in any way attacked the past chapters of German imperialism and militarism.

To be sure, some criticism of the past there was. But, strange though it may appear, all such criticism emanated from the militarist camp and from ideologists most closely associated with it. General Hoffmann called the lost war a "war of forfeited opportunities". Count Reventlow pointed to the gaping disparities between the political aims of the world war and the military means whereby these aims were to be attained.[2] Invariably, however, the conclusion was that the military means were insufficient and that if the political leadership had attached less importance to diplomacy and more to the military system, subordinating all economic and spiritual affairs entirely to the interests of the war, the results would have been different.

Memoirs and historical writings sought to rehabilitate German militarism and toyed with the idea of a "total" war. This was not direct criticism; it was many-faceted, aimed not only against diplomacy, which was blamed for not securing a favourable international climate for the German militarists; it was aimed against the German people, blamed for succumbing to excessive nationalism and overrating its strength, which made it a fertile medium for the idea of a "master people"; elsewhere, and this was more frequent, it was blamed for showing "weakness" at the decisive moment and falling for democratic and revolutionary ideas. Hans Hentig, for example, wrote in his book on the psychological strategy of the world war that

---

[1] Meinecke, *Die Idee der Staatsräson in der neueren Geschichte,* München, 1925, S. 508.
[2] Reventlow, *Deutschlands auswärtige Politik 1888 bis 1914,* Berlin, 1918.

"the self-awareness of a nation grown strong rapidly turned into universal uncritical self-admiration. This frame of mind found expression in the very naive but firm conviction that the more enemies Germany had, the worse it was for its enemies."

The formula that victory drew closer as the number of enemies increased was not a national, not a people's formula. It was proclaimed by Wilhelm II and was a nationalistic formula which flung on the scales not only the interests but also the lives of many millions of Germans.

But the main militarist attack was focused on something else. Having concocted the tale about the "stab in the back",[1] militarism spread the idea that the war was lost because the revolutionary movement erupted behind the lines at a time when victory was round the corner. The main purpose of this story was to implant in the minds of millions of people the myth that the German General Staff was invincible and its strategic principles and warcraft second to none. Militarism had not yet been restored, but its ideology and tradition were back in force. The bourgeois democratic parties, and even the Social-Democrats, pretended not to see it. In the meantime, as General Vincenz Müller, then associated with the politico-military department of the Reichswehr, later testified, "traditions were being cultivated in the Weimar Republic in preparation for a war of revenge."[2]

The functional purport of these ideological variations becomes doubly clear when we recall that the process had just then begun of reviving one of the main aspects, somewhat altered but rigid enough, of the militarist Pan-Germanic ideology, expressed through the traditional and aggressive formula, *Drang nach Osten*. As for the military doctrine, it was one fostered by General Seeckt, advocating a small modern mechanised professional army as the

---

[1] *Der Prozess des Reichspräsidenten*, Berlin, 1925; *Die Dolchstosslegende*, Hrsg. vom Reichsvorstand der Deutschen Republikanischen Reichsbundes, Frankfurt a/M, 1919; *Der Dolchstoss der USPD*, Berlin, 1925; E. Beckmann, *Der Dolchstossprozess im München vom 19. Oktober bis 20. November 1925*, Verhandlungsberichte, München, 1926; *Der Dolchstoss. Warum das deutsche Heer zusammenbrach*, Berlin, 1920. Also see J. Petzold, *Die Dolchstosslegende. Eine Geschichtsfälschung im Dienst des deutschen Imperialismus und Militarismus*, Berlin, 1963
[2] Müller, *Ich fand das wahre Vaterland,* Berlin, 1963, S. 233.

nucleus of a future massive force. Like Schlieffen, father of the war on two fronts strategy[1] (who had whispered on his death-bed in reference to an oblique blow at Paris, "but don't weaken the right flank"), General Seeckt told his contemporaries and successors in *Germany Between West and East*,[2] his politico-strategic will, to avoid a war on two fronts and strike in one direction provided political cover was available in the other. It was in this environment that Field-Marshal Hindenburg, a figurehead which the German school of history put aloft as an "historic image", became the symbol of the militarist tradition.[3]

There was indeed something deeply symbolic in the fact that this Field-Marshal of the Kaiser army became President of the German Republic in the days of Weimar. The Right-wing leaders of the Social-Democratic Party, who split the working class, turned their backs on the mounting danger of militarism, fascism and war. Preoccupied with the propaganda of "economic democracy" and clinging to the theory of "the lesser evil", they helped elect Hindenburg and issued assurances left and right that this inveterate reactionary was a pillar of democracy, that he, this man of limited knowledge who himself confessed to have read nothing since he left military school, was the personification, the champion of the humanistic traditions of German culture. In the mid-twenties huge posters picturing Hindenburg as "our saviour" (*Unser Retter*) were on display in the streets of German cities. Hardly anyone knew, however, whom this idol of the German militarists who helped the nazis seize power "legally" and establish a blood-stained dictatorship in preparation for a world war, had really saved.

That was how the curtain rang down on the Weimar Republic which, through Paragraph 48 of its own Constitution, afforded the militarists and nazis the opportunity to destroy it. The ironies of history can be staggering. None but a great artist, who imposes on us a sense of its tragic truths, can reproduce the twists so generously dispensed by it. The spectacle created by the sinister forces of milit-

---

[1] Groener, *Das Testament des Grafen Schlieffen,* Berlin, 1926; Ritter, *Der Schlieffen-Plan*, München, 1956.

[2] Seeckt, *Deutschland zwischen West und Ost*, Hamburg, 1933.

[3] Ritter, "Hindenburg als historische Gestalt"—*Die Woche* (Sonderheft), 2. VIII. 1934. Quoted from W. Berthold, op. cit., S. 71.

arism and imperialism on the boards of the Weimar stage, ably depicted by Bertolt Brecht in his *Career of Mr. Arturo Ui*, spelled tragedy for Germany and the world whose depth, scale and devastation have still to be fully assessed. German bourgeois historians have not lifted the veil on the secret of fascism. Nor did they ever try, because they, too, in one form or another, personified the ideology of German militarism and imperialism. And they paid the price for it for, to survive in Germany, they had to humble themselves and stoop to the role of apologists, of handmaidens to fascist aggression.

3

On coming to power, Hitler and his nazi clique, who booted out the official bourgeois ideology of Weimar times, tried to create the impression that they were bearers of the old Prusso-German tradition personified by Friedrich II and Hindenburg. That was the purpose of the stilted comedy played out in Potsdam, the Potsdam of the old Prussian traditions, where to the sound of trumpets, beside the tombs of the Prussian electors and kings, Hitler staged his mammoth ceremonial at which red cloths with the black swastika kept company with hundreds of the old Prussian regimental banners, symbolising the intimate alliance between militarism and nazism, the unity of their roots and traditions, their essence and their aims. If anyone today, after Hitler Germany has been conclusively defeated, endeavours to prove that no such alliance existed either sociologically, politically or ideologically, I say that all his efforts are hypocritical to the extreme, despite sounding plausible. Hitler borrowed the old Prusso-German militarist tradition, but he injected it with still greater, universal meaning, geared to the demagogical slogans and candidly piratical practices of national-socialism. He adopted the militarist view that war was a natural state of society, an everlasting function of a "sound" state, maintaining that he considered it a "revolution of sound, peoples" and "the most forceful classical expression of life".

As the *Deutsche Wehr*, mouthpiece of the nazi General Staff, declared, the purpose of propaganda was to create a situation in which the people of Germany would "not dare think of anything but war". "War," the journal said, "should be their sole passion, sole pleasure, vice and sport; in short, an obsession."[1] Unlike the times of the First World War, the German imperialists, espousing the ideology of fascism and racism, made it their aim to win *Lebensraum*, which they intended to "Germanise" by enslaving or exterminating whole nations. Hitler said "national and racial properties run in the blood" and, long before coming to power, proclaimed the man-hating aims of the aggressive, annexationist fascist programme. "You can Germanise only space, not people," he wrote in his *Mein Kampf*. "What was usefully Germanised in the past was the soil which our ancestors obtained with the sword." The nazis launched their "Germanisation" programme by covering Germany with a rash of concentration camps.

But what was uppermost in nazism was its pathological hatred of communism. At home, the nazis embarked on an unheard of reign of terror against Communists, Socialists and all democratic and progressive forces. Also, anti-communism was refracted in the baiting of Jews with the object of physically destroying all of them. In foreign policy, nazi anti-communism was exploited in promoting the so-called Munich policy of the Western powers, in trying to avoid a war on two fronts and assail enemies one by one.

Later, dragging the world into the vortex of war, the nazis spread their "Germanisation" policy to the conquered part of Europe, slaughtering millions of people and inflicting frightful destruction on property and many proud objects of world culture. The policy of conquest was held up as a providential materialisation of the "German mission", which historians accepted as sufficient reason to glorify the *Führer* as the "most brilliant general of all time".[2]

That was the logic of pugnacious nationalism, of the idea of racial superiority and the *Führer* cult, backed up by state terrorism against the German people and a policy of extermination against the peoples of other lands. Cynical and oblivious of the objective truth, nazi imperialism

---

[1] *Deutsche Wehr*, December 1935.
[2] *Das Bild des Krieges in deutschen Denker,* Hrsg. v. A. Faust, Bd. I, Stuttgart-Berlin, 1941, Preface.

trampled underfoot deliberately, according to plan, various scientific concepts, replacing them with irrationalism like Rosenberg's *Twentieth Century Myth*,[1] better suited for their piratical aims and methods.

It was bound to happen in such a climate that out-and-out falsifiers gained prominence in nazi historiography, namely, Otto Westphal, Walter Frank and Christoph Steding,[2] who promptly became peddlers of the maniacal ideas of Hitler, Goebbels and Rosenberg. But that does not absolve the traditional German school of history of guilt for trying to substantiate the fascist policy of aggression and war. "The more fully the state blends with the nation, which is . . . the supreme goal of our present political leadership," Ritter wrote in 1937, "the greater our hope is to enforce in the future Germany's freedom, power and prestige." He stated his conviction that the fascist state would fulfil the predestined German mission and that "never again will the sombre pictures of Germany's impotence and shame reoccur on the Rhine". Ritter predicted the Third Reich a splendid future. "The rapid ascent from the depth of humiliation suffered as a result of our long history," he wrote, "will be but the beginning of still grander and magnificent times."[3] But the future showed that his historical diagnosis was no less false than his historical prognosis was unrealistic. This time, German militarism suffered ignominious defeat not on the Rhine, but chiefly in the open spaces from the Volga to the Spree.

Whereas in Kaiser times the imperialist German concept of world power was concrete and based on definite aims attainable through a world war, Hitler's conception was broad and predicated on a whole era of piratical devastating wars. Hitler said mere victory in a world war would not satisfy him, because nothing but a permanent war, the main and only manifestation of the thousand-year Reich, could elevate the German people to a position of total dominance. This "superior race" would then, he thought, at-

---

[1] Rosenberg, *Der Mythos des 20. Jahrhunderts*, München, 1930.

[2] See A. Norden, *Fälscher. Zur Geschichte der deutsch-sowjetischen Beziehungen*, Berlin, 1966; also see *Protiv fashistskoi falsifikatsii istorii*, ed. by F. O. Notovich, Moscow-Leningrad, 1939 (Russ. ed.).

[3] Ritter, "Der Oberrhein in der deutschen Geschichte"—*Freiburger Universitätsreden*, H. 25, Freiburg, 1937, S. 36, See Berthold, op. cit., S. 76.

tain its natural state—the original form of life resembling that of the cavemen who would, however, enjoy the blessings of an austere, regimented civilisation.

No other example exists in history of a more cynical treatment by the makers of the imperialist ideology of their own progeny. Though Hitler beat the drums of the theory of the Nordic race, a wretched compilation of the quasi-scientific views of several old-time reactionary publicists— the Frenchman Gobineau,[1] the Germanised Frenchman or Frenchified German de Lagarde[2] (Bötticher) and the half-Austrian and half-Anglo-Saxon Chamberlain[3]—he did not believe in it himself and elevated it to an official doctrine merely because he thought it useful for his ends. "I know perfectly well," he admitted one day, "that scientifically nothing like a race exists. . . . But as a politician I need a concept that will enable me to destroy the existing historical foundations and replace them with an entirely new anti-historical order with an intellectual basis." But an intellectual basis was precisely what fascism never had and, by its nature, never could have. That is exactly why it aroused in its followers the basest of instincts, injecting a mass psychosis which, in combination with individual fear of reprisals, found an outlet in a blind, stultifying faith in the "leader's intuition".

Irrationalism and the appeal to baser instincts, a bestial racism, eclipsing even the extreme nationalism of the Pan-Germanists, the chiliastic idea of nazi statehood and Führership and the mystic notions of "blood and soil", combined with a brazen and aggressive bravado cloaked in the reactionary pseudo-romanticism of outwardly appealing symbols that disguised the reign of terror and the highly-organised, deadly system of concentration camps. As for the regimented German National-Socialism, it was no more than a screen for the dictatorship of the big monopolies and the vast close-knit party apparatus whose crude anti-plutocratic propaganda was actually subsidised by the plutocracy. The new order in Europe was designed to vindicate the destruction of states, big and small, the physical

---

[1] Gobineau, *Versuch über die Ungleichheit der Menschenrassen,* Bd. 1-4, Stuttgart, 1898-1902.

[2] P. de Lagarde, *Schriften für Deutschland,* Leipzig, 1933.

[3] H. S. Chamberlain, *Die Grundlagen des 19. Jahrhunderts,* Bd. 1-2, München, 1932.

annihilation of nations and the establishment of German imperialist rule over the world. The rabid anti-communism of the nazis served as a screen for subversive activities and armed aggressions launched on an unprecedented scale in all directions.

Such was this irrational, crude and cynical system of extreme national and social demagogy. Its danger was that it evoked an effective response. Pandering to the basest mob instincts, fanning these instincts, it adjusted itself shrewdly to the psychic mould, the real or imagined needs of various fairly broad sections of the nation. Sustained by the old habit of obedience and the inbred faith in the "truly German" way of life, by nationalist arrogance and the notion of a "true German", haughty and at once obsequious, it fed on the economic rewards created by the war preparations and, later, on the war itself, on the early successes of a policy of conquest, on the tangible results and advantages of the undisguised plunder of conquered lands and of the wholesale transportation to Germany of foreign workers, reduced virtually to slavery.

The history of the Third Reich was short, yet it is the most sinister chapter in the history of the world. Eager to entrench itself by means of an apocalyptic idea, it proclaimed a millennium of power, but died 988 years before its chiliastic term ran out. It lasted 12 years, of which the first six it was preoccupied in preparing for aggression and for seizures in Central Europe, and the last six waging a world war for global power on a scale never seen in history before. A sociological study of the fascist ideology, the monstrous progeny of the imperialism and militarism of its time, its emergence and consolidation, is all the more vital because its downfall in Germany did not occur until the militarist forces collapsed and surrendered.[1]

4

Not surprisingly, the present-day militarists in West Germany are going through the motions of debunking Hitler fascism and its discredited ideology.

---

[1] See the interesting though in many respects debatable book by E. Nolte, *Faschismus in seiner Epoche*, München, 1963.

In the earlier period after the unconditional surrender of 1945, they were ruminating more intensely than after the defeat of 1918 on how and where they should "begin all over again". Their professed "democratic renovation" was no renovation at all, and much less a democratic one. While the "small wheels" of the nazi machine were subjected to a bureaucratic screening facetiously named "denazification", the true masters—the monopolists and militarists who had once nursed Hitler to power and backed his terrorist regime of national and social demagogy—erected a state that, propped up largely by the former Hitler bureaucracy and judiciary, purported to be parliamentary. What they needed most was a political and ideological vehicle promoting their aims and interests in the new environment to the same degree as the fascist Reich did in the past.

So they fell back on political clericalism which, not being discredited by any likeness to nazism, could strut onto the scene as a champion of "democratic renovation" based on the Christian teaching. The clericalists prattled about the "freedom of the individual", professing the ability to supplant class domination and class struggle by a system of "class peace", "social partnership" and collaboration. But their "democratic renovation" was a screen for restoring the political and ideological dominance of the monopolists.[1] The adroit idea of a "free market economy", clothed in professions of "capitalism for all" or "people's capitalism", was really a screen for the revival of the big capitalist monopolies and for recovering home and foreign connections, using the favourable economic climate of the time for certain manoeuvres in social policy. It was considered important to impede the reawakening of class consciousness in the people, to focus their interests on petty day-to-day economic demands and on the chase after petty-bourgeois prosperity. The "social partnership" idea is just a modern version of the "people's community" of nazi times. Both these "social" ideas are equally anti-social, with the one difference that the fascists drummed their demagogy

---

[1] This is registered by a number of West German observers, namely, R. Riemeck, "Wohin geht der Weg?", *Blätter für deutsche und internationale Politik*, 1958, Heft 6, and A. von Borries, "Der demokratische Vorhang", Ibid., 1958, Heft 7.

into the heads of people by frankly terroristic means, while the present clerical system employs a wider, more flexible array of methods. The West German Social-Democrats observed that "at a time of universal contentment the dominant social system needs no ideological defences, for its 'miracles' are attributed to the 'social market economy'. The place of ideologists is then occupied by writers of advertising texts."[1] That, of course, is an exaggeration, but it has a rational grain. On the other hand, the idea of parliamentary democracy put forward by the exponents of political clericalism was essentially a cover for efforts to consolidate a state machine in which nazi cadres occupied many an important post. Soon this was followed by efforts aimed at restoring the traditional military alliances and building up the Bundeswehr as a new powerhouse for aggressive German militarism.

On gaining its legs, the clerico-militarist regime declared a cold war against its real and potential foes, against all progressive forces who expressed their discontent with the come-back of reaction and called for a genuine renovation along democratic lines. There began a political and ideological offensive not only against communist ideas, but against progressive ideas generally. Communism has been officially proclaimed beyond the pale of the law and society, but anti-militarism and anti-fascism, too, are subjected to continuous persecution. Political clericalism and militarism seek to bolster their position as champions of "order" and state "prestige". "Democratic renovation" has gradually become a kind of semi-autocratic regime run by monopolists and militarists.

The élite conception,[2] designed to substantiate "select"

---

[1] Vorwärts, October 31, 1958.

[2] The élite problem was dealt with in a large number of works appearing in West Germany. E.g., see R. Michels, Zur Soziologie des Parteiwesens in der modernen Demokratie. Untersuchungen über die oligarchischen Tendenzen des Gruppenlebens, Leipzig, 1925; M. Weber, Wirtschaft und Gesellschaft, Tübingen, 1921; G. Mosca, Die herrschende Klasse. Grundlagen der politischen Wissenschaft, München, 1950; E. W. Mommsen, Elitebildung in der Wirtschaft, Darmstadt, 1955; H. Zahrnt, Probleme der Elitebildung. Von der Bedrohung und Bewahrung des Einzelnen in der Massenwelt, Hamburg, 1955, etc. Also see Marxist critiques of the West German élite theories: E. Gottschling, " 'Moderne' Elitetheorien in Westdeutschland", Staat und Recht, Berlin,

leadership in economic, social and political affairs, is stridently extolled. True, that is no novelty: time and again we saw it in different garbs in the imperialist epoch: clothed in Nietzsche's aphorisms about the "superman", the only one able to rule and lead the masses, in the form of Spengler's apologia of extreme individualism as the supreme manifestation of the messiahship of the cultured Western select, and as the extremist fascist ideology, which raised the *Führer* cult to an oracular official doctrine, persuading the masses that blind faith and soldierly obedience to the select nazi élite endowed with an iron will, and hence with power, was the true expression of "the national German spirit".

After the Third Reich was defeated and the fascist ideology collapsed, the more discredited of the élite ideas were relegated to the background, especially those contradicting the elementary concepts of bourgeois democracy; German imperialism, after all, was reviving its ideology under the slogan of "freedom" and "democratic renovation". So, at first, the advocates of the élite conception confined themselves to minor researches of a sociological and psychological complexion and to republishing the old Italian elite theorists, the forerunners of the fascist ideology in Italy. But as West Germany was gradually remodelled into a clerico-militarist state, the élite notion reappeared, albeit in a somewhat different form, as part of the general imperialist and militarist ideology. None other than G. Schröder, a Bonn cabinet minister, declared that "neither widespread social resentment nor the terrible deeds of the nazi élite can make us accept the false idea that the élite conception is totally negative".[1]

The many exponents of the élite conception maintain that in contradistinction to the "falsification of the élite idea" in the "totalitarian autocratic systems", they would establish a scientifically grounded conception "inherent in the democratic system". What exactly did they mean?

J. H. Knoll, for example, wrote that "the élite is a dynamic notion, applying to the select group which possesses

---

1957, Heft 7, S. 691-708 and *Herrschaft der Elite? Gegen eine reaktionäre Theorie*, Berlin, 1958.

[1] Schröder, "Elitebildung und soziale Verpflichtung. Ansprache vor der Evangelischen Akademie Bad Boll am 15. Januar 1955" (*Schriftenreihe der Bundeszentrale für Heimatdienst*, 1955, Heft 12, S. 6.).

the faculty to imbue, form and lead a community by means of its exemplary conception of order. . . . The liberal conception of the élite is based on notions best defined with the words 'property and education' ".[1] O. Stammer,[2] on the other hand, held that the élite is an expression less of social and class privilege and much more of the function inherent in certain groups in a democratic environment, while Max zu Solms[3] was inclined to believe that even in a "real democracy" the élite becomes a "qualitatively aristocratic ideal". As for M. Freund, he said the "élite is marked by exclusive qualities which attract like a magnet all people of the same mould. In particular, it applies to people marked out by destiny for active guidance of the affairs of the community."[4]

In this chorus of opinion there stand out two basic points, which, in effect, represent the functional purpose of the élite theory: first, the contraposition of the "élite" to the "masses" which ostensibly "are not people identifiable by profession, status, income or education"[5] (W. Martini, for example, maintains that for this reason an industrialist may come under the head of "masses" alongside an unskilled worker); and second, the definition of the élite as immanent in social and political life but endowed with an inexplicable force. "This force," Freund said, "is an accident, a blessing, a miracle. Human inequality is a fact . . . hardly explicable."[6]

Examining the structure of society at a time of "democratic renovation", the élite-builders have, in essence, veered off to the irrational. The élite theory is, by and large, a new form of social demagogy by ruling classes that have a stake in disguising the depth of the social antagonisms

---

[1] Knoll, *Führungsauslese in Liberalismus und Demokratie,* Stuttgart, 1957, S. 12, 15.

[2] Stammer, "Das Eliteproblem in der Demokratie", *Schmollers Jahrbuch für Gesetzgebung. Verwaltung und Volkswirtschaft,* Berlin, 1951, Heft 5.

[3] M. zu Solms, "Echte Demokratie und Elitegedanke", *Aus der Werkstatt des Sozialforschers,* Frankfurt a/M, 1948, No. 3.

[4] Freund, "Das Eliteproblem in der modernen Politik", *Politische Bildung. Schriftenreihe der Hochschule für Politische Wissenschaften,* München, 1954, Heft 46, S. 237.

[5] Martini, *Das Ende aller Sicherheit, Eine Kritik des Westens,* Stuttgart, 1954, S. 111.

[6] Freund, op. cit., S. 238.

bred by monopoly capital rule. In their efforts to prove that an élite in the economic field does not conflict with liberalism and democracy, Knoll averred that none but "big technicians" can control a modern economy; over are the times, he said, when the big monopolists and industrialists like Stinnes and Krupp[1] could handle things by themselves.

It is childish to assume that these sociological concepts were designed to inhibit the influence of the Western monopolists in economic, social and political affairs. Quite the reverse. The main ideological trend is to prove that the monopolists play first fiddle as top "technicians" of the "economic wonder" irradiating welfare for the masses obliged to put their energy and labour into building "people's capitalism". Alongside the new forms of social demagogy, therefore, apologetics in behalf of the German monopolists have attained unprecedented scope: imitating the U.S. fad for histories of Big Business, the West German book market is flooded with biographies and monographs,[2] singing praises to the accomplishments of Vögler, Krupp, Thyssenn and some of the other prominent German monopolists. Gert von Klass, one of the most fruitful writers of biographies, describes Albert Vögler as "a knight *sans* fear and *sans* reproach".[3] It stands to reason that authors gloss over the role played by these knights in "shining armour" in sponsoring imperialist expansion, aggression and two world wars.

There is a direct link between this and the other side of the clerico-militarist political doctrine: restoration of the ideology of the Holy Alliance as an instrument for combating the progressive forces—now communism, the socialist camp and the democratic movement in Europe and elsewhere. This ideology, represented in the United States by John Foster Dulles and in West Germany by Konrad Adenauer, is based no more on the monarchist principle. While championing legitimism and the immunity of capi-

---

[1] Knoll, op. cit., S. 214.
[2] E.g., see G. v. Klass, *Albert Vögler*, Tübingen, 1957; *Die drei Ringe*, Tübingen, 1953; *Die Wollspindel. Ein schwäbisches Familienporträt*, Tübingen, 1955; *Hugo Stinnes*, Tübingen, 1958; L. Schwerin v. Krosigk, *Die grosse Zeit des Feuers. Der Weg der deutschen Industrie*, Bd. 1-3, Tübingen, 1957-59.
[3] G. v. Klass, *Albert Vögler*, S. 241.

talism, it makes use of the ideas of "freedom" and "democracy" as distinct from "autocracy" and "totalitarianism". The exponents of the Holy Alliance idea have restored to life the mystic contraposition of Christ to Antichrist by counterposing the "Christian West" to the "Communist East" and using it as an excuse for the aggressive politico-military *Nato* system in which West Germany serves as a springboard and the main shock force in Europe. Active and belligerent anti-communism is thus the groundwork for all clericalist political ideas of the cold war period in both home and foreign policy. Revanchism is forging to the forefront more and more candidly as the positions of the German militarists grow firmer in the NATO system, and it would be interesting, therefore, to trace some of the milestones in the evolution of the revenge-seeking ideology through the post-war period.

5

After the 1945 collapse, historico-philosophical and politico-historical thinking in Germany was for a time in a state of profound shock. "German history," wrote Meinecke, patriarch of the liberal wing of the neo-Ranke school, in 1946, "is punctuated by almost insoluble puzzles and sad turns. But the puzzle we face today and the catastrophe we have suffered surpass anything we have seen in the past."[1] Gerhard Ritter, Meinecke's antipode, spoke in the same vein. "A cloud has been cast forever on the sense of our mysterious history by the sudden demise of our national state. Where one cannot see a future there can be no interpretation of the past." He described as "unexampled confusion and bewilderment" the general ideological state of those who, one would think, were called upon to apprehend the past in order to find new ways to the future.[2] But even then, in those early years after the Second World War, the men who pretended to be the bearers of German liberalism, democratism and humanism, found their bearings quickly and, sensing the tasks set them by the im-

---

[1] Meinecke, *Die deutsche Katastrophe*, Wiesbaden, 1946, S. 5.
[2] Ritter, *Geschichte als Bildungsmacht,* Stuttgart, 1946, S. 17, 7; also see W. Berthold, op. cit., S. 135.

perialist rulers of West Germany, cast about for philosophical and historical arguments that would restore the
prestige of the German militarists and their politico-moral
nimbus, to maintain which so much effort had been expend-
ed for decade after decade.

To begin with, they took account of the military defeat
of Hitler Germany and the resultant change in the post-
war balance of forces, revising their previous conceptions
of history. It was farthest from their thoughts, however,
to break loose from militarist tradition; they attempted a
reassessment that would respond to the political tasks of
the present and future.

Shortly before the partition of Germany, anticipating it
from the standpoint of reactionary German nationalism,
Ritter declared that in the post-war environment "a revision of the traditional conception of German history has
become a compulsive political task".[1] True, Ritter proceeded from the main issue of modernity: "Should we consider Hitlerism an inevitable outgrowth of Prusso-German
political thought? Has the crude spirit of conquest and aggression which sparked off the Second World War always
been the distinguishing property of Prusso-German politics?"[2] Yet this approach blocked a genuine solution because, as Ritter's Marxist critic, Werner Berthold, rightly
notes, it evaded the actual problem of fascism, of its socio-
economic and political roots.[3] Limiting himself to the question of ideological tradition, Ritter waded into the set of
notions typical for bourgeois historiography and the political writing in Western Europe and the United States. That,
indeed, was what he wanted. An antipode to Meinecke
(who, as we know, strove for the convergence of German
thought with Western ideas in a treatise written in Weimar
days, *Die Idee der Staatsräson in der neueren Geschichte*),
Ritter now revised his attitude to the West, recognised
Meinecke's view as valid and plunged into the central
problem of modern German history, that of militarism.

Militarism's role was an object of considerable controversy, especially after a German translation of John Wheeler-
Bennett's book, *The Nemesis of Power*, which delved

---

[1] Ritter, *Europa und die deutsche Frage*, München, 1948, S. 7.
[2] Ibid., S. 193.
[3] See Berthold, op. cit., S. 145.

into the role of the German army in the political affairs of recent times (1918-45),[1] appeared on the bookstands. It was not a history of German militarism in the general sense. Neither was it a history of the German army (the *Reichswehr* or the *Wehrmacht*). All it showed, with documentary support, was how the German army, profiting from the 1918 defeat, succeeded in recovering its strength and, moreover, in becoming a prominent political factor in the Weimar Republic. Wheeler-Bennett showed how the German generals who withdrew from the public political scene, actually, to an "amazing degree", built up strength and influence in political matters and then helped the nazis come to power, doing nothing at all to rein in the regime of fascist dictatorship. "It is, in fact, the story of how the German army, having achieved supreme power within the state, threw away the substance for the shadow," Wheeler-Bennett wrote, "and became a victim to the Nemesis of this action."[2] In some respects, the British writer added, it was also "a moral tale". He pointed to the days when the army was a "national industry of Prussia" and thought it historically essential that "the infection of the virus of the *furor Teutonicus*" should be "eradicated from the body politic of Germany". One would think that this entailed the eradication of the entire system of German militarism, the only effective measure that could create a healthy political atmosphere. But the author thought differently; he hoped that the danger of a militarist revival in Germany could be removed by inducting the *Bundeswehr* into the NATO system. He was not quite certain, it is true, that his political conclusions were watertight. After all, he had learned the political methods of the German *Generalität* and feared that at first the *Wehrmacht* would march to the words of the *Wacht am Rhein* and one day finish up with those of *Deutschland über alles*.[3]

The reaction to Wheeler-Bennett's book was violent. Some West German historians attacked his postulate that the *Reichswehr* should remain what it was in General Seeckt's time, that is, a "non-political" factor, and that General Schleicher's departure from this position resulted

---

[1] Wheeler-Bennett, *The Nemesis of Power. The German Army in Politics 1918-1945*, London, 1953.
[2] Wheeler-Bennett, op. cit., p. X.
[3] Ibid.

in the marriage of German militarism and the fascist dictatorship.[1] Others accused him of treating the subject from the standpoint of Britain, that long-time rival of Germany, and underrating or deliberately minimising the politico-national accomplishments of the German army and its generals even at the time of the nazi dictatorship. Later, the Bundeswehr's public relations men averred that the British writer had exaggerated and dramatised the destiny of German militarism as a "Nemesis of power"; much sooner, they maintained, it had been a "Nemesis of impotence". And they drew the conclusion that after its revival German militarism should advance hand in hand with the country's political leadership.[2] The evolution of the views on this score was described as an "enormous exaggeration and glorification of the militarist consciousness in writings about the peace and war of the Third Reich" which in 1945 was replaced by a "devastating verdict against German militarism. . . . Ten years later the pendulum swung back so far that, highlighted by rearmament, soldier newspapers and war memoirs seem to be gaining predominance on the opinion-forming market."[3]

It should be added that the various *Soldatenzeitungen* and the profusion of *Kriegsmemoiren* about the nazi eastern campaign are prominently complemented by reactionary historians posing as critics of the past and seeking to furnish the ideas and the role of German militarism with a scientific firman. Most typical are the efforts of Gerhard Ritter.

Whereas Meinecke's meditation on the nature and causes of the "German catastrophe" and his appeals for self-determination through a regeneration of the classical humanism of Goethe's time[4] mirrored the bewilderment of the German bourgeoisie and intellectuals in the early years

---

[1] H. Herzfeld, "Das Deutsche Heer als geschichtliches Problem", *Zeitschrift für Politik* No. 2, 1954, S. 273 ff; O. E. Schüddekopf, "Wehrmacht und Politik in Deutschland", *Politische Literatur* Nos. 3-4, 1954, K. D. Bracher, *Die Auflösung der Weimarer Republik,* Stuttgart-Düsseldorf, 1955, S. 264, 326.
[2] Ritter, "Nemesis der Ohnmacht", *Frankfurter Allgemeine Zeitung,* April 20, 1955; W. Hubatsch, *Historische Zeitschrift*, 1956, Bd. 182, Heft 2, S. 417.
[3] K. D. Bracher, "Die deutsche Armee zwischen Republik und Diktatur (1918-1945)", *Schicksalsfragen der Gegenwart*, Bd. I, S. 95-120.
[4] Meinecke, *Die deutsche Katastrophe,* S. 172.

after Hitler's collapse, Ritter worked deliberately throughout the post-war period for the restoration and, subsequently, self-assertion of the militarist ideology, as witnessed by his works on the strategic Schlieffen plan, the generals' conspiracy of July 20, 1944, and the basic problems of German militarism.[1] But what is more remarkable still is the politico-ideological content of his works; it shows that Ritter not only reflects and forms, but also anticipates, the general trend of militarist growth.[2] Like Ludwig Dehio,[3] another prominent historian, he is reluctant to discard the *Weltpolitik* idea. He treats it as the basic geopolitical principle in 20th-century world history. In 1947, Ritter held that a "total change" (*totale Wende*) had come about in the world and that the future would depend "only on two world powers or groups of powers of top rank". He was referring to the "Anglo-Saxon sea powers", on the one hand, and the "Russian continental power", on the other. "The natural contraposition of the 'insular' and 'continental' methods and ideals," he concluded, "will thereby enter a global stage."[4]

What bothered Ritter was the place the Western, imperialist part of Germany would occupy in this line-up. He asserted the historical role played by German militarism and used the stratagem of displacement or, more precisely, distortion to declare that militarism and the fascist principle of a "total people's state" were a legacy of the 18th-century French revolution, while the source of the "inherently warlike form of national consciousness" stemmed from the people's movements.[5] Like all reactionaries, he defined humanism as a "rootless cosmopolitanism"[6] and

---

[1] Ritter, *Staatskunst und Kriegshandwerk. Das Problem des "Militarismus" in Deutschland*, Bd. I-II, München, 1959-60; *Der Schlieffen-Plan. Kritik eines Mythos*, München, 1956.

[2] E. Engelberg, "Über das Problem des deutschen Militarismus", *Zeitschrift für Geschichtswissenschaft*, 1956, Heft 6, S. 1113-45; W. Berthold, "Der politisch-ideologische Weg Gerhard Ritters, eines führenden Ideologen der deutschen Bourgeoisie", *Zeitschrift für Geschichtswissenschaft*, 1958, Heft 5, S. 959-89.

[3] Dehio, *Gleichgewicht oder Hegemonie*, Krefeld, 1948; *Deutschland und die Weltpolitik im 20. Jahrhundert*, München, 1955.

[4] Ritter, *Dämonie der Macht*, München, 1947, S. 161.

[5] Ritter, *Staatskunst und Kriegshandwerk,* Bd. I, München, 1959, S. 327.

[6] Ritter, *Dämonie der Macht,* München, 1947, S. 74.

Hitler's "demonism" as a "mixture of good and evil intentions".[1] He called August Bebel a "German nationalist"[2] and Bismarck a "true European",[3] and said that the source of "demoniac power" lay in the irrational impact of nationalist and aggressive mass sentiments, which, he held, had "prompted the leaders" to begin the war,[4] pinpointing as "the real secret" of Hitler's rapid ascent that the nazi *Führer* solved the "problem of the 19th century: the merging of nationalism and socialism".[5] As for Marxism, Ritter avers that ever since its inception it had been an "aggressively expansionist and militarist force".

Need we continue this exposition of mental juggling designed to rehabilitate and reinstate German militarism? As a historian and contemporary, Ritter is perfectly well aware of the political purport behind such rehabilitation. Lamenting the dissolution of the Prussian state (in 1947), he wrote: "He who reflects on the manifestations of the spirit of Friedrich in German history ... will find good cause to think about the impact of the disappearance of the powerful old Prussian military force on the 'West's' easternmost frontier on its present and future."[6] By and large, Ritter pursued his apology along the following lines: firstly, he endeavoured to show that the *Generalität* is not a "militaristic" category, because even under Hitler's "demoniac power" it had allegedly applied the brakes on the nazi war policy and engaged exclusively in rebuilding a defensive army; secondly, he endeavoured to demonstrate that throughout its history, the Prussian, and later the German General Staff, and the corps of generals as a whole, who performed their duties within the "technical" limits, never went beyond the purely military questions and always submitted to political leadership (violations of these tra-

---

[1] H. Picker, *Hitlers Tischgespräche im Führershauptquartier, 1941-1942*. Im Auftrage des Deutschen Instituts für Geschichte der nationalsoziologischen Zeit geordnet, eingeleitet und veröffentlicht von G. Ritter, Bonn, 1951, S. 28.

[2] Ritter, *Europa und die deutsche Frage*, S. 98.

[3] Ritter, *Europa und die deutsche Frage*, S. 205; see Engelberg, "NATO—Politik und die Westdeutsche Historiographie über die Probleme des 19. Jahrhunderts", *Zeitschrift für Geschichtswissenschaft*, 1959, Heft 3.

[4] Ritter, *Europa und die deutsche Frage*, S. 140.

[5] Ibid., S. 191.

[6] Ritter, *Friedrich der Grosse*, Heidelberg, 1954, S. 260.

ditions by Hindenburg and Ludendorff during the First World War therefore had fatal consequences); thirdly, if, in defiance of all tradition, the conspirators of July 20, 1944, had lifted their hand against the head of state, they did so because the situation then was "absolutely exclusive", Germany being enthralled by a group of criminals who were dragging her into the abyss of a military disaster; fourthly, the fact that the conspiracy failed was a disaster whose consequences spread far beyond Germany, because "ever since then the shadow of the Bolshevik world power hovers over Europe".[1]

The general historical conclusion arrived at by Ritter is that German militarism saved "Germany's honour" and, moreover, is destined to "deliver Europe from the communist threat". Clearly, this politico-historical concept is designed not only to whitewash German militarism by contraposing it artificially to nazism, but also to play up the entire political scheme associated with West Germany's admission to the aggressive NATO system.

Those were the aims and results of the revision of one of the traditional conceptions of German history. Spawned by the ideas of Prusso-German militarism, the doctrine, after a certain repatterning, was well geared to the new politico-ideological tasks: it was faithful to its purpose, it served to rehabilitate its component ideas and endeavoured to consolidate and expand their influence throughout the "West". In the final analysis, Ritter's ideas are a somewhat modified variety of the old German nationalism and militarism, peppered with modern anti-communism of the cold war period.

Ritter's conception was criticised, and historians of the neo-Ranke school were the first to do so, but not because of its militarist orientation. To them it looked too traditional. Ludwig Dehio came out with another concept, purporting to cover all the present problems of German history in the context of "20th-century world politics". He took account of the lessons of the two world wars and the two defeats, and in word was ready to renounce the old Prusso-German militarism. It appeared to be an appeal for profound

---

[1] Ritter, "Der 20. Juli 1944. Die Wehrmacht und der politische Wiederstand gegen Hitler", *Schicksalsfragen der Gegenwart*, Bd. I, S. 349-81.

self-criticism. "We Germans," he wrote, "endeavoured by means of a truly Prussian method—that is, by systematic arming—to launch out beyond the narrowly European limits into the cherished system of world balance just as once Prussia ventured into the European balance system. . . . But where did the irreversible results of our undertaking bring us? They put us on the path of world war: we and we alone menaced the vital nerve centres of Britain."[1] Clinging to the primacy of foreign policy and the "battle for hegemony" postulated by the neo-Ranke school as the basic concept of modern history, Dehio said the Second World War was rooted in the results of the First, the victors of which had not renovated the "European system" to the extent to which the reactionary Holy Alliance once had, securing for Europe a period of long peace after the Napoleonic wars. The craving for hegemony that had earlier seized Germany and now coalesced with revanchism, needed an outlet. In Germany, Dehio maintained, on two occasions "there germinated ideas of expansion: the Reformation and Marxism. But it was not German politics that benefited."[2] This is why, sharpened by the fight against Marxism and Bolshevism and equipped with the Prusso-German tradition of power, "a formless revolutionary violence (revolutionärformloser Gewaltsamkeit), hegemonism was transformed into a new fascist dynamism".[3]

Hitler was pictured as a concentrated embodiment of an "extremist struggle for hegemony". "It is simply incomprehensible," Dehio exclaimed, "how Germany could have again risen to such giddy heights without that satanical genius."[4] But the "giddier" the height the harder was the fall, and although Dehio tried to depict it as the typical fate of a "hegemonic power", he pleaded that "in the chain of European wars for hegemony . . . the German fight was the last of the series". In 1945, Dehio claimed, "the path was open to a new world history" highlighted by a "Russo-Anglo-Saxon rivalry for world power".[5] Those are the terms in which Dehio described U.S. imperialism's

---

[1] Dehio, *Deutschland und die Weltpolitik im 20. Jahrhundert,* München, 1955, S. 14-15.
[2] Ibid., S. 34.
[3] Ibid., S. 25.
[4] Ibid., S. 30.
[5] Ibid., S. 32.

efforts to capture hegemony and pursue the policy of "rolling back communism".

With the two world systems locked in struggle, the Federal Republic of Germany was faced from the beginning by the question of what role it should play. The German school of history was naturally aware of this. To use H. Heimpel's words, "the attempt to live with the past"[1] as an attempt to substantiate the role of "history and the science of history in our time" was, in effect, nothing but an attempt to salvage the reactionary ideology and reactionary traditions. In practical terms, it boiled down to disguising the political constructions and aims put forward by the ruling classes, their system of political clericalism and revived militarism, behind a screen of historical sophisms. Medieval Germany was idealised, and the "empire idea" (*Reichsidee*) was championed as a supra-historical absolute, leading particularly to the glorification of the Carolingian empire as the nucleus of the "Romano-Germanic West" and of medieval clericalism. All this, by inference, was designed to justify the imperialist idea of a German *Reich* and *Kleineuropa*.[2] On the other hand, "current history" is described as seeking "a key in studies of the recent past to the big changes" which took place at a critical period in the history of German imperialism and should "entail changes also in the historical and political understanding of the world".[3]

Thus, the ideological task of "current history", Rothfels avers, is profoundly political: not only to overcome the "relativist scepticism" but also to produce "a spiritual discipline as an auxiliary force of cognition and self-education in the sphere of moral solutions".[4]

"Current history" studies assume different organisational forms: ideological work in the subject has spread to uni-

---

[1] Heimpel, "Der Versuch mit der Vergangenheit zu Leben. Über die Geschichte und Geschichtswissenschaft in unserer Zeit", *Frankfurter Allgemeine Zeitung*, March 25, 1959.

[2] T. Büttner, " 'Abendland' Ideologie und Neo-Karolingertum im Dienste der Adenauer-CDU", *Zeitschrift für Geschichtswissenschaft*, 1959, Heft 8, S. 1803 ff.

[3] P. Kluke, "Aufgaben und Methoden zeitgeschichtlicher Forschung", *Europa-Archiv*, April 5, 1955; also see Heimpel, "Der Mensch in seiner Gegenwart", *Die Sammlung*, September 1951.

[4] H. Rothfelt, "Zeitgeschichte als Aufgabe", *Vierteljahrshefte für Zeitgeschichte* No. 1, 1953, S. 8.

versities and specialised institutes, Catholic and Evangelical institutions and "Eastern study" centres. All are largely co-ordinated by the War Ministry and its "psychological warfare agencies".[1] While studies of German fascism are ultimately designed to contrapose nazism and German militarism in order to vindicate the latter, "Eastern studies" (*Ostforschung*) are chiefly aimed at substantiating the revisionist aspirations of German imperialism against Poland, Czechoslovakia and the Soviet Union. "Eastern studies", like "current history", have many hues, variations and aspects—all to prove the advantages of the "Atlantic community", supplemented of late by elaborate disquisitions to prove that Poland and Czechoslovakia historically belong to the "West".

On the other hand, we have seen many attempts to co-ordinate the histories of countries in the system of "European integration", or more broadly, the aggressive NATO system. Historiographers of different countries were deeply engrossed in the subject at special co-ordinating conferences: the most candid nationalist and militarist concepts of German imperialism were relegated to the background, making room for pseudo-democratic ideas which glossed over the contradictions between the different West European countries and proclaimed the common destiny of the "Western world", obscuring the facts and problems related to the aggressive aspirations of German imperialism and the militarist forces and traditions operative in the history of Prussia and Germany. The main effort of the West German historians is concentrated on proving that Germany has always belonged to the "free world", that it is one of the components of "Western culture" and, moreover, on affirming Germany's mission in Europe as that of a shock force in the battle against the East. This is why the "psychological warfare" merchants are so eager to prove the independent role played by German imperialism in the "West" and in Europe. Hermann Aubin maintains that West, Reich, Germany and Europe are politically, culturally and religiously related concepts, and commends Germany for checking the invasion of the East into Europe. Aubin does not deny that the German imperialists were

[1] W. Heide, "Wesen und Funktion der 'psychologischen Kriegführung' der Bonner Machthaber", *Einheit*, 1959, Heft 12, S. 1666.

predatory, but vindicates them, among other things, by qualifying the capture of Czechoslovakia in 1938 as the enforcement of historical German rights recognised by the "West". He would even give credit to the Hitler clique, he says, if it had won the war "against Russia and communism in the interests of the West", but deplores the fact that by starting a war in the West, Hitler "compromised the idea of a Western community". Today, Aubin says, the concept of "Europe" has a new content: "it is the name for the West", epitomised "in the main" by the dominance of the European Coal and Steel Community and Euratom. This new "Europe" and "Russia", he concludes, are at loggerheads, with Germany playing an active role in resolving the contradictions.[1]

It was part of the clericalist ideology of the "Adenauer era" that imperialist Germany's mission was to be the leader of Europe. Aubin dealt with the question from politico-historical positions, while the ruling party hitched its aspirations abroad to the motives of its home and religious policy. P. W. Wenger, one of the Adenauer's experts on ideology, maintained in his book, *Who Will Win Germany?,* that it was high time for Bonn to find ways of exploiting the existing situation and "winning" Europe. "The tragic fault of the Germans for causing a schism is now absolved by the political *Union der Christen,* a coalition of all sections of the population from the standpoint of home policy which faces a great historical task. It must rectify in the heart of Europe the main consequences of the split of the faith, national separation and atheistic materialism. That is how the West will redeem itself as a free Christian and federalist community of nations, as an intermediary of universal peace between the American and Asian systems of states, and show an inspiring example by resolving world problems arising in Europe."[2]

Those are the pretensions of the top West German imperialist party in terms of political clericalism.

True, some of the "psychological warfare" merchants think it wiser to be less candidly nationalist and more quasi-democratic, operating with formulas such as "per-

---

[1] Aubin, "Abendland, Reich, Deutschland und Europa", *Schicksalsfragen der Gegenwart*, Bd. I, S. 29-63.
[2] P. W. Wenger, *Wer gewinnt Deutschland?,* Stuttgart, 1959, S. 47.

sonal freedom", "natural right", "the people", "democratic order", etc. One of them even went so far as to say that the political realities in the Federal Republic embody, of all things, the principles of the 1789 French bourgeois revolution.[1] However, Gerhard Leibholz, writer of a book ordered by the War Ministry for the education of Bundeswehr officers, admits that ideological matters have to be co-ordinated in this interpretation with the interests of the powers of the Atlantic bloc.[2]

The "Europe idea" has been used frequently by the extremists. Before the First World War, the Pan-Germanic Union spoke of a *Mitteleuropa*; the nazis fought the Second World War for the "European idea" and a "new order in Europe", and today the same idea, somewhat refurbished, is used by the "psychological warfare" merchants as a cover for their revenge-seeking aims and interests. This is why Wenger, editor of the Catholic *Rheinischer Merkur*, came out with a plan for a clerico-federalist "new order in Europe". He envisaged an "Alliance of States" east of the Elbe connected with Catholic Western Europe.[3] That is why the "European idea" attracts them all, those who support and represent the regime of political clericalism and warlike militarism and prefer to speak in terms of democracy, and also those who make no bones about proclaiming themselves admirers of Hitler. The neo-fascists in West Germany are now ranging themselves behind the idea of a *Nation Europa*.

It is a striking paradox that the extreme reactionary and aggressive forces who bear the main blame for the untold loss of life, for unheard-of destruction, for ravaging so many human souls, have learned to blend in various proportions their extreme aggressive nationalism with "European" ideas. This is not to say that we deny the immense contribution of the European peoples to world history and culture. On the contrary, it would be a rape of history, a perversion of its essential processes, which are of universal significance, if anyone ever contraposed one of the continents or some regional complex to another, and thereby

[1] M. Göhring, "Die französische Revolution und der Moderne Staat", *Schicksalsfragen der Gegenwart*, Bd. I, S. 217-44.
[2] Leibholz, "Volk, Nation und Staat im 20. Jahrhundert", *Schicksalsfragen der Gegenwart,* Bd. I, S. 64-90.
[3] *Der Spiegel* No. 21, 1958, S. 22.

counterposed one people to another by reason of differences in their historical destinies. Regrettably, the ideology of aggressive nationalism and hegemonic aspirations thrives not only in West Germany, Western Europe and the "Western world", but also on other continents. Mankind reveres the history of India, China, Egypt and all the other regions that were the cradle of civilisation. But credit is also due to the countries of the European continent, where alongside scientific discoveries and lofty works of culture and art there developed the idea of scientific socialism and communism, which absorbed the experience of world history and represents the highest achievement in man's development, its material culture, and, what is most important, its spirit. In this sense, the history of Europe is of truly universal importance no less than the history of other, more ancient civilisations. The awakening of Asia described by Lenin at the beginning of the 20th century as a world-shaking event was influenced by social movements and ideas originating in the working class and other democratic forces of Europe. For this influence to spread it was highly relevant that the centre of the revolutionary movement and the most advanced sociopolitical ideas shifted to Russia at the beginning of the 20th century.

By and large the ideology of "anti-Europeanism" is just as pernicious and dangerous as the "Europocentrist ideology" typical of the European imperialist powers. What is more the "Europe idea" in its various forms—those of *Mitteleuropa,* the "new order in Europe", Little Europe, New Europe, and now *Nation Europa*—is part of the German imperialist ideology at different stages and in differing conditions, working against the national interest of all the European peoples, big and small. It is also working against the national interest of the German people, especially at the present phase, for it has become a tool of the militarist forces waging "psychological war" against the camp of peace, socialism and democracy, when, in a way, it is designed to justify the partition of Germany. The national interest of the German people and the future of Europe are again being sacrificed to German militarism clad now in a new uniform.

6

While the ideology dominant in the German Democratic Republic is designed, among other things, to uphold the democratic tradition of the nation and represents its basic progressive historical conception, the imperialist ideology reigning in West Germany accentuates the militarist tradition geared to the new conditions. This is why not the problem of securing peace, but the problem of coalition war,[1] not the problem of rejecting war for all time, but efforts to vindicate philosophically and historically the imperialist wars of the past and future, are being pushed there to the forefront. This explains why efforts are made to discredit the Nuremberg Tribunal, described not as an act of justice, but of high politics by victors who wished the return to the "law of Versailles".[2] Propaganda is glorifying the more prominent members of the German militarist fraternity, and endeavouring to prove that war, as such, is no crime. Last but not least, some ideologists, sidestepping the question of fascism's social roots, contend that its "totalitarianism" is ostensibly a feature it has in common with communism, to combat which resort should be made to the usual medicine: German militarism equipped with the latest weapons, nuclear included. While justifying Hitler's anti-communism, they contend that the anti-Hitler coalition, in which the Soviet Union and the Western powers fought together, was an unnatural alliance.[3] What they think is a natural alliance is a bloc of the Western powers and German imperialism against the U.S.S.R.

It is hardly surprising that in this climate of rabid anticommunism, blending with the militarist cult, calls are heard again for "German community" with, say, the Flemish and the Dutch, and calls for "hatred"[4] and revenge (against various countries[5]). Not is it surprising that again, as after the First World War, calls are also heard to fight

---

[1] Hubatsch, "Koalitionskriegführung in neuester Zeit, historisch-politisch betrachtet", *Schicksalsfragen der Gegenwart*, Bd. I, S. 245-70.
[2] Kaufmann, "Warum konnte der Krieg zum Verbrechen erklärt werden?", *Schicksalsfragen der Gegenwart*, Bd. I, S. 271-94.
[3] G. Stadtmüller, "Europäische Ostpolitik in der Geschichte", *Schicksalsfragen der Gegenwart*, Bd. I, S. 399.
[4] *Nation Europa* No. 5, 1958, S. 6.
[5] Ibid., No. 1, S. 26.

the "lie" of "war guilt". Small wonder, when Hitler generals like Speidel and Heusinger, heading NATO troops and the *Bundeswehr*, are treated as experienced "war technicians", some of the war criminals pose as "national heroes", while others, like Oberländer and Globke, hold high government offices and aggressive German nationalism and revanchism are extolled as the tool of the "European idea".

At the time of the Weimar Republic, the German imperialists played up the "war guilt question" reckoning to whitewash German imperialism, and the "Adenauer era" gave ample opportunities for pleading in behalf of Hitler fascism. The neo-fascist *Nation Europa*, for example, claims that "Hitler, to whom exaggerated and reckless demands are attributed, actually never made more than very modest demands".[1]

In the cold war climate the aggressive aspirations of some Western publicists considerably transcended the original designs of the Hitler imperialists. The rulers of the "Adenauer era" dissociated themselves from the nazi ideology spelled out in Hitler's *Mein Kampf*, but that did not prevent them from extolling J. Barnick's book, *The German Trumps*,[2] which attempted to adapt Hitler's plans in home and foreign affairs to the present situation. Barnick held that Bonn should abandon its pseudo-democratic front, that it should stop flirting with the masses because, as he put it, the masses are "foolish" and "no serious policy ... has any chance to survive" if the masses are given any sort of say.[3] Barnick contended that "German militarism alone has an ethical basis"[4] and that the old cadres could be relied upon to fulfil the mission for none but "the veteran can do his gory work with calm".[5] He called for an authoritarian regime, that is, a militarist dictatorship.

That is one of Barnick's trumps—the trump of aggressive German imperialist policy. The other trump is all-out preparations for a new war. Barnick declares that even the 1937 borders were "not historical ones"; like Hitler, he wants to capture Czechoslovakia, Austria and Poland, and

---

[1] *Nation Europa* No. 4, 1959, S. 37.
[2] Barnick, *Die deutschen Trümpfe*, Stuttgart, 1958.
[3] Ibidem.
[4] Ibid., S. 279.
[5] Ibid., S. 100-01.

pleads for the return of South Tyrole to the German fold.[1] But that is not all. He wants territories in Central and South-Eastern Europe, and in the Soviet Union too. Like Hitler, Barnick knows that his programme means a new war. But, far from shying away from war, he proclaims it desirable, even necessary. "A third world war," he writes, "is the only way under all circumstances."[2] Like a gambler he stakes everything on his trumps, knowing perfectly well that in any coming war whole towns will be levelled with the ground, and the loss of life literally incalculable.[3]

But that does not deter him. Laying claim to a place in the list of third world war criminals, as it were, he throws down his main trump—a reckless sudden massive nuclear attack against the Soviet Union. His memory is perfectly sound. He has forgotten nothing. But all the lessons of the past have been lost on him. We recall these obtuse ideas because Strauss, Bonn War Minister, found them "highly interesting" and "constructive" and thereby incorporated aggressive revanchism and the idea of a nuclear war into the political arsenal of West German "psychological warfare".

Barnick's German trumps are no novelty. They are the twins of the old, beaten trumps of German imperialism and fascism, and it is high time to discard them. What distinguishes them from Hitler's trumps is the appeal they contain for a nuclear war—a criminal and monstrous appeal stemming from the "atomic ideology" of present-day German imperialism, spelled out by the exponents of existentialism and clericalism, brought together by their common partiality for irrationalism which, having long since burst the confines of pure philosophy, has gained prominence in political thought and action. It has penetrated deep into the Catholic as well as Protestant wings—at least in terms of those leaders who, claiming sole rights to moulding public opinion, saw fit to persecute all dissidents, even within the fold of their own church. Back in 1953, Tillmanns, then prominent in Protestant circles, maintained in the *Evangelische Verantwortung*, a clericalist mouthpiece, that "human cognition, in politics as well, is not the highest

---

[1] Barnick, *Die deutschen Trümphe,* p. 166.
[2] Ibid., S. 27.
[3] Ibid., S. 31.

criterion".[1] Political irrationalism, part and parcel of political clericalism, declared itself from the beginning an aggressive force at war with scientific communism and also with the traditions of German humanism. Hermann Ehlers, former Bundestag president and an ideologist of the Christian-Democratic Union, demanded a "ruthless war on all who still think in terms of the past century, proclaiming the unity of the laws of state and political development and treating man as the measure of all values".[2] Not man and his reason, not knowledge of the objective laws governing social development, but irrationalism is the keynote in the political philosophy of the political clericalism ensconced in West Germany. That is dangerous, and doubly dangerous in our atomic age, because it is kindred to nazism.

7

Georg Mende, eminent thinker of the German Democratic Republic, demonstrated convincingly that existentialism had done much ideological spadework in paving the way for fascism. He showed that post-war German existentialism was as anti-democratic, reactionary and unscientific as ever, but that it had learned to conceal its ability to adapt itself to the general ideological and political aims of the German imperialists.[3] M. Heidegger maintained, for one thing, that the "total" nature of the world wars of our century was due to the solitude of being (*Seinsverlassenheit*) and that the line between war and peace was gradually vanishing. By so doing he linked up the old nazi ideology of "total war" with that of the present-day German imperialists, with their "cold war" against the East. How else to interpret Heidegger's contention that a state of no war germinated during the Second World War and the state of peace that followed was intrinsically senseless?[4] What did he mean by saying that it is "a secondary question whether atomic energy is used for peaceful purposes

---

[1] *Evangelische Verantwortung* No. 10, Bonn, 1953.
[2] *Zeitwende* No. 12, Hamburg, 1954.
[3] Mende, *Studien über die Existenz-Philosophie,* Berlin, 1956.
[4] Heidegger, *Vorträge und Aufsätze,* Pfullingen, 1954, S. 93.

or mobilised for war, whether the one supports or stimulates the other"?[1] Existentialism in West Germany is exerting itself to justify philosophically the cold war policy and that of arming the Bundeswehr with nuclear weapons. The apologia of cold war, it is true, began and continued while it was being put into effect, whereas the apologia of atomic war began long before any formal application was made for nuclear arms. We have to admit, therefore, that the existentialists anticipated this task a long time ahead and endeavoured to substantiate it philosophically and ethically.

One of the more impressive figures among them is Karl Jaspers. By accentuating the notion of "human fate", he forfeited all claim to originality, for he integrated that notion with the fatalistic ideas assiduously cultivated in West Germany after the war by the clericalist philosophers and historians. Fatalism was a kind of graft, a graft of impotence and doom, bred in each individual in regard not only to his own death but also to war. Not surprisingly, the Bonn War Ministry manual for the Bundeswehr is entitled, "The Questions of the Fate of Our Time". Strauss, the War Minister, explained: "The questions of the fate of our time, the answers to which are relevant for the future, cannot be understood without a knowledge of the past."[2]

This appeal to history and the concerted effort of the extreme reactionary historians to revive militarism as the basic question of the "fate of our time" was not isolated. Soon after the war Meinecke noted sadly in great bewilderment that "a radical break with our militarist past, which we must now accomplish, poses the question, however, of what will become of our historical traditions".[3] Ritter later devoted himself to reviving the militarist ideology and substantiating its traditions with regard to the present, and was joined by all reactionary historians in West Germany. Clericalism, on the one hand, and existentialism, on the other, undertook framing the basic categories of an "atomic ideology" for modern warfare. Again the irrational "fate" concept was the springboard. Where

---

[1] Heidegger, *Der Satz vom Grund,* Pfullingen, 1958, S. 199.
[2] *Schicksalsfragen der Gegenwart*, Bd. I, S. 7.
[3] Meinecke, *Die deutsche Katastrophe*, S. 156.

lie the roots of the imperialist wars that heaped on the German people and all mankind so much suffering? The West German historians, along with the sociologists and philosophers, evade the answer deliberately, because a scientific answer would flow from a deep-going study of imperialism and militarism. In that sense the notion of "human fate" devised by the irrationalists is a valuable find, because it explains nothing of the past and inhibits the natural desire to comprehend the present and future. Instead, it offers fertile soil for the notion of the war threat being fatally inevitable, since, as Jaspers maintains, "in all of us there is the violence due to which we always live under the threat of war; and that is our human fate".

We learn, too, that not only the war threat is inevitable, but war also, because it is implicit in human nature, not in the historically transient nature of capitalism and imperialism. Like Heidegger, Jaspers believes that "war takes its source in human being, in its very depth, which cannot be satisfactorily explained either as a characteristic feature, or as an objectively insoluble contradiction between individuals and groups of individuals".[1]

In examining the root and nature of wars and the prospect of peace, Jaspers will not admit bankruptcy. With the cold war in full swing, he sets out to infer from "human fate" the fatal inevitability of the arms race, of nuclear, as well as conventional, arms—a continuous, unbridled race that can end in nothing but universal military disaster. The exponents of the policy from "positions of strength" and cold war were convinced then in the nuclear superiority of the United States. They were sure the Soviet Union would never catch up. In spite of this, or perhaps for this very reason, Jaspers tried to substantiate the necessity of continued nuclear arming, because U.S. superiority, he reckoned, could not be sustained unless the destructive power of its weapons continued to grow, while every new invention, despite efforts to keep it secret, eventually became known to all. His general conclusion was that the arms race is the only possible option, until, finally, the globe is turned to cosmic dust.

Haranguing for nuclear militarism, Jaspers attacked the

---

[1] Jaspers, *Rechenschaft und Ausblick. Reden und Aufsätze*, München, 1958, S. 300.

mass movement opposing the nuclear arming of West Germany. He described it as "polite vituperation against the atom bomb", and from the height of his philosophical Olympus declared senseless state-imposed measures banning the use of nuclear weapons. His conjectures rested on the false premise, or self-deception, that capitalism is superior to socialism in terms of science and technology.

Then this notion was dashed. The policy from "positions of strength" and the arms race became senseless. But German militarism remained true to its aims and, consequently, its ideology, tailored to disguise or justify its designs. What is more, buttressing its position and extending its influence in NATO, it strove to embark on active nuclear arming, evoking sharp protests from the advanced German intellectuals (above all the nuclear physicists) and the foremost section of the working class.

German militarism, chief culprit of the "total" disasters suffered by the German people, is now a potential architect of "total" nuclear annihilation.

The post-war ideology of anti-communism, anti-Sovietism and revanchism needed to be modified. New arguments were needed to suit the new situation. But again the German imperialist ideology revealed its sterility: the idea of death cannot be creative, as borne out by further developments or, more properly, the regeneration of Jasper's existentialist philosophy. Reflecting on the political scene of our time, Jaspers fell back on "human fate" as the irrational substance of world history, in the centre of which he placed Western Europe, describing it as the sole abode of the supreme cultural values and the ideas of "freedom and truth".[1] Juggling with terms and concepts, twisting their meaning, Jaspers identified "totalitarianism" and communism, opposing the latter to the "Western world's" capitalist system based on "freedom". This "freedom", he said, was imperiled by "total domination", of which the material basis was unprecedented "technicalisation" and the ideological basis was "the Marxist-Communist doctrine". All this, he added, combined to create circumstances in which "man ceases to be himself".

What is more, sensing his incapacity for fighting Marx-

---

[1] Jaspers, *Die Atombombe und die Zukunft des Menschen. Politisches Bewusstsein in unserer Zeit*, München, 1958.

ism and communism with truly scientific arguments, Jaspers hastened to draw the "iron curtain" in order to attain complete "freedom"—the freedom of producing truly fantastic fabrications about communism. He averred that communism sought "world-wide totalitarian domination". He inferred that mankind, seeking self-assertion, would be subjected to "total" control by the nuclear bomb, whose dosed use would destroy masses of men without entirely destroying mankind. As if this were not enough, he adds: what could be expected defies the imagination because it seems humanly impossible and therefore impracticable.[1]

Yet his appalling brainchild is loaded with an ideological function transcending the limits of existentialist philosophy. Jaspers holds that "Western solidarity" is the only thing that can guarantee the spiritual "wealth" of capitalism from destruction. He pleads for reinforcing NATO, in which West Germany can and should play an increasingly prominent and active role by virtue of its geographic location and its economic and strategic potential. But that is not all, and not the most important. As Jaspers sees it, any stop to nuclear arming would add to the war peril. In a speech "To Germans: Freedom and Peace", he declared that "peace is not any absence of the ability to fight".[2] But he did not plead for fighting the war threat. On the contrary, what he thought was that in the nuclear age man has to face up to his doom: "For technological reasons man is in a plight he has himself created but not foreseen."[3]

One would think that this should lead to the plea for complete, universal and controlled nuclear disarmament, with atomic energy, that greatest of all human discoveries, being turned solely to peaceful uses and technical progress. But the German existentialist sticks to his irrationalism, leading up to the conclusion that the present-day Westerner has no choice, and, consequently, no future: in protecting his being, he can no longer depend on the divine blessing and must avail himself of the atom bomb, the means of his own destruction. That leads to the sermon of a preventive nuclear war. Existentialism is thus a phi-

[1] Ibid., S. 229.

[2] Jaspers, "An die Deutschen: Freiheit und Frieden", *Die Welt*, Hamburg, Sept. 30, 1958.

[3] Jaspers, *Die Atombombe und die Zukunft des Menschen*, S. 400.

losophy of national despair, of suicide, a monstrous philosophy that eclipses even the fascist theory of "total war", an immoral philosophy of nuclear disaster and global death.

Nor is it purely a construction of the German existentialists. It is disseminated by the Bonn rulers, by the slick press, even by the church. The whole clericalist system is deployed to justifying nuclear weapons for the Bundeswehr and implanting in all minds the idea that nuclear war is both necessary and inevitable. Adenauer, who sought to conceal the truth, said that nuclear arms in Bundeswehr possession are no more than a projection of modern artillery. Strauss called for a nuclear "sword and shield" and the risk of a "lesser war". Influential religious circles, both Protestant and Catholic, are quite prepared to give the nuclear war a theological groundwork and to justify it ethically.

This writer discussed the nuclear threat with a prominent West Berlin Protestant leader, who argued that the "atomic ideology" in West Germany is but a philosophical exercise of individual existentialists, nothing more. He sidestepped the serious issue raised not by philosophers but by the militarists. Prominent Protestants, like Dibelius and Thielicke, have publicly called for nuclear arms. Even official Protestant quarters (the all-German Synod, among others) have, in effect, by elastic theological formulas, ranged themselves behind the idea of a nuclear war. True, pastors, like Niemöller and Mochalski, have taken a courageous stand against nuclear arms, knowing that the "atomic ideology" contradicts the vital interests of the German people, as well as Christian ethics. Naturally, their stand is directed against militarism.

The Catholic Church, for its part, is closely connected with the ruling party both politically and organisationally, and took a hand from the beginning in fertilising the nuclear war idea, covertly at first, but consistently and methodically, and more in the political than the theologico-ethical context. Later, all restraints were cast off. Falling back on the main religious dogmas, the Catholic Church declared itself publicly in favour of the ideology of nuclear war, portraying what is its profound immorality as a supreme postulate of Christian ethics. This was proclaimed from the rostrum of the Catholic Academy in Bavaria to an audience of politicians and Bundeswehr officers, theologians,

504

philosophers, jurists and natural scientists in February 1959.

The papers discussed at that gathering were highly indicative: "Nuclear Physics and the Atom Bomb", "The Atomic Weapon as a Political Instrument", "The Ethical Problems of a Nuclear War", etc. In short, it demonstrated the Catholic intention of mounting a broad ideological campaign for the nuclear arming of the Bundeswehr. The aims nursed by the Catholic ideologists were spelled out in the *Rheinischer Merkur*: "The question of nuclear weapons for the Bundeswehr is a political one; but it is also connected with ethics. Considering the changed situation, a continuous dialogue is essential between politics and ethics."

The dialogue is under way and merits our attention, if only for being an alloy of cynicism and bigotry, of anti-humanism and pleas for destruction—presented with a garnish of Christian ethics and vindicated by identification with the "divine order". The contention is made that atomic war need not be feared, because its terrors transcend human imagination—obviously a green light for the reckless aspirations of German imperialism, its policy of revenge and of a new *Drang nach Osten*. What bothers the gentlemen is that the German Democratic Republic is in the way, meaning that an eastward campaign would inevitably entail a war of German against German. The Catholic ideologists say this should deter no one, because according to the Christian teaching "every war is a war between brothers". Though the conscience of the world may still be troubled by the atomic bombs the United States dropped on Japanese cities in 1945, the West German Catholics deplore only the time and place; dropped elsewhere, at another time, the act could be justified.

As though this were not enough. Professor Gustav Gundlach, Pater and Jesuit, declared that no weapons, no means of warfare, were immoral; one should not differentiate between them, for using them to promote his aims man endowed even means of mass annihilation with a religiously ethical quality. War in the name of the "values" symbolised by the cross, Gundlach said, should be theologically and ethically justified, even if involving nuclear arms. That is his No. 1 argument in favour of a nuclear "crusade".

It should be clear, however, that an atomic "crusade" would doom the German nation to annihilation and turn Germany into a desert. Gundlach is conscious of it, and makes his second and decisive argument. "The very disappearance of the nation," he says, "has a definite sense, provided it remains loyal to God. The Universe is not eternal. It is beyond man's powers to preserve it. God could lead us into a situation where we must display our sense of loyalty regardless of the danger." The conclusion he draws is that "war is the root of the God-established world order".[1]

Bundeswehr spokesmen acclaimed Father Gundlach. Catholic clericalism blended fully with the interests of the German militarists. Suiting their vocabulary to the new historical conditions, the extremists aspire to the same old militarist and revisionist aims and cannot, in effect, put forward any new, let alone constructive, idea.

Never before did the people of Germany need more desperately a realistic historico-philosophical and politico-historical idea that, noting the lessons of the past, would ensure peaceful development. Producing their various philosophical, historical, political and ethical conceptions, mostly unhistorical, unrealistic and reactionary, perverting the basic problem of present and future generations, the imperialist ideologists windowdress or vindicate, formulate or simply refurbish, the reactionary aggressive aspirations of the social and political forces whose interests they represent, express and defend.

Their concept may at times assume different garbs, ascending to the summits of existentialist abstractions[2] or

[1] Gundlach, "Atomverteidigung und gerechter Krieg", *Rheinischer Merkur*, Feb. 27, 1959. Also see "Die Bombe und die Moral der Katoliken", *Frankfurter Allgemeine Zeitung*, Feb. 24, 1959; "Aus moraltheologischer Sicht nicht zulässig", *Frankfurter Rundschau*, Feb. 25, 1959; "Welchen Papstes Meinung vertrat Pater Gundlach?", *Deutsche Woche*, March 4, 1959; P. Nellen, "Gerechter atomarer Krieg?", *Frankfurter Hefte* No. 4, 1959, S. 232-36; "Atomkrieg zur Weltvernichtung", *Neues Deutschland*, Apr. 18, 1959.

[2] Jaspers, *Philosophische Logik*, Bd. I, München, 1947; *Von der Wahrheit*, München, 1958; *Vernunft und Existenz*, Bremen, 1949; *Vernunft und Wiedervernunft in unserer Zeit*, München, 1950; *Vom Ursprung und Ziel der Geschichte*, München, 1952; *Wahrheit, Freiheit, Friede*, München, 1958. Heidegger, *Einführung in die Metaphysik*, Tübingen, 1953; *Idenstität und Differenz*, Pfullingen, 1957; *Zur Seinsfrage*, Frankfurt a/M, 1956.

frigid neo-Thomist[1] categories and dogmas. At other times they may be formulated as dubious historical sophisms and paradoxes about the peaceful role of German militarism, and nazism not having been spawned by German monopoly capital, being rather an extraneous "demoniac" phenomenon. Elsewhere, they endeavour to rehabilitate the Nietzschean ideas in texts purged of Nietzsche's more cynical, defiant and discredited formulas,[2] resorting also to street-corner demagogy and crude propaganda via the morning and evening press, the slick magazines, radio broadcasting and visual pseudo-documentary television programmes expertly run by centralised big-business companies. But in all cases these concepts, whether generalised, complicated, simplistic or even vulgarised, perform the function of consolidating the imperialist ideology of cold war and atomic warfare.

The German school of history, as we have seen, took a hand in shaping this ideology, knowing from the experience of the past two military disasters that it shoulders considerable responsibility for the future. In 1955 Dehio wrote:

"For the third time in 50 years Germany is at the crossroads. Twice it chose wrongly, overrating its capacity and pushing old Europe, and herself as well, to the brink of destruction."

How should Germany choose the third time? If she were not split and militarism were suppressed in her Western part, the people could count on peaceful development. But the country was split into two Germanys by the Western powers jointly with the country's reactionaries. The German Democratic Republic picked a new way—the way of socialism and peaceful development. The Federal Repub-

---

[1] O. v. Niel-Breuning, *Wirtschaft und Gesellschaft heute*, Bd. 1-2, Freiburg, 1956-57; J. Messner, *Das Naturrecht, Innsbruck* (Wien)-München, 1958; E. Welty, *Herders Sozialkatechismus*, Bd. 1, Freiburg, 1957; J. Lotz und J. de Vries, *Die Welt des Menschen*, 2. Aufl., Regensburg, 1951; G. Klaus, *Jesuiten Gott. Materie*, Berlin, 1957; *Philosophie des Verbrechens*, Hrsg. von G. Heyden, M. Klein und A. Kosing, Berlin, 1959.
[2] See F. Nietzsche, *Werke in drei Bänden*, Hrsg. von K. Schlechta, München, 1954-56. A new attempt at interpreting and vindicating Nietzsche was made by Karl Schlechta in his *Der Fall Nietzsche*, München, 1958, criticised from Marxist positions in *Deutsche Zeitschrift für Philosophie* No. 4, Berlin, 1958, S. 653-58; No. 5, 1958, S. 821-22.

lic, which remained capitalist, could, like Austria and Finland, have picked neutralism or at least peaceful coexistence, but did not. It chose to revive militarism, join NATO, pursue the cold war, and leave it to the historians to substantiate its choice. Holding that the establishment of the Federal Republic and Germany's split were "a blessing in disguise" and falling back on the neo-Ranke notion of "power balance", German school of history acclaimed the policy of "Western solidarity" and ranged itself behind the avowed U.S. objective of "rolling back Bolshevism".[1]

German historians know perfectly well, of course, that this is creating insuperable obstacles to reunification on a peaceful basis. "That is the sense of the real crossroads," Dehio writes, "one road leading directly to the national goal and the other via Atlantic solidarity to a long detour."[2] Hence the accent not only on the traditional independent militarist forces, but on "U.S. militarism, which, relying on its superweapon", could at the right moment "launch a preventive war". But Dehio evidently understood that this lacked realism and involved terrible dangers. That is why, appealing for "a definite aim in escaping from our recent history", he pleads for "the Western essence ... to ennoble the national motive power" (*Triebhaftigkeit*), concluding thus: "Impatience and poor judgement ... have twice caused us to choose the wrong road. For us there is no third time."[3]

What historians should do is dig deep into the history of German imperialism and revise their traditional concept of German history, not to rehabilitate militarism and certainly not to justify nuclear arming, but to draw up the accounts and secure truly new paths to the future in line with Europe's peaceful development.

8

No other international political concept has been as universal, as realistic and broad, and, what is most important, as consistent with the spirit of the times and the vital in-

---

[1] Dehio, op. cit., S. 148.
[2] Ibid., S. 146-47.
[3] Ibid., S. 155.

terests of all peoples, as the Leninist concept of the peaceful coexistence of states with different social systems. Lenin formulated it first when the First World War was still on, later making it the cornerstone of Soviet foreign policy. Proclaimed in the historic Decree on Peace, it could not be instantly embodied in reality, but has always been the guideline in the fight for normalising Soviet relations with the capitalist countries, big and small. Ultimately, on passing the test of time in a great and difficult epoch—from October to our day—it won over millions of people in different countries on all continents, turning into a tangible material force that its foes have to reckon with. In that sense the idea of peaceful coexistence, the only possible alternative to nuclear disaster, is truly above all comparison.

But despite this, or precisely because of this, the imperialist cold war architects who want international tension to prevail, reject it. Until recently, there were two distinct lines, outwardly conflicting but, in effect, mutually complementary, of fighting it. It was said, on the one hand, that Lenin repudiated the concept of peaceful coexistence, that, indeed, it appeared after his time, but that his name was associated with it to give it the ultimate historical and politico-ethical vindication. But this line is no longer favoured, even among the cold war warriors in West Germany. W. G. Grewe, for one, admits in his book that Lenin wrote about "the parallel coexistence of states with different class structures", and draws a profound conclusion: in its foreign policy the Soviet Government in recent years "in principle still shares Lenin's views". He adds: "I am inclined to think that it honestly excludes war as a method of settling disputes, but do not think that the kind of competition it offers deserves to be called 'peaceful'."[1]

That is the second, currently dominant line of struggle against peaceful coexistence. Despite being recognised and acclaimed by the Bandung Afro-Asian Conference and later by the United Nations, the cold war architects contend that the principle of peaceful coexistence, finalised by the 20th Congress of the C.P.S.U. in the present conditions, is mere-

---

[1] Grewe, *Deutsche Aussenpolitik der Nachkriegszeit*, Stuttgart, 1960.

ly an ideological and diplomatic stratagem. But that is totally untrue. The idea of peaceful coexistence is neither a stratagem nor an abstraction. Neither does it make the wish father to the thought. It is the fruit of profound meditation about man's future by Lenin's genius, prompted by life and in the name of life. Since Lenin advanced the idea less than half a century ago the correlation between the forces of socialism and peace and the forces of imperialism and war has changed so drastically that Lenin's party, enriched by its own experience and the experience of the international working-class, communist and anti-colonialist movements, made a most significant and promising discovery: whereas in the past, with imperialism ruling undivided, world wars were inevitable, now, when the world socialist system has grown into a mighty force determining the historical progress of mankind, the peaceful coexistence of socialist and capitalist states is objectively possible.

Thus, after two terrible world wars, there is a tangible prospect for the first time to avert a new disaster, one likely to be still more destructive, still more devastating than all the past wars combined. From now on it is no longer self-delusion to think war avoidable. In the nuclear age the chance of interdicting wars can be entirely realistic. The time of the crusades is long over. Peaceful coexistence is a compulsion, one that is turning into reality and shaping international relations that preclude a nuclear disaster.

The idea of peaceful coexistence is truly progressive and abreast of the times, blazing a trail to the future, while all efforts to combat it with the tool of anti-communism are indubitably archaic.

West German critics of the "Adenauer era" observe that it was "tied by a thousand threads to the political, social, economic, military and intellectual past of Germany", to the German history of the mid-nineteenth century. They observe, too, that despite the "somewhat modified style and the changed, extended form of Germany's politico-military alliances", despite the Federal Republic's specific place in the industrialised capitalist world and despite modernised political mores, the basic ideas of the "Adenauer era" dated back to the "historical realities" of more than a hundred years ago.[1] In brief, they are described as a historical and political anachronism. That is, at all events, a fair appraisal of the basic idea of anti-communism, which has for its prototype the legitimist idea advanced in international relations after the French Revolution and the Napoleonic wars. Legitimism, the guideline of the Holy Alliance at the beginning of the 19th century, was indeed aimed against the popular democratic movements, even though these limited themselves to fairly modest aims, and was fashioned to legalise active political interference, even direct armed intervention, by the principal reactionary European powers in the internal affairs of states trying to embark on independent progressive development. But it discredited itself very quickly. However, somewhat refurbished and modernised to suit the new historical conditions, the reactionary Holy Alliance ideology has been pulled out of the mothbag, and modelled into the present-day anti-communism, which Thomas Mann, one of the most honest and far-sighted German intellectuals of our time, described as the greatest folly of the 20th century, under the signboard of which German imperialism, as Dehler, Vice-Chairman of the Bonn Bundestag put it, has waged a "thirty years' war"—from von Papen and Hitler to Adenauer and Strauss—against the Soviet Union.

The facts show that for all the variety of its forms— from the criminal Hitler aggression to the current "cold" variety and "psychological warfare"—this "thirty years' war" was neither local nor isolated. Reviving the archaic Holy Alliance ideology, John Foster Dulles, one of the chief architects of the cold war, produced the concept of "rolling back" the socialist countries in the interest of expanding the domains of capitalism and imperialism. It was this that lay at the back of the revisionist aspirations of the "Adenauer era"[2] and there is no indication yet that the aspirations in question have been abandoned. But even Dulles, shortly before his death, was beginning to realise that his cold war concept, which he endeavoured to oppose to the concept of peaceful coexistence, had neither histor-

---

[1] F. Heer, "Von der Paulskirche nach Bonn, 1848-1963", *Die Ära Adenauer. Einsichten und Ausblicke*, Frankfurt a/M, 1964, S. 94.

[2] This is admitted by West German historians. See K. Bölling, *Die zweite Republik, 15. Jahre Politik in Deutschland*, Köln-Berlin, 1963, S. 361-62.

ical nor practical worth and that the Atlantic policy had to be seriously revised. Anti-communism, revision of borders and cold war, crowned by dreams of "positions of strength" and nuclear weapons were so deeply ingrained in the "Adenauer era" that time and again they were put to use by West Germany to prevent any normalisation between the two main nuclear powers, the United States and the Soviet Union, and even to sharpen their relations.

What is more, other long bankrupt conceptions were revived to back up the cold war idea: one was the "balance of power" doctrine, an old gimmick whereby first Britain and then the United States strove to gain sway over the world by pitting countries against each other. We have shown earlier how this idea, originally framed by the neo-Ranke school, was employed also to justify the hegemonic aspirations of the German imperialists. Now it is being marshalled to justify Bonn's demands for nuclear weapons as a means of maintaining a "power balance" in Europe. But proliferation of nuclear weapons cannot guarantee peaceful international relations. On the contrary, it will only complicate them, especially if it is the German militarists who gain possession of them. The only dependable guarantee of peace is general and complete disarmament and effective international control. But, while rejecting the Soviet disarmament project, the Western powers are in effect offering as a substitute the idea of an armed peace, an old idea which for many decades screened the policy of intensive arming, with the many local and colonial wars, and, above all, the two world wars, as an inevitable sequel.

The post-war race of conventional and nuclear arms has been part of the cold war, and those who say that the latter, conducted under the flag of anti-communism, is the alternative to a new world disaster, are deluding themselves. The "Adenauer era" ideologists, for one thing, have declared in so many words that given nuclear arming, the cold war is no "newspaper expression" but a "real war", or at least a kind of politico-ideological prelude to it. That prelude is inflicting immense damage, straining the resources of the "belligerents" and costing tremendous moral, economic and politico-military effort. Worst of all, it is pregnant with the danger of a nuclear disaster whose probable consequences are incalculable.

Do the cold war zealots, the advocates of a forcible absorption of the German Democratic Republic and of a revision of post-war borders, realise what their ideology of aggressive anti-communism, of "rolling back", can lead to? A prominent West German publicist conversing with this writer in Nuremberg in July 1961, swore by Strauss's policy, but admitted that "unifying Germany the nuclear way would mean unifying a cemetery".

Germany's unification is an internal German problem. The only realistic and peaceful way to resolve it is by negotiations between the two German states. Hence, on German soil, too, the idea of peaceful coexistence—the peaceful coexistence of two states with different socio-economic systems—is vital, creative and realistic. And that is what forms the foundation for the peace doctrine advanced by the German Democratic Republic in the interests of rapprochement and of preventing a third world war from breaking out on German soil.

9

German imperialism's present ideology has nothing in common with peaceful development and the future of the German nation. The imperialists cannot create anything new, so they revert to and combine old or revamped ideas, adapting them to the current conditions and the nearest political tasks. The heroic period of German bourgeois thought is long over. It has, generally speaking, travelled from one pole to the other: from rationalism and the idea of progress to extreme irrationalism and reaction; from faith in man's triumph to the conviction that mass propaganda and Americanised advertising are all-powerful; from Hegel's dialectics and Feuerbach's materialism to existentialism, the revarnished Thomist scholasticism and political clericalism; from the lofty humanism of Herder, Goethe and Schiller to anti-communism and modernised methods of "psychological warfare", and from Kant's treatise on eternal peace to the sinister philosophy of nuclear war.[1] By repudiating the idea of peaceful coexistence, which is

---

[1] See W. S. Schlamm, *Die Grenzen des Wunders. Ein Bericht über Deutschland*, Zürich, 1959.

the most realistic idea of our time, it is slamming the door on Germany's national unification on a democratic basis. By justifying militarism and revenge, it is spurning the realities of the nuclear age or interpreting them in a spirit of extreme irrationalism. All this adds up to the following: despite its bravado, West German ideology is in a profound crisis, one it will never overcome, because any revival of German militarism rules out a German revival and any attempt at achieving aims by wholesale slaughter amounts to suicide. Hence, German imperialist ideology is not only unhumanistic; it is also unrealistic. What it boils down to in the nuclear age is a nuclear conflagration. Therein lies its danger to the German nation, but also to Europe and the rest of the world. It is the *rationale* of a chain reaction, removable not by a philosophy of "deterrence by fear" and not by German nuclear arming, but by a rejection of nuclear arms and by universal disarmament under strict international control. That is an aim worth fighting for, because it would mean the triumph of human reason over its own—one of the greatest but also one of the most terrifying—creation. Yet it will be pushed back far, or made impossible, if German imperialism, the most aggressive force in modern Europe, equipped with an ideology of modernised militarism and revenge, gains access to atomic weapons. The forces of peace and reason cannot reconcile themselves to this possibility, and Peace and Reason are not abstract notions bred by philosophers and moralists, not images created by a poet and not the aberration of a historian accustomed to looking at things through the prism of the past. No, these forces are strong in this difficult age that has endured the terrors of two world wars.

In West Germany they are still disunited, depressed by the reigning ideology, sometimes blinded by the external lustre of the "economic wonder", or simply persecuted. Yet they are casting about for new ideas, for a realistic alternative to the cold war. The main slogans of the "Adenauer era", those of "stability" and "no experiments" no longer suit the objective situation, which is disturbing to those who seek a more realistic approach to the present and are troubled about the future. Thilo Koch, a farsighted and thoughtful observer, notes that the price for the ephemeral stability of the "Adenauer era" is "immobility in foreign policy, especially with regard to the East, autocracy, and the weight of a lingering past in home affairs".[1]

The course did not change when the "Adenauer era" ended. But certain new trends did appear in historico-philosophical and historico-political thinking among those dissociated from political clericalism. Soon after the Third Reich had crashed, some deliberately opposed the fascist ideology, denouncing it, rejecting all its aspects, seeking to resolve important ethical and psychological problems. But that was in the field of fiction. No such school appeared in historiography. Referring to the first year of post-war growth, it is true, Hans Werner Richter, West German publicist and first president of the European Committee Against Atomic Arming formed in 1959, wrote: "The year zero was the year of a new beginning free from the weight of German history.... Germany stood, as people thought then, at a crucial crossroads in her history. She had many opportunities. What she had to do was break through from 'non-existence' as state and nation to an entirely new existence."[2] But West Germany chose a different road, for which its historico-political thinkers are quite considerably to blame, fitting old imperialist ideas to the new conditions and preventing a radical and complete settling of scores with the past, and thereby "an entirely new existence". Yet it turned out that modernising the traditional imperialist ideas did not heal the main sores—neither the split nor the threat of a nuclear disaster on German soil. So new tendencies appeared, highlighting ideas historically and politically realistic. Nor should these be considered simply as an outgrowth of the political situation. Like everything else in the ideological sphere, realistic ideas have their inner logic. Some are a reaction to barren and dangerous extremist trends, others, though they do not depart from these trends, are no more than a timid attempt to steer a more dependable course, seeing that Bonn's post-war course is archaic against the backdrop of change in the world. These realistic ideas are not radical and contain many intrinsic contradictions. All the same, like all other non-conformism, associated with the vital needs of the

[1] Koch, "Stabilität und ihr Preis", *Die Ära Adenauer. Einsichten und Ausblicke*, Frankfurt a/M, 1964, S. 28.

[2] Richter, "Zwischen Freiheit und Quarantäne", *Bestandsaufnahme. Eine deutsche Bilanz 1962*, Hrsg. von H. W. Richter, München-Wien-Basel, 1962, S. 18.

times and fructifying creative thought, they are resisted by reactionaries who see betrayal and danger, a danger more terrible to them than the consequences of the cold war, in any departure from traditional notions and dogmas.

Among historians, realism prompts a search for the truth—even at the price of rejecting the method and categories of the German school of history, the neo-Ranke approach revived in a variety of forms ranging from traditionally nationalist to "European" and "Atlantic" patterns. Fritz Fischer's book, *Drive for World Power*,[1] is the result of just such a search. He examined a vast store of documents and produced a deep and thorough analysis of German annexationist aims at the time of the First World War. Contiguous with his ideas, historically realistic in spirit, are those of his disciple, Imanuel Geiss, set out in papers on the Polish-German frontiers problem during the 1914-18 war[2] and on the July crisis as the prologue to that war.[3] In the first of these papers, Geiss denounces "annexation and use of violence" as too crude for our epoch, and in the second furnishes documentary corroboration of the extremely aggressive role of the German imperialists in the crucial days before the First World War.[4] Although some of the aspects in Fischer's and Geiss's books appear controversial,[5] their basic conclusions deserve merit not only as the fruit of thorough scientific investigation, but as a show of courage and intellectual perspicacity, based on the knowledge that traditional concepts which obstruct a reassessment of German history in the interest of the future, have to be revised.

Replying to his critics, Fischer writes: "Our view is sharpened by the suffering of the two world wars. Here is the question: are we ripe to extract sober-minded conclu-

---

[1] Fischer, *Griff nach der Weltmacht*, Düsseldorf, 1961 (2nd edition, 1962).

[2] Geiss, *Der polnische Grenzstreifen 1914-1918*, Lübeck-Hamburg, 1960.

[3] *Julikrise und Kriegsausbruch 1914*, Bd. I. Bearbeitet und eingeleitet von Geiss. Mit einem Vorwort von Fischer, Hannover, 1963.

[4] Also see Fischer, "Jetzt oder nie—die Julikrise 1914", *Spiegel* No. 21, 1964.

[5] For a Marxist assessment of Fischer's book see F. Klein, "Die Westdeutsche Geschichtsschreibung über die Ziele des deutschen Imperialismus im ersten Weltkrieg", *Zeitschrift für Geschichtswissenschaft*, 1962, Heft. 8.

sions out of the German past from the distance now lying behind us?"[1] This yearning for "sober-minded conclusions", that is, for a realistic approach to the vital historical problem, triggered attacks from the various flanks of the modern "historical school".[2] Ritter accused Fischer of producing a "new war guilt thesis".[3] But even before, bourgeois historians were faced with the problem which Fischer mildly described as the "continuity of error".[4] The exponents of the traditional imperialist conceptions were annoyed. They sensed that a realistic approach to the history of the First World War was bound to influence the "general outline of our time".[5] Ritter, for one thing, feared that historical realism would merge with a politically realistic approach to the vital issues of our time and—though his views are externally mobile—ever faithful to the reactionary nationalist conception, he accused Fischer of national nihilism, placing his thoughts on a par with the politico-historical ideas of Hans Rothfels and the historico-philosophical ideas of Karl Jaspers. This confusion is demagogical[6] and aimed at discrediting everything, be it even mutually exclusive, that reveals the slightest trace of realism.

Rothfels, probably the inspirer of the West German school of "modern history", is trying to modernise and activate ideology, and is prepared to sacrifice many of the traditional nationalist categories, so long as NATO ideology benefits. His school, highly active in both theory and practice, employs an amalgam of liberal, even anti-Hitler notions, on the one hand, and ideas borrowed from the

[1] *Die Welt*, July 7, 1962.
[2] See H. Herzfeld, "Zur deutschen Politik im ersten Weltkrieg. Kontinuität oder permanente Krise?", *Historische Zeitschrift*, 1960, Bd. 161; "Die deutsche Kriegszielpolitik im ersten Weltkrieg", *Vierteljahrshefte für Zeitgeschichte*, 1963, H. 3. E. Hölzle, "Griff nach der Weltmacht?", *Das historisch-politische Buch*, 1962, H. 3.
[3] Ritter, "Eine neue Kriegsschildthese", *Historische Zeitschrift*, 1962, Bd. 194.
[4] Fischer, "Kontinuität des Irrtums. Zum Problem der deutschen Kriegszielpolitik im ersten Weltkrieg", *Historische Zeitschrift*, 1960, Bd. 191.
[5] J. Engel, "Zeitgeschichte-Aussenpolitik", *Geschichte in Wissenschaft und Unterricht* No. 8, 1963.
[6] See W. Berthold, G. Lozek, H. Maier, "Entwicklungstendenzen im historisch-politischen Denken in Westdeutschland", *Zeitschrift für Geschichtswissenschaft*, 1964, H. 4.

anti-communist arsenal and covered by the doctrine of "anti-totalitarianism", on the other. In practice, this blend of contradictory ideas also produces a contradictory and changing historico-political position: recognition of the historic role played by the Communist Party of Germany and other democratic forces in the anti-fascist Resistance movement, and, in the same breath, a repudiation of this fact in order to rehabilitate the Right-wingers of the anti-Hitler plot of July 20, 1944[1]; attempts to justify the "non-recognition" of the German Democratic Republic while rejecting the concept of neutralising Germany as "illusory", and recognition of the need to treat the coexistence problem as "a relationship between two social systems in one country ... and a relationship to the neighbouring Slav peoples".[2]

On the methodological plane, the Rothfels school draws extensively on Max Weber's sociological doctrine which, as we know, was considered a tested weapon against Marxism at the time of the Weimar Republic, while tending to merge with Jaspers's existentialism on the philosophico-historical plane. The rigid traditionalists and the nationalists brand Rothfels's inconsistencies as dangerous experiments, especially after Jaspers, recently an atom-bomb ideologist, somewhat altered his views. They will not suffer with equanimity any changes even in the reactionary camp: their ideal is to freeze ideas and thereby counterpose them to historical development and progress. Yet development is making an imprint on ideas, too, even the reactionary ones.

Jaspers arrived at his sombre philosophy of atomic death by phases. In 1945-46, the "year zero" which began after the collapse of the Third Reich, he meditated on the German nation's responsibility for the criminal nazi system and raised "the question of guilt"—one of the most acute and still valid politico-ethical questions. On returning from his exile, the Heidelberg philosopher told the students of his university at the first congregation after the downfall

---

[1] This is observed by D. E. Melnikov in *Zagovor 20 iyulya 1944 goda v Germanii. Legenda i deistvitelnost*, Moscow, 1962, pp. 284-86 (Russ. ed.).

[2] Rothfels, "Historie und weltpolitische Situation", *Aus Politik und Zeitgeschichte*, December 12, 1962; *Zeitgeschichtliche Betrachtungen*, Göttingen, 1959.

of the fascist state: "We can reach down to the basis of our new life from the depth of our essence only by a complete self-examination."[1] Although he treated the matter not as a socio-political problem, but merely one of individual and national ethics and psychology, his call for settling accounts was bold and impressive. Then, in the Bonn state that embarked on cold war, he passed through the hell of his "atomic ideology". Only now, still revolving within the circle of his old politico-ethical problems, he laments that democracy and freedom as he understands them have not been put into practice. Further, conscious of the realities of our time, he seems to be approaching a proper appreciation of the need for changing the tools of cognition. "The point of departure in our politico-ethical possibilities," he writes, "is lodged in the past experience of disaster and in what brought it about; also, it is lodged in the threat of a coming world disaster. *Both these experiences may change political thinking, though so far this has not taken place.*"[2]

Quite true, no such change has yet taken place, but the search continues with differing intensity, within differing limits, but, by and large, in one direction—that of historical and political realism. It is in this context that we should look at the evolution of Golo Mann. His endeavours to comprehend the German history of the 19th and 20th centuries were, in a way, already a departure from the reactionary traditions of the neo-Ranke historiography towards bourgeois-democratic ideas of a fairly radical complexion.[3] But his articles of more recent years evidenced his readiness to examine critically also the basic historical lines of the "Adenauer era".[4] Mann is aware that in the atomic age revenge is as senseless as the hope to change the socio-economic system in the socialist countries, an object of revisionist aspirations. At first, he thought the Oder-Neisse line was the result of Polish annexations. Now he has arrived at the conclusion, and rightly so, that it is

---

[1] Jaspers, *Lebensfragen der deutschen Politik*, München, 1963, S. 88.

[2] Ibid., S. 12 (italics mine.—*A. Y.*).

[3] Mann, *Deutsche Geschichte des 19. und 20. Jahrhunderts,* Frankfurt a/M, 1958.

[4] Mann, "Der Staatsmann und sein Werk", *Die Ära Adenauer,* S. 170-83.

the historical outcome of Hitler's war. "Asserting the German right to the 1937 borders is bad from the standpoint of power politics and also bad from the ethical standpoint.... It would be good to recognise the Oder-Neisse border by a free decision of the Federal Government and the nation."[1] As he sees it, the Federal Republic would then arrive at broad political and historical horizons, since the removal of international tension in Europe and a realistic approach to the policy of peaceful coexistence with the Soviet Union and the other countries of the socialist community would remove the danger of a new war.[2] He is conscious of obstacles but does not realise that one of them is his own mistaken view about the German Democratic Republic which, he thinks, has no future. But generally speaking, the evolution of his views, affected somewhat by the realistic "Kennedy course",[3] follows in the opposite direction to the unrealistic course of the "Adenauer era". He analysed the general results of this "era" and spotted the many historical contradictions inevitable in any construction in which political aims are at loggerheads with intrinsic logic and objective reality. "Any policy that does not know what it wants, any policy that wants the impossible, will achieve either nothing or war," says Mann.[4] But he concludes: "There must be no war any more."[5]

His stand against war is not a pacifist one. Nor is it merely a good intention that paves the way to hell.

The pacifist ideas prevailing among certain German intellectuals, and in the Protestant and Catholic churches, are also significant. But in our case, the search for ways of evading war is associated with a search for realistic assessments of the times, for historico-political ideas consistent with the correlation of forces and the "spirit of the times",

---

[1] Mann, "Der Verlorene Krieg und die Folgen", *Bestandsaufnahme. Eine deutsche Bilanz 1962*, S. 53-54.

[2] Mann, "Hat Deutschland eine Zukunft?", *Die Zeit*, September 7, 1962; "Krieg darf nicht mehr sein!", *Neue Rundschau* No. 1, 1963.

[3] As rightly noted by Berthold, Lozek and Maier in "Entwicklungstendenzen im historisch-politischen Denken in Westdeutschland", *Zeitschrift für Geschichtswissenschaft*, 1964, H. 4.

[4] Mann, "Der Verlorene Krieg und die Folgen", *Bestandsaufnahme. Eine deutsche Bilanz 1962*, S. 54.

[5] Mann, "Krieg darf nicht mehr sein!" *Neue Rundschau* No. 1, 1963.

an appreciation of which is so essential for resolving vital problems by sophisticated rather than outdated means.

In our time, when development rates grow much more rapidly, political consciousness cannot afford to straggle: any gap between ideas designed to resolve present-day problems and the realities may have dangerous consequences. Yet despite the economic successes of the F.R.G., it is this gap that leaves the deepest imprint on its political development. Since an authoritarian regime of "Kanzler democracy" took root in the F.R.G., from the first, bourgeois historians are still inclined to regard Adenauer as the personification of the ideas that shape Bonn policy. Not only does this apply to the apologists of the ex-Chancellor, but also to his critics, including those who wish to grasp the reasons behind the difference between the old course and the new conditions, and seek possibilities for removing this difference in the interests of peaceful development. "Konrad Adenauer," writes K. H. Flach, a former leader of the Free Democratic Party, "goes back with his roots to the 19th century. He came to power in the Federal Republic when Hiroshima had already been destroyed but when the effect of the super-bomb was not yet measured. Adenauer drew no new lessons from it."

As Flach sees it, this means that after splitting Germany and formalising the split by putting West Germany into the Western military bloc, the ruling circles under Adenauer reverted to the old methods—building military force and making territorial claims. Flach admits thereby that the Federal Republic is "inducing fear of war". He accuses Adenauer and his followers of cultivating "illusions" combined with "despondency" among the West German population, and pleads that the people should be told the actual state of affairs, the fact that any revisionist programme "can only come about at the price of war". And since any new war would mean unprecedented disaster, Flach holds, the main historical task is to find "ways and means for aligning the Federal Republic and its domestic and foreign policies with the atomic age".[1] This means abandoning the ideology and practice of cold war and recognising the realities, social, political and ideological, of our age.

---

[1] Flach, *Erhards schwerer Weg*, Stuttgart, 1963.

The glimmers of historical and political realism observed in West Germany in the early phase of militarist revival grew brighter as the Bonn government gravitated towards atomic arming. But the growth of realistic ideas was sporadic, because the pressures of imperialist ideology continuously increased. The voice of the Communist Party alone, from the underground, reminded continuously of the dangers of cold war and revanchism, militarisation, and the atomic ideology.

Now that the "Adenauer era" is over, its general historical contours and contradictions have come to the surface in bolder relief, and all its profound political miscalculations are being assessed more realistically. So are the dangers which it has created. This is why public opinion is concentrating on the main idea of our time—the idea of preventing an atomic war—though inconsistently, in zigzags, with uncertainty. Among its followers one can find big manufacturers and bankers. "Whether a country situated in the heart of Europe between the giants of East and West, and much closer to the eastern giant," writes Harold Rasch, "should possess such means of mass annihilation as the atomic and hydrogen bombs ... is not a question to be settled by military technical experts, but a vitally important political decision. Whoever wants to support it must ... say candidly that he is prepared to lay the consequences on our people."[1]

That is the problem which the German militarists put before the nation. It calls for a constructive solution, possible and absolutely essential; modern history offers us a good alternative: peaceful coexistence between states with different socio-economic systems. And we have to take advantage of it, because it flows from life. Mankind cannot allow the criminal designs and misjudgements of the imperialists to bring about total destruction. Political anachronisms of the "Adenauer era" type must cease. Political realism consistent with the new epoch must replace them. As rightly noted by Flach, "the period of grace in history has run out; now is the time to think, plan, decide and act."[2]

---

[1] Rasch, *Die Bundesrepublik und Osteuropa. Grundfragen einer künftigen deutschen Ostpolitik*, Köln, 1963, S. 97.
[2] Flach, op. cit.

Could it be that in so responsible a time as now, the German nation, which has created great values of humane culture and attained the summits of scientific and philosophical thought, but which has twice before allowed itself to be pushed into the lower depths of nationalism, racism and aggressive militarism, will lack the courage and moral power to make the sensible choice? Could it be that the German imperialist and anti-communist ideology will again rob the nation of its reason and common sense, and prevent it thereby from understanding the choice of our time between peaceful coexistence and atomic disaster in relation to its own destiny: destruction of the German nation or its revival? The German Democratic Republic has made the choice. Therein lies its incontestable moral strength and its service to history.

History is not a mere chronicle of events of the remote and more recent past. It is interlaced with the present. It is also a judge, and, once its laws are understood, it becomes the guideline in the labyrinth of life, a deep source from which man draws confidence in himself, in his reason, in his future. This is why, meditating on the destiny of nations and on German militarism which, like all militarism, seeks to suppress man's thought and will for living, Bertolt Brecht, a great German 20th-century thinker, departed from this Earth with a sense of historical optimism despite the oppressive experience of the past. He had trust in the reason of the democratic forces, writing a few years before his death:

> General, you need men.
> They can fly and they can kill.
> The one snag is that
> They can also think.

1959-64

ABBREVIATIONS

BD—*British Documents on the Origins of the War, 1898-1914,* Vols. 1-11, London, 1927-38.

DA—*Diplomatische Aktenstücke zur Vorgeschichte des Krieges 1914. Ergänzungen und Nachträge zum österreichisch-ungarischen Bot-buch,* Wien, 1919.

DD—*Die deutschen Dokumente zum Kriegsausbruch Vollständige Sammlung der von K. Kautsky zusammengestellten amtlichen Aktenstücke mit einigen Ergänzungen,* Bd. 1-4. Charlottenburg, 1919.

DDF—*Documents diplomatiques français (1871-1914),* t. 1-42, Paris, 1929-59.

DZA—Deutsches Zentral-Archiv.

GP—*Die Grosse Politik der Europäischen Kabinette, 1871-1914. Sammlung der Diplomatischen Akten des Auswärtigen Amtes,* Bd. 1-40, Berlin, 1922-27.

ÖUA—*Österreichs-Ungarns Aussenpolitik von der Bosnischen Krise 1908 bis zum Kriegsausbruch 1914. Diplomatische Aktenstücke des österreichisch-ungarischen Ministerium des Aussern,* Bd. 1-8, 12, Wien-Leipzig, 1930.

REQUEST TO READERS

Progress Publishers would be glad to have your opinion of this book, its translation and design and any suggestions you may have for future publications.

Please send all your comments to 21, Zubovsky Boulevard, Moscow, U.S.S.R.

Printed in the Union of Soviet Socialist Republics